McDougal Littell

kinetic BOOKS

CONCEPTUAL PHYSICS

ISBN-13: 978-0-618-97610-2
ISBN-10: 0-618-97610-8

1 2 3 4 5 6 7 8 - CKI - 11 10 09 08 07

Table of Contents

CHAPTER 26: CAPACITORS

CHAPTER 27: DIRECT CURRENT CIRCUITS

CHAPTER 28: MAGNETIC FIELDS

0.0 - Welcome to an electronic physics textbook!

Textbooks, like this one, contain words and illustrations. In an ordinary textbook, the words are printed and the illustrations are static, but in this book, many of the illustrations are animations and many words are spoken. Altogether, this textbook contains more than 600,000 words, 150 simulations, 1000 animations, 5000 illustrations, 15 hours of audio narration, and 35,000 lines of Java and JavaScript code.

All this is designed so that you will experience more physics. You will race cars around curves, see the forces between charged particles, dock a space craft, generate electricity by moving a wire through a magnetic field, control waves in a string to "make music", measure the force exerted by an electric field, and much more. These simulations and animations are designed to allow you to "see" more physics and make it easier for you to assess your learning, since many of them pose problems for you to solve.

The foundation of this textbook is the same as a traditional textbook: text like this and illustrations. Concepts like "velocity" or "Newton's second law" are explained as they are in traditional textbooks. From there we go a step further, taking advantage of the computer and giving you additional ways to learn about physics. The textbook has many features: simulations; problems where the computer checks your answers and then works with you step by step; animations that are narrated; search capability; and much more. We will start with some simulations. In subsequent sections, we will show you how we use animations and narration to teach physics, and how a computer will help you solve problems.

At the right are three examples of how we take advantage of an interactive simulation engine. Click on any of the illustrations to start an interactive simulation; it will open a separate window. When you are done, you can close the window. The window that contains this text will remain open.

In the first simulation, you aim the monkey's banana bazooka so that the banana will reach the professor. The instant the banana is fired, the professor lets go of the tree and falls toward the ground. You aim the banana bazooka by dragging the head of the arrow shown on the right. Aim the bazooka and then press GO. Press RESET to try again. (And do not worry: We, too, value physics professors, so the professor will emerge unscathed.)

This is an animated version of a classic physics problem and appears about halfway through a chapter of the textbook. The majority of our simulations require the calculation of precise answers, but like this one, they are all great ways to see a concept at work.

In the second simulation, you can extend a simple circuit. The initial circuit shown on the right contains a battery and a light bulb. You can add light bulbs or more wire segments by dragging them near the desired location. Once there, they will snap into place. You can also use an ammeter to measure the amount of current flowing through a section of a wire, and a voltmeter to measure the potential difference across a light bulb or the battery.

There are many experiments you can conduct with these simple tools. For instance, place a light bulb in the horizontal segment above the one which already contains the light bulb and connect it to the circuit with two additional vertical wire segments. Does this alter the power flowing

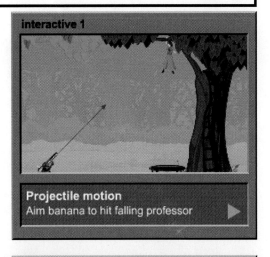

interactive 1

Projectile motion
Aim banana to hit falling professor

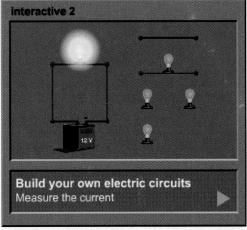

interactive 2

Build your own electric circuits
Measure the current

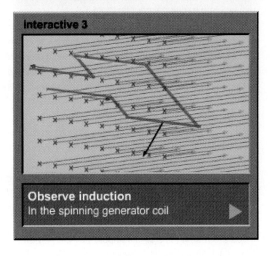

interactive 3

Observe induction
In the spinning generator coil

through the first light bulb? The brightness of each light bulb is roughly proportional to the power the circuit supplies to it.

How do the potential differences across the light bulbs compare to one another? To the potential difference across the battery? Measure the current flowing through a piece of wire immediately adjacent to the battery, and through each of the wire segments that contains a light bulb. Do you see a mathematical relationship between these three values?

You will be asked to make observations in many simulations like this, and as you learn physics, to apply what you have learned to answer problems posed by the simulations. You will use your knowledge to do everything from juggle to dock a spaceship!

In the third simulation, you experiment with a simple electric generator. When the crank is turned, the rectangular wire loop shown in the illustration turns in a magnetic field. The straight lines you see are called magnetic field lines. Turning the handle of the generator creates an electric current and what is called an emf. The emf is measured in volts.

After you launch the simulation, you can change your point-of-view with a slider. The illustration you see to the right provides a conceptual overview of what a generator is. If you change the viewing angle, you can better see the angle between the wire and the field, and how that affects the current. A device called an oscilloscope is used to measure the emf created by the generator.

The electric generator is an advanced topic, and if you are just beginning your study of physics, it presents you with many unfamiliar concepts. However, the simulation shows how we can take advantage of software to allow you to change the viewing angle and to view processes that change over time.

If you want to see more simulations we enjoyed creating: "dragging" a ball to match a graph, sliding a block up a plane, electromagnetic induction, electric potential, space docking mission and wave interference. You can click on any of these topics and the link will take you to that section. There are many simulations; to see even more of them, you can click on the table of contents, pick a chapter, and then click on any section whose name starts with "interactive problem."

To move to the next section, click on the right arrow in the black bar above or below, the arrow to the right of 0.0.

0.1 - Whiteboards

Right now, you are reading the text of this textbook. Its design is similar to that found in traditional textbooks. By "text," we mean the words you are reading and the illustrations and writing you see to the right.

As you read the words, study the illustrations and work the problems, you may feel as though you are using a traditional textbook. (We like to think it is well-conceived and well-written, but that is for you to judge.) You can print out this textbook and use it as you would a traditional print textbook.

When you use the electronic version of this book, however, you have access to an entirely different way of learning the material. It starts with what we call the *whiteboards*. You launch the whiteboards by clicking on the illustrations to the right. They present the same material discussed in the text, but do so using a sequence of narrated animations.

The text and the whiteboards cover essentially the same material. You could learn physics exclusively through the whiteboards, or you could learn it all via the words and pictures you now see. The text sometimes contains additional material: the history of the topic, an application of a principle and so on. Everything found in the whiteboards is always found in the text, so you do **not** have to click through them unless you find them a useful way to learn. The point is: You have a choice. You may also find a combination of the two particularly useful, especially for topics you find challenging.

If you are reading this on a computer, try clicking on the illustration titled "Concept 1" to the right. This will open the whiteboard in a separate window. Each whiteboard is equipped with animations, audio and its own set of controls. Both this textbook and the whiteboards can be used simultaneously. **If you do not have headphones or speakers, click on the "show text" button after you open the whiteboard.** This will allow you to read the whiteboard narration.

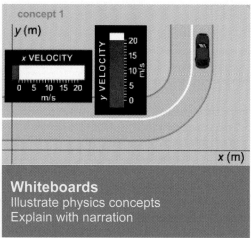

Whiteboards
Illustrate physics concepts
Explain with narration

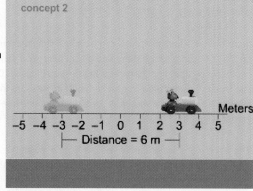

The electronic format provides a visually compelling way for you to learn what can be complex concepts and formulas. For instance, instead of a static diagram that represents a car rounding a curve, our format allows us to actually show the car moving and turning. We can also show you a greater amount of information – for example, how the horizontal and vertical velocities of the car change over time.

Typical sections throughout the book feature three graphic elements on the right side of the page, corresponding to three parts of the whiteboard. The first introduces the **concept**: For instance, what does the term "displacement" mean? The second contains the **equation**: How is displacement calculated? The third, located at the bottom right, then works an **example** problem to test your understanding of the concept and the equation.

The textbook contains hundreds of these whiteboards. If you would like to view some more to get a sense of how animation and audio play together, you can browse any chapter. You can explore topics like displacement, graphing simple harmonic motion, hitting a baseball, electric field diagrams, determining the type of image produced by a mirror and the force of a magnetic field on a moving charged particle.

To move to the next section, click on the right-arrow in the black bar above or below, the arrow to the right of 0.1.

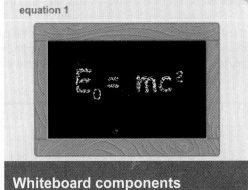

Whiteboard components
Concept slides explain idea

Whiteboard components
Equations provide formula(s)

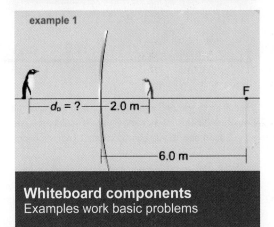

Whiteboard components
Examples work basic problems

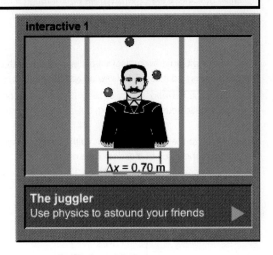

0.2 - Interactive problems

In the first section of this chapter, we encouraged you to try various simulations. We call simulations where you set values and watch the results *interactive problems*. In this section, we explain in more detail how they work.

A sample interactive problem can be launched by clicking on the graphic on the right. When the correct x (horizontal) and y (vertical) velocities are supplied, the juggler will juggle the three balls. Before you proceed, you may wish to read the instructions below for using these interactive simulations.

As mentioned, you launch the simulations by clicking on the graphic. Typically, you will be asked to enter a value in the simulation. Sometimes you fill in a value in a text entry box, and other times you select a value using spin dials that have up and down arrow buttons.

The juggler
Use physics to astound your friends

Then, you typically push the GO button and the simulation begins – things begin to move. Most simulations have a RESET button that allows you to start again. Many have a PAUSE button that makes things go three times faster (just kidding – they pause the simulation so you can record data).

Many simulations, especially those at the beginning of the chapters, just ask you to observe how entering different values changes the results. Simulations often come with gauges that display variables as they change, such as a speedometer to keep track of a car's speed as it goes around a track. You may observe the relationship between mass and the amount of gravitational force, for instance. Other simulations provide direct feedback if you succeed: the juggler juggles, you beat another racecar, and so forth.

Simulations later in the chapter often ask you to perform calculations in order to achieve a particular goal. These simulations are designed to make trial-and-error an ineffective tactic since they require a great amount of precision in the answer.

Enough preamble: Try the juggling simulation to the right. Enter any values you like for the initial y and x velocities, using the spin dials. Then press GO and watch as the juggler begins to juggle. Press RESET to enter a different set of values. A hint: One pair of values that will enable you to juggle is 6.0 m/s (meters per second) for the y velocity and 0.6 m/s for the x velocity.

0.3 - Sample problems and derivations

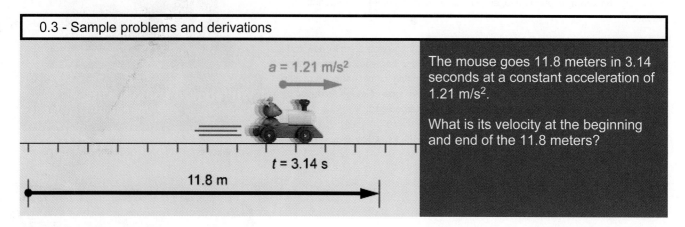

$a = 1.21$ m/s^2

The mouse goes 11.8 meters in 3.14 seconds at a constant acceleration of 1.21 m/s^2.

What is its velocity at the beginning and end of the 11.8 meters?

$t = 3.14$ s

11.8 m

In addition to text and interactive problem sections, this textbook contains sections with *sample problems* and *derivations* of equations. Sample problems often demonstrate a useful problem-solving technique. You see a typical sample problem above. Derivations show how an equation new to you can be created from equations you have already learned.

We follow the same sequence of steps in sample problems and derivations. (You will also follow this same sequence when you work through problems called interactive checkpoints; more on this type of problem in the next section.) Sample problems, derivations and interactive checkpoints all have some or all of the following: a diagram, a table of variables, a statement of the problem-solving strategy, the principles and equations used, and a step-by-step solution.

To show how these are organized, we work through a sample problem from the study of linear motion. The problem is stated above.

Draw a diagram

It is often helpful to draw a diagram of the problem, with important values labeled. Although almost every problem is stated using an illustration, we sometimes find it useful to draw an additional diagram.

Variables

We summarize the variables relating to the problem in a table. Some of these have values given in the problem statement or illustration. If we do not know the value of a variable, we enter the variable symbol. A variable table for the problem stated above is shown.

displacement	$\Delta x = 11.8$ m
acceleration	$a = 1.21$ m/s^2
elapsed time	$t = 3.14$ s
initial velocity	v_i
final velocity	v_f

There are two reasons we write the variables. One is so that if you see a variable with which you are unfamiliar, you can quickly see what it represents. The other is that it is another useful problem-solving technique: Write down everything you know. Sometimes you know more than you think you know! Some variables may also prompt you to think of ways to solve the problem.

After these two steps, we move to strategy.

What is the strategy?

The strategy is a summary of the sequence of steps we will follow in solving the problem. Some students who used this book early in its development called the strategy section "the hints," which is another way to think of the strategy. There are typically many ways to solve a problem; our strategy is the one we chose to employ. (As we point out in the text when we actually solve this problem, there is another efficient manner in which to solve it.)

For the problem above, our strategy was:

1. There are **two** unknowns, the initial and final velocities, so choose **two** equations that include these two unknowns and the values you do know.
2. Substitute known values and use algebra to reduce the two equations to one equation with a single unknown value.

Principles and equations

Principles and equations from physics and mathematics are often used to solve a problem. For the problem above, for example, these two linear motion equations that apply when acceleration is constant are useful:

$$v_f = v_i + at$$

$$\Delta x = \frac{1}{2}(v_i + v_f)t$$

The physics principles are the crucial points that the problems are attempting to reinforce. If they look quite familiar to you at some point: Great!

Step-by-step solution

We solve the problem (or work through the derivation) in a series of steps. We provide a reason for each step. If you want a more detailed explanation, you can click on a step, which causes a more detailed text explanation to appear on the right. Some students find the additional information quite helpful; others prefer the very brief explanation. It also varies depending on the difficulty of the problem – everyone can use a little help sometimes.

Here are the first three steps that we used to solve the problem above.

Step	Reason
1. $v_f = v_i + at$	first motion equation
2. $v_f = v_i + (1.21 \text{ m/s}^2)(3.14 \text{ s})$	substitute values
3. $v_f = v_i + 3.80 \text{ m/s}$	multiply

0.4 - Interactive checkpoints

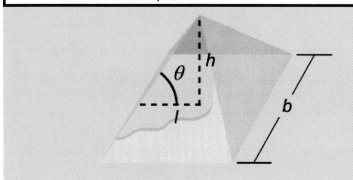

The great pyramid of Cheops has a square base with edges that are almost exactly 230 m long. The side faces of the pyramid make an angle of 51.8° with the ground.
The apex of the pyramid is directly above the center of the base. Find its height.

This section shows you an example of an interactive checkpoint. We chose a problem that uses mathematics you may be familiar with in case you would like to solve the problem yourself.

In interactive checkpoints, all of the problem-solving elements are initially hidden. You can open any element by clicking [Show] below.

You can check your answer at any time by entering it at the top and pressing [Check] to see if you are right. You will find this is far more efficient than keying all the information into the computer, which provides a good motivation for you to solve the problem yourself. However, if you are stuck, you can always have the computer help you.

In the parts called Variables, Strategy, and Physics principles and equations, the computer will show you the information you need when you ask. In the Physics principles and equations section, we show you the principles and equations you need to solve the problem, as well as some that do not apply directly to the problem.

In the Step-by-step solution, you choose from the equations by clicking on the one you think you need to use. You must enter the correct values in each Step-by-step part of the solution to proceed to the next step.

Answer:

$h = $ ☐ m

0.5 - Quizboards

Each chapter has a quizboard containing several multiple-choice conceptual and quantitative problems. There are over 250 quizboard problems throughout the textbook. Quizboards allow you to test your understanding of a chapter. You see a quizboard on the right.

Quizboards appear between the summary section and the problems section in every chapter. The quizboard for a chapter can be launched from the quizboard section by clicking on the image on the right side of the page. The quizboards are designed to enable you to review many of the crucial ideas in a chapter.

Each problem in a quizboard consists of four parts: the question, the answer choices, the hints, and the solution. If you think you know the answer to the problem, choose it and click the "Check answer" button. A message will appear telling you whether you are correct. You can keep trying until you get the problem right. If you are having trouble, click "Give me a hint". Every time you click this button, a new hint appears until there are no more hints available. You can always click "Show solution" if you find yourself completely stuck.

Use the "next" and "previous" buttons on the gray bar at the bottom of the window to navigate between problems. You do not have to answer a problem correctly before moving on, so you can skip problems and come back to them later. If you use the "previous" button to go back to a problem, it will appear unanswered (even if you answered it before) so that you can try the problem again.

Click on the image to the right to use a sample quizboard. You do not need to know any physics to answer these questions. Good luck!

0.6 - Highlighting and notes

You can add notes or highlight text on most sections of the textbook. Notes always appear at the top of the section. You can use a note to write short messages about key elements of a section, or to remind yourself not to forget the extra soccer practice or to pick up the groceries.

As the note above says, you insert notes by pressing Add Note at the bottom of the page. You remove a note by clicking on the Delete button located next to the note. Modify a note by pressing the Edit button.

The text you are reading now is highlighted. To highlight text, click the Highlight button at the bottom of the page to switch it from "Off" to "On". When it is "On", any text you select (by clicking on your mouse and dragging) will be highlighted. You can remove all highlighting from a section by pressing the "Clear" button.

If the text above is **not** highlighted, your operating system or browser does not enable us to offer this feature. For instance, the feature is not available on the Macintosh operating system OS X 10.2.

If you use a shared computer, the highlighting and notes features may be turned off. The preferences page allows you to enable or disable either of these features. You will find the preferences page by clicking on the Preferences button at the bottom of the page.

Notes and highlighting are not supported on our Web Access option or the trial version of the product on our web site.

0.7 - Online Homework

This textbook was designed to support online assessment of homework. Instructors can assign specific problems online, and you submit your responses over the Internet to a central computer. You can work offline and submit the answers when you are ready.

The computer checks the answers, and sends a report about your efforts, and the efforts of your peers, to your instructor. Your instructor can configure this service in a variety of fashions. For instance, they can set deadlines for homework assignments or decide if you are allowed to try answering a question a few times.

Online Homework is an optional feature; not all instructors will use it. If your instructor has supplied you with a login ID or told you to sign up for Online Homework, please log in now. If you are unsure, please check with your instructor.

If you want to learn more about on-line assessment in general, click here.

0.8 - Finding what you need in this book

You can navigate through the book using the Table of Contents button. When you roll your mouse over it, you will see three links.

The Chapter TOC link takes you to the table of contents for the chapter you are currently in. You will see more sections than you might see in a typical physics textbook table of contents. We chose to make it very easy to navigate to each element of the textbook by listing sample problems, derivations and other elements discretely.

The Main TOC link takes you to the list of all the chapters in the textbook. Clicking on the third link, Physics Factbook, opens a reference tool containing useful information including mathematics review topics and formulas, unit conversion factors, fundamental physical constants, properties of the elements, astronomical data, and physics equations. The Factbook also has a built-in search feature to help you find information quickly.

This textbook has no index, but likely you will find that entering text in the "search box" is more useful. Search is located at the bottom of each Web page. Search performs its task by looking at the name of each section, at the first (or essential) time any term is defined, and at some other types of text. Typing in a phrase like "kinetic energy" will produce a number of useful results.

When you use search, you do not have to worry about sequence: You do not have to guess whether we listed something under, say, "average velocity" or "velocity average." Search looks for the terms and presents them to you along with some of their context.

That is it for logistics. The people who worked on this textbook − about 50 of us − hope you enjoy it. We have a passion for physics, and we hope some of that carries on to you.

To explore the rest of the book, move your mouse over a Table of Contents button at the top or bottom of this page, and select the Main TOC.

Measurement and Mathematics

chapter 1

1.0 - Introduction

Heavyweight, lightweight, overweight, slender. Small, tall, vertically impaired, "how's the weather up there?" Gifted, average, 700 math/600 verbal, rocket scientist. Gorgeous, handsome, hunk, babe.

Humans like to measure things. Whether it is our body size, height, IQ or looks, everything seems to be fair game.

Physics will teach you to measure even more things. For example, quantities such as displacement, velocity and acceleration are crucial to understanding motion. Other topics have yet more things to quantify: Mass and period are concepts required to understand the movement of planets; resistance and current are used for analyzing electric circuits. Just as you have developed a vocabulary for the things you measure, so have physicists.

There are many different units for measuring different properties. It is possible to go all the way from A through Z in units: amperes, bars, centimeters, dynes, ergs, farads, grams, hertz, inches, joules, kilograms, liters, meters, newtons, ohms, pascals, quintals, rydbergs, slugs, teslas, unit magnetic poles, volts, webers, x units, years, and zettabars. (OK, we had to stretch for X, but it is a real unit.)

Physicists have so many units of measure at their disposal because they have plenty to measure. Physicists use amperes to tell how much electric current flows through a wire, "pascals" quantify pressure, and "teslas" are used to measure the strength of a magnetic field. If you so desired, you could become a units expert and impress (or worry) your classmates by casually noting that the U.S. tablespoon equals 1.04 Canadian tablespoons, or deftly differentiating between the barrel, U.K. Wine, versus the barrel, U.S. federal spirits, or the barrel, U.S. federal, all of which define slightly different volumes. Or you could become an international sophisticate, telling friends that one German *doppelzentner* equals about 77,162 U.K. *scruples,* which of course equals approximately 101.97 metric *glugs,* which comes out to 3120 *ukies,* a Libyan unit used for the sole purpose of measuring ostrich feathers and wool.

Fortunately, you do not need to learn units such as the ones mentioned immediately above, and you will learn the others over time. Textbooks like this one provide tables that specify the relationships between commonly used units and you will use these tables to convert between units.

1.1 - The metric system and the Système International d'Unités

Metric system: The dominant system of measurement in science and the world.

Historically, people chose units of measure related to everyday life (the "foot" is one example). Scientists continued this tradition, developing units such as "horsepower" to measure power.

The French challenged this philosophy of measurement during their Revolution, when they decided to give measurement a more scientific foundation. Instead of basing their system on things that change – the length of a person's foot changes during her lifetime, for example – the French based their system on what they viewed as constant. To accomplish this, they created units such as the meter, which they defined as a certain fraction of the Earth's circumference. (To be specific: one ten-millionth of the meridian passing through Paris from the equator to the North Pole. It turns out that the distance from the equator to the North Pole does vary, but the metric system's intent of consistency and measurability was exactly on target.)

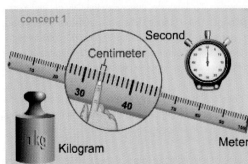

Metric system and the *Système International*
System defines fundamental units
Larger/smaller units based on powers of 10

Copyright 2000-2007 Kinetic Books Co. Chapter 01

The metric system is also based on another inspired idea: units of measurement should be based on powers of 10. This differs from the British system, which provides more variety: 12 inches in a foot, 5280 feet to a mile and so forth.

The metric system makes conversions much simpler to perform. For example, in order to calculate the number of inches in a mile, you would typically multiply by 5280 (for feet in a mile) and then by 12 (for inches in a foot). However, in the metric system, to convert between units, you typically multiply by a power of 10. For instance, to convert from kilometers to meters, you multiply by 1000. The prefix "kilo" means 1000.

The revolutionaries were a little extreme (as revolutionaries tend to be) and they held onto their position of power for only a decade or so. While some of their legacy (including their political art, rather mediocre as is much political art) has been forgotten, their clever and sensible metric system endures. Most scientists, and most countries, use the metric system today.

Scientists continue to update and refine the metric system. This expanded and updated system of measurement used today is called the *Système International d'Unités*, or SI. We typically use SI units in this textbook; several times, though, we refer to different units that may be better known to you or are commonly used in the sciences. We will discuss some of the SI units further in this chapter.

Over the years, scientists have refined measurement systems, making the definition of units ever more precise. For example, instead of being based on the Earth's circumference, the meter is now defined as the distance light travels in a vacuum during the time interval of 1/299,792,458 of a second. Although perhaps not as memorable as the initial standard, this definition is important because it is constant, precise, indestructible, and can be reproduced in laboratories around the world.

In addition to using meters for length, the *Système International* uses seconds (time), kilograms (mass), amperes (electric current), kelvins (temperature), moles (amount of substance) and candelas (luminous intensity). Many other *derived units* are based on these fundamental units. For instance, a newton measures force and is equal to kilograms times meters per second squared. On Earth, the force of gravity on a small apple is about one newton.

At the risk of drowning you in terminology, we should point out that you might also encounter references to the MKS (meter/kilogram/second) and CGS (centimeter/gram/second) systems. These systems are named for the units they use for length, mass and time.

1.2 - Prefixes

Metric units often have prefixes. Kilometers and centimeters both have prefixes before the word "meter." The prefixes instruct you to multiply or divide by a power of 10: **kilo** means multiply by 1000, so a kilometer equals 1000 meters. **Centi** means divide by 100, so a centimeter is one one-hundredth of a meter. In other words, there are 100 centimeters in a meter. The table in Equation 1 on the right lists the values for the most common prefixes.

Prefixes allow you to describe the unimaginably vast and small and everything in between. To illustrate, every day the City of New York produces 10 *giga*grams of garbage. The distance between transistors in a microprocessor is less than a *micro*meter. The power of the Sun is 400 *yotta*watts (a yotta corresponds to the factor of 10^{24}). It takes 3.34 *nano*seconds for light to travel one meter. The electric potential difference across a nerve cell is about 70 *milli*volts.

These prefixes can apply to any unit. You can use gigameters to conveniently quantify a vast distance, gigagrams to measure the mass of a huge object, or gigavolts to describe a large electrical potential difference.

Some of the most common prefixes – kilo, mega, and giga – are commonly used to describe the specifications of computers. The speed of a computer microprocessor is measured by how many computational cycles per second it can perform. Microprocessor speeds used to be specified in *mega*hertz (one million cycles per second) but are now specified in *giga*hertz (one billion cycles per second). Modem speeds have increased from *kilo*bits to *mega*bits per second. (Although bits are not part of the metric system, computer scientists use the same prefixes.)

concept 1

Prefixes
Create larger, smaller units

Philadelphia   New York City
129,000 meters
129 kilometers

0.09 meters
9 centimeters

equation 1

prefix	symbol	factor	prefix	symbol	factor
tera	T	10^{12}	deci	d	10^{-1}
giga	G	10^{9}	centi	c	10^{-2}
mega	M	10^{6}	milli	m	10^{-3}
kilo	k	10^{3}	micro	μ	10^{-6}
hecto	h	10^{2}	nano	n	10^{-9}
deka	da	10^{1}	pico	p	10^{-12}

The units of measurement you use are a matter of both convenience and convention. For example, snow skis are typically measured in centimeters; a ski labeled "170" is 170 centimeters long. However, it could also be called a 1.7-meter ski or a 1700-millimeter ski. The ski industry has decided that centimeters are reasonable units and has settled on their use as a convention.

In this textbook, you are most likely to encounter kilo, mega and giga on the large side of things and centi, milli, micro and nano on the small. Some other prefixes are not as common because they just do not seem that useful. Is it easier to say "a decameter" than the more straightforward 10 meters? And, for the extremely large and small, scientists often use another technique called scientific notation rather than prefixes.

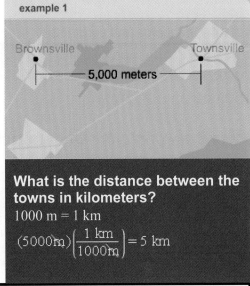

Prefixes
Common prefixes for powers of 10

example 1

What is the distance between the towns in kilometers?

$1000 \text{ m} = 1 \text{ km}$

$(5000 \text{ m})\left(\dfrac{1 \text{ km}}{1000 \text{ m}}\right) = 5 \text{ km}$

1.3 - Scientific notation

Scientific notation: A system, based on powers of 10, most useful for expressing very large and very small numbers.

Physicists like to measure the very big, the very small and everything in between. To express the results efficiently and clearly, they use scientific notation.

Scientific notation expresses a quantity as a number times a power of 10. Why is this useful? Here's an example: the Earth is about 149,000,000,000 meters from the Sun. You could express that distance as we just did, with a long string of zeros, or you could use scientific notation to write it as 1.49×10^{11} meters. The latter method has proven itself to be clearer and less prone to error.

The value on the left (1.49) is called the *leading value*. The power of 10 is typically chosen so the leading value is between one and 10. In the example immediately above, we multiplied by 10^{11} so that we could use 1.49. We also could have written 14.9×10^{10} or 0.149×10^{12} since all three values are equal, but a useful convention is to use a number between one and 10.

In case you have forgotten how to use exponents, here's a quick review. Ten is the *base number*. Ten to the first power is 10; 10^2 is ten to the second (ten squared) or 100; ten to the third is 10 times 10 times 10, or 1000. A positive exponent tells you how many zeros to add after the one. When the exponent is zero, the value is one: 10^0 equals one.

As mentioned, scientists also measure the very small. For example, a particle known as a muon has a mean lifespan of about 2.2 millionths of a second. Scientific notation provides a graceful way to express this number: 2.2×10^{-6} (2.2 times 10 to the negative sixth). To review the mathematics: ten to the minus one is 1/10; ten to the minus two is 1/100; ten to the minus three is 1/1000, and so forth.

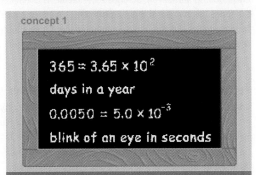

concept 1

$365 = 3.65 \times 10^2$

days in a year

$0.0050 = 5.0 \times 10^{-3}$

blink of an eye in seconds

Scientific notation
Number between 1 and 10 (leading value)
Multiplied by power of 10

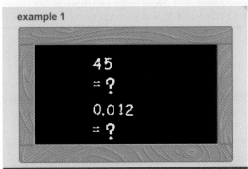

example 1

45
$= ?$

0.012
$= ?$

How do you write the numbers above in scientific notation?

You can also write 1.49×10^{11} as 1.49e11. The two are equivalent. You may have seen this notation in computer spreadsheet programs such as *Microsoft® Excel*. We do not use this "e" notation in the text of the book, but if you submit answers to homework problems or interactive checkpoints, you will use it there.

$$45 = 4.5 * 10 = 4.5 * 10^1$$
$$0.012 = 1.2 * 1/100 = 1.2 * 10^{-2}$$

1.4 - Standards and constants

Standard: A framework for establishing measurement units.

Physical constant: An empirically based value.

Physicists establish standards so they can measure things consistently; how they define a standard can change over time. For example, the length of a meter is now based on how far light travels in a precise interval of time. This replaces a standard based on the wavelength of light emitted by krypton-86. Prior to that, the meter was defined as the distance between enscribed marks on platinum-iridium bars. Advances in technology, and the requirement for increased precision, cause scientists to change the method used to define the standard. Scientists strive for precise standards that can be reproduced as needed and which will not change.

By choosing standards, scientists can achieve consistent results around the globe and compare the results of their experiments. Well-equipped labs can measure time using atomic clocks like the one shown in Concept 1 on the right. These clocks are based on a characteristic frequency of cesium atoms. You can access the official time, as maintained by an atomic clock, by clicking here.

You will encounter two types of constants in this textbook. First, there are mathematical constants like π or the number 2. Second, there are physical constants, such as the gravitational constant, which is represented with a capital G in equations. We show its value in Concept 2 on the right. Devices such as the torsion balance shown are used to gather data to determine the value of G. This is an active area of research, as G is the least precisely known of the major physical constants.

Constants such as G are used in many equations. G is used in Sir Isaac Newton's law of gravitation, an equation that relates the attractive force between two bodies to their masses and the square of the distance between them. You see this equation on the right.

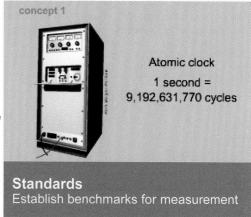

concept 1

Atomic clock
1 second =
9,192,631,770 cycles

Standards
Establish benchmarks for measurement

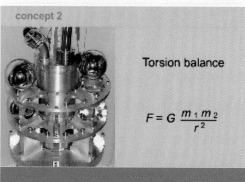

concept 2

Torsion balance

$$F = G \frac{m_1 m_2}{r^2}$$

Physical constants
Empirically determined values
$G = 6.674\ 2 \times 10^{-11}\ \text{N} \cdot \text{m}^2/\text{kg}^2$

1.5 - Length

If you live in a country that uses the metric system, you already have an intuitive sense of how long a meter is. You are likely taller than one meter, and probably shorter than two. If you are a basketball fan, you know that male professional basketball centers tend to be taller than two meters while female professional centers average about two meters.

If you live in a country, such as the United States, that still uses the British system, you may not be as familiar with the meter. A meter equals about 3.28 feet, or 39.4 inches, which is to say a meter is slightly longer than a yard. The kilometer is another unit of length commonly used in metric countries. You may have noticed that cars often have speedometers that show both miles per hour and kilometers per hour. A kilometer (1000 meters) equals about 0.621 miles. In track events, a metric mile is 1.50 kilometers, which is about 93% of a British mile.

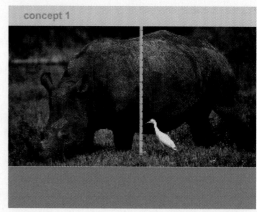

concept 1

Centimeters (one one-hundredth of a meter) are also frequently used metric units. One inch equals 2.54 centimeters, so a centimeter is about four tenths of an inch. One foot equals 30.48 centimeters. You see some common abbreviations in Equation 1 to the right: "m" for meters, "km" for kilometers and "cm" for centimeters.

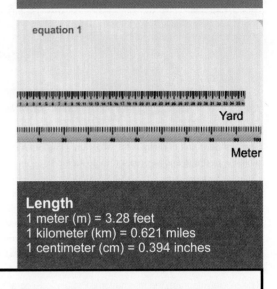

Length
Measured in meters (m)
Distance light travels in
$3.335\ 640\ 95 \times 10^{-9}$ seconds

equation 1

Yard

Meter

Length
1 meter (m) = 3.28 feet
1 kilometer (km) = 0.621 miles
1 centimeter (cm) = 0.394 inches

1.6 - Time

Despite the appeal of measuring a lifetime in daylights, sunsets, midnights, cups of coffee, inches, miles, laughter, or in strife, physicists still choose "seconds." How refreshingly simple!

However, as you might expect, physicists have developed a precise way to define a second. Atomic clocks, such as the one shown in Concept 1 to the right, rely on the fact that cesium-133 atoms undergo a transition when exposed to microwave radiation at a frequency of 9,192,631,770 cycles per second. These clocks are extremely accurate. Thousands of years would pass before two such clocks would differ even by a second. If you are an exceedingly precise person, you might want to consider buying a wristwatch that calibrates itself via radio signals from an atomic clock. For now, though, you can visit a web site that displays the current time as measured by an atomic clock.

In addition to being used to measure a second, atomic clocks are used to keep time. The length of a day on Earth, measured by the time to complete one rotation, is not constant. Why? The frictional force of tides causes the Earth to spin more slowly. This means that the day is getting longer (does it not just feel that way sometimes?). Every fifteen months or so since 1978, a leap second has been added to official time-keeping clocks worldwide to compensate for increased time it takes the Earth to complete a revolution.

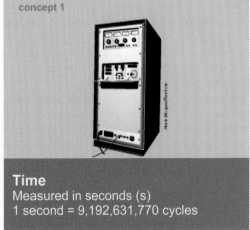

concept 1

Time
Measured in seconds (s)
1 second = 9,192,631,770 cycles

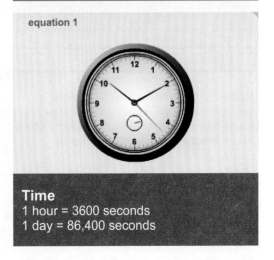

equation 1

Time
1 hour = 3600 seconds
1 day = 86,400 seconds

1.7 - Mass

Mass
Measured in kilograms (kg)
Resistance to change in motion
Not weight!

The standard unit of mass is the *kilogram*. (The British system equivalent is the *slug*, which is perhaps another reason to go metric.)

Physicists define mass as the property of an object that measures its resistance to a change in motion. A car has more mass than a bicycle. The three people shown straining at the car above will cause it to accelerate slowly; if they were pushing a bicycle instead, they could increase its speed much more quickly. Once they do set the car in motion, if they are not careful, its mass might prevent them from stopping it.

The official kilogram, the International Prototype Kilogram, is a cylinder of platinum-iridium alloy that resides at France's International Bureau of Weights and Measures. Copies of this kilogram reside in other secure facilities in different countries and are occasionally brought back for comparison to the original.

A liter of water has a mass of about one kilogram. A typical can of soda contains about 354 milliliters and has a mass of 0.354 kilograms.

equation 1

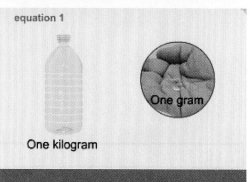

One gram

One kilogram

Mass
One kilogram = one liter of water
One gram = about 25 raindrops

It is tempting to write that one kilogram equals about 2.2 pounds, but this is wrong. The pound is a unit of weight; kilograms and slugs are units for mass. Weight measures the force of gravity that a planet exerts on an object, while mass reflects that object's resistance to change in motion. A classic example illustrates the difference: Your mass is the same on the Earth and the Moon, but you weigh less on the Moon because it exerts less gravitational force on you. On Earth, the force of gravity on one kilogram is 2.2 pounds but the force of gravity on a kilogram is only 0.36 pounds on the Moon.

Kilogram is abbreviated as kg. We typically use kilograms in this book, not grams (which are abbreviated as g).

The three units you need in order to understand motion, force and energy, the topics that start a physics textbook, are meters, kilograms and seconds. Other units used in studying these topics are derived from these fundamental units.

1.8 - Converting units

At times, you will need to convert units. Some conversion factors you know, such as 60 seconds in a minute, 12 inches in a foot, etc. Others, such as the number of seconds in a year, require a bit of calculation.

Keep in mind that if you do not use consistent units, troubles will arise. NASA dramatically illustrated the cost of such errors when it lost a spacecraft in 1999. A company supplied data to NASA based on British units (pounds) when NASA engineers expected metric units (newtons). Oops. That, alas, was the end

Speedometers often show speeds in both mi/h and km/h

of that space probe (and about $125 million and, one suspects, some engineer's NASA career).

As NASA's misfortune indicates, you need to make sure you use the correct units when solving physics problems. If a problem presents information about a quantity like time in different units, you need to convert that information to the same units.

You convert units by:

1. Knowing the conversion factor (say, 12 inches to a foot; 2.54 centimeters to an inch; $125 million to a spacecraft).
2. Multiplying by the conversion factor (such as 3.28 feet/1.00 meter) so that you cancel units in both the numerator and denominator. For example, to convert meters to feet, you multiply by 3.28 ft/m so that the meter units cancel. This may be easier to understand by viewing the example on the right.

In conversions, it is easy to make mistakes so it is good to check your work. To make sure you are applying conversions correctly, make sure the appropriate units cancel. To do this, you note the units associated with each value and each conversion factor.

As is shown on the right, a unit that is in both a denominator and a numerator cancels. You should look to see that the units that remain "uncancelled" are the ones that you desired. For instance, in the example problem, fluid ounces cancel out, and the desired units, milliliters, remain.

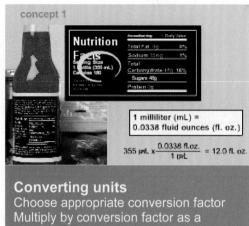

concept 1

1 milliliter (mL) = 0.0338 fluid ounces (fl. oz.)

$$355 \text{ mL} \times \frac{0.0338 \text{ fl.oz.}}{1 \text{ mL}} = 12.0 \text{ fl. oz.}$$

Converting units
Choose appropriate conversion factor
Multiply by conversion factor as a fraction
Make sure units cancel!

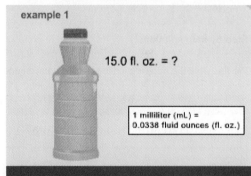

example 1

15.0 fl. oz. = ?

1 milliliter (mL) = 0.0338 fluid ounces (fl. oz.)

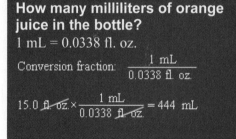

How many milliliters of orange juice in the bottle?
$1 \text{ mL} = 0.0338 \text{ fl. oz.}$

Conversion fraction: $\dfrac{1 \text{ mL}}{0.0338 \text{ fl. oz.}}$

$$15.0 \text{ fl. oz.} \times \frac{1 \text{ mL}}{0.0338 \text{ fl. oz.}} = 444 \text{ mL}$$

1.9 - Sample problem: conversions

$a = 9430 \text{ mi/hr}^2$

Express the car's acceleration in m/s^2, using scientific notation. For an extra challenge, state the result in terameters per second squared.

Variables

We will use a to represent the acceleration we are converting.

What is the strategy?

1. Express the car's acceleration in scientific notation.
2. Using conversion factors in scientific notation, convert miles to yards and then to meters.
3. Convert hours squared to minutes squared and then to seconds squared.
4. Go for the challenge! Convert to terameters.

Conversion factors and prefixes

1 mi = 1760 yd

1 yd = 0.914 m

1 h = 60 min

1 min = 60 s

tera = 10^{12}

Step-by-step solution

We first write the acceleration in scientific notation and convert miles to yards to meters.

Step	Reason
1. $a = 9430 \text{ mi/h}^2 = 9.43 \times 10^3 \text{ mi/h}^2$	scientific notation
2. $a = \left(9.43 \times 10^3 \, \dfrac{\cancel{\text{mi}}}{\text{h}^2}\right)\left(\dfrac{1.76 \times 10^3 \text{ yd}}{1 \, \cancel{\text{mi}}}\right)$ $a = 1.66 \times 10^7 \, \dfrac{\text{yd}}{\text{h}^2}$	multiply by factor converting miles to yards
3. $a = \left(1.66 \times 10^7 \, \dfrac{\cancel{\text{yd}}}{\text{h}^2}\right)\left(\dfrac{9.14 \times 10^{-1} \text{ m}}{1 \, \cancel{\text{yd}}}\right)$ $a = 1.52 \times 10^7 \dfrac{\text{m}}{\text{h}^2}$	multiply by factor converting yards to meters

Now we convert hours squared to minutes squared to seconds squared. Because the units we are converting are squared, we square the conversion factors. As requested, we state the final result in scientific notation.

Step		Reason
4.	$a = \left(1.52 \times 10^7 \ \dfrac{m}{h^2}\right)\left(\dfrac{1 \ h}{6.0 \times 10^1 \ min}\right)^2$ $a = 4.22 \times 10^3 \ \dfrac{m}{min^2}$	multiply by square of factor converting hours to minutes
5.	$a = \left(4.22 \times 10^3 \ \dfrac{m}{min^2}\right)\left(\dfrac{1 \ min}{6.0 \times 10^1 \ s}\right)^2$ $a = 1.17 \times 10^0 \ m/s^2$	multiply by square of factor converting minutes to seconds

Finally, we convert to terameters per second squared, or Tm/s^2. "Tera" means 10^{12}.

Step		Reason
6.	$a = \left(1.17 \times 10^0 \ \dfrac{m}{s^2}\right)\left(\dfrac{1 \ Tm}{10^{12} \ m}\right)$ $a = 1.17 \times 10^{-12} \ Tm/s^2$	multiply by conversion factor for terameters

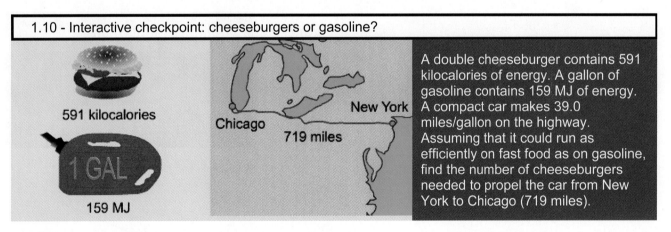

1.10 - Interactive checkpoint: cheeseburgers or gasoline?

591 kilocalories

1 GAL

159 MJ

Chicago
New York
719 miles

A double cheeseburger contains 591 kilocalories of energy. A gallon of gasoline contains 159 MJ of energy. A compact car makes 39.0 miles/gallon on the highway. Assuming that it could run as efficiently on fast food as on gasoline, find the number of cheeseburgers needed to propel the car from New York to Chicago (719 miles).

A kilocalorie is a unit used to measure food energy, and is often called a Calorie, spelled with a capital C. One calorie (small c) is equal to 4.19 J (joules).

Answer:

$N =$ [   ] cheeseburgers

As you proceed through your physics studies, you will find it necessary to understand the Pythagorean theorem, which is reviewed in this section. At the right, you see a right triangle (a triangle with a $90°$ angle). The Pythagorean theorem states that the square of the hypotenuse (the side opposite the right angle) equals the sum of the squares of the two legs. This equation is shown in Equation 1 to the right.

There are two specific right triangles that occur frequently in physics homework problems. In an *isosceles right triangle*, the two legs are the same length and the hypotenuse is the length of either leg times the square root of two. The angles of an isosceles right triangle are 45, 45 and 90 degrees, so it is also called a *45-45-90 triangle*.

When the angles of the triangle measure 30, 60 and 90 degrees, it is called a *30-60-90 triangle*. The shorter leg, the one opposite the $30°$ angle, is one half the length of the hypotenuse. This relationship makes for an easy mathematical calculation and makes this triangle a favorite in homework problems.

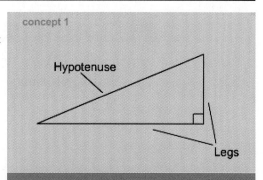

concept 1

Pythagorean theorem
Relates hypotenuse to legs of right triangle

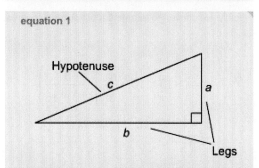

equation 1

Pythagorean theorem

$$c^2 = a^2 + b^2$$

c = length of hypotenuse
a, b = lengths of legs

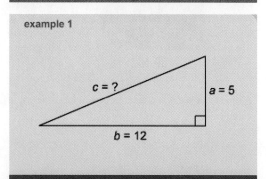

example 1

What is the length of the hypotenuse?
$c^2 = a^2 + b^2 = 5^2 + 12^2 = 25 + 144$
$c^2 = 169$
$c = \sqrt{169} = 13$

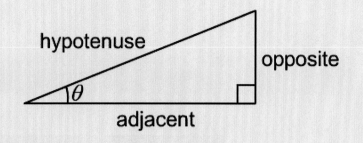

equation 1

Trigonometric functions

$\sin \theta$ = opposite / hypotenuse

$\cos \theta$ = adjacent / hypotenuse

$\tan \theta$ = opposite / adjacent

You will often encounter trigonometric functions in physics. You need to understand the basics of the sine, cosine and tangent, and their inverses: the arcsine, arccosine and arctangent.

The illustration above depicts an angle and three sides of a triangle. The sine (sin) of the angle θ (the Greek letter *theta*, pronounced "thay-tuh") equals the ratio of the side opposite the angle divided by the triangle's hypotenuse. "Opposite" means the leg across from the angle, as the diagram reflects.

The cosine (cos) of θ equals the ratio of the side of the triangle adjacent to the angle, divided by the hypotenuse. "Adjacent" means the leg that forms one side of the angle.

Finally, the tangent (tan) of θ equals the ratio of the opposite side divided by the adjacent side.

These three ratios are constant for a given angle in a right triangle, no matter what the size of the triangle. They are useful because you are often given information such as the length of the hypotenuse and the size of an angle, and then asked to calculate one of the legs of the triangle. For instance, if asked to calculate the opposite leg, you would multiply the sine of the angle by the hypotenuse.

You may also be asked to use the arcsine, the arccosine or the arctangent. These are often written as $\sin^{-1}$, $\cos^{-1}$ and $\tan^{-1}$. These are not the reciprocals of the sine, cosine and tangent! Rather, they supply the size of the angle when the value of the trigonometric function is known. For example, since $\sin 30°$ equals 0.5, the arcsine of 0.5 (or $\sin^{-1} 0.5$) equals $30°$. This is also often written as arcsin(0.5); arccos and arctan are the abbreviations for arccosine and arctangent.

In the old days, scientists consulted tables for these trigonometric values. Today, calculators and spreadsheets can calculate them for you.

example 1

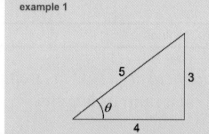

What is sin *θ*? cos *θ*? tan *θ*?

$\sin \theta$ = opposite / hypotenuse = 3/5

$\cos \theta$ = adjacent / hypotenuse = 4/5

$\tan \theta$ = opposite / adjacent = 3/4

equation 1

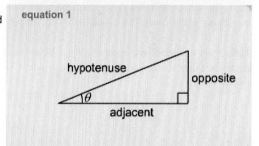

Inverse trigonometric functions

θ = arcsin (opposite / hypotenuse)

θ = arccos (adjacent / hypotenuse)

θ = arctan (opposite / adjacent)

Often written: $\sin^{-1}$, $\cos^{-1}$, $\tan^{-1}$

example 1

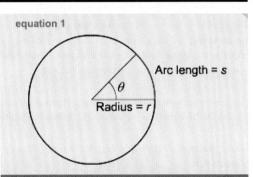

If the tangent of θ is 1, what is θ?
$\theta = \text{arctangent}(1) = 45°$

1.13 - Radians

Radian measure: A measurement of angles based on a ratio of lengths.

Angles are often measured or specified in degrees, but another unit, the *radian*, is useful in many computations. The radian measure of an angle is the ratio of two lengths on a circle. The angle and lengths are perhaps most easily understood by looking at the diagram in Equation 1 on the right. The *arc length* is the length of the arc on the circumference cut off by the angle when it is placed at the circle's center. The other length is the radius of the circle. The radian measure of the angle equals the arc length divided by the radius.

A 360° angle equals 2π radians. Why is this so? The angle 360° describes an entire circle. The arc length in this case equals the circumference ($2\pi r$) of a circle divided by the radius r of the circle. The radius factor cancels out, leaving 2π as the result.

Radians are dimensionless numbers. Why? Since a radian is a ratio of two lengths, the length units cancel out. However, we follow a radian measure with "rad" so it is clear what is meant.

equation 1

Arc length = s
θ
Radius = r

Radian measure

Angle = arc length / radius = s/r

$360° = 2\pi$ rad

· Radians are dimensionless
· Units: radians (rad)

example 1

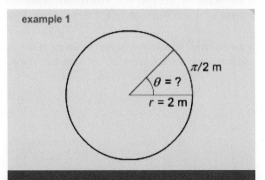

π/2 m
θ = ?
r = 2 m

What is the angle's measure in radians?

Angle = arc length / radius

$\theta = (\pi/2 \text{ m})/(2 \text{ m})$

1.14 - Sample problem: trigonometry

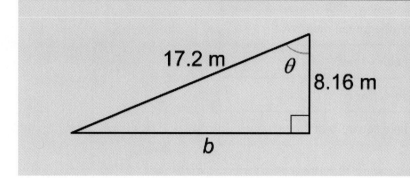

What is the length of side b of this triangle?

What is θ in degrees? in radians?

The lengths of two sides of a right triangle are shown.

Variables

short leg	$a = 8.16$ m
long leg	b
hypotenuse	$c = 17.2$ m
angle	θ

What is the strategy?

1. Use the Pythagorean theorem to calculate the length of the third side.
2. Calculate the cosine of θ and then use the arccosine function on a calculator (or consult a table) to determine θ in degrees.
3. Convert θ to radians.

Mathematics principles

$$c^2 = a^2 + b^2$$

$$\cos \theta = \text{adjacent/hypotenuse}$$

$$360° = 2\pi \text{ rad}$$

Step-by-step solution

First we use the Pythagorean theorem to find the length of the longer leg.

Step	Reason
1. $c^2 = a^2 + b^2$	Pythagorean theorem
2. $(17.2 \text{ m})^2 = (8.16 \text{ m})^2 + b^2$	enter values
3. $b^2 = 17.2^2 - 8.16^2 = 229$	solve for b^2
4. $b = 15.1$ m	take square root

Now, we use the lengths of the sides to find the value of the cosine of θ, and then look up the arccosine of this ratio.

Step	Reason
5. $\cos \theta = $ adjacent/hypotenuse	definition of cosine
6. $\cos \theta = (8.16 \text{ m})/(17.2 \text{ m})$	enter values
7. $\cos \theta = 0.474$	divide
8. $\theta = \arccos(0.474)$	definition of arccosine
9. $\theta = 61.7°$	use calculator

Finally, we convert the angle from degrees to radians.

Step	Reason
10. $\theta = (61.7°)(2\pi \text{ rad}/360°)$	multiply by conversion factor
11. $\theta = 1.08$ rad	multiplication and division

There are other ways to solve this problem. For example, you could first find θ using the arccosine function, and then use the tangent ratio to find the length of the third side.

1.15 - Interactive checkpoint: trigonometry

The great pyramid of Cheops has a square base with edges that are almost exactly 230 m long. The side faces of the pyramid make an angle of 51.8° with the ground.
The apex of the pyramid is directly above the center of the base. Find its height.

Answer:

$h =$ _____ m

1.16 - Gotchas

The goal of "gotchas" is to help you avoid common errors. (Not that your teacher's tests would ever try to make you commit any of these errors!)

Confusing weight and mass. You do not weigh 70 kilograms, or 80, or 60. However, those values could very well be your **mass**, which is an unchanging value that reflects your resistance to a change in motion.

Converting units with factors incorrectly oriented. There could probably be an essay written on this topic. *Make sure the units cancel!* is probably the best advice we can give. For example, if you are converting meters per second to miles per hour, begin by multiplying by a conversion fraction of 3600 seconds over one hour. This will cause the seconds to cancel and hours to be in the right place. (If this is not clear, write it down and strike out units. If it is still unclear, do some practice problems.) In any physics calculation, checking that the units on each side are consistent is a good technique.

Scientists use the *Système International d'Unités*, also known as the metric system of measurement. Examples of metric units are meters, kilograms, and seconds.

In these systems, units that measure the same property, for example units for mass, are related to each other by powers of ten. Unit prefixes tell you how many powers of ten. For example, a kilogram is 1000 grams and a kilometer is 1000 meters, while a milligram is one one-thousandth of a gram, and a millimeter is one-thousandth of a meter.

Numbers may be expressed in scientific notation. Any number can be written as a number between 1 and 10, multiplied by a power of ten. For example, $875.6 = 8.756 \times 10^2$.

A standard is an agreed-on basis for establishing measurement units, like defining the kilogram as the mass of a certain platinum-iridium cylinder that is kept at the International Bureau of Weights and Measures, near Paris. A physical constant is an empirically measured value that does not change, such as the speed of light.

In the metric system, the basic unit of length is the meter; time is measured in seconds; and mass is measured in kilograms.

Sometimes a problem will require you to do unit conversion. Work in fractions so that you can cancel like units, and make sure that the units are of the same type (all are units of length, for instance).

The Pythagorean theorem states that the square of the hypotenuse of a triangle is equal to the sum of the squares of the two legs.

$$c^2 = a^2 + b^2$$

Trigonometric functions, such as sine, cosine and tangent, relate the angles of a right triangle to the lengths of its sides.

Radians (rad) measure angles. The radian measure of an angle located at the center of a circle equals the arc length it cuts off on the circle, divided by the radius of the circle.

Equations

Prefixes

giga (G) $= 10^9$

mega (M) $= 10^6$

kilo (k) $= 10^3$

centi (c) $= 10^{-2}$

milli (m) $= 10^{-3}$

micro (μ) $= 10^{-6}$

nano (n) $= 10^{-9}$

Pythagorean Theorem

$c^2 = a^2 + b^2$

Trigonometric functions

$\sin \theta =$ opposite / hypotenuse

$\cos \theta =$ adjacent / hypotenuse

$\tan \theta =$ opposite / adjacent

Radian measure

Angle $=$ arc length / radius $= s / r$

$360° = 2\pi$ rad

2.0 - Introduction

Objects move: Balls bounce, cars speed, and spaceships accelerate. We are so familiar with the concept of motion that we use sophisticated physics terms in everyday language. For example, we might say that a project has reached "escape velocity" or, if it is going less well, that it is in "free fall."

In this chapter, you will learn more about motion, a field of study called *kinematics*. You will become familiar with concepts such as velocity, acceleration and displacement. For now, the focus is on how things move, not what causes them to move. Later, you will study *dynamics*, which centers on forces and how they affect motion. Dynamics and kinematics make up *mechanics*, the study of force and motion.

Two key concepts in this chapter are velocity and acceleration. Velocity is how fast something is moving (its speed) **and** in what direction it is moving. Acceleration is the rate of change in velocity. In this chapter, you will have many opportunities to learn about velocity and acceleration and how they relate. To get a feel for these concepts, you can experiment by using the two simulations on the right. These simulations are versions of the tortoise and hare race. In this classic parable, the steady tortoise always wins the race. With your help, though, the hare stands a chance. (After all, this is your physics course, not your literature course.)

In the first simulation, the tortoise has a head start and moves at a constant velocity of three meters per second to the right. The hare is initially stationary; it has zero velocity. You set its acceleration − in other words, how much its velocity changes each second. The acceleration you set is constant throughout the race. Can you set the acceleration so that the hare crosses the finish line first and wins the race? To try, click on Interactive 1, enter an acceleration value in the entry box in the simulation, and press GO to see what happens. Press RESET if you want to try again. Try acceleration values up to 10 meters per second squared. (At this acceleration, the velocity increases by 10 meters per second every second. Values larger than this will cause the action to occur so rapidly that the hare may quickly disappear off the screen.)

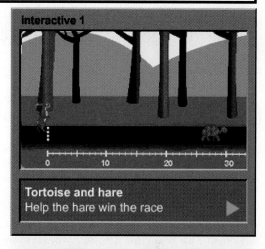

interactive 1

Tortoise and hare
Help the hare win the race ▶

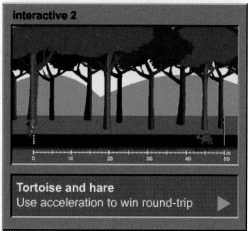

interactive 2

Tortoise and hare
Use acceleration to win round-trip ▶

It does not really matter if you can cause the hare to beat this rather fast-moving tortoise. However, we do want you to try a few different rates of acceleration and see how they affect the hare's velocity. Nothing particularly tricky is occurring here; you are simply observing two basic properties of motion: velocity and acceleration.

In the second simulation, the race is a round trip. To win the race, a contestant needs to go around the post on the right and then return to the starting line. The tortoise has been given a head start in this race. When you start the simulation, the tortoise has already rounded the post and is moving at a constant velocity on the homestretch back to the finish line.

In this simulation, when you press GO the hare starts off moving quickly to the right. Again, you supply a value for its acceleration. The challenge is to supply a value for the hare's acceleration so that it turns around at the post and races back to beat the tortoise. (Hint: Think negative! Acceleration can be either positive or negative.)

Again, it does not matter if you win; we want you to notice how acceleration affects velocity. Does the hare's velocity ever become zero? Negative? To answer these questions, click on Interactive 2, enter the acceleration value for the hare in the gauge, press GO to see what happens, and RESET to try again. You can also use PAUSE to stop the action and see the velocity at any instant. Press PAUSE again to restart the race.

We have given you a fair number of concepts in this introduction. These fundamentals are the foundation of the study of motion, and you will learn much more about them shortly.

Position: The location of an object; in physics, typically specified with graph coordinates.

Position tells you location.

There are many ways to describe location: Beverly Hills 90210; "...a galaxy far, far away"; "as far away from you as possible." Each works in its own context.

Physicists often use numbers and graphs instead of words and phrases. Numbers and graphs enable them (and you) to analyze motion with precision and consistency. In this chapter, we will analyze objects that move in one dimension along a line, like a train moving along a flat, straight section of track.

To begin, we measure position along a *number line*. Two toy figures and a number line are shown in the illustrations to the right. As you can see, the zero point is called the *origin*. Positive numbers are on the right and negative numbers are on the left.

By convention, we draw number lines from left to right. The number line could reflect an object's position in east and west directions, or north and south, or up and down; the important idea is that we can specify positions by referring to points on a line.

When an object moves in one dimension, you can specify its position by its location on the number line. The variable x specifies that position. For example, as shown in the illustration for Equation 1, the hiker stands at position $x = 3.0$ meters and the toddler is at position $x = -2.0$ meters.

Later, you will study objects that move in multiple dimensions. For example, a basketball free throw will initially travel both up and forward. For now, though, we will consider objects that move in one dimension.

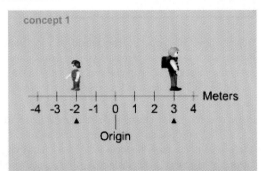

concept 1

Position
Location of an object
Relative to origin

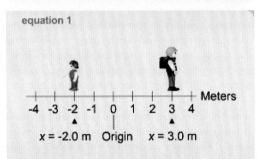

equation 1

$x = -2.0$ m   Origin $x = 3.0$ m

Position
x represents position
Units: meters (m)

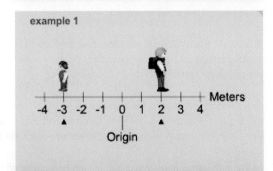

example 1

What are the positions of the figures?
Hiker: $x = 2.0$ m
Toddler: $x = -3.0$ m

Displacement: The direction and distance of the shortest path between an initial and final position.

You use the concept of distance every day. For example, you are told a home run travels 400 ft (122 meters) or you run the metric mile (1.5 km) in track (or happily watch others run a metric mile).

Displacement adds the concept of direction to distance. For example, you go approximately 954 mi (1540 km) **south** when you travel from Seattle to Los Angeles; the summit of Mount Everest is 29,035 ft (8849.9 meters) **above** sea level. (You may have noticed we are using both metric and English units. We will do this only for the first part of this chapter, with the thought that this may prove helpful if you are familiarizing yourself with the metric system.)

Sometimes just distance matters. If you want to be a million miles away from your younger brother, it does not matter whether that's east, north, west or south. The distance is called the magnitude − the amount − of the displacement.

Direction, however, can matter. If you walk 10 blocks north of your home, you are at a different location than if you walk 10 blocks south. In physics, direction often matters. For example, to get a ball to the ground from the top of a tall building, you can simply drop the ball. Throwing the ball back up requires a very strong arm. Both the direction and distance of the ball's movement matters.

The definition of displacement is precise: the direction and length of the **shortest** path from the **initial** to the **final** position of an object's motion. As you may recall from your mathematics courses, the shortest path between two points is a straight line. Physicists use arrows to indicate the direction of displacement. In the illustrations to the right, the arrow points in the direction of the mouse's displacement.

Physicists use the Greek letter Δ (delta) to indicate a change or difference. A change in position is displacement, and since x represents position, we write Δx to indicate displacement. You see this notation, and the equation for calculating displacement, to the right. In the equation, x_f represents the final position (the subscript f stands for final) and x_i represents the initial position (the subscript i stands for initial).

Displacement is a vector. A vector is a quantity that must be stated in terms of its direction and its magnitude. Magnitude means the size or amount. "Move five meters to the right" is a description of a vector. Scalars, on the other hand, are quantities that are stated solely in terms of magnitude, like "a dozen eggs." There is no direction for a quantity of eggs, just an amount.

In one dimension, a positive or negative sign is enough to specify a direction. As mentioned, numbers to the right of the origin are positive, and those to the left are negative. This means displacement to the right is positive, and to the left it is negative. For instance, you can see in Example 1 that the mouse's car starts at the position +3.0 meters and moves to the left to the position −1.0 meters. (We measure the position at the middle of the car.) Since it moves to the left 4.0 meters, its displacement is −4.0 meters.

Displacement measures the distance solely between the beginning and end of motion. We can use dance to illustrate this point. Let's say you are dancing and you take three

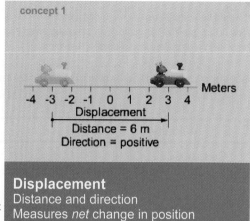

concept 1

Displacement
Distance and direction
Measures *net* change in position

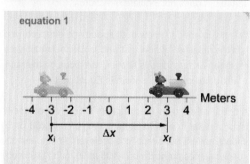

equation 1

Displacement

$$\Delta x = x_f - x_i$$

Δx = displacement
x_f = final position
x_i = initial position
Units: meters (m)

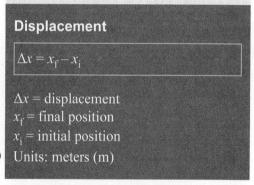

example 1

What is the mouse car's displacement?
$\Delta x = x_f - x_i$

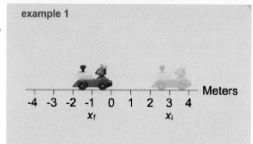
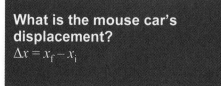

steps forward and two steps back. Although you moved a total of five steps, your displacement after this maneuver is one step forward.

$$\Delta x = -1.0 \ \text{m} - 3.0 \ \text{m}$$
$$\Delta x = -4.0 \ \text{m}$$

It would be better to use signs to describe the dance directions, so we could describe forward as "positive" and backwards as "negative." Three steps forward and two steps back yield a displacement of positive one step.

Since displacement is in part a measure of distance, it is measured with units of length. Meters are the SI unit for displacement.

2.3 - Velocity

Velocity: Speed and direction.

You are familiar with the concept of speed. It tells you how fast something is going: 55 miles per hour (mi/h) is an example of speed. The speedometer in a car measures speed but does not indicate direction.

When you need to know both speed and direction, you use velocity. Velocity is a vector. It is the measure of how fast **and** in which direction the motion is occurring. It is represented by v. In this section, we focus on average velocity, which is represented by v with a bar over it, as shown in Equation 1.

A police officer uses the concepts of both speed and velocity in her work. She might issue a ticket to a motorist for driving 36 mi/h (58 km/h) in a school zone; in this case, speed matters but direction is irrelevant. In another situation, she might be told that a suspect is fleeing **north** on I-405 at 90 mi/h (149 km/h); now velocity is important because it tells her both how fast and in what direction.

To calculate an object's average velocity, divide its displacement by the time it takes to move that displacement. This time is called the elapsed time, and is represented by Δt. The direction for velocity is the same as for the displacement.

For instance, let's say a car moves positive 50 mi (80 km) between the hours of 1 P.M. and 3 P.M. Its displacement is positive 50 mi, and two hours elapse as it moves that distance. The car's average velocity equals +50 miles divided by two hours, or +25 mi/h (+40 km/h). Note that the direction is positive because the displacement was positive. If the displacement were negative, then the velocity would also be negative.

At this point in the discussion, we are intentionally ignoring any variations in the car's velocity. Perhaps the car moves at constant speed, or maybe it moves faster at certain times and then slower at others. All we can conclude from the information above is that the car's **average** velocity is +25 mi/h.

Velocity has the dimensions of length divided by time; the units are meters per second (m/s).

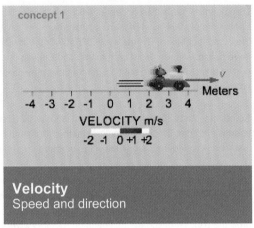

concept 1

Velocity
Speed and direction

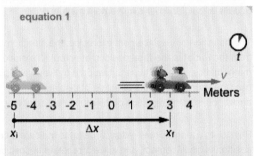

equation 1

Velocity

$$\bar{v} = \Delta x / \Delta t$$

$\bar{v} = $ (average) velocity
$\Delta x = $ displacement
$\Delta t = $ elapsed time
Units: meters/second (m/s)

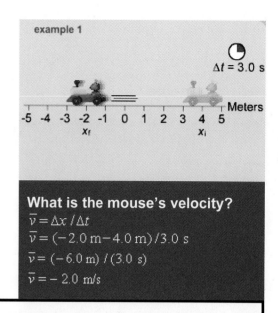

example 1

$\Delta t = 3.0$ s

Meters

-5 -4 -3 -2 -1 0 1 2 3 4 5

x_f x_i

What is the mouse's velocity?

$\bar{v} = \Delta x / \Delta t$

$\bar{v} = (-2.0\,\text{m} - 4.0\,\text{m}) / 3.0\,\text{s}$

$\bar{v} = (-6.0\,\text{m}) / (3.0\,\text{s})$

$\bar{v} = -2.0$ m/s

2.4 - Average velocity

Average velocity: Displacement divided by elapsed time.

Average velocity equals displacement divided by the time it takes for the displacement to occur.

For example, if it takes you two hours to move positive 100 miles (160 kilometers), your average velocity is +50 mi/h (80 km/h). Perhaps you drive a car at a constant velocity. Perhaps you drive really fast, slow down for rush-hour traffic, drive fast again, get pulled over for a ticket, and then drive at a moderate speed. In either case, because your displacement is 100 mi and the elapsed time is two hours, your average velocity is +50 mi/h.

Since the average velocity of an object is calculated from its displacement, you need to be able to state its initial and final positions. In Example 1 on the right, you are shown the positions of three towns and asked to calculate the average velocity of a trip. You must calculate the displacement from the initial to final position to determine the average velocity.

A classic physics problem tempts you to err in calculating average velocity. The problem runs like this: "A hiker walks one mile at two miles per hour, and the next mile at four miles per hour. What is the hiker's average velocity?" If you average two and four and answer that the average velocity is three mi/h, you will have erred. To answer the problem, you must first calculate the elapsed time. You cannot simply average the two velocities. It takes the hiker 1/2 an hour to cover the first mile, but only 1/4 an hour to walk the second mile, for a total elapsed time of 3/4 of an hour. The average velocity equals two miles divided by 3/4 of an hour, which is a little less than three miles per hour.

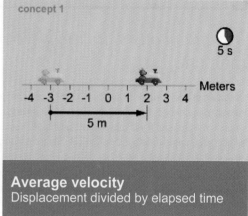

concept 1

5 s

Meters

-4 -3 -2 -1 0 1 2 3 4

5 m

Average velocity
Displacement divided by elapsed time

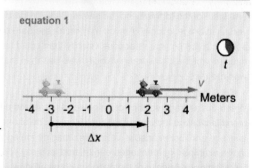

equation 1

t

v

Meters

-4 -3 -2 -1 0 1 2 3 4

Δx

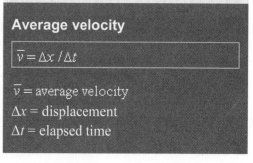

Average velocity

$\bar{v} = \Delta x / \Delta t$

$\bar{v}$ = average velocity

Δx = displacement

Δt = elapsed time

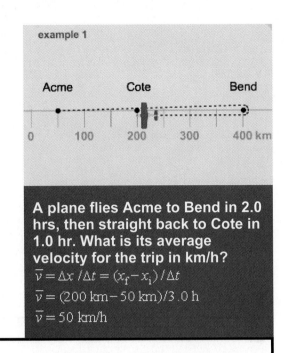

example 1

Acme   Cote   Bend

0   100   200   300   400 km

A plane flies Acme to Bend in 2.0 hrs, then straight back to Cote in 1.0 hr. What is its average velocity for the trip in km/h?

$$\bar{v} = \Delta x / \Delta t = (x_f - x_i)/\Delta t$$
$$\bar{v} = (200\ \text{km} - 50\ \text{km})/3.0\ \text{h}$$
$$\bar{v} = 50\ \text{km/h}$$

2.5 - Instantaneous velocity

Instantaneous velocity: Velocity at a specific moment.

Objects can speed up or slow down, or they can change direction. In other words, their velocity can change. For example, if you drop an egg off a 40-story building, the egg's velocity will change: It will move faster as it falls. Someone on the building's 39th floor would see it pass by with a different velocity than would someone on the 30th.

When we use the word "instantaneous," we describe an object's velocity at a particular instant. In Concept 1, you see a snapshot of a toy mouse car at an instant when it has a velocity of positive six meters per second.

The fable of the tortoise and the hare provides a classic example of instantaneous versus average velocity. As you may recall, the hare seemed faster because it could achieve a greater instantaneous velocity than could the tortoise. But the hare's long naps meant that its average velocity was less than that of the tortoise, so the tortoise won the race.

When the average velocity of an object is measured over a very short elapsed time, the result is close to the instantaneous velocity. The shorter the elapsed time, the closer the average and instantaneous velocities. Imagine the egg falling past the 39th floor window in the example we mentioned earlier, and let's say you wanted to determine its instantaneous velocity at the midpoint of the window.

You could use a stopwatch to time how long it takes the egg to travel from the top to the bottom of the window. If you then divided the height of the window by the elapsed time, the result would be close to the instantaneous velocity. However, if you measured the time for the egg to fall from 10 centimeters above the window's midpoint to 10 centimeters below, and used that displacement and elapsed time, the result would be even closer to the instantaneous velocity at the window's midpoint. As you repeated this process "to the limit" – measuring shorter and shorter distances and elapsed times (perhaps using motion sensors to provide precise values) – you would get values closer and closer to the instantaneous velocity.

To describe instantaneous velocity mathematically, we use the terminology shown in Equation 1. The arrow and the word "lim" mean the limit

concept 1

-4 -3 -2 -1 0 1 2 3 4 Meters

VELOCITY m/s

-6 -5 -4 -3 -2 -1 0 +1 +2 +3 +4 +5 +6

Instantaneous velocity
Velocity at a specific moment

equation 1

Instantaneous velocity

$$v = \lim_{\Delta t \to 0} \frac{\Delta x}{\Delta t}$$

v = instantaneous velocity
Δx = displacement
Δt = elapsed time

as Δt approaches zero. The limit is the value approached by the calculation as it is performed for smaller and smaller intervals of time.

To give you a sense of velocity and how it changes, let's again use the example of the egg. We calculate the velocity at various times using an equation you may have not yet encountered, so we will just tell you the results. Let's assume each floor of the building is four meters (13 ft) high and that the egg is being dropped in a vacuum, so we do not have to worry about air resistance slowing it down.

One second after being dropped, the egg will be traveling at 9.8 meters per second; at three seconds, it will be traveling at 29 m/s; at five seconds, 49 m/s (or 32 ft/s, 96 ft/s and 160 ft/s, respectively.)

After seven seconds, the egg has an instantaneous velocity of 0 m/s. Why? The egg hit the ground at about 5.7 seconds and therefore is not moving. (We assume the egg does not rebound, which is a reasonable assumption with an egg.)

Physicists usually mean "instantaneous velocity" when they say "velocity" because instantaneous velocity is often more useful than average velocity. Typically, this is expressed in statements like "the velocity when the elapsed time equals three seconds."

2.6 - Position-time graph and velocity

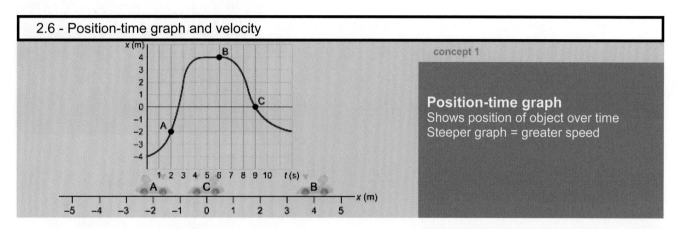

concept 1

Position-time graph
Shows position of object over time
Steeper graph = greater speed

A graph of an object's position over time is a useful tool for analyzing motion. You see such a position-time graph above. Values on the vertical axis represent the mouse car's position, and time is plotted on the horizontal axis. You can see from the graph that the mouse car starts at position $x = -4$ m, then moved to the position $x = +4$ m at about $t = 4.5$ s, stayed ... of seconds, and then reached the position $x = -2$ m ... motion.

Where th... 's position is not
changin... ...ep, position
is chan...

Disp... ...me graph can be
use... ...ope of a straight
lin... ...ocity between them.

... a line is calculated by
... horizontal direction,
... es are the x positions
... the change in position,
... s the elapsed time. This is
... apsed time.

You see this relatio... ...1. Since the slope of the line
shown in this illustration is p... ...between the two points on the
line is positive. Since the mouse mov... ...ween these points, its
displacement is positive, which confirms that it... ge velocity is positive as well.

(handwritten note overlaid)
$t = \dfrac{32.5 \times 2}{9.8}$
$\dfrac{325.2}{659} \div 9.8 = .$

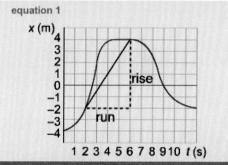

equation 1

Average velocity
Slope of line between two points
$\bar{v} = \text{rise/run} = \Delta x / \Delta t$

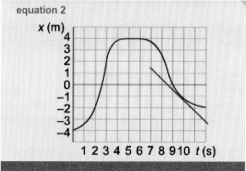

equation 2

The slope of the tangent line for any point on a straight-line segment of a position-time graph is constant. When the slope is constant, the velocity is constant. An example of constant velocity is the horizontal section of the graph that includes the point B in the illustration above.

The slope of a tangent line at different points on a curve is **not** constant. The slope at a single point on a curve is determined by the slope of the tangent line to the curve at that point. You see a tangent line illustrated in Equation 2. The slope as measured by the tangent line equals the **instantaneous** velocity at the point. The slope of the tangent line in Equation 2 is negative, so the velocity there is negative. At that point, the mouse is moving from right to left. The negative displacement over a short time interval confirms that its velocity is negative.

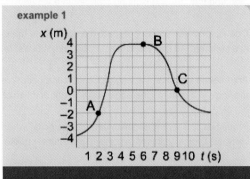

Instantaneous velocity
Slope of tangent line at point

example 1

What is the average velocity between points A and B?

$$\overline{v} = \text{rise/run}$$

$$\overline{v} = \frac{4.0\,\text{m} - (-2.0\,\text{m})}{6.0\,\text{s} - 2.0\,\text{s}}$$

$$\overline{v} = 1.5\,\text{m/s}$$

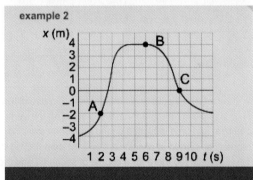

example 2

Consider the points A, B and C. Where is the instantaneous velocity zero? Where is it positive? Where is it negative?

Zero at B

Positive at A

Negative at C

2.7 - Interactive problem: draw a position-time graph

In this section, you are challenged to match a pre-drawn position-time graph by moving a ball along a number line. As you drag the ball, its position at each instant will be graphed. Your challenge is to get as close as you can to the target graph.

When you open the interactive simulation on the right, you will see a graph and a coordinate system with x positions on the vertical axis and time on the horizontal axis. Below the graph is a ball on a number line. Examine the graph and decide how you will move the ball over the 10 seconds to best match the target graph. You may find it helpful to think about the velocity described by the target graph. Where is it increasing? decreasing? zero? If you are not sure, review the section on position-time graphs and velocity.

You can choose to display a graph of the velocity of the motion of the ball as described by the target graph by clicking a checkbox. We encourage you to think first about what the velocity will be and use this checkbox to confirm your hypothesis.

Create your graph by dragging the ball and watching the graph of its motion. You can press RESET and try again as often as you like.

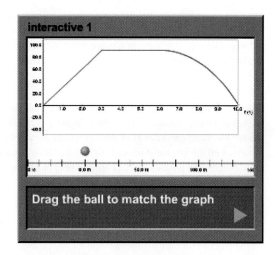

interactive 1

Drag the ball to match the graph

2.8 - Acceleration

Acceleration: Change in velocity.

When an object's velocity changes, it accelerates. Acceleration measures the **rate** at which an object speeds up, slows down or changes direction. Any of these variations constitutes a change in velocity. The letter a represents acceleration.

Acceleration is a popular topic in sports car commercials. In the commercials, acceleration is often expressed as how fast a car can go from zero to 60 miles per hour (97 km/h, or 27 m/s). For example, a current model Corvette® automobile can reach 60 mi/h in 4.9 seconds. There are even hotter cars than this in production.

To calculate average acceleration, divide the change in instantaneous velocity by the elapsed time, as shown in Equation 1. To calculate the acceleration of the Corvette, divide its change in velocity, from 0 to 27 m/s, by the elapsed time of 4.9 seconds. The car accelerates at an average rate of 5.5 m/s per second. We typically express this as 5.5 meters per second squared, or 5.5 m/s^2. (This equals 18 ft/s^2, and with this observation we will cease stating values in both measurement systems, in order to simplify the expression of numbers.) Acceleration is measured in units of length divided by time squared. Meters per second squared (m/s^2) express acceleration in SI units.

Let's assume the car accelerates at a constant rate; this means that each second the Corvette moves 5.5 m/s faster. At one second, it is moving at 5.5 m/s; at two seconds, 11 m/s; at three seconds, 16.5 m/s; and so forth. The car's velocity increases by 5.5 m/s every second.

Since acceleration measures the change in **velocity**, an object can accelerate even while it is moving at a constant **speed**. For instance, consider a car moving around a curve. Even if the car's speed remains constant, it accelerates because the change in the car's direction means its velocity (speed plus direction) is changing.

Acceleration can be positive or negative. If the Corvette uses its brakes to go from +60 to 0 mi/h in 4.9 seconds, its velocity is decreasing just as fast as it was increasing before. This is an example of negative acceleration.

A racing car accelerates.

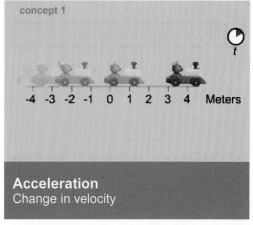

concept 1

Acceleration
Change in velocity

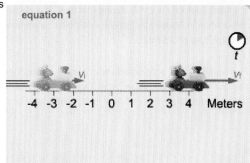

equation 1

You may want to think of negative acceleration as "slowing down," but be careful! Let's say a train has an initial velocity of **negative** 25 m/s and that changes to **negative** 50 m/s. The train is moving at a faster rate (speeding up) but it has negative acceleration. To be precise, its negative acceleration causes an increasingly negative velocity.

Velocity and acceleration are related but distinct values for an object. For example, an object can have **positive** velocity and **negative** acceleration. In this case, it is slowing down. An object can have zero velocity, yet be accelerating. For example, when a ball bounces off the ground, it experiences a moment of zero velocity as its velocity changes from negative to positive, yet it is accelerating at this moment since its velocity is changing.

Acceleration

$$\bar{a} = \Delta v \,/\, \Delta t$$

$\bar{a}$ = (average) acceleration
Δv = change in instantaneous velocity
Δt = elapsed time
Units: meters per second squared
(m/s²)

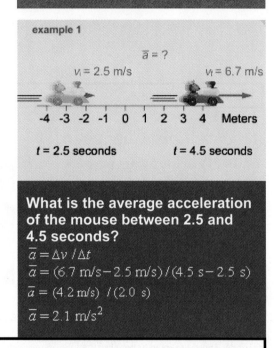

example 1

$\bar{a} = ?$

$v_i = 2.5$ m/s $v_f = 6.7$ m/s

-4 -3 -2 -1 0 1 2 3 4   Meters

$t = 2.5$ seconds $t = 4.5$ seconds

What is the average acceleration of the mouse between 2.5 and 4.5 seconds?

$$\bar{a} = \Delta v \,/\, \Delta t$$
$$\bar{a} = (6.7 \text{ m/s} - 2.5 \text{ m/s}) / (4.5 \text{ s} - 2.5 \text{ s})$$
$$\bar{a} = (4.2 \text{ m/s}) \,/\, (2.0 \text{ s})$$
$$\bar{a} = 2.1 \text{ m/s}^2$$

2.9 - Average acceleration

Average acceleration: The change in instantaneous velocity divided by the elapsed time.

Average acceleration is the change in instantaneous velocity over a period of elapsed time. Its definition is shown in Equation 1 to the right.

We will illustrate average acceleration with an example. Let's say you are initially driving a car at 12 meters per second and 8 seconds later you are moving at 16 m/s. The change in velocity is 4 m/s during that time; the elapsed time is eight seconds. Dividing the change in velocity by the elapsed time determines that the car accelerates at an average rate of 0.5 m/s².

Perhaps the car's acceleration was greater during the first four seconds and less during the last four seconds, or perhaps it was constant the entire eight seconds. Whatever the case, the average acceleration is the same, since it is defined using the initial and final instantaneous velocities.

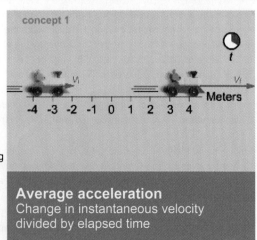

concept 1

v_i v_f

-4 -3 -2 -1 0 1 2 3 4   Meters

Average acceleration
Change in instantaneous velocity divided by elapsed time

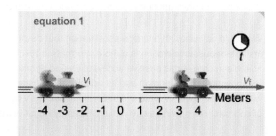

Average acceleration

$$\bar{a} = \Delta v / \Delta t$$

$\bar{a}$ = average acceleration
Δv = change in instantaneous velocity
Δt = elapsed time

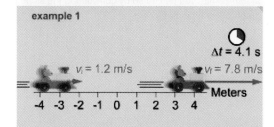

What is the mouse's average acceleration?

$\bar{a} = \Delta v / \Delta t$
$\bar{a} = (7.8 \text{ m/s} - 1.2 \text{ m/s}) / (4.1 \text{ s})$
$\bar{a} = 1.6 \text{ m/s}^2$

2.10 - Instantaneous acceleration

Instantaneous acceleration: Acceleration at a particular moment.

You have learned that velocity can be either average or instantaneous. Similarly, you can determine the average acceleration or the instantaneous acceleration of an object.

We use the mouse in Concept 1 on the right to show the distinction between the two. The mouse moves toward the trap and then wisely turns around to retreat in a hurry. The illustration shows the mouse as it moves toward and then hurries away from the trap. It starts from a rest position and moves to the right with increasingly positive velocity, which means it has a positive acceleration for an interval of time. Then it slows to a stop when it sees the trap, and its positive velocity decreases to zero (this is negative acceleration). It then moves back to the left with increasingly negative velocity (negative acceleration again). If you would like to see this action occur again in the

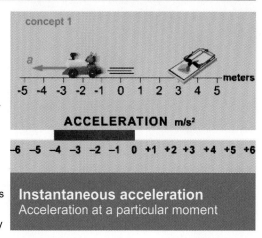

Instantaneous acceleration
Acceleration at a particular moment

Concept 1 graphic, press the refresh button in your browser.

We could calculate an average acceleration, but describing the mouse's motion with instantaneous acceleration is a more informative description of that motion. At some instants in time, it has positive acceleration and at other instants, negative acceleration. By knowing its acceleration and its velocity at an instant in time, we can determine whether it is moving toward the trap with increasingly positive velocity, slowing its rate of approach, or moving away with increasingly negative velocity.

Instantaneous acceleration is defined as the change in velocity divided by the elapsed time as the elapsed time approaches zero. This concept is stated mathematically in Equation 1 on the right.

Earlier, we discussed how the slope of the tangent at any point on a position-time graph equals the instantaneous velocity at that point. We can apply similar reasoning here to conclude that the instantaneous acceleration at any point on a velocity-time graph equals the slope of the tangent, as shown in Equation 2. Why? Because slope equals the rate of change, and acceleration is the rate of change of velocity.

In Example 1, we show a graph of the velocity of the mouse as it approaches the trap and then flees. You are asked to determine the sign of the instantaneous acceleration at four points; you can do so by considering the slope of the tangent to the velocity graph at each point.

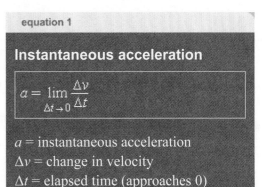

equation 1

Instantaneous acceleration

$$a = \lim_{\Delta t \to 0} \frac{\Delta v}{\Delta t}$$

a = instantaneous acceleration
Δv = change in velocity
Δt = elapsed time (approaches 0)

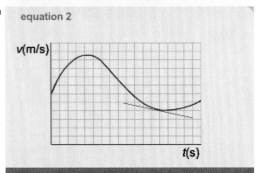

equation 2

v(m/s)

t(s)

Instantaneous acceleration
Slope of line tangent to point on velocity-time graph

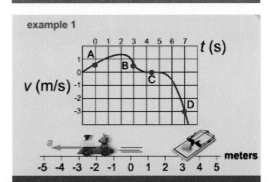

example 1

t (s)

v (m/s)

meters

The graph shows the mouse's velocity versus time. Describe the instantaneous acceleration at A, B, C and D as positive, negative or zero.

a positive at A
a negative at B
a zero at C
a negative at D

2.11 - Sample problem: velocity and acceleration

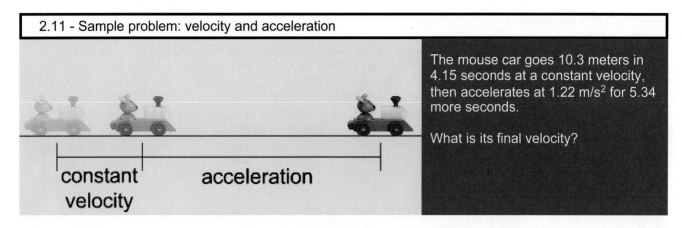

The mouse car goes 10.3 meters in 4.15 seconds at a constant velocity, then accelerates at 1.22 m/s² for 5.34 more seconds.

What is its final velocity?

constant velocity   acceleration

Solving this problem requires two calculations. The mouse car's velocity during the first part of its journey must be calculated. Using that value as the initial velocity of the second part of the journey, and the rate of acceleration during that part, you can calculate the final velocity.

Draw a diagram

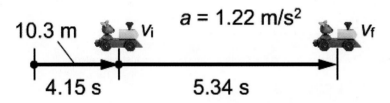

10.3 m ... v_i ... $a = 1.22 \text{ m/s}^2$ ... v_f

4.15 s ... 5.34 s

Variables

Part 1: Constant velocity

displacement	$\Delta x = 10.3 \text{ m}$
elapsed time	$\Delta t = 4.15 \text{ s}$
velocity	v

Part 2: Constant acceleration

initial velocity	$v_i = v$ (calculated above)
acceleration	$a = 1.22 \text{ m/s}^2$
elapsed time	$\Delta t = 5.34 \text{ s}$
final velocity	v_f

What is the strategy?

1. Use the definition of velocity to find the velocity of the mouse car before it accelerates. The velocity is constant during the first part of the journey.

2. Use the definition of acceleration and solve for the final velocity.

Physics principles and equations

The definitions of velocity and acceleration will prove useful. The velocity and acceleration are constant in this problem. In this and later problems, we use the definitions for average velocity and acceleration without the bars over the variables.

$$v = \Delta x/\Delta t$$

$$a = \Delta v/\Delta t = (v_f - v_i)/\Delta t$$

Step-by-step solution

We start by finding the velocity before the engine fires.

Step	Reason
1. $v = \Delta x/\Delta t$	definition of velocity
2. $v = (10.3 \text{ m})/(4.15 \text{ s})$	enter values
3. $v = 2.48 \text{ m/s}$	divide

Next we find the final velocity using the definition of acceleration. The initial velocity is the same as the velocity we just calculated.

Step	Reason
4. $a = (v_f - v_i)/\Delta t$	definition of acceleration
5. $1.22 \text{ m/s}^2 = \dfrac{v_f - 2.48 \text{ m/s}}{5.34 \text{ s}}$	enter given values, and velocity from step 3
6. $6.51 \text{ m/s} = v_f - 2.48 \text{ m/s}$	multiply by 5.34 s
7. $v_f = 8.99 \text{ m/s}$	solve for v_f

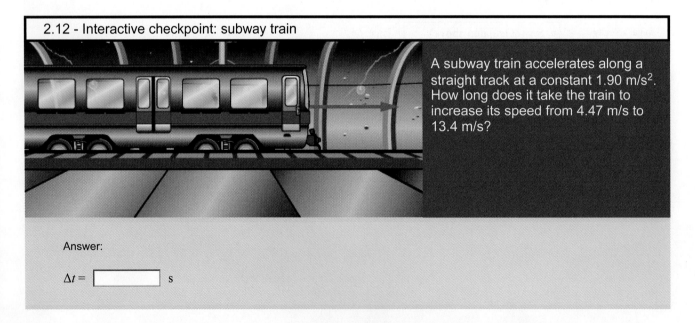

2.12 - Interactive checkpoint: subway train

A subway train accelerates along a straight track at a constant 1.90 m/s². How long does it take the train to increase its speed from 4.47 m/s to 13.4 m/s?

Answer:

$\Delta t =$ [   ] s

2.13 - Interactive problem: what's wrong with the rabbits?

You just bought five rabbits. They were supposed to be constant acceleration rabbits, but you worry that some are the less expensive, non-constant acceleration rabbits. In fact, you think two might be the cheaper critters.

You take them home. When you press GO, they will run or jump for five seconds (well, one just sits still) and then the simulation stops. You can press GO as many times as you like and use the PAUSE button as well.

Your mission: Determine if you were ripped off, and drag the "½ off" sale tags to the cheaper rabbits. The simulation will let you know if you are correct. You may decide to keep the cuddly creatures, but you want to be fairly charged.

interactive 1

Identify the faulty rabbits

Each rabbit has a velocity gauge that you can use to monitor its motion in the simulation. The simplest way to solve this problem is to consider the rabbits one at a time: look at a rabbit's velocity gauge and determine if the velocity is changing at a constant rate. No detailed mathematical calculations are required to solve this problem.

If you find this simulation challenging, focus on the relationship between acceleration and velocity. With a constant rate of acceleration, the velocity must change at a constant rate: no jumps or sudden changes. Hint: No change in velocity is zero acceleration, a constant rate.

2.14 - Derivation: creating new equations

Other sections in this chapter introduced some of the fundamental equations of motion. These equations defined fundamental concepts; for example, average velocity equals the change in position divided by elapsed time.

Several other helpful equations can be derived from these basic equations. These equations enable you to predict an object's motion without knowing all the details. In this section, we derive the formula shown in Equation 1, which is used to calculate an object's final velocity when its initial velocity, acceleration and displacement are known, but **not** the elapsed time. If the elapsed time were known, then the final velocity could be calculated using the definition of velocity, but it is not.

This equation is valid when the acceleration is constant, an assumption that is used in many problems you will be posed.

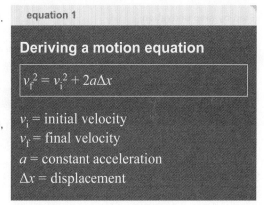

equation 1

Deriving a motion equation

$$v_f^2 = v_i^2 + 2a\Delta x$$

v_i = initial velocity
v_f = final velocity
a = constant acceleration
Δx = displacement

Variables

We use t instead of Δt to indicate the elapsed time. This is simpler notation, and we will use it often.

acceleration (constant)	a
initial velocity	v_i
final velocity	v_f
elapsed time	t
displacement	Δx

Strategy

First, we will discuss our strategy for this derivation. That is, we will describe our overall plan of attack. These strategy points outline the major steps of the derivation.

1. We start with the definition of acceleration and rearrange it. It includes the terms for initial and final velocity, as well as elapsed time.
2. We derive another equation involving time that can be used to eliminate the time variable from the acceleration equation. The condition of constant acceleration will be crucial here.
3. We eliminate the time variable from the acceleration equation and simplify. This results in an equation that depends on other variables, but not time.

Physics principles and equations

Since the acceleration is constant, the velocity increases at a constant rate. This means the average velocity is the sum of the initial and final velocities divided by two.

$$\bar{v} = (v_i + v_f)/2$$

We will use the definition of acceleration,

$$a = (v_f - v_i)/t$$

We will also use the definition of average velocity,

$$\bar{v} = \Delta x / t$$

Step-by-step derivation

We start the derivation with the definition of average acceleration, solve it for the final velocity and do some algebra. This creates an equation with the square of the final velocity on the left side, where it appears in the equation we want to derive.

Step	Reason
1. $a = (v_f - v_i)/t$	definition of average acceleration
2. $v_f = v_i + at$	solve for final velocity
3. $v_f^2 = (v_i + at)^2$	square both sides
4. $v_f^2 = v_i^2 + 2v_i at + a^2 t^2$	expand right side
5. $v_f^2 = v_i^2 + at(2v_i + at)$	factor out at
6. $v_f^2 = v_i^2 + at(v_i + v_i + at)$	rewrite $2v_i$ as a sum
7. $v_f^2 = v_i^2 + at(v_i + v_f)$	substitution from equation 2

The equation we just found is the basic equation from which we will derive the desired motion equation. But it still involves the time variable t – multiplied by a sum of velocities. In the **next** stage of the derivation, we use two different ways of expressing the average velocity to develop a second equation involving time multiplied by velocities. We will subsequently use that second equation to eliminate time from the equation above.

Step		Reason
8.	$\bar{v} = \dfrac{v_i + v_f}{2}$	average velocity is average of initial and final velocities
9.	$\bar{v} = \dfrac{\Delta x}{t}$	definition of average velocity
10.	$\dfrac{v_i + v_f}{2} = \dfrac{\Delta x}{t}$	set right sides of 8 and 9 equal
11.	$t(v_i + v_f) = 2\Delta x$	rearrange equation

We have now developed two equations that involve time multiplied by a sum of velocities. The left side of the equation in step 11 matches an expression appearing in equation 7, at the end of the first stage. By substituting from this equation into equation 7, we eliminate the time variable t and derive the desired equation.

Step		Reason
12.	$v_f^2 = v_i^2 + a(2\Delta x)$	substitute right side of 11 into 7
13.	$v_f^2 = v_i^2 + 2a\Delta x$	rearrange factors

We have now accomplished our goal. We can calculate the final velocity of an object when we know its initial velocity, its acceleration and its displacement, but do not know the elapsed time. The derivation is finished.

2.15 - Motion equations for constant acceleration

The equations above can be derived from the fundamental definitions of motion (equations such as $a = \Delta v / \Delta t$). To understand the equations, you need to remember the notation: Δx for displacement, v for velocity and a for acceleration. The subscripts i and f represent initial and final values. We follow a common convention here by using t for elapsed time instead of Δt. We show the equations above and below on the right.

Note that to hold true these equations all require a constant rate of acceleration. Analyzing motion with a

$$v_f = v_i + at$$

$$\Delta x = v_i t + \frac{1}{2} at^2$$

$$v_f^2 = v_i^2 + 2a\Delta x$$

$$\Delta x = \frac{1}{2}(v_i + v_f)t$$

Δx = displacement, v = velocity, a = acceleration, t = elapsed time

varying rate of acceleration is a more challenging task. When we refer to acceleration in problems, we mean a constant rate of acceleration unless we explicitly state otherwise.

To solve problems using motion equations like these, you look for an equation that includes the values you know, and the one you are solving for. This means you can solve for the unknown variable.

In the example problem to the right, you are asked to determine the acceleration required to stop a car that is moving at 12 meters per second in a distance of 36 meters. In this problem, you know the initial velocity, the final velocity (stopped = 0.0 m/s) and the displacement. You do not know the elapsed time. The third motion equation includes the two velocities, the acceleration, and the displacement, but does not include the time. Since this equation includes only one value you do not know, it is the appropriate equation to choose.

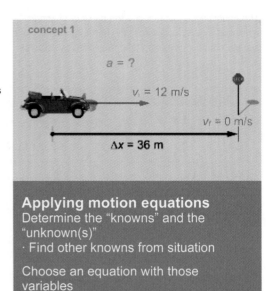

concept 1

$a = ?$

$v_i = 12$ m/s

$v_f = 0$ m/s

$\Delta x = 36$ m

Applying motion equations
Determine the "knowns" and the "unknown(s)"
· Find other knowns from situation

Choose an equation with those variables

equation 1

$$v_f = v_i + at$$

$$\Delta x = v_i t + \frac{1}{2} at^2$$

$$v_f^2 = v_i^2 + 2a\Delta x$$

$$\Delta x = \frac{1}{2} (v_i + v_f)t$$

Motion equations

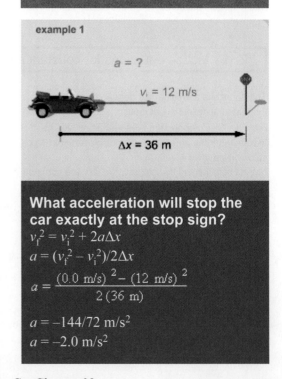

example 1

$a = ?$

$v_i = 12$ m/s

$\Delta x = 36$ m

What acceleration will stop the car exactly at the stop sign?

$v_f^2 = v_i^2 + 2a\Delta x$

$a = (v_f^2 - v_i^2)/2\Delta x$

$a = \dfrac{(0.0 \text{ m/s})^2 - (12 \text{ m/s})^2}{2\,(36 \text{ m})}$

$a = -144/72$ m/s^2

$a = -2.0$ m/s^2

2.16 - Sample problem: a sprinter

What is the runner's velocity at the end of a 100-meter dash?

$a = 0.528$ m/s²

$\Delta x = 100$ m

You are asked to calculate the final velocity of a sprinter running a 100-meter dash. List the variables that you know and the one you are asked for, and then consider which equation you might use to solve the problem. You want an equation with just one unknown variable, which in this problem is the final velocity.

The sprinter's initial velocity is not explicitly stated, but he starts motionless, so it is zero m/s.

Draw a diagram

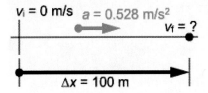

$v_i = 0$ m/s $a = 0.528$ m/s²

$v_f = ?$

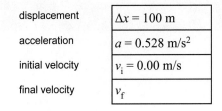

$\Delta x = 100$ m

Variables

displacement	$\Delta x = 100$ m
acceleration	$a = 0.528$ m/s²
initial velocity	$v_i = 0.00$ m/s
final velocity	v_f

What is the strategy?

1. Choose an appropriate equation based on the values you know and the one you want to find.

2. Enter the known values and solve for the final velocity.

Physics principles and equations

Based on the known and unknown values, the equation below is appropriate. We know all the variables in the equation except the one we are asked to find, so we can solve for it.

$$v_f^2 = v_i^2 + 2a\Delta x$$

Step-by-step solution

Step		Reason
1.	$v_f^2 = v_i^2 + 2a\Delta x$	motion equation
2.	$v_f^2 = (0.00\ \text{m/s})^2 + 2(0.528\ \text{m/s}^2)(100\ \text{m})$	enter known values
3.	$v_f^2 = 106\ \text{m}^2/\text{s}^2$	multiplication and addition
4.	$v_f = 10.3\ \text{m/s}$	take square root

In step 4, we take the square root of 106 to find the final velocity. We chose the positive square root, since the runner is moving in the positive direction. When there are multiple roots, you look at the problem to determine the solution that makes sense given the circumstances. If the runner were running to the left, then a negative velocity would be the appropriate choice.

2.17 - Interactive checkpoint: passenger jet

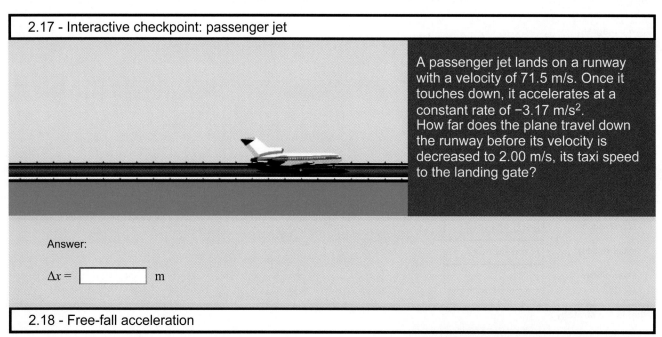

A passenger jet lands on a runway with a velocity of 71.5 m/s. Once it touches down, it accelerates at a constant rate of −3.17 m/s². How far does the plane travel down the runway before its velocity is decreased to 2.00 m/s, its taxi speed to the landing gate?

Answer:

$\Delta x =$ ⬚ m

2.18 - Free-fall acceleration

Free-fall acceleration: Rate of acceleration due to the force of Earth's gravity.

Galileo Galilei is reputed to have conducted an interesting experiment several hundred years ago. According to legend, he dropped two balls with different masses off the Leaning Tower of Pisa and found that both landed at the same time. Their differing masses did not change the time it took them to fall. (We say he was "reputed to have" because there is little evidence that he in fact conducted this experiment. He was more of a "roll balls down a plane" experimenter.)

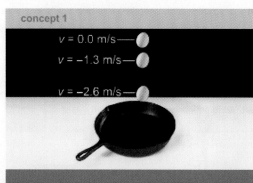

concept 1

$v = 0.0\ \text{m/s}$

$v = -1.3\ \text{m/s}$

$v = -2.6\ \text{m/s}$

Free-fall acceleration
Acceleration due to gravity

Today this experiment is used to demonstrate that free-fall acceleration is constant: that the acceleration of a falling object due solely to the force of gravity is constant, regardless of the object's mass or density. The two balls landed at the same time because they started with the same initial velocity, traveled the same distance and accelerated at the same rate. In 1971, the commander of Apollo 15 conducted a version of the experiment on the Moon, and demonstrated that in the absence of air resistance, a hammer and a feather accelerated at the same rate and reached the surface at the same moment.

In Concept 1, you see a photograph that illustrates free-fall acceleration. Pictures of a freely falling egg were taken every 2/15 of a second. Since the egg's speed constantly increases, the distance between the images increases over time. Greater displacement over the same interval of time means its velocity is increasing in magnitude; it is accelerating.

Free-fall acceleration is the acceleration caused by the force of the Earth's gravity, ignoring other factors like air resistance. It is sometimes stated as the rate of acceleration in a vacuum, where there is no air resistance. Near the Earth's surface, its magnitude is 9.80 meters per second squared. The letter g represents this value. The value of g varies slightly based on location. It is less at the Earth's poles than at the equator, and is also less atop a tall mountain than at sea level.

The acceleration of 9.80 m/s^2 occurs in a vacuum. In the Earth's atmosphere, a feather and a small lead ball dropped from the same height will not land at the same time because the feather, with its greater surface area, experiences more air resistance. Since it has less mass than the ball, gravity exerts less force on it to overcome the larger air resistance. The acceleration will also be different with two objects of the same mass but different surface areas: A flat sheet of paper will take longer to reach the ground than the same sheet crumpled up into a ball.

By convention, "up" is positive, and "down" is negative, like the values on the y axis of a graph. This means when using g in problems, we state free-fall acceleration as **negative** 9.80 m/s^2. To make this distinction, we typically use a or a_y when we are using the negative sign to indicate the direction of free-fall acceleration.

Free-fall acceleration occurs regardless of the direction in which an object is moving. For example, if you throw a ball straight up in the air, it will slow down, accelerating at −9.80 m/s^2 until it reaches zero velocity. At that point, it will then begin to fall back toward the ground and continue to accelerate toward the ground at the same rate. This means its velocity will become increasingly negative as it moves back toward the ground.

The two example problems in this section stress these points. For instance, Example 2 on the right asks you to calculate how long it will take a ball thrown up into the air to reach its zero velocity point (the peak of its motion) and its acceleration at that point.

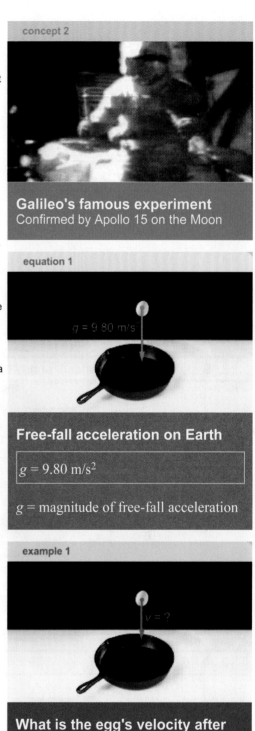

concept 2

Galileo's famous experiment
Confirmed by Apollo 15 on the Moon

equation 1

$g = 9.80$ m/s

Free-fall acceleration on Earth

$g = 9.80$ m/s^2

g = magnitude of free-fall acceleration

example 1

$v = ?$

What is the egg's velocity after falling from rest for 0.10 seconds?
$v_f = v_i + at$
$v_f = (0$ m/s$) + (-9.80$ m/s$^2)(0.10$ s$)$
$v_f = -0.98$ m/s

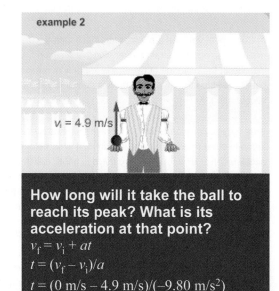

example 2

$v_i = 4.9$ m/s

How long will it take the ball to reach its peak? What is its acceleration at that point?

$v_f = v_i + at$

$t = (v_f - v_i)/a$

$t = (0 \text{ m/s} - 4.9 \text{ m/s})/(-9.80 \text{ m/s}^2)$

$t = 4.9/9.80 \text{ s} = 0.50 \text{ s}$

$\text{acceleration} = -9.80 \text{ m/s}^2$

2.19 - Interactive checkpoint: penny drop

You drop a penny off Taiwan's Taipei 101 tower, which is 509 meters tall. How long does it take to hit the ground? Ignore air resistance, consider down as negative, and the ground as having zero height.

Answer:

$t = $ [   ] s

2.20 - Gotchas

Some errors you might make, or that tests or teachers might try to tempt you to make:

Switching the order in calculating displacement. Remember: It is the final position minus the initial position. If you start at a position of three meters and move to one meter, your displacement is negative two meters. Be sure to subtract three from one, not vice versa.

Confusing distance traveled with displacement. Displacement is the shortest path between the beginning point and final point. It does not matter how the object got there, whether in a straight line or wandering all over through a considerable net distance.

Forgetting the sign. Remember: displacement, velocity and acceleration all have direction. For one-dimensional motion, they require signs indicating the direction. If a problem says that an object moves to the left or down, its displacement is typically negative. Be sure to note the signs of displacement, velocity or acceleration if they are given to you in a problem. Make sure you are consistent with signs. If up is positive, then upward displacement is positive, and the acceleration due to gravity is negative.

Confusing velocity and acceleration. Can an object with zero acceleration have velocity? Yes! A train barreling down the tracks at 150 km/h has velocity. If that velocity is not changing, the train's acceleration is zero.

Can an object with zero velocity have acceleration? Yes again: a ball thrown straight up has zero velocity at the top of its path, but its acceleration at that instant is −9.80 m/s^2.

Confusing constant acceleration with constant velocity. If an object has constant acceleration, it has a constant velocity, right? Quite wrong (unless the constant acceleration is zero). With a constant acceleration other than zero, the velocity is constantly changing.

Misunderstanding negative acceleration. Can something that is "speeding up" also have a negative acceleration? Yes. If something is moving in the negative direction and moving increasingly quickly, it will have a negative velocity and a negative acceleration. When an object has negative velocity and experiences negative acceleration, it will have increasing speed. In other words, negative acceleration is not just "slowing something down." It can also mean an object with negative velocity moving increasingly fast.

2.21 - Summary

Position is the location of an object relative to a reference point called the origin, and is specified by the use of a coordinate system.

Displacement is a measure of the change in the position of an object. It includes both the distance between the object's starting and ending points, and the direction from the starting point to the ending point. An example of displacement would be "three meters west" or "negative two meters".

Similarly, velocity expresses an object's speed **and** direction, as in "three meters per second west." Velocity has a direction. In one dimension, motion in one direction is represented by positive numbers, and motion in the other direction is negative.

An object's velocity may change while it is moving. Its average velocity is its displacement divided by the elapsed time. In contrast, its instantaneous velocity is its velocity at a particular moment. This equals the displacement divided by the elapsed time for a very small interval of time, as the time interval gets smaller and smaller.

Acceleration is a change in velocity. Like velocity, it has a direction and in one dimension, it can be positive or negative. Average acceleration is the change in velocity divided by the elapsed time, and instantaneous acceleration is the acceleration of an object at a specific moment.

There are four very useful motion equations for situations where the acceleration is constant. They are the last four equations shown on the right.

Free-fall acceleration, represented by g, is the magnitude of the acceleration due to the force of Earth's gravity. Near the surface of the Earth, falling objects have a downward acceleration due to gravity of 9.80 m/s^2.

Equations

$$\bar{v} = \Delta x / \Delta t$$

$$\bar{a} = \Delta v / \Delta t$$

$$v_f = v_i + at$$

$$\Delta x = v_i t + \tfrac{1}{2} at^2$$

$$v_f^2 = v_i^2 + 2a\Delta x$$

$$\Delta x = \tfrac{1}{2}(v_i + v_f)t$$

3.0 - Introduction

Knowing "how far" or "how fast" can often be useful, but "which way" sometimes proves even more valuable. If you have ever been lost, you understand that direction can be the most important thing to know.

Vectors describe "how much" **and** "which way," or, in the terminology of physics, magnitude and direction. You use vectors frequently, even if you are not familiar with the term. "Go three miles northeast" or "walk two blocks north, one block east" are both vector descriptions. Vectors prove crucial in much of physics. For example, if you throw a ball up into the air, you need to understand that the initial velocity of the ball points "up" while the acceleration due to the force of gravity points "down."

In this chapter, you will learn the fundamentals of vectors: how to write them and how to combine them using operations such as addition and subtraction.

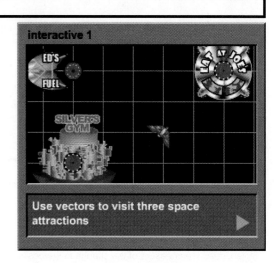

interactive 1

Use vectors to visit three space attractions

On the right, a simulation lets you explore vectors, in this case displacement vectors. In the simulation, you are the pilot of a small spaceship. There are three locations nearby that you want to visit: a refueling station, a diner, and the local gym. To reach any of these locations, you describe the displacement vector of the spaceship by setting its x (horizontal) and y (vertical) components. In other words, you set how far horizontally you want to travel, and how far vertically. This is a common way to express a two-dimensional vector.

There is a grid on the drawing to help you determine these values. You, and each of the places you want to visit, are at the intersection of two grid lines. Each square on the grid is one kilometer across in each direction. Enter the values, press GO, and the simulation will show you traveling in a straight line − along the displacement vector − according to the values you set. See if you can reach all three places. You can do this by entering displacement values to the nearest kilometer, like (3, 4) km. To start over at any time, press RESET.

3.1 - Scalars

Scalar: A quantity that states only an amount.

Scalar quantities state an amount: "how much" or "how many." At the right is a picture of a dozen eggs. The quantity, a dozen, is a scalar. Unlike vectors, there is no direction associated with a scalar − no up or down, no left or right − just one quantity, the amount. A scalar is described by a single number, together with the appropriate units.

Temperature provides another example of a scalar quantity; it gets warmer and colder, but at any particular time and place there is no "direction" to temperature, only a value. Time is another commonly used scalar.

Speed and distance are yet other scalars. A speed like 60 kilometers per hour says how fast but not which way. Distance is a scalar since it tells you how far away something is, but not the direction.

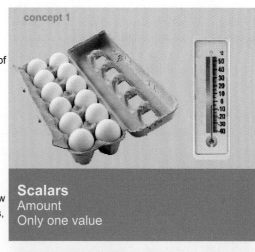

concept 1

Scalars
Amount
Only one value

concept 2

Examples of scalars
12 eggs

3.2 - Vectors

Vector: A quantity specified by both magnitude *and* direction.

Vectors have both magnitude (how much) **and** direction. For example, vectors can be used to supply traveling instructions. If a pilot is told "Fly 20 kilometers due south," she is being given a displacement vector to follow. Its magnitude is 20 kilometers and its direction is south. Vector magnitudes are positive or zero; it would be confusing to tell somebody to drive negative 20 kilometers south.

Many of the fundamental quantities in physics are vectors. For instance, displacement, velocity and acceleration are all vector quantities. Physicists depict vectors with arrows. The length of the arrow is proportional to the vector's magnitude, and the arrow points in the direction of the vector. The horizontal vector in Concept 1 on the right represents the displacement of a car driving from Acme to Dunsville.

You see two displacement vectors in Concept 1. The displacement vector of a drive from Acme to Dunsville is twice as long as the displacement vector from Chester to Dunsville. This is because the distance from Acme to Dunsville is twice that of Chester to Dunsville.

Even if they do not begin at the same point, two vectors are equal if they have the same magnitude and direction. For instance, the vector from Chester to Dunsville in Concept 1 represents a displacement of 100 km southeast. That vector could be moved without changing its meaning. Perhaps it is 100 km southeast from Edwards to Frankville, as well. A vector's meaning is defined by its length and direction, not by its starting point.

Now that we have introduced the concept of vectors formally, we will express vector quantities in boldface. For instance, **F** represents force, **v** stands for velocity, and so on. You will often see F and v, as well, representing the magnitudes of the vectors, without boldface. Why? Because it is frequently useful to discuss the magnitude of the force or the velocity without concerning ourselves with its direction. For instance, there may be several equations that determine the magnitude of a vector quantity like force, but not its direction.

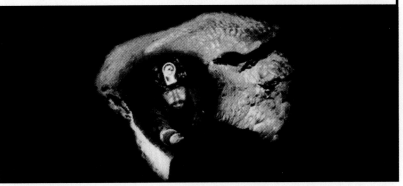

A spelunker (cave explorer) uses both distance and direction to navigate.

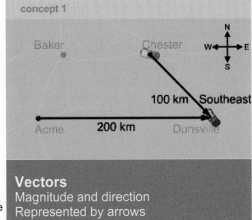

Vectors
Magnitude and direction
Represented by arrows
Length proportional to magnitude

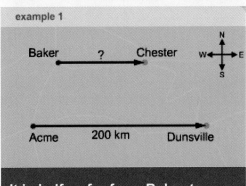

It is half as far from Baker to Chester as from Acme to Dunsville. Describe the displacement vector from Baker to Chester.
Displacement: 100 km, east

Polar notation: Defining a vector by its angle and magnitude.

Polar notation is a way to specify a vector. With polar notation, the magnitude and direction of the vector are stated separately. Three kilometers due north is an example of polar notation. "Three kilometers" is the magnitude and "north" is the direction. The magnitude is always stated as a positive value. Instead of using "compass" or map directions, physicists use angles. Rather than saying "three kilometers north," a physicist would likely say "three kilometers directed at 90 degrees."

The angle is most conveniently measured by placing the vector's starting point at the origin. The angle is then typically measured from the positive side of the x axis to the vector. This is shown in Concept 1 to the right.

Angles can be positive or negative. A positive angle indicates a counterclockwise direction, a negative angle a clockwise direction. For example, $90°$ represents a quarter turn **counterclockwise** from the positive x axis. In other words, a vector with a $90°$ angle points straight up. We could also specify this angle as $-270°$.

The radian is another unit of measurement for angles that you may have seen before. We will use degrees to specify angles unless we specifically note that we are using radians. (Radians do prove essential at times.)

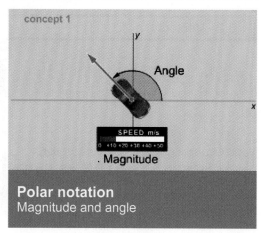

Polar notation
Magnitude and angle

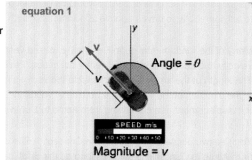

Polar notation
v is magnitude
θ is angle
Written $\mathbf{v} = (v, \theta)$

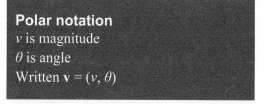

Write the velocity vector of the car in polar notation.
$\mathbf{v} = (v, \theta)$
$\mathbf{v} = (5 \text{ m/s}, 135°)$

Rectangular notation: Defining a vector by its components.

Often what we know, or want to know, about a particular vector is not its overall magnitude and direction, but how far it extends horizontally and vertically. On a graph, we represent the horizontal direction as x and the vertical direction as y. These are called *Cartesian coordinates*. The x component of a vector indicates its extent in the horizontal dimension and the y component its extent in the vertical dimension.

Rectangular notation is a way to describe a vector using the components that make up the vector. In rectangular notation, the x and y components of a vector are written inside parentheses. A vector that extends a units along the x axis and b units along the y axis is written as (a, b). For instance (3, 4) is a vector that extends positive three in the x direction and positive four in the y direction from its starting point.

The components of vectors are scalars with the direction indicated by their sign: x components point right (positive) or left (negative), and y components point up (positive) or down (negative). You see the x and y components of a car's velocity vector in Concept 1 at the right, shown as "hollow" vectors. The x and y values define the vector, as they provide direction and magnitude.

For a vector $\mathbf{A}$, the x and y components are sometimes written as A_x and A_y. You see this notation used for a velocity vector $\mathbf{v}$ in Equation 1 and Example 1 on the right.

Consider the car shown in Example 1 on the right. Its velocity has an x component v_x of 17 m/s and a y component v_y of −13 m/s. We can write the car's velocity vector as (17, −13) m/s.

A vector can extend in more than two dimensions: z represents the third dimension. Sometimes z is used to represent distance toward or away from you. For instance, your computer monitor's width is measured in the x dimension, its height with y and your distance from the monitor with z. If you are reading this on a computer monitor and punch your computer screen, your fist would be moving in the z dimension. (We hope we're not the cause of any such aggressive feelings.) Three-dimensional vectors are written as (x, y, z).

The z component can also represent altitude. A Tour de France bike racer might believe the z dimension to be the most important as he ascends one of the competition's famous climbs of a mountain pass.

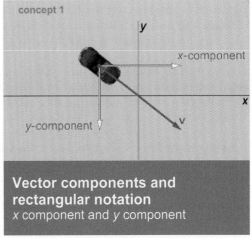

concept 1

Vector components and rectangular notation
x component and y component

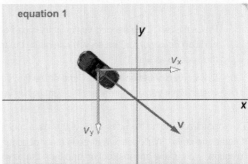

equation 1

Rectangular notation
v_x is horizontal component
v_y is vertical component
Written $\mathbf{v} = (v_x, v_y)$

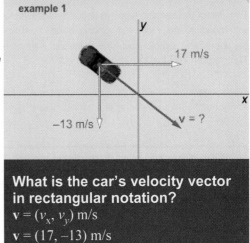

example 1

What is the car's velocity vector in rectangular notation?
$\mathbf{v} = (v_x, v_y)$ m/s
$\mathbf{v} = (17, -13)$ m/s

3.5 - Adding and subtracting vectors graphically

Vectors can be added and subtracted. In this section, we show how to do these operations graphically. For instance, consider the vectors **A** and **B** shown in Concept 1 to the right. The vector labeled **A** + **B** is the sum of these two vectors.

It may be helpful to imagine that these two vectors represent displacement. A person walks along displacement vector **A** and then along displacement vector **B**. Her initial point is the origin, and she would end up at the point at the end of the **A** + **B** vector. The sum represents the displacement vector from her initial to final position.

To be more specific about the addition process: We start with two vectors, **A** and **B**, both drawn starting at the origin (0, 0). To add them, we move the vector **B** so it starts at the head of **A**. The diagram for Equation 1 shows how the **B** vector has been moved so it starts at the head of **A**. The sum is a vector that starts at the tail of **A** and ends at the head of **B**.

In summary, to add two vectors, you:

1. Place the tail of the second vector at the head of the first vector. (The order of addition does not matter, so you can place the tail of the first vector at the head of the second as well.)
2. Draw a vector between the tail end of the first vector and the head of the second vector. This vector represents the sum of two vectors.

To emphasize a point: You can think of this as combining a series of vector instructions. If someone says, "Walk positive three in the x direction and then negative two in the y direction," you follow one instruction and then the other. This is the equivalent of placing one vector's tail at the head of the other. An arrow from where you started to where you ended represents the resulting vector. Any vector is the vector sum of its rectangular components.

When two vectors are parallel and pointing in the same direction, adding them is relatively simple: You just combine the two arrows to form a longer arrow. If the vectors are parallel but pointing in opposite directions, the result is a shorter arrow (three steps forward plus two steps back equals one step forward).

To subtract two vectors, take the opposite of the vector that is being subtracted, and then add. (The opposite or negative of a vector is a vector with the same magnitude but opposite direction.) This is the same as scalar subtraction (for example 20 − 5 is the same as 20 + (−5)). To draw the opposite of a vector, draw it with the same length but the opposite direction. In other words, it starts at the same point but is rotated $180°$. The diagram for Equation 2 shows the subtraction of two vectors.

When a vector is added to its opposite, the result is the *zero vector*, which has zero magnitude and no direction. This is analogous to adding a scalar number to its opposite, like adding +2 and −2 to get zero.

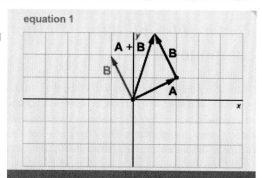

Adding vectors A + B graphically
Move tail of B to head of A
Draw vector from tail of A to head of B

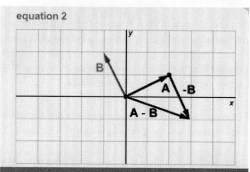

Subtracting A – B graphically
Take the opposite of B
Move it to head of A
Draw vector from tail of A to head of –B

3.6 - Adding and subtracting vectors by components

You can combine vectors graphically, but it may be more precise to add up their components.

You perform this operation intuitively outside physics. If you were a dancer or a cheerleader, you would easily understand the following choreography: "Take two steps forward, four steps to the right and one step back." These are vector instructions. You can add them to determine the overall result. If asked how far **forward** you are after this dance move, you would say "one step," which is two steps forward plus one step back. You realize that your progress forward or back is unaffected by steps to the left or right. You correctly process left/right and forward/back separately. If a physics-oriented dance instructor asked you to describe the results of your "dancing vector" math, you would say, "One step forward, four steps to the right."

You have just learned the basics of vector addition, which is reasonably straightforward: Break the vector into its components and add each component independently. In physics though, you concern yourself with more than dance steps. You might want to add the vector (20, −40, 60) to (10, 50, 10). Let's assume the units for both vectors are meters. As with the dance example, each component is added independently. You add the first number in each set of parentheses: 20 plus 10 equals 30, so the sum along the x axis is 30. Then you add −40 and 50 for a total of 10 along the y axis. The sum along the z axis is 60 plus 10, or 70. The vector sum is (30, 10, 70) meters. If following all this in the text is hard, you can see another problem worked in Example 1 on the right.

Although we use displacement vectors in much of this discussion since they may be the most intuitive to understand, it is important to note that all types of vectors can be added or subtracted. You can add two velocity vectors, two acceleration vectors, two force vectors and so on. As illustrated in the example problem, where two velocity vectors are added, the process is identical for any type of vector.

Vector subtraction works similarly to addition when you use components. For example, (5, 3) minus (2, 1) equals 5 minus 2, and 3 minus 1; the result is the vector (3, 2).

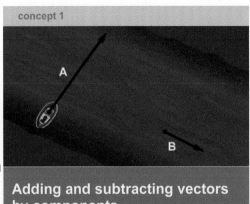

concept 1

Adding and subtracting vectors by components
Add (or subtract) each component separately

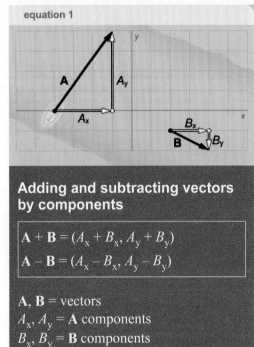

equation 1

Adding and subtracting vectors by components

$$A + B = (A_x + B_x, A_y + B_y)$$
$$A - B = (A_x - B_x, A_y - B_y)$$

A, B = vectors
A_x, A_y = A components
B_x, B_y = B components

A = (3, 4) m/s

B = (2,–1) m/s

The boat has the velocity A in still water. Calculate its velocity as the sum of A and the velocity B of the river's current.

$\mathbf{v} = \mathbf{A} + \mathbf{B}$

$\mathbf{v} = (3, 4)$ m/s $+ (2, -1)$ m/s

$\mathbf{v} = (3 + 2, 4 + (-1))$ m/s

$\mathbf{v} = (5, 3)$ m/s

3.7 - Interactive checkpoint: vector addition

$$\mathbf{v}_1 = (5, 6)$$
$$\mathbf{v}_2 = (a, 4)$$
$$\mathbf{v}_1 + \mathbf{v}_2 = (2, b)$$

What are the number values of the constants a and b?

Answer:

$a = $ [　　　　] , $b = $ [　　　　]

You can multiply vector quantities by scalar quantities. Let's say an airplane, as shown in Concept 1 on the right, travels at a constant velocity represented by the vector (40, 10) m/s. Let's say you know its current position and want to know where it will be if it travels for two seconds. Time is a scalar. To calculate the displacement, multiply the velocity vector by the time.

To multiply a vector by a scalar, multiply each component of the vector by the scalar. In this example, (2 s)(40, 10) m/s = (80, 20) m. This is the plane's displacement vector after two seconds of travel.

If you wanted the opposite of this vector, you would multiply by negative one. The result in this case would be (−40, −10) m/s, representing travel at the same speed, but in the opposite direction.

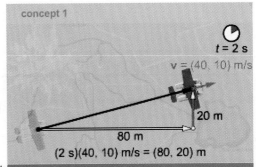

concept 1

$t = 2$ s

$v = (40, 10)$ m/s

20 m

80 m

$(2\ s)(40, 10)\ m/s = (80, 20)\ m$

Multiplying a rectangular vector by a scalar
Multiply each component by scalar
Positive scalar does not affect direction

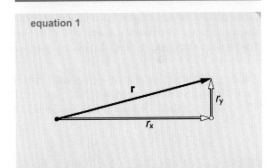

equation 1

$\mathbf{r}$

r_y

r_x

Multiplying a rectangular vector by a scalar

$$s\mathbf{r} = (sr_x, sr_y)$$

s = a scalar
$\mathbf{r}$ = a vector
r_x, r_y = $\mathbf{r}$ components

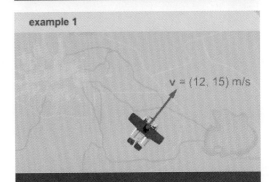

example 1

$v = (12, 15)$ m/s

What is the displacement d of the plane after 5.0 seconds?
$\mathbf{d} = (5.0\ s)\mathbf{v}$

$\mathbf{d} = (5.0\ \text{s})\ (12\ \text{m/s},\ 15\ \text{m/s})$

$\mathbf{d} = (\ (5.0\ \text{s})(12\ \text{m/s}),\ (5.0\ \text{s})(15\ \text{m/s})\ )$

$\mathbf{d} = (60, 75)\ \text{m}$

3.9 - Multiplying polar vectors by a scalar

Multiplying a vector represented in polar notation by a positive scalar requires only one multiplication operation: Multiply the magnitude of the vector by the scalar. The angle is unchanged.

Let's say there is a vector of magnitude 50 km with an angle of $30°$. You are asked to multiply it by positive three. This situation is shown in Example 1 to the right. Since you are multiplying by a positive scalar, the angle stays the same at $30°$, and so the answer is 150 km at $30°$.

If you multiply a vector by a negative scalar, multiply its magnitude by the absolute value of the scalar (that is, ignore the negative sign). Then change the direction of the vector by $180°$ so that it points in the opposite direction. In polar notation, since the magnitude is always positive, you add $180°$ to the vector's angle to take its opposite. The result of multiplying $(50\ \text{km}, 30°)$ by negative three is $(150\ \text{km}, \mathbf{210°})$.

If adding $180°$ would result in an angle greater than $360°$, then subtract $180°$ instead. For instance, in reversing an angle of $300°$, subtract $180°$ and express the result as $120°$ rather than $480°$. The two results are identical, but $120°$ is easier to understand.

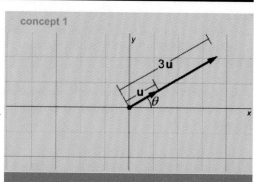

Multiplying polar vector by positive scalar
Multiply vector's magnitude by scalar
Angle unchanged

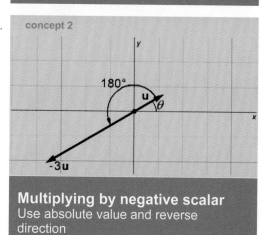

Multiplying by negative scalar
Use absolute value and reverse direction

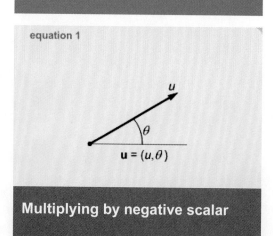

$\mathbf{u} = (u, \theta)$

Multiplying by negative scalar

$s\mathbf{u} = (su, \theta)$, if s positive
$s\mathbf{u} = (|s|u, \theta + 180°)$, if s negative

s = a scalar, $\mathbf{u}$ = a vector
u = magnitude of vector
θ = angle of vector

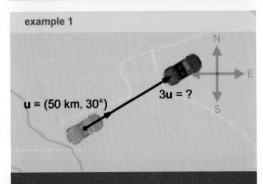

example 1

$\mathbf{u} = (50 \text{ km}, 30°)$

$3\mathbf{u} = ?$

What is the displacement vector if the car travels three times as far?

$s\mathbf{u} = (su, \theta)$
$3\mathbf{u} = (3(50 \text{ km}), 30°)$
$3\mathbf{u} = (150 \text{ km}, 30°)$

3.10 - Gotchas

Stating a value as a scalar when a vector is required. This happens in physics and everyday life as well. You need to use a vector when direction is required. Throwing a ball up is different than throwing a ball down; taking highway I-5 south is different than taking I-5 north.

Vectors always start at the origin. No, they can start at any location.

3.11 - Summary

A scalar is a quantity, such as time, temperature, or speed, which indicates only amount.

A vector is a quantity, like velocity or displacement, which has both magnitude and direction. Vectors are represented by arrows that indicate their direction. The arrow's length is proportional to the vector's magnitude. Vectors are represented with **boldface** symbols, and their magnitudes are represented with *italic* symbols.

One way to represent a vector is with polar notation. The direction is indicated by the angle between the positive x axis and the vector (measured in the counterclockwise direction). For example, a vector pointing in the negative y direction would have a direction of $270°$ in polar notation. The magnitude is expressed separately. A polar vector is expressed in the form (r, θ) where r is the magnitude and θ is the direction angle.

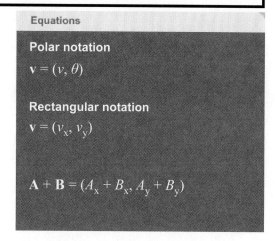

Equations

Polar notation

$$\mathbf{v} = (v, \theta)$$

Rectangular notation

$$\mathbf{v} = (v_x, v_y)$$

$$\mathbf{A} + \mathbf{B} = (A_x + B_x, A_y + B_y)$$

Another way to represent a vector is by using rectangular notation. The vector's x and y components are expressed as an ordered pair of numbers (x, y). The components of a vector $\mathbf{A}$ are also written as A_x and A_y.

To add vectors graphically, place the tail of one on the head of the other, then draw a vector that goes from the free tail to the free head: The new vector is the sum. To subtract, first take the opposite of the vector being subtracted, then add. (The opposite of a vector has the same magnitude, but it points in the opposite direction.)

4.0 - Introduction

Imagine that you are standing on the 86th floor observatory of the Empire State Building, holding a baseball. A friend waits in the street below, ready to catch the ball. You toss it forward and watch it move in that direction at the same time as it plummets toward the ground. Although you have not thrown the ball downward at all, common sense tells you that your friend had better be wearing a well-padded glove!

When you tossed the ball, you subconsciously split its movement into two dimensions. You supplied the initial forward velocity that caused the ball to move out toward the street. You did not have to supply any downward vertical velocity. The force of gravity did that for you, accelerating the ball toward the ground. If you had wanted to, you could have simply leaned over and dropped the ball off the roof, supplying no initial velocity at all and allowing gravity to take over.

To understand the baseball's motion, you need to analyze it in two dimensions. Physicists use x and y coordinates to discuss the horizontal and vertical motion of the ball. In the horizontal direction, along the x axis, you supply the initial forward velocity to the ball. In the vertical direction, along the y axis, gravity does the work. The ball's vertical velocity is completely independent of its horizontal velocity. In fact, the ball will land on the ground at the same time regardless of whether you drop it straight off the building or hurl it forward at a Randy Johnson-esque 98 miles per hour.

To get a feel for motion in two dimensions, run the simulations on the right. In the first simulation, you try to drive a race car around a circular track by controlling its x and y component velocities separately, using the arrow keys on your keyboard. The right arrow increases the x velocity and the left arrow decreases it. The up arrow key increases the y velocity, and yes, the down arrow decreases it. Your mission is to stay on the course and, if possible, complete a lap using these keys.

Your car will start moving when you press any of the arrow keys. On the gauges, you can observe the x and y velocities of your car, as well as its overall speed. Does changing the x velocity affect the y velocity, or vice-versa? How do the two velocities seem to relate to the overall speed?

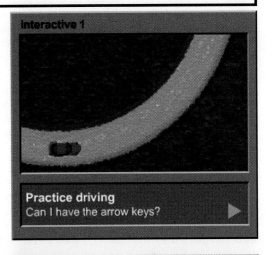

Practice driving
Can I have the arrow keys?

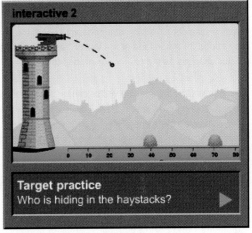

Target practice
Who is hiding in the haystacks?

There is also a clock, so you can see which among your friends gets the car around the track in the shortest time. There is no penalty for driving your car off the track, though striking a wall is not good for your insurance rates. Press RESET to start over. Happy motoring!

In the second simulation, you can experiment with motion in two dimensions by firing the cannon from the castle. The cannon fires the cannonball horizontally from the top of a tower. You change the horizontal velocity of the cannonball by dragging the head of the arrow. Try to hit the two haystacks on the plain to see who is hiding inside.

As the cannonball moves, look at the gauges in the control panel. One displays the horizontal velocity of the cannonball, its displacement per unit time along the x axis. The other gauge displays the cannonball's vertical velocity, its displacement per unit time along the y axis. As you use the simulation, consider these important questions: Does the cannonball's horizontal velocity change as it moves through the air? Does its vertical velocity change? The simulation pauses when a cannonball hits the ground, and the gauges display the values from an instant before that moment.

The simulation also contains a timer that starts when the ball is fired and stops when it hits a haystack or the ground. Note the values in the timer as you fire shots of varying horizontal velocity. Does the ball stay in the air longer if you increase the horizontal velocity, or does it stay in the air the same amount of time regardless of that velocity?

The answers to these questions are the keys to understanding what is called projectile motion, motion where the acceleration occurs due to gravity alone. This chapter will introduce you to motion in two and three dimensions; projectile motion is one example of this type of motion.

4.1 - Velocity in two dimensions

Velocity is a vector quantity, meaning it contains two pieces of information: how fast something is traveling and in which direction. Both are crucial for understanding motion in multiple dimensions.

Consider the car on the track to the right. It starts out traveling parallel to the x axis at a constant speed. It then reaches a curve and continues to travel at a constant speed through the curve. Although its speed stays the same, its direction changes. Since velocity is defined by speed **and** direction, the change in direction means the car's velocity changes.

Using vectors to describe the car's velocity helps to illustrate its change in velocity. The velocity vector points in the direction of the car's motion at any moment in time. Initially, the car moves horizontally, and its velocity vector points to the right, parallel to the x axis. As the car goes around the curve, the velocity vector starts to point upward as well as to the right. You see this shown in the illustration for Concept 1.

When the car exits the curve, its velocity vector will be straight up, parallel to the y axis. Because the car is moving at a constant speed, the length of the vector stays the same: The speed, or magnitude of the vector, remains constant. However, the direction of the vector changes as the car moves around the curve.

Like any vector, the velocity vector can be written as the sum of its components, the velocities along the x and y axes. This is also shown in the Concept 1 illustration. The gauges display the x and y velocities. If you click on Concept 1 to see the animated version of the illustration, you will see the gauges constantly changing as the car rounds the bend. At the moment shown in the illustration, the car is moving at 17 m/s in the horizontal direction and 10 m/s in the vertical direction. The components of the vector shown also reflect these values. The horizontal component is longer than the vertical one.

Equations 1 and 2 show equations useful for analyzing the car's velocity. Equation 1 shows how to break the car's overall velocity into its components. (These equations employ the same technique used to break any vector into its components.) The illustration shows the car's velocity vector. The angle θ is the angle the velocity vector makes with the positive x axis. The product of the cosine of that angle and the magnitude of the car's velocity (its speed) equals the car's horizontal velocity component. The sine of the angle times the speed equals the vertical velocity component.

The first equation in Equation 2 shows how to calculate the car's average velocity when its displacement and the elapsed time are known. The displacement $\Delta \mathbf{r}$ divided by the elapsed time Δt equals the average velocity.

The equations for determining the average velocity components when the components of the displacement are known are also shown in Equation 2. Dividing the displacement along the x axis by the elapsed time yields the horizontal component of the car's average velocity. The displacement along the y axis divided by the elapsed time equals the vertical component of the average velocity. A demonstration of these calculations is shown in Example 1.

The distinction between average and instantaneous velocity parallels the discussion of these two topics in the study of motion in one dimension. To determine the instantaneous velocity, $\Delta \mathbf{r}$ is measured during a very short increment of time and divided by that increment.

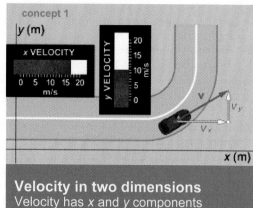

Velocity in two dimensions
Velocity has x and y components
Analyze x and y components separately
Two component vectors sum to equal total velocity

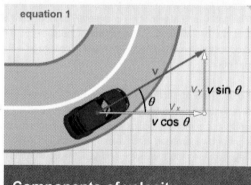

Components of velocity

$$v_x = v \cos \theta$$
$$v_y = v \sin \theta$$

v = speed
θ = angle with positive x axis
v_x = x component of velocity
v_y = y component of velocity

As with linear motion, the velocity vector points in the direction of motion. On the curved part of the track, the instantaneous velocity vector is tangent to the curve, since that is the direction of the car's motion at any instant in time. The average velocity vector points in the same direction as the displacement vector used to determine its value.

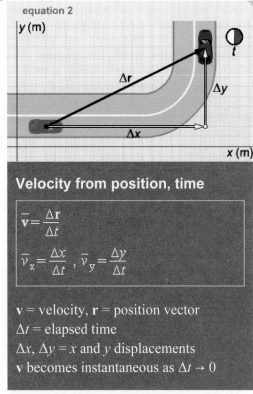

equation 2

Velocity from position, time

$$\bar{\mathbf{v}} = \frac{\Delta \mathbf{r}}{\Delta t}$$

$$\bar{v}_x = \frac{\Delta x}{\Delta t} \; , \; \bar{v}_y = \frac{\Delta y}{\Delta t}$$

$\mathbf{v}$ = velocity, $\mathbf{r}$ = position vector
Δt = elapsed time
$\Delta x, \Delta y = x$ and y displacements
$\mathbf{v}$ becomes instantaneous as $\Delta t \rightarrow 0$

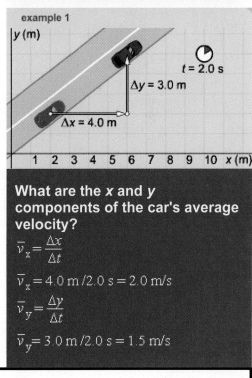

example 1

$t = 2.0$ s
$\Delta y = 3.0$ m
$\Delta x = 4.0$ m

What are the x and y components of the car's average velocity?

$$\bar{v}_x = \frac{\Delta x}{\Delta t}$$

$$\bar{v}_x = 4.0 \text{ m} / 2.0 \text{ s} = 2.0 \text{ m/s}$$

$$\bar{v}_y = \frac{\Delta y}{\Delta t}$$

$$\bar{v}_y = 3.0 \text{ m} / 2.0 \text{ s} = 1.5 \text{ m/s}$$

4.2 - Acceleration in two dimensions

Analyzing acceleration in two dimensions is analogous to analyzing velocity in two dimensions. Velocity can change independently in the horizontal and vertical dimensions. Because acceleration is the change in velocity per unit time, it follows that acceleration also can change independently in each dimension.

The cannonball shown to the right is fired with a horizontal velocity that remains constant throughout its flight. Constant velocity means zero acceleration. The cannonball has zero horizontal acceleration.

The cannonball starts with zero vertical velocity. Gravity causes its vertical velocity to become an increasingly negative number as the cannonball accelerates toward the ground. The vertical acceleration component due to gravity equals −9.80 m/s².

As with velocity, there are several ways to calculate the acceleration and its components.

The average acceleration can be calculated using the definition of acceleration, dividing the change in velocity by the elapsed time. The components of the average acceleration can be calculated by dividing the changes in the velocity components by the elapsed time. These equations are shown in Equation 1. Instantaneous acceleration is defined using the limit as Δt gets close to zero.

If the overall acceleration is known, in both magnitude and direction, you can calculate its x and y components by using the cosine and sine of the angle θ that indicates its direction. These equations are shown in Equation 2.

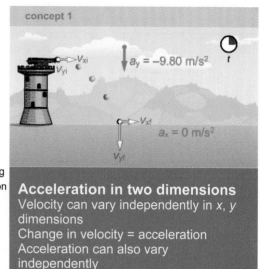

concept 1

Acceleration in two dimensions
Velocity can vary independently in x, y dimensions
Change in velocity = acceleration
Acceleration can also vary independently

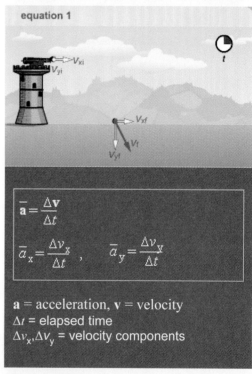

equation 1

$$\overline{\mathbf{a}} = \frac{\Delta \mathbf{v}}{\Delta t}$$

$$\overline{a}_x = \frac{\Delta v_x}{\Delta t} \quad , \quad \overline{a}_y = \frac{\Delta v_y}{\Delta t}$$

$\mathbf{a}$ = acceleration, $\mathbf{v}$ = velocity
Δt = elapsed time
$\Delta v_x, \Delta v_y$ = velocity components

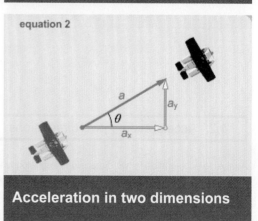

equation 2

Acceleration in two dimensions

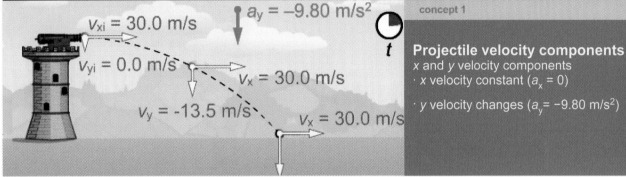

$$a_x = a \cos \theta$$
$$a_y = a \sin \theta$$

θ = angle with positive x axis
a_x = x component of acceleration
a_y = y component of acceleration

4.3 - Projectile motion

$v_{xi} = 30.0$ m/s

$a_y = -9.80$ m/s^2

t

$v_{yi} = 0.0$ m/s

$v_x = 30.0$ m/s

$v_y = -13.5$ m/s

$v_x = 30.0$ m/s

concept 1

Projectile velocity components
x and y velocity components
· x velocity constant ($a_x = 0$)

· y velocity changes ($a_y = -9.80$ m/s^2)

Projectile motion: Movement determined by an object's initial velocity and the constant acceleration of gravity.

The path of a cannonball provides a classic example of projectile motion.

The cannonball leaves the cannon with an initial velocity and, ignoring air resistance, that initial velocity changes during the flight of the cannonball due solely to the acceleration due to the Earth's gravity.

The cannon shown in the illustrations fires the ball horizontally. After the initial blast, the cannon no longer exerts any force on the cannonball. The cannonball's horizontal velocity does not change until it hits the ground.

Once the cannonball begins its flight, the force of gravity accelerates it toward the ground. The force of gravity does not alter the cannonball's horizontal velocity; it only affects its vertical velocity, accelerating the cannonball toward the ground. Its y velocity has an increasingly negative value as it moves through the air.

The time it takes for the cannonball to hit the ground is completely unaffected by its horizontal velocity. It makes no difference if the cannonball flies out of the cannon with a horizontal velocity of 300 m/s or if it drops out of the cannon's mouth with a horizontal velocity of 0 m/s. In either case, the cannonball will take the same amount of time to land. Its vertical motion is determined solely by the acceleration due to gravity, −9.80 m/s^2.

The equations to the right illustrate how you can use the x and y components of the cannonball's velocity and acceleration to determine how long it will take to reach the ground (its *flight time*) and how far it will travel horizontally (its *range*). These are standard motion equations applied in the x and y directions. They hold true when the acceleration is constant, as is the case with projectile motion, where the acceleration

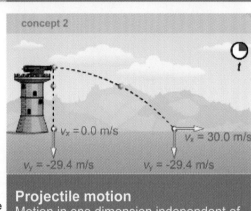

concept 2

$v_x = 0.0$ m/s

$v_x = 30.0$ m/s

$v_y = -29.4$ m/s

$v_y = -29.4$ m/s

Projectile motion
Motion in one dimension independent of motion in other

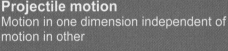

equation 1

$a_y = -9.80$ m/s^2

t

Δy

Projectile flight time

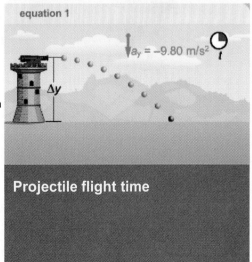

along each dimension is constant.

In Equation 1, we show how to determine how long it takes a projectile to reach the ground. This equation holds true when the initial vertical velocity is zero, as it is when a cannon fires horizontally. To derive the equation, we use a standard linear motion equation applied to the vertical, or y, dimension. You see that equation in the second line in Equation 1. We substitute zero for the initial vertical velocity and then solve for t, the elapsed time.

Equation 2 shows how to solve for the range. The horizontal displacement of the ball equals the product of its horizontal velocity and the elapsed time. Since its horizontal velocity does not change, it equals the initial horizontal velocity. Together, the two equations describe the flight of a projectile that is fired horizontally.

$$v_{yi} = 0$$

$$\Delta y = v_{yi}t + \frac{1}{2}a_y t^2$$

$$t = \sqrt{\frac{2\Delta y}{a_y}}$$

v_{yi} = initial y velocity
Δy = vertical displacement
$a_y = -9.80 \text{ m/s}^2$
t = time when projectile hits ground

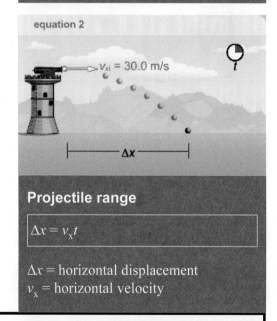

equation 2

$v_{xi} = 30.0 \text{ m/s}$

Δx

Projectile range

$$\Delta x = v_x t$$

Δx = horizontal displacement
v_x = horizontal velocity

4.4 - Sample problem: a horizontal cannon

What horizontal firing (muzzle) velocity splashes the cannonball into the pond?

Variables

vertical displacement	$\Delta y = -40.0 \text{ m}$
vertical acceleration	$a_y = -9.80 \text{ m/s}^2$
horizontal displacement	$\Delta x = 95.0 \text{ m}$
elapsed time	t
horizontal velocity	v_x

What is the strategy?

1. Calculate how long the cannonball remains in the air. This can be done with a standard motion equation.

2. Use the elapsed time and the specified horizontal displacement to calculate the required horizontal firing velocity.

Physics principles and equations

$$\Delta y = v_{yi}t + \tfrac{1}{2}a_y t^2$$

$$v_x = \frac{\Delta x}{t}$$

The amount of time the ball takes to fall is independent of its horizontal velocity.

Step-by-step solution

We start by determining how long the cannonball is in the air. We can use a linear motion equation to find the time it takes the cannonball to drop to the ground.

Step	Reason
1. $\Delta y = v_{yi}t + \tfrac{1}{2}a_y t^2$	linear motion equation
2. $\Delta y = (0)t + \tfrac{1}{2}a_y t^2$	initial vertical velocity zero
3. $t = \sqrt{\dfrac{2\Delta y}{a_y}}$	solve for time
4. $t = \sqrt{\dfrac{2(-40.0 \text{ m})}{-9.80 \text{ m/s}^2}}$	enter values
5. $t = 2.86 \text{ s}$	evaluate

Now that we know the time the cannonball takes to fall to the ground, we can calculate the required horizontal velocity.

Step		Reason
6.	$v_x = \dfrac{\Delta x}{t}$	definition of velocity
7.	$v_x = \dfrac{95.0 \text{ m}}{2.86 \text{ s}}$	enter values
8.	$v_x = 33.2 \text{ m/s}$	divide

4.5 - Interactive problem: the monkey and the professor

The monkey at the right has a banana bazooka and plans to shoot a banana at a hungry physics professor. He has a glove to catch the banana. The professor is hanging from the tree, and the instant he sees the banana moving, he will drop from the tree in his eagerness to dine.

Can you correctly aim the monkey's bazooka so that the banana reaches the professor's glove as he falls? Should you aim the shot above, below or directly at the professor? As long as the banana is fired fast enough to reach the professor before it hits the ground, does its initial speed matter? (Note: The simulation has a minimum speed so the banana will reach the professor when correctly aimed.)

Give it a try in the interactive simulation to the right. No calculations are required to solve this problem. As you ponder your answer, consider the two key concepts of projectile motion: (1) all objects accelerate toward the ground at the same rate, and (2) the horizontal and vertical components of motion are independent. (The effect of air resistance is ignored.)

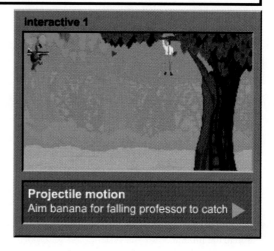

Interactive 1

Projectile motion
Aim banana for falling professor to catch ▶

Aim the banana by dragging the vector arrow at the end of the bazooka. You can increase the firing speed of the banana by making the arrow longer, and you can change the angle at which the banana is fired by moving the arrow up or down. Stretching out the vector makes it easy to aim the banana.

To shoot the banana, press GO. Press RESET to try again. (Do not worry: We, too, value physics professors, so the professor will emerge unscathed.)

If you have trouble with this problem, review the section on projectile motion.

4.6 - Interactive checkpoint: golfing

A golfer is on the edge of a 12.5 m high bluff overlooking the eighteenth hole, which is located 67.1 m from the base of the bluff. She launches a horizontal shot that lands in the hole on the fly, and the gallery erupts into cheers. How long was the ball in the air? What was the ball's horizontal velocity? Take upward to be the positive y direction.

Answer:

$t =$ [   ] s

$v_x =$ [   ] m/s

4.7 - Projectile motion: juggling

Juggling is a form of projectile motion in which the projectiles have initial velocities in both the vertical and horizontal dimensions. This motion takes more work to analyze than when a projectile's initial vertical velocity is zero, as it was with the horizontally fired cannonball.

Jugglers throw balls from one hand to the other and then back. To juggle multiple balls, the juggler repeats the same simple toss over and over. An experienced juggler's ability to make this basic routine seem so effortless stems from the fact that the motion of each ball is identical. The balls always arrive at the same place for the catch, and in roughly the same amount of time.

A juggler throws each ball with an initial velocity that has both x and y components. Ignoring the effect of air resistance, the x component of the velocity remains constant as the ball moves in the air from one hand to another.

The initial y velocity is upward, which means it is a positive value. At all times, the ball accelerates downward at -9.80 m/s^2. This means the ball's velocity decreases as it rises until it has a vertical velocity of zero. The ball then accelerates back toward the ground. When the ball plops down into the other hand, the magnitude of the y velocity will be the same as when the ball was tossed up, but its sign will be reversed. If the ball is thrown up with an initial y velocity of $+5$ m/s, it will land with a y velocity of -5 m/s. This symmetry is due to the constant rate of vertical acceleration caused by gravity.

Because the vertical acceleration is constant, the ball takes as much time to reach its peak of motion as it takes to fall back to the other hand. This also means it has covered half of the horizontal trip when it is at its peak. The path traced by the ball is a *parabola*, a shape symmetrical around its midpoint.

We said the juggler chooses the y velocity so that the ball takes the right amount of time to rise and then fall back to the other hand. What, exactly, is the right amount of time? It is the time needed for the ball to move the horizontal distance between the juggler's hands.

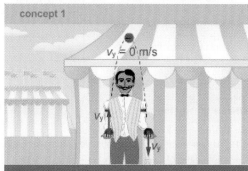

Projectile motion: y velocity
y velocity = zero at peak
Initial y velocity equal but opposite to final y velocity

Projectile motion: x velocity
x velocity constant

If a juggler's hands are 0.5 meters apart, and the horizontal velocity of the ball is 0.5 m/s, it will take one second for the ball to move that horizontal distance. (Remember that the horizontal velocity is constant.) The juggler must throw the ball with enough vertical velocity to keep it in the air for one second.

4.8 - Sample problem: calculating initial velocity in projectile motion

A juggler throws each ball so it hangs in the air for 1.20 seconds before landing in the other hand, 0.750 meters away.

What are the initial vertical and horizontal velocity components?

Variables

elapsed time	$t = 1.20$ s
horizontal displacement	$\Delta x = 0.750$ m
initial vertical velocity	v_y
horizontal velocity	v_x
acceleration due to gravity	$a_y = -9.80$ m/s^2

What is the strategy?

1. Use a linear motion equation to determine the initial vertical velocity that will result in a final vertical velocity of 0 m/s after 0.60 s (half the total time of 1.20 s).

2. Use the definition of velocity to calculate the horizontal velocity, since the displacement and the elapsed time are both provided.

Physics principles and equations

We rely on two concepts. First, the motion of a projectile is symmetrical, so half the time elapses on the way up and the other half on the way down. Second, the vertical velocity of a projectile is zero at its peak.

We also use the two equations listed below.

$$v_{yf} = v_{yi} + a_y t$$

$$v_x = \frac{\Delta x}{t}$$

Step-by-step solution

We start by calculating the vertical component of the initial velocity. We use the fact that gravity will slow the ball to a vertical velocity of 0 m/s at the peak, 0.60 seconds (halfway) into the flight.

Step	Reason
1. $v_{yf} = v_{yi} + a_y t$	motion equation
2. $0 = v_{yi} + a_y t$	vertical velocity at peak equals zero
3. $v_{yi} = -a_y t$	rearrange
4. $v_{yi} = -(-9.80 \text{ m/s}^2)(0.600 \text{ s})$	enter values
5. $v_{yi} = 5.89 \text{ m/s}$	multiply

Now we solve for the horizontal velocity component. We could have solved for this first; these steps require no results from the steps above.

Step	Reason
6. $v_x = \dfrac{\Delta x}{t}$	definition of velocity
7. $v_x = \dfrac{0.750 \text{ m}}{1.20 \text{ s}}$	enter values
8. $v_x = 0.625 \text{ m/s}$	divide

From our perspective, the horizontal velocity of the ball when it is going from our left to our right is positive. From the juggler's, it is negative.

4.9 - Interactive problem: the monkey and the professor, part II

The monkey is at it again with his banana bazooka. Another hungry professor drops from the tree the instant the banana leaves the tip of the bazooka. (Are professors paid enough? Answer: No.)

Can you correctly aim the banana so that it hits the professor's glove as she falls? Should you aim the shot above, below or directly at the glove? Does the banana's initial speed matter? (Note: The simulation has a minimum speed so the banana will reach the professor when correctly aimed.) Air resistance is ignored in this simulation.

Give it a try in the interactive simulation to the right. No calculations are needed to solve this problem.

To find an answer, think about the key concepts of projectile motion: Objects accelerate toward the ground at the same rate, and the horizontal and vertical components of motion are independent.

interactive 1

Projectile motion
Aim banana to hit falling professor

Once you launch the simulation, aim the banana by dragging the vector arrow at the end of the bazooka. You can increase the firing speed of the banana by making the arrow longer. Moving the arrow up or down changes the angle at which the banana is fired. Stretching out the vector makes it easy to aim the banana.

To shoot the banana, press GO. Press RESET to try again. Keep trying until the banana reaches the professor!

4.10 - Projectile motion: aiming a cannon

The complexities of correctly aiming artillery pieces have challenged leaders as famed as Napoleon and President Harry S. Truman. Because a cannon typically fires projectiles at a particular speed, aiming the cannon to hit a target downfield involves adjusting the cannon's angle relative to the ground. If you break the motion into components, you can determine how far a projectile with a given speed and angle will travel.

To determine when and where a cannonball will land, you must consider horizontal and vertical motion separately. To start, convert its initial speed and angle into x and y velocity components. The horizontal velocity will equal the initial speed of the ball multiplied by the cosine of the angle at which the cannonball is launched. The horizontal velocity will not change as the cannonball flies toward the target.

The initial y velocity equals the initial speed times the sine of the launch angle. The y velocity is not constant. It changes at the rate of −9.80 m/s². When the cannonball lands at the **same height** at which it was fired, its final y velocity is equal but opposite to its initial y velocity.

The initial y velocity of the projectile determines how long it stays in the air. As mentioned, the cannonball lands with a final y velocity equal to the negative of the initial y velocity, that is, $y_f = -y_i$. This means the **change** in y velocity equals $-2y_i$. Knowing this, and the value for acceleration due to gravity, enables us to rearrange a standard motion equation ($v_f = v_i + at$) and solve for the elapsed time. The equation for the flight time of a projectile is the third one in Equation 1.

Once you know how long the ball stays in the air, you can determine how far it travels by multiplying the horizontal velocity by the ball's flight time. This is the final equation on the right.

You can use these equations to solve projectile motion problems, but understanding the analysis that led to the equations is more important than knowing the equations. Recall the basic principles of projectile motion: The x velocity is constant, the y velocity changes at the rate of −9.80 m/s², and the projectile's final y velocity is the opposite of its initial y velocity.

concept 1

Aiming a projectile, step 1
Start with initial angle, speed
Separate into x and y components

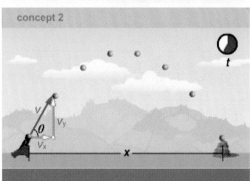

concept 2

Aiming a projectile, step 2
Use initial y velocity and a_y to calculate flight time
Use initial x velocity and flight time to calculate range

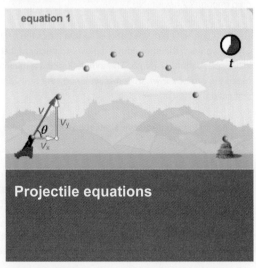

equation 1

Projectile equations

Becca Fox

1. a. X rays, ultraviolet, infrared, Microwaves,
   radio waves.
   b.

$$v_x = v \cos \theta$$
$$v_y = v \sin \theta$$
$$t = -2v_y / a_y \ \ \text{(same-height landing)}$$
$$\Delta x = v_x t$$

$v_x = x$ velocity
$v_y = $ initial y velocity
$t = $ time projectile is in air
$\Delta x = $ horizontal displacement
$a_y = -9.80$ m/s^2

4.11 - Sample problem: a cannon's range

How far away is the haystack from the cannon?

Draw a diagram

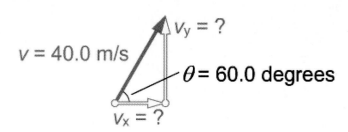

$v = 40.0$ m/s
$v_y = ?$
$\theta = 60.0$ degrees
$v_x = ?$

Variables

speed	$v = 40.0$ m/s
angle	$\theta = 60.0°$
initial y velocity	v_{yi}
final y velocity	v_{yf}
x velocity	v_x
elapsed time	t
horizontal displacement	Δx
acceleration due to gravity	$a_y = -9.80$ m/s^2

What is the strategy?

1. Use trigonometry to determine the x and y components of the cannonball's initial velocity.
2. The final y velocity is the opposite of the initial y velocity. Use that fact and a linear motion equation to determine how long the cannonball is in the air.
3. The x velocity is constant. Rearrange the definition of constant velocity to solve for horizontal displacement (range).

Physics principles and equations

The projectile's final y velocity is the opposite of its initial y velocity. The x velocity is constant.

We use the following motion equations.

$$v_{yf} = v_{yi} + a_y t$$

$$v_x = \frac{\Delta x}{t}$$

Step-by-step solution

Use trigonometry to determine the x and y components of the initial velocity from the initial speed and the angle.

Step	Reason
1. $v_y = v \sin \theta$	trigonometry
2. $v_y = (40.0 \text{ m/s}) \sin 60.0°$	enter values
3. $v_y = 34.6 \text{ m/s}$	evaluate
4. $v_x = v \cos \theta$	trigonometry
5. $v_x = (40.0 \text{ m/s}) \cos 60.0°$	enter values
6. $v_x = 20.0 \text{ m/s}$	evaluate

Copyright 2000-2007 Kinetic Books Co. Chapter 04

Now we focus on the vertical dimension of motion, using the initial y velocity to determine the time the cannonball is in the air. We calculated the initial y velocity in step 3.

Step	Reason
7. $v_{yf} = v_{yi} + a_y t$	linear motion equation
8. $-v_{yi} = v_{yi} + a_y t$	final y velocity is negative of initial y velocity
9. $-2v_{yi} = a_y t$	rearrange
10. $t = \dfrac{-2v_{yi}}{a_y}$	solve for time
11. $t = \dfrac{-2(34.6 \text{ m/s})}{-9.80 \text{ m/s}^2}$	enter values
12. $t = 7.07$ s	evaluate

Now we use the time and the x velocity to solve for the cannonball's range. We calculated the constant x velocity in step 6.

Step	Reason
13. $v_x = \dfrac{\Delta x}{t}$	definition of velocity
14. $\Delta x = v_x t$	rearrange
15. $\Delta x = (20.0 \text{ m/s})(7.07 \text{ s})$	enter values
16. $\Delta x = 141$ m	multiply

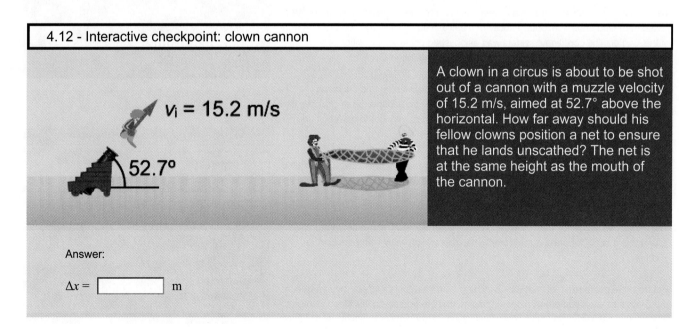

4.12 - Interactive checkpoint: clown cannon

$v_i = 15.2$ m/s

52.7°

A clown in a circus is about to be shot out of a cannon with a muzzle velocity of 15.2 m/s, aimed at 52.7° above the horizontal. How far away should his fellow clowns position a net to ensure that he lands unscathed? The net is at the same height as the mouth of the cannon.

Answer:

$\Delta x = $ _____ m

4.13 - Interactive problem: test your juggling!

Much of this chapter focuses on projectile motion: specifically, how objects move in two dimensions. If you have grasped all the concepts, you can use what you have learned to make the person at the right juggle.

The distance between the juggler's hands is 0.70 meters and the acceleration due to gravity is −9.80 m/s². You have to calculate the initial x and y velocities to send each ball from one hand to the other. If you do so correctly, he will juggle three balls at once.

There are many possible answers to this problem. A good strategy is to pick an initial x or y component of the velocity, and then determine the other velocity component so that the balls, once thrown, will land in the juggler's opposite hand. You want to pick an initial y velocity above 2.0 m/s to give the juggler time to make his catch and throw. For similar reasons, you do not want to pick an initial x velocity that exceeds 2.0 m/s.

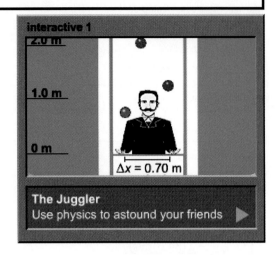

interactive 1

2.0 m
1.0 m
0 m
$\Delta x = 0.70$ m

The Juggler
Use physics to astound your friends

Make your calculations and then click on the diagram to the right to launch the simulation. Enter the values you have calculated to the nearest 0.1 m/s and press the GO button. Do not worry about the timing of the juggler's throws. They are calculated for you automatically.

If you have difficulty with this problem, refer to the sections on projectile motion.

4.14 - Reference frames

Reference frame: A coordinate system used to make observations.

The choice of a reference frame determines the perception of motion. A reference frame is a coordinate system used to make observations. If you stand next to a lab table and hold out a meter stick, you have established a reference frame for making observations.

The choice of reference frames was a minor issue when we considered juggling: We chose to measure the horizontal velocity of a ball as you saw it when you stood in front of the juggler. The coordinate system was established using your position and orientation, assuming you were stationary relative to the juggler.

As the juggler sees the horizontal velocity of the ball, however, it has the same magnitude you measure, but is opposite in sign. It does so because when you see it moving from your left to your right, he sees it moving from his right to his left. If you measure the velocity as 1.1 m/s, he measures it as −1.1 m/s.

In the analysis of motion, it is commonly assumed that you, the observer, are standing still. To pursue this further, we ask you to sit or stand still for a moment. Are you moving? Likely you will answer: "No, you just asked me to be still!"

That response is true for what you are implicitly using as your reference frame, your coordinate system for making measurements. You are implicitly using the Earth's surface.

But from the perspective of someone watching from the Moon, you are moving due to the Earth's rotation and orbital motion. Imagine that the person on the Moon wanted to launch a rocket to pick you up. Unless the person factored in your velocity as the Earth

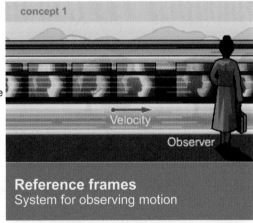

concept 1

Velocity
Observer

Reference frames
System for observing motion

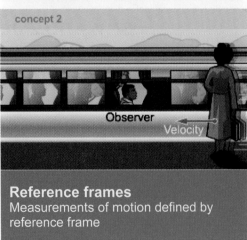

concept 2

Observer
Velocity

Reference frames
Measurements of motion defined by reference frame

spins about its axis, as well as the fact that the Earth orbits the Sun and the Moon orbits the Earth, the rocket surely would miss its target. If you truly think you are stationary here on Earth, you must also conclude that the entire universe revolves around the Earth (a dubious conclusion, though a common one for centuries).

Reference frames define your perception and measurements of motion. If you are in a car moving at 80 km/h, another car moving alongside you with the same velocity will appear to you as if it is not moving at all. As you drive along, objects that you ordinarily think of as stationary, such as trees, seem to move rapidly past you. On the other hand, someone sitting in one of the trees would say the tree is stationary and you are the one moving by.

A reference frame is more than just a viewpoint: It is a coordinate system used to make measurements. For instance, you establish and use a reference frame when you do lab exercises. Consider making a series of measurements of how long it takes a ball to roll down a plane. You might say the ball's starting point is the top of the ramp. Its x position there is 0.0 meters. You might define the surface of the table as having a y position of 0.0 meters, and the ball's initial y position is its height above the table. Typically you consider the plane and table to be stationary, and the ball to be moving.

Two reference frames are shown on the right. One is defined by Joan, the woman standing at a train station. As the illustration in Concept 1 shows, from Joan's perspective, she is stationary and the train is moving to the right at a constant velocity.

Another reference frame is defined by the perspective of Ted who is inside the train, and considers the train stationary. This reference frame is illustrated in Concept 2. Ted in the train perceives himself as stationary, and would see Joan moving backward at a constant velocity. He would assign Joan the velocity vector shown in the diagram.

It is important to note there is no correct reference frame; Joan cannot say her reference frame is better than the reference frame used by Ted. Measurements of velocity and other values made by either observer are equally valid.

Reference frames are often chosen for the sake of convenience (choosing the Earth's surface, not the surface of Jupiter, is a logical choice for your lab exercises). Once you choose a reference frame, you must use it consistently, making all your measurements using that reference frame's coordinate system. You cannot measure a ball's initial position using the Earth's surface as a reference frame, and its final position using the surface of Jupiter, and still easily apply the physics you are learning.

4.15 - Relative velocity

Observers in reference frames moving past one another may measure different velocities for the same object. This concept is called *relative velocity*.

In the illustrations to the right, two observers are measuring the velocity of a soccer ball, but from different vantage points: The man is standing on a moving train, while the woman is standing on the ground. The man and the woman will measure different velocities for the soccer ball.

Let's discuss this scenario in more depth. Fred is standing on a train car and kicks a ball to the right. The train is moving along the track at a constant velocity. The train is Fred's reference frame, and, to him, it is stationary. In Fred's frame of reference, his kick causes the ball to move at a constant velocity of positive 10 m/s.

concept 1

10 m/s

Observer on train
Measures ball velocity relative to train

The train is passing Sarah, who is standing on the ground. Her reference frame is the ground. From her perspective, the train with the man on it moves by at a constant velocity of positive 5 m/s.

What velocity would Sarah measure for the soccer ball in her reference frame? She adds the velocity vector of the train, 5 m/s, to the velocity vector of the ball as measured on the train, 10 m/s. The sum is positive 15 m/s, pointing along the horizontal axis. Summing the velocities determines the velocity as measured by Sarah.

Note that there are two different answers for the velocity of one ball. Each answer is correct in the reference frame of that observer. For someone standing on the ground, the ball moves at 15 m/s, and for someone standing on the train, it moves at 10 m/s.

The equation in Equation 1 shows how to relate the velocity of an object in one reference frame to the velocity of an object in another frame.

The variable $\mathbf{v}_{OA}$ is the velocity vector of the object as measured in reference frame A (which in this diagram is the ground). The variable $\mathbf{v}_{OB}$ is the velocity of an object as measured in reference frame B (which in this diagram is the train). Finally, the variable $\mathbf{v}_{BA}$ is the velocity of frame B (the train) relative to frame A (the ground). $\mathbf{v}_{OA}$ is the **vector** sum of $\mathbf{v}_{OB}$ and $\mathbf{v}_{BA}$.

An important caveat is that this equation can be used to solve relative velocity problems only when the frames are moving at constant velocity relative to one another. If one or both frames are accelerating, the equation does not apply.

We use this equation in the example problem on the right. Now Sarah sees the train moving in the opposite direction, at **negative** 5 m/s. It is negative because to Sarah, the train is moving to the left along the x axis. Fred is on the train, again kicking the ball from left to right as before. Here he kicks the ball at +5 m/s, as measured in his reference frame. To Sarah, how fast and in what direction is the ball moving now?

The answer is that she sees the ball as stationary. The sum of the velocities equals zero, because it is the sum of +5 m/s (the velocity of the object as measured in reference frame B) and −5 m/s (the velocity of frame B as measured from frame A).

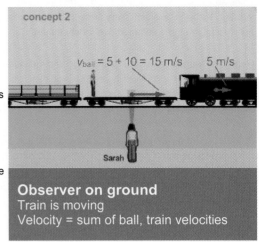

Observer on ground
Train is moving
Velocity = sum of ball, train velocities

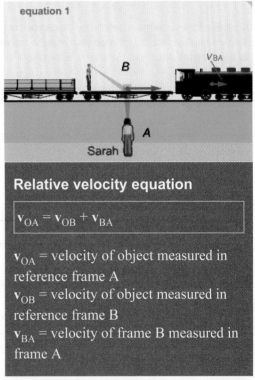

Relative velocity equation

$$\mathbf{v}_{OA} = \mathbf{v}_{OB} + \mathbf{v}_{BA}$$

$\mathbf{v}_{OA}$ = velocity of object measured in reference frame A
$\mathbf{v}_{OB}$ = velocity of object measured in reference frame B
$\mathbf{v}_{BA}$ = velocity of frame B measured in frame A

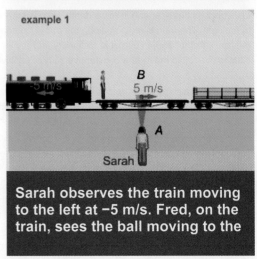

Sarah observes the train moving to the left at −5 m/s. Fred, on the train, sees the ball moving to the

right at +5 m/s. What is the ball's velocity in Sarah's reference frame?

$$\mathbf{v}_{OA} = \mathbf{v}_{OB} + \mathbf{v}_{BA}$$
$$\mathbf{v}_{OA} = (5 \text{ m/s}) + (-5 \text{ m/s}) = 0 \text{ m/s}$$

4.16 - Gotchas

A ball will land at the same time if you drop it straight down from the top of a building or if you throw it out horizontally. Yes, the ball will hit the ground at the same time in both cases. Velocity in the y direction is independent of velocity in the x direction.

An object has positive velocity along the x and y axes. Along the y axis, it accelerates, has a constant velocity for a while, then accelerates some more. What happens along the x axis? You have no idea. Information about motion along the y axis tells you nothing about motion along the x axis, because they can change independently.

A projectile has zero acceleration at its peak. No, a projectile has zero y velocity at its peak. Even though it briefly comes to rest in the vertical dimension, the projectile is always accelerating at −9.80 m/s^2 due to the force of gravity.

4.17 - Summary

Like any vector, velocity can be broken into its component vectors in the x and y dimensions using trigonometry. These components sum to equal the velocity vector. The components can also be analyzed separately, reducing a two-dimensional problem to two separate one-dimensional problems. The same principle applies to the acceleration vector.

Objects that move solely under the influence of gravity are called projectiles. To analyze projectile motion, consider the motion along each dimension separately.

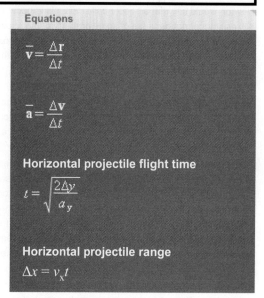

Equations

$$\bar{\mathbf{v}} = \frac{\Delta \mathbf{r}}{\Delta t}$$

$$\bar{\mathbf{a}} = \frac{\Delta \mathbf{v}}{\Delta t}$$

Horizontal projectile flight time

$$t = \sqrt{\frac{2\Delta y}{a_y}}$$

Horizontal projectile range

$$\Delta x = v_x t$$

5.0 - Introduction

Objects can speed up, slow down, and change direction while they move. In short, they accelerate.

A famous scientist, Sir Isaac Newton, wondered how and why this occurs. Theories about acceleration existed, but Newton did not find them very convincing. His skepticism led him to some of the most important discoveries in physics.

Before Newton, people who studied motion noted that the objects they observed on Earth always slowed down. According to their theories, objects possessed an internal property that caused this acceleration. This belief led them to theorize that a force was required to keep things moving.

This idea seems like common sense. Moving objects do seem to slow down on their own: a car coasts to a stop, a yo-yo stops spinning, a soccer ball rolls to a halt. Newton, however, rejected this belief, instead suggesting the opposite: The nature of objects is to continue moving unless some force acts on them. For instance, Newton would say that a soccer ball stops rolling because of forces like friction and air resistance, not because of some property of the soccer ball. He would say that if these forces were **not** present, the ball would roll and roll and roll. A force (a kick) is required to start the ball's motion, and a force such as the frictional force of the grass is required to stop its motion.

Newton proposed several fundamental principles that govern forces and motion. Nearly 300 years later, his insights remain the foundation for the study of forces and much of motion. This chapter stands as a testament to a brilliant scientist.

At the right, you can use a simulation to experience one of Newton's fundamental principles: his law relating a net force, mass and acceleration. In the simulation, you can attempt some of the basic tasks required of a helicopter pilot. To do so, you control the **net** force upward on the helicopter. When the helicopter is in the air, the net force equals the lift force minus its weight. (The lift force is caused by the interaction of the spinning blades with the air, and is used to propel the helicopter upward.) The net force, like all forces, is measured in newtons (N).

When the helicopter is in the air, you can set the net force to positive, negative, or zero values. The net force is negative when the helicopter's lift force is less than its weight. When the helicopter is on the ground, there cannot be a negative net force because the ground opposes the downward force of the helicopter's weight and does not allow the helicopter to sink below the Earth's surface.

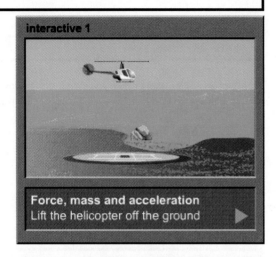

interactive 1

Force, mass and acceleration
Lift the helicopter off the ground ▶

Sir Isaac Newton, 1642 -1727

The simulation starts with the helicopter on the ground and a net force of 0 N. To increase the net force on the helicopter, press the up arrow key (↑) on your keyboard; to decrease it, press the down arrow key (↓). This net force will continue to be applied until you change it.

To start, apply a positive net force to cause the helicopter to rise off the ground. Next, attempt to have the helicopter reach a constant vertical velocity. For an optional challenge, have it hover at a constant height of 15 meters, and finally, attempt to land (not crash) the helicopter.

Once in the air, you may find that controlling the craft is a little trickier than you anticipated – it may act a little skittish. Welcome to (a) the challenge of flying a helicopter and (b) Newton's world.

Here are a few hints: Start slowly! Initially, just use small net forces. You can look at the acceleration gauge to see in which direction you are accelerating. Try to keep your acceleration initially between plus or minus 0.25 m/s^2.

This simulation is designed to help you experiment with the relationship between force and acceleration. If you find that achieving a constant velocity or otherwise controlling the helicopter is challenging – read on! You will gain insights as you do.

5.1 - Force

Force: Loosely defined as "pushing" or "pulling."

Your everyday conception of force as pushing or pulling provides a good starting point for explaining what a force is.

There are many types of forces. Your initial thoughts may be of forces that require direct contact: pushing a box, hitting a ball, pulling a wagon, and so on.

Some forces, however, can act without direct contact. For example, the gravitational force of the Earth pulls on the Moon even though hundreds of thousands of kilometers separate the two bodies. The gravitational force of the Moon, in turn, pulls on the Earth.

Electromagnetic forces also do not require direct contact. For instance, two magnets will attract or repel each other even when they are not touching each other.

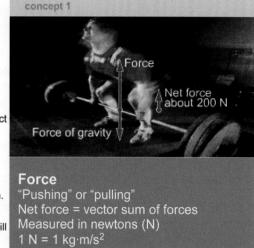

concept 1

Force
about 200 N
Net force
Force of gravity

Force
"Pushing" or "pulling"
Net force = vector sum of forces
Measured in newtons (N)
$1 \text{ N} = 1 \text{ kg·m/s}^2$

We have discussed a few forces above, and could continue to discuss more of them: static friction, kinetic friction, weight, air resistance, electrostatic force, tension, buoyant force, and so forth. This extensive list gives you a sense of why a general definition of force is helpful.

These varied types of forces do share some essential attributes. Newton observed that a force, or to be precise, a net force, causes acceleration.

All forces are vectors: their direction matters. The weightlifter shown in Concept 1 must exert an upward force on the barbell in order to accelerate it off the ground. For the barbell to accelerate upward, the force he exerts must be greater than the downward force of the Earth's gravity on the barbell. The *net force* (the vector sum of all forces on an object) and the object's mass determine the direction and amount of acceleration.

The SI unit for force is the newton (N). One newton is defined as one kg·m/s^2. We will discuss why this combination of units equals a newton shortly.

We have given examples where a net force causes an object to accelerate. Forces can also be in equilibrium (balance), which means there is no net force and no acceleration. When a weightlifter holds a barbell steady over his head after lifting it, his upward force on the barbell exactly balances the downward gravitational force on it, and the barbell's acceleration is zero. The net force would also be zero if he were lifting the barbell at constant velocity.

5.2 - Newton's first law

Newton's first law: "Every body perseveres in its state of being at rest or of moving uniformly straight forward except insofar as it is compelled to change by forces impressed."

This translation of Newton's original definition (Newton wrote it in Latin) may seem antiquated, but it does state an admirable amount of physics in a single sentence. Today, we are more likely to summarize Newton's first law as saying that **an object remains at rest, or maintains a constant velocity, unless a net external force acts upon it**. (Newton's formulation even includes an "insofar" to foreshadow his second law, which we will discuss shortly.)

To state his law another way: An object's velocity changes − it accelerates − when a net force acts upon it. In Concept 1, a puck is shown gliding across the ice with nearly constant velocity because there is little net force acting upon it. The puck that is stationary in Concept 2 will not move until it is struck by the hockey stick.

The hockey stick can cause a great change in the puck's velocity: a professional's slap shot can travel 150 km/hr. Forces also cause things to slow down. As a society, we spend a fair amount of effort trying to minimize these forces. For example, the grass of a soccer field is specially cut to reduce the force of friction to ensure that the ball travels a good distance when passed or shot.

Top athletes also know how to reduce air resistance. Tour de France cyclists often bike single file. The riders who follow the leader encounter less air resistance. Similarly, downhill ski racers "tuck" their bodies into low, rounded shapes to reduce air resistance, and they coat the bottoms of their skis with wax compounds to reduce the slowing effect of the snow's friction.

Newton's first law states that an object will continue to move "uniformly straight" unless acted upon by a force. Today we state this as "constant velocity," since a change in direction is acceleration as much as a change in speed. In either formulation, the point is this: Direction matters. An object not only continues at the same speed, it also moves in the same direction unless a net force acts upon it.

You use this principle every day. Even in as basic a task as writing a note, your fingers apply changing forces to alter the direction of the pen's motion even as its speed is approximately constant.

There is an important fact to note here: Newton's laws hold true in an *inertial reference frame*. An object that experiences no net force in an inertial reference frame moves at a constant velocity. Since we assume that observations are made in such a reference frame, we will be terse here about what is meant. The surface of the Earth (including your physics lab) approximates an inertial reference frame, certainly closely enough for the typical classroom lab experiment. (The motion of the Earth makes it less than perfect.)

Newton's first law
Objects move at constant velocity unless acted on by net force

Newton's first law
Objects at rest remain at rest in absence of net force

A car rounding a curve provides an example of a *non-inertial reference frame*. If you decided to conduct your experiments inside such a car, Newton's laws would **not** apply. Objects might seem to accelerate (a coffee cup sliding along the dashboard, for example) yet you would observe no net force acting on the cup. However, the nature of observations made in an accelerating reference frame is a topic far removed from this chapter's focus, and this marks the end of our discussion of reference frames in this chapter.

5.3 - Mass

Mass: A property of an object that determines how much it will resist a change in velocity.

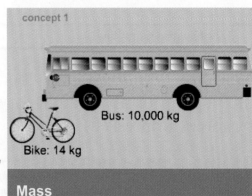

Bus: 10,000 kg
Bike: 14 kg

Mass
Measures an object's resistance to

Newton's second law summarizes the relationship of force, mass and acceleration. Mass is crucial to understanding the second law because an object's mass determines how much it resists a change in velocity.

More massive objects require more net force to accelerate than less massive objects. An object's resistance to a change in velocity is called its *inertial mass.* It requires more force to accelerate the bus on the right at, say, five m/s² than the much less massive bicycle.

A common error is to confuse mass and weight. Weight is a force caused by gravity and is measured in newtons. Mass is an object's resistance to change in velocity and is measured in kilograms. An object's weight can vary: Its weight is greater on Jupiter's surface than on Earth's, since Jupiter's surface gravity is stronger than Earth's. In contrast, the object's mass does not change as it moves from planet to planet. The kilogram (kg) is the SI unit of mass.

change in velocity
Measured in kilograms (kg)

5.4 - Gravitational force: weight

Weight: The force of gravity on an object.

We all experience weight, the force of gravity. On Earth, by far the largest component of the gravitational force we experience comes from our own planet. To give you a sense of proportion, the Earth exerts 1600 times more gravitational force on you than does the Sun. As a practical matter, an object's weight on Earth is defined as the gravitational force the Earth exerts on it.

Weight is a force; it has both magnitude and direction. At the Earth' surface, the direction of the force is toward the center of the Earth.

The magnitude of weight equals the product of an object's mass and the rate of freefall acceleration due to gravity. On Earth, the rate of acceleration *g* due to gravity is 9.80 m/s². The rate of freefall acceleration depends on a planet's mass and radius, so it varies from planet to planet. On Jupiter, for instance, gravity exerts more force than on Earth, which makes for a greater value for freefall acceleration. This means you would weigh more on Jupiter's surface than on Earth's.

Scales, such as the one shown in Concept 1, are used to measure the magnitude of weight. The force of Earth's gravity pulls Kevin down and compresses a spring. This scale is calibrated to display the amount of weight in both newtons and pounds, as shown in Equation 1. Forces like weight are measured in pounds in the British system. One newton equals about 0.225 pounds.

A quick word of caution: In everyday conversation, people speak of someone who "weighs 100 kilograms," but kilograms are units for mass, not weight. Weight, like any force, is measured in newtons. A person with a mass of 100 kg weighs 980 newtons.

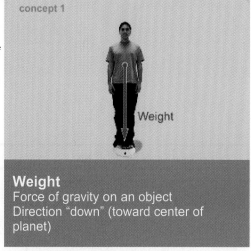

concept 1

Weight
Force of gravity on an object
Direction "down" (toward center of planet)

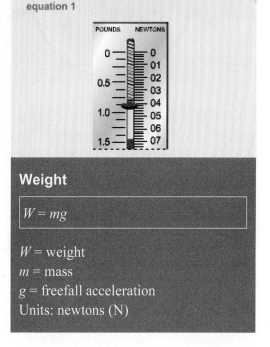

equation 1

Weight

$$W = mg$$

W = weight
m = mass
g = freefall acceleration
Units: newtons (N)

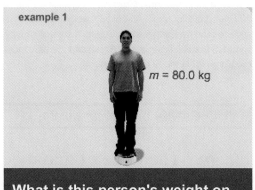

example 1

$m = 80.0$ kg

What is this person's weight on Earth?

$W = mg$

$W = (80.0 \text{ kg})(9.80 \text{ m/s}^2)$

$W = 784$ N

5.5 - Newton's second law

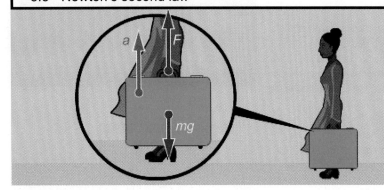

concept 1

Newton's second law
Net force equals mass times acceleration

Newton's second law: "A change in motion is proportional to the motive force impressed and takes place along the straight line in which that force is impressed."

Newton stated that a change in motion (acceleration) is proportional to force. Today, physicists call this Newton's second law, and it is stated to explicitly include mass. Physicists state that **acceleration is proportional to the net force on an object and inversely proportional to its mass**.

To describe this in the form of an equation: net force equals mass times acceleration, or $\Sigma\mathbf{F} = m\mathbf{a}$. It is the law. The Σ notation means the vector sum of all the forces acting on an object: in other words, the net force. Both the net force and acceleration are vectors that point in the same direction, and Newton's formulation stressed this point: "The change in motion...takes place along the straight line in which that force is impressed." The second law explains the units that make up a newton (kg·m/s^2); they are the result of multiplying mass by acceleration.

In the illustrations, you see an example of forces and the acceleration caused by the net force. The woman who stars in these illustrations lifts a suitcase. The weight of the suitcase opposes this motion. This force points down. Since the force supplied by the woman is greater than the weight, there is a net force up, which causes the suitcase to accelerate upward.

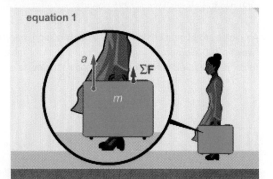

equation 1

Newton's second law

$$\Sigma\mathbf{F} = m\mathbf{a}$$

$\Sigma\mathbf{F}$ = net force

m = mass

$\mathbf{a}$ = acceleration

Units of force: newtons (N, kg·m/s^2)

In Example 1, the woman lifts the suitcase with a force of 158 N upward. The weight of the suitcase opposes the motion with a downward force of 147 newtons. The two forces act along a line, so we use the convention that up is positive and down is negative, and subtract to find the net force. (If both forces were not acting along a line, you would have to use trigonometry to calculate their components.)

The net force is 11 N, upward. The mass of the suitcase is 15 kg. Newton's second law can be used to determine the acceleration: It equals the net force divided by the mass. The suitcase accelerates at 0.73 m/s² in the direction of the net force, upward.

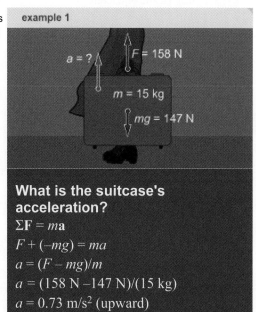

example 1

What is the suitcase's acceleration?

$$\Sigma \mathbf{F} = m\mathbf{a}$$
$$F + (-mg) = ma$$
$$a = (F - mg)/m$$
$$a = (158 \text{ N} - 147 \text{ N})/(15 \text{ kg})$$
$$a = 0.73 \text{ m/s}^2 \text{ (upward)}$$

5.6 - Sample problem: Rocket Guy

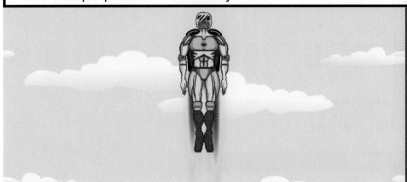

Rocket Guy weighs 905 N and his jet pack provides 1250 N of thrust, straight up. What is his acceleration?

Above you see "Rocket Guy," a superhero who wears a jet pack. The jet pack provides an upward force on him, while Rocket Guy's weight points downward.

Variables

All the forces on Rocket Guy are directed along the y axis.

thrust	$F_T = 1250$ N
weight	$-mg = -905$ N
mass	m
acceleration	a

What is the strategy?

1. Determine the net force on Rocket Guy.
2. Determine Rocket Guy's mass.
3. Use Newton's second law to find his acceleration.

Physics principles and equations

Newton's second law

$$\Sigma \mathbf{F} = m\mathbf{a}$$

Step-by-step solution

We start by determining the net force on Rocket Guy.

Step	Reason
1. $\Sigma \mathbf{F} = \mathbf{F}_T + m\mathbf{g}$	calculate net vertical force
2. $\Sigma F = F_T + (-mg)$	apply sign conventions
3. $\Sigma F = 1250 \text{ N} + (-905 \text{ N})$ $\Sigma F = 345 \text{ N}$	enter values and add

Now we find Rocket Guy's mass.

Step	Reason
4. $m = weight / g$	definition of weight
5. $m = (905 \text{ N}) / (9.80 \text{ m/s}^2)$ $m = 92.3 \text{ kg}$	calculate m

Finally we use Newton's second law to calculate Rocket Guy's acceleration.

Step	Reason
6. $\Sigma \mathbf{F} = m\mathbf{a}$	Newton's second law
7. $a = \Sigma F/m$	solve for a
8. $a = (345 \text{ N}) / (92.3 \text{ kg})$ $a = 3.74 \text{ m/s}^2$ (upward)	enter values from steps 3 and 5, and divide

5.7 - Interactive checkpoint: heavy cargo

A helicopter of mass 3770 kg can create an upward lift force F. When empty, it can accelerate straight upward at a maximum of 1.37 m/s². A careless crewman overloads the helicopter so that it is just unable to lift off. What is the mass of the cargo?

Answer:

$m_c =$ [   ] kg

5.8 - Interactive checkpoint: pushing a box

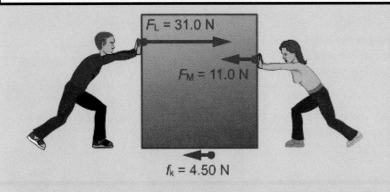

$F_L = 31.0$ N

$F_M = 11.0$ N

$f_k = 4.50$ N

Len pushes toward the right on a 12.0 kg box with a force of magnitude 31.0 N. Martina applies a 11.0 N force on the box in the opposite direction. The magnitude of the kinetic friction force between the box and the very smooth floor is 4.50 N as the box slides toward the right. What is the box's acceleration?

Answer:

$a =$ [   ] m/s²

5.9 - Interactive problem: flying in formation

The simulation on the right will give you some practice with Newton's second law. Initially, all the space ships have the same velocity. Their pilots want all the ships to accelerate at 5.15 m/s². The red ships have a mass of 1.27×10^4 kg, and the blue ships, a mass of 1.47×10^4 kg. You need to set the amount of force supplied by the ships' engines so that they accelerate equally. The masses of the ships do not change significantly as they burn fuel.

Apply Newton's second law to calculate the engine forces needed. The simulation uses scientific notation; you need to enter three-digit leading values. Enter your values and press GO to start the simulation. If all the ships accelerate at 5.15 m/s², you have succeeded. Press RESET to try again.

If you have difficulty solving this problem, review Newton's second law.

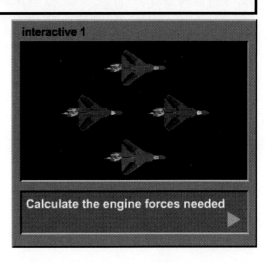

interactive 1

Calculate the engine forces needed

$F_{on\ person}$ $F_{on\ wall}$

Newton's third law
Forces come in pairs
Equal in strength, opposite in direction
The forces act on different objects

Newton's third law: "To any action there is always an opposite and equal reaction; in other words, the actions of two bodies upon each other are always equal and always opposite in direction."

Newton's third law states that forces come in pairs and that those forces are equal in magnitude and opposite in direction. When one object exerts a force on another, the second object exerts a force equal in magnitude but opposite in direction on the first.

For instance, if you push a button, it pushes back on you with the same amount of force. When someone leans on a wall, it pushes back, as shown in the illustration above.

To illustrate this concept, we use an example often associated with Newton, the falling apple shown in Example 1. The Earth's gravitational force pulls an apple toward the ground and the apple pulls upward on the Earth with an equally strong gravitational force. These pairs of forces are called *action-reaction* pairs, and Newton's third law is often called the action-reaction law.

If the forces on the apple and the Earth are equal in strength, do they cause them to accelerate at the same rate? Newton's second law enables you to answer this question. First, objects accelerate due to a net force, and the force of the apple on the Earth is minor compared to other forces, such as those of the Moon or Sun. But, even if the apple were exerting the sole force on the Earth, its acceleration would be very, very small because of the Earth's great mass. The forces are equal, but the acceleration for each body is inversely proportional to its mass.

equation 1

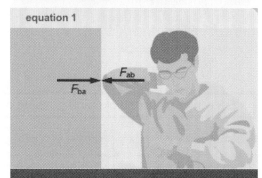

F_{ba} F_{ab}

Newton's third law

$$F_{ab} = -F_{ba}$$

Force of a on b = opposite of force of b on a

example 1

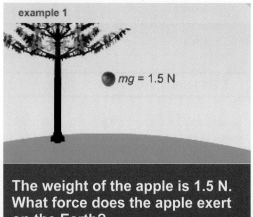

$mg = 1.5\ N$

The weight of the apple is 1.5 N. What force does the apple exert on the Earth?
1.5 N upward

Normal force: When two objects are in direct contact, the force one object exerts in response to the force exerted by the other. This force is perpendicular to the objects' contact surface.

The normal force is a force exerted by one object in direct contact with another. The normal force is a *response force*, one that appears in response to another force. The direction of the force is perpendicular to the surfaces in contact. (One meaning of "normal" is perpendicular.)

A normal force is often a response to a gravitational force, as is the case with the block shown in Concept 1 to the right. The table supports the block by exerting a normal force upward on it. The normal force is equal in magnitude to the block's weight but opposite in direction. The normal force is perpendicular to the surface between the block and the table.

You experience the normal force as well. The force of gravity pulls you down, and the normal force of the Earth pushes in the opposite direction. The normal force prevents you from being pulled to the center of the Earth.

Let's consider the direction and the amount of the normal force when you are standing in your classroom. It is equal in magnitude to the force of gravity on you (your weight) and points in the opposite direction. If the normal force were greater than your weight, the net force would accelerate you upward (a surprising result), and if it were less, you would accelerate toward the center of the Earth (equally surprising and likely more distressing). The two forces are equal in strength and oppositely directed, so the amount of the normal force is the same as the magnitude of your weight.

What is the source of the normal force? The weight of the block causes a slight deformation in the table, akin to you lying on a mattress and causing the springs to compress and push back. With a normal force, the deformation occurs at the atomic level as atoms and molecules attempt to "spring back."

Normal forces do not just oppose gravity, and they do not have to be directed upward. A normal force is always perpendicular to the surface where the objects are in contact. When you lean against a wall, the wall applies a normal force on you. In this case, the normal force opposes your push and is acting horizontally.

We have discussed normal forces that are acting solely vertically or horizontally. The normal force can also act at an angle, as shown with the block on a ramp in Example 1. The normal force opposes a component of the block's weight, not the full weight. Why? Because the normal force is always perpendicular to the contact surface. The normal force opposes the component of the weight perpendicular to the surface of the ramp.

Example 2 makes a similar point. Here again the normal force and weight are not equal in magnitude. The string pulls up on the block, but not enough to lift it off the surface. Since this reduces the force the block exerts on the table, the amount of the normal force is correspondingly reduced. The force of the string reduces the net downward force on the table to 75 N, so the amount of the normal force is 75 N, as well. The direction of the normal force is upward.

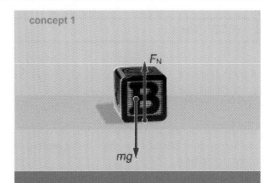

concept 1

Normal force
Occurs with two objects in direct contact
Perpendicular to surface of contact
Normal force opposes force

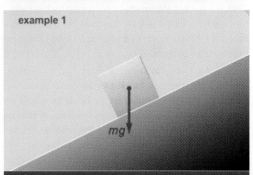

example 1

What is the direction of the normal force?
Perpendicular to the surface of the ramp

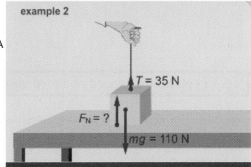

example 2

The string supplies an upward force on the block which is resting on the table. What is the normal force of the table on the block?

$$\Sigma \mathbf{F} = m\mathbf{a} = 0$$
$$F_N + T + (-mg) = 0$$
$$F_N + 35\,N - 110\,N = 0$$

5.12 - Tension

Tension: Force exerted by a string, cord, twine, rope, chain, cable, etc.

In physics textbooks, tension means the pulling force conveyed by a string, rope, chain, tow-bar, or other form of connection. In this section, we will use a rope to illustrate the concept of tension.

The rope in Concept 1 is shown exerting a force on the block; that force is called tension. This definition differs slightly from the everyday use of the word tension, which often refers to forces within a material or object − or a human brain before exams.

In physics problems, two assumptions are usually made about the nature of tension. First, the force is transmitted unchanged by the rope. The rope does not stretch or otherwise diminish the force. Second, the rope is treated as having no mass (it is massless). This means that when calculating the acceleration of a system, the mass of the rope can be ignored.

Example 1 shows how tension forces can be calculated using Newton's second law. There are two forces acting on the block: its weight and the tension. The vector sum of those forces, the net force, equals the product of its mass and acceleration. Since the mass and acceleration are stated, the problem solution shows how the tension can be determined.

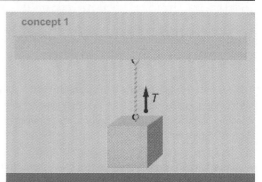

concept 1

Tension
Force through rope, string, etc.

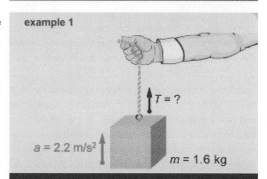

example 1

$T = ?$

$a = 2.2$ m/s^2

$m = 1.6$ kg

What is the amount of tension in the rope?

$\Sigma \mathbf{F} = m\mathbf{a}$

$T + (-mg) = ma$

$T - (1.6 \text{ kg})(9.8 \text{ m/s}^2) = (1.6 \text{ kg})(2.2 \text{ m/s}^2)$

$T = 19$ N (upward)

5.13 - Newton's second and third laws

It might seem that Newton's third law could lead to the conclusion that forces do **not** cause acceleration, because for every force there is an equal but opposite force. If for every force there is an equal but opposite force, how can there be a net non-zero force? The answer lies in the fact that the forces do not act on the same object. The pair of forces in an action-reaction pair acts on **different** objects. In this section, we illustrate this often confusing concept with an example.

Consider the box attached to the rope in Concept 1. We show two pairs of action-reaction forces. Normally, we draw all forces in the same color, but in this illustration, we draw each pair in a different color. One pair is caused by the force of gravity. The force of the Earth pulls the box down. In turn, the box exerts an upward gravitational force of equal strength on the Earth.

There is also a pair of forces associated with the rope. The tension of the rope pulls up on the box. In response, the box pulls down on the rope. These forces are equal but

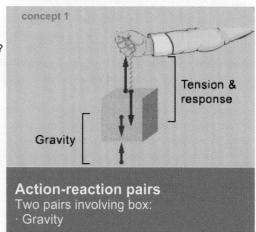

concept 1

Tension & response

Gravity

Action-reaction pairs
Two pairs involving box:
· Gravity

opposite and form a second action-reaction pair. (Here we only focus on pairs that include forces acting on the box or caused by the box. We ignore other action-reaction pairs present in this example, such as the hand pulling on the rope, and the rope pulling on the hand.)

Now consider only the forces acting **on** the box. This means we no longer consider the forces the box exerts on the Earth and on the rope. The two forces on the box are gravity pulling it down and tension pulling it up. In this example, we have chosen to make the force of tension greater than the weight of the box.

The Concept 2 illustration reflects this scenario: The tension vector is longer than the weight vector, and the resulting net force is a vector upward. Because there is a net upward force on the box, it accelerates in that direction.

Now we will clear up another possible misconception: that the weight of an object resting on a surface and the resulting normal force are an action-reaction pair. They are **not**. Since they are often equal but opposite, they are easily confused with an action-reaction pair. Consider a block resting on a table. The action-reaction pair is the Earth pulling the block down and the block pulling the Earth up. It is not the weight of the block and the normal force.

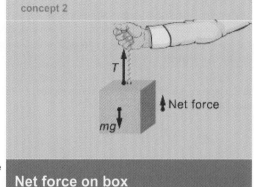

· Tension & response

concept 2

Net force on box
Tension minus weight
Causes acceleration

Here is one way to confirm this: Imagine the block is attached to a rope pulling it up so that it just touches the table. The normal force is now near zero, yet the block's weight is unchanged. If the weight and the normal force are supposed to be equal but opposite, how could the normal force all but disappear? The answer is that the action-reaction pair in question is what is stated above: the equal and opposite forces of gravity between the Earth and the block.

5.14 - Free-body diagrams

Free-body diagram: A drawing of the external forces exerted on an object.

Free-body diagrams are used to display multiple forces acting on an object. In the drawing above, the free body is a monkey, and the free-body diagram in Concept 1 shows the forces acting upon the monkey: the tension forces of the two ropes and the force of gravity.

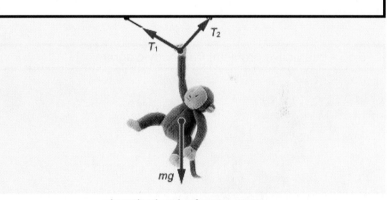

A monkey hanging from two ropes.

The diagram only shows the external forces acting on the monkey. There are other forces present in this configuration, such as forces within the monkey, and forces that the monkey exerts. Those forces are not shown; a free-body diagram shows just the forces that act **on** a single object like the monkey.

Although we often draw force vectors where they are applied to an object, in free-body diagrams it is useful to draw the vectors starting from a single point, typically the origin. This allows the components of the vectors to be more easily analyzed. You see this in Concept 1.

Free-body diagrams are useful in a variety of ways. They can be used to determine the magnitudes of forces. For instance, if the mass of the monkey and the orientations of the ropes are known, the tension in each rope can be determined.

When forces act along multiple dimensions, the forces and the resulting acceleration

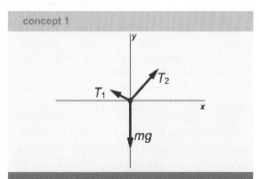

concept 1

Free-body diagrams
Shows all external forces acting on body
Often drawn from the origin

need to be considered independently in each dimension. In the illustration, the monkey is stationary, hanging from two ropes. Since there is no vertical acceleration, there is no **net** force in the vertical dimension. This means the downward force of gravity on the monkey must equal the upward pull of the ropes.

The two ropes also pull horizontally (along the x axis). Because the monkey is not accelerating horizontally, these horizontal forces must balance as well. By considering the forces acting in both the horizontal and vertical directions, the tensions of the ropes can be determined.

In Example 1, one of the forces shown is friction, f. Friction acts to oppose motion when two objects are in contact.

example 1

Draw a free-body diagram of the forces on the box.

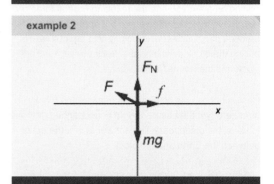

example 2

Free-body diagram of forces on box

5.15 - Interactive problem: free-body diagram

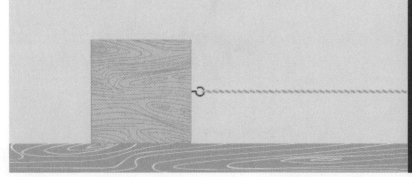

A rope pulls the block against friction. Draw a free-body diagram. The block accelerates at 11 m/s² if the diagram is correct.

In this section, you practice drawing a free-body diagram. Above, you see the situation: A block is being pulled horizontally by a rope. It accelerates to the right at 11 m/s². In the simulation on the right, the force vectors on the block are drawn, but each one points in the wrong direction, has the wrong magnitude, or both. We ignore the force of air resistance in this simulation.

Your job is to fix the force vectors. You do this by clicking on the heads of the vectors and dragging them to point in the correct direction. (To simplify your work, they "snap" to vertical and horizontal orientations, but you do need to drag them close before they will snap.) You change both their lengths (which determine their magnitudes) and their directions with the mouse.

The mass of the block is 5.0 kg. The tension force T is 78 N and the force of friction f is 23 N. The friction force acts opposite to the direction of the motion. Calculate the magnitudes of the weight mg and the normal force F_N to the nearest newton, and then drag the heads of the vectors to the correct positions, or click on the up and down arrow buttons, and press GO. If you are correct, the block will accelerate to the right at 11 m/s². If not, the block will move based on the net force as determined by your vectors as well as its mass. Press RESET to try again.

Copyright 2000-2007 Kinetic Books Co. Chapter 05

There is more than one way to arrange the vectors to create the same acceleration, but there is only one arrangement that agrees with all the information given.

If you have difficulty solving this problem, review the sections on weight and normal force, and the section on free-body diagrams.

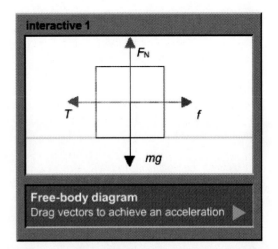

interactive 1

F_N

T f

mg

Free-body diagram
Drag vectors to achieve an acceleration ▶

5.16 - Friction

Friction: A force that resists the motion of one object sliding past another.

If you push a cardboard box along a wooden floor, you have to push to overcome the force of friction. This force makes it harder for you to slide the box. The force of friction opposes any force that can cause one object to slide past another. There are two types of friction: static and kinetic. These forces are discussed in more depth in other sections. In this section, we discuss some general properties of friction.

Friction between the buffalo's back and the tree scratches an itch.

The amount of friction depends on the materials in contact. For example, the box would slide more easily over ice than wood. Friction is also proportional to the normal force. For a box on the floor, the greater its weight, the greater the normal force, which increases the force of friction.

Humans expend many resources to combat friction. Motor oil, Teflon™, WD-40™, Tri-Flo™ and many other products are designed to reduce this force. However, friction can be very useful. Without it, a nail would slip out of a board, the tires of a car would not be able to "grip" the road, and you would not be able to walk.

concept 1

Normal

Friction

Friction
Force that opposes "sliding" motion
Varies by materials in contact
Proportional to normal force

Friction exists even between seemingly smooth surfaces. Although a surface may appear smooth, when magnified sufficiently, any surface will look bumpy or rough, as the illustration in Concept 2 on the right shows. The magnified picture of the "smooth" crystal reveals its microscopic "rough" texture. Friction is a force caused by the interaction of molecules in two surfaces.

You might think you can defeat friction by creating surfaces that are highly polished. Instead, you may get an effect called *cold welding*, in which the two highly polished materials fuse together. Cold welding can be desirable, as when an aluminum connector is crimped onto a copper wire to create a strong electrical connection.

Objects can also move in a fashion that is called *slip and slide*. They slide for a while, stick, and then slide some more. This phenomenon accounts for both the horrid noise generated by fingernails on a chalkboard and the joyous noise of a violin. (Well, joyous when played by some, chalkboard-like when played by others.)

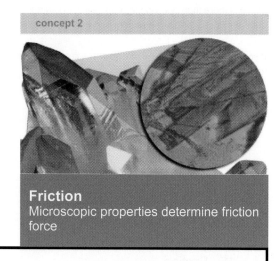

Friction
Microscopic properties determine friction force

Static friction: A force that resists the sliding motion of two objects that are stationary relative to one another.

Imagine you are pushing a box horizontally but cannot move it due to friction. You are experiencing a response force called static friction. If you push harder and harder, the amount of static friction will increase to exactly equal – but not exceed – the amount of horizontal force you are supplying. For the two surfaces in contact, the friction will increase up to some maximum amount. If you push hard enough to exceed the maximum amount of static friction, the box will slide.

For instance, let's say the maximum amount of static friction for a box is 30 newtons. If you push with a force of 10 newtons, the box does not move. The force of static friction points in the opposite direction of your force and is 10 newtons as well. If it were less, the box would slide in the direction you are pushing. If it were greater, the box would accelerate toward you. The box does not move in either direction, so the friction force is 10 newtons. If you push with 20 newtons of force, the force of static friction is 20 newtons, for the same reasons.

You keep pushing until your force is 31 newtons. You have now exceeded the maximum force of static friction and the box accelerates in the direction of the net force. The box will continue to experience friction once it is sliding, but this type of friction is called kinetic friction.

Static friction occurs when two objects are motionless relative to one another. Often, we want to calculate the maximum amount of static friction so that we know how much force we will have to apply to get the object to move. The equation in Equation 1 enables you to do so. It depends on two values. One is the normal force, the perpendicular force between the two surfaces. The second is called the *coefficient of static friction*.

Engineers calculate this coefficient empirically. They place an object (say, a car tire) on top of another surface (perhaps ice) and measure how hard they need to push before the object starts to move. Coefficients of friction are specific to the two surfaces. Some examples of coefficients of static friction are shown in the table in Equation 2.

You might have noticed a fairly surprising fact: The amount of surface area between the

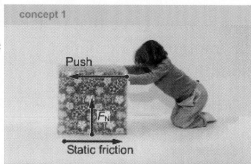

Static friction
Force opposing sliding when no motion
Balances "pushing" force until object slides
Maximum static friction proportional to:
· coefficient of static friction

· normal force

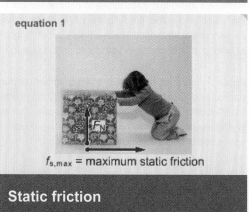

$f_{s,max}$ = maximum static friction

Static friction

$$f_{s,max} = \mu_s F_N$$

$f_{s,max}$ = maximum static friction

two objects does not enter into the calculation of maximum static friction. In principle, whether a box of a given mass has a surface area of one square centimeter or one square kilometer, the maximum amount of static friction is constant. Why? With the greater contact area, the normal and frictional forces per unit area diminish proportionally.

μ_s = coefficient of static friction
F_N = normal force

equation 2

Coefficient of static friction

Tires on dry pavement	0.90
Tires on wet pavement	0.42
Glass on glass	0.94
Steel on steel	0.78
Oak on oak	0.54
Waxed ski on dry snow	0.04
Teflon™ on Teflon™	0.04

Coefficients of static friction

example 1

Anna is pushing but the box does not move. What is the force of static friction?
f_s = 7 N to the right

example 2

What is the maximum static friction force? The coefficient of static friction for these materials is 0.31.
$f_{s,max} = \mu_s F_N$
$f_{s,max} = (0.31)(27 \text{ N})$
$f_{s,max} = 8.4 \text{ N}$

Kinetic friction: Friction when an object slides along another.

Kinetic friction occurs when two objects slide past each other. The magnitude of kinetic friction is less than the maximum amount of static friction for the same objects. Some values for coefficients of kinetic friction are shown in Equation 2 to the right. These are calculated empirically and do not vary greatly over a reasonable range of velocities.

Like static friction, kinetic friction always opposes the direction of motion. It has a constant value, the product of the normal force and the coefficient of kinetic friction.

In Example 1, we state the normal force. Note that the normal force in this case does **not** equal the weight; instead, it equals a component of the weight. The other component of the weight is pulling the block down the plane.

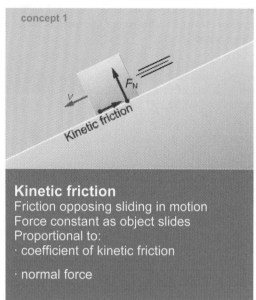

concept 1

Kinetic friction
Friction opposing sliding in motion
Force constant as object slides
Proportional to:
· coefficient of kinetic friction

· normal force

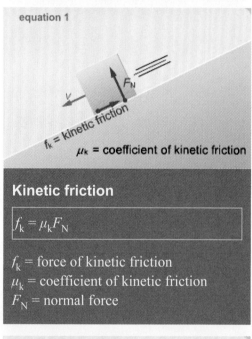

equation 1

μ_k = coefficient of kinetic friction

Kinetic friction

$$f_k = \mu_k F_N$$

f_k = force of kinetic friction
μ_k = coefficient of kinetic friction
F_N = normal force

equation 2

Coefficient of kinetic friction	
Tires on dry pavement	0.85
Tires on wet pavement	0.36
Glass on glass	0.40
Steel on steel	0.42
Oak on oak	0.32
Waxed ski on dry snow	0.03
Teflon® on Teflon®	0.04

Coefficients of kinetic friction

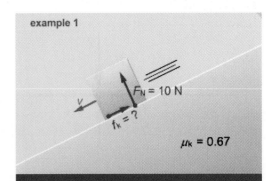

example 1

$\mu_k = 0.67$

What is the force of friction?

$f_k = \mu_k F_N$

$f_k = (0.67)(10\ N)$

$f_k = 6.7\ N$ (pointing up the ramp)

5.19 - Interactive checkpoint: moving the couch

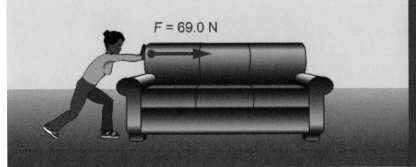

F = 69.0 N

While rearranging your living room, you push your couch across the floor at a constant speed with a horizontal force of 69.0 N. You are using special pads on the couch legs that help it slide easier. If the couch has a mass of 59.5 kg, what is the coefficient of kinetic friction between the pads and the floor?

Answer:

$\mu_k = $ _____

5.20 - Sample problem: friction and tension

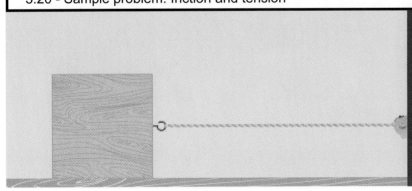

The coefficient of kinetic friction is 0.200. What is the magnitude of the tension force in the rope?

Above, you see a block accelerating to the right due to the tension force applied by a rope. What is the magnitude of tension the rope applies to the block?

Starting this type of problem with a free-body diagram usually proves helpful.

Draw a free-body diagram

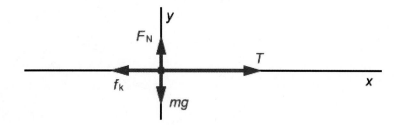

Variables

	x component	y component
normal force	0	$F_N = mg$
acceleration	$a = 2.20$ m/s^2	0
tension	T	0
friction force	$-f_k$	0
mass	$m = 1.60$ kg	
coefficient of kinetic friction	$\mu_k = 0.200$	

What is the strategy?

1. Draw a free-body diagram.
2. Find an expression for the net force on the block.
3. Substitute the net force into Newton's second law to find the tension.

Are there any useful relationships?

Since the surface is horizontal, the amount of normal force equals the weight of the block.

Physics principles and equations

Newton's second law

$$\Sigma \mathbf{F} = m\mathbf{a}$$

The magnitude of the force of kinetic friction is found by

$$f_k = \mu_k F_N$$

Copyright 2000-2007 Kinetic Books Co. Chapter 05

Step-by-step solution

We begin by determining the net horizontal force on the block.

Step	Reason
1. $\Sigma F = T + (-f_k)$	net horizontal force
2. $f_k = \mu_k F_N$	equation for kinetic friction
3. $\Sigma F = T - \mu_k F_N$	substitute equation 2 into 1
4. $\Sigma F = T - \mu_k mg$	enter value of F_N

Now we substitute the net force just found into Newton's second law. This allows us to solve for the tension force.

Step	Reason
5. $\Sigma F = ma$	Newton's second law
6. $T - \mu_k mg = ma$	substitute equation 4 into 5
7. $T = \mu_k mg + ma$	solve for tension
8. $T = (0.200)(1.60 \text{ kg})(9.80 \text{ m/s}^2) + (1.60 \text{ kg})(2.20 \text{ m/s}^2)$	enter values
9. $T = 6.66 \text{ N}$	evaluate

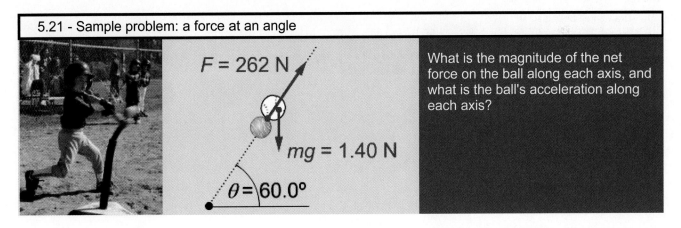

5.21 - Sample problem: a force at an angle

$F = 262$ N

$mg = 1.40$ N

$\theta = 60.0°$

What is the magnitude of the net force on the ball along each axis, and what is the ball's acceleration along each axis?

Above, you see a bat hitting a ball at an angle. You are asked to find the net force and the acceleration of the ball along the x and y axes.

Draw a free-body diagram

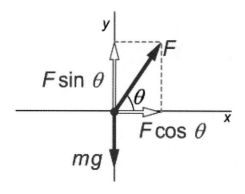

The forces on the ball are its weight down and the force of the bat at the angle θ to the x axis.

Variables

	x component	y component
weight	0	$mg \sin 270° = -1.40$ N
force	$F \cos \theta$	$F \sin \theta$
acceleration	a_x	a_y
force	$F = 262$ N	
angle	$\theta = 60.0°$	
mass	$m = mg/g = (1.40 \text{ N}) / (9.80 \text{ m/s}^2) = 0.143$ kg	

What is the strategy?

1. Draw a free-body diagram.
2. Use trigonometry to calculate the net force on the ball along each axis.
3. Use Newton's second law to find the acceleration of the ball along each axis. The mass of the ball is not given, but you can determine it because you are told its weight. We do this in the variables table.

Physics principles and equations

Newton's second law

$$\Sigma \mathbf{F} = m\mathbf{a}$$

Step-by-step solution

We begin by calculating the net force along the x axis.

Step	Reason
1. $\Sigma F_x = F \cos \theta$	net force along x axis
2. $\Sigma F_x = (262 \text{ N})(\cos 60.0°)$	x component of force
3. $\Sigma F_x = 131$ N	evaluate

Copyright 2000-2007 Kinetic Books Co. Chapter 05

We next calculate the force along the *y* axis. In this case, there are two forces to consider.

Step	Reason
4. $\Sigma F_y = F \sin \theta + (-1.40 \text{ N})$	net force along *y* axis
5. $\Sigma F_y = (262 \text{ N})(\sin 60.0°) + (-1.40 \text{ N})$	enter values
6. $\Sigma F_y = 225 \text{ N}$	evaluate

Now we calculate the acceleration along the *x* axis, using Newton's second law.

Step	Reason
7. $\Sigma F_x = ma_x$	Newton's second law
8. $a_x = \Sigma F_x / m$	solve for a_x
9. $a_x = (131 \text{ N}) / (0.143 \text{ kg})$	enter values from step 3 and table
10. $a_x = 916 \text{ m/s}^2$	division

We calculate the acceleration along the *y* axis.

Step	Reason
11. $\Sigma F_y = ma_y$	Newton's second law
12. $a_y = \Sigma F_y / m$	solve for a_y
13. $a_y = (225 \text{ N})/(0.143 \text{ kg})$	enter values from step 6, table
14. $a_y = 1570 \text{ m/s}^2$	division

The acceleration values may seem very large, but this is the acceleration during the brief moment the bat is in contact with the ball.

5.22 - Interactive problem: forces on a sliding block

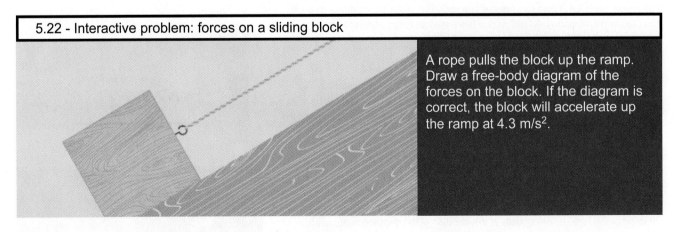

A rope pulls the block up the ramp. Draw a free-body diagram of the forces on the block. If the diagram is correct, the block will accelerate up the ramp at 4.3 m/s².

Above, you see an illustration of a block that is being pulled up a ramp by a rope. In the simulation on the right, the force vectors on the block are drawn, but they are in the wrong directions, have the wrong magnitudes, or both. Your job is to fix the force vectors. If you do this correctly, the block will accelerate up the ramp at a rate of 4.3 m/s². If not, the block will move due to the net force as determined by your vectors as well as its mass.

The mass of the block is 6.0 kg. The amount of tension from the rope is 78 N and the coefficient of kinetic friction is 0.45. The angle the ramp makes with the horizontal is $30°$. Calculate (to the nearest newton) the directions and magnitudes of the weight, normal force and friction force. Drag the head of a vector to set its magnitude and direction. You can also set the magnitudes in the control panel. The vectors will "snap" to angles.

When you have arranged all the vectors, press the GO button. If your free-body diagram is accurate, the block will accelerate up the ramp at 4.3 m/s². Press RESET to try again.

There is more than one way to set the vectors to produce the same acceleration, but only one arrangement agrees with all the information given. If you have difficulty solving this problem, review the sections on kinetic friction and the normal force, and the sample problem involving a force at an angle.

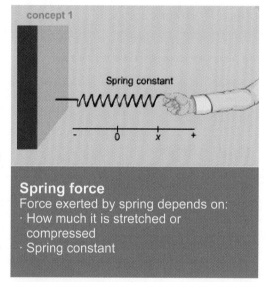

interactive 1

Forces on a sliding block
Drag vectors to achieve an acceleration ▶

5.23 - Hooke's law and spring force

You probably already know a few basic things about springs: You stretch them, they pull back on you. You compress them, they push back.

As a physics student, though, you are asked to study springs in a more quantitative way. Let's consider the force of a spring using the configuration shown in Concept 1. Initially, no force is applied to the spring, so it is neither stretched nor compressed. When no force is applied, the end of the spring is at a position called the rest point (sometimes called the equilibrium point).

Then we stretch the spring. In the illustration to the right, the hand pulls to the right, so the end of the spring moves to the right, away from its rest point, and the spring pulls back to the left.

Hooke's law is used to determine how much force the spring exerts. It states that the amount of force is proportional to how far the end of the spring is stretched or compressed away from its rest point. Stretch the end of the spring twice as far from its rest point, and the amount of force is doubled.

The amount of force is also proportional to a spring constant, which depends on the construction of the spring. A "stiff" spring has a greater spring constant than one that is easier to stretch. Stiffer springs can be made from heavier gauge materials. The units for spring constants are newtons per meter (N/m).

The equation for Hooke's law is shown in Equation 1. The spring constant is represented by k. The displacement of the end of the spring is represented by x. At the rest position, $x = 0$. When the spring is stretched, the displacement of the end of the spring has a positive x value. When it is compressed, x is negative.

Hooke's law calculates the magnitude of the spring force. The equation has a negative sign to indicate that the force of a spring is a *restoring force*, which means it acts to restore the end of the spring to its rest point. Stretch a spring and it will pull back toward the rest position; compress a spring, and it will push back toward the rest position. The direction of the force is the opposite of the direction of the displacement.

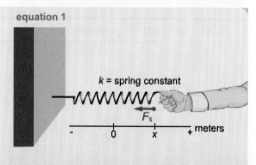

concept 1

Spring constant

Spring force
Force exerted by spring depends on:
· How much it is stretched or compressed
· Spring constant

equation 1

k = spring constant

F_s

Hooke's law

$$F_s = -kx$$

F_s = spring force
k = spring constant
x = displacement of end from rest point

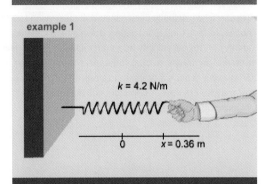

example 1

$k = 4.2$ N/m

0   $x = 0.36$ m

What is the force exerted by the spring?
$$F_s = -kx$$
$$F_s = -(4.2\text{ N/m})(0.36\text{ m})$$
$$F_s = -1.5\text{ N (to the left)}$$

5.24 - Air resistance

Air resistance: A force that opposes motion in air.

If you parachute, or bike or ski, you have experienced air resistance. In each of these activities, you move through a fluid – air – that resists your motion. As you move through the air, you collide with the molecules that make up the atmosphere. Although air is not very dense and the molecules are very small, there are so many of them that their effects add up to a significant force. The sum of all these collisions is the force called air resistance.

Unlike kinetic friction, air resistance is not constant but increases as the speed of the object increases. The force created by air resistance is called *drag*.

The formula in Equation 1 supplies an approximation of the force of air resistance for objects moving at relatively high speeds through air. For instance, it is a relevant equation for the skysurfer shown in Concept 1, or for an airplane. The resistance is proportional to the square of the speed and to the cross sectional area of the moving object. (For the skysurfer, the board would constitute the main part of the cross sectional area.) It is also proportional to an empirically determined constant called the *drag coefficient*.

The shape of an object determines its drag coefficient. A significant change in speed can change the drag coefficient, as well. Aerospace engineers definitely earn their keep by analyzing air resistance using powerful computers. They also use wind tunnels to check their computational results.

Another interesting implication of the drag force equation is that objects will reach what is called *terminal velocity*. Terminal velocity is the maximum speed an object reaches when falling. The drag force increases with speed while the force of gravity is constant;

concept 1

Drag force

Air resistance
Drag force opposes motion in air
Force increases as speed increases

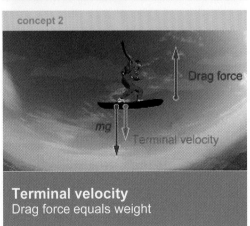

concept 2

Drag force

mg

Terminal velocity

Terminal velocity
Drag force equals weight

at some point, the upward drag force equals the downward force of gravity. When this occurs, there is no net force and the object ceases to accelerate and maintains a constant speed. The equation for calculating terminal velocity is shown in Equation 2. It is derived by setting the drag force equal to the object's weight and solving for the speed.

Research has actually determined that cats reach terminal velocity after falling six stories. In fact, they tend to slow down after six stories. Here's why this occurs: The cat achieves terminal velocity and then relaxes a little, which expands its cross sectional area and increases its drag force. As a result, it slows down. One has to admire the cat for relaxing in such a precarious situation (or perhaps doubt its intelligence). If you think this may be an urban legend, consult the *Journal of the American Veterinary Association*, volume 191, page 1399.

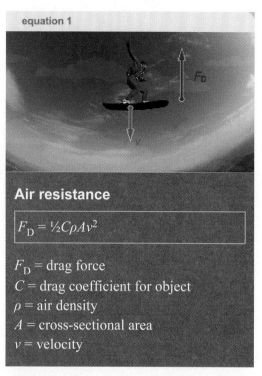

equation 1

Air resistance

$$F_D = \tfrac{1}{2}C\rho A v^2$$

F_D = drag force
C = drag coefficient for object
ρ = air density
A = cross-sectional area
v = velocity

equation 2

Terminal velocity

$$v_T = \sqrt{\frac{2mg}{C\rho A}}$$

v_T = terminal velocity
mg = weight

equation 3

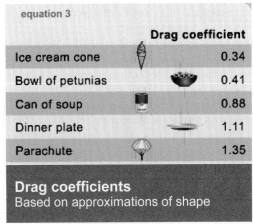

		Drag coefficient
Ice cream cone		0.34
Bowl of petunias		0.41
Can of soup		0.88
Dinner plate		1.11
Parachute		1.35

Drag coefficients
Based on approximations of shape

example 1

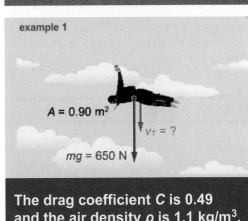

$A = 0.90 \ m^2$

$v_T = ?$

$mg = 650 \ N$

The drag coefficient C is 0.49 and the air density ρ is 1.1 kg/m^3. What is the skydiver's terminal velocity?

$$v_T = \sqrt{\frac{2mg}{C\rho A}}$$

$$v_T = \sqrt{\frac{2(650 \ N)}{(0.49)(1.1 \ kg/m^3)(0.90 \ m^2)}}$$

$$v_T = 52 \ m/s$$

5.25 - Interactive Problem: Forces in Multiple Dimensions

Now, you will get some additional practice applying Newton's laws. More specifically, you will use them in situations where multiple forces are acting on a single object.

If the application of multiple forces results in a net force acting on an object, it accelerates. On the other hand, if the forces acting on it sum to zero in every dimension, the result is equilibrium. The object does not accelerate; it either maintains a constant velocity, or remains stationary. (Forces can also cause an object to rotate, but rotational motion is a later topic in mechanics.)

Equilibrium is an important topic in engineering. The school buildings you study in, the bridges you travel across − all such structures require careful design to ensure that they remain in equilibrium.

The simulation on the right will help you develop an understanding for how forces in

interactive 1

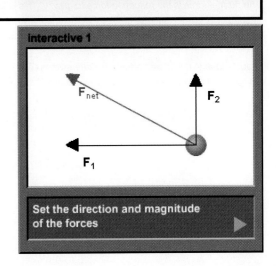

Set the direction and magnitude of the forces

different directions combine when applied to an object. The 5.0 kg ball has two forces acting on it, $\mathbf{F}_1$ and $\mathbf{F}_2$. They act on it as long as the ball is on the screen.

You control the direction and magnitude of each force. In the simulation, you set a force vector's direction and magnitude by dragging its arrowhead; You will notice the angles are restricted to multiples of $90°$. You can also adjust the magnitude of each vector with a controller in the control panel. The net force is shown in the simulation; it is the vector sum of $\mathbf{F}_1$ and $\mathbf{F}_2$.

You can check the box "Display vectors head to tail" if you would like to see them graphically combined in that fashion. Press GO to start the simulation and set the ball moving in response to the forces on it.

Here are some challenges for you. First, set the forces so that the ball does not move at all when you press GO. The individual forces must be at least 10 newtons, so setting them both to zero is not an option!

Next, hit each of the three animated targets. The center of one is directly to the right of the ball and the center of another is at a $45°$ angle above the horizontal from the ball. Set the individual vectors and press GO to hit the center of each target in turn.

The target to the left is at a $150°$ angle. It is the "extra credit" target. Determining the correct ratio of vectors will require a little thought. We allow for rounding with this target; if you set one of the vectors to 10 N, you can solve the problem by setting the other one to the appropriate closest integer value.

5.26 - Gotchas

An object has a speed of 20 km/h. It swerves to the left but maintains the same speed. Was a force involved? Yes. A change in speed **or** direction is acceleration, and acceleration requires a force.

An object is moving. A net force must be acting on it. No. Only if the object is accelerating (changing speed or direction) is there a net force. Constant velocity means there is no net force.

No acceleration means no forces are present. Close. No acceleration means no **net** forces. There can be a balanced set of forces and no acceleration.

"I weigh 70 kilograms." False. Kilograms measure mass, not weight.

"I weigh the same on Jupiter as I do on Mars." Not unless you dieted (lost mass) as you traveled from Jupiter to Mars. Weight is gravitational force, and Mars exerts less gravitational force.

"My mass is the same on Jupiter and Mars." Yes.

The normal force is the response force to gravity. This is too specific of a definition. The normal force appears any time two objects are brought in contact. It is not limited to gravity. For instance, if you lean against a wall, the force of the wall on you is a normal force. If you stand on the ground, the normal force of the ground is a response force to gravity.

"I push against a wall with a force of five newtons. The wall pushes back with the same force." Close, but it is better to say, "The same amount (magnitude) of force but in the opposite direction."

"I pull on the Earth with the same amount of gravitational force that the Earth exerts on me." True. You are an action-reaction pair.

Force, and Newton's laws which describe force, are fundamental concepts in the study of physics. Force can be described as a push or pull. It is a vector quantity that is measured in newtons (1 N = 1 kg·m/s^2). Net force is the vector sum of all the external forces on an object.

Free-body diagrams depict all the external forces on an object. Even though the forces may act on different parts of the object, free-body diagrams are drawn so that the forces are shown as being applied at a single point.

Newton's first law states that an object maintains a constant velocity (including remaining at rest) until a net force acts upon it.

Mass is the property of an object that determines its resistance to a change in velocity, and it is a scalar, measured in kilograms. Mass should not be confused with weight, which is a force caused by gravity, directed toward the center of the Earth.

Newton's second law states that the net force on an object is equal to its mass times its acceleration.

Newton's third law states that the forces that two bodies exert on each other are always equal in magnitude and opposite in direction.

The normal force is a force that occurs when two objects are in direct contact. It is always directed perpendicular to the surface of contact.

Equations

$$\text{weight} = mg$$

Newton's second law

$$\Sigma \mathbf{F} = m\mathbf{a}$$

Newton's third law

$$\mathbf{F}_{ab} = -\mathbf{F}_{ba}$$

Static friction

$$f_{s,max} = \mu_s F_N$$

Kinetic friction

$$f_k = \mu_k F_N$$

Hooke's law

$$F_s = -kx$$

Tension is a force exerted by a means of connection such as a rope, and the tension force always pulls on the bodies to which the rope is attached.

Friction is a force that resists the sliding motion of two objects in direct contact. It is proportional to the magnitude of the normal force and varies according to the composition of the objects.

Static friction is the term for friction when there is no relative motion between two objects. It balances any applied pushing force that tends to slide the body, up to a maximum determined by the normal force and the coefficient of static friction between the two objects, μ_s. If the applied pushing force is greater than the maximum static friction force, then the object will move.

Once an object is in motion, kinetic friction applies. The force of kinetic friction is determined by the magnitude of the normal force multiplied by μ_k, the coefficient of kinetic friction between the two objects.

Hooke's law describes the force that a spring exerts when stretched or compressed away from its equilibrium position. The force increases linearly with the displacement from the equilibrium position. The equation for Hooke's law includes k, the spring constant; a value that depends on the particular spring. The negative sign indicates that the spring force is a restoring force that points in the opposite direction as the displacement, that is, it resists both stretching and compression.

Air resistance, or drag, is a force that opposes motion through a fluid such as air. Drag increases as speed increases. Terminal velocity is reached when the drag force on a falling object equals its weight, so that it ceases to accelerate.

chapter

6 Work, Energy, and Power

□ Conceptual

physics

kinetic
BOOKS

6.0 - Introduction

The use of energy has played an important role in defining much of human history. Fire warmed and protected our ancestors. Coal powered the Industrial Revolution. Gasoline enabled the proliferation of the automobile, and electricity led to indoor lighting, then radio, television and the computer. The enormous energy unleashed by splitting the atom was a major factor in ending World War II. Today, businesses involved in technology or media may garner more newspaper headlines, but energy is a larger industry.

Humankind has long studied how to harness and transform energy. Early machines used the energy of flowing water to set wheels spinning to mill grain. Machines designed during the Industrial Revolution used energy unleashed by burning coal to create the steam that drove textile looms and locomotives. Today, we still use these same energy sources – water and coal – but often we transform the energy into electric energy.

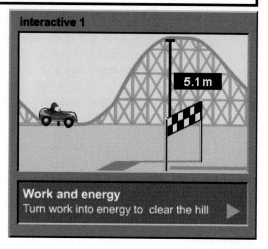

interactive 1

5.1 m

Work and energy
Turn work into energy to clear the hill ▶

Scientists continue to study energy sources and ways to store energy. Today, environmental concerns have led to increased research in areas including atomic fusion and hydrogen fuel cells. Even as scientists are working to develop new energy technologies, there is renewed interest in some ancient energy sources: the Sun and the wind. They too can provide clean energy via photovoltaic cells and wind turbines.

Why is energy so important? Because humankind uses it to do work. It no longer requires as much human labor to plow fields, to travel, or to entertain ourselves. We can tap into other energy sources to serve those needs.

This chapter is an introduction to work and energy. It appears in the mechanics section of the textbook, because we focus here on what is called *mechanical energy*, energy arising from the motion of particles and objects, and energy due to the force of gravity. Work and energy also are major topics in thermodynamics, a topic covered later. Thermodynamics adds the topic of heat to the discussion. We will only mention heat briefly in this chapter.

Whatever the source and ultimate use of energy, certain fundamental principles always apply. This chapter begins your study of those principles, and the simulation to the right is your first opportunity to experiment with them.

Your mission in the simulation is to get the car over the hill on the right and around a curve that is beyond the hill. You do this by dragging the car up the hill on the left and releasing it. If you do not drag it high enough, it will fail to make it over the hill. If you drag it too high, it will fly off the curve after the hill. The height of the car is shown in a gauge in the simulation.

Only the force of gravity is factored into this simulation; the forces of friction and air resistance are ignored. In this chapter, we consider only the kinetic energy due to the object moving as a whole and ignore rotational energy, such as the energy of the car wheels due to their rotational motion. (Taxes, title and dealer prep are also not factored into the simulation; contact your local dealership for any other additional restrictions or limitations.)

Make some predictions before you try the simulation. If you release the car at a higher point, will its speed at the bottom of the hill be greater, the same or less? How high will you have to drag the car to have it just reach the summit of the other hill: to the same height, higher or lower? You can use PAUSE to see the car's speed more readily at any point.

When you use this simulation, you are experimenting with some of the key principles of this chapter. You are doing work on the car as you drag it up the hill, and that increases the car's energy. That energy, called potential energy, is transformed into kinetic energy as the car moves down the hill. Energy is conserved as the car moves down the hill. It may change forms from potential energy to kinetic energy, but as the car moves on the track, its total energy remains constant.

Work: The product of displacement and the force in the direction of displacement.

You may think of work as homework, or as labor done to earn money, or as exercise in a demanding workout.

But physicists have a different definition of work. To them, work equals the component of force exerted on an object along the direction of the object's displacement, times the object's displacement.

When the force on an object is in the same direction as the displacement, the magnitude of the force and the object's displacement can be multiplied together to calculate the work done by the force. In Concept 1, a woman is shown pushing a crate so that all her force is applied in the same direction as the crate's motion.

All the force need not be in the direction of the displacement. When the force and displacement vectors are not in the same direction, only the component of the force in the direction of the displacement contributes to work. Consider the woman pulling the crate at an angle with a handle, as shown in Concept 2. Again, the crate slides along the ground. The component of the force perpendicular to the displacement contributes nothing to the work because there is no motion up or down.

Perhaps subconsciously, you may have applied this concept. When you push on a heavy object that is low to the floor, like a sofa, it is difficult to slide it if you are mostly pushing down on top of it. Instead, you bend low so that more of your force is horizontal, parallel to the desired motion.

The equation on the right is used to calculate how much work is done by a force. It has notation that may be new to you. The equation states that the work done equals the "dot product" of the force and displacement vectors (the name comes from the dot between the **F** and the Δ**x**).

The equation is also expressed in a fashion that you will find useful: $(F \cos \theta)\Delta x$. The angle θ is the angle between the force and displacement vectors when they are placed tail to tail. The vectors and the angle are shown in Equation 1.

By multiplying the amount of force by $\cos \theta$, you calculate the component of the force parallel to the displacement. You may recall other cases in which you used the cosine or sine of an angle to calculate a component of a vector. In this case, you are calculating the component of one vector that is parallel to another.

The equation to the right is for a constant or average force. If the force varies as the motion occurs, then you have to break the motion into smaller intervals within which the force is constant in order to calculate the total work.

The everyday use of the word "work" can lead you astray. In physics, if there is no displacement, there is no work. Suppose the woman on the right huffed and puffed and pushed the crate as hard as she could for ten minutes, but it did not move. She would certainly believe she had done work. She would be exhausted. But a physicist would say she has done zero work on the crate because it did not move. No displacement means no work, regardless of how much force is exerted.

Work can be a positive or negative value. Positive work occurs when the force and displacement vectors point in the same direction. Negative work occurs when the force

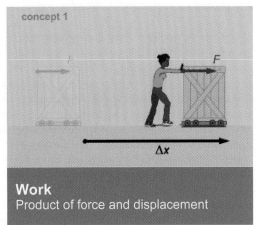

Work
Product of force and displacement

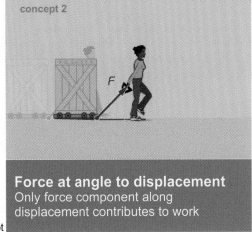

Force at angle to displacement
Only force component along displacement contributes to work

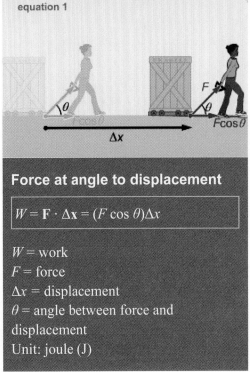

Force at angle to displacement

$$W = \mathbf{F} \cdot \Delta \mathbf{x} = (F \cos \theta)\Delta x$$

W = work
F = force
Δx = displacement
θ = angle between force and displacement
Unit: joule (J)

and displacement vectors point in opposite directions. If you kick a stationary soccer ball, propelling it downfield, you have done positive work on the ball because the force and the displacement are in the same direction.

When a goalie catches a kicked ball, negative work is done by the force from the goalie's hands on the ball. The force on the ball is in the opposite direction of the ball's displacement, with the result that the ball slows down.

The sign of work can be calculated with the equation to the right. When force and displacement point in the same direction, the angle between them is $0°$, and the cosine of $0°$ is positive one. When force and displacement point in opposite directions, the angle between the vectors is $180°$, and the cosine of $180°$ is negative one. This mathematically confirms the points made above: Force in the direction of motion results in positive work; force opposing the motion results in negative work.

Work is a scalar quantity, which means it has magnitude but no direction. The *joule* is the unit for work. The units that make up the joule are $kg·m^2/s^2$ and come from multiplying the unit for force ($kg·m/s^2$) by the unit for displacement (m).

If several forces act on an object, each of them can do work on the object. You can calculate the *net work* done on the object by all the forces by calculating the net force and using the equation in Equation 1.

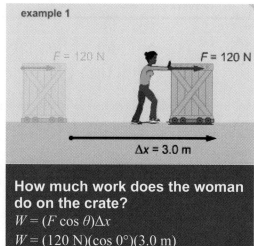

example 1

$F = 120$ N $F = 120$ N

$\Delta x = 3.0$ m

How much work does the woman do on the crate?
$W = (F \cos \theta)\Delta x$
$W = (120 \text{ N})(\cos 0°)(3.0 \text{ m})$
$W = (120 \text{ N})(1)(3.0 \text{ m}) = 360 \text{ J}$

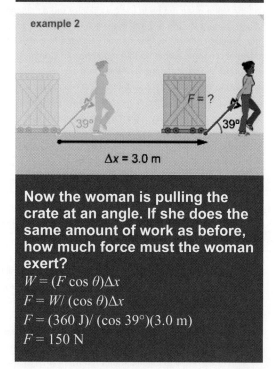

example 2

39° $F = ?$ 39°

$\Delta x = 3.0$ m

Now the woman is pulling the crate at an angle. If she does the same amount of work as before, how much force must the woman exert?
$W = (F \cos \theta)\Delta x$
$F = W/ (\cos \theta)\Delta x$
$F = (360 \text{ J})/ (\cos 39°)(3.0 \text{ m})$
$F = 150 \text{ N}$

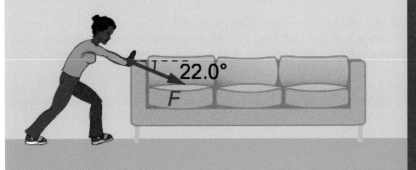

Sally does 401 J of work moving a couch 1.30 meters. If she applies a constant force at an angle of 22.0° to the horizontal as shown, what is the magnitude of this force?

Answer:

$F =$ ☐ N

6.3 - Energy

Before delving into some specific forms of energy, in this section we address the general topic of energy. Although it is a very important concept in physics, and an important topic in general, energy is notoriously hard to define.

Why? There are several reasons. Many forms of energy exist: electric, atomic, chemical, kinetic, potential, and so on. Finding a definition that fits all these forms is challenging. You may associate energy with motion, but not all forms of energy involve motion. A very important class of energy, potential energy, is based on the position or configuration of objects, not their motion.

Energy is a property of an object, or of a system of objects. However, unlike many other properties covered so far in this textbook, is hard to observe and measure directly. You can measure most forces, such as the force of a spring. You can see speed and decide which of two objects is moving faster. You can use a stopwatch to measure time. Quantifying energy is more elusive, because energy depends on multiple factors, such as an object's mass and the square of its speed, or the mass and positions of a system of objects.

Despite these caveats, there are important principles that concern all forms of energy. First, there is a relationship between work and energy. For instance, if you do work by kicking a stationary soccer ball, you increase a form of its energy called kinetic energy, the energy of motion.

Second, energy can transfer between objects. When a cue ball in the game of pool strikes another ball, the cue ball slows or stops, and the other ball begins to roll. The cue ball's loss of energy is the other ball's gain.

Third, energy can change forms. When water falls over a dam, its energy of position becomes the energy of motion (kinetic energy). The kinetic energy from the moving water can cause a turbine to spin in a dam, generating electric energy. If that electricity is used to power a blender to make a milkshake, the energy is transformed again, this time into the rotational kinetic energy of the blender's spinning blades.

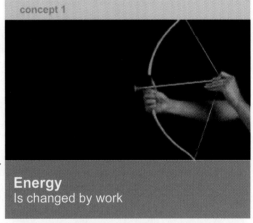

concept 1

Energy
Is changed by work

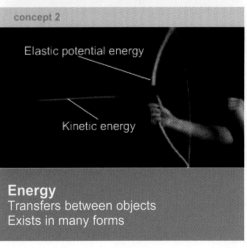

concept 2

Elastic potential energy

Kinetic energy

Energy
Transfers between objects
Exists in many forms

In Concept 1, an archer does work by applying a force to pull a bowstring. This work increases the elastic potential energy of the bow. When the string is released, it accelerates the arrow, transferring and transforming the bow's elastic potential energy into the kinetic energy of the arrow.

One can trace the history of the energy in the bow and arrow example much farther back. Maybe the chemical energy in the archer that was used by his muscles to stretch the bow came from the chemical energy of a hamburger, and the cow acquired that energy by digesting plants, which got energy via photosynthesis by tapping electromagnetic energy, which came from nuclear reactions in the Sun. We could go on, but you get the idea.

Energy is a scalar. Objects can have more or less energy, and some forms of energy can be positive or negative, but energy does not have a direction, only a value. The joule is the unit for energy, just as it is for work. The fact that work and energy share the same unit is another indication that a fundamental relationship exists between them.

6.4 - Kinetic energy

Kinetic energy: The energy of motion.

Physicists describe the energy of objects in motion using the concept of kinetic energy (*KE*). Kinetic energy equals one-half an object's mass times the square of its speed.

To the right is an arrow in motion. The archer has released the bowstring, causing the arrow to fly forward. A fundamental property of the arrow changes when it goes from motionless to moving: It gains kinetic energy.

The kinetic energy of an object increases with mass and the square of speed. A 74,000 kg locomotive barreling along at 40 m/s has four times as much kinetic energy as when it is going 20 m/s, and about five million times the kinetic energy of a 6-kg bowling ball rolling at 2 m/s.

With kinetic energy, only the magnitude of the velocity (the speed) matters, not direction. The locomotive, whether heading east or west, north or south, has the same kinetic energy.

Objects never have negative kinetic energy, only zero or positive kinetic energy. Why? Kinetic energy is a function of the speed squared and the square of a value is never negative.

Because it is a type of energy, the unit for kinetic energy is the joule, which is one kg· (m/s)^2. This is the product of the units for mass and the square of the units for velocity.

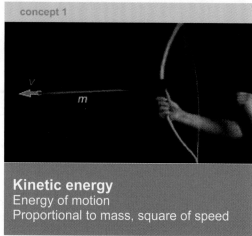

concept 1

Kinetic energy
Energy of motion
Proportional to mass, square of speed

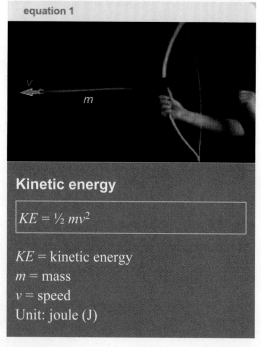

equation 1

Kinetic energy

$$KE = \tfrac{1}{2}\, mv^2$$

KE = kinetic energy
m = mass
v = speed
Unit: joule (J)

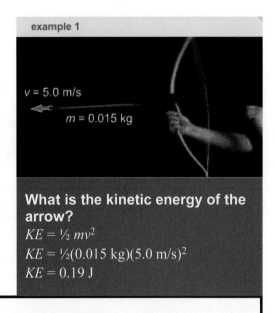

$v = 5.0$ m/s

$m = 0.015$ kg

What is the kinetic energy of the arrow?

$KE = \frac{1}{2}\,mv^2$

$KE = \frac{1}{2}(0.015\ \text{kg})(5.0\ \text{m/s})^2$

$KE = 0.19$ J

6.5 - Work-kinetic energy theorem

Work-kinetic energy theorem: The net work done on a particle equals its change in kinetic energy.

Consider the foot kicking the soccer ball in Concept 1. We want to relate the work done by the force exerted by the foot on the ball to the ball's change in kinetic energy. To focus solely on the work done by the foot, we ignore other forces acting on the ball, such as friction.

Initially, the ball is stationary. It has zero kinetic energy because it has zero speed. The foot applies a force to the ball as it moves through a short displacement. This force accelerates the ball. The ball now has a speed greater than zero, which means it has kinetic energy. The work-kinetic energy theorem states that the work done by the foot on the ball equals the change in the ball's kinetic energy. In this example, the work is positive (the force is in the direction of the displacement) so the work increases the kinetic energy of the ball.

As shown in Concept 2, a goalie catches a ball kicked directly at her. The goalie's hands apply a force to the ball, slowing it. The force on the ball is opposite the ball's displacement, which means the work is negative. The negative work done on the ball slows and then stops it, reducing its kinetic energy to zero. Again, the work equals the change in energy; in this case, negative work on the ball decreases its energy.

In the scenarios described here, the ball is the object to which a force is applied. But you can also think of the soccer ball doing work. The ball applies a force on the goalie, causing the goalie's hands to move backward. The ball does positive work on the goalie because the force it applies is in the direction of the displacement of the goalie's hands.

When stated precisely, which is always worthwhile, the work-kinetic energy theorem is defined to apply to a particle: The net work done on a particle equals the change in its KE. A *particle* is a small, indivisible point of mass that does not rotate, deform, and so on. Various properties of the particle can be observed at any point in time, and by recording those properties at any instant, its *state* can be defined.

The only form of energy that a single particle can possess is kinetic energy. Stating the work-kinetic energy theorem for a particle means that

Work done on a particle
Net work equals change in kinetic energy
Positive work on object increases its *KE*

Δx

Δx

Negative work on object
Decreases object's kinetic energy

the work contributes solely to the change in the particle's kinetic energy. A soccer ball is **not** a particle. When you kick a soccer ball, the surface of the ball deforms, the air particles inside move faster, and so forth.

Having said this, we (and others) apply the work-kinetic energy theorem to objects such as soccer balls. A textbook filled solely with particles would be a drab textbook indeed. We simplify the situation, modeling the ball as a particle, so that we can apply the work-kinetic energy theorem. We can always make it more complicated (have the ball rotate or lift off the ground, so rotational KE and gravitational potential energy become factors), but the work-kinetic energy theorem provides an essential starting point.

For instance, in Example 1, we first calculate the work done on the ball by the foot. We then use the work-kinetic energy theorem to equate the work to the change in KE of the ball. Using the definition of KE, we can calculate the ball's speed immediately after being kicked.

It is important that the theorem applies to the **net** work done on an object. Here, we ignore the force of friction, but if it were being considered, we would have to first calculate the net force being applied on the ball in order to consider the net work that is done on it.

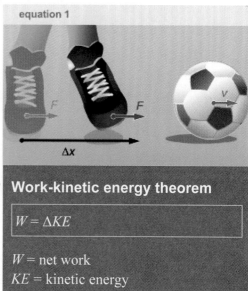

equation 1

Work-kinetic energy theorem

$$W = \Delta KE$$

W = net work
KE = kinetic energy

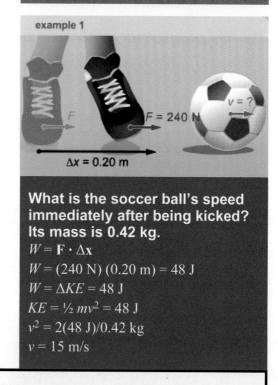

example 1

$F = 240$ N

$\Delta x = 0.20$ m

What is the soccer ball's speed immediately after being kicked? Its mass is 0.42 kg.

$W = \mathbf{F} \cdot \Delta \mathbf{x}$

$W = (240 \text{ N})(0.20 \text{ m}) = 48$ J

$W = \Delta KE = 48$ J

$KE = \frac{1}{2}mv^2 = 48$ J

$v^2 = 2(48 \text{ J})/0.42 \text{ kg}$

$v = 15$ m/s

6.6 - Sample problem: work-kinetic energy theorem

Four bobsledders push their 235 kg sled with a constant force, moving it from rest to a speed of 10.0 m/s along a flat, 50.0-meter-long icy track. Ignoring friction and air resistance, what force does the team exert on the sled?

We assume here that all the work done by the athletes goes to increasing the kinetic energy of the sled.

Variables

mass of sled	$m = 235 \text{ kg}$
displacement	$\Delta x = 50.0 \text{ m}$
sled's initial speed	$v_i = 0 \text{ m/s}$
sled's final speed	$v_f = 10.0 \text{ m/s}$
work	W
force	F

What is the strategy?

1. Calculate the change in kinetic energy of the sled, using the sled's mass and its initial and final speeds.
2. Use the work-kinetic energy theorem and the definition of work to find the force exerted on the sled.

Physics principles and equations

The definition of work, applied when the force is in the direction of the displacement

$$W = F\Delta x$$

The definition of kinetic energy

$$KE = \tfrac{1}{2}\, mv^2$$

The work-kinetic energy theorem

$$W = \Delta KE$$

Step-by-step solution

Start by calculating the change in kinetic energy of the sled.

Step	Reason
1. $\Delta KE = KE_f - KE_i$	definition of change in kinetic energy
2. $\Delta KE = \tfrac{1}{2}mv_f^2 - \tfrac{1}{2}mv_i^2$	definition of kinetic energy
3. $\Delta KE = \tfrac{1}{2}m(v_f^2 - v_i^2)$	factor
4. $\Delta KE = \tfrac{1}{2}(235 \text{ kg})((10.0 \text{ m/s})^2 - (0 \text{ m/s})^2)$	enter values
5. $\Delta KE = 11{,}800 \text{ J}$	solve

Use the work-kinetic energy theorem to find the work done on the sled. Then, use the definition of work to determine how much force was exerted on the sled.

Step	Reason
6. $W = \Delta KE$	work-kinetic energy theorem
7. $W = (F \cos \theta)\Delta x$	definition of work
8. $(F \cos \theta)\Delta x = \Delta KE$	set two work equations equal
9. $F \cos \theta = \Delta KE/\Delta x$	rearrange
10. $F = \Delta KE/\Delta x$	force in direction of displacement
11. $F = 11{,}800 \text{ J}/50.0 \text{ m}$	enter values
12. $F = 236 \text{ N}$	solve

6.7 - Interactive problem: work-kinetic energy theorem

In this simulation, you are a skier and your challenge is to do the correct amount of work to build up enough energy to soar over the canyon and land near the lip of the slope on the right.

You, a 50.0 kg skier, have a flat 12.0 meter long runway leading up to the lip of the canyon. In that stretch, you must apply a force such that at the end of the straightaway, you are traveling with a speed of 8.00 m/s. Any slower, and your jump will fall short. Any faster, and you will overshoot.

How much force must you apply, in newtons, over the 12.0 meter flat stretch? Ignore other forces like friction and air resistance.

Enter the force, to the nearest newton, in the entry box and press GO to check your result.

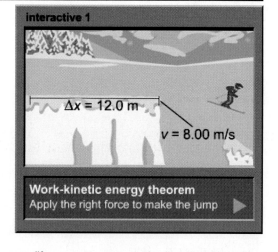

interactive 1

$\Delta x = 12.0 \text{ m}$

$v = 8.00 \text{ m/s}$

Work-kinetic energy theorem
Apply the right force to make the jump ▷

If you have trouble with this problem, review the section on the work-kinetic energy theorem. (If you want to, you can check your answer using a linear motion equation and Newton's second law.)

2560 km

13,100 m/s   15,700 m/s

m = 45,500 kg

A 45,500 kg spaceship is far from any significant source of gravity. It accelerates at a constant rate from 13,100 m/s to 15,700 m/s over a distance of 2560 km. What is the magnitude of the force on the ship due to the action of its engines? Use equations involving work and energy to solve the problem, and assume that the mass is constant.

Answer:

$F =$ [_____] N

6.9 - Power

Power: Work divided by time; also the rate of energy output or consumption.

The definition of work − the dot product of force and displacement − does not say anything about how long it takes for the work to occur. It might take a second, or a year, or any interval of time. Power adds the concept of time to the topics of work and energy. Power equals the amount of work divided by the time it took to do the work. You see this expressed as an equation in Equation 1.

One reason we care about power is because more power means that work can be accomplished faster. Would you rather have a car that accelerated you from zero to 100 kilometers per hour in five seconds, or five minutes? (Some of us have owned cars of the latter type.)

The unit of power is the watt (W), which equals one joule per second. It is a scalar unit. Power can also be expressed as the rate of change of energy. For instance, a 100 megawatt power plant supplies 100 million joules of energy to the electric grid every second.

Sometimes power is expressed in terms of an older unit, the horsepower. This unit comes from the days when scientists sought to establish a standard for how much work a horse could do in a set amount of time. They then compared the power of early engines to the power of a horse. One horsepower equals 550 foot-pounds/second, which is the same as 746 watts.

We still measure the power of cars in horsepower. For instance, a 300-horsepower Porsche is more powerful than a 135-horsepower Toyota. The Porsche's engine is capable of doing more work in a given period of time than the Toyota's.

As with other values that include time, such as velocity or acceleration, there is average

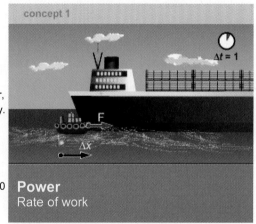
concept 1

$\Delta t = 1$

Power
Rate of work

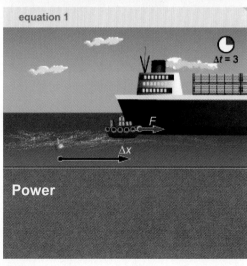
equation 1

$\Delta t = 3$

Power

and instantaneous power. Average power measures the total amount of work done over a period of time, divided by the time. Instantaneous power has the same definition, but the time interval must be a brief instant.

Equation 2 shows two other useful equations for power. Power can be expressed as the rate of change of energy, as you see in the first equation in Equation 2. Sometimes this is stated as "energy consumption", as in a 100-watt light bulb "consumes" 100 joules of energy each second. In other words, the light bulb converts 100 joules of electrical energy each second into other forms of energy, such as light and heat.

The companies that provide electrical power to homes measure each household's energy consumption in kilowatt·hours. You can check that this is a unit of energy. The companies multiply power (thousands of joules per second, or kilowatts) by time (hours). The result is that one kilowatt·hour equals 60 kilojoules, a unit of energy.

The second equation in Equation 2 shows that when there is a constant force **in the direction of an object's displacement**, the power can be measured as the product of the force and the velocity. This equation can be derived from the definition of work: $W = F\Delta x$. Dividing both sides of that equation by time yields power on the left (work divided by time). On the right side, dividing displacement by time yields velocity.

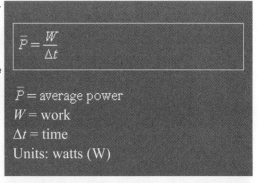

$$\bar{P} = \frac{W}{\Delta t}$$

$\bar{P}$ = average power
W = work
Δt = time
Units: watts (W)

equation 2

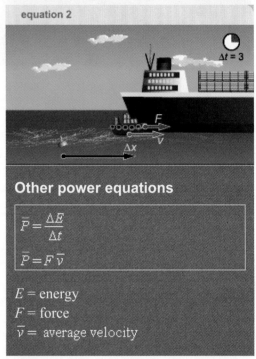

$\Delta t = 3$

Other power equations

$$\bar{P} = \frac{\Delta E}{\Delta t}$$

$$\bar{P} = F\,\bar{v}$$

E = energy
F = force
$\bar{v}$ = average velocity

example 1

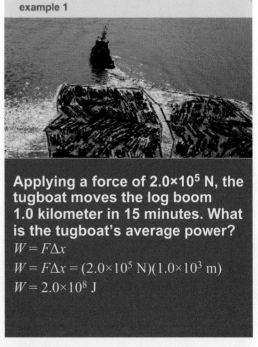

Applying a force of 2.0×10^5 N, the tugboat moves the log boom 1.0 kilometer in 15 minutes. What is the tugboat's average power?

$W = F\Delta x$
$W = F\Delta x = (2.0 \times 10^5 \text{ N})(1.0 \times 10^3 \text{ m})$
$W = 2.0 \times 10^8 \text{ J}$

$$\bar{P} = \frac{W}{\Delta t} = \frac{2.0 \times 10^8 \text{ J}}{9.0 \times 10^2 \text{ s}}$$

$$\bar{P} = 2.2 \times 10^5 \text{ W}$$

6.10 - Potential energy

Potential energy: Energy related to the positions of and forces between the objects that make up a system.

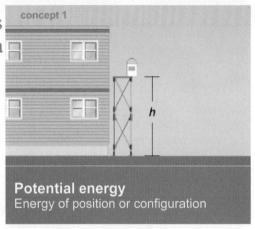

Potential energy
Energy of position or configuration

Although the paint bucket in Concept 1 is not moving, it makes up part of a system that has a form of energy called potential energy. In general, potential energy is the energy due to the configuration of objects that exert forces on one other.

In this section, we focus on one form of potential energy, *gravitational potential energy*. The paint bucket and Earth make up a system that has this form of potential energy.

A *system* is some "chunk" of the universe that you wish to study, such as the bucket and the Earth. You can imagine a boundary like a bubble surrounding the system, separating it from the rest of the universe. The particles within a system can interact with one another via internal forces or fields. Particles outside the system can interact with the system via external forces or fields.

Gravitational potential energy is due to the gravitational force between the bucket and Earth. As the bucket is raised or lowered, its **change** in potential energy (ΔPE) equals the magnitude of its weight, mg, times its vertical displacement, Δh. (We follow the common convention of using Δh for change in height, instead of Δy.) The weight is the amount of force exerted on the bucket by the Earth (and vice versa). This formula is shown in Equation 1.

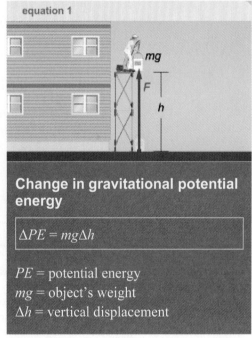

Change in gravitational potential energy

$$\Delta PE = mg\Delta h$$

PE = potential energy
mg = object's weight
Δh = vertical displacement

A change in PE can be positive or negative. The magnitude of weight is a positive value, but change in height can be positive (when the bucket moves up) or negative (when it moves down).

To define a system's PE, we must define a configuration at which the system has zero PE. Unlike kinetic energy, where zero KE has a natural value (when an object's speed is zero), the configuration with zero PE is defined by you, the physicist.

In the diagrams to the right, it is convenient to say the system has zero PE when the bucket is on the Earth's surface. This convention means its PE equals its weight times its height above the ground, mgh. Only the bucket's distance above the Earth, h, matters here; if the bucket moves left or right, its PE does not change.

In Example 1, we calculate the paint bucket's gravitational potential energy as it sits on the scaffolding, four meters above the ground.

There are other types of potential energy. One you will frequently encounter is *elastic potential energy*, which is the energy stored in a compressed or stretched object such as a spring. As you may recall, this form of energy was present in the bow that was used to fire an arrow.

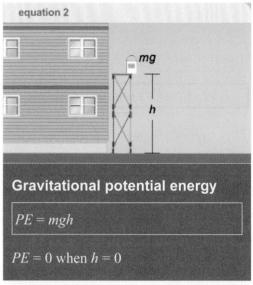

equation 2

Gravitational potential energy

$$PE = mgh$$

$PE = 0$ when $h = 0$

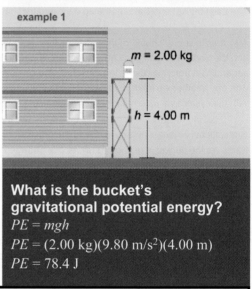

example 1

$m = 2.00$ kg

$h = 4.00$ m

What is the bucket's gravitational potential energy?
$$PE = mgh$$
$$PE = (2.00 \text{ kg})(9.80 \text{ m/s}^2)(4.00 \text{ m})$$
$$PE = 78.4 \text{ J}$$

6.11 - Work and gravitational potential energy

Potential energy is the energy of a system due to forces between the particles or objects that make up the system. It can be related to the amount of work done on a system by an external force. We will use gravitational force and gravitational potential energy as an example of this general principle. Our discussion applies to what are called conservative forces, a type of force we will later discuss in more detail.

The system we consider consists of two objects, the bucket and the Earth, illustrated to the right. The painter applies an external force to this system (via a rope) when she raises or lowers the bucket. The bucket starts at rest on the ground, and she raises it up and places it on the scaffolding. That means the work she does as she moves the bucket from its initial to its final position changes only its gravitational PE. The system's kinetic energy is zero at the beginning and the end of this process.

As she raises the bucket, the painter does work on it. She pulls the bucket up against the force of gravity, which is equal in magnitude to the bucket's weight, mg. She pulls in the direction of the bucket's displacement, Δh. The work equals the force multiplied by the displacement: $mg\Delta h$. The paint bucket's change in gravitational potential energy also equals $mg\Delta h$. The analysis lets us reach an important conclusion: The work done on the system, against

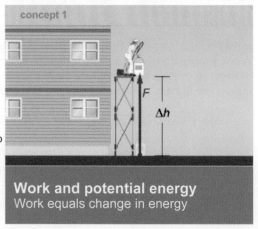

concept 1

Work and potential energy
Work equals change in energy

gravity, equals the system's increase in gravitational potential energy.

Earlier, we stated the work-kinetic energy theorem: The net work done on a particle equals its change in kinetic energy. Here, where there is no change in kinetic energy, we state that the work done on a system equals its change in potential energy.

Are we confused? No. Work performed on a system can change its mechanical energy, which consists of its kinetic energy and its potential energy. Either or both of these forms of energy can change when work is applied to the system.

As the painter does work against the force of gravity, the force of gravity itself is also doing work. The work done by gravity is the negative of the work done by the painter. This means the work done by gravity is also the negative of the change in potential energy, as seen in Equation 2.

Imagine that the painter drops the bucket from the scaffolding. Only the force of gravity does work on the bucket as it falls. The system has more potential energy when the bucket is at the top of the scaffolding than when it is at the bottom, so the work done by gravity has lowered the system's PE: the change in PE due to the work done by gravity is negative.

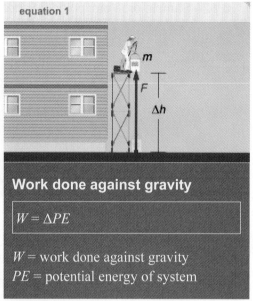

Work done against gravity

$$W = \Delta PE$$

W = work done against gravity
PE = potential energy of system

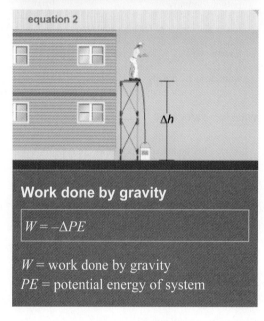

Work done by gravity

$$W = -\Delta PE$$

W = work done by gravity
PE = potential energy of system

In its natural state, an average of 5.71×10^6 kg of water flowed per second over Niagara Falls, falling 51.0 m. If all the work done by gravity could be converted into electric power as the water fell to the bottom, how much power would the falls generate?

Variables

height of falls	$h = 51.0$ m
magnitude of acceleration due to gravity	$g = 9.80$ m/s^2
potential energy	PE
mass of water over falls per unit time	$m/t = 5.71\times10^6$ kg/s
power	P
work done by gravity	W

What is the strategy?

1. Use the definition of power as the rate of work done to define an equation for the power of the falls.

2. Use the fact that work done by gravity equals the negative of the change in gravitational potential energy to solve for the power.

Physics principles and equations

Power is the rate at which work is performed.

$$P = \frac{W}{\Delta t}$$

Change in gravitational PE

$$\Delta PE = mg\Delta h$$

Work done by gravity

$$W = -\Delta PE$$

Step-by-step solution

We start with the definition of power – work done per unit time – and then substitute in the definition of work done by gravity and the definition of gravitational potential energy to solve the problem.

Step	Reason
1. $\quad P = \dfrac{W}{\Delta t}$	power equation
2. $\quad P = \dfrac{-\Delta PE}{\Delta t}$	work done by gravity lowers PE
3. $\quad P = \dfrac{-(mg\Delta h)}{\Delta t} = \dfrac{-mg\,(h_f - h_i)}{\Delta t}$ $\quad P = \dfrac{mg\,(h_i - h_f)}{\Delta t}$	definition of gravitational potential energy
4. $\quad P = \dfrac{m\left(9.80\ \text{m/s}^2\right)(51.0\ \text{m} - 0\ \text{m})}{\Delta t}$	enter values for g and h
5. $\quad P = \left(5.71\times10^6\ \tfrac{\text{kg}}{\text{s}}\right)\left(9.80\ \text{m/s}^2\right)(51.0\ \text{m})$	enter value for m/t
6. $\quad P = 2.85\times10^9\ \text{W}$	solve

This is the theoretical maximum power that could be generated. A real power plant cannot be 100% efficient.

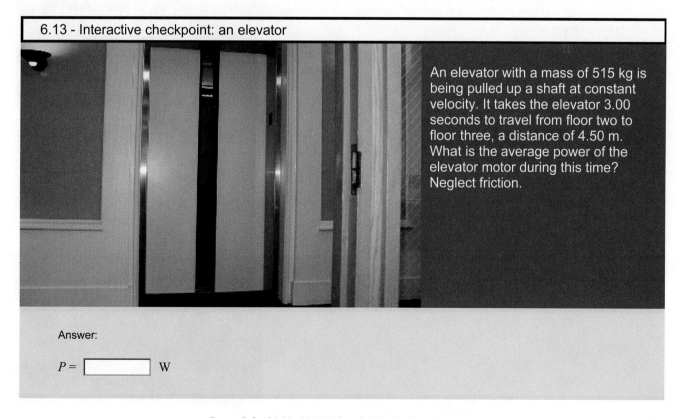

6.13 - Interactive checkpoint: an elevator

An elevator with a mass of 515 kg is being pulled up a shaft at constant velocity. It takes the elevator 3.00 seconds to travel from floor two to floor three, a distance of 4.50 m. What is the average power of the elevator motor during this time? Neglect friction.

Answer:

$P = \boxed{}$ W

We have discussed work on a particle increasing its KE, and work on a system increasing its PE. Now we discuss what happens when work increases both forms of mechanical energy.

Because we are considering only KE and PE in this chapter, we can say the net work done on an object equals the change in the sum of its KE and PE. Positive work done on an object increases its energy; negative work decreases its energy.

Let's also consider what happens when an object does work, and how that affects the object's energy. Consider a soccer ball slamming into the hands of a goalie. The ball is doing work, forcing the goalie's hands backwards. The ball slows down; its energy decreases. Work done **by** an object **decreases** its energy. At the same time, this work on the goalie increases her energy. Work has transferred energy from one system (the ball) to another (the goalie).

We will use the scenario in Example 1 to show how both an object's KE and PE can change when work is done on it. A cannon shoots a 3.20 kg cannonball straight up. The barrel of the cannon is 2.00 m long, and it exerts an average force of 6,250 N while the cannonball is in the cannon. We will ignore air resistance. Can we determine the cannonball's velocity when it has traveled 125 meters upward?

As you may suspect, the answer is "yes".

The cannon does 12,500 J of work on the cannonball, the product of the force (6,250 N) and the displacement (2.00 m). (We assume the cannon does no work on the cannonball after it leaves the cannon.)

At a height of 125 meters, the cannonball's increase in PE equals $mg\Delta h$, or 3,920 J. Since a total of 12,500 J of work was done on the ball, the rest of the work must have gone into raising the cannonball's KE: The change in KE is 8,580 J.

Applying the definition of kinetic energy, we determine that its velocity at 125 m is 73.2 m/s. We could further analyze the cannonball's trip if we were so inclined. At the peak of its trip, all of its energy is potential since its velocity (and KE) there are zero. The PE at the top is 12,500 J. Again applying the formula $mg\Delta h$, we can determine that its peak height above the cannon is about 399 m.

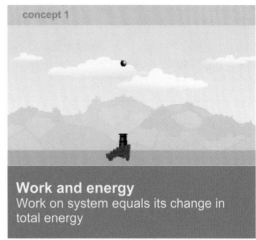

concept 1

Work and energy
Work on system equals its change in total energy

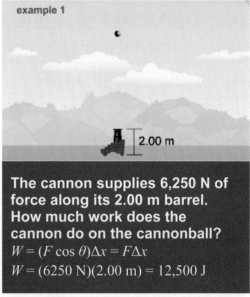

example 1

2.00 m

The cannon supplies 6,250 N of force along its 2.00 m barrel. How much work does the cannon do on the cannonball?
$W = (F\cos\theta)\Delta x = F\Delta x$
$W = (6250\ \text{N})(2.00\ \text{m}) = 12{,}500\ \text{J}$

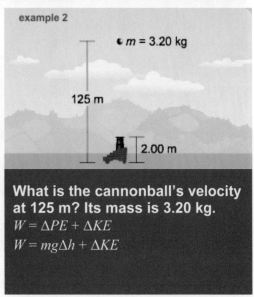

example 2

$m = 3.20$ kg

125 m

2.00 m

What is the cannonball's velocity at 125 m? Its mass is 3.20 kg.
$W = \Delta PE + \Delta KE$
$W = mg\Delta h + \Delta KE$

6.15 - Conservative and non-conservative forces

Earlier, when discussing potential energy, we mentioned that we would explain conservative forces later. The concept of potential energy only applies to conservative forces.

Gravity is an example of a *conservative force*. It is conservative because the total work it does on an object that starts and finishes at the same point is zero. For example, if a 20 kg barbell is raised 2.0 meters, gravity does −40 J of work, and when the barbell is lowered 2.0 meters back to its initial position, gravity does +40 J of work. When the barbell is returned to its initial position, the sum of the work done by gravity on the barbell equals zero.

You can confirm this by considering the barbell's gravitational potential energy. Since that equals mgh, it is the same at the beginning and end because the height is the same. Since there is no change in gravitational PE, there is no work done by gravity on the barbell.

We illustrate this with the roller coaster shown in Concept 1. For now, we ignore other forces, such as friction, and consider gravity as the only force doing work on the roller coaster car. When the roller coaster car goes down a hill, gravity does positive work. When the roller coaster car goes up a hill, gravity does negative work. The sum of the work done by gravity on this journey equals zero.

When a roller coaster car makes such a trip, the roller coaster car travels on what is called a closed path, a trip that starts and stops at the same point. Given a slight push at the top of the hill, the roller coaster would make endless trips around the roller coaster track.

Kinetic friction and air resistance are two examples of *non-conservative forces*. These forces oppose motion, whatever its direction. Friction and air resistance do negative work on the roller coaster car, slowing it regardless of whether it is going uphill or downhill.

We show non-conservative forces at work in Concept 2. The roller coaster glides down the hill, but it does not return to its initial position because kinetic friction and air resistance dissipate some of its energy as it goes around the track. The presence of these forces dictates that net work must be done on the roller coaster car by some other force to return it to its initial position. A mechanism such as a motorized pulley system can accomplish this.

A way to differentiate between conservative and non-conservative forces is to ask: Does the amount of work done by the force depend on the path?

Consider only the force of gravity, a conservative force, as it acts on the skier shown in Concept 3. When considering the work done by gravity, it does not matter in terms of work and energy whether the skier goes down the longer, zigzag route (path A), or the straight route (path B). The work done by gravity is the same along either path. All that

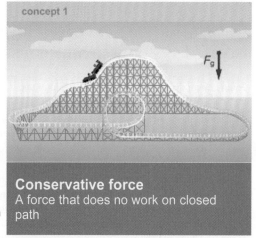

Conservative force
A force that does no work on closed path

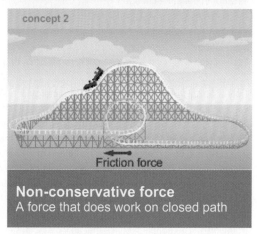

Non-conservative force
A force that does work on closed path

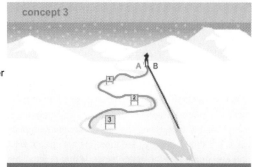

Effect of path on work and energy

matters are the locations of the initial and final points of the path. The conservative force is *path independent*.

However, with non-conservative forces, the path does influence the amount of work done by a force. Consider the skier in the context of kinetic friction, a non-conservative force. The amount of force of kinetic friction is the same along either route, but it acts along a greater distance if the skier chooses the longer route. The amount of work done by the force of kinetic friction increases with the path length. A non-conservative force is *path dependent*.

6.16 - Conservation of energy

Conservation of energy: The total energy in an isolated system remains constant.

Energy never disappears. It only changes form and transfers between objects.

To illustrate this principle, we use the boy to the right who is swinging on a rope. We consider his mechanical energy, the sum of his kinetic and gravitational potential energy. When he jumps from the riverbank and swings toward the water, his gravitational potential energy becomes kinetic energy. The decrease in gravitational PE (shown in the gauge labeled PE in Concept 1) is matched by an increase in his kinetic energy (shown in the gauge labeled KE). Ignoring air resistance or any other non-conservative forces, the sum of KE and PE is a constant at any point. The total amount of energy (labeled TE, for total energy) stays the same. The total energy is conserved; its amount does not change.

The law of conservation of energy applies to an isolated system. An *isolated system* is one that has no interactions with its environment. The particles within the system may interact with one another, but no net external force or field acts on an isolated system.

Only external forces can change the total energy of a system. If a giant spring lifts a car, you can say the spring has increased the energy of the car. In this case, you are considering the spring as supplying an external force and not as part of the system. If you include the spring in the system, the increase in the energy of the car is matched by a decrease in the potential energy contained of the spring, and the total energy of the system remains the same. For the law of conservation of energy to apply, there can be no non-conservative forces like friction within the system.

The law of conservation of energy can be expressed mathematically, as shown in Equation 1. The equation states that an isolated system's total energy at any final point in time is the same as its total energy at an initial point in time. When considering mechanical energy, we can state that the sum of the kinetic and potential energies at some final moment equals the sum of the kinetic and potential energies at an initial moment.

In the case of the boy on the rope, if you know his mass and height on the riverbank, you can calculate his gravitational potential energy. In this example, rather than saying his PE equals zero on the ground, we say it equals zero at the bottom of the arc. This simplifies matters. Using the law of conservation of energy, you can then determine what his kinetic energy, and therefore his speed, will be when he reaches the bottom of the arc, nearest to the water, since at that point all his energy is kinetic.

Let's leave the boy swinging for a while and switch to another example: You drop a weight. When the weight hits the ground it will stop moving. At this point, the weight has neither kinetic energy nor potential energy because it has no motion and its height off

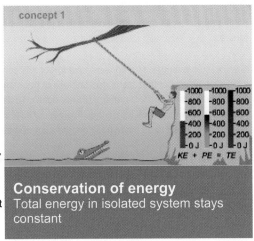

Conservation of energy
Total energy in isolated system stays constant

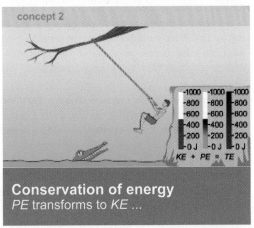

Conservation of energy
PE transforms to *KE* ...

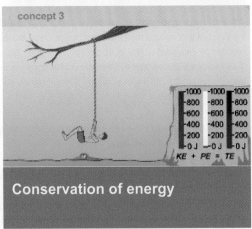

Conservation of energy

the Earth's surface is zero. Does the law of conservation of energy still hold true?

Yes, it does, although we need to broaden the forms of energy included in the discussion. With careful observation you might note that the ground shakes as the weight hits it (more energy of motion). The weight and the ground heat up a bit (thermal energy). The list can continue: energy of the motion of flying dirt, the energy of sound and so on. The amount of mechanical energy does decline, but when you include all forms of energy, the overall energy stays constant.

There is a caveat to the law of conservation of energy. Albert Einstein demonstrated that there is a relationship between mass and energy. Mass can be converted into energy, as it is inside the Sun or a nuclear reactor, and energy can be converted into mass. It is the sum of mass and energy that remains constant. Our current focus is on much less extreme situations.

Using the principle of conservation of energy can have many practical benefits, as automotive engineers are now demonstrating. When it comes to energy and cars, the focus is often on how to cause the car to accelerate, how fast they will reach say a speed of 100 km/h.

Of course, cars also need to slow down, a task assigned to the brakes. As conventional cars brake, the energy is typically dissipated as heat as the brake pads rub on the rotors. Innovative new cars, called hybrids, now capture some of the kinetic energy and convert it to chemical energy stored in batteries or mechanical energy stored in flywheels. The engine then recycles that energy back into kinetic energy when the car needs to accelerate, saving gasoline.

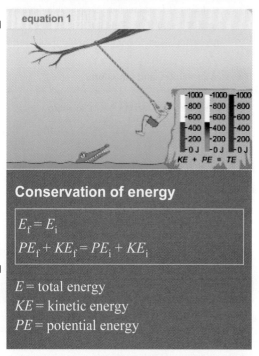

... but total energy remains the same

equation 1

$KE + PE = TE$

Conservation of energy

$$E_f = E_i$$
$$PE_f + KE_f = PE_i + KE_i$$

E = total energy
KE = kinetic energy
PE = potential energy

6.17 - Sample problem: conservation of energy

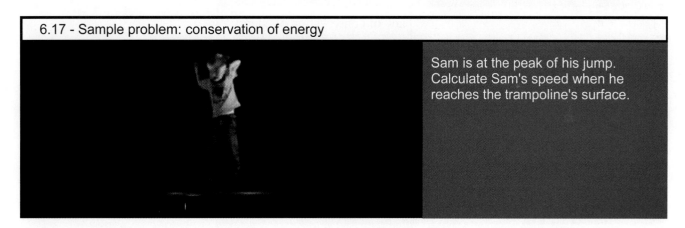

Sam is at the peak of his jump. Calculate Sam's speed when he reaches the trampoline's surface.

Sam is jumping up and down on a trampoline. He bounces to a maximum height of 0.25 m above the surface of the trampoline. How fast will he be traveling when he hits the trampoline? We define Sam's potential energy at the surface of the trampoline to be zero.

Variables

Sam's height at peak	$h = 0.25$ m
Sam's speed at peak	$v_{peak} = 0$ m/s
Sam's speed at bottom	v

What is the strategy?

1. Use the law of conservation energy, to state that Sam's total energy at the peak of his jump is the same as his total energy at the surface of the trampoline. Simplify this equation, using the facts that his kinetic energy is zero at the peak, and his potential energy is zero at the surface of the trampoline.
2. Solve the resulting equation for his speed at the bottom.

Physics principles and equations

The definition of gravitational potential energy

$$PE = mgh$$

The definition of kinetic energy

$$KE = \tfrac{1}{2}\, mv^2$$

Total energy is conserved in this isolated system.

$$E_f = E_i$$

Step-by-step solution

We start by stating the law of conservation of energy in equation form, and then adapting it to fit the specifics of Sam's trampoline jump.

Step	Reason
1. $E_f = E_i$	law of conservation of energy
2. $KE_f + PE_f = KE_i + PE_i$	energy is mechanical energy
3. $KE_f + 0 = 0 + PE_i$	enter values
4. $KE_f = PE_i$	simplify

Now we have a simpler equation for Sam's energy. The task now is to solve it for the one unknown variable, his speed at the surface of the trampoline.

Step	Reason
5. $KE_f = PE_i$	state equation again
6. $\tfrac{1}{2}\, mv^2 = mgh$	definitions of KE, PE
7. $v = \sqrt{2gh}$	solve for v
8. $v = \sqrt{2\,(9.80 \ \text{m}/\text{s}^2)\,(0.25 \ \text{m})}$	enter values
9. $v = 2.2$ m/s	evaluate

6.18 - Interactive checkpoint: conservation of energy

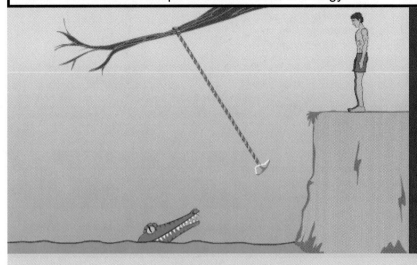

A boy releases a pork chop on a rope. The chop is moving at a speed of 8.52 m/s at the bottom of its swing. How much higher than this point is the point from which the pork chop is released? Assume that it has no initial speed when starting its swing.

Answer:

$h =$ [   ] m

6.19 - Interactive problem: conservation of energy

The law of conservation of energy states that the total energy in an isolated system remains constant. In the simulation on the right, you can use this law and your knowledge of potential and kinetic energies to help a soapbox derby car make a jump.

A soapbox derby car has no engine. It gains speed as it rolls down a hill. You can drag the car to any point on the hill. A gauge will display the car's height above the ground. Release the mouse button and the car will fly down the hill.

In this interactive, if the car is traveling 12.5 m/s at the bottom of the ramp, it will successfully make the jump through the hoop. Too slow and it will fall short; too fast and it will overshoot.

You can use the law of conservation of energy to figure out the vertical position needed for the car to nail the jump.

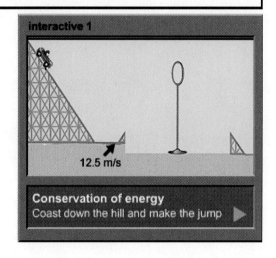

interactive 1

12.5 m/s

Conservation of energy
Coast down the hill and make the jump ▶

6.20 - Friction and conservation of energy

In this section, we show how two principles we have discussed can be combined to solve a typical problem. We will use the principle of conservation of energy and how work done by an external force affects the total energy of a system to determine the effect of friction on a block sliding down a plane.

Suppose the 1.00 kg block shown to the right slides down an inclined wooden plane. Since the block is released from rest, it has no initial velocity. It loses 2.00 meters in height as it slides, and it slides 6.00 meters along the surface of the inclined plane. The force of kinetic friction is 2.00 N. You want to know the block's speed when it reaches the bottom position.

To solve this problem, we start by applying the principle of conservation of energy. The block's initial energy is all potential, equal to the product of its mass, g and its height (mgh). At a height of 2.00 meters, the block's PE equals 19.6 J. The potential energy will be zero when the block reaches the bottom of the plane. Ignoring friction, the PE of the block at the top equals its KE at the bottom.

Now we will factor in friction. The force of friction opposes the block's motion down the inclined plane. The work it does is negative, and that work reduces the energy of the block. We calculate the work done by friction on the block as the force of friction times the displacement along the plane, which equals −12.0 J. The block's energy at the top (19.6 J) plus the −12.0 J means the block has 7.6 J of kinetic energy at the bottom. Using the definition of kinetic energy, we can conclude that the 1.00 kg block is moving at 3.90 m/s.

You can also calculate the effect of friction by determining how fast the block would be traveling if there were no friction. All 19.6 J of PE would convert to KE, yielding a speed of 6.26 m/s. Friction reduces the speed of the block by approximately 38%.

In general, non-conservative forces like friction and air resistance are *dissipative forces*: They reduce the energy of a system. They do negative work since they act opposite the direction of motion. (There are a few cases where they do positive work, such as when the force of friction causes something to move, as when you step on a moving sidewalk.)

concept 1

Effect of non-conservative forces
Reduce object's energy

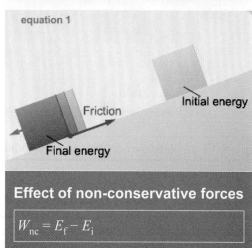

equation 1

Initial energy

Friction

Final energy

Effect of non-conservative forces

$$W_{nc} = E_f - E_i$$

W_{nc} = work by non-conservative force
E_f = final energy
E_i = initial energy

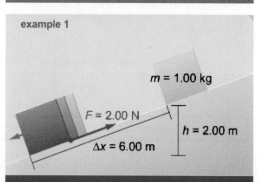

example 1

$m = 1.00$ kg

$F = 2.00$ N

$h = 2.00$ m

$\Delta x = 6.00$ m

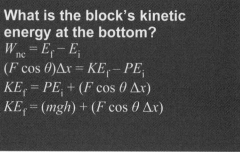

What is the block's kinetic energy at the bottom?
$W_{nc} = E_f - E_i$
$(F \cos \theta)\Delta x = KE_f - PE_i$
$KE_f = PE_i + (F \cos \theta \, \Delta x)$
$KE_f = (mgh) + (F \cos \theta \, \Delta x)$

$$KE_f = (1.00 \text{ kg} * 9.80 \text{ m/s}^2 * 2.00 \text{ m}) +$$
$$(2.00 \text{ N} \times \cos 180° \times 6.00 \text{ m})$$
$$KE_f = 19.6 \text{ J} + (-12.0 \text{ J})$$
$$KE_f = 7.60 \text{ J}$$

6.21 - Gotchas

You are asked to push two wheelbarrows up a hill. One wheelbarrow is empty, and you are able to push it up the hill in one minute. The other is filled with huge rocks, and even after you push it for an hour, you cannot budge it. In which case do you do more work on the wheelbarrow? You do more work on the empty wheelbarrow because it is the only one that moves. You do no work on the wheelbarrow filled with rocks because you do not move it; its displacement is zero.

Two 1/4 kg cheeseburgers are moving in opposite directions. One is rising at three m/s, the other is falling at three m/s. Which has more kinetic energy? They are the same. The direction of velocity does not matter for kinetic energy; only the magnitude of velocity (the speed) matters.

You start on a beach. You go to the moon. You come back. You go to Hollywood. You then go to the summit of Mount Everest. Have you increased your gravitational potential energy more than if you had climbed to this summit without all the other side trips? No, the increase in energy is the same. In both cases, the increase in gravitational potential energy equals your mass times the height of Mount Everest times g.

You are holding a cup of coffee at your desk, a half-meter above the floor. You extend your arm laterally out a nearby third-story window so that the cup is suspended 10 meters above the ground. Have you increased the cup's gravitational potential energy? No. Assume you choose the floor as the zero potential energy point. The potential energy is the same because the cup remains the same distance above the floor.

An apple falls to the ground. Because the Earth's gravity did work on it, the apple's energy has increased. It depends on how you define "the system." If you said the apple had gravitational potential energy, then you are including the Earth as part of the system. In this case, the Earth's gravity is not an external force. Energy is conserved: The system's decreased PE is matched by an increase in KE. You could also say "the system" is solely the apple. In that case, it has no PE, since PE requires the presence of a force between objects in a system, and this system has only one object. Gravity is now an external force acting on the apple, and it does increase the apple's KE. This is not, perhaps, the typical way to think about it, but it is valid.

It is impossible for a system to have negative PE. Wrong: Systems can have negative PE. For instance, if you define the system to have zero PE when an object is at the Earth's surface, the object has negative PE when it is below the surface. Its PE has decreased from zero, so it must be negative. Negative PE is common in some topics, such as orbital motion.

6.22 - Summary

Work is the product of the force on an object and its displacement in the direction of that force. It is a scalar quantity with units of joules (1 J = 1 kg·m²/s²).

Work and several other scalar quantities can be computed by taking the dot product of two vectors. The dot product is a scalar equal to the product of the magnitudes of the two vectors and the cosine of the angle between them. Loosely, it tells you how much of one vector is in the direction of another.

Energy is a property of an object or a system. It has units of joules and is a scalar quantity. Energy can transfer between objects and change forms. Work on an object or system will change its energy.

One form of energy is kinetic energy. It is the energy possessed by objects in motion and is proportional to the object's mass and the square of its speed.

The work-kinetic energy theorem states that the work done on a particle or an object modeled as a particle is equal to its change in kinetic energy. Positive work increases the energy, while negative work decreases it.

Equations

$$W = \mathbf{F} \cdot \Delta \mathbf{x} = (F \cos \theta)\Delta x$$

$$KE = \tfrac{1}{2}\, mv^2$$

$$W = \Delta KE, \text{ for a particle}$$

$$P = \frac{W}{\Delta t} = \frac{\Delta E}{\Delta t}$$

$$\Delta PE = mg\Delta h$$

$$E_f = E_i$$

Power is work divided by time. The unit of power is the watt (1 W = 1 J/s), a scalar quantity. It is often expressed as a rate of energy consumption or output. For example, a 100-watt light bulb converts 100 joules of electrical energy per second into light and heat.

Another form of energy is potential energy. It is the energy related to the positions of the objects in a system and the forces between them. Gravitational potential energy is an object's potential energy due to its position relative to a body such as the Earth.

Forces can be classified as conservative or non-conservative. An object acted upon only by conservative forces, such as gravitational and spring forces, requires no *net* work to return to its original position. An object acted upon by non-conservative forces, such as kinetic friction, will not return to its initial position without additional work being done on it.

When only conservative forces are present, the work to move an object between two points does not depend on the path taken. The work is path independent. When non-conservative forces are acting, the work does depend on the path taken, and the work is path dependent.

The law of conservation of energy states that the total energy in an isolated system remains constant, though energy may change form or be transferred from object to object within the system.

Mechanical energy is conserved only when there are no non-conservative forces acting in the system. When a non-conservative force such as friction is present, the mechanical energy of the system decreases. The law of conservation of energy still holds, but we have not yet learned to account for the other forms into which the mechanical energy might be transformed, such as thermal (heat) energy.

chapter
7 Momentum
physics
□ Conceptual
kinetic
BOOKS

7.0 - Introduction

"The more things change, the more they stay the same" is a well-known French saying.

However, though witty and perhaps true for many matters on which the French have great expertise, this saying is simply not good physics.

Instead, a physicist would say: "Things stay the same, period. That is, unless acted upon by a net force." Perhaps a little less *joie de vivre* than your average Frenchman, but nonetheless the key to understanding momentum.

What we now call momentum, Newton referred to as "quantity of motion." The linear momentum of an object equals the product of its mass and velocity. (In this chapter, we focus on linear momentum. Angular momentum, or momentum due to rotation, is a topic in another chapter.) Momentum is a useful concept when applied to collisions, a subject that can be a lot of fun. In a collision, two or more objects exert forces on each other for a brief instant of time, and these forces are significantly greater than any other forces they may experience during the collision.

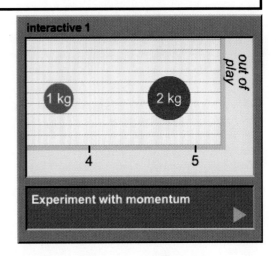

interactive 1

out of play

1 kg   2 kg

4   5

Experiment with momentum

At the right is a simulation − a variation of shuffleboard − that you can use to begin your study of momentum and collisions. You can set the initial velocity for both the blue and the red pucks and use these velocity settings to cause them to collide. The blue puck has a mass of 1.0 kg, and the red puck a mass of 2.0 kg. The shuffleboard has no friction, but the pucks stop moving when they fall off the edge. Their momenta and velocities are displayed in output gauges.

Using the simulation, answer these questions. First, is it possible to have negative momentum? If so, how can you achieve it? Second, does the collision of the pucks affect the sum of their velocities? In other words, does the sum of their velocities remain constant? Third, does the collision affect the sum of their momenta? Remember to consider positive and negative signs when summing these values. Press PAUSE before and after the collisions so you can read the necessary data. For an optional challenge: Does the collision conserve the total kinetic energy of the pucks? If so, the collision is called an elastic collision. If it reduces the kinetic energy, the collision is called an inelastic collision.

7.1 - Momentum

Momentum (linear): Mass times velocity.

An object's linear momentum equals the product of its mass and its velocity. A fast moving locomotive has greater momentum than a slowly moving ping-pong ball.

The units for momentum are kilogram·meters/second (kg·m/s). A ping-pong ball with a mass of 2.5 grams moving at 1.0 m/s has a momentum of 0.0025 kg·m/s. A 100,000 kg locomotive moving at 5 m/s has a momentum of 5×10^5 kg·m/s.

Momentum is a vector quantity. The momentum vector points in the same direction as the velocity vector. This means that if two identical locomotives are moving at the same speed and one is heading east and the other west, they will have equal but **opposite** momenta, since they have equal but oppositely directed velocities.

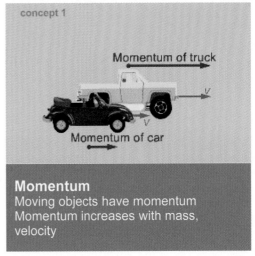

concept 1

Momentum of truck

v

v

Momentum of car

Momentum
Moving objects have momentum
Momentum increases with mass, velocity

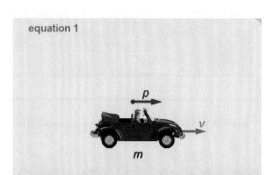

equation 1

Momentum

$$\mathbf{p} = m\mathbf{v}$$

$\mathbf{p}$ = momentum
m = mass
$\mathbf{v}$ = velocity
Momentum same direction as velocity
Units: kg·m/s

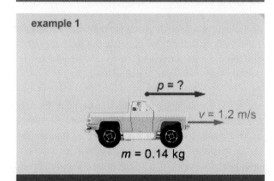

example 1

What is the toy truck's momentum?

$p = mv$
$p = (0.14 \text{ kg})(1.2 \text{ m/s})$
$\mathbf{p} = 0.17$ kg·m/s to the right

7.2 - Momentum and Newton's second law

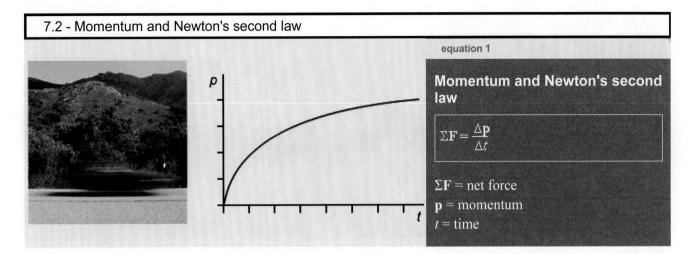

equation 1

Momentum and Newton's second law

$$\Sigma \mathbf{F} = \frac{\Delta \mathbf{p}}{\Delta t}$$

$\Sigma \mathbf{F}$ = net force
$\mathbf{p}$ = momentum
t = time

Although you started your study of physics with velocity and acceleration, early physicists such as Newton focused much of their attention on momentum.

The equation on the right may remind you of Newton's second law. In fact, it is equivalent to the second law (as we show below) and Newton stated his law in this form. This equation is useful when you know the change in the momentum of an object (or, equivalently for an object of constant mass, the change in velocity). This equation as stated assumes an average or constant external net force.

Below, we show that this equation is equivalent to the more familiar version of Newton's second law based on mass and acceleration. We state that version of Newton's law, and then use the definition to restate the law as you see it here.

Step	Reason
1. $\quad \Sigma \mathbf{F} = m\,\mathbf{a} = m\frac{\Delta \mathbf{v}}{\Delta t}$	Newton's second law; definition of acceleration
2. $\quad \mathbf{p} = m\mathbf{v}$	definition of momentum
3. $\quad \frac{\Delta \mathbf{p}}{\Delta t} = m\frac{\Delta \mathbf{v}}{\Delta t}$	divide equation 2 by Δt
4. $\quad \Sigma \mathbf{F} = \frac{\Delta \mathbf{p}}{\Delta t}$	substitute equation 3 into equation 1

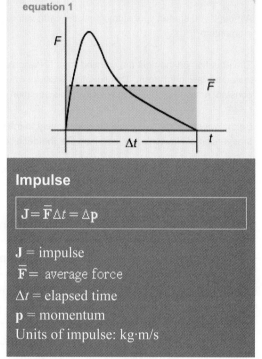

concept 1

Impulse
Force times elapsed time
Change in momentum

Impulse: Change in momentum.

In the prior section, we stated that net force equals change in momentum per unit time. We can rearrange this equation and state that the change in momentum equals the product of the average force and the elapsed time, which is shown in Equation 1.

This quantity is called the impulse of the force, and is represented by **J**. Impulse is a vector, has the same units as momentum, and points in the same direction as the change in momentum and as the force. The relationship shown is called the *impulse-momentum theorem*.

In this section, we focus on the case when a force is applied for a brief interval of time, and is stated or approximated as an average force. This is a common and important way of applying the concept of impulse.

A net force is required to accelerate an object, changing its velocity and its momentum. The greater the net force, or the longer the interval of time it is applied, the more the object's momentum changes, which is the same as saying the impulse increases.

Engineers apply this concept to the systems they design. For instance, a cannon barrel is long so that the cannonball is exposed to the force of the explosive charge longer, which causes the cannonball to experience a greater impulse, and a greater change in momentum.

Even though a longer barrel allows the force to be applied for a longer time interval, it is still brief. Measuring a rapidly changing force over such an interval may be difficult, so the force is often modeled as an average force. For example, when a baseball player swings a bat and hits the ball, the duration of the collision can be as short as 1/1000th of a second and the force averages in the thousands of newtons.

The brief but large force that the bat exerts on the ball is called an *impulsive force*. When analyzing a collision like this, we ignore other forces (like gravity) that are acting upon the ball because their effect is minimal during this brief period of time.

In the illustration for Equation 1, you see a force that varies with time (the curve) and the average of that force (the straight dashed line). The area under the curve and the area of the rectangle both equal the impulse, since both equal the product of force and time.

The nature of impulse explains why coaches teach athletes like long jumpers, cyclists, skiers and martial artists to relax when they land or fall, and why padded mats and sand

equation 1

Impulse

$$J = \bar{F}\Delta t = \Delta p$$

$\mathbf{J}$ = impulse
$\bar{\mathbf{F}}$ = average force
Δt = elapsed time
$\mathbf{p}$ = momentum
Units of impulse: kg·m/s

example 1

68 kg

The long jumper's speed just before landing is 7.8 m/s. What is the impulse of her landing?
$$J = \mathbf{p}_f - \mathbf{p}_i$$
$$J = mv_f - mv_i$$

pits are used. In Example 1 on the right, we calculate the (one-dimensional) impulse experienced by a long jumper on landing in the sand pit, from her change in momentum.

$$J = 0.0 - (68 \text{ kg})(7.8 \text{ m/s})$$
$$J = -530 \text{ kg·m/s}$$

Her impulse (change in momentum) is the same, however long it takes her to stop when she hits the ground. In the example, that impulse is −530 kg·m/s.

Why does she want to extend the time of her landing? She wants to make this time as long as possible (by landing in the sand, by flexing her knees), since it means the collision lasts longer. Since impulse equals force multiplied by elapsed time, the average force required to produce the change in momentum **decreases** as the time **increases**. The reduced average force lessens the chance of injury. Padded mats are another application of this concept: The impulse of landing is the same on a padded or unpadded floor, but a mat increases the duration of a landing and reduces its average force.

There are also numerous applications of this principle outside of sports. For example, cars have "crumple zones" designed into them that collapse upon impact, extending the duration of the impulse during a collision and reducing the average force.

7.4 - Physics at play: hitting a baseball

When a professional baseball player swings a bat and hits a ball square on, he will dramatically change its velocity in a millisecond. A fastball can approach the plate at around 95 miles per hour, and in a line drive shot, the ball can leave the bat in roughly the opposite direction at about 110 miles per hour, a change of about 200 mph in about a millisecond.

The bat exerts force on the baseball in the very brief period of time they are in contact. The amount of force varies over this brief interval, as the graph to the right reflects.

At the moment of contact, the bat and ball are moving toward each other. The force on the ball increases as they come together and the ball compresses against the bat. The force applied to the ball during the time it is in contact with the bat is responsible for the ball's change in momentum.

How long the bat stays in contact with the ball is much easier to measure than the average force the bat exerts on the ball, but by applying the concept of impulse, that force can be calculated. Impulse equals both the average force times the elapsed time and the change in momentum. Since the velocities of the baseball can be observed (say, with a radar gun), and the baseball's mass is known, its change in momentum can be calculated, as we do in Example 1. The time of the collision can be observed using stroboscopic photography and other techniques. This leaves one variable − average force − and we solve for that in the example problem.

The average force equals 2.5×10^4 N. A barrier that stops a car moving at 20 miles per hour in half a second exerts a comparable average amount of force.

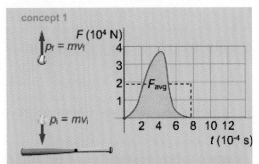

concept 1

Baseballs, bats and impulse
Force applied over time changes momentum
Impulse = change in momentum
Impulse = average force × elapsed time

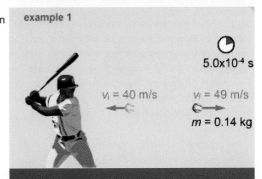

example 1

5.0×10^{-4} s

$v_i = 40$ m/s

$v_f = 49$ m/s

$m = 0.14$ kg

The ball arrives at 40 m/s and leaves at 49 m/s in the opposite direction. The contact time is 5.0×10^{-4} s. What is the average force on the ball?

$$J = F_{avg}\,\Delta t = \Delta p = m\Delta v$$
$$F_{avg} = m\Delta v / \Delta t$$

$$F_{avg} = \frac{(0.14\ \text{kg})(49 - (-40)\ \text{m/s})}{5.0 \times 10^{-4}\ \text{s}}$$

$$F_{avg} = 2.5 \times 10^4\ \text{N}$$

7.5 - Conservation of momentum

Momentum before = Momentum after

concept 1

Conservation of momentum
No net external force on system:
Total momentum is conserved

Conservation of momentum: The total momentum of an isolated system is constant.

Momentum is conserved in an isolated system. An *isolated system* is one that does not interact with its environment. Momentum can transfer from object to object within this system but the vector sum of the momenta of all the objects remains constant.

Excluding deep space, it can be difficult to find locations where a system has no interaction with its environment. This makes it useful to state that momentum is conserved in a system that has no net force acting on it.

We will use pool balls on a pool table to discuss the conservation of momentum. To put it more formally, the pool balls are the system.

In pool, a player begins play by striking the white cue ball. To use the language of physics, a player causes there to be a net external force acting on the cue ball.

Once the cue ball has been struck, it may collide with another ball, and more collisions may ensue. However, there is **no** net external force acting on the balls after the cue ball has been struck (ignoring friction which we will treat as negligible). The normal force of the table balances the force of gravity on the balls. Since there is now no net external force acting on the balls, the total amount of their momentum remains constant. When they collide, the balls exert forces on one another, but this is a force internal to the system, and does not change its total momentum.

In the scenario you see illustrated above, the cue ball and another ball are shown before and after a collision. The cue ball initially has positive momentum since it is moving to the right. The ball it is aimed at is initially stationary and has zero momentum.

When the cue ball strikes its target, the cue ball slows down and the other ball speeds up. In fact, the cue ball may stop moving. You see this shown on the right side of the illustration above. During the collision, momentum transfers from one ball to another. The law of conservation of momentum states that the combined momentum of both remains constant: One ball's loss equals the other ball's gain.

A rifle also provides a notable example of the conservation of momentum. Before it is fired, the initial momentum of a rifle and the bullet it fires are both zero (since neither

equation 1

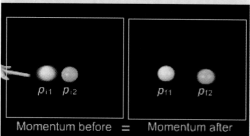

Momentum before = Momentum after

Conservation of momentum

$$\mathbf{p}_{i1} + \mathbf{p}_{i2} + \ldots + \mathbf{p}_{in} = \mathbf{p}_{f1} + \mathbf{p}_{f2} + \ldots + \mathbf{p}_{fn}$$

$\mathbf{p}_{i1}, \mathbf{p}_{i2}, \ldots, \mathbf{p}_{in}$ = initial momenta
$\mathbf{p}_{f1}, \mathbf{p}_{f2}, \ldots, \mathbf{p}_{fn}$ = final momenta

example 1

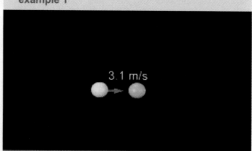

3.1 m/s

The balls have the same mass. The cue ball strikes the stationary yellow ball head on, and stops. What is the yellow ball's resulting velocity?

has any velocity). When the rifle is fired, the bullet moves in one direction and the rifle recoils in the opposite direction. The bullet and the rifle each now have nonzero momentum, but the vector sum of their momenta must remain at zero.

Two factors account for this. First, the rifle and the bullet are moving in opposite directions. In the case of the rifle and bullet, all the motion takes place along a line, so we can use positive and negative to indicate direction. Let's assume the bullet has positive velocity; since the rifle moves (recoils) in the opposite direction, it has negative velocity. The momentum vector of each object points in the same direction as its velocity vector. This means the bullet has positive momentum while the rifle has negative momentum.

$$\mathbf{p}_{i,cue} + \mathbf{p}_{i,yel} = \mathbf{p}_{f,cue} + \mathbf{p}_{f,yel}$$
$$m\mathbf{v}_{i,cue} + m\mathbf{v}_{i,yel} = m\mathbf{v}_{f,cue} + m\mathbf{v}_{f,yel}$$
$$\mathbf{v}_{i,cue} + \mathbf{v}_{i,yel} = \mathbf{v}_{f,cue} + \mathbf{v}_{f,yel}$$
$$v_{i,cue} + v_{i,yel} = v_{f,cue} + v_{f,yel}$$
$$3.1 \text{ m/s} + 0.0 \text{ m/s} = 0.0 \text{ m/s} + v_{f,yel}$$
$$\mathbf{v}_{f,yel} = 3.1 \text{ m/s to the right}$$

Second, for momentum to be conserved, the sum of these momenta must equal zero, since the sum was zero before the rifle was fired. The amount of momentum of the faster moving but less massive bullet equals the amount of momentum of the more massive but slower moving rifle. When the two are added together, the total momentum continues to equal zero.

7.6 - Derivation: conservation of momentum from Newton's laws

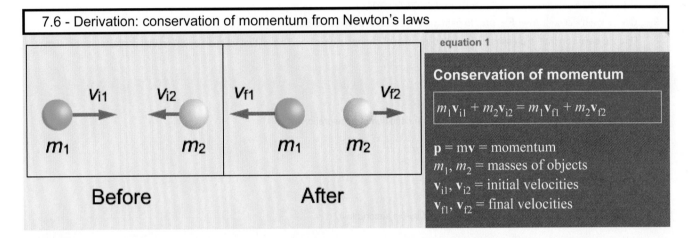

equation 1

Conservation of momentum

$$m_1\mathbf{v}_{i1} + m_2\mathbf{v}_{i2} = m_1\mathbf{v}_{f1} + m_2\mathbf{v}_{f2}$$

$\mathbf{p} = m\mathbf{v} = $ momentum
$m_1, m_2 = $ masses of objects
$\mathbf{v}_{i1}, \mathbf{v}_{i2} = $ initial velocities
$\mathbf{v}_{f1}, \mathbf{v}_{f2} = $ final velocities

Before   After

Newton formulated many of his laws concerning motion using the concept of momentum, although today his laws are stated in terms of force and acceleration. The law of conservation of momentum can be derived from his second and third laws.

The derivation uses a collision between two balls of masses m_1 and m_2 with velocities v_1 and v_2. You see the collision illustrated above, along with the conservation of momentum equation we will prove for this situation.

To derive the equation, we consider the forces on the balls during their collision. During the time Δt of the collision, the balls exert forces $\mathbf{F}_1$ and $\mathbf{F}_2$ on each other. ($\mathbf{F}_1$ is the force on ball 1 and $\mathbf{F}_2$ the force on ball 2.)

Diagram

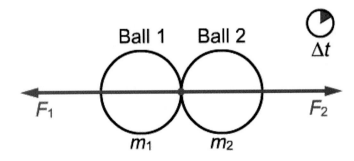

This diagram shows the forces on the balls during the collision.

Variables

<table>
<tr><td>duration of collision</td><td colspan="2">Δt</td></tr>
<tr><td></td><td>ball 1</td><td>ball 2</td></tr>
<tr><td>force on ball</td><td>$\mathbf{F}_1$</td><td>$\mathbf{F}_2$</td></tr>
<tr><td>mass</td><td>m_1</td><td>m_2</td></tr>
<tr><td>acceleration</td><td>$\mathbf{a}_1$</td><td>$\mathbf{a}_2$</td></tr>
<tr><td>initial velocity</td><td>$\mathbf{v}_{i1}$</td><td>$\mathbf{v}_{i2}$</td></tr>
<tr><td>final velocity</td><td>$\mathbf{v}_{f1}$</td><td>$\mathbf{v}_{f2}$</td></tr>
</table>

Strategy

1. Use Newton's third law: The forces will be equal but opposite.
2. Use Newton's second law, $\mathbf{F} = m\mathbf{a}$, to determine the acceleration of the balls.
3. Use the definition that expresses acceleration in terms of change in velocity. This will result in an equation that contains momentum ($m\mathbf{v}$) terms.

Physics principles and equations

In addition to Newton's laws cited above, we will use the definition of acceleration.

$$\mathbf{a} = \Delta\mathbf{v}/\Delta t$$

Step-by-step derivation

In these first steps, we use Newton's third law followed by his second law.

Step	Reason
1. $\mathbf{F}_1 = -\mathbf{F}_2$	Newton's third law
2. $m_1\mathbf{a}_1 = -m_2\mathbf{a}_2$	Newton's second law
3. $m_1\dfrac{\Delta\mathbf{v}_1}{\Delta t} = -m_2\dfrac{\Delta\mathbf{v}_2}{\Delta t}$	definition of acceleration

In the next steps, we apply the definition of the change Δv in velocity. After some algebraic simplification we obtain the result we want: The sum of the initial momenta equals the sum of the final momenta.

Step	Reason
4. $m_1\dfrac{\mathbf{v}_{f1} - \mathbf{v}_{i1}}{\Delta t} = -m_2\dfrac{\mathbf{v}_{f2} - \mathbf{v}_{i2}}{\Delta t}$	definition of change in velocity
5. $m_1\mathbf{v}_{f1} - m_1\mathbf{v}_{i1} = -m_2\mathbf{v}_{f2} + m_2\mathbf{v}_{i2}$	multiply both sides by Δt
6. $m_1\mathbf{v}_{i1} + m_2\mathbf{v}_{i2} = m_1\mathbf{v}_{f1} + m_2\mathbf{v}_{f2}$	rearrange

The 55.0 kg astronaut is stationary in the spaceship's reference frame. She wants to move at 0.500 m/s to the left. She is holding a 4.00 kg bag of dehydrated astronaut chow. At what velocity must she throw the bag to achieve her desired velocity? (Assume the positive direction is to the right.)

Answer:

$v_{fb} = $ [   ] m/s

7.8 - Collisions

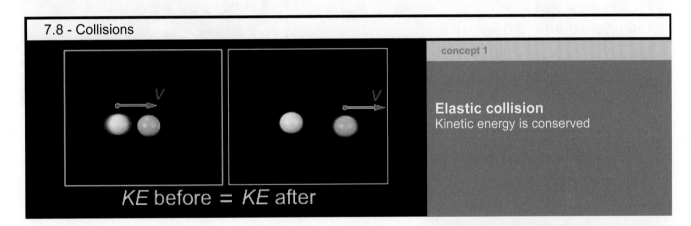

concept 1

Elastic collision
Kinetic energy is conserved

KE before = *KE* after

Elastic collision: The kinetic energy of the system is unchanged by the collision.

Inelastic collision: The kinetic energy of the system is changed by the collision.

concept 2

KE before ≠ *KE* after

Inelastic collision
Kinetic energy is not conserved

In a collision, one moving object briefly strikes another object. During the collision, the forces the objects exert on each other are much greater than the net effect of other forces acting on them, so we may ignore these other forces.

Elastic and inelastic are two terms used to define types of collisions. These types of collisions differ in whether the total amount of **kinetic** energy in the system stays constant or is reduced by the collision. In any collision, the system's total amount of energy must be the same before and after, because the law of conservation of energy must be obeyed. But in an inelastic collision, some of the kinetic energy is transformed by the collision into other types of energy, so the total kinetic energy decreases.

For example, a car crash often results in dents. This means some kinetic energy compresses the car permanently; other KE becomes thermal energy, sound energy and so on. This means that an **inelastic** collision reduces the total amount of KE.

In contrast, the total kinetic energy is the same before and after an **elastic** collision. None of the kinetic energy is transformed into other forms of energy. The game of pool provides a good example of nearly elastic collisions. The collisions between balls are almost completely elastic and little kinetic energy is lost when they collide.

In both elastic and inelastic collisions occurring within an isolated system, momentum is conserved. This important principle enables you to analyze any collision.

We will mention a third type of collision briefly here: *explosive collisions*, such as what occurs when a bomb explodes. In this type of collision, the kinetic energy is greater after the collision than before. However, since momentum is conserved, the explosion does not change the total momentum of the constituents of the bomb.

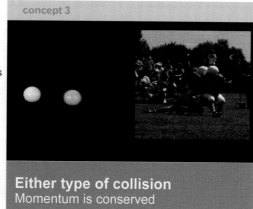

concept 3

Either type of collision
Momentum is conserved

7.9 - Sample problem: elastic collision in one dimension

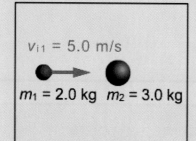

$v_{i1} = 5.0$ m/s

$m_1 = 2.0$ kg $m_2 = 3.0$ kg

Before

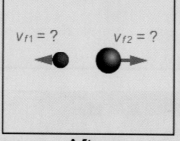

$v_{f1} = ?$ $v_{f2} = ?$

After

The small purple ball strikes the stationary green ball in an elastic collision. What are the final velocities of the two balls?

The picture and text above pose a classic physics problem. Two balls collide in an elastic collision. The balls collide head on, so the second ball moves away along the same line as the path of the first ball. The balls' masses and initial velocities are given. You are asked to calculate their velocities after the collision. The strategy for solving this problem relies on the fact that both the momentum and kinetic energy remain unchanged.

Variables

	ball 1 (purple)	ball 2 (green)
mass	$m_1 = 2.0$ kg	$m_2 = 3.0$ kg
initial velocity	$v_{i1} = 5.0$ m/s	$v_{i2} = 0$ m/s
final velocity	v_{f1}	v_{f2}

What is the strategy?

1. Set the momentum before the collision equal to the momentum after the collision.

2. Set the kinetic energy before the collision equal to the kinetic energy after the collision.

3. Use algebra to solve two equations with two unknowns.

Physics principles and equations

Since problems like this one often ask for values **after** a collision, it is convenient to state the following conservation equations with the final values on the left.

Conservation of momentum

$$m_1\mathbf{v}_{f1} + m_2\mathbf{v}_{f2} = m_1\mathbf{v}_{i1} + m_2\mathbf{v}_{i2}$$

Conservation of kinetic energy

$$\tfrac{1}{2}\,m_1 v_{f1}{}^2 + \tfrac{1}{2}\,m_2 v_{f2}{}^2 = \tfrac{1}{2}\,m_1 v_{i1}{}^2 + \tfrac{1}{2}\,m_2 v_{i2}{}^2$$

Step-by-step solution

First, we use the conservation of momentum to find an equation where the only unknown values are the two final velocities. Since all the motion takes place on a horizontal line, we use sign to indicate direction.

Step		Reason
1.	$m_1 v_{f1} + m_2 v_{f2} = m_1 v_{i1} + m_2 v_{i2}$	conservation of momentum
2.	$(2.0\,\mathrm{kg})v_{f1} + (3.0\,\mathrm{kg})v_{f2}$ $= (2.0\,\mathrm{kg})(5.0\,\mathrm{m/s}) + (3.0\,\mathrm{kg})(0.0\,\mathrm{m/s})$	enter values
3.	$v_{f1} = (-1.5)v_{f2} + 5.0$	solve for v_{f1}

The conservation of kinetic energy gives us another equation with these two unknowns.

Step		Reason
4.	$\tfrac{1}{2}m_1 v_{f1}^2 + \tfrac{1}{2}m_2 v_{f2}^2 = \tfrac{1}{2}m_1 v_{i1}^2 + \tfrac{1}{2}m_2 v_{i2}^2$	elastic collision: KE conserved
5.	$m_1 v_{f1}^2 + m_2 v_{f2}^2 = m_1 v_{i1}^2 + m_2 v_{i2}^2$	simplify
6.	$(2.0\,\mathrm{kg})v_{f1}^2 + (3.0\,\mathrm{kg})v_{f2}^2$ $= (2.0\,\mathrm{kg})(5.0\,\mathrm{m/s})^2 + (3.0\,\mathrm{kg})(0.0\,\mathrm{m/s})^2$	enter values
7.	$(2.0)v_{f1}^2 + (3.0)v_{f2}^2 - 50.0 = 0$	re-arrange as quadratic equation

We substitute the expression for the first ball's final velocity found in equation 3 into the quadratic equation, and solve. This gives us the second ball's final velocity. Then we use equation 3 again to find the first ball's final velocity. One velocity is negative, and one positive − one ball moves to the left after the collision, the other to the right.

Step	Reason
8. $(2.0)[(-1.5)v_{f2}+(5.0)]^2+(3.0)v_{f2}^2-50=0$	substitute equation 4 into equation 8
9. $15v_{f2}^2-60v_{f2}=0$	simplify
10. $v_{f2}=4.0$ m/s (to the right)	solve equation
11. $v_{f1}=(-1.5)v_{f2}+5.0$ $v_{f1}=-1.0$ m/s (to the left)	use equation 3 to find v_{f1}

A quick check shows that the total momentum both before and after the collision is 10 kg·m/s. The kinetic energy is 25 J in both cases. This verifies that we did the computations correctly.

There is a second solution to this problem: You can see that $v_{f2}=0$ is also a solution to the quadratic equation in step 9, and then using step 3, you see that v_{f1} would equal 5.0 m/s. This solution satisfies the conditions that momentum and KE are conserved, and it describes what happens if the balls do not collide. In other words, the purple ball passes by the green ball without striking it.

7.10 - Interactive checkpoint: another one dimensional collision problem

$v_{i1}=3.0$ m/s $v_{i2}=-1.0$ m/s $v_{f1}=-2.0$ m/s $v_{f2}=$?

$m_1=4.0$kg m_2 $m_2=$?

Before   After

Two balls move toward each other and collide head-on in an elastic collision. What is the mass and final velocity of the green ball?

Answer:

$m_2=$ [ ] kg

$v_{f2}=$ [ ] m/s

7.11 - Physics at play: clicky-clack balls

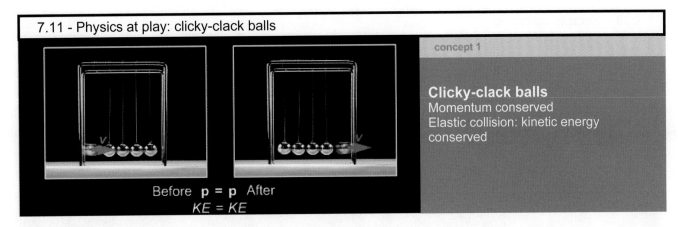

concept 1

Clicky-clack balls
Momentum conserved
Elastic collision: kinetic energy conserved

Before **p = p** After
$KE = KE$

The law of conservation of momentum and the nature of elastic collisions underlie the functioning of a desktop toy: a set of balls of equal mass hanging from strings. This toy is shown in the photograph above.

You may have seen these toys in action but if you have not, imagine pulling back one ball and releasing it toward the pack of balls. (Click on Concept 1 to launch a video.) The one ball strikes the pack, stops, and a ball on the far side flies up, comes back down, and strikes the pack. The ball you initially released now flies back up again, returns to strike the pack, and so forth. The motion continues in this pattern for quite a while.

Interestingly, if you pick up two balls and release them, then two balls on the far side of the pack will fly off, resulting in a pattern of two balls moving. This pattern obeys the principle of the conservation of momentum as well as the definition of an elastic collision: kinetic energy remains constant. Other scenarios that on the surface might seem plausible fail to meet both criteria. For instance, if one ball moved off the pack at twice the speed of the two balls striking, momentum would be conserved, but the KE of the system would increase, since KE is a function of the **square** of velocity. Doubling the velocity of one ball quadruples its KE. One ball leaving at twice the velocity would have twice the combined KE of the two balls that struck the pack.

However, it turns out this is not the only solution which obeys the conservation of momentum and of kinetic energy. For instance, the striking ball could rebound at less than its initial speed, and the remaining four balls could move in the other direction as a group. With certain speeds for the rebounding ball and the pack of four balls, this would provide a solution that would obey both principles. Why the balls behave exactly as they do has inspired plenty of discussion in physics journals.

7.12 - Interactive problem: shuffleboard collisions

The simulation at the right shows a variation of the game of shuffleboard. The red puck has an initial velocity of −2.0 m/s. You want to set the initial velocity of the blue puck so that after the two pucks collide head on in an elastic collision, the red puck moves with a velocity of +2.0 m/s. This will cause the red puck to stop at the scoring line, since the friction in the green area on the right side of the surface will cause it to slow down and perhaps stop.

The blue puck has a mass of 1.0 kilograms. The red puck's mass is 3.0 kilograms. Use the fact that the collision is elastic to calculate and enter the initial velocity of the blue puck to the nearest 0.1 m/s and press GO to see the results. Press RESET to try again.

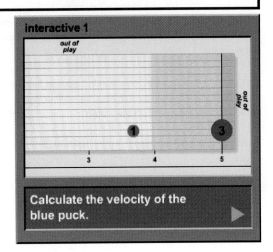

interactive 1

out of play

out of play

Calculate the velocity of the blue puck.

concept 1

Inelastic collisions
Collision reduces total KE
Momentum conserved
Completely inelastic collisions:
· Objects "stick together"

· Have common velocity after collision

Inelastic collision: The collision results in a decrease in the system's total kinetic energy.

In an inelastic collision, momentum is conserved. But **kinetic** energy is not conserved. In inelastic collisions, kinetic energy transforms into other forms of energy. The kinetic energy after an inelastic collision is **less** than the kinetic energy before the collision. When one boxcar rolls and connects with another, as shown above, some of the kinetic energy of the moving car transforms into elastic potential energy, thermal energy and so forth. This means the kinetic energy of the system of the two boxcars decreases, making this an inelastic collision.

A *completely inelastic* collision is one in which two objects "stick together" after they collide, so they have a common final velocity. Since they may still be moving, completely inelastic does not mean there is zero kinetic energy after the collision. For instance, after the boxcars connect, the two "stick together" and move as one unit. In this case, the train combination continues to move after the collision, so they still have kinetic energy, although less than before the collision.

As with elastic collisions, we assume the collision occurs in an isolated system, with no net external forces present. You can think of elastic collisions and completely inelastic collisions as the extreme cases of collisions. Kinetic energy is not reduced at all in an elastic collision. In a completely inelastic collision, the total amount of kinetic energy after the collision is reduced as much as it can be, consistent with the conservation of momentum.

In Equation 1, you see an equation to calculate the final velocity of two objects, like the snowballs shown, after a completely inelastic collision. This equation is derived below. The derivation hinges on the two objects having a common velocity after the collision.

In this derivation, two objects, with masses m_1 and m_2, collide in a completely inelastic collision.

equation 1

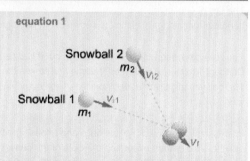

Completely inelastic collision

$$\mathbf{v}_f = \frac{m_1\mathbf{v}_{i1} + m_2\mathbf{v}_{i2}}{m_1+m_2}$$

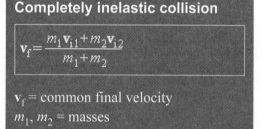

$\mathbf{v}_f$ = common final velocity
m_1, m_2 = masses
$\mathbf{v}_{i1}, \mathbf{v}_{i2}$ = initial velocities

example 1

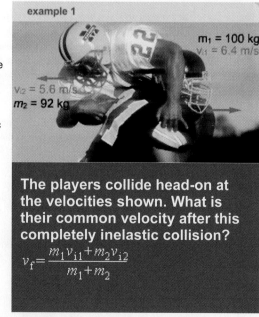

$m_1 = 100$ kg
$v_{i1} = 6.4$ m/s
$v_2 = 5.6$ m/s
$m_2 = 92$ kg

The players collide head-on at the velocities shown. What is their common velocity after this completely inelastic collision?

$$v_f = \frac{m_1 v_{i1} + m_2 v_{i2}}{m_1+m_2}$$

Step		Reason
1.	$\mathbf{v}_{f1} = \mathbf{v}_{f2} = \mathbf{v}_f$	final velocities equal
2.	$m_1\mathbf{v}_f + m_2\mathbf{v}_f = m_1\mathbf{v}_{i1} + m_2\mathbf{v}_{i2}$	conservation of momentum
3.	$\mathbf{v}_f(m_1+m_2) = m_1\mathbf{v}_{i1} + m_2\mathbf{v}_{i2}$	factor out v_f
4.	$\mathbf{v}_f = \dfrac{m_1\mathbf{v}_{i1} + m_2\mathbf{v}_{i2}}{m_1+m_2}$	divide

$$v_f = \frac{(100 \text{ kg})(6.4 \text{ m/s}) + (92 \text{ kg})(-5.6 \text{ m/s})}{100 + 92 \text{ kg}}$$

$$\mathbf{v}_f = 0.65 \text{ m/s to the right}$$

Example 1 on the right applies this equation to a collision seen on many fall weekends: a football tackle.

7.14 - Center of mass

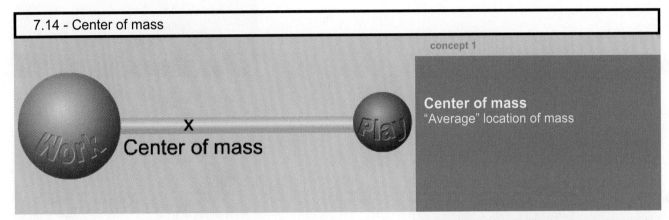

concept 1

Center of mass
"Average" location of mass

Center of mass: Average location of mass. An object can be treated as though all its mass were located at this point.

The center of mass is useful when considering the motion of a complex object, or system of objects. You can simplify the analysis of motion of such an object, or system of objects, by determining its center of mass. An object can be treated as though all its mass is located at this point. For instance, you could consider the force of a weightlifter lifting the barbell pictured above as though she applied all the force at the center of mass of the bar, and determine the acceleration of the center of mass.

You may react: "But we have been doing this in many sections of this book," and yes, implicitly we have been. If we asked earlier how much force was required to accelerate this barbell, we assumed that the force was applied at the center of mass, rather than at one end of the barbell, which would cause it to rotate.

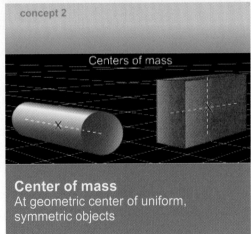

concept 2

Centers of mass

Center of mass
At geometric center of uniform, symmetric objects

In this section, we focus on how to calculate the center of mass of a system of objects. Consider the barbell above. Its center of mass is on the rod that connects the two balls, nearer the ball labeled "Work," because that ball is more massive.

When an object is symmetrical and made of a uniform material, such as a solid sphere of steel, the center of mass is at its geometric center. So for a sphere, cube or other symmetrical shape made of a uniform material, you can use your sense of geometry and decide where the center of the object is. That point will be the center of the mass. (We can relax the condition of uniformity if an object is composed of different parts, but each one of them is symmetrical, like a golf ball made of different substances in spherically symmetrical layers.)

The center of mass does not have to lie inside the object. For example, the center of mass of a doughnut lies in the middle of its hole.

The equation to the right can be used to calculate the overall center of mass of a set of objects whose individual centers of mass lie along a line. To use the equation, place the center of mass of each object on the x axis. It helps to choose for the origin a point where one of the centers of mass is located, since this will simplify the calculation. Then, multiply the mass of each object times its center's x position and divide the sum of these products by the sum of the masses. The resulting value is the x position of the center of mass of the set of objects.

If the objects do not conveniently lie along a line, you can calculate the x and y positions of the center of mass by applying the equation in each dimension separately. The result is the x, y position of the system's center of mass.

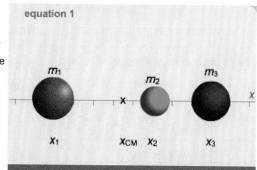

equation 1

Center of mass

$$x_{CM} = \frac{m_1 x_1 + m_2 x_2 + \ldots + m_n x_n}{m_1 + m_2 + \ldots + m_n}$$

$x_{CM} = x$ position of center of mass
$m_i = $ mass of object i
$x_i = x$ position of object i

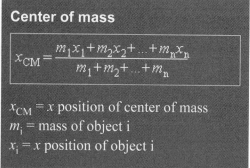

example 1

What is the location of the center of mass?

$$x_{CM} = \frac{m_1 x_1 + m_2 x_2}{m_1 + m_2}$$

$$x_{CM} = \frac{(3.0\,\text{kg})(0.0\,\text{m}) + (2.0\,\text{kg})(16\,\text{m})}{3.0\,\text{kg} + 2.0\,\text{kg}}$$

$$x_{CM} = 32/5.0$$
$$x_{CM} = 6.4\,\text{m}$$

7.15 - Center of mass and motion

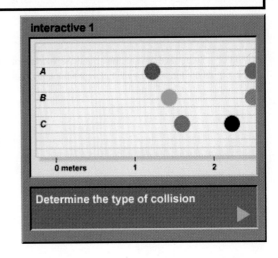

concept 1

Center of mass and motion
Laws of mechanics apply to center of mass
Shifting center of mass creates "floating" illusion

Above, you see a ballet dancer performing a *grand jeté*, a "great leap." When a ballet dancer performs this leap well, she seems to float through the air. In fact, if you track the dancer's motion by noting the successive positions of her head, you can see that its path is nearly horizontal. She seems to be defying the law of gravity. This seeming physics impossibility is explained by considering the dancer's center of mass. An object (or a system of objects) can be analyzed by considering the motion of its center of mass.

concept 2

Look carefully at the locations of the dancer's center of mass in the diagram. The center of mass follows the parabolic path of projectile motion.

To achieve the illusion of floating – moving horizontally – the dancer alters the location of her center of mass relative to her body as she performs the jump. As she reaches the peak of her leap, she raises her legs, which places her center of mass nearer to her head. This decreases the distance from the top of her head to her center of mass, so her head does not rise as high as it would otherwise. This allows her head to move in a straight line while her center of mass moves in the mandatory parabolic projectile arc.

Center of mass
Center of mass follows projectile path

At the right, we use another example to make a similar point. A cannonball explodes in midair. Although the two resulting fragments move in different directions, the center of mass continues along the same trajectory the cannonball would have followed had it not exploded. The two fragments have different masses. The path of the center of mass is closer to the path of the more massive fragment, as you might expect.

7.16 - Interactive summary problem: types of collisions

On the right is a simulation featuring three collisions. Each collision is classified as one of the following: an elastic collision, a completely inelastic collision, an inelastic (but not completely inelastic) one, or an impossible collision that violates the laws of physics. The colliding disks all have the same mass, and there is no friction. Each disk on the left has an initial velocity of 1.00 m/s. The disks on the right have an initial velocity of −0.60 m/s.

Press GO to watch the collisions. Use the PAUSE button to stop the action after the collisions and record data, then make whatever calculations you need to classify each collision using the choices in the drop-down controls labeled "Collision type." Press RESET if you want to start the simulation from the beginning.

If you have difficulty with this, review the sections on elastic and inelastic collisions.

interactive 1

A

B

C

0 meters   1   2

Determine the type of collision

7.17 - Gotchas

One object has a mass of 1 kg and a speed of 2 m/s, and another object has a mass of 2 kg and a speed of 1 m/s. The two objects have identical momenta. Only if they are moving in the same direction. You **can** say they have equal magnitudes of momentum, but momentum is a vector, so direction matters. Consider what happens if they collide. The result will be different depending on whether they are moving in the same or opposite directions.

In inelastic collisions, momentum is not conserved. No. Kinetic energy decreases, but momentum **is** conserved.

Two objects are propelled by equal constant forces, and the second one is exposed to its force for three times as long. The second object's change in momentum must be greater than the first's. This is true. It experienced a greater impulse, and impulse equals the change in momentum.

7.18 - Summary

An object's momentum is the product of its mass and velocity. It is a vector quantity with units of kg·m/s.

Like energy, momentum is conserved in an isolated system. If no net external force acts on a system, its total momentum is constant.

A change in momentum is called impulse. It is a vector with the same units as momentum. Impulse can be calculated as the difference between the final and initial momenta, or as an average applied force times the duration of the force.

The conservation of momentum is useful in analyzing collisions between objects, since the total momentum of the objects involved must be the same before and after the collision. In an elastic collision, kinetic energy is also conserved. In an inelastic collision, the kinetic energy is reduced during the collision as some or all of it is converted into other forms of energy.

A collision is completely inelastic if the kinetic energy is reduced as much as possible, consistent with the conservation of momentum. The two objects "stick together" after the collision.

Equations

$$\mathbf{p} = m\mathbf{v}$$

$$\Sigma \mathbf{F} = \frac{\Delta \mathbf{p}}{\Delta t}$$

$$\mathbf{J} = \bar{\mathbf{F}} \Delta t = \Delta \mathbf{p}$$

Conservation of momentum

$$\mathbf{p}_{i1} + \mathbf{p}_{i2} + ... + \mathbf{p}_{in} = \mathbf{p}_{f1} + \mathbf{p}_{f2} + ... + \mathbf{p}_{fn}$$

Center of mass

$$x_{CM} = \frac{m_1 x_1 + m_2 x_2 + ... + m_n x_n}{m_1 + m_2 + ... + m_n}$$

The center of mass of an object (or system of objects) is the average location of the object's (or system's) mass. For a uniform object, this is the object's geometric center. For more complicated objects and systems, center of mass equations must be applied.

Moving objects behave as if all their mass were concentrated at their center of mass. For example, a hammer thrown into the air may rotate as it falls, but its center of mass will follow the parabolic path followed by any projectile.

8.0 - Introduction

A child riding on a carousel, you riding on a Ferris wheel: Both are examples of uniform circular motion. When the carousel or Ferris wheel reaches a constant rate of rotation, the rider moves in a circle at a constant **speed**. In physics, this is called uniform circular motion.

Developing an understanding of uniform circular motion requires you to recall the distinction between speed and velocity. Speed is the magnitude, or how fast an object moves, while velocity includes both magnitude and direction. For example, consider the car in the graphic on the right. Even as it moves around the curve at a constant speed, its velocity constantly changes as its direction changes. A change in velocity is called acceleration, and the acceleration of a car due to its change in direction as it moves around a curve is called centripetal acceleration.

interactive 1

r = 18 m

Centripetal acceleration
Vary the car's speed

▶

Although the car moves at a constant speed as it moves around the curve, it is accelerating. This is a case where the everyday use of a word – acceleration – and its use in physics differ. A non-physicist would likely say: If a car moves around a curve at a constant speed, it is not accelerating. But a physicist would say: It most certainly is accelerating because its direction is changing. She could even point out, as we will discuss later, that a net external force is being applied on the car, so the car must be accelerating.

Uniform circular motion begins the study of rotational motion. As with linear motion, you begin with concepts such as velocity and acceleration and then move on to topics such as energy and momentum. As you progress, you will discover that much of what you have learned about these topics in earlier lessons will apply to circular motion.

In the simulation shown to the right, the car moves around the track at a constant speed. The red velocity vector represents the direction and magnitude of the car's instantaneous velocity.

The simulation has gauges for the x and y components of the car's velocity. Note how they change as the car travels around the track. These changes are reflected in the centripetal acceleration of the car. You can also have the car move at different constant speeds, and read the corresponding centripetal acceleration in the appropriate gauge. Is the centripetal acceleration of the car higher when it is moving faster? Note: If you go too fast, you can spin off the track. Happy motoring!

8.1 - Uniform circular motion

Uniform circular motion: Movement in a circle at a constant speed.

The toy train on the right moves on a circular track in uniform circular motion. The identical lengths of the velocity vectors in the diagram indicate a constant magnitude of velocity – a constant speed. When an object is moving in uniform circular motion, its speed is uniform (constant) and its path is circular.

The train does **not** have constant velocity; in fact, its velocity is constantly changing. Why? As you can also see in the diagram to the right, the direction of the velocity vector changes as the train moves around the track. A change in the direction of velocity means a change in velocity. The velocity vector is tangent to the circle at every instant because the train's displacement is tangent to the circle during every small interval of time.

concept 1

Uniform circular motion
Motion in a circle with constant speed
· *Velocity* changes!

Uniform circular motion is important in physics. For instance, a satellite in a circular orbit around the Earth moves in uniform circular motion.

8.2 - Period

Period: The amount of time it takes for an object to return to the same position.

The concept of period is useful in analyzing motion that repeats itself. We use the example of the toy train shown in Concept 1 to illustrate a period. The train moves around a circular track at a constant rate, which is to say in uniform circular motion. It returns to the same position on the track after equal intervals of time. The period measures how long it takes the train to complete one revolution. In this example, it takes the train six seconds to make a complete lap around the track.

When an object like a train moves in uniform circular motion, that motion is often described in terms of the period. Many other types of motion can be discussed using the notion of a period, as well. For example, the Earth follows an elliptical path as it moves around the Sun, and its period is called a year. A metronome is designed to have a constant period that provides musicians with a source of rhythm.

The equation on the right enables you to calculate the period of an object moving in uniform circular motion. The period is the circumference of the circle, $2\pi r$, divided by the object's speed. To put it more simply, it is distance divided by speed.

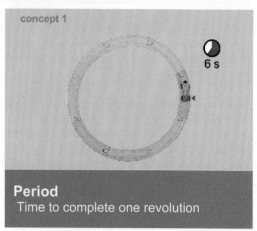

concept 1

Period
Time to complete one revolution

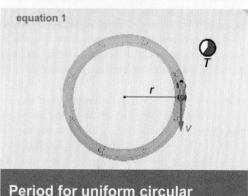

equation 1

Period for uniform circular motion

$$T = \frac{2\pi r}{v}$$

T = period
r = radius
v = speed

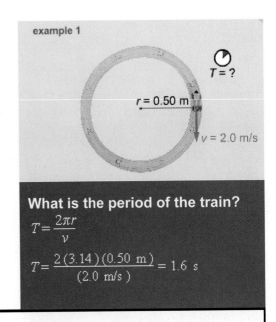

example 1

$T = ?$

$r = 0.50$ m

$v = 2.0$ m/s

What is the period of the train?

$$T = \frac{2\pi r}{v}$$

$$T = \frac{2(3.14)(0.50\ \text{m})}{(2.0\ \text{m/s})} = 1.6\ \text{s}$$

8.3 - Centripetal acceleration

Centripetal acceleration: The centrally directed acceleration of an object due to its circular motion.

An object moving in uniform circular motion constantly accelerates because its direction (and therefore its velocity) constantly changes. This type of acceleration is called centripetal acceleration. Any object moving along a circular path has centripetal acceleration.

In Concept 1 at the right is a vector analysis of centripetal acceleration that uses a toy train as an example of an object moving along a circular path. As the drawing indicates, the train's velocity is tangent to the circle.

In uniform circular motion, the acceleration vector always points toward the center of the circle, perpendicular to the velocity vector. In other words, the object accelerates toward the center. This can be proven by considering the change in the velocity vector over a short period of time and using a geometric argument (an argument that is not shown here).

The equation for calculating centripetal acceleration is shown in Equation 1 on the right. The magnitude of centripetal acceleration equals the speed squared divided by the radius. Since both the speed and the radius are constant in uniform circular motion, the magnitude of the centripetal acceleration is also constant.

With uniform circular motion, the only acceleration is centripetal acceleration, but for circular motion in general, there may be both centripetal acceleration, which changes the object's direction, and acceleration in the direction of the object's motion (tangential acceleration), which changes its speed. If you ride on a Ferris wheel which is starting up, rotating faster and faster, you are experiencing both centripetal and tangential acceleration. For now, we focus on uniform circular motion and centripetal acceleration, leaving tangential acceleration as another topic.

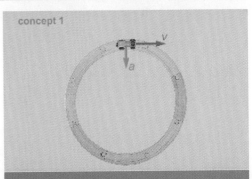

concept 1

Centripetal acceleration
Acceleration due to change in direction in circular motion
In uniform circular motion, acceleration:
· Has constant magnitude
· Points toward center

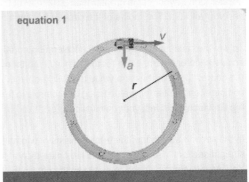

equation 1

Centripetal acceleration

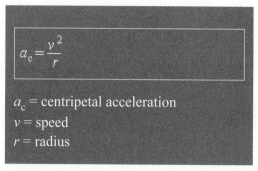

$a_c = $ centripetal acceleration
$v = $ speed
$r = $ radius

example 1

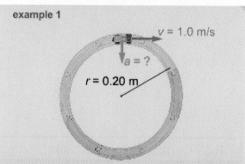

$v = 1.0$ m/s
$a = ?$
$r = 0.20$ m

What is the centripetal acceleration of the train?

$$a_c = \frac{v^2}{r}$$

$$a_c = \frac{1.0^2}{0.2} = 5.0 \text{ m/s}^2$$

Accelerates toward center

8.4 - Interactive problems: racing in circles

The two simulations in this section let you experience uniform circular motion and centripetal acceleration as you race your car against the computer's.

In the first simulation, you race a car around a circular track. Both your car and the computer's move around the loop at constant speeds. You control the speed of the blue car. Halfway around the track, you encounter an oil slick. If the centripetal acceleration of your car is greater than 3.92 m/s² at this point, it will leave the track and you will lose. The radius of the circle is 21.0 m.

To win the race, set the centripetal acceleration equal to 3.92 m/s² in the centripetal acceleration equation, solve for the velocity, and then round **down** the velocity to the nearest 0.1 m/s; this is a value that will keep your car on the track and beat the computer car. Enter this value using the controls in the simulation. Press GO to start the simulation and test your calculations.

interactive 1

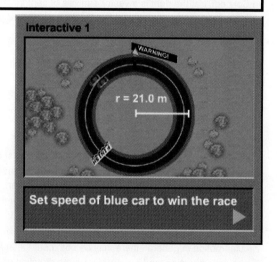

$r = 21.0$ m

Set speed of blue car to win the race

In the second simulation, the track consists of two half-circle curves connected by a straight section. Your blue car runs the entire race at the speed that you set for it.
You want to set this speed to just keep the car on the track. The first curve has a radius of 14.0 meters; the second, 8.50 meters. On either curve, if the centripetal acceleration of your car exceeds 9.95 m/s², its tires will lose traction on the curve, causing it to leave the track. If your car moves at the fastest speed possible without leaving the track, it will win. Again, calculate the speed of the blue car on each curve but using a centripetal acceleration value of 9.95 m/s², and round down to the nearest 0.1 m/s. Since the car will go the same speed on both curves, you need to decide which curve determines your maximum speed. Enter this value, then press GO.

If you have difficulty solving these interactive problems, review the equation relating centripetal acceleration, circle radius, and speed.

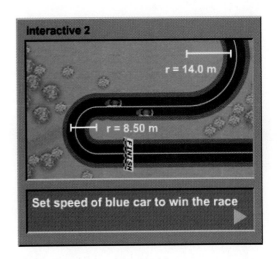

8.5 - Newton's second law and centripetal forces

If you hold onto the string of a yo-yo and twirl it in a circle overhead, as illustrated in Concept 1, you know you must hold the string firmly or the yo-yo will fly away from you. This is true even when the toy moves at a constant speed. A force must be applied to keep the yo-yo moving in a circle.

A force is required because the yo-yo is accelerating. Its change in direction means its velocity is changing. Using Newton's second law, $F = ma$, we can calculate the amount of force as the product of the object's mass and its centripetal acceleration. That equation is shown in Equation 1. It applies to any object moving in uniform circular motion. The force, called a *centripetal force*, points in the same direction as the acceleration, toward the center of the circle.

The term "centripetal" describes any force that causes circular motion. A centripetal force is not a new type of force. It can be the force of tension exerted by a string, as in the yo-yo example, or it can be the force of friction, such as when a car goes around a curve on a level road. It can also be a normal force; for example, the walls of a clothes dryer supply a normal force that keeps the clothes moving in a circle, while the holes in those walls allow water to "spin out" of the fabric. Or, as in the case of the motorcycle rider in Example 1, the centripetal force can be a combination of forces, such as the normal force from the wall and the force of friction.

Sometimes the source of a centripetal force is easily seen, as with a string or the walls of a dryer. Sometimes that force is invisible: The force of gravity cannot be directly seen, but it keeps the Earth in its orbit around the Sun. The centripetal force can also be quite subtle, such as when an airplane tilts or banks; the air passing over the plane's angled wings creates a force inward. In each of these examples, a force causes the object to accelerate toward the center of its circular path.

Identifying the force or forces that create the centripetal acceleration is a key step in solving many problems involving circular motion.

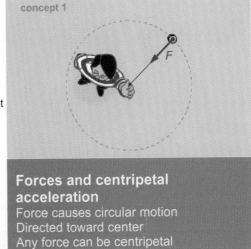

concept 1

F

Forces and centripetal acceleration
Force causes circular motion
Directed toward center
Any force can be centripetal

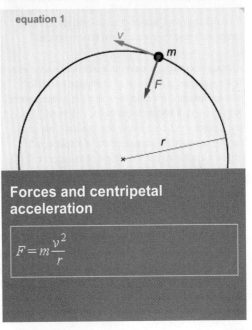

equation 1

v

m

F

r

Forces and centripetal acceleration

$$F = m\frac{v^2}{r}$$

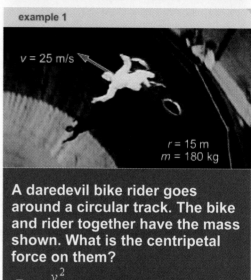

F = net force
m = mass
v = speed
r = radius

example 1

$v = 25$ m/s

$r = 15$ m
$m = 180$ kg

A daredevil bike rider goes around a circular track. The bike and rider together have the mass shown. What is the centripetal force on them?

$$F = m\frac{v^2}{r}$$

$F = (180 \text{ kg})(25 \text{ m/s})^2/15 \text{ m}$
$F = (180)(625)/15$
$F = 7500$ N
Force directed toward center

8.6 - Artificial gravity

When a spacecraft is far away from the Earth and any other massive body, the force of gravity is near zero. As a result of this lack of gravitational force, the astronauts and their equipment float in space.

Although perhaps amusing to watch and experience, floating presents an unusual challenge because humans are accustomed to working in environments with enough gravity to keep them, and their equipment, anchored to the floor. (Note: This same feeling of weightlessness occurs in a spacecraft orbiting the Earth, but the cause of the apparent weightlessness in this case arises from the free-fall motion of the craft and the astronaut, not from a lack of gravitational force.)

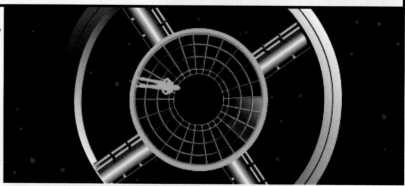

A rotating space station provides an illusion of gravity.

A number of science fiction books and films have featured spacecraft that rotate very slowly as they travel through the universe. Arthur C. Clarke's science fiction novel *Rendezvous with Rama* is set in a massive rotating spacecraft, as is part of the movie *2001*, which is also based on his work. This rotation supplies *artificial gravity* – the illusion of gravity – to the astronauts and their equipment. Artificial gravity has effects similar to true gravity, and as a result can mislead the people riding in such machines to believe they are experiencing true gravitational force.

Why does the rotation of a spacecraft produce the **sensation** of gravity? Consider what happens when an airplane takes off from a runway: You feel a force pulling you back into your seat, as if the force of gravity were increasing. The force of gravity has not been significantly altered (in fact, it decreases a bit as you gain elevation). However, while the airplane accelerates upward, you feel a greater normal force pushing up from your seat, and you may interpret this subconsciously as increased gravity.

A roughly analogous situation occurs on a rotating spaceship. The astronauts are rotating in uniform circular motion. The outside wall of the station (the floor, from the astronauts' perspective) provides the centrally directed normal force that is the centripetal force. This force keeps the astronauts moving in a circle. From the astronauts' perspective, this force is upwards, and they relate it to the upward normal force of the ground they feel when standing on the Earth. On Earth, the normal force is equal but opposite to the force of gravity. Because they typically associate the normal force with gravity, the astronauts may erroneously perceive this force from the spacecraft floor as being caused by some form of artificial or simulated gravity.

Artificial gravity is a pseudo, or fictitious, force. The astronauts assume it exists because of the normal force. The perception of this fictitious force is a function of the acceleration of the astronauts as they move in a circle. It would disappear if the spacecraft stopped rotating.

Although discussed as the realm of science fiction, real-world carnival rides (like the "Gravitron") use this effect. Riders are placed next to the wall of a cylinder. The cylinder then is rotated at a high speed and the floor (or seats) below the riders is lowered. The walls of the cylinder supply a normal force and the force of friction keeps the riders from slipping down.

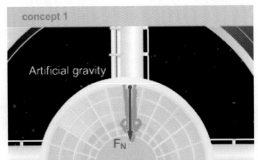

concept 1

Artificial gravity

Artificial gravity
Space station rotates
Floor of craft provides centripetal force
Person (incorrectly) assumes normal force counters force of gravity

example 1

$T = 60$ s

F_N $r = ?$

To simulate Earth's gravity, what should the radius of the space station be?

$$\frac{v^2}{r} = g \text{ and } v = \frac{2\pi r}{T}$$

$$\frac{4\pi^2 r^2}{T^2 r} = g$$

$$r = \frac{gT^2}{4\pi^2}$$

$$r = \frac{(9.80 \text{ m/s}^2)(60 \text{ s})^2}{(4)(3.14^2)} = 890 \text{ m}$$

8.7 - Interactive summary problem: race curves

In the simulation on the right, you are asked to race a truck on an S-shaped track against the computer. This time, the first curve is covered with snow and you are racing against a snowmobile. As you go around the track, the static friction between the tires of your truck and the snow or pavement provides the centripetal force. If you go too fast, you will exceed the maximum force of friction and your truck will leave the track. If you go as fast as you can without sliding, you will beat the snowmobile.

The snowmobile runs the entire race at its maximum speed. The blue truck negotiates each curve at a constant speed, but these speeds must be different for you to win the race. You set the speed of the blue truck on each curve. Straightaway sections are located at the start of the race and between the two curves. The simulation will automatically supply the acceleration you need on the straightaway sections.

The blue truck has a mass of 1,800 kg. The first curve is icy, and the coefficient of static friction of the truck on this curve is 0.51. (The snowmobile has a greater coefficient thanks to its snow-happy treads.) On the second curve, the coefficient of static friction is 0.84. The radius of the first curve is 13 m, and the second curve is 11 m. Set the speed of the blue truck on each curve as fast as it can go without sliding off the track, and you will win.

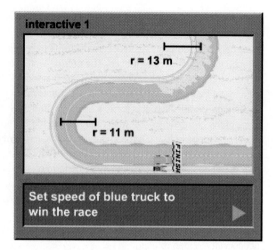

interactive 1

r = 13 m

r = 11 m

FINISH

Set speed of blue truck to win the race

You set the speed in increments of 0.1 m/s in the simulation. If you need to round a value after your calculations, make sure you round down to the nearest 0.1 m/s. (If you round up, you will be exceeding the maximum safe speed.) Press GO to begin the race, and RESET if you need to try again.

If you have difficulty with this problem, you may want to review the section on static friction in a previous chapter and the section on centripetal acceleration in this chapter.

8.8 - Gotchas

A car is moving around a circular track at a constant speed of 20 km/h. This means its velocity is constant, as well. Wrong. The car's velocity changes because its direction changes as it moves.

Since an object moving in uniform circular motion is constantly changing direction, it is hard at any point in time to know the direction of its velocity and the direction of its acceleration. This is not true. The velocity vector is always tangent to the circle at the location of the object. Centripetal acceleration always points toward the center of the circle.

No force is required for an object to move in uniform circular motion. After all, its speed is constant. Yes, but its velocity is changing due to its change in direction, which means it is accelerating. By Newton's second law, this means there must be a net force causing this acceleration.

Centripetal force is another type of force. No, rather it is a way to describe what a force is "doing." The normal force, gravity, tension – each of these forces can be a centripetal force if it is causing an object to move in uniform circular motion.

8.9 - Summary

Uniform circular motion is movement in a circle at a constant speed. But while speed is constant in this type of motion, velocity is not. Since instantaneous velocity in uniform circular motion is always tangent to the circle, its direction changes as the object's position changes.

The period is the time it takes an object in uniform circular motion to complete one revolution of the circle.

Since the velocity of an object moving in uniform circular motion changes, it is accelerating. The acceleration due to its change in direction is called centripetal acceleration. For uniform circular motion, the acceleration vector has a constant magnitude and always points toward the center of the circle.

Equations

$$T = \frac{2\pi r}{v}$$

$$a_c = \frac{v^2}{r}$$

$$F = m\frac{v^2}{r}$$

Newton's second law can be applied to an object in uniform circular motion. The net force causing centripetal acceleration is called a centripetal force. Like centripetal acceleration, it is directed toward the center of the circle.

A centripetal force is not a new type of force; rather, it describes a role that is played by one or more forces in the situation, since there must be *some* force that is changing the velocity of the object. For example, the force of gravity keeps the Moon in a roughly circular orbit around the Earth, while the normal force of the road and the force of friction combine to keep a car in circular motion around a banked curve.

9.0 - Introduction

If you feel as though you spend your life spinning around in circles, you may be pleased to know that an entire branch of physics is dedicated to studying that kind of motion. This chapter is for you! More seriously, this chapter discusses motion that consists of rotation about a fixed axis. This is called *pure rotational motion*. There are many examples of pure rotational motion: a spinning Ferris wheel, a roulette wheel, or a music CD are three instances of this type of motion.

In this chapter, you will learn about rotational displacement, rotational velocity, and rotational acceleration: the fundamental elements of what is called *rotational kinematics*.

The simulation on the right features the "Angular Surge," an amusement park ride you will be asked to operate in order to gain insight into rotational kinematics. The ride has a rotating arm with a "rocket" where passengers sit. You can move the rocket closer to or farther from the center by setting the distance in the simulation. You can also change the rocket's period, which is the amount of time it takes to complete one revolution.

By changing these parameters, you affect two values you see displayed in gauges: the rocket's angular velocity and its linear speed. The rocket's angular velocity is the change per second in the angle of the ride's arm, measured from its initial position. Its units are radians per second. For instance, if the rocket completes one revolution in one second, its angular velocity is 2π radians ($360°$) per second.

This simulation has no specific goal for you to achieve, although you may notice that you can definitely have an impact on the passengers! What you should observe is this: How do changes in the period affect the angular velocity? The linear speed? And how does a change in the distance from the center (the radius of the rocket's motion) affect those values, if at all? Can you determine how to maximize the linear speed of the rocket?

To run the ride, you start the simulation, set the values mentioned above, and press GO. You can change the settings while the ride is in motion.

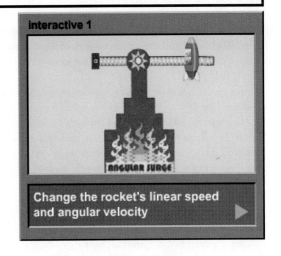

interactive 1

Change the rocket's linear speed and angular velocity ▶

9.1 - Angular position

Angular position: The amount of rotation from a reference position, described with a positive or negative angle.

When an object such as a bicycle wheel rotates about its axis, it is useful to describe this motion using the concept of angular position. Instead of being specified with a linear coordinate such as x, as linear position is, angular position is stated as an angle.

In Concept 1, we use the location of a bicycle wheel's valve to illustrate angular position. The valve starts at the 3 o'clock position (on the positive x axis), which is zero radians by convention. As the illustration shows, the wheel has rotated one-eighth of a turn, or $\pi/4$ radians ($45°$), in a counterclockwise direction away from the reference position. In other words, angular position is measured from the positive x axis.

Note that this description of the wheel's position used radians, not degrees; this is

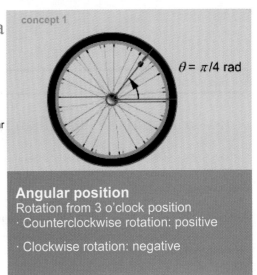

concept 1

$\theta = \pi/4$ rad

Angular position
Rotation from 3 o'clock position
· Counterclockwise rotation: positive

· Clockwise rotation: negative

because radians are typically used to describe angular position. The two lines we use to measure the angle radiate from the point about which the wheel rotates.

The *axis of rotation* is a line also used to describe an object's rotation. It passes through the wheel's center, since the wheel rotates about that point, and it is perpendicular to the wheel. The axis is assumed to be stationary, and the wheel is assumed to be rigid and to maintain a constant shape. Analyzing an object that changes shape as it rotates, such as a piece of soft clay, is beyond the scope of this textbook. We are concerned with the wheel's rotational motion here: its motion around a fixed axis. Its linear motion when moving along the ground is another topic.

As mentioned, angular position is typically measured with *radians* (rad) instead of degrees. The formula that defines the radian measure of an angle is shown in Equation 1. The angle in radians equals the arc length s divided by the radius r. As you may recall, 2π radians equals one revolution around a circle, or $360°$. One radian equals about $57.3°$. To convert radians to degrees, multiply by the conversion factor $360°/2\pi$. To convert degrees to radians, multiply by the reciprocal: $2\pi/360°$. The Greek letter θ (theta) is used to represent angular position.

The angular position of zero radians is defined to be at 3 o'clock, which is to say along a horizontal line pointing to the right. Let's now consider what happens when the wheel rotates a quarter turn **counterclockwise**, moving the valve from the 3 o'clock position to 12 o'clock. A quarter turn is $\pi/2$ rad (or $90°$). The valve's angular position when it moves a quarter turn counterclockwise is $\pi/2$ rad. By convention, angular position **increases** with counterclockwise motion.

The valve can be placed in the same angular position, $\pi/2$ rad, by rotating the wheel in the other direction, by rotating it **clockwise** three quarters of a turn. By convention, angular position **decreases** with clockwise motion, so this rotation would be described as an angular position of $-3\pi/2$ rad.

An angular position can be greater than 2π rad. An angular position of 3π rad represents one and a half counterclockwise revolutions. The valve would be at 9 o'clock in that position.

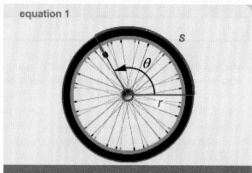

Units are radians

equation 1

Radian measure

$$\theta = \frac{s}{r}$$

θ = angle in radians
s = arc length
r = radius

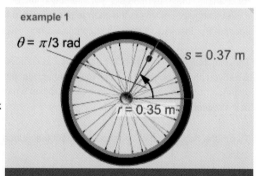

example 1

$\theta = \pi/3$ rad

$s = 0.37$ m

$r = 0.35$ m

What is the arc length?

$$\theta = \frac{s}{r}$$

$s = r\theta = (0.35 \text{ m})(\pi/3 \text{ rad})$
$s = 0.37 \text{ m}$

9.2 - Angular displacement

Angular displacement: Change in angular position.

In Concept 1 you see a pizza topped with a single mushroom (we are not going back to that pizzeria!). We use a mushroom to make the rotational motion of the pizza easier to see. As the pizza rotates, its angular position changes. This change in angular position is called angular displacement.

To calculate angular displacement, you subtract the initial angular position from the final position. For instance, the mushroom in the Equation illustration moves from $\pi/2$ rad to π rad, a displacement of $\pi/2$ rad. As you can see in this example, angular displacement in the counterclockwise direction is positive.

Revolution is a common term in the study of rotational motion. It means one complete rotational cycle, with the object starting and returning to the same position. One counterclockwise revolution equals 2π radians of angular displacement.

The angular displacement is the **total** angle "swept out" during rotational motion from an initial to a final position. If the pizza turns counterclockwise three complete revolutions, its angular displacement is 6π radians.

The definition of angular displacement resembles that of linear displacement. However, the discussion above points out a difference. A mushroom that makes a complete revolution has an angular displacement of 2π rad. On the other hand, its linear displacement equals zero, since it starts and stops at the same point.

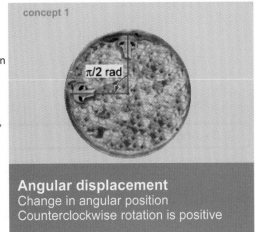

concept 1

Angular displacement
Change in angular position
Counterclockwise rotation is positive

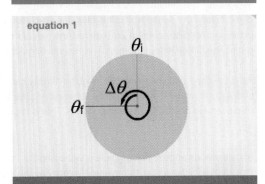

equation 1

Angular displacement

$$\Delta\theta = \theta_f - \theta_i$$

$\Delta\theta$ = angular displacement
θ_f = final angular position
θ_i = initial angular position
Units: radians (rad)

example 1

At 12:10, the initial angular position of the minute hand is $\pi/6$. After 15 minutes have passed, what is the minute hand's angular displacement?

$$\Delta\theta = \theta_f - \theta_i$$

$$\Delta\theta = \left(-\frac{\pi}{3} \text{ rad}\right) - \left(\frac{\pi}{6} \text{ rad}\right)$$

$$\Delta\theta = -\frac{\pi}{2} \text{ rad}$$

9.3 - Angular velocity

Angular velocity: Angular displacement per unit time.

In Concept 1, a ball attached to a string is shown moving counterclockwise around a circle. Every four seconds, it completes one revolution of the circle. Its angular velocity is the angular displacement 2π radians (one revolution) divided by four seconds, or $\pi/2$ rad/s. The Greek letter ω (omega) represents angular velocity.

As is the case with linear velocity, angular velocity can be discussed in terms of average and instantaneous velocity. *Average angular velocity* equals the total angular displacement divided by the elapsed time. This is shown in the first equation in Equation 1.

Instantaneous angular velocity refers to the angular velocity at a precise moment in time. It equals the limit of the average velocity as the increment of time approaches zero. This is shown in the second equation in Equation 1.

The sign of angular velocity follows that of angular displacement: positive for counterclockwise rotation and negative for clockwise rotation. The magnitude (absolute value) of angular velocity is *angular speed*.

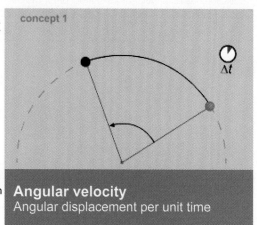

concept 1

Angular velocity
Angular displacement per unit time

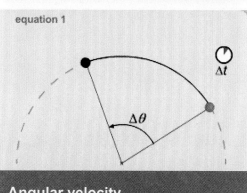

equation 1

Angular velocity

$$\overline{\omega} = \frac{\Delta\theta}{\Delta t}$$

$\overline{\omega}$ = average angular velocity

$$\omega = \lim_{\Delta t \to 0} \frac{\Delta\theta}{\Delta t}$$

ω = instantaneous angular velocity
$\Delta\theta$ = angular displacement
Δt = elapsed time
Units: rad/s

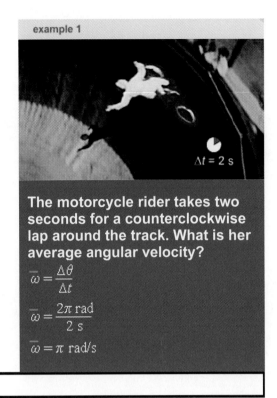

example 1

$\Delta t = 2$ s

The motorcycle rider takes two seconds for a counterclockwise lap around the track. What is her average angular velocity?

$$\bar{\omega} = \frac{\Delta\theta}{\Delta t}$$

$$\bar{\omega} = \frac{2\pi \text{ rad}}{2 \text{ s}}$$

$$\bar{\omega} = \pi \text{ rad/s}$$

9.4 - Angular acceleration

Angular acceleration: The change in angular velocity per unit time.

By now, you might be experiencing a little *déjà vu* in this realm of angular motion. Angular velocity equals angular displacement per unit time, but if you drop the word "angular" you are stating that velocity equals displacement per unit time, an equation that should be familiar to you from your study of linear motion.

So it is with angular acceleration. Angular acceleration equals the change in angular velocity divided by the elapsed time. The toy train shown in Concept 1 is experiencing angular acceleration. This is reflected in the increasing separation between the images you see. Its angular **velocity** is becoming increasingly negative since it is moving in the clockwise direction. It is moving faster and faster in the negative angular direction.

Average angular acceleration equals the change in angular velocity divided by the elapsed time. The *instantaneous angular acceleration* equals the limit of this ratio as the increment of time approaches zero. These two equations are shown in Equation 1 to the right. The Greek letter α (alpha) is used to represent angular acceleration.

With rotational kinematics, we often pose problems in which the angular acceleration is constant; this helps to simplify the mathematics involved in solving problems. We made similar use of constant acceleration for the same reason in the linear motion chapter.

concept 1

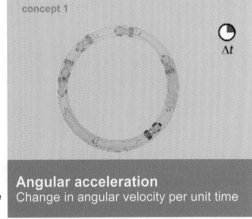

Δt

Angular acceleration
Change in angular velocity per unit time

equation 1

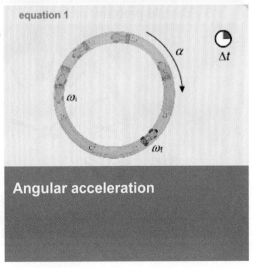

α

Δt

ω_i

ω_f

Angular acceleration

$$\overline{\alpha} = \frac{\Delta\omega}{\Delta t}$$

$\overline{\alpha}$ = average acceleration

$$\alpha = \lim_{\Delta t \to 0} \frac{\Delta\omega}{\Delta t}$$

α = instantaneous angular acceleration
ω = angular velocity
Δt = elapsed time
Units: rad/s^2

example 1

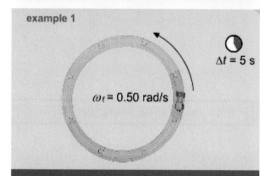

$\omega_f = 0.50$ rad/s

$\Delta t = 5$ s

The toy train starts from rest and reaches the angular velocity shown in 5.0 seconds. What is its average angular acceleration?

$$\overline{\alpha} = \frac{\Delta\omega}{\Delta t}$$

$$\overline{\alpha} = \frac{0.50 \text{ rad/s} - 0.00 \text{ rad/s}}{5.0 \text{ s}}$$

$$\overline{\alpha} = 0.10 \text{ rad/s}^2$$

9.5 - Sample problem: a clock

Over the course of 1.00 hour, what is (a) the angular displacement, (b) the angular velocity and (c) the angular acceleration of the minute hand?

Think about the movement of the minute hand over the course of an hour. Be sure to consider the direction!

Variables

elapsed time	$\Delta t = 1.00 \text{ h}$
angular displacement	$\Delta\theta$
angular velocity	ω
angular acceleration	α

What is the strategy?

1. Calculate the angular displacement.
2. Convert the elapsed time to seconds.
3. Use the angular displacement and time to determine the angular velocity and angular acceleration.

Physics principles and equations

Definition of angular velocity

$$\omega = \frac{\Delta\theta}{\Delta t}$$

Definition of angular acceleration

$$\alpha = \frac{\Delta\omega}{\Delta t}$$

Step-by-step solution

We start by calculating the angular displacement of the minute hand over 1.00 hour. We then calculate the angular velocity.

Step	Reason
1. $\Delta\theta = -2\pi \text{ rad}$	minute hand travels clockwise one revolution
2. $\Delta t = 1.00 \text{ h}\left(\dfrac{3600 \text{ s}}{1.00 \text{ h}}\right) = 3600 \text{ s}$	convert to seconds
3. $\omega = \dfrac{\Delta\theta}{\Delta t}$	definition of angular velocity
4. $\omega = \dfrac{-2\pi \text{ rad}}{3600 \text{ s}}$	substitute
5. $\omega = -1.75 \times 10^{-3} \text{ rad/s}$	evaluate

The angular displacement is calculated in step 1, and the angular velocity in step 5. Since the angular velocity is constant, the angular acceleration is zero.

9.6 - Interactive checkpoint: a potter's wheel

At a particular instant, a potter's wheel rotates clockwise at 12.0 rad/s; 2.50 seconds later, it rotates at 8.50 rad/s clockwise. Find its average angular acceleration during the elapsed time.

Answer:

$\bar{\alpha} =$ [＿＿＿＿＿] rad/s^2

9.7 - Tangential velocity

Tangential velocity: The instantaneous linear velocity of a point on a rotating object.

Concepts such as angular displacement and angular velocity are useful tools for analyzing rotational motion. However, they do not provide the complete picture. Consider the salt and pepper shakers rotating on the lazy Susan shown to the right. The containers have the same angular velocity because they are on the same rotating surface and complete a revolution in the same amount of time.

However, at any instant, they have different **linear** speeds and velocities. Why? They are located at different distances from the axis of rotation (the center of the lazy Susan), which means they move along circular paths with different radii. The circular path of the outer shaker is longer, so it moves farther than the inner one in the same amount of time. At any instant, its linear speed is greater. Because the direction of motion of an object moving in a circle is always tangent to the circle, the object's linear velocity is called its tangential velocity.

To reinforce the distinction between linear and angular velocity, consider what happens if you decide to run around a track. Let's say you are asked to run one lap around a circular track in one minute flat. Your angular velocity is 2π radians per minute.

Could you do this if the track had a radius of 10 meters? The answer is yes. The circumference of that track is $2\pi r$, which equals approximately 63 meters. Your pace would be that distance divided by 60 seconds, which works out to an easy stroll of about 1.05 m/s (3.78 km/h).

What if the track had a radius of 100 meters? In this case, the one-minute accomplishment would require the speed of a world-class sprinter capable of averaging more than 10 m/s. (If the math ran right past you, note that we are again multiplying the radius by 2π to calculate the circumference and dividing by 60 seconds to calculate the tangential velocity.) Even though the angular velocity is the same in both cases, 2π radians per minute, the tangential speed changes with the radius.

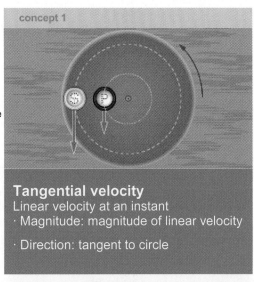

concept 1

Tangential velocity
Linear velocity at an instant
· Magnitude: magnitude of linear velocity
· Direction: tangent to circle

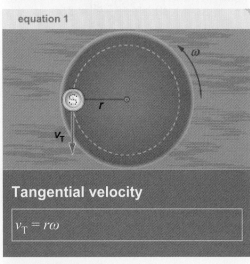

equation 1

Tangential velocity

$v_T = r\omega$

As you see in Equation 1, tangential speed equals the product of the distance to the axis of rotation, r, and the angular velocity, ω. The units for tangential velocity are meters per second. The direction of the velocity is always tangent to the path of the object.

Confirming the direction of tangential velocity can be accomplished using an easy home experiment. Let's say you put a dish on a lazy Susan and then spin the lazy Susan faster and faster. Initially, the dish moves in a circle, constrained by static friction. At some point, though, it will fly off. The dish will always depart in a straight line, tangent to the circle at its point of departure.

The tangential speed equation can also be used to restate the equation for centripetal acceleration in terms of angular velocity. Centripetal acceleration equals v^2/r. Since $v = r\omega$, centripetal acceleration also equals $\omega^2 r$.

We derive the equation for tangential speed using the diagram below.

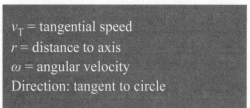

v_T = tangential speed
r = distance to axis
ω = angular velocity
Direction: tangent to circle

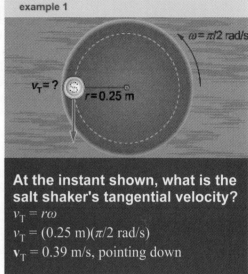

$\omega = \pi/2$ rad/s

$v_T = ?$ $r = 0.25$ m

At the instant shown, what is the salt shaker's tangential velocity?
$v_T = r\omega$
$v_T = (0.25 \text{ m})(\pi/2 \text{ rad/s})$
$\mathbf{v}_T = 0.39$ m/s, pointing down

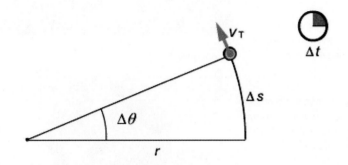

To understand the derivation, you must recall that the arc length Δs (the distance along the circular path) equals the angular displacement $\Delta\theta$ in radians times the radius r. Also recall that the instantaneous speed v_T equals the displacement divided by the elapsed time for a very small increment of time. Combining these two facts, and the definition of angular velocity, yields the equation for tangential speed.

Step	Reason
1. $v_T = \lim\limits_{\Delta t \to 0} \dfrac{\Delta s}{\Delta t}$	definition of instantaneous velocity
2. $\Delta s = r\Delta\theta$	definition of radian measure
3. $v_T = \lim\limits_{\Delta t \to 0} \dfrac{r\Delta\theta}{\Delta t} = r\left(\lim\limits_{\Delta t \to 0} \dfrac{\Delta\theta}{\Delta t}\right)$	substitute equation 2 into equation 1
4. $v_T = r\omega$	definition of angular velocity

Tangential acceleration: A vector tangent to the circular path whose magnitude is the rate of change of tangential speed.

As discussed earlier, an object moving in a circle at a constant speed is accelerating because its direction is constantly changing. This is called centripetal acceleration.

Now consider the mushroom on the pizza to the right. Let's say the pizza has a positive angular acceleration. Since it is rotating faster and faster, its angular velocity is increasing. Since tangential speed is the product of the radius and the angular velocity, the magnitude of its tangential velocity is also increasing.

The magnitude of the tangential acceleration vector equals the rate of change of tangential speed. The tangential acceleration vector is always parallel to the linear velocity vector. When the object is speeding up, it points in the same direction as the tangential velocity vector; when the object is slowing down, tangential acceleration points in the opposite direction.

Since the centripetal acceleration vector always points toward the center, the centripetal and tangential acceleration vectors are perpendicular to each other. An object's overall acceleration is the sum of the two vectors. To put it another way: The centripetal and tangential acceleration are perpendicular components of the object's overall acceleration.

Like tangential velocity, tangential acceleration increases with the distance from the axis of rotation. Consider again the pizza and its toppings in Concept 1. Imagine that the pizza started stationary and it now has positive angular acceleration. Since tangential velocity is proportional to radius, at any moment in time the mushroom near the outer edge of the pizza has greater tangential velocity than the piece of pepperoni closer to the center. Since the mushroom's change in tangential velocity is greater, it must have accelerated at a greater rate.

Tangential acceleration can be calculated as the product of the radius and the angular acceleration. This relationship is stated in Equation 1. The units for tangential acceleration are meters per second squared, the same as for linear acceleration. Note that it only makes sense to calculate the tangential acceleration for an object (or really a point) on the pizza. You cannot speak of the tangential acceleration of the entire pizza because it includes points that are at different distances from its center and have different rates of tangential acceleration.

Because it is easy to confuse angular and linear motion, we will now review a few fundamental relationships.

An object rotating at a constant angular velocity has zero angular acceleration and zero tangential acceleration. An example of this is a car driving around a circular track at a constant speed, perhaps at 100 km/hr. This means the car completes a lap at a constant rate, so its angular velocity is constant. A constant angular velocity means zero angular acceleration. Since the angular acceleration is zero, so is the tangential acceleration.

In contrast, the car's linear (or tangential) velocity is changing since it changes direction as it moves along the circular path. This accounts for the car's centripetal acceleration, which equals its speed squared divided by the radius of the track. The direction of

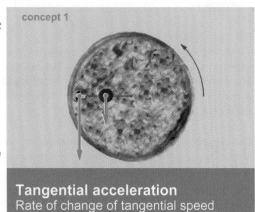

Tangential acceleration
Rate of change of tangential speed
Increases with distance from center
Direction of vector is tangent to circle

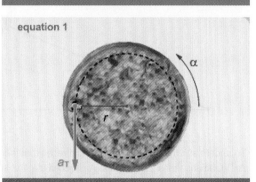

Tangential acceleration

$$a_T = r\alpha$$

a_T = tangential acceleration
r = distance to axis
α = angular acceleration
Direction: tangent to circle

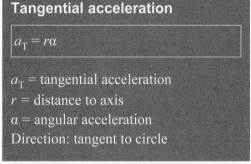

$\alpha = \pi/10$ rad/s²
$a_T = ?$
$r = 0.15$ m

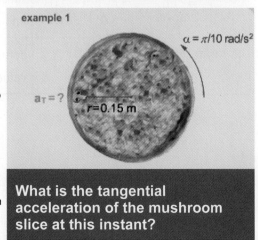

What is the tangential acceleration of the mushroom slice at this instant?

centripetal acceleration is always toward the center of the circle.

Now imagine that the car speeds up as it circles the track. It now completes a lap more quickly, so its angular velocity is increasing, which means it has positive angular acceleration (when it is moving counterclockwise; it is negative in the other direction). The car now has tangential acceleration (its linear speed is changing), and this can be calculated by multiplying its angular acceleration by the track's radius.

$$a_T = r\alpha$$
$$a_T = (\pi/10 \text{ rad/s}^2)(0.15 \text{ m})$$
$$\mathbf{a}_T = 0.047 \text{ m/s}^2, \text{ pointing down}$$

The equation for tangential acceleration is derived below from the equations for tangential velocity and angular acceleration. We begin with the basic definition of linear acceleration and substitute the tangential velocity equation. The result is an expression which contains the definition of angular acceleration. We replace this expression with α, angular acceleration, which yields the equation we desire.

Step	Reason
1. $\quad a_T = \lim\limits_{\Delta t \to 0} \dfrac{\Delta v_T}{\Delta t}$	definition of linear acceleration
2. $\quad \Delta v_T = r\Delta\omega$	tangential velocity equation
3. $\quad a_T = \lim\limits_{\Delta t \to 0} \dfrac{r\Delta\omega}{\Delta t} = r\left(\lim\limits_{\Delta t \to 0} \dfrac{\Delta\omega}{\Delta t}\right)$	substitute equation 2 into equation 1
4. $\quad a_T = r\alpha$	definition of angular acceleration

9.9 - Interactive checkpoint: a marching band

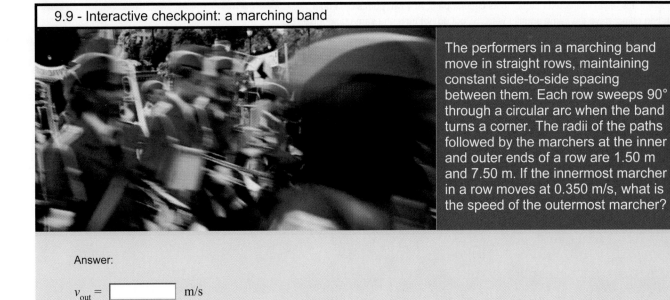

The performers in a marching band move in straight rows, maintaining constant side-to-side spacing between them. Each row sweeps 90° through a circular arc when the band turns a corner. The radii of the paths followed by the marchers at the inner and outer ends of a row are 1.50 m and 7.50 m. If the innermost marcher in a row moves at 0.350 m/s, what is the speed of the outermost marcher?

Answer:

$v_{out} =$ [   ] m/s

9.10 - Gotchas

A potter's wheel rotates. A location farther from the axis will have a greater angular velocity than one closer to the axis. Wrong. They all have the same angular displacement over time, which means they have the same angular velocity, as well. In contrast, they do have different **linear** (tangential) velocities.

A point on a wheel rotates from 12 o'clock to 3 o'clock, so its angular displacement is 90 degrees, correct? No. This would be one definite error and one "units police" error. The displacement is negative because clockwise motion is negative. And, using radians is preferable and sometimes essential in the study of angular motion, so the angular displacement should be stated as $-\pi/2$ radians.

9.11 - Summary

Rotational kinematics applies many of the ideas of linear motion to rotational motion.

Angular position is described by an angle θ, measured from the positive *x* axis. Radians are the typical units.

Angular displacement is a change $\Delta\theta$ in angular position. By convention, the counterclockwise direction is positive.

Angular velocity is the angular displacement per unit time. It is represented by ω and has units of radians per second.

Angular acceleration is the change in angular velocity per unit time. It is represented by α and has units of radians per second squared.

As with linear motion, physicists define instantaneous and average angular velocity and angular acceleration. Instantaneous and average are defined in ways analogous to those used in the study of linear motion.

The linear velocity of a point on a rotating object is called its tangential velocity, because it is always directed tangent to its circular path. Any two points on a rigid rotating object have the same angular velocity, but do not have the same tangential velocity unless they are the same distance from the rotational axis. Tangential speed increases as the distance from the axis of rotation increases.

Tangential acceleration is the change in tangential speed per unit time. Its magnitude increases as the radius increases. Its direction is the same as the tangential velocity if the object is speeding up, and in the opposite direction as the velocity if it is slowing down.

Equations

$$\theta = \frac{s}{r}$$

$$\Delta\theta = \theta_f - \theta_i$$

$$\bar{\omega} = \frac{\Delta\theta}{\Delta t}$$

$$\bar{\alpha} = \frac{\Delta\omega}{\Delta t}$$

$$v_T = r\omega$$

$$a_T = r\alpha$$

chapter

10 Rotational
Dynamics

physics
□ Conceptual

kinetic
BOOKS

10.0 - Introduction

In the study of rotational kinematics, you analyze the motion of a rotating object by determining such properties as its angular displacement, angular velocity or angular acceleration. In this chapter, you explore the origins of rotational motion by studying *rotational dynamics*.

At the right is a simulation that lets you conduct some experiments in the arena of rotational dynamics. In it, you play the role of King Kong, and your mission is to save the day, namely, the bananas on the truck. The bridge is initially open, and the truck loaded with bananas is heading toward it. You must rotate the bridge to a closed position. You determine where on the bridge you push and with how much force. If you cause the bridge to rotate too slowly, it will not close in time, and the truck will fall into the river. If you accelerate the bridge at too great a rate, the bridge will smash through the pilings.

In this simulation, you are experimenting with torque, the rotational analog to force. A net force causes linear acceleration, and a net torque causes angular acceleration. The greater the torque you apply on the bridge, the greater the angular acceleration of the bridge. You control two of the elements that determine torque: the amount of force and how far it is applied from the axis of rotation. The third factor, the angle at which the force is applied, is a constant $90°$ in this simulation.

Try pushing with the same amount of force at different points on the bridge. Is the angular acceleration the same or different? Where do you push to create the maximum torque and angular acceleration? Select a combination of force and location that swings the bridge closed before the truck arrives, but not so hard that the pilings get smashed.

interactive 1

Set Kong's force and his distance from the pivot to close the bridge in time

10.1 - Torque

Torque: A force that causes or opposes rotation.

A net force causes linear acceleration: a change in the linear velocity of an object. A net torque causes angular acceleration: a change in the angular velocity. For instance, if you push hard on a wrench like the one shown in Concept 1, you will start it and the nut rotating.

We will use a wrench that is loosening a nut as our setting to explain the concept of torque in more detail. In this section, we discuss two of the factors that determine the amount of torque. One factor is how much force F is exerted and the other is the distance r between the axis of rotation and the location where the force is applied. We assume in this section that the force is applied perpendicularly to the line from the axis of rotation and the location where the force is applied. (If this description seems cryptic, look at Concept 1, where the force is being applied in this manner.)

When the force is applied as stated above, the torque equals the product of the force F and the distance r. In Equation 1, we state this as an equation. The Greek letter τ (tau) represents torque.

Your practical experience should confirm that the torque increases with the amount of force and the distance from the axis of rotation. If you are trying to remove a "frozen" nut, you either push harder or you get a longer wrench so you can apply the force at a greater distance.

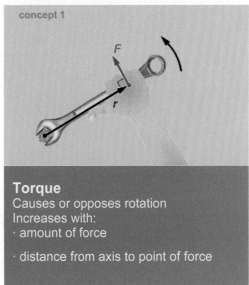

concept 1

Torque
Causes or opposes rotation
Increases with:
· amount of force
· distance from axis to point of force

The location of a doorknob is another classic example of factoring in where force is applied. A torque is required to start a door rotating. The doorknob is placed far from the axis of rotation at the hinges so that the force applied to opening the door results in as much torque as possible. If you doubt this, try opening a door by pushing near its hinges.

The wrench and nut scenario demonstrates another aspect of torque. The angular acceleration of the nut is due to a **net** torque. Let's say the nut in Concept 1 is stuck: the force of static friction between it and the bolt creates a torque that opposes the torque caused by the force of the hand. If the hand pushes hard enough and at a great enough distance from the nut, the torque it causes will exceed that caused by the force of static friction, and the nut will accelerate and begin rotating. The torque caused by the force of kinetic friction will continue to oppose the motion.

A net torque can cause an object to start rotating clockwise or counterclockwise. By convention, a torque that would cause counterclockwise rotation is a positive torque. A negative torque causes clockwise rotation. In Example 1, the torque caused by the hand on the wrench is positive, and the torque caused by friction between the nut and bolt is negative.

The unit for torque is the newton-meter (N·m). You might notice that work and energy are also measured using newton-meters, or, equivalently, joules. Work (and energy) and torque are different, however, and to emphasize that difference, the term "joule" is not used when discussing torque, but only when analyzing work or energy.

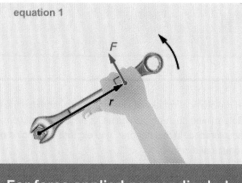
equation 1

For force applied perpendicularly

$$\tau = rF$$

τ = magnitude of torque
r = distance from axis to force
F = force
Counterclockwise +, clockwise −
Units: newton-meters (N·m)

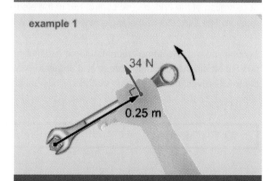
example 1

The hand applies a force of 34 N as shown. Static friction creates an opposing torque of 8.5 N·m. Does the nut rotate?

$\tau = rF$
$\tau = (0.25 \text{ m})(34 \text{ N})$
$\tau = 8.5$ N·m
No, the nut does not rotate

10.2 - Torque, moment of inertia and angular acceleration

Moment of inertia: The measure of resistance to angular acceleration.

An object's moment of inertia is the measure of its resistance to a change in its angular velocity. It is analogous to mass for linear motion; a more massive object requires more net force to accelerate at a given rate than a less massive object. Similarly, an object with a greater moment of inertia requires more net torque to angularly accelerate at a given rate than an object with a lesser moment of inertia. For example, it takes more torque to accelerate a Ferris wheel than it does a bicycle wheel, for the same rate of acceleration.

To state this as an equation: The net torque equals the moment of inertia times the angular acceleration. This equation, $\Sigma\tau = I\alpha$, resembles

Newton's second law, $\Sigma F = ma$. We sometimes refer to this equation as *Newton's second law for rotation*. The moment of inertia is measured in kilogram·meters squared (kg·m²). Like mass, the moment of inertia is always a positive quantity.

We show how the moment of inertia of an object could be experimentally determined in Example 1. A block, attached to a massless rope, is causing a pulley to accelerate. The angular acceleration and the net torque are stated in the problem. (The net torque could be determined by multiplying the tension by the radius of the pulley, keeping in mind that the tension is less than the weight of the block since the block accelerates downward.) With these facts known, the moment of inertia of the pulley can be determined.

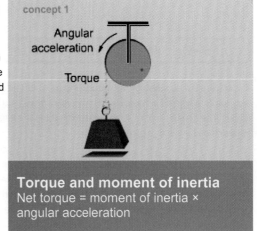

concept 1

Torque and moment of inertia
Net torque = moment of inertia ×
angular acceleration

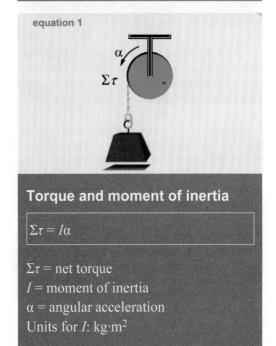

equation 1

Torque and moment of inertia

$$\Sigma\tau = I\alpha$$

$\Sigma\tau$ = net torque
I = moment of inertia
α = angular acceleration
Units for I: kg·m²

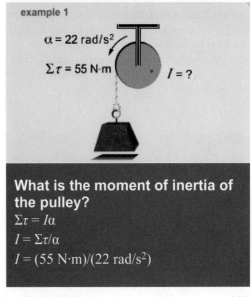

example 1

What is the moment of inertia of the pulley?
$\Sigma\tau = I\alpha$
$I = \Sigma\tau/\alpha$
$I = (55 \text{ N·m})/(22 \text{ rad/s}^2)$

$$I = 2.5 \ \text{kg·m}^2$$

10.3 - Calculating the moment of inertia

If you were asked whether the same amount of torque would cause a greater angular acceleration with a Ferris wheel or a bicycle wheel, you would likely answer: the bicycle wheel. The greater mass of the Ferris wheel means it has a greater moment of inertia. It accelerates less with a given torque.

But more than the amount of mass is required to determine the moment of inertia; the distribution of the mass also matters. Consider the case of a boy sitting on a seesaw. When he sits close to the axis of rotation, it takes a certain amount of torque to cause him to have a given rate of angular acceleration. When he sits farther away, it takes more torque to create the same rate of acceleration. Even though the boy's (and the seesaw's) mass stays constant, he can increase the system's moment of inertia by sitting farther away from the axis.

When a rigid object or system of particles rotates about a fixed axis, each particle in the object contributes to its moment of inertia. The formula in Equation 1 to the right shows how to calculate the moment of inertia. The moment equals the sum of each particle's mass times the square of its distance from the axis of rotation.

A single object often has a different moment of inertia when its axis of rotation changes. For instance, if you rotate a baton around its center, it has a smaller moment of inertia than if you rotate it around one of its ends. The baton is harder to accelerate when rotated around an end. Why is this the case? When the baton rotates around an end, more of its mass on average is farther away from the axis of rotation than when it rotates around its center.

If the mass of a system is concentrated at a few points, we can calculate its moment of inertia using multiplication and addition. You see this in Example 1, where the mass of the object is concentrated in two balls at the ends of the rod. The moment of inertia of the rod is very small compared to that of the balls, and we do not include it in our calculations. We also consider each ball to be concentrated at its own center of mass when measuring its distance from the axis of rotation (marked by the ×). This is a reasonable approximation when the size of an object is small relative to its distance from the axis.

Not all situations lend themselves to such simplifications. For instance, let's assume we want to calculate the moment of inertia of a CD spinning about its center. In this case the mass is uniformly distributed across the entire CD. In such a case, we need to use calculus to sum up the contribution that each particle of mass makes to the moment, or we must take advantage of a table that tells us the moment of inertia for a disk rotating around its center.

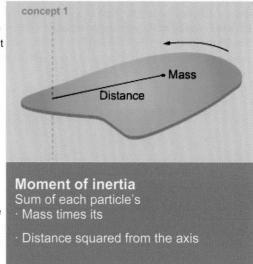

concept 1

Moment of inertia
Sum of each particle's
· Mass times its

· Distance squared from the axis

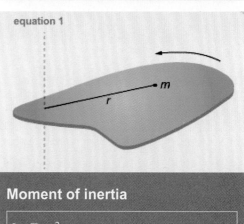

equation 1

Moment of inertia

$$I = \Sigma m r^2$$

I = moment of inertia
m = mass of a particle
r = distance of particle from axis
Units: kg·m^2

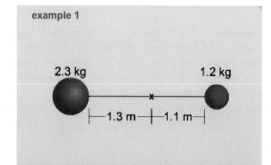

2.3 kg   1.2 kg

├─1.3 m─┼─1.1 m─┤

What is the system's moment of inertia? Ignore the rod's mass.

$$I = \Sigma mr^2 = m_1 r_1^2 + m_2 r_2^2$$
$$I = (2.3 \text{ kg})(1.3 \text{ m})^2 + (1.2 \text{ kg})(1.1 \text{ m})^2$$
$$I = 5.3 \text{ kg·m}^2$$

10.4 - A table of moments of inertia

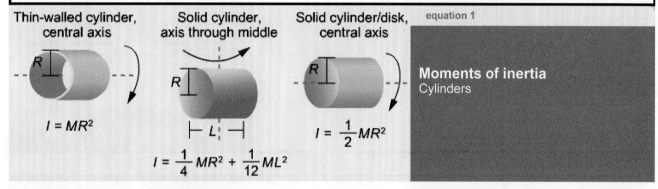

Thin-walled cylinder, central axis
$$I = MR^2$$

Solid cylinder, axis through middle
$$I = \frac{1}{4}MR^2 + \frac{1}{12}ML^2$$

Solid cylinder/disk, central axis
$$I = \frac{1}{2}MR^2$$

equation 1

Moments of inertia
Cylinders

Sets of objects are shown in the illustrations above and to the right. Above each object is a description of it and its axis of rotation. Below each object is a formula for calculating its moment of inertia, I.

The variable M represents the object's mass. It is assumed that the mass is distributed uniformly throughout each object.

If you look at the formulas in each table, they will confirm an important principle underlying moments of inertia: The distribution of the mass relative to the axis of rotation matters. For instance, consider the equations for the hollow and solid spheres, each of which is rotating about an axis through its center. A hollow sphere with the same mass and radius as a solid sphere has a greater moment of inertia. Why? Because the mass of the hollow sphere is on average farther from its axis of rotation than that of the solid sphere.

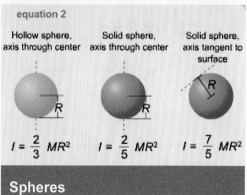

equation 2

Hollow sphere, axis through center
$$I = \frac{2}{3}MR^2$$

Solid sphere, axis through center
$$I = \frac{2}{5}MR^2$$

Solid sphere, axis tangent to surface
$$I = \frac{7}{5}MR^2$$

Spheres

Note also that the moment of inertia for an object depends on the location of the axis of rotation. The same object will have different moments of inertia when rotated around differing axes. As shown on the right, a thin rod rotated around its center has one-fourth the moment of inertia as the same rod rotated around one end. Again, the difference is due to the distribution of mass relative to the axis of rotation. On average, the mass of the rod is further away from the axis when it is rotated around one end.

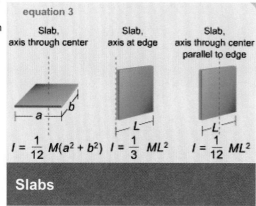

equation 3

Slab, axis through center $\quad$ Slab, axis at edge $\quad$ Slab, axis through center parallel to edge

$I = \dfrac{1}{12} M(a^2 + b^2)$ $\quad$ $I = \dfrac{1}{3} ML^2$ $\quad$ $I = \dfrac{1}{12} ML^2$

Slabs

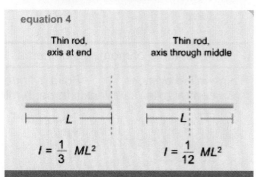

equation 4

Thin rod, axis at end $\qquad$ Thin rod, axis through middle

$I = \dfrac{1}{3} ML^2$ $\qquad$ $I = \dfrac{1}{12} ML^2$

Thin Rods

10.5 - Sample problem: a seesaw

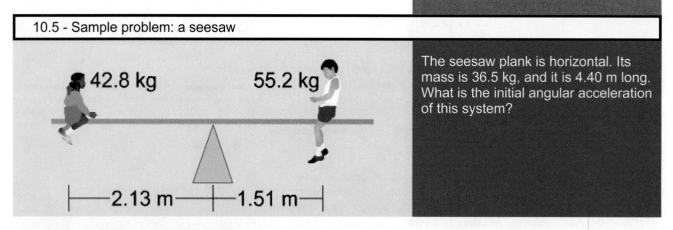

42.8 kg $\qquad$ 55.2 kg

2.13 m $\qquad$ 1.51 m

The seesaw plank is horizontal. Its mass is 36.5 kg, and it is 4.40 m long. What is the initial angular acceleration of this system?

The axis of rotation is the point where the fulcrum touches the midpoint of the plank. The plank itself creates no net torque since it is balanced at its middle. For every particle at a given distance from the axis that creates a clockwise torque, there is a matching particle at the same distance creating a counterclockwise torque. However, the plank does factor into the moment of inertia.

Draw a diagram

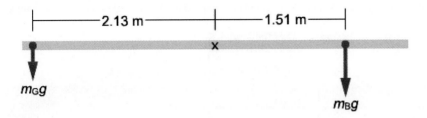

Variables

mass of seesaw plank	$m_S = 36.5$ kg
seesaw plank's moment of inertia	I_S

	girl	boy
mass	$m_G = 42.8$ kg	$m_B = 55.2$ kg
distance from axis	$r_G = 2.13$ m	$r_B = 1.51$ m
moment of inertia	I_G	I_B

What is the strategy?

1. Calculate the moment of inertia of the system: the sum of the moments for the children, and the moment of the plank.

2. Calculate the net torque by summing the torques created by each child. The torques of the left and right sides of the plank cancel, so you do not have to consider them.

3. Divide the net torque by the moment of inertia to determine the initial angular acceleration.

Physics principles and equations

We will use the definitions of torque and moment of inertia.

$$\tau = rF \sin \theta, I = \Sigma mr^2$$

To calculate the moments of inertia of the children, we consider the mass of each to be concentrated at one point.

The plank can be considered as a slab rotating on an axis parallel to an edge through the center, with moment of inertia

$$I = \frac{1}{12} ML^2$$

The equation relating net torque and moment of inertia is Newton's second law for rotation,

$$\Sigma \tau = I\alpha$$

Step-by-step solution

First, we add the moments of inertia for the two children and the seesaw plank. The sum of these values equals the system's moment of inertia.

Step	Reason
1. $I = I_G + I_B + I_S$	total moment is sum
2. $I = m_G r_G{}^2 + m_B r_B{}^2 + I_S$	definition of moment of inertia
3. $I = m_G r_G^2 + m_B r_B^2 + \frac{1}{12} m_S L^2$	moment of slab
4. $I = (42.8)(2.13)^2 + (55.2)(1.51)^2 + \frac{1}{12}(36.5)(4.40)^2$	enter values
5. $I = 379 \text{ kg·m}^2$	evaluate

The children create torques, and to calculate the net torque, we sum their torques, being careful about signs. The plank creates no net torque since its midpoint is at the fulcrum.

Step	Reason
6. $\Sigma\tau = \tau_G + \tau_B$	net torque equals sum of torques
7. $\Sigma\tau = m_G g r_G + (-m_B g r_B)$	equation for torque
8. $\Sigma\tau = (42.8)(9.80)(2.13) - (55.2)(9.80)(1.51)$	enter values
9. $\Sigma\tau = 76.6 \text{ N·m}$	evaluate

Now we use the values we calculated for the net torque and the moment of inertia to calculate the angular acceleration.

Step	Reason
10. $\alpha = \Sigma\tau / I$	Newton's second law for rotation
11. $\alpha = (76.6 \text{ N·m})/(379 \text{ kg·m}^2)$	substitute equations 5 and 9 into equation 10
12. $\alpha = 0.202 \text{ rad/s}^2$ (counterclockwise)	solve for α

Because various quantities change, such as the angle between the direction of each child's weight and the seesaw, the angular acceleration changes as the seesaw rotates. This is why we asked for the **initial** angular acceleration.

10.6 - Interactive problem: close the bridge

Once again, you are King Kong, and your task is to close the bridge you see on the right in order to save an invaluable load of bananas (well, invaluable to you at least). Here, we ask you to be a more precise gorilla than you may have been in the introductory exercise.

To close the bridge quickly enough to save the fruit without breaking off the bumper pilings, you need to apply a torque so that the bridge's angular acceleration is $\pi/16.0$ rad/s^2. The moment of inertia of the rotating part of the bridge is 45,400,000 kg·m^2.

Two trucks are parked on this part of the bridge, and you must include them when you calculate the total moment of inertia. Each truck has a mass of 4160 kg; the midpoint of one is 20.0 m and the midpoint of the other is 30.0 m from the pivot (axis of rotation) of the swinging bridge. The trucks will increase the bridge's moment of inertia. To solve the problem, consider all the mass of each truck to be concentrated at its midpoint.

You apply your force 35.0 m from the pivot and your force is perpendicular to the rotating component of the bridge. Enter the amount of force you wish to apply to the nearest 0.01×10^5 N and press GO to start the simulation. Press RESET if you need to try again.

If you have difficulty solving this problem, review the sections on calculating the moment of inertia, and the relation between torque, angular acceleration, and moment of inertia.

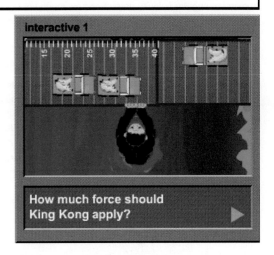

interactive 1

How much force should King Kong apply?

10.7 - Physics at work: flywheels

Flywheels are rotating objects used to store energy as rotational kinetic energy. Recently, environmental and other concerns have caused flywheels to receive increased attention. Many of these new flywheels serve as mechanical "batteries," replacing traditional electric batteries.

Why the interest? Traditional chemical batteries, rechargeable or not, have a shorter total life span than flywheels and can cause environmental problems when disposed of incorrectly. On the other hand, flywheels cost more to produce than traditional batteries, and their ability to function in demanding situations is unproven.

This advanced flywheel is being developed by NASA as a source of stored energy for use by satellites and spacecraft.

Flywheels can be powered by "waste" energy. For instance, when a bus slows down, its brakes warm up. The bus's kinetic energy becomes thermal energy, which the vehicle cannot re-use efficiently. Some buses now use a flywheel to convert a portion of that linear kinetic energy into rotational energy, and then later transform that rotational energy back into linear kinetic energy as the bus speeds up.

Flywheels can receive power from more traditional sources, as well. For instance, uninterruptible power sources (UPS) for computers use rechargeable batteries to keep computers powered during short-term power outages. Flywheels are being considered as an alternative to chemical batteries in these systems. Less traditional sources can also supply energy to a flywheel: NASA uses solar power to energize flywheels in space.

concept 1

Flywheels
Spinning objects "store" rotational *KE*
Energy depends on

The equation for rotational KE is shown to the right. The moment of inertia and maximum angular velocity determine how much energy a flywheel can store. The moment of inertia, in turn, is a function of the mass and its distance (squared) from the axis of rotation.

In Concept 1, you see a traditional flywheel. It is large, massive, and constructed with most of its mass at the outer rim, giving it a large moment of inertia and allowing it to store large amounts of rotational KE. In Concept 2, you see a modern flywheel, which is much smaller and less massive, but capable of rotating with a far greater angular velocity. Flywheels in these systems can rotate at 60,000 revolutions per minute (6238 rad/s). Air drag and friction losses are greatly reduced by enclosing the flywheel in a near vacuum and by employing magnetic bearings.

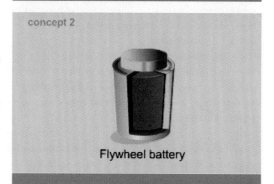

· angular velocity
· moment of inertia (mass, radius)

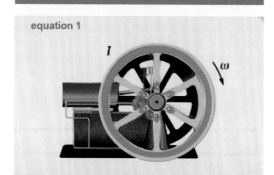

concept 2

Flywheel battery

Flywheels
Serve as mechanical batteries

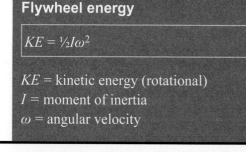

equation 1

Flywheel energy

$$KE = \tfrac{1}{2}I\omega^2$$

KE = kinetic energy (rotational)
I = moment of inertia
ω = angular velocity

10.8 - Angular momentum of a particle in circular motion

The concepts of linear momentum and conservation of linear momentum prove very useful in understanding phenomena such as collisions. *Angular momentum* is the rotational analog of linear momentum, and it too proves quite useful in certain settings. For instance, we can use the concept of angular momentum to analyze an ice skater's graceful spins.

In this section, we focus on the angular momentum of a single particle revolving in a circle. Angular momentum is always calculated using a point called the origin. With circular motion, the simple and intuitive choice for the origin is the center of the circle, and that is the point we will use here. The letter $\mathbf{L}$ represents angular momentum.

As with linear momentum, angular momentum is proportional to mass and velocity. However, with rotational motion, the distance of the particle from the origin must be taken into account, as well. With circular motion, the amount of angular momentum equals the product of mass, speed and the radius of the circle: mvr. Another way to

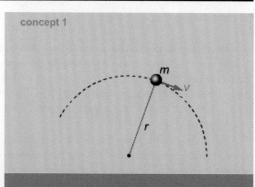

concept 1

Angular momentum of a particle
Proportional to mass, speed, and distance from origin

Copyright 2000-2007 Kinetic Books Co. Chapter 10

state the same thing is to say that the amount of angular momentum equals the linear momentum mv times the radius r.

Like linear momentum, angular momentum is a vector. When the motion is counterclockwise, by convention, the vector is positive. The angular momentum of clockwise motion is negative. The units for angular momentum are kilogram-meter^2 per second (kg·m^2/s).

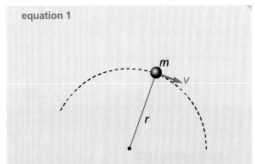

equation 1

Angular momentum of a particle

$L = mvr$

L = angular momentum
m = mass
v = speed
r = distance from origin (radius)
Counterclockwise +, clockwise −
Units: kg·m^2/s

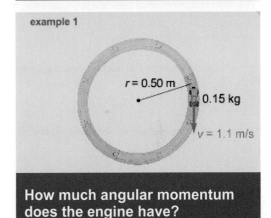

example 1

$r = 0.50$ m
0.15 kg
$v = 1.1$ m/s

How much angular momentum does the engine have?
$L = -mvr$
$L = -(0.15 \text{ kg})(1.1 \text{ m/s})(0.50 \text{ m})$
$L = -0.083$ kg·m^2/s

10.9 - Angular momentum of a rigid body

On the right, you see a familiar sight: a rotating compact disc. In the prior section, we defined the angular momentum of a single particle as the product of its mass, speed and radial distance from the axis of revolution. A CD is more complex than that. It consists of many particles rotating at different distances from a common axis of rotation. The CD is rigid, which means the particles all rotate with the same angular velocity, and each remains at a constant radial distance from the axis.

We can determine the angular momentum of the CD by summing the angular momenta of all the particles that make it up. The resulting sum can be expressed concisely using the concept of moment of inertia. The magnitude of the angular momentum of the CD equals the product of its moment of inertia, I, and its angular velocity, ω.

We derive this formula for calculating angular momentum below. In Equation 1, you see one of the rotating particles drawn, with its mass, velocity and radius indicated.

Variables

mass of a particle	m_i
tangential (linear) speed of a particle	v_i
radius of a particle	r_i
angular momentum of particle	L_i
angular momentum of CD	L
angular velocity of CD	ω
moment of inertia of CD	I

Strategy

1. Express the angular momentum of the CD as the sum of the angular momenta of all the particles of mass that compose it.
2. Replace the speed of each particle with the angular velocity of the CD times the radial distance of the particle from the axis of rotation.
3. Express the sum in concise form using the moment of inertia of the CD.

Physics principles and equations

The angular momentum of a particle in circular motion

$$L = mvr$$

We will use the equation that relates tangential speed and angular velocity.

$$v = r\omega$$

The formula for the moment of inertia of a rotating body

$$I = \Sigma m_i r_i^2$$

Step-by-step derivation

First, we express the angular momentum of the CD as the sum of the angular momenta of the particles that make it up.

Step	Reason
1. $L_i = m_i v_i r_i$	definition of angular momentum
2. $L = \Sigma m_i v_i r_i$	angular momentum of object is sum of particles

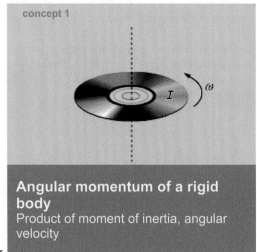

concept 1

Angular momentum of a rigid body
Product of moment of inertia, angular velocity

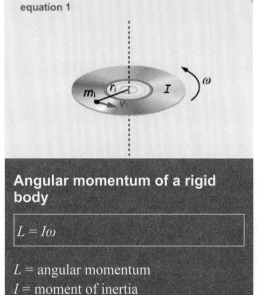

equation 1

Angular momentum of a rigid body

$$L = I\omega$$

L = angular momentum
I = moment of inertia
ω = angular velocity

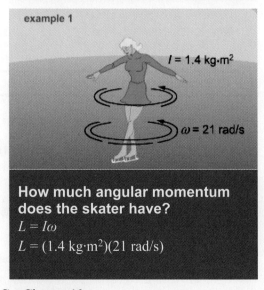

example 1

$I = 1.4$ kg·m²

$\omega = 21$ rad/s

How much angular momentum does the skater have?
$L = I\omega$
$L = (1.4 \text{ kg·m}^2)(21 \text{ rad/s})$

Copyright 2000-2007 Kinetic Books Co. Chapter 10

We now express the speed of the *i*th particle as its radius times the constant angular velocity ω, which we then factor out of the sum. The angular velocity is the same for all particles in a rigid body.

$$L = 29 \text{ kg} \cdot \text{m}^2/\text{s}$$

Step	Reason
3. $v_i = r_i\omega$	tangential speed and angular velocity
4. $L = \Sigma m_i(r_i\omega)r_i$	substitute equation 3 into equation 2
5. $L = (\Sigma m_i r_i^2)\omega$	factor out ω

In the final steps we express the above result concisely, replacing the sum in the last equation by the single quantity I.

Step	Reason
6. $I = \Sigma m_i r_i^2$	moment of inertia
7. $L = I\omega$	substitute equation 6 into equation 5

10.10 - Torque and angular momentum

A net force changes an object's velocity, which means its linear momentum changes as well. Similarly, a net torque changes a rotating object's angular velocity, and this changes its angular momentum.

As Equation 1 shows, the product of torque and an interval of time equals the change in angular momentum. This equation is analogous to the equation from linear dynamics stating that the impulse (the product of average force and elapsed time) equals the change in linear momentum.

In the illustration to the right, we show a satellite rotating at a constant angular velocity and then firing its thruster rockets, which changes its angular momentum. The thrusters apply a constant torque τ to the satellite for an elapsed time Δt. In Example 1, the satellite's change in angular momentum is calculated using the equation. (The change in the satellite's mass and moment of inertia resulting from the expelled fuel are small enough to be ignored.)

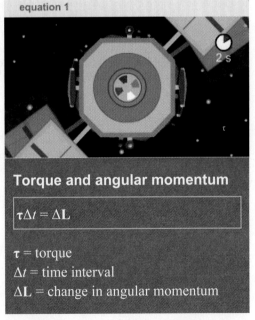

equation 1

Torque and angular momentum

$$\tau\Delta t = \Delta \mathbf{L}$$

τ = torque
Δt = time interval
$\Delta \mathbf{L}$ = change in angular momentum

example 1

The rockets provide 56 N·m of torque for 3.0 s. What is the amount of change in the

satellite's angular momentum?

$\tau \Delta t = \Delta L$

$(56 \text{ N·m})(3.0 \text{ s}) = \Delta L$

$\Delta L = 168 \text{ kg·m}^2/\text{s}$

10.11 - Conservation of angular momentum

concept 1

Angular momentum conserved
No external torque
Angular momentum is constant

Linear momentum is conserved when there is no external net force acting on a system. Similarly, angular momentum is conserved when there is no net external torque. To put it another way, if there is no net external torque, the initial angular momentum equals the final angular momentum. This is stated in Equation 1.

The principle of conservation of linear momentum is often applied to collisions, and the masses of the colliding objects are assumed to remain constant. However, with angular momentum, we often examine what occurs when the moment of inertia of a body changes. Since angular momentum equals the product of the moment of inertia and angular velocity, if one of these properties changes, the other must as well for the angular momentum to stay the same. This principle is used both in classroom demonstrations and in the world of sports. In a common classroom demonstration, a student is set rotating on a stool. The student holds weights in each hand, and as she pushes them away from her body, she slows down. In doing so, she demonstrates the conservation of angular momentum: As her moment of inertia increases, her angular velocity decreases. In contrast, pulling the weights close in to her body decreases her moment of inertia and increases her angular velocity.

Ice skaters apply this principle skillfully. When they wish to spin rapidly, they wrap their arms tightly around their bodies. They decrease their moment of inertia to increase their angular velocity. You can see images of a skater applying this principle to the right and above.

equation 1

Conservation of angular momentum

$$L_i = L_f$$
$$I_i \omega_i = I_i \omega_f$$

L = angular momentum
I = moment of inertia
ω = angular velocity

example 1

The skater pulls in her arms,

cutting her moment of inertia in half. How much does her angular velocity change?

$$I_i\omega_i = I_f\omega_f$$
$$I_i\omega_i = (\tfrac{1}{2}I_i)\omega_f$$
$$\omega_f = 2\omega_i \text{ (it doubles)}$$

10.12 - Gotchas

A torque is a force. No, it is not. A net torque causes **angular** acceleration. It requires a force.

A torque that causes counterclockwise acceleration is a positive torque. Yes, and a torque that causes clockwise acceleration is negative.

I have a baseball bat. I shave off some weight from the handle and put it on the head of the bat. A baseball player thinks I have changed the bat's moment of inertia. Is he right? Yes. A baseball player swings from the handle, so you have increased the amount of mass at the farthest distance, changing the bat's moment. The player will find it harder to apply angular acceleration to the bat.

A skater begins to rotate more slowly, so his angular momentum must be changing. Not necessarily. An external torque is required to change the angular momentum. The slower rotation could instead be caused by the skater altering his moment of inertia, perhaps by moving his hands farther from his body. On the other hand, if he digs the tip of a skate into the ice, that torque would reduce his angular momentum.

10.13 - Summary

Torque is a force that causes rotation. Torque is a vector quantity with units N·m.

An object's moment of inertia is a measure of its resistance to angular acceleration, just as an object's mass is a measure of its resistance to linear acceleration. The moment of inertia is measured in kg·m^2 and depends not only upon an object's mass, but also on the distribution of that mass around the axis of rotation. The farther the distribution of the mass from the axis, the greater the moment of inertia.

Another linear analogy applies: Just as Newton's second law states that net force equals mass times linear acceleration, the net torque on an object equals its moment of inertia times its angular acceleration.

Rotational kinetic energy depends upon the moment of inertia and the angular velocity. Mechanical devices called flywheels can store rotational kinetic energy.

Angular momentum is the rotational analog to linear momentum. Its units are kg·m^2/s. The magnitude of the angular momentum of an object in circular motion is the product of its mass, tangential velocity, and the radius of its path. The angular momentum of a rigid rotating body equals its moment of inertia multiplied by its angular velocity.

Just as a change in linear momentum (impulse) is equal to a force times its duration, a change in angular momentum is equal to a torque times its duration.

Angular momentum is conserved in the absence of a net torque on the system.

Equations

Torque
$$\tau = rF$$

Newton's second law for rotation
$$\Sigma\tau = I\alpha$$

Moment of inertia
$$I = \Sigma mr^2$$

Angular momentum
$$L = I\omega$$
$$\tau\Delta t = \Delta L$$

Conservation of angular momentum
$$L_i = L_f$$
$$I_i\omega_i = I_f\omega_f$$

11.0 - Introduction

Although much of physics focuses on motion and change, the topic of how things stay the same − equilibrium − also merits study. Bridges spanning rivers, skyscrapers standing tall… None of these would be possible without engineers having achieved a keen understanding of the conditions required for equilibrium. In this chapter, we focus on static equilibrium. To do so, we must consider both forces and torques, since for an object to be in static equilibrium, the net force and net torque on it must both equal zero.

A tightrope walker balances forces and torques to maintain equilibrium.

The forces and masses involved in equilibrium can be stupendous. The Brooklyn Bridge was the engineering marvel of its day; it gracefully spans the East River between Brooklyn and Manhattan. The anchorages at the ends of the bridge each have a mass of almost 55 million kilograms, while the suspended superstructure between the anchorages has a mass of 6 million kilograms. Supporting those 6 million kilograms are four cables of 787,000 kilograms apiece. A five-year construction effort resulted in the largest suspension bridge of its time, and one that over 200,000 vehicles pass over daily.

Engineers who design structures such as bridges must concern themselves with forces that cause even a material like steel to change shape, to lengthen or contract. If the material returns to its initial dimensions when the force is removed, it is called elastic.

11.1 - Static equilibrium

Static equilibrium: No net torque, no net force and no motion.

In California, equilibrium is achieved either by renouncing one's possessions, moving to a commune and selecting a guru, or by becoming extremely rich, moving to Malibu and choosing a personal trainer.

In physics, static equilibrium also requires a threefold path. First, there is no net force acting on the body. Second, there is no net torque on it about any axis of rotation. Finally, in the case of static equilibrium, there is no motion. An object moving with a constant linear and rotational velocity is also in equilibrium, but not in *static* equilibrium.

Let's see how we can apply these concepts to the seesaw at the right. There are two children of different weights on the seesaw. They have adjusted their positions so that the seesaw is stationary in the position you now see. (We will only concern ourselves with the weights of the children, and will ignore the weight of the seesaw.)

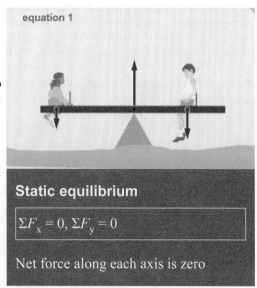

equation 1

Static equilibrium

$$\Sigma F_x = 0,\ \Sigma F_y = 0$$

Net force along each axis is zero

In Equation 2, we examine the torques. The fulcrum is the axis of rotation. Since the system is stationary, there is no angular acceleration, which means there is no net torque.

Let's consider the torques in more detail. They must sum to zero since the net torque equals zero. We choose to use an axis of rotation that passes through the point where the fulcrum touches the seesaw. The normal force of the fulcrum creates no torque because its distance to this axis is zero. The boy exerts a clockwise (negative) torque. The girl exerts a counterclockwise (positive) torque. Since the girl weighs less than the boy, she sits farther from the fulcrum to make their torques equal but opposite. In sum, there are no net forces, no net torques, and the system is not moving: It is in static equilibrium.

Note that in analyzing the seesaw, we used the fulcrum as the axis of rotation. This seems natural, since it is the point about which the seesaw rotates when the children are "seesawing." However, in problems you will encounter later, it is not always so easy to determine the axis of rotation. In those cases, it is helpful to remember that if the net torque is zero about one axis, it will be zero about any axis, so the choice of axis is up to you. However, this trick only works for cases when the net torque is zero. In general, the torque depends on one's choice of axis.

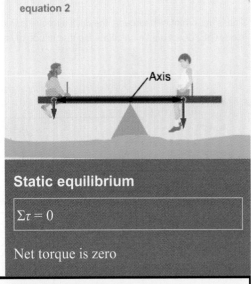

equation 2

Axis

Static equilibrium

$$\Sigma \tau = 0$$

Net torque is zero

11.2 - Sample problem: a witch and a duck balance

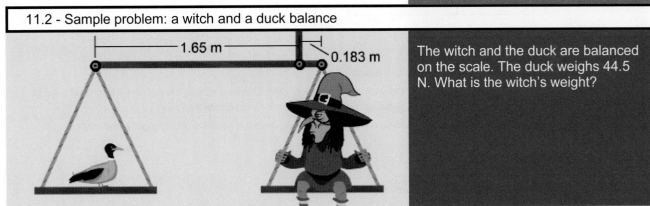

1.65 m

0.183 m

The witch and the duck are balanced on the scale. The duck weighs 44.5 N. What is the witch's weight?

Since the system is stationary, it is in static equilibrium. This means there is no net torque and no net force. We use the pivot point of the scale as the axis of rotation. We start by drawing a diagram for the problem. (The diagrams in this section are not drawn to scale; we also are not really sure witches exist, but then we do assume objects to be massless and frictionless and so on, so who are we to complain?) We ignore the masses of the various parts of the balance in this problem.

Draw a Diagram

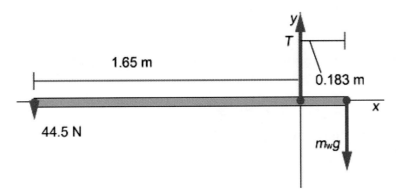

y

T

1.65 m

0.183 m

x

44.5 N

$m_w g$

Variables

Sign is important with torques: the duck's torque is in the positive (counterclockwise) direction while the witch's torque is in the negative (clockwise) direction. To calculate the magnitude of each torque, we can multiply the force by the lever arm, since the two are perpendicular.

Forces	x	y
weight, duck	0 N	$-m_d g = -44.5$ N
weight, witch	0 N	$-m_w g$
tension	0 N	T

Torques	lever arm (m)	torque (N·m)
weight, duck	1.65	$(1.65)(44.5)$
weight, witch	0.183	$-(0.183)(m_w g)$
tension	0	0

What is the strategy?

1. Draw a free-body diagram that shows the forces on the balance beam.
2. Place the axis of rotation at the location of an unknown force (the tension). This simplifies solving the problem. There is no need to calculate the amount of this force since a force applied at the axis of rotation does not create a torque.
3. Use the fact that there is no net torque to solve the problem. The only unknown in this equation is the weight of the witch.

Physics Principles and Equations

There is no net torque since there is no angular acceleration.

$$\Sigma\tau = 0$$

The weights are perpendicular to the beam, so we calculate the torques they create using

$$\tau = rF$$

A force (like tension) applied at the axis of rotation creates no torque.

Step-by-step solution

We use the fact that the torques sum to zero to solve this problem. There are only two torques in the problem due to the location of the axis of rotation: The tension creates no torque.

Step	Reason
1. torque of witch + torque of duck = 0	no net torque
2. $-(0.183 \text{ m})(m_w g) + (1.65 \text{ m})(44.5 \text{ N}) = 0 \text{ N·m}$	substitute values
3. $m_w g = (1.65 \text{ m})(44.5 \text{ N}) / (0.183 \text{ m})$	solve for $m_w g$
4. $m_w g = 401$ N	evaluate

Copyright 2000-2007 Kinetic Books Co. Chapter 11

Center of gravity: The force of gravity effectively acts at a single point of an object called the center of gravity.

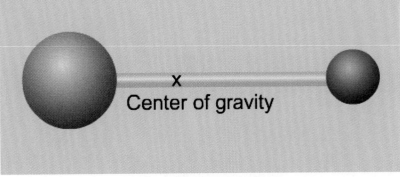

The center of gravity of a barbell.

The concept of center of gravity complements the concept of center of mass. When working with torque and equilibrium problems, the concept of center of gravity is highly useful.

Consider the barbell shown above. The sphere on the left is heavier than the one on the right. Because the spheres are not equal in weight, if you hold the barbell exactly in the center, the force of gravity will create a torque that causes the barbell to rotate. If you hold it at its center of gravity however, which is closer to the left ball than to the right, there will be no net torque and no rotation.

When a body is symmetric and uniform, you can calculate its center of gravity by locating its geometric center. Let's consider the barbell for a moment as three distinct objects: the two balls and the bar. Because each of the balls on the barbell is a uniform sphere, the geometric center of each coincides with its center of gravity. Similarly, the center of gravity of the bar connecting the two spheres is at its midpoint.

When we consider the entire barbell, however, the situation gets more complicated. To calculate the center of gravity of this entire system, you use the equation to the right. This equation applies for any group of masses distributed along a straight line. To apply the equation, pick any point (typically, at one end of the line) as the origin and measure the distance to each mass from that point. (With a symmetric, uniform object like a ball, you measure from the origin to its geometric center.)

Then, multiply each distance by the corresponding weight, add the results, and divide that sum by the sum of the weights. The result is the distance from the origin you selected to the center of gravity of the system. The center of gravity of an object does not have to be within the mass of the object: For example, the center of gravity of a doughnut is in its hole.

If you have studied the center of mass, you may think the two concepts seem equivalent. They are. When g is constant across an object, its center of mass is the same as its center of gravity. Unless the object is enormous (or near a black hole where the force of gravity changes greatly with location), a constant g is a good assumption.

You can empirically determine the center of gravity of any object by dangling it. In Concept 1, you see the center of gravity of a painter's palette being determined by dangling. To find the center of gravity of an object using this method, hang (dangle) the object from a point and allow it to move until it naturally stops and rests in a state of equilibrium. The center of gravity lies directly below the point where the object is suspended, so you can draw an imaginary line through the object straight down from the point of suspension. The object is then dangled again, and you draw another line down from the suspension point. Since both of these lines go through the center of gravity, the center of gravity is the point where the lines intersect.

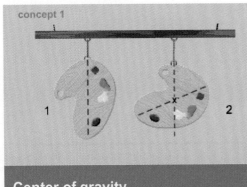

concept 1

Center of gravity
One point where weight effectively acts
Can be found by "dangling" object twice

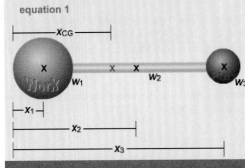

equation 1

Center of gravity

$$x_{CG} = \frac{w_1 x_1 + w_2 x_2 + \ldots + w_n x_n}{w_1 + w_2 + \ldots + w_n}$$

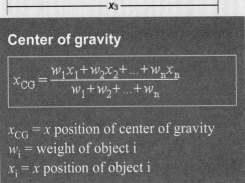

$x_{CG} = x$ position of center of gravity
w_i = weight of object i
x_i = x position of object i

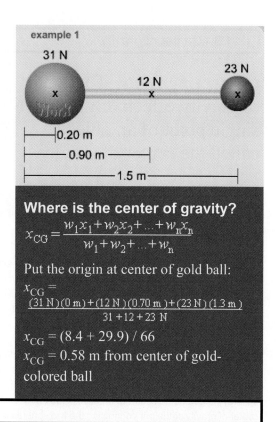

example 1

31 N

23 N

12 N

0.20 m

0.90 m

1.5 m

Where is the center of gravity?

$$x_{CG} = \frac{w_1 x_1 + w_2 x_2 + \ldots + w_n x_n}{w_1 + w_2 + \ldots + w_n}$$

Put the origin at center of gold ball:

$$x_{CG} = \frac{(31 \text{ N})(0 \text{ m}) + (12 \text{ N})(0.70 \text{ m}) + (23 \text{ N})(1.3 \text{ m})}{31 + 12 + 23 \text{ N}}$$

$x_{CG} = (8.4 + 29.9) / 66$

$x_{CG} = 0.58$ m from center of gold-colored ball

11.4 - Interactive problem: achieve equilibrium

In the simulation on the right, you are asked to apply three forces to a rod so that it will be in static equilibrium. Two of the forces are given to you and you have to calculate the magnitude, position, and direction of the third force. If you do this correctly, when you press GO, the rod will not move.

The rod is 2.00 meters long, and is horizontal. A force of 323 N is applied to the left end, straight up. A force of 627 N is applied to the right end, also straight up. You are asked to apply a force to the rod that will balance these two forces and keep it in static equilibrium.

Here is a free-body diagram of the situation. We have **not** drawn the third force where it should be!

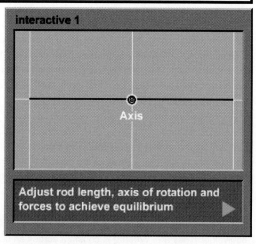

interactive 1

Axis

Adjust rod length, axis of rotation and forces to achieve equilibrium

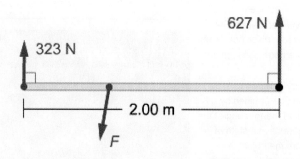

627 N

323 N

2.00 m

F

After you calculate the third vector's magnitude, position and direction, follow these steps to set up the simulation.

1. Adjust the rod length so it is 2.00 m.

2. Drag the axis of rotation to an appropriate position.

3. Apply all the forces. Drag a force vector by its tail from the control panel and attach the tail to the rod. You can then move the tail of the vector along the rod to the correct position, and drag the head of the vector to change its length and angle.

The control panel will show you the force's magnitude, direction and distance to the axis of rotation. The vector whose properties are being displayed has its head in blue.

When you have the simulation set up, press GO. If everything is set up correctly, the rod will be in equilibrium and will not move. Press RESET if you need to make any adjustments. If you have trouble, refer to the section on static equilibrium in this chapter, and the section on torque in the Rotational Dynamics chapter.

After you solve this interactive problem, consider the following additional challenge. What do you think will happen in the simulation if you change the position of the axis of rotation? Make a guess, and test your hypothesis with the simulation.

11.5 - Elasticity

Elastic: An elastic object returns to its original dimensions when a deforming force is removed.

In much of physics, the object being analyzed is assumed to be rigid and its dimensions are unchanging. For instance, if a homework problems asks: "What is the effect of a net force on a car?" and you answer, "The net force on the car caused a dent in its fender and enraged the owner," then you are thinking a little too much outside the box. The question anticipates that you will apply Newton's second law, not someone's insurance policy.

However, objects do stretch or compress when an external force is applied to them. They may return to their original dimensions when that force is removed: Objects with this property are called elastic. The external force causes the bonds between the molecules that make up the material to stretch or compress, and when that force is removed, the molecules can "spring back" to their initial configuration. The extent to which the dimensions of an object change in response to a *deforming force* is a function of the object's original dimensions, the material that makes it up, and the nature of the force that is applied.

concept 1

Elastic
Shape changes under force
Elastic: when force is removed, original shape is restored

It is also possible to stretch or compress an object to the point where it is unable to spring back. When this happens, the object is said to be *deformed*.

It can require a great deal of force to cause significant stretching. For instance, if you hang a 2000 kg object, like a midsize car, at the end of a two-meter long steel bar with a radius of 0.1 meters, the bar will stretch only about 6×10^{-6} meters.

There are various ways to change the dimensions of an object. For instance, it can be stretched or compressed along a line, like a vertical steel column supporting an overhead weight. Or, an object might experience compressive forces from all dimensions, like a ball submerged in water. Calculating the change of dimensions is a slightly different exercise in each case.

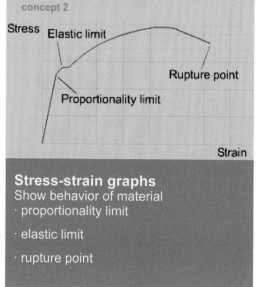

concept 1

Stress and strain
Stress: force per unit area
Strain: fractional change in dimension due to stress
Modulus of elasticity: relates stress, strain for given material

Stress: External force applied per unit area.

Strain: Fractional change in dimension due to stress.

concept 2

Stress-strain graphs
Show behavior of material
· proportionality limit
· elastic limit
· rupture point

Above, you see a machine that tests the behavior of materials under stress. Stress is the external force applied **per unit area** that causes deformation of an object. The machine above stretches the rod, increasing its length. Although we introduce the topic of stress and strain by discussing changes in length, stress can alter the dimensions of objects in other fashions as well.

Strain measures the **fractional** change in an object's dimensions: the object's change in dimension divided by its original dimension. This means that strain is dimensionless. For instance, if a force stretches a two-meter rod by 0.001 meters, the resulting strain is 0.001 meters divided by two meters, which is 0.0005.

Stress measures the force applied per unit area. If a rod is being stretched, the area equals the surface area of the end of the rod, called its cross-sectional area. If the force is being applied over the entirety of an object, such as a ball submerged in water, then the area is the entire surface area of the ball.

For a range of stresses starting at zero, the strain of a material (fractional change in size) is linearly proportional to the stress on it. When the stress ends, the material will resume its original shape: That is, it is elastic. The *modulus of elasticity* is a proportionality constant, the ratio of stress to strain. It differs by material, and depends upon what kind of stress is applied.

Values for modulus of elasticity apply only for a range of stress values. Here, we specifically use changes in length to illustrate this point. If you stress an object beyond its material's *proportionality limit*, the strain ceases to be linearly proportional to stress. A "mild steel" rod will exhibit a linear relation between stress and strain for a stress on it up to about 230,000,000 N/m^2. This is its proportionality limit.

Beyond a further point called the *elastic limit*, the object becomes permanently deformed and will not return to its original shape when the stress ceases to be applied. You have exceeded its *yield strength*. At some point, you pull so far it ruptures. At that *rupture point*, you have exceeded the material's *ultimate strength*.

Concept 2 shows a stress-strain graph typical of a material like soft steel (a type of steel that is easily cut or bent) or copper. Graphs like these are commonly used by engineers. They are created with testing machines similar to the one above by carefully applying force to a material over time. The graph plots the minimum stress required to achieve a certain amount of strain, which in this case is measured as the lengthening of a rod of the material. (We say "minimum stress" because the strain may vary depending on whether a given amount of stress is applied suddenly or is slowly increased to the same value.)

You may notice that the graph has an interesting property: Near the end, the curve flattens and its slope decreases. Less stress is required to generate a certain strain. The material has become *ductile*, or stretchy like taffy, and it is easier to stretch than it was before. Soft steel and copper are ductile. Other materials will reach the rupture point without becoming stretchy; they are called *brittle*. Concrete and glass are two brittle materials, and hardened steel is more brittle than soft steel.

Tensile stress: A stress that stretches.

On the right, you see a rod being stretched. Tensile forces cause materials to lengthen. Tensile stress is the force per cross-sectional unit area of the object. Here, the cross-sectional area equals the surface area of the end of the rod. The strain is measured as the rod's change in length divided by its initial length.

Young's modulus equals tensile stress divided by strain. The letter Y denotes Young's modulus, which is measured in units of newtons per square meter. The value for Young's modulus for various materials is shown in Concept 2. Note the scale used in the table: billions of newtons per square meter.

To correctly apply the equation in Equation 1 on the right, you must be careful with the definitions of stress and strain. First, stress is force **per unit area**. Second, strain is the **fractional** change in size. The relevant area for a rod in calculating tensile stress is the area of its end, as the diagrams on the right reflect.

The equation on the right can be used for compression as well as expansion. When a material is compressed, ΔL is the decrease in length. For some materials, Young's modulus is roughly the same for compressing (shortening) as for stretching, so you can use the same modulus when a *compressive force* is applied.

In addition to supplying the values for Young's modulus, we supply values for the yield strength (elastic limit) of a few of the materials. The table can give you a sense of why certain materials are used in certain settings. Steel, for example, has both a high Young's modulus and high yield strength. This means it requires a lot of stress to stretch steel elastically, as well as a lot of stress to deform it permanently.

Some materials have different yield strengths for compression and tension. Bone, for instance, resists compressive forces better than tensile forces. The value listed in the table is for compressive forces.

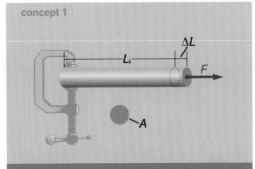

concept 1

Tensile stress
Causes stretching/compression along a line
Stress: force per cross-section unit area
Strain: fractional change in length

concept 2

	Young's modulus 10^9 (N/m²)	Yield strength 10^7 (N/m²)
Aluminum alloys	70	3 to 50
Bone	14	10
Brass	110	6 to 55
Concrete	21	
Copper	108	3 to 40
Glass	70	
Stainless steel	190	20 to 24
Titanium	100	83

Young's modulus
Relates stress, strain

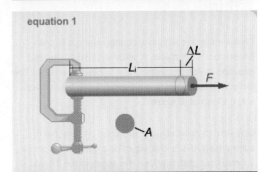

equation 1

Young's modulus

$$\frac{F}{A} = Y\frac{\Delta L}{L_i}$$

F = force
A = cross-sectional area

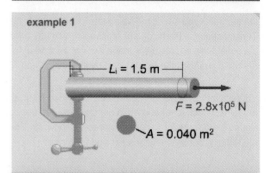

Y = Young's modulus (N/m^2)
ΔL = change in length
L_i = initial length

example 1

L_i = 1.5 m

$F = 2.8 \times 10^5$ N

$A = 0.040$ m^2

How much does this aluminum rod stretch under the force?

$$\frac{F}{A} = Y\frac{\Delta L}{L_i}, \text{ so } \Delta L = \frac{L_i F}{YA}$$

$$\Delta L = \frac{(1.5\,\text{m})\,(2.8 \times 10^5\,\text{N})}{(70 \times 10^9\,\text{N/m}^2)(0.040\,\text{m}^2)}$$

$$\Delta L = 1.5 \times 10^{-4}\,\text{m}$$

11.8 - Volume stress

Volume stress: A stress that acts on the entire surface of an object, changing its volume.

The effect of volume stress on a Styrofoam cup submerged 7875 feet underwater (with an un-stressed cup also shown for comparison). The stress on the cup exceeded its elastic limit: It is permanently deformed.

Tensile stress results in a change along a single dimension of an object. A volume stress is one that exposes the entire surface of an object to a force. The force is assumed to be perpendicular to the surface and uniform at all points.

One way to exert volume stress on an object is to submerge it in a fluid (a liquid or a gas). For example, submersible craft that visit the wreck of the Titanic travel four kilometers below the surface, experiencing a huge amount of volume stress on their hulls.

In all cases, stress is force per unit area, which is also the definition of pressure. With volume stresses, the term pressure is used explicitly, since the pressure of fluids is a commonly measured property.

Volume strain is measured as a fractional change in the volume of an object. The modulus of elasticity that relates volume stress and strain is called the *bulk modulus*, and is represented with the letter B.

The equation in Equation 1 states that the change in pressure equals the bulk modulus times the strain. The negative sign means that an **increase** in pressure results in a **decrease** in volume. Unlike the equation for tensile stress, this equation does not have an explicit term for area, because the pressure term already takes this factor into account. Notice that the equation is stated in terms of the **change** in pressure.

At the right is a table that lists values for the bulk modulus for some materials. To give you a sense of the deformation, the increase in pressure at 100 meters depth of water, as compared to the surface, is about 1.0×10^6 N/m^2. The volume of water will be reduced by 0.043% at this depth; steel, only 0.00063%.

At a depth of 11 km, approximately the maximum depth of the Earth's oceans, the increased pressure is 1.1×10^8 N/m^2. At this depth, a steel ball with a radius of 1.0 meter will compress to a radius of 0.997 m.

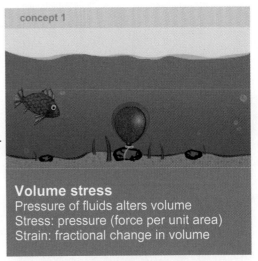

concept 1

Volume stress
Pressure of fluids alters volume
Stress: pressure (force per unit area)
Strain: fractional change in volume

concept 2

	Bulk modulus (10^9 N/m^2)
Aluminum alloys	69
Air	0.000144
Brass	110
Copper	120
Glass	37
Mercury	24.8
Saltwater	2.34
Stainless steel	160

Bulk modulus
Relates stress, strain

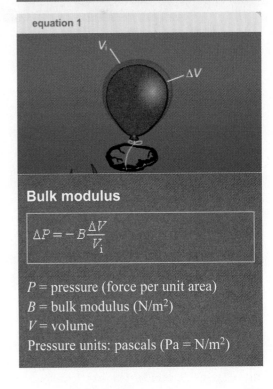

equation 1

V_i

ΔV

Bulk modulus

$$\Delta P = -B \frac{\Delta V}{V_i}$$

P = pressure (force per unit area)
B = bulk modulus (N/m^2)
V = volume
Pressure units: pascals (Pa = N/m^2)

example 1

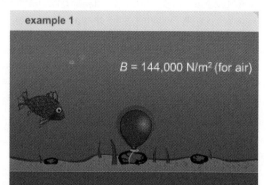

$B = 144,000$ N/m² (for air)

The increase in water pressure is $3.2×10^3$ Pa. The balloon's initial volume was 0.50 m³. What is it now?

$$\Delta P = - B\frac{\Delta V}{V_i}, \text{ so } \Delta V = - \frac{V_i \Delta P}{B}$$

$$\Delta V = - \frac{(0.50 \text{ m}^3)(3.2 \times 10^3 \text{ Pa})}{144,000 \text{ N/m}^2}$$

$$\Delta V = -0.011 \text{ m}^3$$
$$V_f = V_i + \Delta V = 0.50 - 0.011 \text{ m}^3$$
$$V_f = 0.49 \text{ m}^3$$

11.9 - Interactive checkpoint: stress and strain

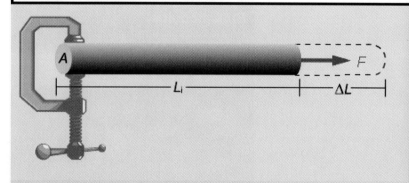

A 3.50 meter-long rod, composed of a titanium alloy, has a cross-sectional area of $4.00×10^{-4}$ m². It increases in length by 0.0164 m under a force of $2.00×10^5$ N. What is the stress on the rod? What is the strain? What is Young's modulus for this titanium alloy?

Answer:

$stress =$ [　　　　　] N/m²

$strain =$ [　　　　　]

$Y =$ [　　　　　] N/m²

11.10 - Gotchas

Stress equals force. No, stress is always a measure of force per unit surface area.

A force stretches a rod by 0.01 meters, so the strain is 0.01 meters. No, strain is always the fractional change (a dimensionless ratio). To calculate the strain, you need to divide this change in length by the initial length of the rod. This is not stated here, so you cannot determine the strain without more information.

11.11 - Summary

An object is in equilibrium when there are no net forces or torques on it. Static equilibrium is a special case where there is also no motion.

The center of gravity is the average location of the weight of an object. The force of gravity effectively acts on the object at this point. The concept of center of gravity is very similar to the concept of center of mass. The two locations differ only when an object is so large that the pull of gravity varies across it.

Elasticity refers to an object's shape changing when forces are applied to it. Objects are called elastic when they return to their original shape as forces are removed.

Related to elasticity are stress and strain. Stress is the force applied to an object per unit area. The area used to determine stress depends on how the force is applied. Strain is the fractional change in an object's dimensions due to stress.

Equations

Static equilibrium

$$\Sigma F_x = 0, \ \Sigma F_y = 0, \ \Sigma \tau = 0$$

Tensile stress

$$\frac{F}{A} = Y\frac{\Delta L}{L_i}$$

Volume stress

$$\Delta P = -B\frac{\Delta V}{V_i}$$

The relationship between stress and strain is determined by a material's modulus of elasticity up to the proportionality limit. An object will become permanently deformed if it is stressed past its elastic limit. It will finally break at its rupture point. Ductile materials are easily deformed, while brittle materials tend to break rather than stretch.

Tensile stress is the application of stress causing stretching or compression along a line. Strain under tensile stress is measured as a fractional change in length and stress is measured as the force per unit cross-sectional area. Young's modulus is the tensile stress on a material divided by its strain.

Volume stress acts over the entire surface of an object. The amount of volume stress is calculated as the force per unit surface area, while the strain is the fractional change in volume. The bulk modulus relates volume stress and strain.

12.0 - Introduction

The topic of gravity has had a starring role in some of the most famous tales in the history of physics. Galileo Galilei was studying the acceleration due to the Earth's gravity when he dropped two balls from the Leaning Tower of Pisa. A theory to explain the force of gravity came to Isaac Newton shortly after an apple fell from a tree and knocked him in the head. Although historians doubt whether these events actually occurred, the stories have come to symbolize how a simple experiment or a sudden moment of insight can lead to important and lasting scientific progress.

Galileo is often said to have dropped two balls of different masses from the tower so that he could see if they would land at the same time. Most scientists of his era would have predicted that the heavier ball would hit the ground first. Instead, the balls landed at the same instant, showing that the acceleration due to gravity is a constant for differing masses. While it is doubtful that Galileo actually dropped balls off that particular tower, his writings show that he performed many experiments studying the acceleration due to gravity.

In another famous story, Newton formed his theory of gravity after an apple fell and hit him on the head. At least one person (the daughter of French philosopher Voltaire) said that Newton mentioned that watching a falling apple helped him to comprehend gravity. Falling apple or no, his theory was not the result of a momentary insight; Newton pondered the topic of gravity for decades, relying on the observations of contemporary astronomers to inform his thinking. Still, the image of a scientist deriving a powerful scientific theory from a simple physical event has intrigued people for generations.

The interactive simulations on the right will help you begin your study of gravity.

Interactive 1 permits you to experiment with the gravitational forces between objects. In its control panel, you will see five point masses. There are three identical red masses of mass m. The green mass is twice as massive as the red, and the blue mass is four times as massive.

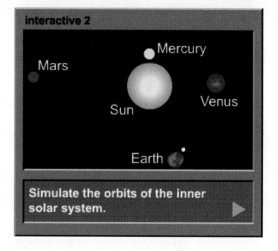

interactive 1

$F = 31.2$ N

$F = 31.2$ N

Observe gravitational force between masses ▶

interactive 2

Mars
Mercury
Sun
Venus
Earth

Simulate the orbits of the inner solar system. ▶

You can start your experimentation by dragging two masses onto the screen. The purple vectors represent the gravitational forces between them. You can move a mass around the screen and see how the gravitational forces change. What is the relationship between the magnitude of the forces and the distances between the masses?

Experiment with different masses. Drag out a red mass and a green mass. Do you expect the force between these two masses to be smaller or larger than it would be between two red masses situated the same distance apart? Make a prediction and test it. You can also drag three or more masses onto the screen to see the gravitational force vectors between multiple bodies. There is yet more to do: You can also press GO and see how the gravitational forces cause the masses to move.

The other major topic of this chapter is orbital motion. The force of gravity keeps bodies in orbit. Interactive 2 is a reproduction of the inner part of our solar system. It shows the Sun, fixed at the center of the screen, along with the four planets closest to it: Mercury, Venus, Earth and Mars.

Press GO to watch the planets orbit about the Sun. You can experiment with our solar system by changing the position of the planets prior to pressing GO, or by altering the Sun's mass as the planets orbit.

In the initial configuration of this system, the period of each planet's orbit (the time it takes to complete one revolution around the Sun) is proportional to its actual orbital period. Throughout this chapter, as in this simulation, we will often not draw diagrams to scale, and will speed up time. If we drew diagrams to scale, many of the bodies would be so small you could not see them, and taking 365 days to show the Earth completing one revolution would be asking a bit much of you.

12.1 - Newton's law of gravitation

Newton's law of gravitation: The attractive force of gravity between two particles is proportional to the product of their masses and inversely proportional to the square of the distance between them.

Newton's law of gravitation states that there is a force between every pair of particles, of any mass, in the universe. This force is called the gravitational force, and it causes objects to attract one another. The force does not require direct contact. The Earth attracts the Sun, and the Sun attracts the Earth, yet 1.5×10^{11} meters of distance separate the two.

The strength of the gravitational force increases with the masses of the objects, and weakens proportionally to the square of the distance between them. Two masses exert equal but opposite attractive forces on each other. The forces act on a line between the two objects. The magnitude of the force is calculated using the equation on the right. The symbol G in the equation is the *gravitational constant*.

It took Newton about 20 years and some false starts before he arrived at the relationship between force, distance and mass. Later scientists established the value for G, which equals $6.674\ 2 \times 10^{-11}$ N·m²/kg². This small value means that a large amount of mass is required to exert a significant gravitational force.

The example problems on the right provide some sense of the magnitude of the gravitational force. First, we calculate the gravitational force the Earth exerts on the Moon (and the Moon exerts on the Earth). Although separated by a vast distance (on average, their midpoints are separated by about 384,000,000 meters), the Earth and the Moon are massive enough that the force between them is enormous: 1.98×10^{20} N.

In the second example problem, we calculate the gravitational force between an 1100-kg car and a 2200-kg truck parked 15 meters apart. The force is 0.00000072 N. When you press a button on a telephone, you press with a force of about one newton, 1,400,000 times greater than this force.

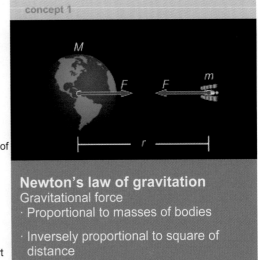

concept 1

Newton's law of gravitation
Gravitational force
· Proportional to masses of bodies
· Inversely proportional to square of distance

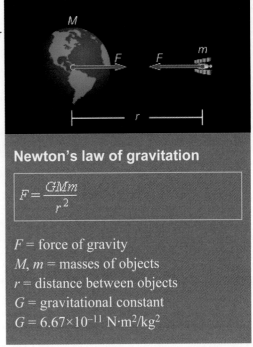

equation 1

Newton's law of gravitation

$$F = \frac{GMm}{r^2}$$

F = force of gravity
M, m = masses of objects
r = distance between objects
G = gravitational constant
$G = 6.67 \times 10^{-11}$ N·m²/kg²

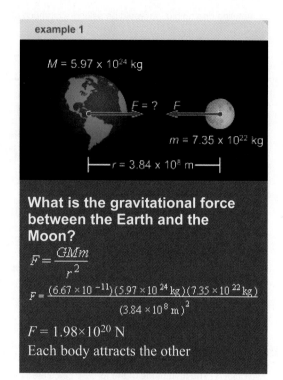

example 1

$M = 5.97 \times 10^{24}$ kg

$F = ?$

$m = 7.35 \times 10^{22}$ kg

$r = 3.84 \times 10^8$ m

What is the gravitational force between the Earth and the Moon?

$$F = \frac{GMm}{r^2}$$

$$F = \frac{(6.67 \times 10^{-11})(5.97 \times 10^{24}\,\text{kg})(7.35 \times 10^{22}\,\text{kg})}{(3.84 \times 10^8\,\text{m})^2}$$

$$F = 1.98 \times 10^{20}\,\text{N}$$

Each body attracts the other

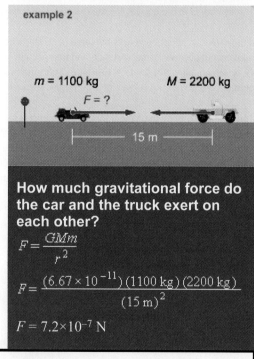

example 2

$m = 1100$ kg $\qquad$ $M = 2200$ kg

$F = ?$

15 m

How much gravitational force do the car and the truck exert on each other?

$$F = \frac{GMm}{r^2}$$

$$F = \frac{(6.67 \times 10^{-11})(1100\,\text{kg})(2200\,\text{kg})}{(15\,\text{m})^2}$$

$$F = 7.2 \times 10^{-7}\,\text{N}$$

12.2 - G and g

Newton's law of gravity includes the gravitational constant G.

In this section, we discuss the relationship between G and g, the rate of freefall acceleration in a vacuum near the Earth's surface.

The value of g used in this textbook is 9.80 m/s², an average value that varies slightly by location on the Earth. Both a 10-kg object and a 100-kg object will accelerate toward the ground at 9.80 m/s². The rate of freefall acceleration does not vary with mass.

Newton's law of gravitation, however, states that the Earth exerts a stronger gravitational force on the more massive object. If the force on the more massive object is greater, why does gravity cause both objects to accelerate at the same rate?

The answer becomes clear when Newton's second law of motion, $F = ma$, is applied. The acceleration of an object is proportional to the force acting on it, divided by the object's mass. The Earth exerts ten times the force on the 100-kg object that it does on the 10-kg object. But that tenfold greater force is acting on an object with a mass ten times greater, meaning the object has ten times more resistance to acceleration. The result is that the mass term cancels out and both objects accelerate toward the center of the Earth at the same rate, g.

If the gravitational constant G and the Earth's mass and radius are known, then the acceleration g of an object at the Earth's surface can be calculated. We show this calculation in the following steps. The distance r used below is the average distance from the surface to the center of the Earth, that is, the Earth's average radius. We treat the Earth as a particle, acting as though all of its mass is at its center.

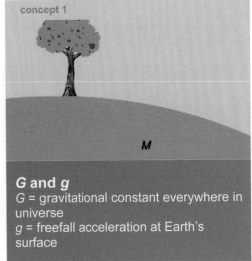

G and g
G = gravitational constant everywhere in universe
g = freefall acceleration at Earth's surface

Variables

gravitational constant	$G = 6.67 \times 10^{-11}$ N·m^2/kg^2
mass of the Earth	$M = 5.97 \times 10^{24}$ kg
mass of object	m
Earth-object distance	$r = 6.38 \times 10^6$ m
acceleration of object	g

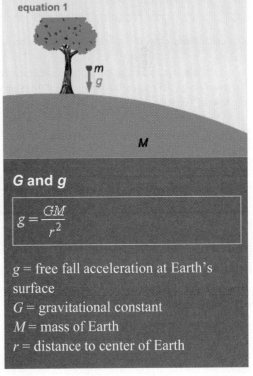

G and g

$$g = \frac{GM}{r^2}$$

g = free fall acceleration at Earth's surface
G = gravitational constant
M = mass of Earth
r = distance to center of Earth

Strategy

1. Set the expressions for force from Newton's second law and his law of gravitation equal to each other.
2. Solve for the acceleration of the object, and evaluate it using known values for the other quantities in the equation.

Physics principles and equations

We will use Newton's second law of motion and his law of gravitation. In this case, the acceleration is g.

$$F = ma = mg, \quad F = \frac{GMm}{r^2}$$

Step-by-step derivation

Here we use two of Newton's laws, his second law ($F = ma$) and his law of gravitation ($F = GMm/r^2$). We use g for the acceleration instead of a, because they are equal. We set the right sides of the two equations equal and solve for g.

Step		Reason
1.	$mg = \dfrac{GMm}{r^2}$	Newton's laws
2.	$g = \dfrac{GM}{r^2}$	simplify
3.	$g = \dfrac{(6.67 \times 10^{-11}\ \frac{\text{N} \cdot \text{m}^2}{\text{kg}^2})(5.97 \times 10^{24}\ \text{kg})}{(6.38 \times 10^6\ \text{m})^2}$	substitute known values
4.	$g = 9.78\ \text{m/s}^2$	evaluate

Our calculations show that g equals 9.78 m/s^2. The value for g varies by location on the Earth for reasons you will learn about later.

In the steps above, the value for G, the gravitational constant, is used to calculate g, with the mass of the Earth given in the problem. However, if g and G are both known, then the mass of the Earth can be calculated, a calculation performed by the English physicist Henry Cavendish in the late 18th century.

Physicists believe G is the same everywhere in the universe, and that it has not changed since the Big Bang some 13 billion years ago. There is a caveat to this statement: some research indicates the value of G may change when objects are extremely close to each other.

12.3 - Shell theorem

Shell theorem: The force of gravity outside a sphere can be calculated by treating the sphere's mass as if it were concentrated at the center.

concept 1

The shell theorem
Consider sphere's mass to be concentrated at center
· r is distance between centers of spheres

Newton's law of gravitation requires that the distance between two particles be known in order to calculate the force of gravity between them. But applying this to large bodies such as planets may seem quite daunting. How can we calculate the force between the Earth and the Moon? Do we have to determine the forces between all the particles that compose the Earth and the Moon in order to find the overall gravitational force between them?

Fortunately, there is an easier way. Newton showed that we can assume the mass of each body is concentrated at its center.

Newton proved mathematically that a uniform sphere attracts an object outside the sphere as though all of its mass were concentrated at a point at the sphere's center. Scientists call this the shell theorem. (The word "shell" refers to thin shells that together make up the sphere and which are used to mathematically prove the theorem.)

Consider the groundhog on the Earth's surface shown to the right. Because the Earth is approximately spherical and the matter that makes up the planet is distributed in a spherically symmetrical fashion, the shell theorem can be applied to it. To use Newton's law of gravitation, three values are required: the masses of two objects and the distance between them. The mass of the groundhog is 5.00 kg, and the Earth's mass is

Copyright 2000-2007 Kinetic Books Co. Chapter 12

5.97×10²⁴ kg. The distance between the groundhog and the center of the Earth is the Earth's radius, which averages $6.38×10^6$ meters.

In the example problem to the right, we use Newton's law of gravitation to calculate the gravitational force exerted on the groundhog by the Earth. The force equals the groundhog's weight (mg), as it should.

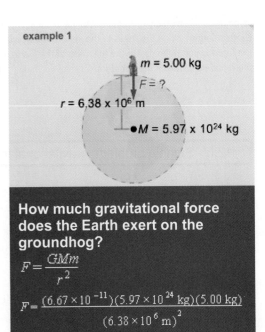

example 1

$m = 5.00$ kg

$F = ?$

$r = 6.38 \times 10^6$ m

$M = 5.97 \times 10^{24}$ kg

How much gravitational force does the Earth exert on the groundhog?

$$F = \frac{GMm}{r^2}$$

$$F = \frac{(6.67 \times 10^{-11})(5.97 \times 10^{24} \text{ kg})(5.00 \text{ kg})}{(6.38 \times 10^6 \text{ m})^2}$$

$$F = 48.9 \text{ N}$$

12.4 - Shell theorem: inside the sphere

Another section discussed how to calculate the force of gravity exerted on an object on the surface of a sphere (a groundhog on the Earth). Now imagine a groundhog burrowing halfway to the center of the Earth, as shown to the right. For the purposes of calculating the force of gravity, what is the distance between the groundhog and the Earth? And what mass should be used for the Earth in the equation?

The first question is easier: The distance used to calculate gravity's force remains the distance between the groundhog and the Earth's center. Determining what mass to use is trickier. We use the sphere defined by the groundhog's position, as shown to the right. The mass inside this new sphere, and the mass of the groundhog, are used to calculate the gravitational force. (Again, we assume that the Earth's mass is symmetrically distributed.)

If the groundhog is 10 meters from the Earth's center, the mass enclosed in a sphere with a radius of 10 meters is used in Newton's equation. If the animal moves to the center of the Earth, then the radius of the sphere is zero. At the center, no mass is enclosed, meaning there is no net force of gravity. The groundhog is perhaps feeling a little claustrophobic and warm, but is effectively weightless at the Earth's center.

The volume of a sphere is proportional to the cube of the radius, as the equation to the right shows. If the groundhog burrows halfway to the center of the Earth, then the sphere encloses one-eighth the volume of the Earth and one-eighth the Earth's mass.

Let's place the groundhog at the Earth's center and have him burrow back to the planet's surface. The gravitational force on him increases linearly as he moves back out to the Earth's surface. Why? The force increases proportionally to the mass enclosed by the sphere, which means it increases as the cube of his distance from the center. But the force also decreases as the square of the distance. When the cube of a quantity is divided by its square, the result is a linear relationship.

If the groundhog moves back to the Earth's surface and then somehow moves above the surface (perhaps he boards a plane and flies to an altitude of 10,000 meters), the

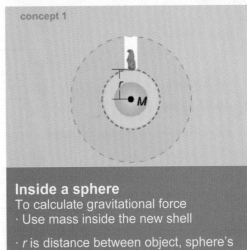

concept 1

Inside a sphere
To calculate gravitational force
· Use mass inside the new shell

· r is distance between object, sphere's center

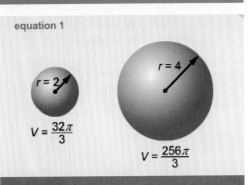

equation 1

$r = 2$

$r = 4$

$$V = \frac{32\pi}{3}$$

$$V = \frac{256\pi}{3}$$

Volume of a sphere

force again is inversely proportional to the square of the groundhog's distance from the Earth's center. Since the mass of the sphere defined by his position no longer varies, the force is computed using the full mass of the Earth, the mass of the groundhog, and the distance between their centers.

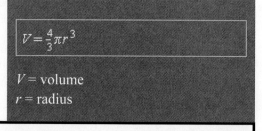

$$V = \frac{4}{3}\pi r^3$$

V = volume
r = radius

12.5 - Sample problem: gravitational force inside the Earth

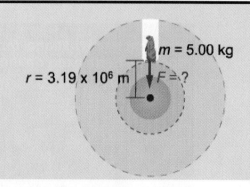

$m = 5.00$ kg

$r = 3.19 \times 10^6$ m $F = ?$

What is the gravitational force on the groundhog after it has burrowed halfway to the center of the Earth?

Assume the Earth's density is uniform. The Earth's mass and radius are given in the table of variables below.

Variables

gravitational force	F
mass of Earth	$M_E = 5.97 \times 10^{24}$ kg
radius of Earth	$r_E = 6.38 \times 10^6$ m
mass of inner sphere	M_s
distance between groundhog and Earth's center	$r_s = 3.19 \times 10^6$ m
mass of groundhog	$m = 5.00$ kg
gravitational constant	$G = 6.67 \times 10^{-11}$ N·m²/kg²

What is the strategy?

1. Use the shell theorem. Compute the ratio of the volume of the Earth to the volume of the sphere defined by the groundhog's current position. Use this comparison to calculate the mass of the inside sphere.

2. Use the mass of the inside sphere, the mass of the groundhog and the distance between the groundhog and the center of the Earth to calculate the gravitational force.

Physics principles and equations

Newton's law of gravitation

$$F = \frac{GMm}{r^2}$$

Mathematics principles

The equation for the volume of a sphere is

$$V = \frac{4}{3}\pi r^3$$

Step-by-step solution

First, we calculate the mass enclosed by the sphere.

Step		Reason
1.	$\dfrac{M_s}{M_E} = \dfrac{V_s}{V_E}$	ratio of masses proportional to ratio of volumes
2.	$M_s = \dfrac{V_s M_E}{V_E}$	rearrange
3.	$M_s = \dfrac{\left(\frac{4}{3}\pi r_s^3\right)(M_E)}{\frac{4}{3}\pi r_E^3}$	volume of a sphere
4.	$M_s = \dfrac{\left(r_s^3\right)(M_E)}{r_E^3}$	cancel common factors
5.	$M_s = \dfrac{\left(3.19\times10^6\ \mathrm{m}\right)^3\left(5.97\times10^{24}\ \mathrm{kg}\right)}{\left(6.38\times10^6\ \mathrm{m}\right)^3}$	enter values
6.	$M_s = 7.46\times10^{23}\ \mathrm{kg}$	evaluate

Now that we know the mass of the inner sphere, the shell theorem states that we can use it to calculate the gravitational force on the groundhog using Newton's law of gravitation.

Step		Reason
7.	$F = \dfrac{GMm}{r^2}$	law of gravitation
8.	$F = \dfrac{\left(6.67\times10^{-11}\frac{\mathrm{N}\cdot\mathrm{m}^2}{\mathrm{kg}^2}\right)\left(7.46\times10^{23}\,\mathrm{kg}\right)(5.00\,\mathrm{kg})}{\left(3.19\times10^6\,\mathrm{m}\right)^2}$	enter values
9.	$F = 24.4\ \mathrm{N}$	solve for the force

This calculation also confirms a point made previously: Inside the Earth, the groundhog's weight increases linearly with distance from the planet's center. At half the distance from the center, his weight is half his weight at the surface.

Copyright 2000-2007 Kinetic Books Co. Chapter 12

12.6 - Earth's composition and g

The force of gravity differs slightly at different locations on the Earth. These variations mean that g, the acceleration due to the force of gravity, also differs by location. Why do the force of gravity and g vary?

First, the surface of the Earth can be slightly below sea level (in Death Valley, for example), and it can be more than 8000 meters above it (on peaks such as Everest and K2). Compared to an object at sea level, an object at the summit of Everest is 0.14% farther from the center of the Earth. This greater distance to the Earth's center means less force (Newton's law of gravitation), which in turn reduces acceleration (Newton's second law). If you summit Mt. Everest and jump with joy, the force of gravity will accelerate you toward the ground about 0.03 m/s² slower than if you were jumping at sea level.

Second, the Earth has a paunch of sorts: It bulges at the equator and slims down at the poles, making its radius at the equator about 21 km greater than at the poles. This is shown in an exaggerated form in the illustration for Concept 3. The bulge is caused by the Earth's rotation and the fact that it is not entirely rigid. This bulge means that at the equator, an object is farther from the Earth's center than it would be at the poles and, again, greater distance means less force and less acceleration.

Finally, the density of the planet also varies. The Earth consists of a jumble of rocks, minerals, metals and water. It is denser in some regions than in others. The presence of materials such as iron that are denser than the average increases the local gravitational force by a slight amount. Geologists use *gravity gradiometers* to measure the Earth's density. Variations in the density can be used to prospect for oil or to analyze seismic faults.

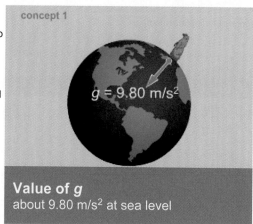

Value of g
about 9.80 m/s² at sea level

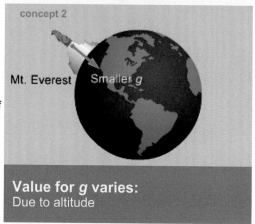

Value for g varies:
Due to altitude

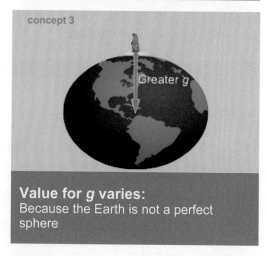

Value for g varies:
Because the Earth is not a perfect sphere

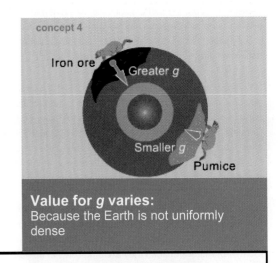

concept 4

Iron ore

Greater *g*

Smaller *g*

Pumice

Value for *g* varies:
Because the Earth is not uniformly dense

12.7 - Newton's cannon

In addition to noting that the Earth exerts a force on an apple, Newton also pondered why the Moon circles the Earth. He posed a fundamental question: Is the force the Earth exerts on the Moon the same type of force that it exerts on an apple? He answered yes, and his correct answer would forever change humanity's understanding of the universe.

Comparing the orbit of the distant Moon to the fall of a nearby apple required great intellectual courage. Although the motion of the Moon overhead and the fall of the apple may not seem to resemble one another, Newton concluded that the same force dictates the motion of both, leading him to propose new ways to think about the Moon's orbit.

To explain orbital motion, Newton conducted a thought experiment: What would happen if you used a very powerful cannon to fire a stone from the top of a very tall mountain? He knew the stone would obey the basic precepts of projectile motion, as shown in the diagrams to the right.

But, if the stone were fired fast enough, could it just keep going, never touching the ground? (Factors such as air resistance, the Earth's rotation, and other mountains that might block the stone are ignored in Newton's thought experiment.)

Newton concluded that the stone would not return to the Earth if fired fast enough. As he wrote in his work, *Principia*, published in 1686:

> " ... the greater the velocity with which [a stone] is projected, the farther it goes before it falls to the earth. We may therefore suppose the velocity to be so increased, that it would describe an arc of 1, 2, 5, 10, 100, 1000 miles before it arrived at earth, till at last, exceeding the limits of the earth, it should pass into space without touching."

Newton correctly theorized that objects in orbit – moons, planets and, today, artificial satellites – are in effect projectiles that are falling around a central body but moving fast enough that they never strike the ground. He could use his theory of gravity and his knowledge of circular motion to explain orbits. (In this section, we focus exclusively on circular orbits, although orbits can be elliptical, as well.)

Why is it that the stone does not return to the Earth when it is fired fast enough? Why can it remain in orbit, forever circling the Earth, as shown to the right?

First, consider what happens when a cannon fires a cannonball horizontally from a mountain at a relatively slow speed, say 100 m/s. In the

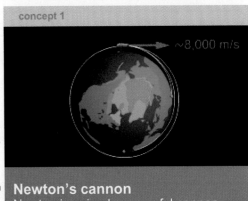

concept 1

~8,000 m/s

Newton's cannon
Newton imagined a powerful cannon
The faster the projectile, the farther it travels
At ~8,000 m/s, projectile never touches ground

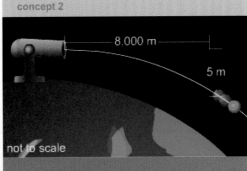

concept 2

8,000 m

5 m

not to scale

Close-up of Newton's cannon
At high speeds, Earth's curvature affects whether projectile lands
At ~8,000 m/s, ground curves away at same rate that object falls

vertical direction, the cannonball accelerates at *g* toward the ground. In the horizontal direction, the ball continues to move at 100 m/s until it hits the ground. The force of gravity pulls the ball down, but there is neither a force nor a change in speed in the horizontal direction (assuming no air resistance).

Now imagine that the cannonball is fired much faster. If the Earth were flat, at some point the ball would collide with the ground. But the Earth is a sphere. Its approximate curvature is such that it loses five meters for every 8000 horizontal meters, as shown in Concept 2. At the proper horizontal (or more properly, tangential) velocity, the cannonball moves in an endless circle around the planet. For every 8000 meters it moves forward, it falls 5 meters due to gravity, resulting in a circle that wraps around the globe.

In this way, satellites in orbit actually are falling around the Earth. The reason astronauts in a space shuttle orbiting close to the Earth can float about the cabin is **not** because gravity is no longer acting on them (the Earth exerts a force of gravity on them), but rather because they are projectiles in freefall.

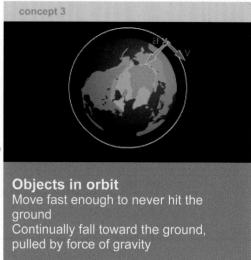

concept 3

Objects in orbit
Move fast enough to never hit the ground
Continually fall toward the ground, pulled by force of gravity

12.8 - Interactive problem: Newton's cannon

Imagine that you are Isaac Newton. It is the year 1680, and you are staring up at the heavens. You see the Moon passing overhead.

You think: Perhaps the motion of the Moon is related to the motion of Earth-bound objects, such as projectiles. Suppose you threw a stone very, very fast. Is there a speed at which the stone, instead of falling back to the Earth, would instead circle the planet, passing around it in orbit like the Moon?

You devise an experiment in your head, a type of experiment called a thought experiment. A thought experiment is a way physicists can test or explain valuable concepts even though they cannot actually perform the experiment. You ask: "What if I had an extremely powerful cannon mounted atop a mountain. Could I fire a stone so fast it would never hit the ground?"

interactive 1

Fire Newton's cannon to put cannonball into orbit ▶

Try Newton's cannon in the simulation to the right. You control the initial speed of the cannonball by clicking the up and down buttons in the control panel. The cannon fires horizontally, tangent to the surface of the Earth. See if you can put the stone into orbit around the Earth. You can create a nearly perfect circular orbit, as well as orbits that are elliptical.

(In this simulation we ignore the rotation of the Earth, as Newton did in his thought experiment. When an actual satellite is launched, it is fired in the same direction as the Earth's rotation to take advantage of the tangential velocity provided by the spinning Earth.)

12.9 - Circular orbits

The Moon orbits the Earth, the Earth orbits the Sun, and today artificial satellites are propelled into space and orbit above the Earth's surface. (We will use the term *satellite* for any body that orbits another body.)

These satellites move at great speeds. The Earth's orbital speed around the Sun averages about 30,000 m/s (that is about 67,000 miles per hour!) A communications satellite in circular orbit 250 km above the surface of the Earth moves at 7800 m/s.

In this section, we focus on circular orbits. Most planets orbit the Sun in roughly circular paths, and artificial satellites typically travel in circular orbits around the Earth as well.

The force of gravity is the centripetal force that along with a tangential velocity keeps the body moving in a circle. We use an equation for centripetal force on the right to derive the relationship between the mass of the body being orbited, orbital radius, and satellite speed. As shown in Equation 1, we first set the centripetal force equal to the gravitational force and then we solve for speed.

This equation has an interesting implication: The mass of the satellite has no effect on its orbital speed. The speed of an object in a circular orbit around a body with mass M is determined solely by the orbital radius, since M and G are constant. Satellite speed and radius are linked in circular orbits. A satellite cannot increase or decrease its speed and stay in the same circular orbit. A change in speed **must** result in a change in orbital radius, and vice versa.

At the same orbital radius, the speed of a satellite increases with the square root of the mass of the body being orbited. A satellite in a circular orbit around Jupiter would have to move much faster than it would if it were in an orbit of the same radius around the Earth.

concept 1

Circular orbits
Satellites in circular orbit have constant speed

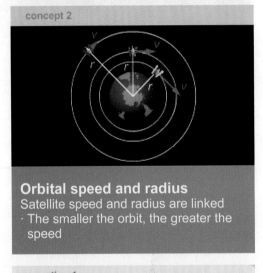

concept 2

Orbital speed and radius
Satellite speed and radius are linked
· The smaller the orbit, the greater the speed

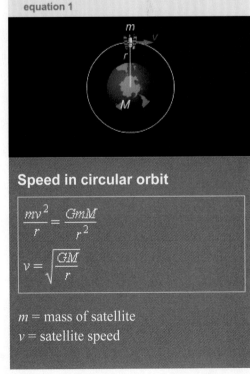

equation 1

Speed in circular orbit

$$\frac{mv^2}{r} = \frac{GmM}{r^2}$$

$$v = \sqrt{\frac{GM}{r}}$$

m = mass of satellite
v = satellite speed

G = gravitational constant
M = mass of body being orbited
r = orbital radius

12.10 - Sample problem: speed of an orbiting satellite

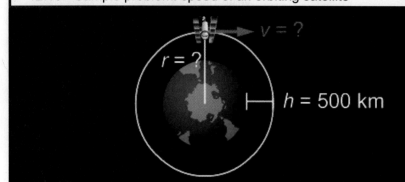

What is the speed of a satellite in circular orbit 500 kilometers above the Earth's surface?

h = 500 km

The illustration above shows a satellite in circular orbit 500 km above the Earth's surface. The Earth's radius is stated in the variables table.

Variables

satellite speed	v
satellite orbital radius	r
satellite height	$h = 500$ km
Earth's radius	$r_E = 6.38 \times 10^6$ m
Earth's mass	$M_E = 5.97 \times 10^{24}$ kg
gravitational constant	$G = 6.67 \times 10^{-11}$ N·m^2/kg^2

What is the strategy?

1. Determine the satellite's orbital radius, which is its distance from the center of the body being orbited.
2. Use the orbital speed equation to determine the satellite's speed.

Physics principles and equations

The equation for orbital speed is

$$v = \sqrt{\frac{GM}{r}}$$

Copyright 2000-2007 Kinetic Books Co. Chapter 12

Step-by-step solution

We start by determining the satellite's orbital radius. Careful: this is not the satellite's height above the surface of the Earth, but its distance from the center of the planet.

Step	Reason
1. $r = r_E + h$	equation for satellite's orbital radius
2. $r = 6.38 \times 10^6 \text{ m} + 5.00 \times 10^5 \text{ m}$	enter values
3. $r = 6.88 \times 10^6 \text{ m}$	add

Now we apply the equation for orbital speed.

Step	Reason
4. $v = \sqrt{\dfrac{GM_E}{r}}$	orbital speed equation
5. $v = \sqrt{\dfrac{(6.67 \times 10^{-11} \frac{N \cdot m^2}{kg^2})(5.97 \times 10^{24} kg)}{6.88 \times 10^6 m}}$	enter values
6. $v = 7610 \text{ m/s}$	evaluate

12.11 - Interactive problem: intercept the orbiting satellite

In this simulation, your mission is to send up a rocket to intercept a rogue satellite broadcasting endless *Barney*® reruns. You can accomplish this by putting the rocket into an orbit with the same radius and speed as that of the satellite, but traveling in the opposite direction. The resulting collision will destroy the satellite (and your rocket, but that is a small price to pay to save the world's sanity).

The rogue satellite is moving in a counterclockwise circular orbit 40,000 kilometers (4.00×10^7 m) above the center of the Earth. Your rocket will automatically move to the same radius and will move in the correct direction.

You must do a calculation to determine the proper speed to achieve a circular orbit at that radius. You will need to know the mass of the Earth, which is 5.97×10^{24} kg. Enter the speed (to the nearest 10 m/s) in the control panel and press GO. Your rocket will rise from the surface of the Earth to the same orbital radius as the satellite, and then go into orbit with the speed specified. You do not have to worry about how the rocket gets to the orbit; you just need to set the speed once the rocket is at the radius of the satellite. If you fail to destroy the satellite, check your calculations, press RESET and try a new value.

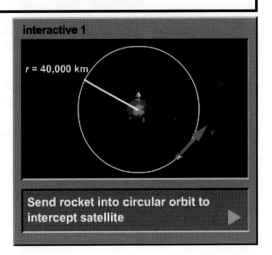

interactive 1

$r = 40,000$ km

Send rocket into circular orbit to intercept satellite

12.12 - Interactive problem: dock with an orbiting space station

In this simulation, you are the pilot of an orbiting spacecraft, and your mission is to dock with a space station. As shown in the diagram to the right, your ship is initially orbiting in the same circular orbit as the space station. However, it is on the far side of the Earth from the space station.

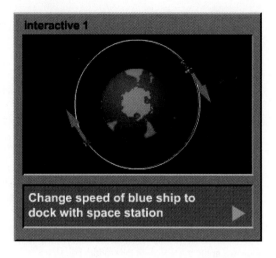

interactive 1

Change speed of blue ship to dock with space station ▶

In order to dock, your ship must be in the same orbit as the space station, and it must touch the space station. To dock, your speed and radius must be very close to that of the space station. A high speed collision does not equate to docking!

You have two buttons to control your ship. The "Forward thrust" button fires rockets out the back of the ship, accelerating your spacecraft in the direction of its current motion. The other button, labeled "Reverse thrust," fires retrorockets in the opposite direction. To use more "professional" terms, the forward thrust is called *prograde* and the reverse thrust is called *retrograde*.

Using these two controls, can you figure out how to dock with the space station?

To assist in your efforts, the current orbital paths for both ships are drawn on the screen. Your rocket's path is drawn in yellow, and the space station's is drawn in white.

This simulation requires no direct mathematical calculations, but some thought and experimentation are necessary. If you get too far off track, you may want to press RESET and try again from the beginning.

There are a few things you may find worth observing. You will learn more about them when you study orbital energy. First, what is the change in the speed of the rocket after firing its rear (Forward thrust) engine? What happens to its speed after a few moments? If you **qualitatively** consider the total energy of the ship, can you explain you what is going on? You may want to consider it akin to what happens if you throw a ball straight up into the sky.

If you cannot dock but are able to leave and return to the initial circular orbit, you can consider your mission achieved.

12.13 - Kepler's first law

The law of orbits: Planets move in elliptical orbits around the Sun.

The reason Newton's comparison of the Moon's motion to the motion of an apple was so surprising was that many in his era believed the orbits of the planets and stars were "divine circles:" arcs across the cosmic sky that defied scientific explanation. Newton used the fact that the force of gravity decreases with the square of the distance to explain the geometry of orbits.

Scientists had been proposing theories about the nature of orbits for centuries before Newton stated his law of gravitation. Numerous theories held that all bodies circle the Earth, but subsequent observations began to point to the truth: the Earth and other planets orbit the Sun. The conclusion was controversial; in 1633 the Catholic Church forced Galileo to repudiate his writings that implied this conclusion.

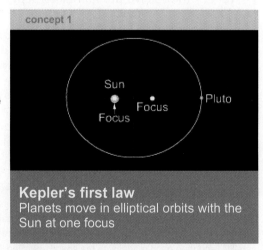

concept 1

Sun
Focus
Focus
Pluto

Kepler's first law
Planets move in elliptical orbits with the Sun at one focus

Even earlier, in 1609, the astronomer and astrologer Johannes Kepler began to propose what are now three basic laws of astronomy. He developed these laws through careful mathematical analysis, relying on the detailed observations of his mentor, Tycho Brahe, a talented and committed observational astronomer.

Kepler and Brahe formed one of the most productive teams in the history of astronomy. Brahe had constructed a state of the art observatory on an island off the coast of Denmark. "State of the art" is always a relative term − the telescope had not yet been invented, and Brahe might well have traded his large observatory for a good pair of current day binoculars. However, Brahe's records of years of observations allowed Kepler, with his keen mathematical insight, to derive the fundamental laws of planetary motion. He accomplished this decades before Newton published his law of gravitation.

Kepler, using Brahe's observations of Mars, demonstrated what is now known as Kepler's first law. This law states that all the planets move in elliptical orbits, with the Sun at one focus of the ellipse.

The planets in the solar system all move in elliptical motion. The distinctly elliptical orbit of Pluto is shown to the right, with the Sun located at one focus of the ellipse. Had Kepler been able to observe Pluto, the elliptical nature of orbits would have been more obvious.

The other planets in the solar system, some of which he could see, have orbits that are very close to circular. (If any of them moved in a perfectly circular orbit, they would still be moving in an ellipse, since a circle is an ellipse with both foci at its center.) Some of the orbits of these other planets are shown in Concept 2.

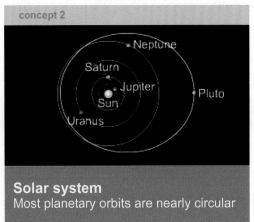

Solar system
Most planetary orbits are nearly circular

12.14 - More on ellipses and orbits

The ellipse shape is fundamental to orbits and can be described by two quantities: the semimajor axis a and the eccentricity e. Understanding these properties of an ellipse proves useful in the study of elliptical orbits.

The *semimajor axis,* represented by a, is one-half the width of the ellipse at its widest, as shown in Concept 1. You can calculate the semimajor axis by averaging the maximum and minimum orbital radii, as shown in Equation 1.

The *eccentricity* is a measure of the elongation of an ellipse, or how much it deviates from being circular. (The word eccentric comes from "ex-centric," or off-center.) Mathematically, it is the ratio of the distance d between the ellipse's center and one focus to the length a of its semimajor axis. You can see both these lengths in Equation 2. Since a circle's foci are at its center, d for a circle equals zero, which means its eccentricity equals zero.

Pluto has the most eccentric orbit in our solar system, with an eccentricity of 0.25, as calculated on the right. By comparison, the eccentricity of the Earth's orbit is 0.0167. Most of the planets in our solar system have nearly circular orbits.

Comets have extremely eccentric orbits. This means their distance from the Sun at the *aphelion,* the point when they are farthest away, is much larger than their distance at the *perihelion,* the point when they are closest to the Sun. (Both terms come from the Greek, "far from the Sun" and "near the Sun" respectively.)

Halley's comet has an eccentricity of 0.97. We show the comet's orbit in Example 1, but for visual clarity it is not drawn to scale. The comet's orbit is so eccentric that its maximum distance from the Sun is 70 times greater than its minimum distance. In Example 1, you calculate the perihelion of this object in *AU*. The AU (*astronomical unit*) is a unit of measurement used in planetary astronomy. It is equal to the average radius of the Earth's orbit around the Sun: about 1.50×10^{11} meters.

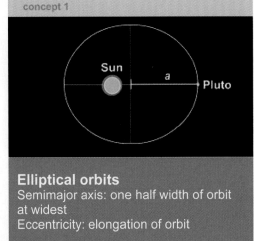

Elliptical orbits
Semimajor axis: one half width of orbit at widest
Eccentricity: elongation of orbit

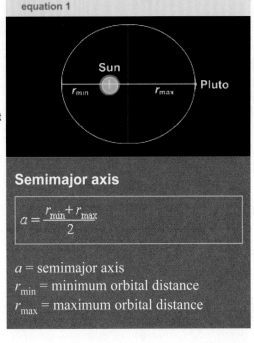

Semimajor axis

$$a = \frac{r_{min} + r_{max}}{2}$$

a = semimajor axis
r_{min} = minimum orbital distance
r_{max} = maximum orbital distance

equation 2

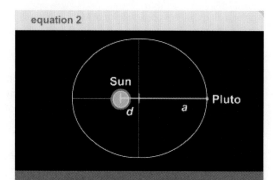

Eccentricity

$$e = \frac{d}{a}$$

e = eccentricity
d = distance from center to focus
a = semimajor axis

example 1

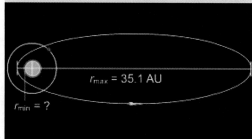

r_{max} = 35.1 AU

r_{min} = ?

What is the perihelion distance of Halley's Comet? The comet's semimajor axis is 17.8 AU.

$$a = \frac{r_{min} + r_{max}}{2}$$

$r_{min} = 2a - r_{max}$
$r_{min} = 2(17.8 \text{ AU}) - 35.1 \text{ AU}$
$r_{min} = 0.5 \text{ AU}$

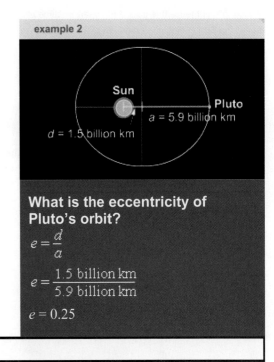

example 2

What is the eccentricity of Pluto's orbit?

$$e = \frac{d}{a}$$

$$e = \frac{1.5 \text{ billion km}}{5.9 \text{ billion km}}$$

$$e = 0.25$$

12.15 - Kepler's second law

The law of areas: An orbiting body sweeps out equal areas in equal amounts of time.

In his second law, Kepler used a geometrical technique to show that the speed of an orbiting planet is related to its distance from the Sun. (We use the example of a planet and the Sun; this law applies equally well for a satellite orbiting the Earth, or for Halley's comet orbiting the Sun.)

Kepler used the concept of a line connecting the planet to the Sun, moving like a second hand on a watch. As shown to the right, the line "sweeps out" slices of area over time. His second law states that the planet sweeps out an equal area in an equal amount of time in any part of an orbit. In an elliptical orbit, planets move slowest when they are farthest from the Sun and move fastest when they are closest to the Sun.

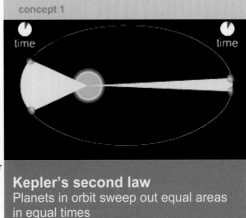

Kepler's second law
Planets in orbit sweep out equal areas in equal times

Kepler established his second law nearly a century before Newton proposed his theory of gravitation. Although Kepler did not know that gravity varied with the inverse square of the distance, using Brahe's data and his own keen quantitative insights he determined a key aspect of elliptical planetary motion.

12.16 - Kepler's third law

The law of periods: The square of the period of an orbit is proportional to the cube of the semimajor axis of the orbit.

Kepler's third law, proposed in 1619, states that the period of an orbit around a central body is a function of the semimajor axis of the orbit and the mass of the central body. The semimajor axis a is one half the width of the orbit at its widest. In a circular orbit, the semimajor axis is the same as the radius r of the orbit.

We illustrate this in Concept 1 using the Earth and the Sun. Given the scale of illustrations in this section, the Earth's nearly circular orbit appears as a circle.

The length of the Earth's period − a year, the time required to complete a revolution about the Sun − is solely a function of the mass of the Sun and the distance a shown in Concept 2.

Kepler's third law states that the square of the period is proportional to the cube of the semimajor axis, and inversely proportional to the mass of the central body. The law is shown in Equation 1. For the equation to hold true, the mass of the central body must be much greater than that of the satellite.

This law has an interesting implication: The square of the period divided by the cube of the semimajor axis has the same value for all the bodies orbiting the Sun. In our solar system, that ratio equals about 3×10^{-34} years^2/meters^3 (where "years" are Earth years) or 3×10^{-19} s^2/m^3. This is demonstrated in the graph in Concept 3. The horizontal and vertical scales of the coordinate system are logarithmic, with semimajor axis measured in AU and period measured in Earth years.

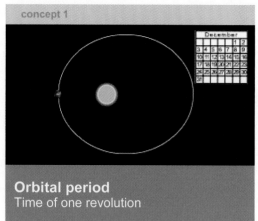

concept 1

Orbital period
Time of one revolution

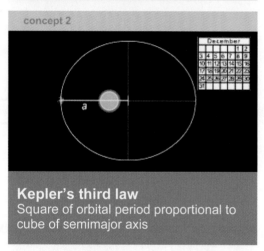

concept 2

Kepler's third law
Square of orbital period proportional to cube of semimajor axis

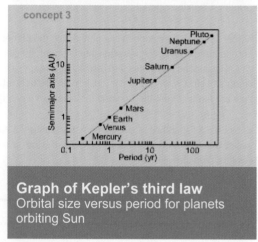

concept 3

Graph of Kepler's third law
Orbital size versus period for planets orbiting Sun

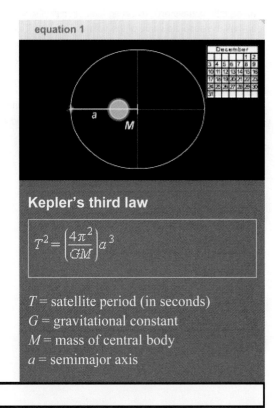

equation 1

Kepler's third law

$$T^2 = \left(\frac{4\pi^2}{GM}\right)a^3$$

T = satellite period (in seconds)
G = gravitational constant
M = mass of central body
a = semimajor axis

12.17 - Orbits and energy

Satellites have both kinetic energy and potential energy. The KE and PE of a satellite in elliptical orbit both change as it moves around its orbit. This is shown in Concept 1. Energy gauges track the satellite's changing PE and KE. When the satellite is closer to the body it orbits, Kepler's second law states that it moves faster, and greater speed means greater KE.

The PE of the system is less when the satellite is closer to the body it orbits. When discussing gravitational potential energy, we must choose a reference point that has zero PE. For orbiting bodies, that reference point is usually defined as infinite separation. As two bodies approach each other from infinity, potential energy decreases and becomes increasingly negative as the value declines from zero.

Concept 2 shows that even while the PE and KE change continuously in an elliptical orbit, the total energy TE stays constant. Because there are no external forces acting on the system consisting of the satellite and the body it orbits, nor any internal dissipative forces, its total mechanical energy must be conserved. Any increase in kinetic energy is matched by an equivalent loss in potential energy, and vice versa.

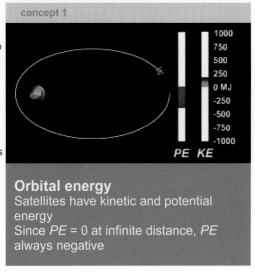

concept 1

Orbital energy
Satellites have kinetic and potential energy
Since $PE = 0$ at infinite distance, PE always negative

In a circular orbit, a satellite's speed is constant and its distance from the central body remains the same, as shown in Concept 3. This means that both its kinetic and potential energies are constant.

The total energy of a satellite increases with the radius (in the case of circular orbits) or the semimajor axis (in the case of elliptical orbits). Moving a satellite into a larger orbit requires energy; the source of that energy for a satellite might be the chemical energy present in its rocket fuel.

Equations used to determine the potential and kinetic energies and the total energy of a satellite in **circular** orbit are shown in Equation 1. These equations can be used to determine the energy required to boost a satellite from one circular orbit to another with a different radius. The KE equation can be derived from the equation for the velocity of a satellite. The PE equation holds true for any two bodies, and can be derived by calculating the work done by gravity as the satellite moves in from infinity.

The equations have an interesting relationship: The kinetic energy of the satellite equals one-half the absolute value of the potential energy. This means that when the radius of a satellite's orbit increases, the total energy of the satellite increases. Its kinetic energy decreases since it is moving more slowly in its higher orbit, but the potential energy increases twice as much as this decrease in KE.

Equation 2 shows the total energy equation for a satellite in an elliptical orbit. This equation uses the value of the semimajor axis a instead of the radius r.

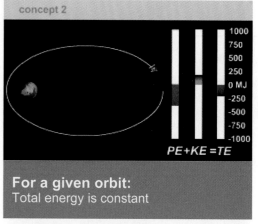

concept 2

$PE + KE = TE$

For a given orbit:
Total energy is constant

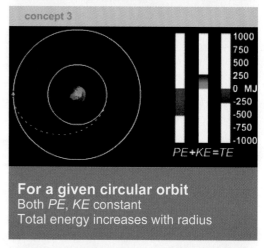

concept 3

$PE + KE = TE$

For a given circular orbit
Both PE, KE constant
Total energy increases with radius

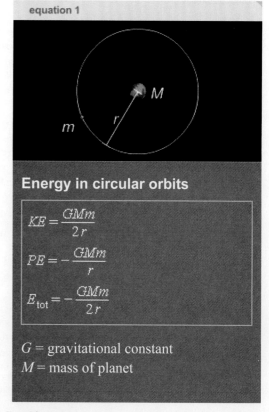

equation 1

M

r

m

Energy in circular orbits

$$KE = \frac{GMm}{2r}$$

$$PE = -\frac{GMm}{r}$$

$$E_{\text{tot}} = -\frac{GMm}{2r}$$

G = gravitational constant
M = mass of planet

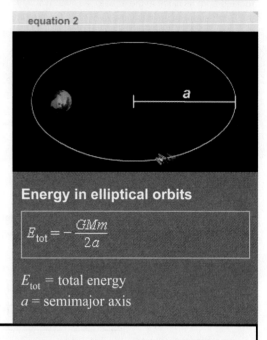

m = mass of satellite
r = orbit radius

equation 2

Energy in elliptical orbits

$$E_{\text{tot}} = -\frac{GMm}{2a}$$

E_{tot} = total energy
a = semimajor axis

12.18 - Escape speed

Escape speed: The minimum speed required for an object to escape a planet's gravitational attraction.

You know that if you throw a ball up in the air, the gravitational pull of the Earth will cause it to fall back down. If by some superhuman burst of strength you were able to hurl the ball up fast enough, it could have enough speed that the force of Earth's gravity would never be able to slow it down enough to cause it to return to the Earth.

The speed required to accomplish this feat is called the escape speed. Space agencies frequently fire rockets with sufficient speed to escape the Earth's gravity as they explore space.

Given enough speed, a rocket can even escape the Sun's gravitational influence, allowing it to explore outside our solar system. As an example, the Pioneer 10 spacecraft, launched in 1972, was nearly 8 billion miles away from the Earth by 2003, and is projected by NASA to continue to coast silently through deep space into the interstellar reaches indefinitely.

At the right is an equation for calculating the escape speed from a planet of mass M. As the example problem shows, the escape speed for the Earth is about 11,200 m/s, a little more than 40,000 km/h. The escape **speed** does not depend on the mass of the object being launched. However, the **energy** given to the object to make it escape is a function of its mass, since the object's kinetic energy is proportional to its mass.

The rotation of the Earth is used to assist in the gaining of escape speed. The Earth's rotation means that a rocket will have tangential speed (except at the poles, an unlikely launch site for other reasons as well). The tangential speed equals the product of the

concept 1

Escape speed
Minimum speed to escape planet's gravitational attraction

concept 2

Body	Mass (kg)	Radius (km)	Escape speed (km/s)
Pluto	1.5×10^{22}	1151	1.1
Earth's Moon	7.35×10^{22}	1738	2.37
Mars	6.42×10^{23}	3397	5.02
Earth	5.97×10^{24}	6378	11.2
Jupiter	1.90×10^{27}	71,492	59.6
Sun	1.99×10^{30}	695,990	618

Some escape speeds

Earth's angular velocity and the distance from the Earth's axis of rotation.

An object will have a greater tangential speed near the equator because there the distance from the Earth's axis of rotation is greatest. The United States launches its rockets from as close to the equator as is convenient: southern Florida. The rotation of the Earth supplies an initial speed of 1469 km/h (408 m/s) to a rocket fired east from Cape Canaveral, about 4% of the required escape speed.

Derivation. We will derive the escape speed equation by considering a rocket launched from a planet of mass M with initial speed v. The rocket, pulled by the planet's gravity, slows as it rises. Its launch speed is just large enough that it never starts falling back toward the planet; instead, its speed approaches zero as it approaches an infinite distance from the planet. If the initial speed is just a little less, the rocket will eventually fall back toward the planet. If the speed is greater than or equal to the escape speed, the rocket will never return.

Variables

We will derive the escape speed by comparing the potential and kinetic energies of the rocket as it blasts off (subscript 0), and as it approaches infinity (subscript ∞).

	initial	final	change
potential energy	PE_0	PE_∞	ΔPE
kinetic energy	KE_0	KE_∞	ΔKE
gravitational constant	G		
mass of planet	M		
mass of rocket	m		
radius of planet	r		
initial speed of rocket	v		

Strategy

1. Calculate the change in potential energy of the Earth-rocket system between launch and an infinite separation of the two.
2. Calculate the change in kinetic energy between launch and an infinite separation.
3. The conservation of mechanical energy states that the total energy after the engines have ceased firing equals the total energy at infinity. State this relationship and solve for v, the initial escape speed.

Physics principles and equations

We use the equation for the potential energy of an object at a distance r from the center of the planet.

$$PE = -\frac{GMm}{r}$$

We use the definition of kinetic energy.

Escape speed equation

$$v = \sqrt{\frac{2GM}{r}}$$

v = escape speed
G = gravitational constant
M = mass of planet
r = radius of planet

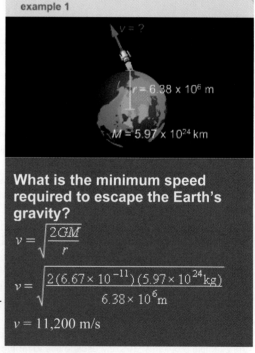

example 1

What is the minimum speed required to escape the Earth's gravity?

$$v = \sqrt{\frac{2GM}{r}}$$

$$v = \sqrt{\frac{2(6.67 \times 10^{-11})(5.97 \times 10^{24}\,\text{kg})}{6.38 \times 10^{6}\,\text{m}}}$$

$$v = 11{,}200 \text{ m/s}$$

$$KE = \frac{1}{2}mv^2$$

Finally, we will use the equation that expresses the conservation of mechanical energy.

$$\Delta PE + \Delta KE = 0$$

Step-by-step derivation

In the first steps we find the potential energy of the rocket at launch and at infinity, and subtract the two values.

Step		Reason
1.	$PE_0 = -\dfrac{GMm}{r}$	potential energy at launch
2.	$PE_\infty = -\dfrac{GMm}{\infty} = 0$	potential energy at infinity
3.	$\Delta PE = \dfrac{GMm}{r}$	change in potential energy

In the following steps we find the kinetic energy of the rocket at launch and at infinity, and subtract the two values.

Step		Reason
4.	$KE_0 = \dfrac{mv^2}{2}$	kinetic energy
5.	$KE_\infty = 0$	assumption
6.	$\Delta KE = -\dfrac{mv^2}{2}$	change in kinetic energy

To complete the derivation, we will substitute both changes in energy into the equation for the conservation of energy, and solve for the critical speed v.

Step		Reason
7.	$\Delta PE + \Delta KE = 0$	conservation of energy
8.	$\dfrac{GMm}{r} + \left(-\dfrac{mv^2}{2}\right) = 0$	substitute equations 3 and 6 into equation 7
9.	$v = \sqrt{\dfrac{2GM}{r}}$	solve for v

12.19 - Gotchas

The freefall acceleration rate, g, does not depend on the mass that is falling. If you say yes, you are agreeing with Galileo and you are correct.

A satellite can move faster and yet stay in the same circular orbit. No, it cannot. The speed is related to the dimensions of the orbit.

12.20 - Summary

Newton's law of gravitation states that the force of gravity between two particles is proportional to the product of their masses and inversely proportional to the square of the distance between them.

The gravitational constant G appears in Newton's law of gravitation and is the same everywhere in the universe. It should not be confused with g, the acceleration due to gravity near the Earth's surface. The value of g varies slightly according to the location on the Earth. This is due to local variations in altitude and to the Earth's bulging shape, nonuniform density and rotation.

A circular orbit is the simplest type of orbit. The speed of an object in a circular orbit is inversely proportional to the square root of the orbital radius. The speed is also proportional to the square root of the mass of the object being orbited, so orbiting a more massive object requires a greater speed to maintain the same radius.

Johannes Kepler set forth three laws that describe the orbital motion of planets. Kepler's first law says that the planets move in elliptical orbits around the Sun, which is located at one focus of the ellipse. Most of the planets' orbits in the solar system are only slightly elliptical.

Kepler's second law, the law of areas, says that an orbiting body such as a planet sweeps out equal areas in equal amounts of time. This means that the planet's speed will be greater when it is closer to the Sun.

Kepler's third law, the law of periods, states that the square of the period of an orbit is proportional to the cube of the semimajor axis a, which is equal to one half the width of the orbit at its widest. For a circular orbit, a equals the radius of the orbit.

The orbital energy of a satellite is the sum of its gravitational potential energy (which is negative) and its kinetic energy. The total energy is constant, though the PE and KE change continuously if the satellite moves in an elliptical orbit.

The escape speed is the minimum speed necessary to escape a planet's gravitational attraction. It depends on the mass and radius of the planet, but not on the mass of the escaping object.

Equations

Newton's law of gravitation

$$F = \frac{GMm}{r^2}$$

Gravitational acceleration

$$g = \frac{GM}{r^2}$$

Circular orbit

$$v = \sqrt{\frac{GM}{r}}$$

Kepler's second law

$$A = \frac{L}{2m}\Delta t$$

Kepler's third law

$$T^2 = \left(\frac{4\pi^2}{GM}\right)a^3$$

Energy in circular orbits

$$KE = \frac{GMm}{2r}$$

$$PE = -\frac{GMm}{r}$$

$$E_{\text{tot}} = -\frac{GMm}{2r}$$

Energy in elliptical orbits

$$E_{\text{tot}} = -\frac{GMm}{2a}$$

Escape speed

$$v = \sqrt{\frac{2GM}{r}}$$

13.0 - Introduction

The study of physics typically begins with the study of solid objects: You learn how to determine the velocity of a car as it accelerates down a street, what happens when two pool balls collide, and so on.

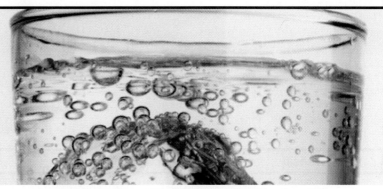

This chapter introduces the study of fluids. Liquids and gases are both fluids. Fluids change shape much more readily than solids. Pour soda from a can into a glass and the liquid will change shape to conform to the shape of the glass. Push on a balloon full of air or water and you can easily change the shape of the balloon and the fluid it contains. In contrast to liquids, gases expand to fill all the space available to them.

The glass and the ice cube in this photo are solid objects. The water is a liquid. The bubbles and the surrounding air are gasses.

One reason astronauts wear spacesuits is to keep their air near them, and not let it expand limitlessly into the near vacuum of space.

This chapter focuses on the characteristics exhibited by fluids when their temperature and density remain nearly constant. It covers topics such as the method of calculating how much pressure water will exert on a submerged submarine, and why a boat floats. Some of the topics apply to liquids alone, while others apply to both liquids and gases.

13.1 - Fluid

Fluid: A substance that can flow and conform to the shape of a container. Liquids and gases are fluids.

A fluid alters its shape to conform to the shape of the container that surrounds and holds it. The molecules of a fluid can "flow" because they are not fixed into position as they would be in a solid. Liquids and gases are fluids, and they are two of the common forms of matter, with solids being the third. There are other forms of matter as well, such as plasma (created in fusion reactors) and degenerate matter (found in neutron stars).

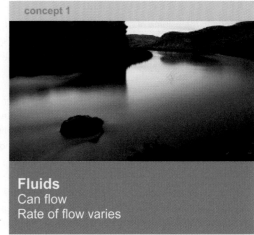

Fluids
Can flow
Rate of flow varies

A substance can exist as a solid, a liquid or a gas depending on the surrounding physical conditions. Factors such as temperature and pressure determine its state. For the purposes of a physics textbook, we need to be specific about what state of matter we are discussing at any given time. However, whether a substance is considered a solid or a fluid may depend on factors such as the time scale under consideration. For instance, the ice in a glacier can seem quite solid, but glaciers do flow slowly over time, so treating glacier ice as a fluid is useful to geologists.

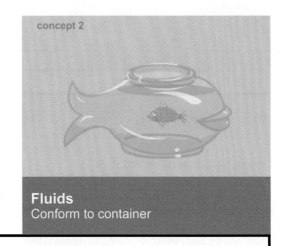

Fluids
Conform to container

13.2 - Density

Density: Mass per unit volume.

Density – to be precise, *mass density* – equals mass divided by volume. The Greek letter ρ (rho, pronounced "roe") represents density. The SI unit for density is the kilogram per cubic meter. The gram per cubic centimeter is also a common unit, useful in part because the density of water is close to one gram per cubic centimeter.

Liquids and solids retain a fairly constant density. It requires a great deal of force to compress water or a piece of clay into a more compact form. A given mass of liquid will change shape in order to conform to the shape of the container you pour it into, but its volume will remain nearly constant over a great variety of conditions.

In contrast, the volume of a sample of gas changes readily, which means its density changes easily, as well. For example, when you pump a stroke of air into a bicycle tire, the volume of air in the pump cylinder is reduced to "squeeze" it into the tire, increasing the air's density.

Much larger changes can be accomplished using larger increases in pressure. Machinery compresses the air fed into a scuba diving tank, causing its contents to be at a density on the order of 200 times greater than the density of the atmosphere you breathe. Before a diver breathes this air, its density (and pressure) are reduced. It would be lethal at the pressure maintained in the tank.

The density of an object can vary at different points based on its composition. A precise way to state the definition of density is $\Delta m/\Delta V$: The mass of a small volume of material is measured to establish its local density. However, unless otherwise stated, we will assume that the substances we deal with have *uniform density*, the same density at all points. This means that the density can be established by dividing the total mass by the total volume.

The table on the right shows the densities of various materials. Their densities are given at $0°C$ and one standard atmosphere of pressure (the density of the air around you can vary, depending on atmospheric conditions). Exceptions to this are the super-dense neutron star, which has no temperature in the ordinary sense, and liquid water, whose density is given at $4°C$, the temperature at which it is the greatest. We also supply some common equivalents for water, for instance relating a liter of water to its mass.

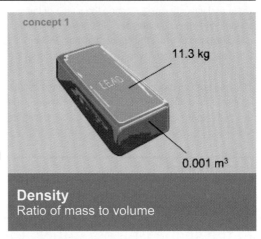

Density
Ratio of mass to volume

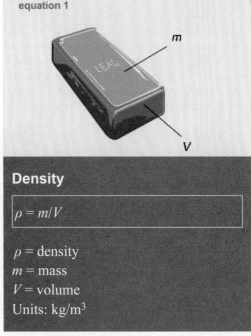

Density

$$\rho = m/V$$

ρ = density
m = mass
V = volume
Units: kg/m^3

The concept of *specific gravity* provides a useful tool for understanding and comparing various materials' densities. Specific gravity divides the density of one material by that of a reference material, usually water at $4°C$. For instance, if a material has a specific gravity of two, it is twice as dense as water.

Density of various substances

For water at 4° C:

· 1 liter has mass of 1 kg

· 1 cm³ has mass of 1 g

example 1

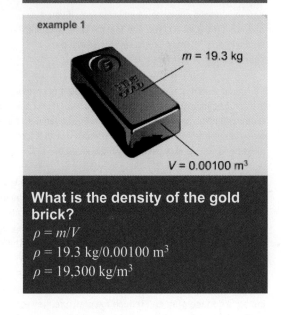

$m = 19.3$ kg

$V = 0.00100$ m³

What is the density of the gold brick?

$\rho = m/V$

$\rho = 19.3 \text{ kg} / 0.00100 \text{ m}^3$

$\rho = 19{,}300 \text{ kg/m}^3$

Pressure: Final exams, SATs, free throws in the last 30 seconds of a tight game, and driver's license tests.

Pressure: Force divided by the surface area over which the force acts.

Big feet distribute this lynx's weight over a larger surface area, lowering the pressure they exert on the snow.

The first definition of pressure above speaks for itself, but the second deserves further explanation.

You experience pressure when you swim. If you dive deep under the water, you can feel the water pushing against you with more pressure, more force per square meter of your body.

For a surface immersed in a fluid, the amount of pressure at a given location in the fluid is the same for any orientation of the surface. If you place your hand thirty centimeters underwater, the pressure on your palm is the same no matter how you rotate it. In the aquarium illustrated on the right, the water exerts a force on the bottom of the tank, but it exerts force − and pressure − on the sides as well.

Pressure equals the amount of force divided by the surface area to which it is applied. As the photograph above shows, some animals, such as the lynx, are able to travel easily across the surface of snow because their large paws spread the force of their weight over a large area. This reduces the pressure they exert on the snow, enabling them to walk on its surface. Animals of similar weight, but with smaller paws, sink into the snow.

People who need to travel across the snow may likewise use snowshoes or skis to increase surface area and reduce the pressure they exert. In contrast, spike-heeled shoes concentrate almost all the weight of their wearers over a very small surface area, and can exert a pressure large enough to damage wood or vinyl floors.

The water in the aquarium exerts force on the walls of the tank as well as its bottom. This is shown in Concept 1. Why does the water exert a force on the sides of the aquarium? Consider squishing down on a water balloon: The balloon bulges out on its sides. The additional force you exert on the top is translated into a force on the sides. To return to the aquarium, the downward weight of the water results in a force on the walls as well as the bottom.

The formula in Equation 1 shows how to calculate pressure. It equals the magnitude of the force divided by the area and is a scalar quantity. The SI unit for pressure is the newton per square meter, called a *pascal* (Pa). One pascal is a very small amount of pressure. The Earth's atmosphere exerts about 100,000 pascals of air pressure at the planet's surface. A *bar* of pressure equals 100,000 (10^5) pascals and is another commonly used unit. Bars are informally called "atmospheres" (atm) of pressure. You may have heard references to "millibars" in weather reports.

In the British system, force is measured in pounds. Pounds per square inch, *psi*, is a

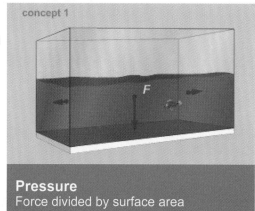

concept 1

Pressure
Force divided by surface area

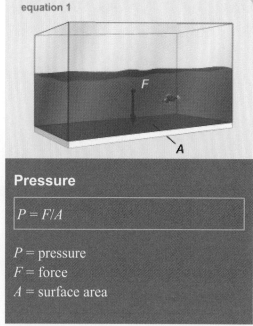

equation 1

Pressure

$$P = F/A$$

P = pressure
F = force
A = surface area

common measure of force. At the Earth's surface, typical atmospheric pressure is 14.7 psi. Automobile tires are normally inflated to a pressure of about 24 psi, while road bicycle tires are inflated to pressures as high as 120 psi. The tire readings reflect the amount of pressure inside the tires **over** atmospheric pressure. The total (absolute) pressure inside a tire is the sum of atmospheric pressure and the gauge reading (a total of about 135 psi for the bicycle tire).

Units: pascal (Pa), newton/meter^2

equation 2

Atmospheric pressure at sea level
$P_{atm} = 101{,}300 \text{ Pa} \approx 1 \text{ bar}$

example 1

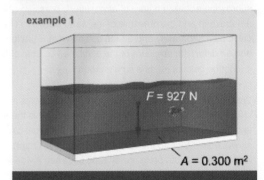

$F = 927 \text{ N}$

$A = 0.300 \text{ m}^2$

What is the pressure inside the bottom of the aquarium caused solely by the weight of the water?

$P = F/A$

$P = 927 \text{ N} / 0.300 \text{ m}^2$

$P = 3090 \text{ Pa}$

13.4 - Pressure and fluids

As a submarine dives deeper and deeper into the sea, it encounters increasing pressure. The nightmare of any submariner is that his craft goes so deep it collapses under the tremendous pressure of the water. (Rent the movie *U-571* if you want to watch a Hollywood thriller that deals with pressure at great depths.)

Physicists prefer a little less drama and a little more measurement in their dealings with pressure. They have developed an equation to describe the pressure of a fluid as a function of the fluid's depth.

Navy personnel performing under pressure.

Why does water pressure increase as a submarine descends? The pressure increases because the amount of water on top of the submarine increases as the vessel does down. The weight of the water exerts a force over the entire surface area of the submarine's hull. The water pressure does not depend on the orientation of the surface. It exists all over the craft: on its top, bottom and sides.

The first equation on the right shows how to calculate the pressure at a point underneath the surface of a fluid. The pressure equals the product of the fluid's density, the constant acceleration of gravity, and the height of the column of fluid above the point. "Height" means the distance from the point to the surface of the fluid. The equation states that pressure increases linearly with depth. The water pressure at 200 meters down is twice as great as it is at 100 meters. This equation applies when the fluid is static.

The fluid pressure varies solely as a function of the density ρ and the depth in the fluid, not with the shape of the container holding the fluid. If you fill a swimming pool and a Coke bottle with water, the water pressure at 0.1 meters below the surface will be the same in both containers. The pressure will also be the same at the bottom of the bottle and on the wall of the pool at the same depth. Whether the surface area is horizontal or vertical, the pressure is the same.

You can add pressures. The **total** pressure exerted on the exterior of the hull of the submarine equals the sum of *atmospheric pressure* (the pressure exerted by the Earth's air above it) and the pressure of the water above it. The two pressures must be calculated separately and added as shown in Equation 2. Since the densities of water and air differ, the pressure of the combined column of fluids above the submarine cannot be calculated as a single product ρgh.

We have implicitly described two types of pressure: absolute and gauge pressure. The total pressure is called the *absolute pressure*. It is the sum of the atmospheric pressure and the pressure of the fluid in question, in this case water. The photograph below shows how a Styrofoam® cup (as shown on the right) was crushed (as shown on the left) by an absolute pressure of 3288 psi when it was submerged to a depth of more than two kilometers below the ocean's surface.

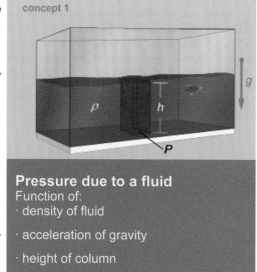

Pressure due to a fluid
Function of:
· density of fluid

· acceleration of gravity

· height of column

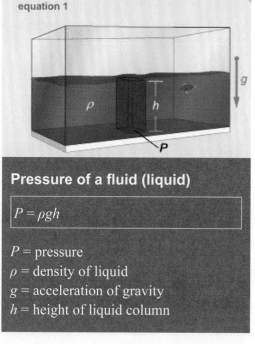

Pressure of a fluid (liquid)

$$P = \rho gh$$

P = pressure
ρ = density of liquid
g = acceleration of gravity
h = height of liquid column

The term *gauge pressure* describes the pressure caused solely by the water (or other fluid), ignoring the atmospheric pressure. The gauge pressure equals ρgh, where ρ, g and h are measured for the fluid alone. To state the same concept in another way: Gauge pressure equals the absolute pressure minus the atmospheric pressure.

Pressures can oppose one other, when they act on opposite sides of the same surface. For example, the "atmospheric" pressure inside an airplane cabin is allowed to decrease as the plane climbs. The pressure inside your ear can be higher than the pressure of the cabin, since it may remain at the higher pressure of the atmosphere at the Earth's surface. In this case, the pressure in parts of your ears is greater than the pressure outside them, producing a net outward pressure (and force) on your eardrums. The result is that your ear begins to ache.

You can reduce the pressure inside your ears by chewing gum or yawning to "pop" them. This stretches and opens the Eustachian tubes, passages between your ears and throat. Air flows out of your ear into the cabin, balancing the pressures, and your earache disappears.

If you look at the large value calculated in the example problem for the absolute pressure on the inner surface of the aquarium's bottom, you might wonder why the tank does not burst. Remember that atmospheric pressure is pushing inward on its exterior surfaces as well. The net pressure on the bottom plate is the gauge pressure due solely to the water, which is not large enough to cause the tank to burst.

The density of a liquid does not vary significantly with depth, so using an average density figure in the formula $\rho g h$ provides a good approximation of the pressure at any depth. The density of gases can vary greatly, so the formula is not as applicable to them, especially if h is large. For instance, the density of the Earth's atmosphere is about 1.28 kg/m³ at sea level (and $0°C$), but only 0.38 kg/m³ at an altitude of 10,600 m (35,000 ft) above sea level (at $-20°C$). The lower layers of the atmosphere are significantly compressed by the weight of the air above them. Mountain climbers note this difference, remarking that the air is "thinner" at higher altitudes.

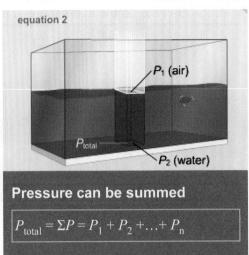

equation 2

Pressure can be summed

$$P_{total} = \Sigma P = P_1 + P_2 + ... + P_n$$

Total pressure = sum of pressures

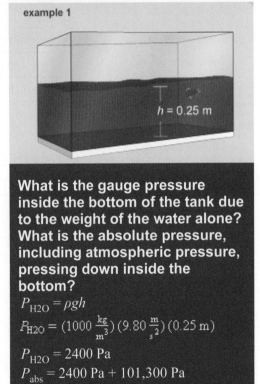

example 1

What is the gauge pressure inside the bottom of the tank due to the weight of the water alone? What is the absolute pressure, including atmospheric pressure, pressing down inside the bottom?

$$P_{H2O} = \rho g h$$
$$P_{H2O} = (1000 \tfrac{kg}{m^3})(9.80 \tfrac{m}{s^2})(0.25 \text{ m})$$

$$P_{H2O} = 2400 \text{ Pa}$$
$$P_{abs} = 2400 \text{ Pa} + 101,300 \text{ Pa}$$
$$P_{abs} = 103,700 \text{ Pa}$$

13.5 - Sample problem: pressure at the bottom of a lake

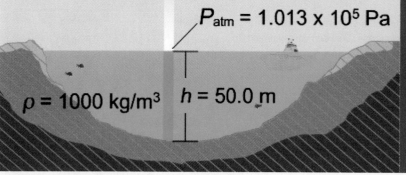

$P_{atm} = 1.013 \times 10^5$ Pa

$\rho = 1000$ kg/m³ $h = 50.0$ m

This lake is at sea level. What is the absolute pressure at the bottom of the lake?

Variables

absolute pressure	P_{abs}
atmospheric pressure	$P_{atm} = 1.013 \times 10^5$ Pa
gauge pressure due to water	P_{H2O}
density of water	$\rho = 1000$ kg/m³
acceleration of gravity	$g = 9.80$ m/s²
height of water column	$h = 50.0$ m

Strategy

1. The atmospheric pressure is given. Find the gauge pressure of the water in the lake.
2. Add the atmospheric and gauge pressures to get the absolute pressure.

Physics principles and equations

The gauge pressure of the water at the bottom of the lake is

$$P_{H2O} = \rho g h$$

The absolute pressure at the bottom of the lake is

$$P_{abs} = P_{H2O} + P_{atm}$$

P_{atm} is known. We find P_{H2O} and add the two quantities together to find the absolute pressure P_{abs}.

Step	Reason
1. $P_{atm} = 1.013 \times 10^5$ Pa	standard value
2. $P_{H2O} = \rho g h$	gauge pressure equation
3. $P_{H2O} = (1000 \, \frac{kg}{m^3})(9.80 \, \frac{m}{s^2})(50.0 \text{ m})$	substitute values
4. $P_{H2O} = 4.90 \times 10^5$ Pa	evaluate
5. $P_{abs} = P_{H2O} + P_{atm}$	absolute pressure
6. $P_{abs} = 5.91 \times 10^5$ Pa $P_{abs} \approx 6$ atm (bars)	substitute equations 1 and 4 into equation 5

13.6 - Physics at work: measuring pressure

Atmospheric pressure is not constant, even at a fixed height like sea level. In Concept 1, you see a simple *barometer*. Barometers measure atmospheric pressure. The terms "barometer" and "barometric pressure" are sometimes heard in weather reports because changes in atmospheric pressure often indicate that a change of weather is on the way.

Dial-type barometer, calibrated in millimeters of mercury and millibars.

The barometer depicted on the right consists of a vertical tube, closed at the top. This tube is partially filled with a liquid, commonly the liquid metal mercury, and is placed in a container that serves as a reservoir. The mercury in the tube stands in a column, with the space at the top of the tube occupied by a near vacuum, which exerts negligible pressure.

Increased air pressure pushing down on the surface of the reservoir causes the column of mercury to rise, until the air pressure and the pressure due to the mercury column reach equilibrium. The pressure exerted by this liquid column, the product of its density, the acceleration of gravity, and its height, equals the external air pressure.

On a typical day at sea level, air pressure causes the mercury to rise to a height of about 760 millimeters, or about 30 inches. (The pressure of a one-millimeter column of mercury is called a *torr*, after the physicist Evangelista Torricelli.) The design of this instrument should give you a sense of how strong atmospheric pressure is: It is able to force a column of mercury, which is denser than lead, to rise more than three-quarters of a meter.

In Concept 2 you see an *open-tube manometer*, a device for measuring the gauge pressure of a gas confined in a spherical vessel. The vessel that contains the gas is connected to a U-shaped tube partially filled with mercury and open to the atmosphere at its far end. This apparatus allows physicists to accurately determine the gauge pressure of the gas.

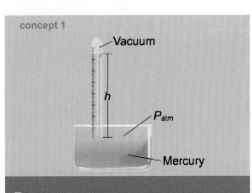

concept 1

Vacuum

h

P_{atm}

Mercury

Barometer
Air pressure equals pressure of mercury
· Height of mercury reflects air pressure

The pressure inside the spherical vessel on the left-hand side is an absolute pressure. It presses down on the surface of the left-hand column of mercury, but the higher column of mercury and the air pressure on the right side push back. When the two columns of mercury are in equilibrium, the absolute pressure of the gas equals the sum of the atmospheric pressure and the pressure exerted by the extra mercury on the right-hand side of the instrument. This equality is shown in Equation 2. In the equation, the product $\rho g h$ represents the pressure exerted by a column of mercury of height h.

The height h of the extra mercury, indicated in the diagram, equals the amount by which the mercury level on the right is higher than the mercury level on the left. It can be used with the density of mercury and the acceleration of gravity to calculate the product $\rho g h$. This product equals the difference between the absolute pressure of the gas in the vessel and atmospheric pressure. In other words, the product $\rho g h$ gives the gauge pressure of the gas, in pascals. When the gauge pressure is expressed in "millimeters of mercury," or torr, then its numeric value equals the numeric value of the height h, measured in millimeters.

Traditional blood pressure gauges (*sphygmomanometers*) are open-tube manometers. The gauge has an inflatable cuff that is wrapped around your upper arm. Like the sphere in the diagram, the cuff can be filled with pressurized air. This restricts the flow of blood to the lower parts of your arm. Air is then released from the cuff until the first flow of blood can be heard with a stethoscope. At this point, the gauge pressure of the blood being pumped by your heart equals the cuff's gauge pressure. This blood pressure, the *systolic pressure*, occurs when the heart generates its maximum pressure.

The sphygmomanometer operator (try saying that quickly!) then listens for the part of the heartbeat cycle when the pressure is the lowest, releasing pressure from the cuff until its pressure is the same as the lowest blood pressure, and the flow of blood can be heard continuously. This lower pressure is the *diastolic pressure*. A young, healthy human has a systolic blood gauge pressure of about 120 millimeters of mercury and a diastolic pressure equal to about 80 millimeters of mercury.

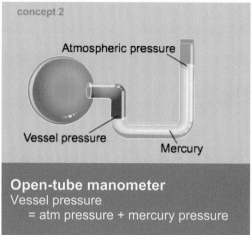

concept 2

Atmospheric pressure

Vessel pressure

Mercury

Open-tube manometer
Vessel pressure
= atm pressure + mercury pressure

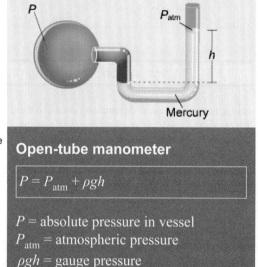

equation 1

P

P_{atm}

h

Mercury

Open-tube manometer

$$P = P_{atm} + \rho g h$$

P = absolute pressure in vessel
P_{atm} = atmospheric pressure
$\rho g h$ = gauge pressure

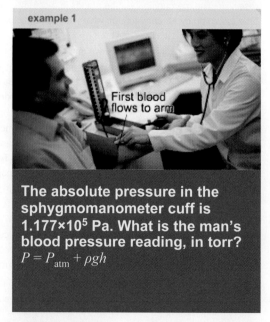

example 1

First blood flows to arm

The absolute pressure in the sphygmomanometer cuff is 1.177×10^5 Pa. What is the man's blood pressure reading, in torr?
$P = P_{atm} + \rho g h$

$$h = \frac{P - P_{\text{atm}}}{\rho g}$$

$$h = \frac{1.177 \times 10^5 \text{ Pa} - 1.013 \times 10^5 \text{ Pa}}{(13{,}600 \text{ kg/m}^3)(9.80 \text{ m/s}^2)}$$

$h = 0.123$ m $= 123$ mm

systolic blood pressure $= 123$ torr

13.7 - Archimedes' principle

Archimedes' principle: An object in a fluid experiences an upward force equal to the weight of the fluid it displaces.

Archimedes (287-212 BCE) explained why objects float. His principle states that *buoyancy*, the upward force caused by the displacement of fluid, equals the weight of the volume of the fluid displaced. For instance, if a boat displaces 300 tons of water, then it experiences an upward buoyant force of 300 tons. If this buoyant force is greater than the weight of the boat, the boat floats.

Archimedes' principle can be used to explain why a small stone sinks, while a large block of Styrofoam® floats, even if the Styrofoam block is much heavier than the stone. Stone is denser than water, so the weight of the water it displaces is less than its own weight. This means that the stone's weight, directed down, is greater than the upward buoyant force on it. The net force on an underwater stone is downward.

In contrast, Styrofoam is less dense than water. A Styrofoam block displaces a weight of water equal to its own weight when it is only partially submerged. It is in a state of equilibrium since the buoyant force up equals the weight down. In short, it floats.

Archimedes' principle applies at any water depth. The buoyancy of a submerged submarine is the same whether it is 50 meters or 300 meters below the water's surface, since the density (and weight) of the displaced water changes only slightly with depth. If this is so, how can a submarine dive or surface? The submarine changes its weight: It either adds weight by allowing water into its ballast tanks or reduces its weight by blowing the water out with compressed air.

Fish approach the issue in a slightly different way. They change their volume by inflating or deflating an organ called a swim bladder, filled with gas released from the blood of the fish. When they increase their volume, they rise because they displace more water and experience increased upward buoyancy.

Archimedes' principle can also be used to analyze the buoyancy of human beings. People with a high percentage of body fat float more easily than do their slimmer counterparts. This is because fat is less dense than water, while muscle is denser than water. In one test for lean body mass, a person is weighed out of water, and then weighed again while submerged. The difference in the two weights equals the buoyant force, which allows a calculation of the volume of the displaced water. The average density of the person, based on his volume and his dry weight, can be used to determine what percentage of his body is fat.

Triathletes, whose body fat is likely to be very low, demonstrate their appreciation of the principles of buoyancy by preferring to wear wetsuits during swimming events. Lean people tend to sink, and a wetsuit helps an athlete float since it is less dense than water, reducing the energy

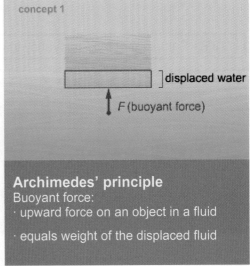

concept 1

displaced water

F (buoyant force)

Archimedes' principle
Buoyant force:
· upward force on an object in a fluid

· equals weight of the displaced fluid

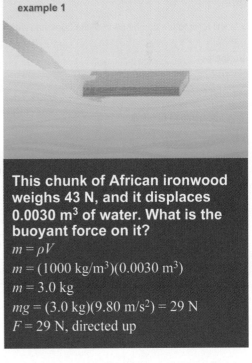

example 1

This chunk of African ironwood weighs 43 N, and it displaces 0.0030 m³ of water. What is the buoyant force on it?

$m = \rho V$

$m = (1000 \text{ kg/m}^3)(0.0030 \text{ m}^3)$

$m = 3.0$ kg

$mg = (3.0 \text{ kg})(9.80 \text{ m/s}^2) = 29$ N

$F = 29$ N, directed up

spent on staying up and allowing more to be spent on moving forward. Because of this effect, triathlons ban wetsuits in warm water events where they are not strictly necessary for survival. You wouldn't want to give those triathletes any breaks before they bike 180 kilometers and then run over 40 kilometers!

Objects fabricated from materials denser than water can float. A steel boat floats since its hull encloses air, which means the average density of the volume enclosed by the boat is less than that of water. Observe what happens when someone steps into a small boat: It sinks slightly as more water is displaced to balance the person's weight. If the boat is overloaded with cargo, or if water enters the hull, its average density will surpass that of water and the boat will sink (fast-forward to the end of the film *A Perfect Storm* for a graphic example of the latter problem).

Often, the concept of buoyancy is applied to water, but it also applies to other fluids, such as the atmosphere. Blimps and hot air balloons use buoyancy to float in the air. A blimp contains helium, a gas lighter than air. The weight of the air it displaces is greater than the weight of the blimp, so it floats upward until it reaches a region of the atmosphere where the air is less dense and the weight of the blimp equals the weight of the displaced air.

13.8 - Sample problem: buoyancy in water

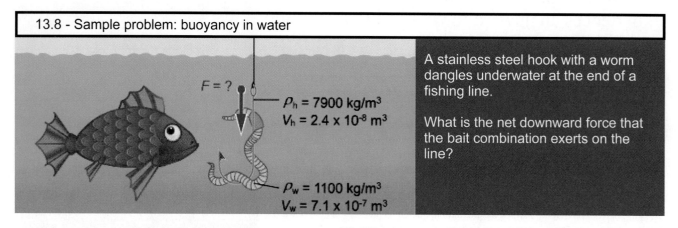

A stainless steel hook with a worm dangles underwater at the end of a fishing line.

$\rho_h = 7900 \text{ kg/m}^3$
$V_h = 2.4 \times 10^{-8} \text{ m}^3$

What is the net downward force that the bait combination exerts on the line?

$\rho_w = 1100 \text{ kg/m}^3$
$V_w = 7.1 \times 10^{-7} \text{ m}^3$

A stainless steel fishing hook with a worm is in the water at the end of a line, dangled with the intent of attracting the wily fish. For the density of the hook we use the density of stainless steel, 7900 kg/m³.

We will refer to the combination of the hook and worm as "the bait."

Variables

net force of bait on line	F
acceleration of gravity	$g = 9.80 \text{ m/s}^2$
buoyant force on bait combination	F_b

	hook	worm	displaced water
density	$\rho_h = 7900 \text{ kg/m}^3$	$\rho_w = 1100 \text{ kg/m}^3$	$\rho_{H2O} = 1000 \text{ kg/m}^3$
volume	$V_h = 2.4 \times 10^{-8} \text{ m}^3$	$V_w = 7.1 \times 10^{-7} \text{ m}^3$	V_{H2O}
mass	m_h	m_w	m_{H2O}
weight	$m_h g$	$m_w g$	$m_{H2O}\, g$

Strategy

1. Calculate the weight of the hook, a downward force.

2. Calculate the weight of the worm, another downward force.

3. From the combined volumes of the hook and worm, compute the volume and the weight of the displaced water. Use this value for the

Copyright 2000-2007 Kinetic Books Co. Chapter 13

upward buoyant force F_b on the bait combination.

4. With all the contributing downward and upward forces known, calculate the net force exerted by the bait on the line.

Physics principles and equations

Use the definitions of density and weight,

$$\rho = \frac{m}{V}, \quad \text{weight} = mg$$

Archimedes' principle states that the upward buoyant force on the bait equals the weight of the water it displaces.

Step-by-step solution

Calculate the weight of the hook.

Step	Reason
1. $m_h = \rho_h V_h$	definition of density
2. $m_h g = \rho_h V_h g$	multiply by g
3. $m_h g = (7900 \, \frac{kg}{m^3})(2.4 \times 10^{-8} m^3)(9.80 \, \frac{m}{s^2})$ $m_h g = 1.9 \times 10^{-3} \, N$	evaluate

Calculate the weight of the worm.

Step	Reason
4. $m_w g = \rho_w V_w g$	equation 2, for the worm
5. $m_w g = (1100 \, \frac{kg}{m^3})(7.1 \times 10^{-7} m^3)(9.80 \, \frac{m}{s^2})$ $m_w g = 7.7 \times 10^{-3} \, N$	evaluate

Calculate the weight of the displaced water, and from that the buoyancy of the bait combination.

Step	Reason
6. $V_{H2O} = V_h + V_w$	add volumes
7. $m_{H2O} g = \rho_{H2O}(V_h + V_w)g$	substitute equation 6 into equation 2
8. $m_{H2O} g = (1000 \, \frac{kg}{m^3})(7.3 \times 10^{-7} m^3)(9.80 \, \frac{m}{s^2})$ $m_{H2O} g = 7.2 \times 10^{-3} \, N$	evaluate
9. $F_b = 7.2 \times 10^{-3} \, N$	Archimedes' principle

Finally, the net force is the sum of the buoyancy upward and the weight of the bait downward.

Step	Reason
10. $F = F_b + (-m_h g) + (-m_w g)$	net force
11. $F = (7.2 \times 10^{-3} - 1.9 \times 10^{-3} - 7.7 \times 10^{-3})$ N $F = -2.4 \times 10^{-3}$ N	evaluate

The negative value of the net force indicates that the bait combination is pulling down on the line.

The quantities involved in this problem are rather small: The weight of the bait, its buoyancy and the net downward force all have magnitudes in the thousandths of newtons. Bait like this will sink, but not very quickly, due to the resistance of water to its motion. For this reason, fishermen often use lead weights called "sinkers" to cause the bait to sink faster to a depth where fish are feeding.

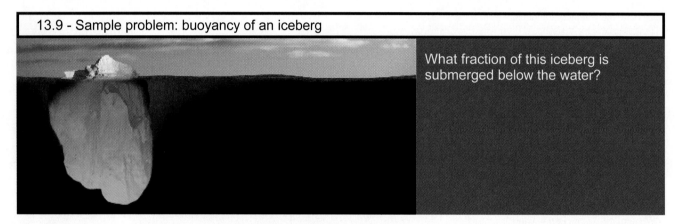

13.9 - Sample problem: buoyancy of an iceberg

What fraction of this iceberg is submerged below the water?

You may have heard the expression "it's just the tip of the iceberg"; icebergs are infamous for having nine-tenths of their volume submerged below the surface of the sea. The composite photograph above shows just how dangerous icebergs can be for navigation. The submerged portion not only extends downward a great distance, it may also extend sideways to an extent that is not evident from above. A ship might easily strike the submerged portion without passing especially close to the visible ice.

Use the values stated below for the densities of ice and of seawater at $-1.8°C$, which is the freezing point of seawater in the arctic. The iceberg is in static equilibrium, moving neither up nor down.

Variables

The upward buoyant force on the iceberg is F_b.

	iceberg	displaced water
density	$\rho_{ice} = 917$ kg/m^3	$\rho_{H2O} = 1030$ kg/m^3
volume	V_{ice}	V_{H2O}
mass	m_{ice}	m_{H2O}

Strategy

1. Use equilibrium to state that the buoyant force acting on the iceberg equals its weight. Archimedes' principle allows you to express the buoyant force in terms of the weight of the displaced water. Replace the equilibrium equation with one stating that the mass of the iceberg equals the mass of the displaced water.

2. Use the definition of density to replace the masses in the previous equation by products of density and volume. Solve for the ratio V_{H2O}/V_{ice}, and evaluate it.

Physics principles and equations

Newton's second law.

$$\Sigma F = ma$$

Archimedes' principle states that the buoyant force on an object in a fluid equals the weight of the fluid it displaces.

The definition of density is

$$\rho = \frac{m}{V}$$

Step-by-step solution

We begin by stating the condition for static equilibrium, and then we apply Archimedes' principle.

Step	Reason
1. $F_b + (-m_{ice}g) = 0$ $F_b = m_{ice}g$	equilibrium
2. $m_{H2O}\, g = m_{ice}\, g$	Archimedes
3. $m_{H2O} = m_{ice}$	simplify

Now we replace the masses in the previous equation by products of densities and volumes, solve for a ratio of volumes, and evaluate.

Step	Reason
4. $\rho_{H2O} V_{H2O} = \rho_{ice} V_{ice}$	definition of density
5. $\dfrac{V_{H2O}}{V_{ice}} = \dfrac{\rho_{ice}}{\rho_{H2O}}$	rearrange
6. $\dfrac{V_{H2O}}{V_{ice}} = \dfrac{917 \text{ kg/m}^3}{1030 \text{ kg/m}^3} = 89.0\%$	evaluate

Since the volume V_{H2O} of the displaced water equals the volume of the submerged portion of the iceberg, we have shown that 89.0% of the iceberg is submerged.

For most substances, the solid phase is denser than the liquid phase, meaning a solid sinks when immersed in a liquid composed of the same substance. Water is very unusual in this respect: the solid phase (ice) floats in liquid water. This proves crucial to life on Earth for a variety of reasons.

13.10 - Interactive problem: Eureka!

In this simulation you play the role of the ancient Greek mathematician and physicist Archimedes. As the story goes, in olden Syracuse the tyrant Hieron suspected that a wily goldsmith had adulterated one of his kingly crowns during manufacture by adding some copper and zinc to the precious gold. His Royal Highness asked Archimedes to discover whether this was indeed the case.

Archimedes pondered the problem for days. Then, one day, in the public bath, he observed how the water level in the pool rose as he eased himself in for a good soak, and suddenly realized that the answer was right in front of his eyes. Ecstatic, he supposedly leapt from the bath and ran dripping through the streets of the city crying "*Eureka!*" (I have found it!) The adulterated crown was quickly identified, and the goldsmith roundly punished.

Your task is to determine the nature of Archimedes' insight and apply it in the simulation to the right. You have two crowns and a bar of pure gold. You have already observed their masses using a balance scale. You can measure the volume of a crown or bar in the simulation by dragging it to the bath and noting how much water it displaces. You see the tube that measures the displaced liquid in the illustration at the right. Decide which crown has been altered and drag it to the king's palace. The appropriate consequences will be enacted.

interactive 1

Archimedes' bath
Find the adulterated crown

13.11 - Pascal's principle

Pascal's principle: Pressure in a confined fluid is transmitted unchanged to all parts of the fluid and to the containing walls.

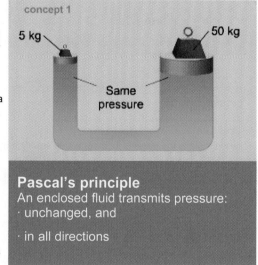

concept 1

5 kg   50 kg

Same
pressure

Pascal's principle
An enclosed fluid transmits pressure:
· unchanged, and
· in all directions

If you jump down on one side of a waterbed, a person sitting on the other side will get a jolt up. This illustrates Pascal's principle: A variation in pressure in the enclosed fluid is being transmitted unchanged throughout the fluid.

In the illustration to the right, you see a five-kilogram mass "balancing" a 50-kilogram mass. How does something that seems so counterintuitive – a small mass balancing a large mass – occur?

First, Pascal's principle asserts that the **pressure** exerted by the weight of the first mass on the fluid is transmitted to the second mass unchanged. The two masses "balance" because the surface area of the fluid under the 50-kilogram mass is 10 times larger than the surface area under the five-kilogram mass. The pressure is the same under both masses, but since the surface area is 10 times larger under the more massive object, the upward force, the pressure times the area, is 10 times greater than it is under the less massive object, so the system is in equilibrium. Although we focus on the pressures supporting the weights, according to Pascal's principle the pressure acts in all directions at every point in the fluid, so it presses on the walls of the hydraulic system as well.

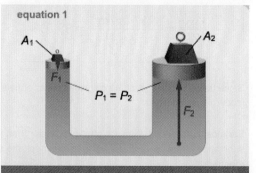

equation 1

A_1 A_2

F_1

$P_1 = P_2$

F_2

In some ways, the equilibrium in such a system is similar to a small mass located at the end of a long lever arm balancing a large mass located close to the lever's pivot point. In fact, this similarity has caused systems like those shown to the right to be called *hydraulic levers.* You may be familiar with them from the "racks" in car repair shops: they are the gleaming metal pistons that lift cars.

Illustrations of hydraulic levers are shown to the right. In each case the pressure on both pistons must be the same in order to conform to Pascal's principle, but the **force** will depend on the areas of the pistons. In the example problem you are asked to calculate the downward force needed on the left piston to lift the small automobile on the right. It turns out that this force is about 20 newtons (only 4½ pounds)!

Do you get "something for nothing" when you raise a heavy car with such a small force?

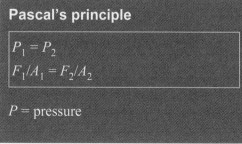

Pascal's principle

$$P_1 = P_2$$
$$F_1/A_1 = F_2/A_2$$

P = pressure

Copyright 2000-2007 Kinetic Books Co. Chapter 13

No, the amount of work you do equals the work the piston on the right does on the car. You apply less force, but through a greater displacement. If you press your piston down a meter in the scenario shown in Example 1, the car will rise only about 1.6 millimeters, as you can verify by considering the incompressible volume of water displaced on each side.

F = force

A = surface area

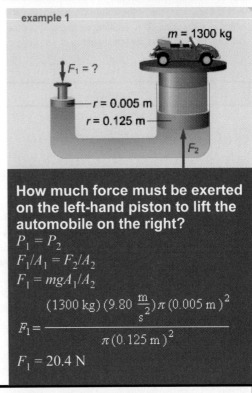

example 1

$m = 1300$ kg

$F_1 = ?$

$r = 0.005$ m

$r = 0.125$ m

F_2

How much force must be exerted on the left-hand piston to lift the automobile on the right?

$P_1 = P_2$

$F_1/A_1 = F_2/A_2$

$F_1 = mgA_1/A_2$

$$F_1 = \frac{(1300 \text{ kg})(9.80 \frac{\text{m}}{\text{s}^2})\pi(0.005 \text{ m})^2}{\pi(0.125 \text{ m})^2}$$

$F_1 = 20.4$ N

13.12 - Streamline flow

Streamline flow: A fluid flow in which the fluid's velocity remains constant at any particular point.

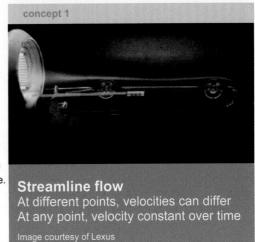

concept 1

Streamline flow
At different points, velocities can differ
At any point, velocity constant over time

Image courtesy of Lexus

Steady, or streamline, flow is one of the characteristics of ideal fluid flow. Streamline flow is particularly easy to demonstrate with the flow of a gas, although since gasses are compressible they are not ideal fluids.

At the right, you see one *streamline* traced by smoke in the diagram, flowing around an automobile. As long as the car does not rotate, the streamline stays the same over time. Any particle of the fluid will follow some streamline, visible or not, as it flows past the car. As the car is rotated in the video, you get a chance to see the paths followed by different streamlines of air flowing around various parts of its body.

Engineers use wind tunnels to photograph streamlines. Powerful fans blow air past an object like a car or an airplane, and dyes or smoke are injected into the airflow at several points and carried downstream so that the streamlines are made visible. Engineers analyze the streamlines to investigate the air resistance of a particular car design, or the amount of lift (upward force) generated by an airplane wing.

The velocity of streamline fluid flow can vary from point to point. Air moves past an airplane wing or auto body with different velocities at different points (for example, it moves faster over the tops of these objects than beneath them). The tangent to a streamline at a point coincides with the direction of the velocity vectors of the fluid particles passing by the point.

In streamline flow, the fluid has a constant velocity at all times **at a given point**. The velocity of any given air particle in the visible streamline on the right may change as the flow carries it downstream past the stationary automobile. In particular, a change in the direction of the streamline reflects a change in velocity. However, all the particles in the streamline pass the same point with the same velocity.

How can you conclude that the velocity remains constant at each point? Consider what would happen if the speed of the fluid flow at a point were to vary over time. If the speed increased, the affected particles would collide with particles ahead of them; if it decreased, particles from behind would collide. The resulting collisions would cause an erratic flow, changing the streamline, as would changes in the direction of the particles' motions. The constancy of the streamlines over time indicates that the velocity at each point does not change.

13.13 - Fluid continuity

Fluid equation of continuity: The volume flow rate of an ideal fluid flowing through a closed system is the same at every point.

Fluid continuity
Fluid flows past each point at same rate

Turn on a hose and watch the water flow out, and then cover half the hose end with your thumb. The water flows faster through the narrower opening. You have just demonstrated the fluid equation of continuity: How much volume flows per unit time – the volume rate of flow – stays constant in a closed system. The increased speed of the flow at the opening balances the decreased cross sectional area there. Of course after the water leaves the hose with its new speed, it is no longer in the closed system, and you cannot apply the equation of continuity to the resulting spray of droplets. They spread out without slowing down.

The fluid equation of continuity can be observed in rivers, whose courses approximate closed systems. River water flows more quickly through narrow or shallow channels, called rapids, and more slowly where riverbeds are wider and deeper. This relationship is alluded to by the proverb, "Still waters run deep."

The constancy of fluid flow rate is summarized in the continuity equation that appears as the first line in Equation 1. In this equation, stated for two arbitrary points P_1 and P_2, the rate of flow is measured as the *mass flow rate*. The mass flow rate equals the product of the speed of the fluid, its density, and the cross sectional area it flows through. It is measured in kilograms per second (kg/s). In a closed system (no leaks, no inflows) the mass flow rate is the same past all points.

Since we assume that an ideal fluid is incompressible, having a density that is constant, we can cancel the density factor from both sides of the first continuity equation. This enables us to say that the speed of the fluid times its cross sectional area is everywhere the same. This is stated by the second equation, which expresses continuity in terms of the *volume flow rate*, represented by R. The volume flow rate is measured in cubic meters per second (m³/s). If the cross sectional area decreases (as when the pipe illustrated in Equation 1 narrows), the speed of the fluid flow increases, and R remains the same.

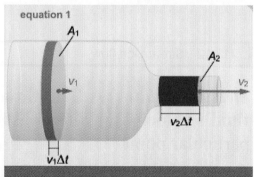

Mass and volume flow rates constant

$$v_1 \rho_1 A_1 = v_2 \rho_2 A_2$$
$$v_1 A_1 = v_2 A_2 = R$$

v = speed of fluid
ρ = density of fluid
A = cross-sectional area of flow
Fluid is incompressible
R = volume flow rate

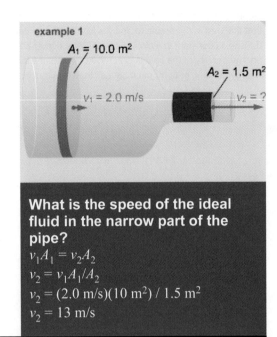

$A_1 = 10.0 \text{ m}^2$

$A_2 = 1.5 \text{ m}^2$

$v_1 = 2.0$ m/s

$v_2 = ?$

What is the speed of the ideal fluid in the narrow part of the pipe?

$$v_1 A_1 = v_2 A_2$$
$$v_2 = v_1 A_1 / A_2$$
$$v_2 = (2.0 \text{ m/s})(10 \text{ m}^2) / 1.5 \text{ m}^2$$
$$v_2 = 13 \text{ m/s}$$

13.14 - Bernoulli's equation

Bernoulli's equation applies to ideal fluids. It was developed by the Swiss mathematician and physicist Daniel Bernoulli (1700-1782). The equation is used to analyze fluid flow at different points in a closed system. It states that the sum of the pressure, the KE per unit volume, and the PE per unit volume has a constant value. Concept 1 shows an idealized apparatus for determining these three values at various points in such a system.

A simplified form of Bernoulli's equation is shown in Equation 1. It applies to horizontal flow, in which the PE of the fluid is everywhere the same. In such a system, the sum of just the pressure and the kinetic energy per unit volume is constant. Since the expression for the "KE" uses the density ρ of the fluid in place of mass, it describes energy per unit volume: the *kinetic energy density*.

To illustrate the simplified equation, we use the horizontal-flow configuration shown in the diagram of Equation 1. The pressure of the fluid is measured where it passes the gauges. If the speed of the fluid is known at the first gauge, its speed at the second gauge can be calculated using Bernoulli's equation.

When the sum of the pressure and kinetic energy density equals a constant in a system, as in the case of horizontal flow, it is often useful to set the sum of these values at one point equal to the sum of the values at another point. This is stated for points P_1 and P_2 in Equation 2. An implication of the simplified form of Bernoulli's equation is the *Bernoulli effect*: When a fluid flows faster, its pressure decreases.

Airplane wings, like the one shown in Equation 2, take advantage of the Bernoulli effect. Air travels faster over the upper surface of the wing than the lower, because it must traverse a longer path in the same amount of time. A faster fluid is a lower pressure fluid; the result is that there is more pressure below the wing than above. This causes a net force up, which is called *lift*. (The Bernoulli effect is only one way to explain how wings work. Lift can also be explained using Newton's third law in conjunction with a fluid phenomenon called the *Coanda effect*. The topic of wing lift engenders much discussion.)

In Equation 3 you see a general form of Bernoulli's equation, which also accounts for

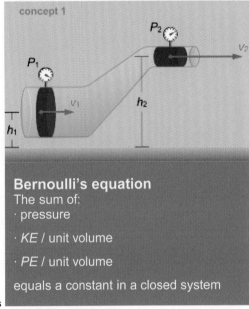

concept 1

P_2

v_2

P_1

v_1

h_2

h_1

Bernoulli's equation
The sum of:
· pressure

· KE / unit volume

· PE / unit volume

equals a constant in a closed system

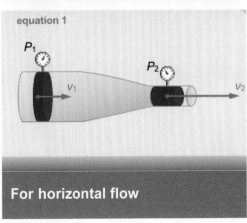

equation 1

P_1

P_2

v_1

v_2

For horizontal flow

differences in height and the resulting differences in potential energy density. It states that the sum of the pressure and the kinetic energy density, plus the potential energy density, is constant in a closed system. At a higher point in such a system, the potential energy density of the fluid is greater. At that point either the pressure or the kinetic energy density, or both, must be less than they are at lower points.

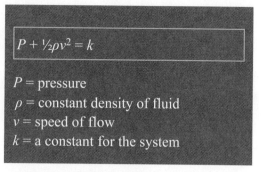

$$P + \tfrac{1}{2}\rho v^2 = k$$

P = pressure
ρ = constant density of fluid
v = speed of flow
k = a constant for the system

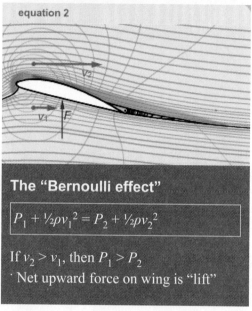

equation 2

The "Bernoulli effect"

$$P_1 + \tfrac{1}{2}\rho v_1{}^2 = P_2 + \tfrac{1}{2}\rho v_2{}^2$$

If $v_2 > v_1$, then $P_1 > P_2$
∴ Net upward force on wing is "lift"

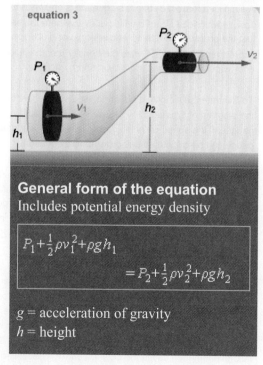

equation 3

General form of the equation
Includes potential energy density

$$P_1 + \tfrac{1}{2}\rho v_1^2 + \rho g h_1$$
$$= P_2 + \tfrac{1}{2}\rho v_2^2 + \rho g h_2$$

g = acceleration of gravity
h = height

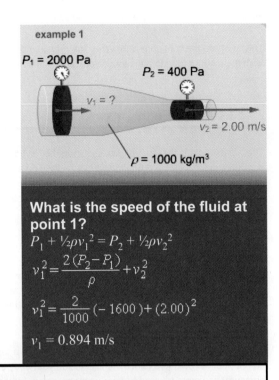

example 1

$P_1 = 2000$ Pa

$P_2 = 400$ Pa

$v_1 = ?$

$v_2 = 2.00$ m/s

$\rho = 1000$ kg/m³

What is the speed of the fluid at point 1?

$$P_1 + \tfrac{1}{2}\rho v_1^2 = P_2 + \tfrac{1}{2}\rho v_2^2$$

$$v_1^2 = \frac{2\,(P_2 - P_1)}{\rho} + v_2^2$$

$$v_1^2 = \frac{2}{1000}\,(-1600) + (2.00)^2$$

$$v_1 = 0.894 \text{ m/s}$$

13.15 - Physics at work: Bernoulli effect and plumbing

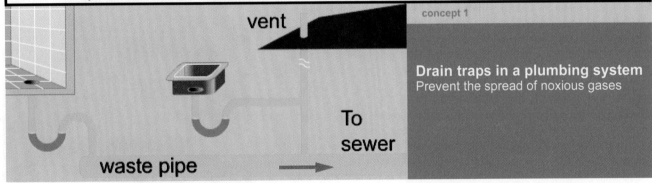

vent

To sewer

waste pipe

Plumbing system with vented sink trap.

concept 1

Drain traps in a plumbing system
Prevent the spread of noxious gases

The Bernoulli effect can help you understand not only the lofty topic of how airplanes fly, but also the more mundane topic of venting in household plumbing systems.

The illustration above shows a shower, a sink, their wastewater pipe, and a "vent" pipe. Water can flow down the shower drain, through a P-shaped "water trap," and from there to a wastewater pipe that connects to a sewer line. The water trap retains a seal of water that prevents noxious sewer gas from flowing up the waste pipe into the house. The sink in the illustration is likewise connected through a protective P-trap to the waste pipe.

In the illustration, the sink drain is "vented" by an air pipe that extends through the roof of the house. Because it is called a vent pipe, you might think it allows air to leave, but it actually allows air in. Several such vents can be seen on the roofs of most houses. The vents work in conjunction with the water traps that protect the home. What purpose does a vent serve?

concept 2

Traps are vented
To counter Bernoulli effect in wastewater pipes

Waste pipes are not pressurized like water supply pipes, and they are always at least slightly inclined so that they ordinarily stand empty. Imagine that someone turns on the shower, causing a stream of water to flow through the waste pipe. As the flow increases, the pressure decreases, in accordance with the Bernoulli effect. If the pressure in the waste pipe were to decrease enough, it could "suck" the water out of the sink's P-trap, thwarting its protective function.

This is where the vent comes in: When the pressure decreases at the bottom of the sink's waste connection due to the shower flow, air flows in from the exterior (due to atmospheric pressure), restoring the pressure in the connection. The water remains in place in the trap.

13.16 - The Earth's atmosphere

The *atmosphere* is the layer of gas, including the oxygen we need in order to survive, surrounding the Earth and bound to it by gravity. The atmosphere receives a great deal of press these days due to environmental concerns such as global warming and ozone holes. Understanding the nature and dynamics of the atmosphere is proving increasingly important to human life.

In this section we give a brief overview of three topics relating to the Earth's atmosphere. The first is the magnitude of atmospheric pressure, and how its existence was first demonstrated. Next, we discuss briefly why there is no hydrogen in the Earth's atmosphere (unlike the atmosphere of Jupiter). Finally, we provide a general sense of the range of pressures, densities and temperatures of the Earth's atmosphere at different altitudes.

The very existence of atmospheric pressure was once a topic of debate. After all, you do not "feel" air pressure (since the fluid inside your body exerts an equal and opposite pressure) any more than a fish feels water pressure. (At least no fish has ever told us that it feels this pressure.) In a famous demonstration that showed the existence of atmospheric pressure, the German scientist Otto von Guericke created a near vacuum between two copper hemispheres, as shown in Concept 1. Von Guericke, also the mayor of the town of Magdeburg, where he conducted the demonstration in 1654, challenged teams of horses to pull the hemispheres apart. The horses failed: The force of the air pressure was too great for them to overcome.

This clever demonstration of air pressure may seem incredible until you consider that the air pressure on the Earth's surface is about 101 kilopascals (14.7 pounds per square inch). To get an approximate value for the pressure holding the hemispheres together, we can simplify matters and assume they acted like halves of a cube, one meter on a side. We will further assume that a perfect vacuum was created inside them, so the pressure inside was zero. Each team of horses would then have had to overcome 101,000 N of force, more than 10 tons. Whoa, Nellie!

Von Guericke demonstrated the surprisingly large magnitude of atmospheric pressure. He might have been startled to know how fast the particles that make up the atmosphere move. Sunlight energizes the molecules in the atmosphere, keeping it in a gaseous state, and causes them to fly energetically about, reaching speeds of up to 1600 km/h. The gravitational force of the Earth keeps most of these molecules from flying off into space, but some molecules – especially the lightest ones – do reach escape velocity and leave the planet's atmosphere. This is why there is little or no hydrogen, or any other light gas, in the Earth's atmosphere. On the average, a lighter molecule moves faster than a heavier molecule of the same energy, meaning the lightest molecules most easily reach the 11.2 km/s required to escape the Earth's gravitational pull. The escape velocity is greater on Jupiter, allowing that planet to keep hydrogen in its atmosphere.

The Earth's atmosphere is a gas, which makes it a fluid. However, since it is a gas, its density changes with its height above the planet's surface. The weight of the atmosphere above "compacts" the atoms and molecules below, increasing their concentration (density). We live in an ocean of air, just as fish dwell in an ocean of water. An important difference between the two is that water is relatively incompressible and the ocean has essentially the same density, although different temperatures and pressures, at any depth.

The diagram in Concept 2 shows the Earth's atmosphere schematically. The pressure and density of the atmosphere lessen, as does its temperature, with height. The density of air at sea level and $15°C$ equals 1.23 kg/m³; at the higher and chillier altitude of 30,000 meters, where the temperature is $−63°C$, the density equals 0.092 kg/m³. At the summit of Mount Everest, a human can breathe barely enough oxygen to stay alive.

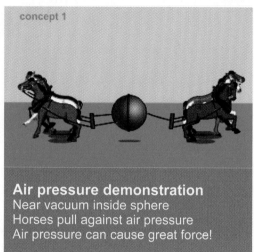

concept 1

Air pressure demonstration
Near vacuum inside sphere
Horses pull against air pressure
Air pressure can cause great force!

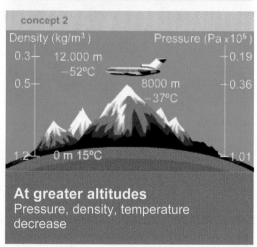

concept 2

Density (kg/m³)   Pressure (Pa x10⁵)
0.3 — 12,000 m   — 0.19
       −52°C
0.5 —   8000 m   — 0.36
                         −37°C
1.2   0 m 15°C   1.01

At greater altitudes
Pressure, density, temperature decrease

Conversely, in deep diamond mines, air pressure and density both increase, and the temperature rises rapidly with depth. In the deepest mines, it would be impossible for miners to work without the introduction of refrigerated air.

13.17 - Surface tension

Surface tension: A cohesive effect at the surface of a liquid due to the forces between the liquid's atoms or molecules.

Dewdrops on rose petals form tiny spheres.

Above, you see a dewy rose. The drops of water do not spread and flow to cover the petals on which they rest. Instead they contract into tiny spheroids. They do this because the surface tension of water causes each drop to try to minimize its own surface area. The bristles of a wet paintbrush contract into a sleek shape for the same reason. The surface tension of the water on the bristles causes them to pull in. You see this in Concept 1.

Surface tension also enables an insect called a water strider to walk on water. The creature's weight, transmitted to the water's surface through its feet, causes tiny depressions, but the feet do not break through. The surface tension of the deformed liquid surface provides an elastic-like restoring force that balances the insect's weight. A video of this interesting phenomenon is shown in Concept 2.

What causes surface tension? In some liquids like water, the molecules that make up the liquid attract each other. These molecules are dipoles; they have regions of positive and negative electrostatic charge. The positive pole of each molecule is attracted to the negative poles of neighboring molecules, and vice versa.

Molecules in the interior of the liquid experience equal attractions in all directions, and so they experience no net intermolecular force. Molecules at the surface of the liquid, however, are pulled on only by the molecules below, and by their neighbors in the surface, so there is a net force pulling them into the interior of the liquid. Because of this, the surface of the liquid tends to contract and consequently to minimize its own area. You see the intermolecular forces illustrated in Concept 1.

In the case of liquid dewdrops, the minimum surface area is roughly spherical. In the case of the water strider, the elastic-like upward force of surface tension on its feet results from the water's tendency to flatten, and so minimize the area, of its surface.

Water has a strong surface tension, but that tension can be reduced. For example, when you heat water, you reduce its surface tension because the faster moving molecules do not attract each other as much as they would at cooler temperatures. Diminished surface tension allows other substances that might be in the water – say, butter – to rise to the surface. Cooks know this (at least implicitly), and they serve soups hot because they will be more flavorful. Adding soap to water also reduces its surface tension – and it can cause a water strider to sink!

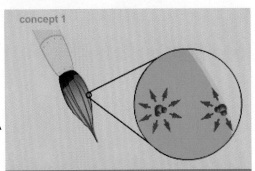

Surface tension
Contraction of surface of liquid
Due to mutual attraction of molecules

Water strider
Surface tension lets insect walk on water
Restoring force balances weight

Pressure increases with depth in a fluid. Yes, it does. The farther below the surface of a fluid an object is, the more fluid above it and the greater the pressure on it.

Buoyant force increases with an object's depth in water. Only if more of the object is getting submerged, in which case the buoyant force does increase. But a soda can five meters below the surface, and one 500 meters below the surface, both experience the same buoyant force. This force is equal in magnitude to the weight of the displaced water.

Two surfaces have the same pressure on them, so the pressure must exert the same force on each. No, pressure is force divided by area, so if one surface has a greater area, it experiences a greater force.

Pressure acts in every direction. Yes, this is stated by Pascal's principle. For instance, water pressure pushes both down on the top and up on the bottom of a scuba diver exploring under the sea.

Fluids are substances, liquids and gases, that can flow and conform to the shape of the container that holds them.

A material's density is the amount of mass it contains, per unit volume. Density is represented by the Greek letter ρ and has units of kg/m^3. Unless otherwise stated, substances are assumed to be of uniform density, which means they have the same density at all points.

Pressure is the amount of force on a surface per unit area. The unit of pressure is the pascal (Pa), which is equal to 1 N/m^2.

Fluids can exert forces, and therefore pressure, just as solid objects can. For an object immersed in a liquid, the pressure is the product of the liquid's density, the acceleration of gravity g, and the object's depth. Gauge pressure is the pressure due solely to the liquid, while absolute pressure is the pressure of the liquid plus atmospheric pressure.

Buoyancy is the upward force that results when an object is placed in a fluid, the force that causes a ship to float. Archimedes' principle states that the magnitude of the buoyant force is equal to the weight of the fluid displaced by the object.

Pascal's principle applies to confined fluids. It states that an enclosed fluid will transmit pressure unchanged in all directions.

To simplify the study of fluid flow, we often assume an ideal fluid flow. This means that the flow is streamline flow − it has a constant velocity at every fixed point − and that it is irrotational. The fluid is also assumed to be incompressible and nonviscous.

One property of ideal fluid flow is stated by the fluid equation of continuity. The amount of fluid flowing past every point in a closed system is the same. In other words, the volume flow rate is constant regardless of the size of the area through which the fluid flows.

Another property of ideal fluid flow is described by Bernoulli's equation. The sum of the pressure, kinetic energy density, and potential energy density is constant in a closed system. For horizontal flow, the faster a fluid flows, the lower its pressure. This is called the Bernoulli effect.

Equations

Definition of density

$$\rho = m/V$$

Definition of pressure

$$P = F/A$$

Pressure of a liquid

$$P = \rho g h$$

Pascal's principle

$$P_1 = P_2$$

$$F_1/A_1 = F_2/A_2$$

Fluid equation of continuity

$$v_1 \rho A_1 = v_2 \rho A_2$$

$$v_1 A_1 = v_2 A_2 = R$$

Bernoulli's equation

For horizontal flow: $P + \frac{1}{2} \rho v^2 = k$

$$P_1 + \frac{1}{2} \rho v_1^2 = P_2 + \frac{1}{2} \rho v_2^2$$

General form:

$$P_1 + \frac{1}{2} \rho v_1^2 + \rho g h_1$$
$$= P_2 + \frac{1}{2} \rho v_2^2 + \rho g h_2$$

The atmosphere exerts pressure because it is a fluid. But since it is a gas, air density and pressure decrease noticeably with altitude. Despite often being ignored in day-to-day life, air pressure is actually (and demonstrably) quite large.

Surface tension is an effect seen with certain liquids such as water. Polar molecules on the surface of the liquid are attracted toward the interior by unbalanced intermolecular forces, causing the surface to contract, and consequently to minimize its own area and exhibit some elastic-like properties.

14.0 - Introduction

This chapter will give you a new take on the saying, "What goes around comes around."

An oscillation is a motion that repeats itself. There are a myriad of examples of oscillations: a child playing on a swing, the motion of the Earth in an earthquake, a car bouncing up and down on its shock absorber, the rapid vibration of a tuning fork, the diaphragm of a loudspeaker, a quartz in a digital watch, the amount of electric current flowing in certain electric circuits, etc.!

Motion that repeats itself at regular intervals is called periodic motion. A traditional metronome provides an excellent example of periodic motion: Its periodic nature is used by musicians for timing purposes. Simple harmonic motion (SHM) describes a specific type of periodic motion. SHM provides an essential starting point for analyzing many types of motion you often see, such as the ones mentioned above.

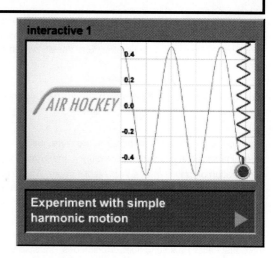

interactive 1

Experiment with simple harmonic motion

SHM has several interesting properties. For instance, the time it takes for an object to return to an endpoint in its motion is independent of how far the object moves. Galileo Galilei is said to have noted this phenomenon during an apparently less-than-engrossing church service. He sat in the church, watching a chandelier swing back and forth during the service, and noticed that the distance the chandelier moved in its oscillations decreased over time as friction and air resistance took their toll. According to the story, he timed its period − how long it took to complete a cycle of motion − using his pulse. To his surprise, the period remained constant even as the chandelier moved less and less. (Although this is a well-known anecdote, apparently the chandelier was actually installed too late for the story to be true.)

To begin your study of simple harmonic motion, you can try the simulation to the right. A mass (an air hockey puck) is attached to a spring, and glides without friction or air resistance over an air hockey table, which you are viewing from overhead. When the puck is pushed or pulled from its rest position and released, it will oscillate in simple harmonic motion.

A pen is attached to the puck, and paper underneath it scrolls to the left over time. This enables the system to produce a graph of displacement versus time. A sample graph is shown in the illustration to the right. A mass attached to a spring is a classic configuration used to explain SHM, and the graph of the mass's displacement over time is an important element in analyzing this form of motion.

Using the controls, you can change the amplitude and period of the puck's motion. The amplitude is the maximum displacement of the puck from its rest position. The period is the time it takes the puck to complete one full cycle of motion.

As you play with the controls, make a few observations. First, does changing the amplitude change the period, or are these quantities independent? Second, does the shape of the curve look familiar to you? To answer this question, think back to the graphs of some of the functions you studied in mathematics courses.

14.1 - Simple harmonic motion

Simple harmonic motion: Motion that follows a repetitive pattern, caused by a restoring force that is proportional to displacement from the equilibrium position.

At the right, you see an overhead view of an air hockey table with a puck attached to a spring. Friction is minimal and we ignore it. The only force we concern ourselves with is the force of the spring on the puck.

Initially, the puck is stationary and the spring is relaxed, neither stretched nor compressed. This means the puck is at its equilibrium (rest) position. Imagine that you reach out and pull the puck toward you. You see this situation in Concept 1 to the right. The spring is pulling the puck back toward its equilibrium position but the puck is stationary since you are holding onto it.

Now, you release the puck. The spring pulls on the puck until it reaches the equilibrium point. At this point, the spring exerts no force on the puck, since the spring is neither stretched nor compressed. As it reaches the equilibrium point, the puck's speed will be at its maximum. You see this in Concept 2.

The puck's momentum means it will continue to move to the left beyond the equilibrium point. This compresses the spring, and the force of the spring now slows the puck until it stops moving. You see this in Concept 3. At this point, the puck's velocity is zero.

Both the displacement of the puck from the equilibrium position and the force on it are now the opposites of their starting values. The puck is as far from the equilibrium point as it was when you released it, but on the opposite side. The spring exerts an equal amount of force on the puck as it initially did, but in the opposite direction. The force will start to accelerate the puck back to the right.

The motion continues. The spring expands, pushing the puck to the equilibrium point. The puck passes this point and continues on, stretching the spring. It will return to the position from which you released it. There, the force of the stretched spring causes the puck to accelerate to the left again. Without any friction or air resistance, the puck would oscillate back and forth forever.

As you may have noted, "equilibrium" means there is no net force present. It does not mean "at rest" since the puck is moving as it passes through the equilibrium position. It is where the spring is neither stretched nor compressed.

The motion of the puck is called simple harmonic motion (SHM). The force of the spring plays an essential role in this motion. Two aspects of this force are required for SHM to occur. First, the spring exerts a *restoring force*. This force always points toward the equilibrium point, opposing any displacement of the puck. This is shown in the diagrams to the right: The force vectors point toward the equilibrium position.

Second, for SHM to occur, the amount of the restoring force must increase linearly with the puck's displacement from the equilibrium point. Why can a spring cause SHM? Springs obey Hooke's law, which states that $F = -kx$. The factor k is the spring constant and it does not vary for a given spring. As x (the displacement from equilibrium) increases in absolute value, so does the force. For instance, as the puck moves from $x = 0.25$ m to $x = 0.50$ m, the amount of force doubles. In sum, since a spring causes a restoring force that increases linearly with displacement, it can cause SHM.

We have extensively used the example of a puck on an air hockey table here, but this is just one configuration that generates SHM. For example, we could also hang the puck from a vertical spring and allow the puck's weight to stretch the spring until an equilibrium position was reached. If the puck were then pulled down from this position, it would oscillate in SHM, since the net force on the puck would be proportional to its displacement from equilibrium but opposite in sign.

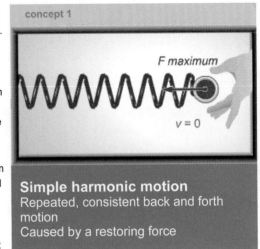

concept 1

Simple harmonic motion
Repeated, consistent back and forth motion
Caused by a restoring force

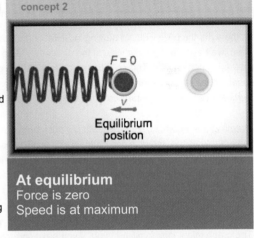

concept 2

At equilibrium
Force is zero
Speed is at maximum

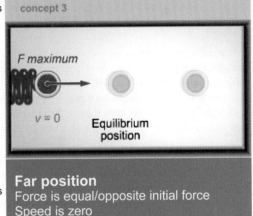

concept 3

Far position
Force is equal/opposite initial force
Speed is zero

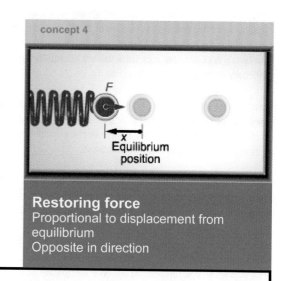

Restoring force
Proportional to displacement from equilibrium
Opposite in direction

14.2 - Simple harmonic motion: graph and equation

At the right, the puck is again moving in SHM, and a graph of its motion is shown. In this case, we have changed our view of the air hockey table so the puck moves vertically instead of horizontally. This puts the graph in the usual orientation. We continue to measure the displacement of the puck with the variable x, which is plotted on the vertical axis. The horizontal axis is the time t.

Unrolling the graph paper underneath the puck as it moves up and down would create the graph you see, the blue line on the white paper. The graph traces out the displacement from equilibrium of the puck over time as it moves from "peaks" where its displacement is most positive, to "troughs" where it is most negative. It starts at a peak, passes through equilibrium, moves to a trough, and so on. After four seconds, it has returned to its initial position for the second time.

The graph might look familiar to you. If you have correctly recognized the graph of a cosine function, congratulations! A cosine function describes the displacement of the puck over time. You see this function in Equation 1.

This graph represents the puck starting at its maximum displacement. When $t = 0$ seconds, the argument of the cosine function is zero radians and the cosine is one, its maximum value. (In describing SHM, the units of the argument of the cosine must be specified as radians.) Because the function used for this graph multiplies the cosine function by an amplitude of three meters, the maximum displacement of the puck (this is always measured from equilibrium) is also three meters.

Equation 2 shows the general form of the equation for SHM. The parameters A, ω, and φ are called the *amplitude*, *angular frequency*, and *phase constant*, respectively. The argument of the cosine function, $\omega t + \varphi$, is called the *phase*. In sections that follow we will explain how these parameters are used to describe SHM.

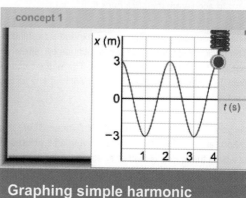

Graphing simple harmonic motion
Cosine (or sine) function describes displacement

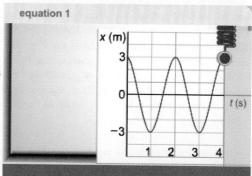

equation 1

Graphing simple harmonic motion
For *this* graph:
$x(t) = 3 \cos{(\pi t)}$ meters

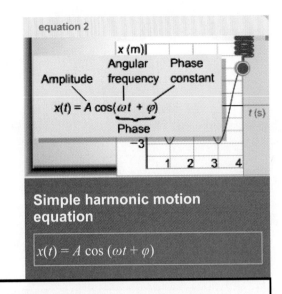

equation 2

Amplitude | Angular frequency | Phase constant

$$x(t) = A \cos(\omega t + \varphi)$$

Phase

Simple harmonic motion equation

$$x(t) = A \cos(\omega t + \varphi)$$

14.3 - Period and frequency

Period: Time to complete one full cycle of motion.

Frequency: Number of cycles of motion per second.

The period specifies how long it takes an object to complete one full cycle of motion. The letter T represents period, which is measured in seconds. A convenient way to calculate the period is to measure the time interval between two adjacent peaks, as we do in Equation 1. In the example shown there, it takes two seconds for the puck to complete one full cycle of motion.

The frequency, represented by f, specifies how many cycles are completed each second. It is the reciprocal of the period. The graph in Equation 2 is the same as in Equation 1. Its frequency is 0.5 cycles per second.

Frequency has its own units. One cycle per second equals one hertz (Hz). This unit is named after the German physicist Heinrich Hertz (1857–1894). You may be familiar with the hertz units from computer terminology: The speed of computer microprocessors used to be specified in megahertz (one million internal clock cycles per second) but microprocessors now operate at over one gigahertz (one billion cycles per second). Radio stations are also known by their frequencies. If you tune into an AM station shown on the dial at 950, the frequency of the radio waves transmitted by the station is 950 kHz.

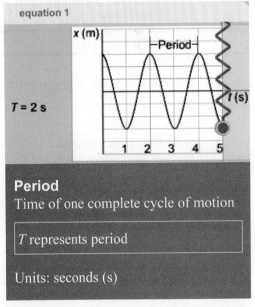

equation 1

$T = 2$ s

Period

Time of one complete cycle of motion

T represents period

Units: seconds (s)

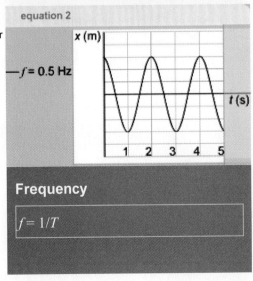

equation 2

$f = 0.5$ Hz

Frequency

$$f = 1/T$$

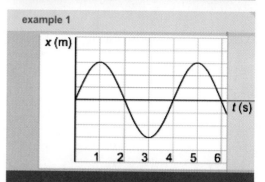

Cycles per second
Units: hertz (Hz)

example 1

What is the period? What is the
frequency?

$T = 4.0$ s

$f = 1/T = 0.25$ Hz

14.4 - Angular frequency

Angular frequency: Frequency measured in radians/second.

In the equation for SHM shown in Equation 1, the parameter ω is the angular frequency and it is the coefficient of time in the equation for SHM. Its units are radians per second.

The angular frequency equals 2π times the frequency. The relationship between frequency and period can be used to restate this equation in terms of the period. Both these equations are shown in Equation 2.

You may have noticed that ω also stands for the angular speed of an object moving in a circle, which is measured in radians per second, as well. If an object makes a complete loop around a circle in one second, its angular speed will be 2π radians per second. Similarly, an object in SHM that completes a cycle of motion in one second has an angular frequency of 2π radians per second. This is indicative of a relationship between circular motion and SHM that can be productively explored elsewhere.

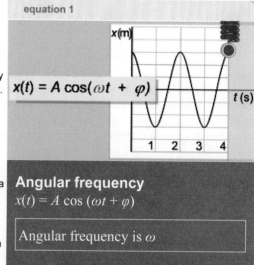

equation 1

$$x(t) = A \cos(\omega t + \varphi)$$

Angular frequency

$x(t) = A \cos(\omega t + \varphi)$

Angular frequency is ω

Units: radians per second (rad/s)

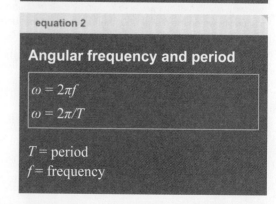

equation 2

Angular frequency and period

$\omega = 2\pi f$

$\omega = 2\pi/T$

$T =$ period
$f =$ frequency

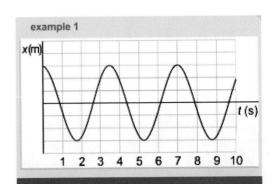

The function $x(t) = A \cos(\omega t)$ describes this graph. What is the angular frequency, ω?

$\omega = 2\pi/T$

$T = 3.5$ seconds

$\omega = 2\pi/3.5$

$\omega = 1.8$ rad/s

14.5 - Amplitude

Amplitude: Maximum displacement from equilibrium.

The amplitude describes the greatest displacement of an object in simple harmonic motion from its equilibrium position.

In Concept 1, you see the now familiar air hockey puck and spring, as well as a graph of its motion. The amplitude is indicated. It is the farthest distance of the puck from the equilibrium point.

The equation for SHM is shown again in Equation 1, with the amplitude term highlighted. The amplitude is the absolute value of the coefficient of the cosine function. The letter A stands for amplitude. Since the amplitude represents a displacement, it is measured in meters.

Why does the amplitude equal the factor outside the cosine function? The values of the cosine range from +1 to −1. Multiplying the maximum value of the cosine by the amplitude (for example, four meters for the function shown in Example 1) yields the maximum displacement.

concept 1

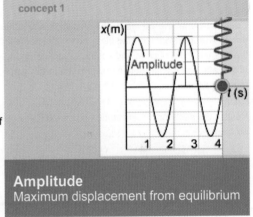

Amplitude
Maximum displacement from equilibrium

equation 1

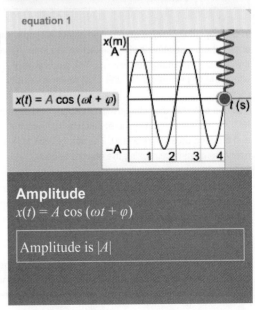

$x(t) = A \cos(\omega t + \varphi)$

Amplitude
$x(t) = A \cos(\omega t + \varphi)$

Amplitude is $|A|$

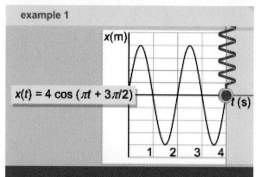

Units: meters (m)

example 1

$$x(t) = 4\cos(\pi t + 3\pi/2)$$

What is the amplitude?
Amplitude $= |A| = 4$ m

14.6 - Interactive problem: match the curve

In the simulation on the right, you control the amplitude and period for a puck on a spring moving in simple harmonic motion. With the right settings, the motion of the puck will create a graph that matches the one shown on the paper.

Determine what the values for the amplitude and period should be by examining the graph. Assume you can read the graph to the nearest 0.1 m of displacement and the nearest 0.1 s of time, and set the values accordingly. Press GO to start the action and see if your motion matches the target graph. If it does not, press RESET to try again.

Review the sections on amplitude and period if you have difficulty solving this problem.

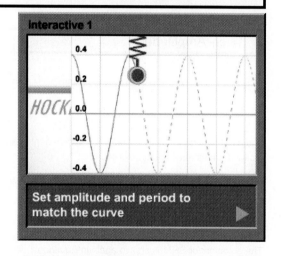

interactive 1

HOCK

Set amplitude and period to match the curve

14.7 - Velocity

In Concept 1, you see a graph of an object in simple harmonic motion. The graph shows the displacement of the object versus time. At any point the slope of the graph is the object's instantaneous velocity. The slope equals $\Delta y/\Delta x$. In this graph, this is the change in displacement per unit time, which is velocity.

You can consider the relationship of velocity and displacement by reviewing the role of force in SHM. Consider an object attached to a spring, where the spring is stretched and then the object is released. The spring force pulls the object until it reaches the equilibrium point, increasing the object's speed.

Once the object passes through the equilibrium point, the spring is compressed and its force resists the object's motion, slowing it down. Because the object speeds up as it approaches the equilibrium point and slows down as it moves away from equilibrium, its greatest speed is at the equilibrium point.

When the spring reaches its maximum compression, the object stops for an instant. At this point, its speed equals zero. The spring then expands until the object returns to its initial position, with the spring fully extended. Again, the object stops for an instant, and

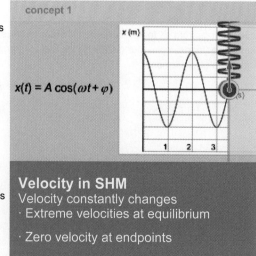

concept 1

$$x(t) = A\cos(\omega t + \varphi)$$

Velocity in SHM
Velocity constantly changes
· Extreme velocities at equilibrium

· Zero velocity at endpoints

its speed is zero.

In the paragraphs above, we discussed the motion in terms of speed, not velocity, so we could ignore the sign and focus on how fast the object moves. The object's velocity will be both positive and negative as it moves back and forth. You see this alternating pattern of positive and negative velocities in the graph in Equation 1.

When the displacement is at an extreme, the velocity is zero, and vice-versa. One way to state the relationship between the displacement and velocity functions is to say they are $\pi/2$ radians ($90°$) out of phase. An equivalent way to express this without a phase constant is to use a cosine function for displacement and a sine function for velocity, and this is what we do. This relationship can also be derived using calculus. In Equation 1, you see both a velocity graph and the function for velocity.

The second equation shown in Equation 1 states that the maximum speed v_{max} is the amplitude of the displacement function times the angular frequency. To understand the source of this equation, recall that the maximum magnitude of the sine function is one. When the sine has a value of -1 in the velocity equation, the velocity reaches its maximum value of $A\omega$.

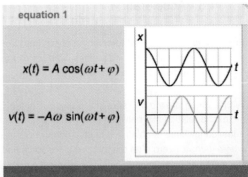

equation 1

$$x(t) = A \cos(\omega t + \varphi)$$

$$v(t) = -A\omega \sin(\omega t + \varphi)$$

Velocity in SHM

$$v(t) = -A\omega \sin(\omega t + \varphi)$$
$$v_{max} = A\omega$$

v = velocity
A = amplitude
ω = angular frequency
t = time
φ = phase constant

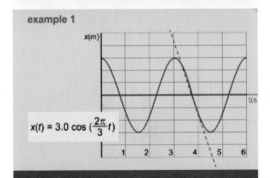

example 1

$$x(t) = 3.0 \cos\left(\frac{2\pi}{3}t\right)$$

What is the velocity at $t = 4.0$ seconds?

$$v(t) = -A\omega \sin(\omega t + \varphi)$$
$$v(4.0 \text{ s}) = (-3.0 \text{ m})\left(\frac{2\pi}{3}\frac{\text{rad}}{\text{s}}\right)\sin\left(\left(\frac{2\pi}{3}\frac{\text{rad}}{\text{s}}\right)(4.0 \text{ s})\right)$$

$$v(4.0 \text{ s}) = (-2\pi)\sin(8\pi/3) \text{ m/s}$$
$$v(4.0 \text{ s}) = (-6.28)(0.866) \text{ m/s}$$
$$v(4.0 \text{ s}) = -5.4 \text{ m/s}$$

For SHM to occur, the net force on an object has to be proportional and opposite in sign to its displacement. Again, we use the example of a mass attached to a spring on a friction-free surface, like an air hockey table.

With a spring like the one shown in Concept 1 to the right, Hooke's law ($F = -kx$) states the relationship between net force and displacement from equilibrium. This equation for force enables you to determine where the acceleration is the greatest, and where it equals zero. The magnitudes of the force and the acceleration are greatest at the extremes of the motion, where x itself is the greatest. This is the point where the object is changing direction. Conversely, $x = 0$ at the equilibrium point, so $F = 0$ and the object is not accelerating there.

The first equation shown in Equation 1 enables you to calculate the acceleration of an object in SHM as a function of time. This equation can be simplified by noting that the amplitude times the cosine function, the rightmost term in the equation, is the function for the object's displacement, $x(t)$. We replace the terms $A \cos \omega t$ by $x(t)$ to derive the second equation, which relates the acceleration directly to the object's displacement. This equation says that the acceleration at a particular time equals the negative of the angular frequency squared times the object's displacement at that time.

Finally, the third equation reveals that the maximum acceleration of the object is the amplitude times the square of the angular frequency. This equation is a consequence of the first equation.

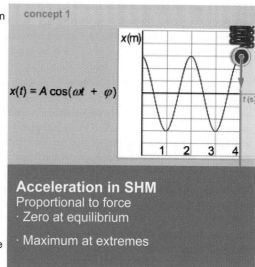

concept 1

$$x(t) = A \cos(\omega t + \varphi)$$

Acceleration in SHM
Proportional to force
· Zero at equilibrium
· Maximum at extremes

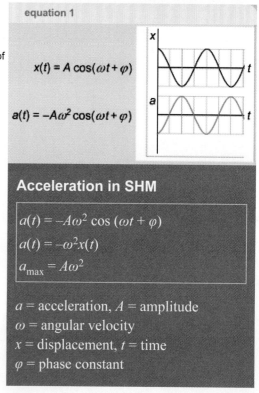

equation 1

$$x(t) = A \cos(\omega t + \varphi)$$

$$a(t) = -A\omega^2 \cos(\omega t + \varphi)$$

Acceleration in SHM

$$a(t) = -A\omega^2 \cos(\omega t + \varphi)$$
$$a(t) = -\omega^2 x(t)$$
$$a_{max} = A\omega^2$$

a = acceleration, A = amplitude
ω = angular velocity
x = displacement, t = time
φ = phase constant

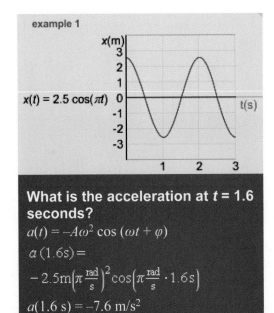
14.9 - A torsional pendulum

The *torsional pendulum* shown in Concept 1 is another device that exhibits simple harmonic motion. A torsional pendulum consists of a mass suspended at the end of a stiff rod, wire or spring. It does not swing back and forth. Instead, the mass at the bottom is initially rotated by an external torque away from its equilibrium position. The elasticity of the rod supplies a *restoring torque*, causing the mass to rotate back to the equilibrium position and beyond. The mass rotates in an angular version of simple harmonic motion.

Earlier, we stated that for SHM to occur, the force must be proportional to displacement. Since torsional pendulums rotate, we must use angular concepts to analyze them. With a torsional pendulum, a restoring torque, not a force, acts to return the system to its equilibrium position. The restoring torque is proportional to angular displacement, just as a restoring force is proportional to (linear) displacement. The moment of inertia of the system takes on the role that mass plays in linear SHM.

The same analysis that applies to linear displacement, velocity and acceleration applies equally well to angular displacement, angular velocity and angular acceleration. In Equation 1, you see an equation that states the nature of the restoring torque. It equals the negative of the product of the *torsion constant* and the angular displacement.

The formula in Equation 2 calculates the period of the pendulum. When the period and the torsion constant are known, the moment of inertia can be calculated, as shown in Example 1. This makes torsional pendulums useful tools for experimentally determining the moments of inertia of complex objects.

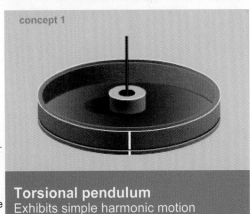

concept 1

Torsional pendulum
Exhibits simple harmonic motion
Use rotational concepts to analyze

equation 1

κ

θ

Restoring torque

$\tau = -\kappa\theta$

$\tau = $ torque

κ = torsion constant
θ = angular displacement
Units for κ: N·m/rad

equation 2

Period

$$T = 2\pi\sqrt{\frac{I}{\kappa}}$$

T = period
I = moment of inertia
κ = torsion constant

example 1

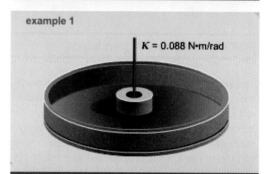

$\kappa = 0.088$ N·m/rad

The torsional pendulum has a period of 3.0 s. What is its moment of inertia?

$$T = 2\pi\sqrt{\frac{I}{\kappa}}$$

$$I = \frac{\kappa T^2}{4\pi^2}$$

$I = (0.088 \text{ N·m/rad})(3.0 \text{ s})^2/4\pi^2$
$I = 0.020 \text{ kg·m}^2$

14.10 - A simple pendulum

Old-fashioned "grandfather" clocks, like the one you see in Concept 1, rely on the regular motion of their pendulums to keep time. A typical pendulum is constructed with a heavy weight called a "bob" attached to a long, thin rod. The bob swings back and forth at the end of the rod in a regular motion.

We approximate such a system as a *simple pendulum*. In a simple pendulum, the bob is assumed to be concentrated at a single point located at the very end of a cable, and the cable itself is treated as having no mass. The system is assumed to have no friction and to experience no air resistance. When such a pendulum swings back and forth with a small amplitude, its angular displacement closely approximates simple harmonic motion. This means the period does not vary much with the pendulum's amplitude. This regularity of period is what makes pendulums useful in clocks.

For SHM to occur, the restoring force or torque needs to vary linearly with displacement. In the case of a pendulum, the motion is rotational, so the torque must be linearly proportional to the angular displacement.

In Equation 1, you see a free-body diagram of the forces on the pendulum bob. The tension in the cable exerts no torque on the pendulum since it passes through its center of rotation, so the weight mg of the bob exerts the only torque. The lever arm of this weight equals the length L of the cable times $\sin \theta$. For small angles, the angle expressed in radians is a very close approximation of the sine of the angle. (The error is less than 1% for angles less than $14°$.) This means that the resulting torque is roughly proportional to the angular displacement, and the condition for SHM is approximated, with a torsion constant of mgL.

In Equation 2, you see the equation for the period of a simple pendulum. When the angular amplitude is small and the approximation mentioned above is used, the period depends solely on the length of the cable and the acceleration of gravity.

A pendulum can be an effective tool for measuring the acceleration caused by gravity using the equation just mentioned. The length L of the cable is measured and the pendulum is set swinging with a small amplitude. The period T is then measured. The value of g can be calculated using the rearranged equation $g = 4L(\pi/T)^2$.

concept 1

Simple pendulum
Point mass at end of massless rod
Approximates simple harmonic motion

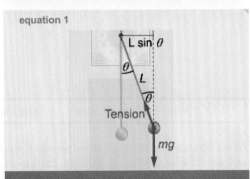

equation 1

Restoring torque

$$\tau = -mgL \sin \theta \approx -mgL\theta$$

τ = torque
m = mass
g = acceleration of gravity
L = length of pendulum
θ = angular displacement

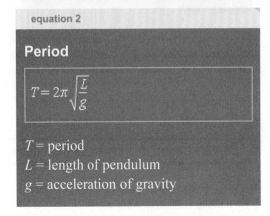

equation 2

Period

$$T = 2\pi \sqrt{\frac{L}{g}}$$

T = period
L = length of pendulum
g = acceleration of gravity

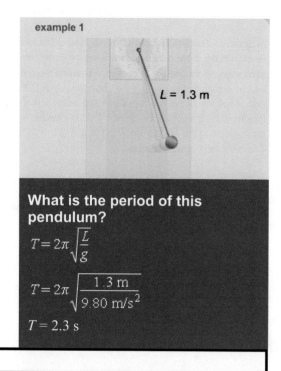

example 1

L = 1.3 m

What is the period of this pendulum?

$$T = 2\pi \sqrt{\frac{L}{g}}$$

$$T = 2\pi \sqrt{\frac{1.3 \text{ m}}{9.80 \text{ m/s}^2}}$$

$$T = 2.3 \text{ s}$$

14.11 - Interactive problem: a pendulum

On the right is a simulation of a simple pendulum: a bob at the end of a string. You can control the length of the string, and in doing so change the period of the pendulum. Your goal is to set the length so that the period is 2.20 seconds. As the pendulum swings, you will see a graph reflecting the **angular** displacement of the bob.

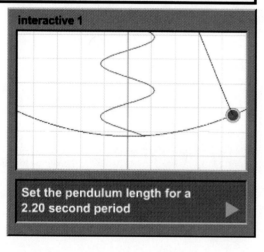

interactive 1

Set the pendulum length for a 2.20 second period

Calculate and set the value for the string length to the nearest 0.05 m using the dial, then use your mouse to drag the bob to one side and release it to start the pendulum swinging. There may not be enough room in the window to show the entire length of the string, but we will show the motion of the bob and the resulting period. If you do not set the length correctly, press RESET to try again. Refer to the section on simple pendulums if you do not remember the equation for the period.

You may want to double-check your work by creating an actual pendulum with a string of the correct length. You can time it: Ten cycles of its motion should take about 22 seconds.

For small angles, the angular displacement of a pendulum approximates simple harmonic motion and the graph looks sinusoidal. Try smaller and larger angles and observe the graphs. How sinusoidal do they look to you? (In the simulation, decreasing the string length makes it easier to create large angular displacements.) You can check the box labeled "SHM" to draw a sinusoidal graph of SHM motion in black underneath your red graph. The black graph shows simple harmonic motion for the amplitude you choose and the period calculated by the pendulum equation. If the amplitude is small, you might not see the black graph, because the two graphs match so closely.

14.12 - Period of a physical pendulum

Not all pendulums are simple. A *physical pendulum* is a rigid extended object (not a point mass) pivoting around a point. In Concept 1, you see a violin acting as a physical pendulum.

The equation for the period of a physical pendulum is shown in Equation 1. The distance h is the distance from the pivot point to the center of mass of the object. As always, the moment of inertia must be calculated about the pivot point.

The example problem shows how to calculate the period of a meter stick used as a pendulum in the Earth's gravitational field. The period is 1.6 seconds. With the use of a meter stick, this is a result you can verify for yourself. If the stick has a hole close to one end, put an unbent paper clip through the hole (otherwise, pinch the end very loosely between your fingers), and set the stick swinging. Ten swings should take approximately 16 seconds.

concept 1

Physical pendulum
Mass is distributed
Motion approximates SHM

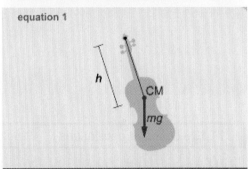

equation 1

h

CM

mg

Physical pendulum period

$$T = 2\pi \sqrt{\frac{I}{mgh}}$$

T = period
I = moment of inertia
m = mass, g = acceleration of gravity
h = distance from pivot to center of mass

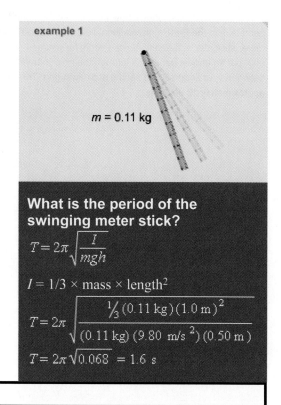

example 1

What is the period of the swinging meter stick?

$$T = 2\pi\sqrt{\frac{I}{mgh}}$$

$$I = 1/3 \times \text{mass} \times \text{length}^2$$

$$T = 2\pi\sqrt{\frac{\frac{1}{3}(0.11\text{ kg})(1.0\text{ m})^2}{(0.11\text{ kg})(9.80\text{ m/s}^2)(0.50\text{ m})}}$$

$$T = 2\pi\sqrt{0.068} = 1.6\text{ s}$$

14.13 - Damped oscillations

We have considered many types of oscillations, and up until now assumed the periodic motion continued without change. But most real-world oscillations are *damped*, which means they are subject to forces like friction that cause the amplitude of the motion to decrease over time.

Mountain bike shock absorbers provide an excellent demonstration of damped oscillations. A shock absorber often combines a spring with a sealed container of fluid. Shock absorbers lessen the jolts of a bumpy trail.

To explain this in more detail, let's consider what happens when a bike equipped with such a shock absorber hits a bump. The force from the bump compresses the spring, with the result that less of the force from the bump passes to the rest of the bike (and the rider).

The spring then supplies a restoring force. In the absence of any other force, the rider and bike would in principle then move forever in simple harmonic motion. However, inside a shock absorber, the spring moves a piston in a sealed cylinder of fluid. The fluid supplies what is called a *damping force*.

In Concepts 1 and 2, you see a diagram of this system. The fluid (typically oil) provides a force that opposes the motion of the piston. The damping force always opposes (resists) the motion of an object, which means sometimes it acts in the same direction as the restoring force (when the object moves away from equilibrium), and sometimes in the opposite direction (when the object moves toward equilibrium). At all times, however, it is opposing the motion.

Instead of moving in SHM, the system moves back to its equilibrium point and stops, or it may oscillate a few times with smaller and smaller amplitude before resting at its equilibrium point. The fluid "dampens" the motion, reducing the amplitude of the oscillations. The result is a relatively fast yet smooth return to the equilibrium position.

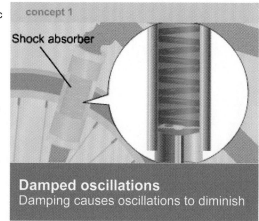

concept 1

Shock absorber

Damped oscillations
Damping causes oscillations to diminish

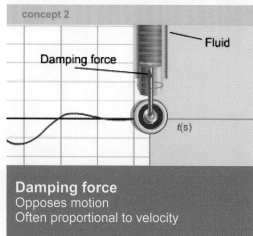

concept 2

Fluid

Damping force

$t(s)$

Damping force
Opposes motion
Often proportional to velocity

The resistive force of the fluid in a system like this is often proportional to the velocity, and opposite in direction. In Equation 1, you see the equation for the damping force. It equals the negative of b (the *damping coefficient*) times the velocity. (You may note that this is similar to the formula for air resistance, where the drag force depends on the square of the velocity.) The negative sign indicates that the damping force opposes the motion that causes it.

In Equation 2, you also see the equation for the net force F_N. The net force is the sum of the restoring forces and the damping force. (If you look at the equation, it may seem that two negatives combine to make a larger number, but the sign of the velocity is the opposite of the displacement as the system moves toward equilibrium.)

The graph in Equation 3 illustrates three types of damping. The blue line represents a *critically damped* system. The damping force is such that the system returns to equilibrium as quickly as possible and stops at that point.

The green line represents a system that is *overdamped*. The damping force is greater than the minimum needed to prevent oscillations. The system returns to equilibrium without oscillating, but it takes longer to do so than a critically damped system.

The red line is a system that is *underdamped*. It oscillates about the equilibrium point, with ever diminishing amplitude.

With certain shock absorbers, the system can be adjusted, which means that the damping coefficient can be tuned based on rider preferences. Beginners often prefer an underdamped system. The bike bounces a bit but there is less of a "jolt" because the shock absorber acts more slowly. Advanced riders sometimes prefer a critically damped or overdamped "harder" ride, trading off a less smooth ride in exchange for regaining control of the bicycle more quickly.

equation 1

Damping force

$$F_d = -bv$$

F_d = damping force
b = damping coefficient
v = velocity

equation 2

Net force

$$\Sigma F = -kx - bv$$

ΣF = net force
k = spring constant
x = displacement
b = damping coefficient
v = velocity

equation 3

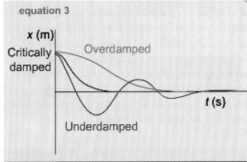

Types of damped harmonic motion
Critically damped: blue line
Overdamped: green line
Underdamped: red line

14.14 - Forced oscillations and resonance

Forced oscillation: A periodic external force acts on an object, increasing the amplitude of its motion.

External forces can dampen, or reduce, the amplitude of harmonic motion. For instance, in a mass-spring system, friction reduces the amplitude of the mass's motion over time. External forces can also maintain or increase the amplitude of an oscillation, counteracting damping forces.

Consider a child on a swing. Friction and air resistance are damping forces that reduce the amplitude of the motion. On the other hand, an external force like a person pushing, as you see in Concept 1, can increase the amplitude. When an external force increases the amplitude, *forced oscillation* occurs.

An external force that acts to increase the amplitude of oscillations is called a *driving force*. The driving force oscillates at a frequency called the *driving frequency*.

The natural frequency of a system is the frequency at which it will oscillate in the absence of any external force. Systems have natural frequencies based on their structure. The closer the driving frequency is to the natural frequency, the more efficiently the driving force transfers energy to the system, and the greater the resulting amplitude. This is why you push a child on a swing "in sync" with the swing's motion. The resulting phenomenon is called *resonance*. When the driving and natural frequencies are the same, the result is called *perfect resonance*.

There are several famous/infamous cases of forced oscillations and resonance. In Equation 1, you see a movie of the Tacoma Narrows Bridge. A few months after it was built in 1940, strong winds caused the bridge to oscillate at its natural frequency, and the amplitude of the oscillations increased over time until the bridge collapsed. The precise cause of the collapse is a matter of some debate, but the resonant oscillations played a large part.

The Bay of Fundy in Nova Scotia provides another famous example. The tides vary greatly in the bay with the water level changing by as much as 16 meters. One reason for the dramatic tides is that the natural frequency of the bay, the time it takes for a wave to go from one end to the other, is close to the driving frequency of the tide cycle, which is about 12.5 hours.

As a third example, the natural frequency of one- to three-story buildings is close to the driving frequency supplied by some earthquakes, which is why these buildings (very common in San Francisco) often sustain the heaviest damage during quakes.

In Equation 2, you see a graph called a *resonance curve*. It is a graph of amplitude versus frequency for a system that has both a damping force and an external driving force. We call the natural (angular) frequency ω_n and use ω to indicate the driving frequency. As the driving frequency ω approaches the natural frequency ω_n, the amplitude increases dramatically.

Natural frequencies can be "natural," but in some cases they can also be controlled. Electric circuits, such as those used to tune radios to stations of different frequencies, are designed so that humans can change the natural frequency of the circuit. As you turn the radio dial, you are changing the natural frequency of the circuit. It then "tunes in" a driving frequency from a radio station that matches the natural frequency of the circuit. These concepts have entered everyday language. People say that "an idea resonates with me." Such everyday speech is good physics; they mean the "driving frequency" of the idea is close to the "natural frequency" of their own beliefs.

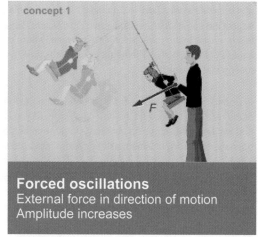

concept 1

Forced oscillations
External force in direction of motion
Amplitude increases

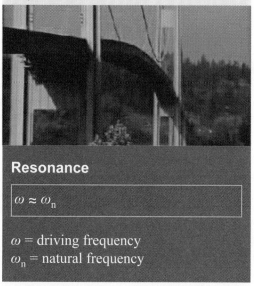

equation 1

Resonance

$$\omega \approx \omega_n$$

ω = driving frequency
ω_n = natural frequency

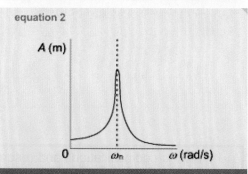

equation 2

A (m)

0 ω_n ω (rad/s)

Frequency and amplitude
Amplitude increases as ω approaches ω_n

14.15 - Gotchas

To calculate the amplitude of an object moving in SHM, measure the difference between two successive peaks of its graph. No, that is the period you just measured. The amplitude is the height of a peak of the graph above the horizontal (time) axis.

The slope at any point on the displacement graph of an object in SHM is its velocity. Yes, you are correct. This is a point that is true of any displacement graph, not just an SHM graph.

14.16 - Summary

Simple harmonic motion (SHM) is a kind of repeated, consistent back and forth motion, like the swinging of a pendulum. It is caused by a restoring force that varies linearly with displacement.

The displacement associated with such motion can be described with a sinusoidal function, typically a cosine. The displacement is zero at equilibrium and maximum at the extreme positions.

Just as with other types of repetitive motion, the period of SHM is the amount of time required to complete one cycle of motion. The frequency is the number of cycles completed per second. It is the reciprocal of the period. The unit of frequency is the hertz (Hz), equal to one inverse second.

Angular frequency is the frequency measured in radians per second. It is represented by the Greek letter ω and is seen in the function for harmonic motion.

Equations

$$x(t) = A \cos (\omega t + \varphi)$$

$$f = 1/T$$

$$\omega = 2\pi f$$

$$v(t) = -A\omega \sin (\omega t + \varphi)$$

$$a(t) = -A\omega^2 \cos (\omega t + \varphi)$$

The amplitude of harmonic motion is the maximum displacement from equilibrium. It is represented by A and appears as the coefficient of the cosine in the displacement function for SHM.

The velocity and acceleration functions for SHM are also sinusoidal. The maximum velocity occurs at equilibrium, and it is zero at the extremes. Acceleration is the opposite: zero at equilibrium and maximum at the extremes. These relationships follow from the general nature of velocity as the instantaneous slope of the displacement graph, and acceleration as the slope of velocity.

A simple pendulum displays simple harmonic motion in its angular displacement, provided that the amplitude of the motion is small. Instead of a restoring force, there is a restoring torque due to gravity. The period of a pendulum depends upon the length of the pendulum and the acceleration of gravity.

The simple pendulum is a special case of the more complicated physical pendulum. In general, the period of a physical pendulum depends upon its moment of inertia, mass, and the distance from the pivot point to its center of mass, as well as the acceleration of gravity.

Sometimes a damping force opposes oscillatory motion. A typical damping force is proportional to the velocity of the object, which changes with time.

A force that acts **with** the restoring force can maintain or increase the amplitude of oscillations. Forced oscillations occur when such a driving force is present. The natural frequency of a system is the frequency at which it will oscillate in the absence of external force. As the frequency of the driving force approaches the natural frequency, energy is transferred more efficiently and the system's oscillation amplitude increases. When these frequencies are approximately equal, resonance occurs.

15.0 - Introduction

Waves can be as plain to see as the ripples in a pond or as invisible as the electromagnetic waves emanating from a cellular phone. Mechanical waves, like those in a pond, require a medium in order to propagate. Electromagnetic waves – including radio waves and light – require no medium and can travel in the near vacuum of space. Electromagnetic waves rely on the interaction of electric and magnetic fields to propagate through space.

In this chapter, we focus on mechanical waves. These are waves in which a vibration causes a disturbance to travel through a medium. You are familiar with a variety of mechanical waves: water waves in the ocean, sound waves in the air, or waves along a string if you shake an end up and down. These waves exist due to the movement of particles that make up a medium, such as water molecules in the ocean or gas molecules in the air.

Waves carry energy from place to place: a relatively small amount with a sound wave, a much larger amount with a tsunami wave.

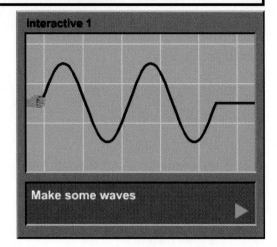

Interactive 1

Make some waves

Although many mechanical waves travel, sometimes across great distances, there is no net movement of the medium through which they propagate. The 15th century Italian scientist and artist Leonardo da Vinci described this key attribute when he said: "It often happens that the wave flees the place of its creation, while the water does not."

Use the simulation to the right to begin your exploration of waves. It consists of a string stretched across the screen. A hand on the left holds the string. By shaking the hand up and down, you can generate a variety of waves in the string.

When you open the simulation, press GO to send a wave down the string. You will see the hand begin to shake the string, causing a wave to travel from left to right.

The control panel has two input gauges that allow you to vary the amplitude and frequency of the wave. As you may remember from your study of simple harmonic motion, amplitude is the maximum displacement of a wave from equilibrium. Frequency is the number of cycles per second. You can vary these parameters and observe changes in the shape of the wave. Also in the control panel is an output gauge that displays the wavelength, the distance between successive peaks of the wave.

The string's tension and other properties remain constant.

When you run the simulation, make sure you observe the differences between a wave with higher frequency and one with lower frequency. This is an important fundamental characteristic of a wave.

Then try three quick experiments. First, does changing the frequency of a wave also change its wavelength? Change the frequency and observe what happens to the wavelength.

Second, does changing the frequency result in any change in amplitude? Again, you can vary the frequency and note any change.

Finally, as you change the frequency and amplitude, does the wave travel down the string any faster or slower? For example, does a wave with a very large amplitude travel noticeably faster than one with a very small amplitude?

The simulation is intended to let you conduct a preliminary exploration of topics that will be presented in this chapter. Answer what questions you can above and then proceed to the rest of the chapter, which covers the topics in more depth.

Mechanical waves: Vibrations in a medium.

Ocean breakers, the rolling wave of a crowd in a sports stadium, the back and forth vibrations in a Slinky®: These are a few of the many kinds of waves you can see. Some mechanical waves are invisible to the eye but detectable by the ear, such as the sound waves generated by musical instruments.

Mechanical waves are vibrations in a medium, traveling from place to place without causing any net movement of the medium. You may be familiar with "the wave" in a football or baseball stadium. The wave travels around the stadium, the result of spectators standing and then sitting in a rolling succession. As the fans oscillate up and down, they create what is called a *disturbance* or *waveform*. The location of the disturbance changes as the wave moves through the stadium, but the wave's medium, the crowd, stays put.

A wave in a stadium is a useful example, but it is not a true mechanical wave. Mechanical waves, such as a wave in a string, result from an initial force (a vibration up and down or to and fro) followed by a continuing sequence of interactions between particles in the medium. In a stadium wave, the particles of the medium (the people) do not typically exert physical forces on one another to propagate the wave (since peer pressure is not a physical force).

Mechanical waves have some common properties. First, they require a physical medium, such as air, a string or a body of water. Mechanical waves cannot move through a vacuum.

Second, mechanical waves require a driving excitation to get the wave started. The vibrations then propagate, via interactions between particles, through the medium.

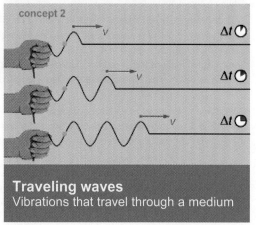

concept 1

Mechanical waves
Disturbances in a medium

concept 2

Traveling waves
Vibrations that travel through a medium

In this fashion, waves transfer energy from place to place. When you hear a sound, you are hearing energy that has been transferred by a wave through air or water (or even, if you are listening for buffalo, the ground).

All of the waves in this chapter are *traveling waves* in which the disturbance moves from one point to another. Concept 2 shows a wave moving down a string, caused by a hand shaking the string. The illustration shows three successive moments in time. You can track the position of the first peak as it moves down the string over time. It moves with a constant speed v. The other peaks also move down the string with the same speed.

The peaks do not move through the medium in all waves. In what are called standing waves, the locations in the medium where peaks and troughs (the "low" parts of the wave) occur are fixed. These waves, caused by the reflection or interaction of traveling waves, are discussed in a later chapter.

Transverse wave: Particles in a medium vibrating perpendicular to the direction the wave is traveling.

Longitudinal wave: Particles in a medium vibrating parallel to the direction the wave is traveling.

Waves can be classified by the relationship between their direction of travel, and the direction of the motion of the particles in the medium.

Imagine that two people stretch a Slinky between them, and one shakes the Slinky up and down. This causes a wave to move along the Slinky, as shown in Concept 1. The wave moves to the right with a velocity called v_{wave} in the diagram.

Although the wave moves to the right, the particles that make up the medium move up and down. An individual particle of the Slinky is highlighted in red in the diagram to the right, and its movement is shown with the vertically directed arrows. The direction of the wave is **perpendicular** to the motion of the particles of the medium. This type of wave is called a *transverse wave*.

Many types of mechanical waves are transverse waves, including those caused by shaking a Slinky up and down, the vibrations of a violin string, and certain types of earthquake waves.

Now imagine that instead of shaking the Slinky up and down, a person pulls the Slinky to the left and then pushes it to the right, as shown in Concept 2. This causes the spring to be stretched and then compressed.

This disturbance again travels horizontally along the Slinky, and again we show its velocity as v_{wave}. The wave consists of regions in which the coils of the spring are tightly packed, followed by regions in which the coils are widely spaced. A particle of the Slinky, again marked with a red dot, oscillates horizontally, **parallel** to the direction the wave is traveling. This type of wave is called a *longitudinal wave*.

Sound is a longitudinal wave that consists of alternate compressions and rarefactions of air. Individual air particles oscillate back and forth, and a sound wave travels through the air, where it can be detected by a sophisticated instrument: the human ear.

In both transverse and longitudinal waves, the particles do move, but there is no **net** motion of the particles after each cycle. A particle moves up and down, or back and forth, but it returns to its initial position. It oscillates like a mass attached to a spring.

A single source of vibration, such as an earthquake, can create both transverse and longitudinal waves. In an earthquake, the longitudinal waves (*P waves*, for primary waves) travel at about 8 km/s, while the transverse waves (*S waves,* for secondary waves) are slower, moving at about 5 km/s. By noting when each type of wave arrives at a given seismographic station, a seismologist can determine the distance of the earthquake from that station. Using data from several stations, the seismologist can triangulate the location of the earthquake's epicenter.

The motion of the particles that make up a wave can be complex, with ocean waves serving as one example. You can see this in Concept 3, where the wave moves to the left and the water molecules near the surface move in circles. This means the molecules' motion involves vertical and horizontal components. Their motion is both perpendicular and parallel to the direction of the wave. An ocean wave displays both longitudinal and transverse properties.

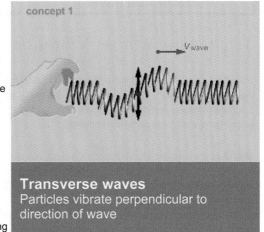

Transverse waves
Particles vibrate perpendicular to direction of wave

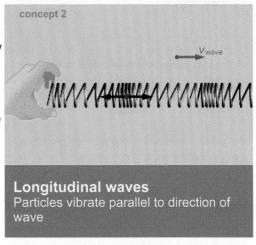

Longitudinal waves
Particles vibrate parallel to direction of wave

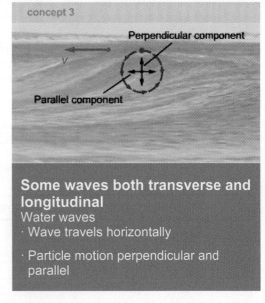

Some waves both transverse and longitudinal
Water waves
· Wave travels horizontally

· Particle motion perpendicular and parallel

Wave pulse: A single disturbance caused by a one-time excitation.

Periodic wave: A continuing wave caused by a repeated vibration.

Two types of transverse waves are shown to the right. Concept 1 shows a single wave pulse in a string. The hand shakes up and down once and the wave pulse moves from left to right along the string.

Concept 2 shows a periodic wave. The hand moves continuously up and down. In a periodic wave, each particle in the string moves through a repeated cycle of rising to a peak, falling to a trough, and then returning again to a peak. The procession of wavefronts moving down the string is called a *wave train*.

If you observe a particular crest in the periodic wave, it will move horizontally along the string over time. This is more apparent in an animation. In a static diagram, the wave can appear to be stationary, though it is moving down the string as the velocity vector indicates. Click on the illustration to see an animation.

In this chapter, we focus on waves in which the particles are vibrating in simple harmonic motion. This vibration will be caused by something (in this case, a hand) moving or vibrating in simple harmonic motion. The result is the type of sinusoidal wave you see to the right.

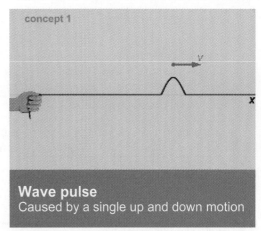

Wave pulse
Caused by a single up and down motion

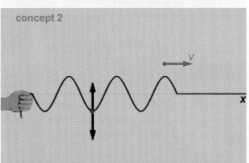

Periodic wave
Continuing wave caused by a repetitive vibration

Amplitude: The maximum displacement of a particle in a wave from its equilibrium position.

Several terms discussed in earlier topics such as simple harmonic motion also apply to waves, including *amplitude*.

At the right, you see a transverse wave caused by a hand shaking a string. The amplitude of the wave is the distance between a particle at its maximum displacement − a peak or trough − and the particle at its rest or equilibrium position. The horizontal line in the diagram is the equilibrium position for the particles in the string. The amplitude by convention is positive. Since amplitude is a distance, it is measured in meters.

A wave's amplitude is related to the energy it carries. Waves with greater amplitude carry more energy. You can experience this relationship at the beach; you may barely notice a small-amplitude wave crashing into you, while a large-amplitude wave may knock you off your feet!

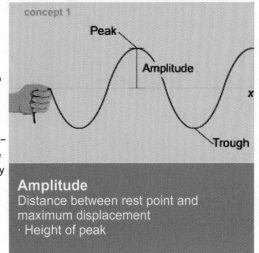

Amplitude
Distance between rest point and maximum displacement
· Height of peak

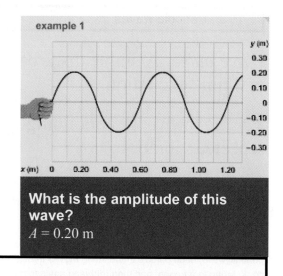

example 1

What is the amplitude of this wave?

$A = 0.20$ m

15.5 - Wavelength

Wavelength: The distance between adjacent peaks.

The wavelength of a wave is the distance between adjacent peaks in the wave. This will be the same distance as that between adjacent troughs, or any two successive points on the wave with the same vertical displacement and direction of particle motion.

The Greek letter lamda (λ) represents wavelength. At the right, you see the wavelength measured for a transverse periodic wave in a string. The unit for wavelength is the meter.

Also on the right is a table that shows the wavelengths of a variety of waves.

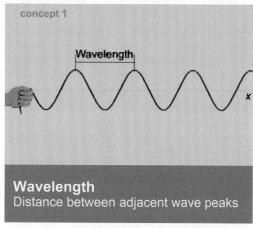

concept 1

Wavelength

Wavelength
Distance between adjacent wave peaks

concept 2

	Wavelength (m)
Tsunami	$\sim 5.0 \times 10^5$
AM radio waves	$\sim 3.0 \times 10^2$
Low range whale call (100Hz)	1.5×10^1
4th octave A (440 Hz)	7.7×10^{-1}
Bat sonar	$\sim 5.0 \times 10^{-3}$
X-ray waves	10^{-10}

A variety of wavelengths

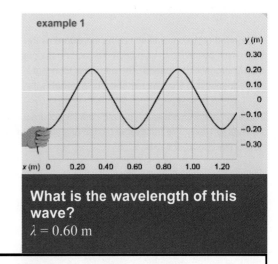

example 1

y (m)
0.30
0.20
0.10
0
−0.10
−0.20
−0.30

x (m) 0   0.20   0.40   0.60   0.80   1.00   1.20

What is the wavelength of this wave?
$\lambda = 0.60$ m

15.6 - Period and frequency

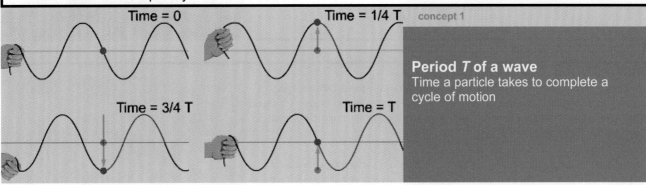

Time = 0   Time = 1/4 T   concept 1

Time = 3/4 T   Time = T

Period *T* of a wave
Time a particle takes to complete a cycle of motion

Period: Amount of time for a particle in a wave to complete a cycle of motion.

Frequency: Number of wave cycles per second.

The definitions of period and frequency may look familiar from your study of simple harmonic motion.

The period of a wave equals the amount of time required for a particle of the medium to move through a complete cycle of motion.

At the top of this section are four time-lapse "snapshots" of a transverse wave moving through a string. The particle marked in red moves vertically up and down. The amount of time it takes to rise to a peak, fall to a trough and return to its initial position is the period. Because the period is an interval of time, its unit is the second.

As the particle oscillates up and down through a full cycle of motion, the wave travels to the right a distance of one wavelength. Frequency is the number of full cycles of motion per second. Frequency (cycles/second) equals the reciprocal of the period (seconds/cycle). The unit for frequency is the hertz (Hz), equal to one cycle per second.

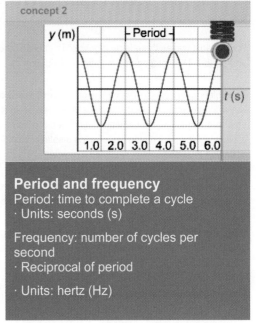

concept 2

y (m)   ⊢ Period ⊣

t (s)

1.0 2.0 3.0 4.0 5.0 6.0

Period and frequency
Period: time to complete a cycle
· Units: seconds (s)

Frequency: number of cycles per second
· Reciprocal of period

· Units: hertz (Hz)

In Concept 2, we show a graph related to the transverse wave, which is not a depiction of the wave itself, but a graph of the motion of a particle over time. The scale of its horizontal axis is time, **not** position. The particle oscillates up and down in SHM, like the red particle used in the wave illustration at the top of this section. This graph could be generated in a fashion akin to the graphs you saw in the chapter on simple harmonic motion, where we rolled graph paper below a mass that had a "pen" attached to it. In this case, we would roll the paper under the red circle to record its location over time.

The period of the wave itself can be measured as the difference in time between two equivalent points (such as adjacent peaks) on the graph. The frequency of the wave is the reciprocal of the period. The particle in Concept 2 has a period of 2.0 seconds, so its frequency is 0.5 cycles per second, and that is the frequency of the associated wave.

The example problem asks you to determine the frequency and period of another transverse wave. The transverse motion of a single particle in this wave is graphed with time on the horizontal axis.

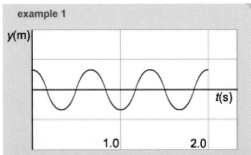

example 1

What are the frequency f and the period T of the wave?
$f = 3.0$ cycles/2.0 s
$f = 1.5$ Hz
$T = 1/f = 1/1.5$ cycles
$T = 0.67$ s

15.7 - Wave speed

How fast a wave moves through a medium is called its wave speed. Different types of waves have vastly different speeds, from 300,000,000 m/s for light to 343 m/s for sound in air to less than 1 m/s for a typical ocean wave. The wave in the string to the right might be moving at, say, 15 m/s.

The speed of a mechanical wave depends solely on the properties of the medium through which it travels. For example, the speed of a wave in a string depends on the linear mass density and tension of the string. This relationship is explored in another section.

For periodic waves there is an algebraic relationship between wave speed, wavelength and period. This relationship is shown in Equation 1.

This relationship can be derived by considering some of the essential properties of a wave. Wavelength is the distance between two adjacent wave peaks. The period is the time that elapses when the wave travels a distance of one wavelength. If you divide wavelength by period, you are dividing displacement by elapsed time. This is the definition of speed.

Because frequency is the reciprocal of period, the speed of a wave also equals the wavelength times its frequency. Both of these formulations are shown to the right.

Since the speed of a wave is dictated by the physical characteristics of its medium, its speed must be constant in that medium. In the example of the string mentioned above, the constant speed is determined by the linear density and tension of the string.

Because the speed of a wave in a medium is constant, the product of its wavelength and frequency is a constant. This means that for a wave in a given medium the wavelength is inversely proportional to the frequency. Increase the frequency of the wave and the wavelength decreases. Decrease the frequency and the wavelength increases.

Consider sound waves. Different sounds can have different frequencies. If this were not the case, there would be no music. For example, consider the first four notes of Beethoven's Fifth Symphony (the famous "dut dut dut daaah"). As played by the violins,

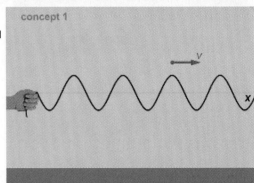

concept 1

Wave speed
How fast a wave travels

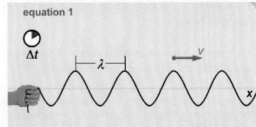

equation 1

Δt

Wave speed

$$v = \frac{\lambda}{T} = \lambda f$$

$v = $ wave speed

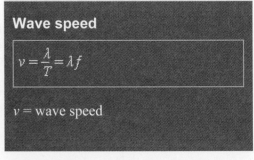

Copyright 2000-2007 Kinetic Books Co. Chapter 15

the first three identical notes are the G above middle C and have a frequency of 784.3 Hz and a wavelength of 0.434 m, while the fourth note (E flat) has a frequency of 622.4 Hz and wavelength of 0.547 m.

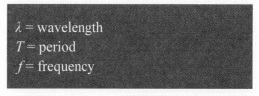

λ = wavelength
T = period
f = frequency

example 1

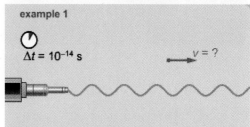

$\Delta t = 10^{-14}$ s

$v = ?$

The light's wavelength is 6.0×10^{-7} m. The light completes 5.0 cycles in 10^{-14} seconds. What is the light's wave speed?

$v = \lambda f$

$f = \dfrac{5.0 \text{ cycles}}{10^{-14} \text{ s}} = 5.0 \times 10^{14} \text{ Hz}$

$v = (6.0 \times 10^{-7} \text{ m})(5.0 \times 10^{14} \text{ Hz})$

$v = 3.0 \times 10^{8}$ m/s

15.8 - Wave speed in a string

This section examines in detail the physical factors that determine the speed of a transverse wave in a string. The factors are the force on the string (the string's tension) and the string's linear density. Linear density is the mass per unit length, m/L. It is represented with the Greek letter μ (pronounced "mew").

The relationship of wave speed to the string's tension and linear density is expressed in Equation 1. The equation states that the wave speed equals the square root of the string tension divided by the linear density of the string.

Your physics intuition may help you understand why wave speed increases with string tension and decreases with string density.

Consider Newton's second law, $F = ma$. If the mass of a particle is fixed, a larger force on the particle will result in a greater acceleration. When a string under tension is shaken up and down, the tension acts as a restoring force on the string, pulling its particles back toward their rest positions. The greater the tension, the greater this restoring force and the faster the string will return to equilibrium. This means the string will oscillate faster (its frequency increases). Because wave speed is proportional to frequency, the speed will increase with the tension.

concept 1

m/L

v

F

Wave speed in a string
Increases with string's tension
Decreases with string's linear density

Now let's assume that the tension is fixed, and compare wave speeds in strings that have differing linear densities (mass per unit length). Newton's second law says that for a given restoring force (tension), the particles in the more massive string will have less acceleration and move back to their rest positions more slowly. The wave frequency and wave speed will be less.

The equation on the right is a good approximation when the amplitude of the wave is significantly smaller than the overall length of the medium though which the wave moves. The force that causes the wave must also be significantly less than the tension for this equation to be accurate. The equation can be derived using the principles discussed in this section.

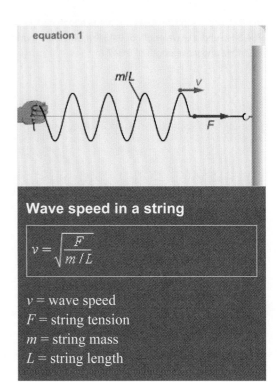

equation 1

Wave speed in a string

$$v = \sqrt{\frac{F}{m/L}}$$

v = wave speed
F = string tension
m = string mass
L = string length

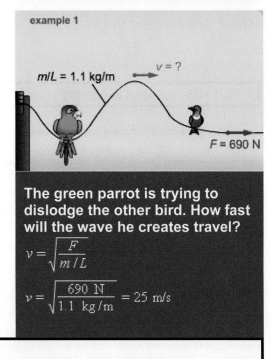

example 1

m/L = 1.1 kg/m   v = ?

F = 690 N

The green parrot is trying to dislodge the other bird. How fast will the wave he creates travel?

$$v = \sqrt{\frac{F}{m/L}}$$

$$v = \sqrt{\frac{690 \text{ N}}{1.1 \text{ kg}/\text{m}}} = 25 \text{ m/s}$$

15.9 - Interactive problem: wave speed in a string

In this interactive problem, two strings are tied together with a knot and stretched between two hooks. String 1, on the left, is twice as long as string 2, on the right. Both strings have the same tension.

In the simulation, each string is plucked at its hook at the same instant. The resulting wave pulses travel inward toward the knot. The wave pulse in string 1 starts at twice the distance from the knot as the wave pulse in string 2.

You want the wave pulses to meet at the knot at the same instant. To accomplish this, set the linear density of each segment of string. When you increase a string segment's linear density in this simulation, the string gets thicker.

Copyright 2000-2007 Kinetic Books Co. Chapter 15

The minimum linear densities you can set are 0.010 kg/m. Set a convenient linear density for string 1; your choice for this linear density determines the appropriate linear density for string 2, which you must calculate.

Enter these values using the dials in the control panel and press GO to start the wave pulses. If they do not meet at the knot at the same instant, the simulation will pause when either of the pulses reaches the knot. Press RESET and enter different values for the linear densities to try again.

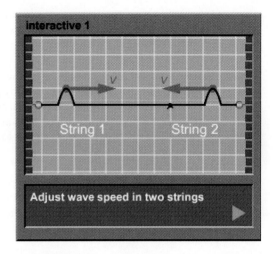

interactive 1

String 1   String 2

Adjust wave speed in two strings

15.10 - Mathematical description of a wave

When a mechanical wave travels through a medium, the particles in the medium oscillate. Consider the diagram in Concept 1 showing a transverse periodic wave. The particles of the string oscillate vertically and the wave moves horizontally.

The vertical displacement of the highlighted particle will change over time as it oscillates. We show its displacement in Concept 1 at an instant in time.

In this section, we analyze a wave in which the particles oscillate in simple harmonic motion. An equation that includes the sine function is used to describe a particle's displacement. The equation relates the vertical displacement of the particle to various factors: the horizontal position of the particle, the elapsed time, and the wave's amplitude, frequency and wavelength. When all these factors are known, the vertical position of a point can be determined at any time t.

Equation 1 describes a wave moving from left to right. The variable y in the equation is the vertical displacement of a particle at a given horizontal position away from its equilibrium position at a particular time. To use the equation, you must assume the wave has traveled the length of the string, and the time t is some time after this has occurred.

In the equation, the variable x is the particle's position along the x axis, which does not change for a given particle. The variable A is the wave's amplitude; the variable λ is the wavelength; and the variable f is the wave's frequency.

The argument of the sine function is called the *phase*. As a wave sweeps past a particle located at a horizontal position x, the phase changes linearly with respect to the elapsed time t. **The phase is an angle measured in radians**. The angle in the wave equation must be expressed in radians.

The equation in Equation 1 describes a transverse wave moving from left to right. For a wave moving from right to left, the minus sign inside the phase is switched to a plus sign, reversing the sign of the coefficient of time.

Equation 1 assumes that a particle at position $x = 0$ at time $t = 0$ is at the equilibrium position $y = 0$. You can add what is called a phase constant to the equation to create a new equation describing a wave with a different initial state. For example, suppose a constant angle such as $\pi/2$ radians were added to the argument of the sine function. Then, the particle at $x = 0$ at time $t = 0$ would be at its maximum positive displacement, because the sine of $\pi/2$ equals one. A phase constant does not change the shape of a wave, but rather shifts

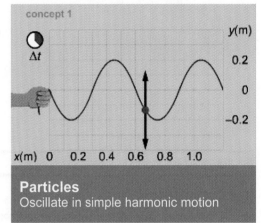

concept 1

y(m)

Δt

0.2

0

-0.2

x(m)   0   0.2   0.4   0.6   0.8   1.0

Particles
Oscillate in simple harmonic motion

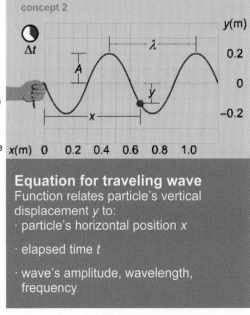

concept 2

y(m)

Δt

λ

A

y

0.2

0

-0.2

x

x(m)   0   0.2   0.4   0.6   0.8   1.0

Equation for traveling wave
Function relates particle's vertical displacement y to:

· particle's horizontal position x

· elapsed time t

· wave's amplitude, wavelength, frequency

it back or forward along the horizontal axis by the same amount at all times. Note that as the phase is increased by an integer multiple of 2π radians, the sine function describing the wave behaves as if there were no change at all.

If you contrast the equation here to the equation for simple harmonic motion, you will note that the equation for a traveling wave requires two inputs to determine the vertical displacement of a particle. Both equations include time, but the equation in this section also requires knowing the x position of a particle in the medium. With a wave, the vertical displacement is a function not only of time, but also of position in the medium, while the position is not a factor in SHM.

The equations to the right can be used with either transverse or longitudinal waves. When applied to longitudinal waves, the oscillation of the particles occurs parallel to the direction of travel of the wave, and then we would use the variable s instead of y to represent the horizontal displacement of a particle away from its equilibrium position.

equation 1

$$y = A \sin \left(\frac{2\pi x}{\lambda} - 2\pi ft \right)$$

Equation for traveling wave

$y = A \sin (2\pi x/\lambda - 2\pi ft)$

y = particle's vertical displacement
A = amplitude of wave
x = particle's horizontal position
λ = wavelength, f = frequency
t = elapsed time

For wave motion toward $-x$:

$y = A \sin (2\pi x/\lambda + 2\pi ft)$

15.11 - Gotchas

A mechanical wave can travel with or without a medium. No. Mechanical waves must have a medium. This is why, in the vacuum of space, there is total silence. Sound, a mechanical wave, cannot travel without a medium such as air.

The medium carrying a wave does not move along with the wave. That is correct. The medium oscillates, but it does not travel with the wave. This differentiates wind, which consists of moving air, from a sound wave. With a sound wave, the air remains in place after the sound wave has passed through.

The amplitude of a wave has no effect on the speed of the wave. That is correct. The speed of a wave is determined by the properties of the medium. This means that if you are in a hurry, it is no use yelling at people!

Wave speed in a string is a function of frequency, so if I increase the wave frequency, the wave speed will increase, too. No. The speed of a wave in a string is fixed by the tension and linear density of the string. Increasing wave frequency will cause a decrease in wavelength, but no change in wave speed.

Amplitude is the same as the vertical displacement y of a particle in a wave. No, the amplitude A is the maximum positive vertical displacement of a particle, while at a time t the instantaneous vertical displacement y can be anywhere between $+A$ and $-A$.

15.12 - Summary

Mechanical waves are oscillations in a medium. This chapter discussed traveling waves: disturbances that move through a medium.

There are two basic wave types. In a transverse wave, the particles in the medium oscillate perpendicularly to the direction that the wave travels. In a longitudinal wave, the particles oscillate parallel to the direction the wave travels. Some waves, such as water waves, exhibit both transverse and longitudinal oscillation.

A wave can come as a single pulse, or as a periodic (repeating) wave. In this chapter, we analyze periodic waves whose particles oscillate in simple harmonic motion.

The amplitude of a wave is the distance from its equilibrium position to its peak. The wavelength is the distance between two adjacent peaks. The period is the time it takes for a particle to complete one cycle of motion, for example, moving from peak to peak. Frequency is the number of cycles that are completed per second.

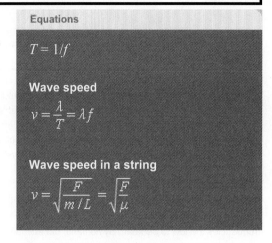

Equations

$$T = 1/f$$

Wave speed

$$v = \frac{\lambda}{T} = \lambda f$$

Wave speed in a string

$$v = \sqrt{\frac{F}{m/L}} = \sqrt{\frac{F}{\mu}}$$

Wave speed is the speed with which a wave moves through a medium. It is equal to the wavelength of the wave times its frequency.

The wave speed in a string increases with the tension of the string and decreases with the string's linear density.

The wave equation may be written using the angular wave number and angular frequency of the wave, which differ from the reciprocal of its wavelength and from its frequency by a factor of 2π.

Waves transfer energy through a medium. The rate of this transfer is the wave's power. In a string, the power depends upon the string's linear density and the speed, angular frequency and amplitude of the wave.

16.0 - Introduction

Sounds are so commonplace that it is easy to take them for granted, but they are a central part of the human experience. When you think of sound, you may think of your favorite song or an alarm clock that goes off early and loud. To a physicist, though, both a pleasant song and a shrill alarm are mechanical longitudinal waves consisting of regions of high and low pressure. The physics of sound waves is the topic of this chapter.

Sounds can be classified as audible, infrasonic or ultrasonic. Audible sounds are in the frequency range that can be heard by humans. *Infrasonic* sounds are at frequencies too low to be heard by humans, but animals such as elephants and whales use them to communicate over great distances. *Ultrasonic* sounds are at frequencies too high to be perceived by humans. They are used by bats for sonar and by doctors to see inside the human body.

interactive 1

Air particles

Speaker

Make some sound waves

You may have used the speed of sound in air to estimate the distance to a thunderstorm. The flash from the lightning reaches you almost instantaneously, while the sound from the thunder takes more time. Sound travels at approximately 343 m/s in air at $20°C$, so for every third of a kilometer of distance to the lightning, the sound of the thunder lags the flash of light by about one second.

Sound travels slowly enough in air that manmade objects such as airplanes can catch and pass their own sound waves. You may have heard the result when a plane is flying faster than the speed of sound: a sonic boom. A small sonic boom is also the cause of the "crack" of a whip, as the tip of the whip travels faster than the speed of sound.

You may begin your study of sound with the simulation to the right, which allows you to experiment with a loudspeaker that causes sound waves to travel through a tube filled with air particles. One set of particles is colored red to emphasize that all the particles just oscillate back and forth; they do not travel along with the wave.

Sound waves can be described with the same parameters that are used to describe transverse mechanical waves: amplitude, frequency and wavelength. Recognizing these parameters in a longitudinal wave may require some practice.

When you open the simulation, press GO to send a sound wave through the air. You will see the loudspeaker's diaphragm vibrate horizontally. This causes the nearby air particles to vibrate and a longitudinal wave to travel from left to right along the length of the tube.

Observe the differences between this wave and the transverse waves you saw in strings. You should be able to see how the particles of the medium (air) oscillate **parallel** to the direction the wave travels in a longitudinal wave, as opposed to the perpendicular motion of the particles in a transverse wave.

The simulation lets you control the loudspeaker to determine the amplitude and frequency of the wave. As with any wave, the amplitude is the maximum displacement of a particle from its rest position, and the frequency is the number of cycles per second. You can vary these parameters and observe changes in the motion of the loudspeaker and in the properties of the sound wave. You can also observe how the wavelength changes when you alter the frequency.

Humans can identify different sound waves by pitch, which is related to frequency. If you have audio on your computer, turn it on and listen to the pitch created by a particular wave. Then increase the frequency and hear how the pitch changes. The loudness of a sound wave is related to its amplitude. Increase the amplitude of the wave in the simulation and note what you hear.

Sound waves are longitudinal mechanical waves in a medium like air generated by vibrations such as the plucking of a guitar string or the oscillations of a loudspeaker.

Sound waves are caused by alternating compression and decompression of a medium. In Concept 1, a loudspeaker is shown. As the loudspeaker diaphragm moves forward, it compresses the air in front of it, causing the air particles there to be closer together. This region of compressed air is called a *condensation*. The pressure and density of particles is greater in a region of condensation. This compressed region travels away from the loudspeaker at the speed of sound in air.

The diaphragm then pulls back, creating a region in which there are fewer particles. This region is a *rarefaction*, and the pressure there is lower. The rarefaction also travels away from the loudspeaker at the speed of sound. The velocity of the wave is indicated with the orange vector **v** in the diagram. The back-and-forth motion of an individual particle is indicated with the black arrows.

The illustration for Concept 2 also shows the alternating regions of condensation and rarefaction as the loudspeaker oscillates back and forth. The wavelength is the distance between two successive areas of maximum condensation or rarefaction. As with transverse waves, the wavelength is measured along the direction of travel. The wavelength can be readily visualized as the distance between the midpoints of the two regions of condensation shown in the diagram.

With a wave in a string, a complete cycle of motion occurs when a particle in the string starts at a point (perhaps a peak), moves to a trough, and returns to a peak. With a sound wave, an analogous cycle passes from compression to rarefaction and then returns to compression.

To measure the period, you can note how long it takes for an air particle to pass through a complete cycle at a given location. As with transverse waves, the frequency of a sound wave is the number of cycles completed per second.

Concept 3 illustrates the motion of an individual particle in a sound wave. Refresh the browser page to see an animation of the particle's motion. The particle oscillates back and forth horizontally as regions of high and low pressure pass by, also horizontally. The particle is first pushed to the right as an area of higher pressure passes, and then pulled to the left by a region of lower pressure. As high and low pressure regions pass by, the individual particles oscillate in simple harmonic motion.

The harmonic oscillation of the particles distinguishes a sound wave from wind. Wind causes particles to have net displacement; it moves them from one location to another. There is no net movement of air particles over time due to sound waves. The particles oscillate back and forth around their original locations.

Two aspects of the behavior of gas molecules will help you understand sound waves. First, we have used increased density and increased pressure to define condensation, and decreased density and decreased pressure to define rarefaction. Density and pressure are correlated. The ideal gas law (which you may study in a later chapter) states that, everything else being equal, pressure increases with the number of gas molecules in a system. This means that the pressure is greater in regions of condensation than in regions of rarefaction. Other factors (such as temperature) also influence pressure, but in this discussion we treat them as constant.

Second, the speed of sound can be understood in terms of the behavior of air molecules. The speed *v* of a sound wave does not equal the speed of the loudspeaker's motion. That may seem odd. How could the waves move faster or slower than the object that causes them?

The diagram we use simplifies the nature of the motion of air molecules in a wave. Air molecules at room temperature move at high speeds

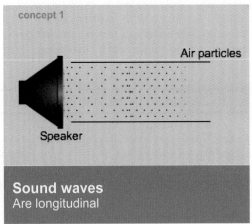

concept 1

Air particles

Speaker

Sound waves
Are longitudinal

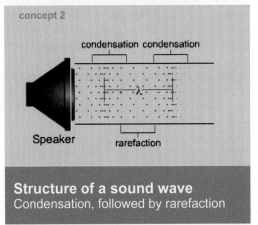

concept 2

condensation condensation

λ

Speaker   rarefaction

Structure of a sound wave
Condensation, followed by rarefaction

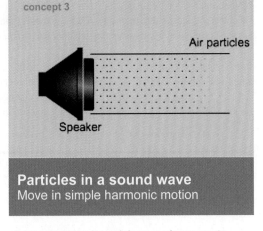

concept 3

Air particles

Speaker

Particles in a sound wave
Move in simple harmonic motion

(hundreds of meters per second) and frequently collide. On average, their location is stationary since their motion is random, so we can draw them as stationary to reflect their average position. On the other hand, they are always moving, and when the loudspeaker moves, it changes the velocity of molecules that are already in motion. The change in velocity caused by the loudspeaker is transmitted through the air by multiple collisions as a function of the random speeds of the molecules. The faster the molecules are moving, the more frequently they will collide. As the air becomes warmer, for example, the average thermal speed of the molecules increases, as does the speed of sound. Properties of the medium itself, not the speed of the loudspeaker, determine the speed of sound.

16.2 - Human perception of sound frequency

When a sound wave composed of alternating high and low pressure regions reaches a human ear, the wave vibrates the eardrum, a thin membrane in the outer ear. The vibrations are then carried through a series of structures to generate signals that are transmitted by the auditory nerve to the brain, which interprets them as sound.

There is a subjective relationship between the frequency of a sound wave and the *pitch* of the sound you hear. Pitch is the distinctive quality of the sound that determines whether it sounds relatively high or low within a range of musical notes. A home smoke alarm issues a high-pitched beep, while a foghorn emits a low-pitched rumble. The human ear is extremely sensitive to differences in the frequency of sound waves.

concept 1

Human	20 - 20,000
Dog	60 - 45,000
Cat	45 - 60,000
Bat	2,000 - 110,000
Dolphin	75 - 150,000

0Hz   50,000Hz   100,000Hz   150,000Hz

Audible frequencies

A *pure tone* sound consists of a sound of a single frequency. The tones produced by musical instruments combine waves with several frequencies, but each note has a fundamental frequency that predominates. The note middle C on a piano has a fundamental frequency of 262 cycles per second (Hz); the lowest and highest notes of a piano have frequencies of 27.5 and 4186 Hz, respectively. Orchestras tune to a note of 440 Hz (the A above middle C). To experiment with frequency and pitch yourself, try the interactive simulation in the next section.

A young person can hear sounds that range from 20 to 20,000 Hz. With age, the ability of humans to perceive higher frequency sounds diminishes. Middle-aged people can hear sounds with a maximum frequency of about 14,000 Hz.

The human ear is sensitive to a wide range of frequencies, but other animals can perceive frequencies that humans cannot. Whales emit and hear sounds with a frequency as low as 15 Hz. Bats emit sounds in a frequency range from 20,000 Hz up to 100,000 Hz and then listen to the reflected sound to locate their prey. Dogs (and cats) can detect frequencies more than twice as high as humans can hear, and some dog whistles operate at frequencies that the animals can hear but humans cannot.

Interestingly, when it comes to certain sounds, the ear is not the most sensitive part of the human body. Sometimes you can feel sounds even when you cannot hear them. Some contrabass musical instruments are designed to play notes below the lowest limit of human hearing (20 Hz). For example, the organ in the Sydney (Australia) Town Hall can play a low, low C that vibrates at only 8 Hz, a rumbling that can only be felt by the audience members. Low frequency sounds are also used in movies and some arcade games to increase tension and suspense.

16.3 - Interactive problem: sound frequency

In this interactive simulation, you can experience the relationship between sound wave frequency and pitch.

The simulation includes a virtual keyboard. (As you might expect, your computer must have a sound card and speakers or a headphone for you to be able to hear the musical notes.)

Above the keyboard is an oscilloscope, used to display the sound wave. The oscilloscope graphs the waves with time on the horizontal axis. Each division on the horizontal axis represents one millisecond.

On the vertical axis, the oscilloscope graphs an air particle's displacement from equilibrium as a function of time, as the sound wave passes by. The wave is longitudinal, and peaks and troughs on the graph correspond to the particle's maximum displacement, which occurs along the direction of the wave's motion. Although we do not provide units on the vertical axis, displacements of the particles in audible sound waves are generally in the micrometer range.

The frequency of ordinary musical notes is high enough that the oscilloscope graphs time in milliseconds. The middle C on the keyboard (a white key near its midpoint) has a frequency of about 262 Hz (cycles per second), or 0.262 cycles per millisecond. A full cycle of this sound wave would span slightly less than four squares on the horizontal axis of the oscilloscope.

When you start the simulation, the instrument is set to "synthesizer." When you press a key, you will hear a tone that plays at the same intensity for as long as you hold down the key. Even this simple synthesizer tone consists of several frequencies, but one fundamental frequency predominates, and it is displayed on the oscilloscope.

You can use the oscilloscope to compare the frequencies of various sound waves, as well as using your ears to compare various pitches. Do they relate? Specifically, do higher pitched musical notes have a higher or lower frequency than lower pitched musical notes? If you know how to play notes on the piano that are an octave apart, compare the frequencies and wavelengths of these sounds. What are the relationships?

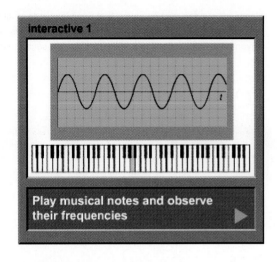

interactive 1

Play musical notes and observe their frequencies

You can also set the simulation to hear notes from a grand piano. These tones are even more complex than the synthesizer and again we display just the fundamental frequency. To simulate a piano's sound, the notes will fade away even if you hold down the key, but the oscilloscope will continue to display the initial sound wave.

This simulation is designed to give you an intuitive sense of the frequencies of different musical notes. If you know how to play the piano, even something as simple as "Chopsticks," play a song and observe the waves that make up that tune. You can also play a note and see how close a friend can come to guessing it. Some people have a capability called *perfect pitch*, and can tell the note or frequency correctly every time.

16.4 - Sound intensity

Sound intensity: The sound power per unit area.

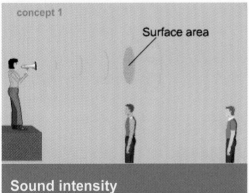

concept 1

Surface area

Sound intensity
Sound power that passes perpendicularly through a surface area
Diminishes with square of distance from sound source

Sound carries energy. It may be a small amount, as when someone whispers in your ear, or it may be much more, as when the sonic boom of an airplane rattles windows, or when a guitar amplifier goes to 11.

Sound intensity is used to characterize the power of sound. It is defined as the power of the sound passing perpendicularly through a surface area. Watts per square meter are typical units for sound intensity.

The definition of sound intensity is shown in Equation 1. An intensity of approximately 1×10^{-12} W/m^2 is the minimum perceptible by the human ear. An intensity greater than 1 W/m^2 can damage the ear.

As a sound wave travels, it typically spreads out. You perceive the loudness of the sound of a loudspeaker at an outdoor concert differently at a distance of one meter than you do at 100 meters. The intensity of the sound diminishes with distance.

Equation 2 is used to calculate the intensity of sound when it spreads freely from a single source. The intensity diminishes with the square of the distance from the source. It does so because the sound energy in this case is treated as being distributed over the surface of a sphere whose radius increases with time. The denominator of the expression for intensity is $4\pi r^2$, the expression for the surface area of a sphere.

The example problem to the right asks you to find the relative sound intensities experienced by two listeners, one twice as far as the other from the fireworks. In this scenario, the sound is four times as intense for the closer listener, but this does not mean he hears the sound as four times louder. The loudness of sounds as perceived by human beings has a logarithmic relationship to sound intensity. This topic is explored in another section.

Here we have focused on sound that freely expands in all directions. However, sound can also reflect off surfaces such as walls. Concert halls are designed to take advantage of this reflection to deliver a full, rich sound to the audience.

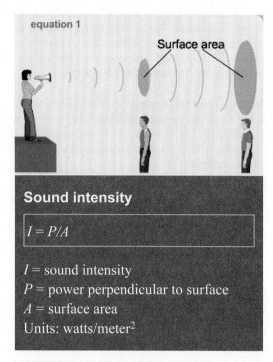

Sound intensity

$$I = P/A$$

I = sound intensity
P = power perpendicular to surface
A = surface area
Units: watts/meter^2

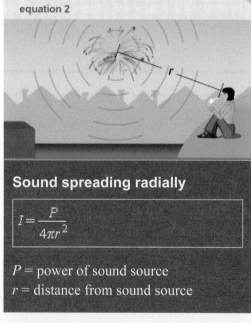

Sound spreading radially

$$I = \frac{P}{4\pi r^2}$$

P = power of sound source
r = distance from sound source

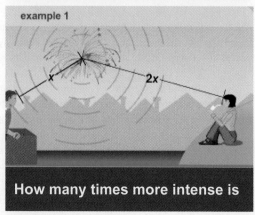

How many times more intense is

16.5 - Sound level in decibels

Sound level: A scale for measuring the perceived intensity of sounds.

To compare the intensity of two sounds, you could directly calculate the ratio of their intensities. However, humans do not perceive a sound with twice the intensity as being twice as loud, so a different system may be used. Loudness is subjective, and having an objective measurement that corresponds to human perception is convenient. This measurement is called the *sound level* (or sometimes, more confusingly, the *intensity level*).

The human ear is sensitive to an extraordinary range of sound intensities; at the extremes, humans can perceive sounds whose intensities differ by a factor of 1,000,000,000,000. Although they can hear a broad range of intensities, people do not distinguish between them finely. For instance, the human ear cannot very well distinguish a sound that has an intensity of 1.0 W/m² from one with an intensity of 0.50 W/m².

To reflect humans' perception of differences in sound intensity, scientists use a logarithmic scale. The common unit for the sound level is the decibel (dB), or one-tenth of a "bel," a unit named after Alexander Graham Bell. A logarithmic scale provides an appropriate tool for describing the human perception of sounds.

In calculating a sound level β, you start by dividing the intensity of the sound being measured by a reference sound intensity that approximates the lowest intensity humans can hear. This reference intensity is 1×10^{-12} W/m². Then you calculate the common logarithm (to the base 10) of this ratio, which gives the sound level in bels, and finally you multiply that value by 10 to express the level in decibels. This is the first equation shown to the right.

To practice calculating sound levels in decibels, consider a sound with an intensity of 1.5×10^{-11} W/m². It has 15 times the sound intensity of the reference intensity of 1×10^{-12} W/m². The base-10 logarithm of 15 is 1.2. Multiplying this value by 10 decibels yields a sound level of 12 decibels. A sound level increase of 10 dB means the intensity increases by a factor of 10. In calculations of sound levels, both the numbers 1×10^{-12} W/m² and 10 (decibels) are considered exact.

You may note that the reference intensity of 1×10^{-12} W/m² corresponds to a decibel reading of zero. At zero decibels, a human ear can still barely hear sound. The pressure exerted by this sound is very, very slight: It displaces particles of air by about one hundred-billionth of a meter. It is possible to have negative decibel sounds,

concept 1

Sound	Sound level (decibels, dB)
Jet aircraft engine	160
Threshold of pain	140
Pneumatic drill	100
Subway train	90
Vacuum cleaner	85
Heavy auto traffic	75
Conversational speech	65
Whispered speech	40
Threshold of hearing	0

Sound level
Used to measure perceived loudness
· Units: decibels (dB)

· Logarithmic scale (20 dB is ten times more intense than 10 dB)

equation 1

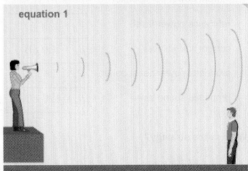

Sound level

$$\beta = (10 \text{ dB}) \log \frac{I}{I_0}$$

β = sound level
I = intensity of sound
reference intensity $I_0 = 1\times10^{-12}$ W/m²

perturbations in air pressure so slight the human ear cannot detect them.

Tests indicate that a one to three decibel change in sound level is about the smallest change most humans can perceive. A general rule of thumb is that a human will perceive a tenfold increase in intensity as sounding twice as loud. A 50 dB sound is 10 times more intense than a 40 dB sound – remember, it is a logarithmic scale – and a typical human would say it sounds twice as loud.

The sound level equation can be recast in terms of sound power, as shown in the second equation to the right. If you know the relative power of two sound sources, you can use this equation to compare their relative loudness to the human ear, provided the listener is equidistant from the two sound sources. The reference power P_0 in this equation is the power at the source that results in the reference intensity at the location of interest. For instance, you might determine this value for a loudspeaker for an audience member 75 meters away.

$$\beta = (10 \text{ dB}) \log \frac{P}{P_0}$$

P = sound power of source
P_0 = reference sound power
Units: decibels (dB)

16.6 - Sample problem: sound level

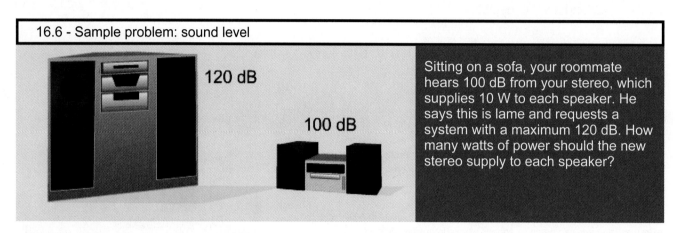

120 dB

100 dB

Sitting on a sofa, your roommate hears 100 dB from your stereo, which supplies 10 W to each speaker. He says this is lame and requests a system with a maximum 120 dB. How many watts of power should the new stereo supply to each speaker?

Assume the sound power of the loudspeakers equals the power supplied by the stereo.

Variables

current power per speaker	$P_1 = 10 \text{ W}$
reference power level	P_0
current sound level	$\beta_1 = 100 \text{ dB}$
proposed power per speaker	P_2
proposed sound level	$\beta_2 = 120 \text{ dB}$

What is the strategy?

1. State two equations that relate sound level to power, for both the current system and the proposed system.
2. Subtract the two equations and solve the resulting equation to determine the power of the new stereo.

Physics principles and equations

The equation for sound level with respect to the power of the sound source is

$$\beta = (10 \text{ dB}) \log \frac{P}{P_0}$$

Mathematics principles

$$\log(a) - \log(b) = \log(a/b)$$

Step-by-step solution

Step	Reason
1. $\beta_1 = (10 \text{ dB}) \log \dfrac{P_1}{P_0}$	sound level power equation
2. $100 \text{ dB} = (10 \text{ dB}) \log \dfrac{10 \text{ W}}{P_0}$	current system
3. $120 \text{ dB} = (10 \text{ dB}) \log \dfrac{P_2}{P_0}$	proposed system
4. $20 = 10 \log \dfrac{P_2}{P_0} - 10 \log \dfrac{10}{P_0}$	subtract
5. $20 = 10 \log \dfrac{P_2/P_0}{10/P_0}$	difference of logarithms
6. $2 = \log \dfrac{P_2}{10}$	divide and simplify
7. $10^2 = \dfrac{P_2}{10}$	take antilogarithm
8. $P_2 = 1000 \text{ W}$	solve

To increase the sound level by 10 decibels, the sound power (and sound intensity) must increase tenfold. Raising the maximum sound intensity of the system by 20 decibels requires a 100-fold increase in sound power and stereo power. The result will be loud enough to ensure the entire dormitory hears your music!

We hope they appreciate your taste.

16.7 - Doppler effect: moving sound source

Doppler effect: A change in the frequency of a wave due to motion of the source and/or the listener.

You experience the Doppler effect when a train races past you while sounding its whistle. As the train is approaching, you perceive the whistle as emitting sound of one frequency, and as it moves away, the perceived frequency of the whistle drops to a lower pitch.

This effect is named for the Austrian physicist who first analyzed it, Christian Doppler (1803-1853). Doppler's research concerned light from stars, but his principles apply to sound also.

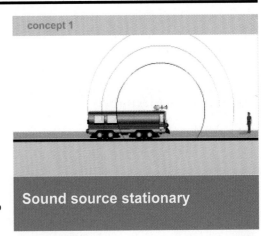

concept 1

Sound source stationary

In the example described above, the frequency of the sound emitted by the train is constant. The Doppler effect occurs because of the motion of the source of the sound, the train whistle. It is moving first toward and then away from you, and you are standing still. (What is moving and what is still is relative to sound's medium, the air.)

You see this situation illustrated on the right. In Concept 1, the train and listener are both stationary. The diagram shows the peaks of the sound waves as they emanate from the train and radiate in all directions, including toward the listener. They are equally spaced, which means their wavelength is constant, as is their frequency.

In Concept 2, the train is moving to the right, toward the listener, at a source velocity $\mathbf{v}_s$. As you see, the peaks of the sound waves at the listener are closer together than in Concept 1, which means the wavelength is shorter and the frequency at the listener is higher.

The motion of the train causes these changes in wavelength and frequency. To understand this, consider two successive regions of condensation generated by the train's horn. The first moves toward the listener. The train continues to move forward, and the next time the horn creates a region of condensation, it will be closer to the prior one than if the train were stationary. The regions arrive more frequently because of the motion of the train toward the listener.

Concept 3 shows the effect perceived by a listener for whom the train is moving away. The sound waves reach this listener less frequently, and he hears a lower pitched sound.

The Doppler effect is quantified using the two equations shown to the right. (They apply when the sound source is moving; a different set of equations is used when the listener is moving.) The first equation shows how to calculate the frequency when the source of the sound moves directly toward a stationary listener; the second is used when the source moves directly away. If the source is moving in some other direction, the component of its velocity directly toward or away from the listener must be used in the formulas. The speed of sound changes with temperature, air density and so on; a value of 343 m/s is often used.

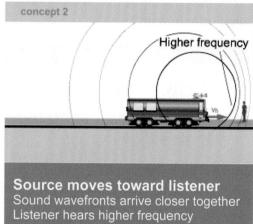

Wavelength, frequency constant

concept 2

Higher frequency

Source moves toward listener
Sound wavefronts arrive closer together
Listener hears higher frequency

concept 3

Lower frequency

Source moves away from listener
Sound wavefronts arrive farther apart
Listener hears lower frequency

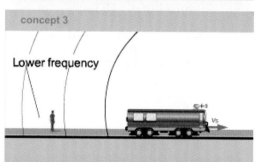

equation 1

Source moves toward listener

$$f_L = f_s \frac{1}{1 - v_s/v}$$

f_L = frequency perceived by listener
f_s = frequency emitted by source
v_s = speed of the source
v = speed of sound in air ≈ 343 m/s

equation 2

Source moves away from listener

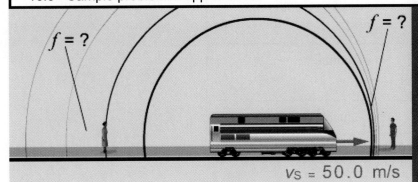

$$f_L = f_s \frac{1}{1 + v_s / v}$$

16.8 - Sample problem: Doppler effect

$f = ?$ $f = ?$

The frequency of the train whistle when the train is not moving is 495 Hz. What sound frequency does each person hear?

$v_S = 50.0$ m/s

Variables

speed of train	$v_s = 50.0$ m/s
speed of sound	$v = 343$ m/s
frequency of train whistle when train is motionless	$f_s = 495$ Hz
frequency heard by front listener	f_{L1}
frequency heard by rear listener	f_{L2}

What is the strategy?

1. Use the equation for determining the Doppler effect when a sound-emitting object is moving toward a listener.

2. Then use the equation for determining the Doppler effect when a sound-emitting object is moving away from a listener.

Physics principles and equations

The equation for a sound source approaching a listener

$$f_L = f_s \frac{1}{1 - v_s / v}$$

The equation for a sound source moving away from a listener

$$f_L = f_s \frac{1}{1 + v_s / v}$$

Step-by-step solution

We start by calculating the frequency perceived by the front listener. The train is approaching that listener.

Step	Reason
1. $f_{L1} = f_s \dfrac{1}{1 - v_s/v}$	Doppler equation
2. $f_{L1} = 495 \text{ Hz} \dfrac{1}{1 - \left(\left(50.0 \text{ }^{m}\!/_{s}\right) / \left(343 \text{ }^{m}\!/_{s}\right)\right)}$	substitute values
3. $f_{L1} = 579 \text{ Hz}$	evaluate

Now we calculate the frequency perceived by the rear listener, for whom the train is moving away.

Step	Reason
4. $f_{L2} = f_s \dfrac{1}{1 + v_s/v}$	Doppler equation
5. $f_{L2} = 495 \text{ Hz} \dfrac{1}{1 + \left(\left(50.0 \text{ }^{m}\!/_{s}\right) / \left(343 \text{ }^{m}\!/_{s}\right)\right)}$	substitute values
6. $f_{L2} = 432 \text{ Hz}$	evaluate

This is quite a noticeable Doppler effect. The listener on the right hears a frequency roughly one-third higher than the listener on the left. If the train were playing a musical note, the listener on the right would hear a pitch about five semitones (piano keys) higher than the listener on the left.

16.9 - Supersonic speed and shock waves

After studying the Doppler effect equations, you might wonder: What happens if the speed of the sound source equals the speed of sound? The relevant Doppler equation shows that you would have to divide by zero, yielding infinite frequency, a troubling result.

Equally troubling was the result when aircraft first tried to break the *sound barrier* (the speed of sound). In the first half of the 20th century, the planes tended to fall apart as much as the equation does. It was not until 1947 that a plane was able to fly faster than the speed of sound, as excitingly shown in the movie *The Right Stuff*, proving that sound was not a barrier after all.

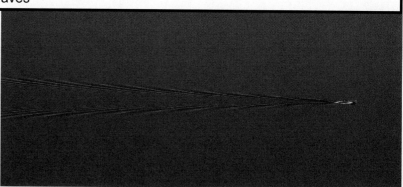

This boat is traveling faster than the speed of waves in water. Its wake forms a two-dimensional "Mach cone" on the water's surface.

The Doppler effect equations do not apply if the sound source is moving at or above the speed of sound. Concept 1 shows the result when a sound source moves at the speed of sound. The leading edges of the sound waves bunch up at the tip of the aircraft as the plane travels as fast as its own sound waves.

Concept 2 shows the result when an aircraft exceeds the speed of sound. Aircraft capable of flying that fast are called *supersonic*. The plane travels faster than its own sound waves, and the waves spool out behind the plane creating a *Mach cone*.

The surface of the Mach cone is called a *shock wave*. Supersonic jets produce shock waves, which in turn create sounds called *sonic booms*. As long as a jet exceeds the speed of sound, it will create this sound. A rapid change in air pressure causes the sonic boom. Shock waves may be visible to the human eye because a rapid pressure decrease lowers temperature and causes water molecules to condense, resulting in fog. You may have heard other sonic booms, such as the report of a rifle or the crack of a well-snapped whip. The boom indicates that the bullet or the tip of the whip has moved faster than the speed of sound. The example of the whip shows that the moving object can be silent and still create a shock wave.

Equation 1 shows how the sine of the angle of a Mach cone can be calculated as a ratio of speeds. The inverse ratio, of the speed of the object to the speed of sound, is known as the *Mach number*. A fighter jet described as a "Mach 1.6 plane" can move as fast as 1.6 times the speed of sound, or about 550 m/s (more than 1200 mph). You see this described mathematically in Equation 2. Because the speed of sound varies with factors like temperature, the exact speed of a Mach 1.6 plane depends on its environment.

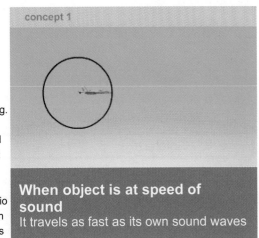

concept 1

When object is at speed of sound
It travels as fast as its own sound waves

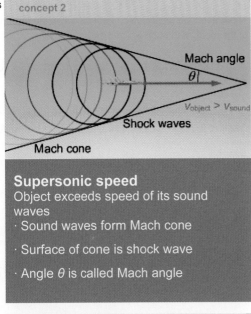

concept 2

Mach angle

θ

$v_{object} > v_{sound}$

Shock waves

Mach cone

Supersonic speed
Object exceeds speed of its sound waves
· Sound waves form Mach cone

· Surface of cone is shock wave

· Angle θ is called Mach angle

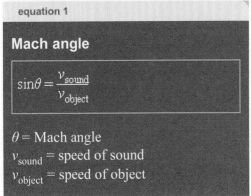

equation 1

Mach angle

$$\sin\theta = \frac{v_{sound}}{v_{object}}$$

θ = Mach angle
v_{sound} = speed of sound
v_{object} = speed of object

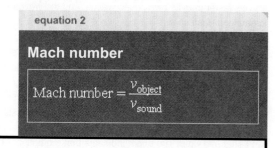

equation 2

Mach number

$$\text{Mach number} = \frac{v_{object}}{v_{sound}}$$

16.10 - Gotchas

You hear sound because air molecules move from the sound's source to your ears. No. Air molecules oscillate back and forth as a sound wave passes by, but there need be no net motion of the particles that make up the medium.

The speed of sound can vary significantly depending on the medium it travels through. Yes. The speed of sound varies widely. Sound travels nearly five times faster through water than through air, for instance, and faster still through solids, including many metals.

The greater the amplitude of a sound wave, the faster the wave moves. No. The speed of a sound wave is dependent solely on the properties of the medium through which it moves.

A 20 dB sound is twice as intense as a 10 dB sound. No, the decibel measurement system is logarithmic. The 20 dB sound has ten times the intensity: ten times as many watts per square meter. A typical person perceives it as twice as loud.

The degree of Doppler shift experienced by a listener is independent of how far the listener is from a moving sound source. This is true: Distance is not a factor in determining the Doppler shift.

Sound waves are longitudinal mechanical waves. Instead of the peaks and troughs of transverse waves, sound waves are composed of condensations and rarefactions of the medium through which they travel. Particles in a sound wave move in simple harmonic motion along the direction that the wave travels.

The intensity of a sound is the sound power passing perpendicularly through a unit area. For a sound that spreads radially, such as from a fireworks explosion in midair, the sound intensity is inversely proportional to the square of the distance from the source.

Do not confuse sound intensity with the sound level. The sound level takes into account the logarithmic perception of sound by the human ear.

The Doppler effect is the change in frequency of a wave due to the relative motion of the source and/or the listener. A common example is the change in frequency heard as the siren on a fire engine races by you. As the fire engine moves toward you, the sound waves "pile up" and their wavelength decreases. Since the speed of sound remains the same, this results in you hearing a higher frequency.

Equations

Speed of sound in air

$$v = (331 \text{ m/s})\sqrt{1 + \frac{T_C}{273\ ^\circ\text{C}}}$$

Sound intensity

$$I = P/A$$

Sound spreading radially

$$I = \frac{P}{4\pi r^2}$$

Sound level

$$\beta = (10 \text{ dB})\log\frac{I}{I_0}$$

Doppler effect, source moves toward listener

$$f_L = f_s \frac{1}{1 - v_s/v}$$

Doppler effect, source moves away from listener

$$f_L = f_s \frac{1}{1 + v_s/v}$$

Mach angle

$$\sin\theta = \frac{v_{sound}}{v_{object}}$$

$$\text{Mach number} = \frac{v_{object}}{v_{sound}}$$

chapter
17
Wave Superposition
and Interference
physics
Conceptual
kinetic
BOOKS

17.0 - Introduction

In this chapter, we will discuss what happens when two or more traveling waves combine with each other, as when waves meet in a pond, a pool or even a bathtub. The result is higher peaks and lower troughs. These waves can "pass through" each other and then regain their original shape and direction, in contrast to the collision of two particles, such as tennis balls, which alters the motion of the balls.

A stringed musical instrument like a violin or a guitar uses the reflection and recombination of waves from the end of a bowed or plucked string to create its magical sound. You also hear the result of waves combining when you listen to music on loudspeakers or as a live performance of a band or a symphony. Music halls are designed to take advantage of the reflection and combination of sound waves to produce an effect that audience members will find particularly pleasing.

You can begin your study of the result of combining waves with the simulations to the right. In Interactive 1, you control two wave pulses traveling on the same string. One pulse starts on the left and moves right, and the other starts on the right and moves left. You determine the amplitude and width of each pulse, as well as whether it is a peak or a trough. Set the parameters for each pulse and press GO to see what happens when the pulses meet. If you want to see the pulses combining in slow motion, press the "time step" arrow to advance or reverse time in small increments.

A challenge for you: Can you set the pulses so that when they meet they exactly cancel each other out, causing the string to be completely flat for an instant?

In Interactive 2, two traveling waves combine as they move toward one another. You determine the amplitudes and wavelengths of these waves. Again, set the parameters of the waves and press GO to see the result of combining the waves. Can you create a single combined wave that does not move either to the left or to the right? If you do, you will have created what is called a standing wave. You will find that by making the settings of the two waves identical, except for travel direction, you can create such a wave.

Intersecting ripples from two different wave sources in a pond.

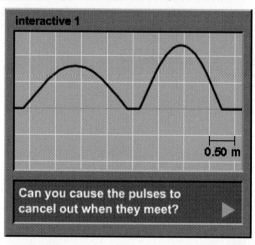

interactive 1

0.50 m

Can you cause the pulses to cancel out when they meet?

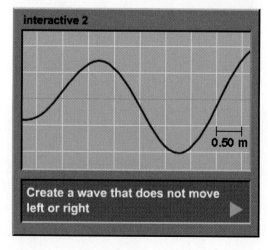

interactive 2

0.50 m

Create a wave that does not move left or right

17.1 - Combining waves: the principle of superposition

In much of this chapter, we discuss what happens when traveling waves combine. In this section, we consider the less complicated case of what occurs when two wave pulses combine in a string, as you see above. This will help us illustrate the principle of superposition, which is more readily viewed with pulses than with traveling waves.

In Concept 1 below, we show what occurs when two peaks like the ones in the illustration above combine. We show the result at four successive times. A blue pulse is traveling from left to right and a red pulse is traveling in the opposite direction. You can see that at each instant the combined pulse is determined by adding the vertical displacements of the two pulses at every point along the string.

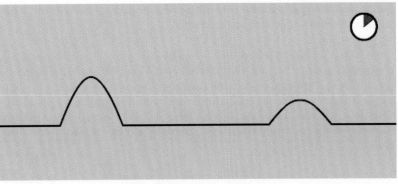

Two traveling wave pulses on a string.

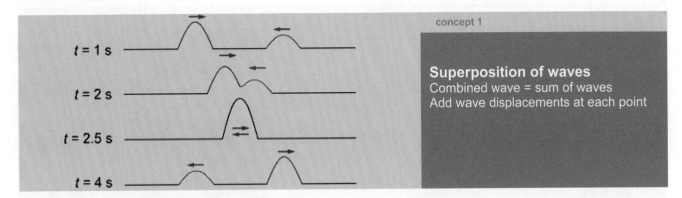

concept 1

Superposition of waves
Combined wave = sum of waves
Add wave displacements at each point

In the description above, we are applying the *principle of superposition*: The wave that results when two or more waves combine can be determined by adding the displacements of the individual waves at every point in the medium. This is sometimes more tersely stated as: The resulting wave is the algebraic sum of the displacements of the waves that cause it. ("Algebraic" means that you add positive and negative displacements as you would any signed numbers; no trigonometry is required.)

You see this principle in play in Concept 1. For instance, when the two peaks meet at time $t = 2.5$ s, the resulting peak's displacement equals the sum of the displacements of the two separate peaks. This is an example of *constructive interference*, which occurs when the amplitude of a combined pulse or wave is greater than the amplitude of any individual pulse or wave.

In Concept 2 below, a peak meets a trough. Except for the different directions of displacement, the pulses are identical. The two pulses cancel out completely when they occupy the same location on the string, and the string momentarily has zero displacement at each point. Positive and negative displacements of the same magnitude sum to zero. This is *destructive interference*: The amplitude of the combined pulse or wave is less than the amplitude of either individual pulse or wave.

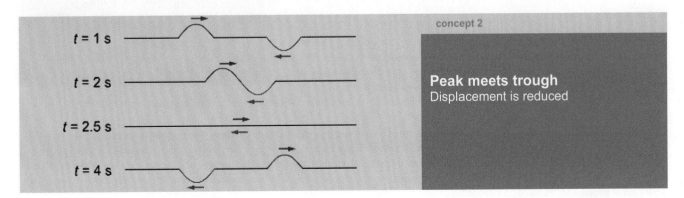

concept 2

Peak meets trough
Displacement is reduced

You may have experimented with this in the introduction simulation, but if you did not, you can go back and see what happens when peak meets peak, when peak meets trough, and finally, when two troughs meet. The result in each case is that the combined displacement is the sum of the displacements of all the pulses.

When the string is "flat" in Concept 2, it may seem there is no motion because you are looking at a static diagram. In fact, some of the string particles are moving up and some are moving down. The particles that were part of a peak are moving down and will be part of a trough. This is readily witnessed in the introductory simulation.

In this section, we used transverse wave pulses on a string to illustrate superposition, but the principle of superposition can also be applied to longitudinal waves (for instance, the combined sound wave produced by two stereo speakers). Acoustical (sound) engineers rely on constructive interference to create louder sounds and destructive interference to mask noises. For instance, noise-reducing headphones contain a microphone that detects unwanted noise from the environment. A circuit then creates a sound wave that is an inverted version of the noise wave, with peaks where the noise has troughs, and vice-versa. When this wave is played through the headphones, it destructively interferes with the unwanted ambient noise. The same technique is used to reduce the noise from fans in commercial heating and ventilation systems.

17.2 - Standing waves

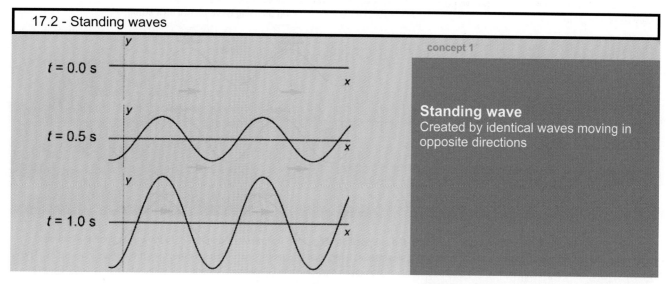

concept 1

Standing wave
Created by identical waves moving in opposite directions

Standing wave: Oscillations with a stationary outline produced by the combination of two identical waves moving in opposite directions.

When two identical traveling waves move in opposite directions through a medium, the resulting combined wave stays in the same location. The resulting wave is called a standing wave. Individual particles oscillate up and down, but unlike the case of a traveling wave, the locations of the peaks and troughs of a standing wave stay at fixed positions.

Consider the illustration above, showing waves on a string. The standing wave is formed by the combination of two traveling waves. We show three "snapshots" in time of two identical waves traveling in opposite directions, and the combined wave they create. The traveling waves are shown in colors. These waves have the same frequency and amplitude, but are traveling in opposite directions. The result is a standing wave that does not move along the string.

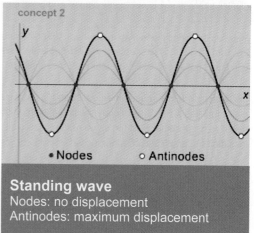

concept 2

• Nodes   ○ Antinodes

Standing wave
Nodes: no displacement
Antinodes: maximum displacement

In the first snapshot above, the two traveling waves are out of phase, and they destructively interfere. The combined standing wave has a constant zero displacement. In the second snapshot, the traveling waves have moved slightly, and the standing wave exhibits some peaks and troughs. In the third snapshot, the traveling waves exactly coincide, in phase, to constructively interfere, and the standing wave has its largest peaks and troughs. As the traveling waves continue to move, the standing wave's peaks and troughs will diminish until the traveling waves are again out of phase and the standing wave is flat.

If you find this difficult to visualize, you can see a simulation of the creation of a standing wave by clicking on the whiteboard above. You can have the simulation move slowly, step by step, by pressing the arrow buttons. You can also press "show components" if you want to see the component traveling waves. Press REPLAY to restart the simulation.

Along a standing wave, there are some fixed positions where there is no displacement and others where there is the maximum displacement. The positions with no displacement are called *nodes*. The positions where the wave has the greatest displacement (the peaks and troughs) are called *antinodes*. Adjacent nodes (and antinodes) are separated by a constant distance. Looking at the illustration for Concept 2, you can see that two adjacent nodes are separated by one half the wavelength of the wave. The same is true for two adjacent antinodes.

The standing wave depicted above is created by the combination of transverse waves. Longitudinal waves, such as sound waves, can combine to form standing waves as well.

17.3 - Reflected waves and resonance

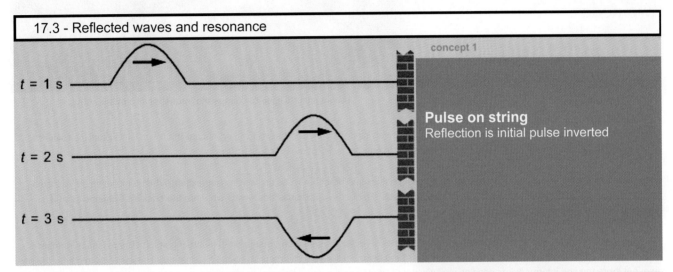

concept 1

$t = 1$ s

$t = 2$ s

$t = 3$ s

Pulse on string
Reflection is initial pulse inverted

concept 2

Wave on string
Reflects at wall
Creates standing wave

We have considered standing waves formed by two waves generated by separate sources, but they can also be formed by a single wave reflecting off a fixed point. This is the basis behind the sound production of many musical instruments. We will discuss this topic using the example of a piece of string, with one end connected to a wave-making machine that vibrates sinusoidally, moving the string up and down, and the other end fixed to a wall.

To start, consider what happens when the wave machine generates a single pulse, as illustrated above. We show the pulse at three positions over time. When the pulse reaches the wall, it "yanks" on the wall. Newton's third law dictates that there will be an equal "yank" in the opposite direction, which sends a reflected pulse back down the string. The reflected pulse is inverted from the original, so when a peak reaches a wall, a trough returns in the opposite direction.

A wave is a continuous series of pulses. When the wave machine vibrates continuously, each pulse will reflect off the wall, resulting in an inverted wave moving at the same speed in the direction opposite to the original wave. The reflected wave travels down the string toward the wave machine. We also consider the wave machine as fixed, which is reasonable if its vibrations are small in amplitude. The wave then reflects off that piece of machinery just as it reflected off the wall.

The wave machine continues to vibrate, sending wave pulses down the string. If it vibrates in synchronization with the reflected wave, the result will be two traveling waves of equal amplitude, frequency and speed, moving in opposite directions on the same string. This system has created the condition for a standing wave: two identical traveling waves moving in opposite directions. You see this illustrated in Concept 2.

On the other hand, if the wave machine is not in sync with the reflected wave, it will continue to add "new" waves to the string that will combine in more complicated ways, and there may be no obvious pattern of movement on the string.

If the wave machine works in synchronization with the reflected waves to create a standing wave, we say that it is working in *resonance*. Its motion reinforces the waves, and the amplitude of the resulting standing wave will be greater than the amplitude of the vibrations of the wave machine. This is akin to you pushing a friend on a swing. If you time the frequency of your "pushes" correctly, you will send your friend higher. We will discuss next how this frequency is determined.

Fundamental frequency: The frequency of a standing wave in a vibrating string that has two nodes.

Harmonic: A frequency of a standing wave in a string that has more than two nodes.

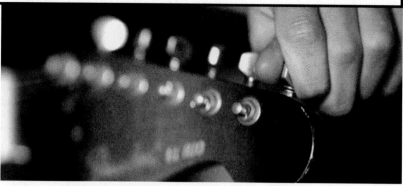

A tuning peg is used to change the frequency of a guitar string.

We have considered vibrating strings fairly abstractly. However, strings connected to two fixed points are the basis for musical instruments such as violins, cellos and so forth. To put it another way: Orchestras have "string" sections.

In this section, we want to put your knowledge of standing waves into practice. To do so, we ask a question: When a musician plays a note, what determines the frequency at which the string will vibrate? To put the question another way, what are the possible frequencies of a standing wave on a string fixed at both ends?

To answer this question, we begin by considering the number of nodes that must be present on the vibrating string. The minimum number of nodes is two: There must be a node at each end of the string because the string is attached to two fixed points. These nodes might be the only two, but there may be intermediate nodes as well. Drawings of standing waves with zero, one and two intermediate nodes are shown in Concept 1 below.

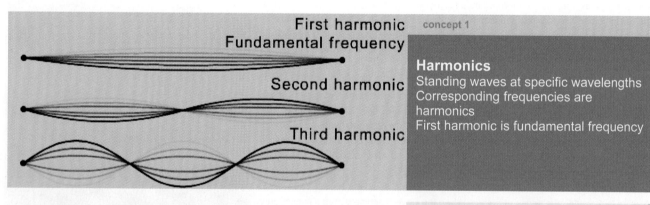

First harmonic
Fundamental frequency

Second harmonic

Third harmonic

concept 1

Harmonics
Standing waves at specific wavelengths
Corresponding frequencies are harmonics
First harmonic is fundamental frequency

The fundamental frequency of the string occurs when the only nodes are at the ends of the string. The fundamental frequency is also called the *first harmonic*. The second harmonic has one additional node in the middle of the string, the third harmonic two such nodes, the fourth harmonic three such nodes, and so on. Each harmonic is created by a particular *mode of vibration* of the string.

The fundamental frequency occurs when the wavelength of the standing wave is twice the length of the string, because two adjacent nodes represent half a wave. In general, the wavelength of the *n*th harmonic is twice the length of the string divided by *n*, with *n* being a positive integer. That is, the wavelength of the *n*th harmonic on a string of length L is $\lambda_n = 2L/n$.

The frequency of a wave is its speed divided by the wavelength, which lets us restate the equation above in terms of frequency. The equation to the right is the basic equation for harmonic frequencies. The harmonic frequencies are positive integer multiples of the fundamental frequency $v/2L$. Let's say the fundamental frequency f_1 of a string is 30

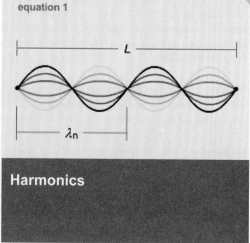

equation 1

L

λ_n

Harmonics

hertz (Hz). The second harmonic f_2 will be 60 Hz, the third harmonic f_3 90 Hz, and so forth.

You see these principles in play in musical instruments like the piano. Its strings are of different lengths, which is one factor in determining their fundamental frequency. Other factors that you see in the equations are also employed in musical instruments to determine a string's fundamental frequency. Pianos have thicker and thinner strings. A string's mass per unit length (its linear density) will partly determine its fundamental frequency, by changing the wave speed on the string.

In addition, string instruments are "tuned" by changing the tension in a string. You will see a guitarist frequently adjusting her instrument by turning a tuning peg, as you see at the top of this page, which determines the tension in a string. Along with linear density, this is the other factor that determines wave speed. A guitarist will also press her finger on a single string to temporarily create a string with a specific length and fundamental frequency.

A harmonic is sometimes called a *resonance frequency* or a *natural frequency*. Musicians also use other terms dealing with frequencies and harmonics. An *overtone* or a *partial* is any frequency produced by a musical device that is higher than the fundamental frequency. Unlike a harmonic, the frequency of an overtone does not necessarily bear any simple numerical relationship to the fundamental.

Some overtones are harmonics – that is, whole-number multiples of the fundamental – but some are not. Musical instruments such as drums, whose modes of vibration can be very complex, create non-harmonic overtones. Although harmonic overtones are "simple" integer multiples of the fundamental, they are often referred to by numbers that are, confusingly, "one off" from the numbers for harmonics: The first overtone is the second harmonic, and so on. Each musical instrument has a characteristic set of overtones that creates its distinctive timbre.

$$f_n = \frac{v}{\lambda_n} = n\frac{v}{2L}$$

for $n = 1, 2, 3, \ldots$

$f_n = n^{\text{th}}$ harmonic, v = wave speed

λ_n = wavelength of nth harmonic

L = string length

example 1

A tension of 417 N is applied to a 1.56 m string of mass 0.00133 kg. What is the fundamental frequency?

$$v = \sqrt{\frac{F}{m/L}}$$

$$v = \sqrt{\frac{417 \text{ N}}{(0.00133 \text{ kg})/(1.56 \text{ m})}}$$

$$v = 699 \text{ m/s}$$

$$f_n = n\frac{v}{2L}$$

$$f_1 = (1)(699 \text{ m/s})/2(1.56 \text{ m})$$

$$f_1 = 224 \text{ Hz}$$

17.5 - Interactive problem: tune the string

Let's say you play an unusual instrument in the orchestra, the alto pluck, an instrument specifically designed for physics students. The concert is underway and your big moment is coming up, when you get to play a particular note on the pluck.

You are supposed to play the G above middle C, a note that has a frequency of 392 Hz. You produce the correct note by setting the string length and the harmonic number. Remember that harmonic numbers are multiples of the fundamental frequency of the string. For this instrument, you are limited to harmonic numbers in the range of one to four.

When you set a harmonic number higher than one, a finger will touch the string at a position that will cause the string to vibrate with the harmonic number you selected. It does so by creating a standing wave node at the appropriate location. For instance, if you choose a harmonic number of four, there will be three nodes between the two ends of the string, and the finger will be one-fourth of the way along the string. If you see a musician such as a cellist performing, you will see that he sometimes lightly places his fingers at locations along a string to create harmonics in just this way. He also frequently presses a string firmly against the fingerboard to create a different, shorter, string length.

The string length of the alto pluck can range from 1.00 to 2.00 meters, but within that range, you are restricted to values that will produce frequencies found on the musical scale. You will find that as you click on the arrows for length, the values will move between appropriate string lengths. The harmonic values are easy to set: Just choose a number from one to four!

The description above is reasonably complicated; it is impressive that musicians with some instruments must make similar determinations as they play. In terms of approaching this problem, you will want to start with the equation

$$f_n = nv/2L$$

that enables you to calculate the frequency of the nth harmonic. The wave speed in your stringed instrument is 588 m/s.

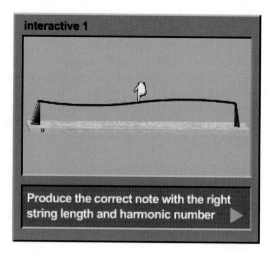

There is only one solution to the problem we pose, given the range of string lengths and harmonics together with the wave speed we provide.

If you are not sure how to proceed, try solving the equation above for the string length and entering the known values. You will still have another variable, n, left in the equation. However, since you know the range of string lengths, and that n must be an integer from one to four, you will be able to solve the problem.

To test your answer, set a string length and harmonic number and press GO to see a hand come down and pluck the string so you can hear the resulting note and see its frequency. The resulting musical note is displayed on the sounding board. Press RESET to start over.

17.6 - Sample problem: string tension

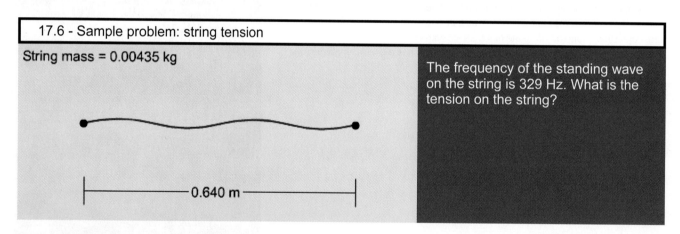

String mass = 0.00435 kg

The frequency of the standing wave on the string is 329 Hz. What is the tension on the string?

0.640 m

The values shown in the problem are representative of the lowest frequency string on a guitar. To answer the question, you must first determine the harmonic of the standing wave. You can do so by inspecting the diagram above. We exaggerated the amplitude of the wave to make the nodes and antinodes more visible.

Variables

string length	$L = 0.640$ m
string mass	$m = 0.00435$ kg
frequency	$f = 329$ Hz
harmonic number	n
wave speed	v
tension	T

What is the strategy?

1. Determine the harmonic by counting the number of nodes shown in the string above.
2. Calculate the wave speed from the frequency, string length and harmonic number.
3. Calculate the tension using the equation for wave speed on a string.

Physics principles and equations

Nodes are locations where there is no displacement. The harmonic number is one less than the number of nodes, including the nodes at the ends of the string.

The equation for the nth harmonic

$$f_n = \frac{nv}{2L}$$

The wave speed on a stretched string

$$v = \sqrt{\frac{T}{m/L}}$$

Step-by-step solution

First, we determine the harmonic number by looking at the wave above. Then, we calculate the wave speed using the equation for the frequency of the nth harmonic.

Step	Reason
1. $n = 4$	harmonic is one less than number of nodes
2. $f_n = \dfrac{nv}{2L}$	frequency of nth harmonic
3. $v = \dfrac{2Lf_n}{n}$	solve for wave speed
4. $v = \dfrac{2\,(0.640\ \text{m})(329\ \text{Hz})}{4}$	substitute values
5. $v = 105$ m/s	evaluate

Now we use the equation that relates wave speed to tension, mass, and string length.

Step		Reason
6.	$v = \sqrt{\dfrac{T}{m/L}}$	wave speed on string
7.	$T = \dfrac{v^2 m}{L}$	solve for tension
8.	$T = \dfrac{(105 \text{ m/s})^2 (0.00435 \text{ kg})}{0.640 \text{ m}}$	substitute values
9.	$T = 74.9 \text{ N}$	evaluate

17.7 - Wave interference and path length

We described wave interference resulting from a phase difference, or differing initial conditions for two waves moving in the same direction. Interference also results when two waves travel from different starting points and meet. To illustrate this, we use the example of two longitudinal traveling waves produced by two loudspeakers.

To the right, we show a person listening to the loudspeakers. The vibrating speakers create regions of pressure that are greater than atmospheric pressure (condensation) and less (rarefaction). We show this pattern of oscillation emanating from each speaker in Concept 1. We assume the speakers create waves with the same amplitude and wavelength, and that there is no phase difference between them. We focus on the point where the two waves combine just as they reach the listener's ear.

In Concept 1, we position the two speakers so that the listener is equidistant from them. The distance from a speaker to the ear is called the *path length*. Since the waves travel the same distance, they will be in phase when they arrive. This means peaks and troughs exactly coincide with each other.

When two peaks combine, they double the pressure increase. When two troughs combine, they also add, and the pressure decrease is doubled. The listener hears a louder sound. In short, the waves constructively interfere.

The waves would also constructively interfere if one speaker were placed one wavelength farther away. Peaks would still meet peaks and troughs would still meet troughs. In fact, if the difference in the distances between the loudspeakers and the listener is any integer multiple of the wavelength, the waves constructively interfere. (This does assume that the loudspeakers vibrate at a constant frequency, an unusual assumption for most music.) You see this condition for constructive interference stated in Equation 1.

Can we arrange the speakers so that the waves **destructively** interfere? Yes, by moving one speaker one-half wavelength away from the listener. This is shown in Concept 2. When the waves combine, peaks will meet troughs and vice versa. This will also occur if the speaker/listener distances differ by half a wavelength, or 1.5 wavelengths, or any half-integer multiple of the wavelength. This condition for destructive interference is stated as an equation on the right. If the waves have the same amplitude at the ear and destructively interfere completely, the result is silence at the listener's position.

The principle of conservation of energy applies to sound waves. When two waves destructively interfere at some position, the energy does not

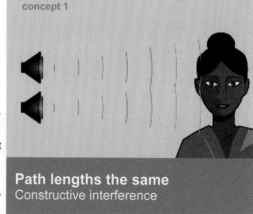

concept 1

Path lengths the same
Constructive interference

concept 2

$\left|\dfrac{\lambda}{2}\right|$

Path lengths differ by one-half wavelength
Destructive interference

disappear. Rather, there must be another area where the waves are constructively interfering, as well. For any area of silence, there must be a louder area. Positioning loudspeakers or designing concert halls to minimize the severity of these "dead spots" and "hot spots" is a topic of interest to audiophiles and sound engineers alike.

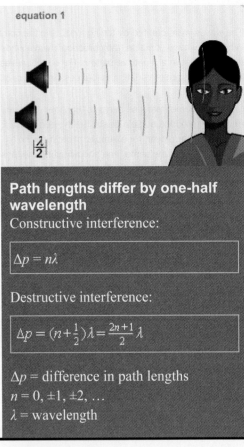

equation 1

Path lengths differ by one-half wavelength

Constructive interference:

$$\Delta p = n\lambda$$

Destructive interference:

$$\Delta p = (n + \tfrac{1}{2})\lambda = \frac{2n+1}{2}\lambda$$

Δp = difference in path lengths
$n = 0, \pm 1, \pm 2, \ldots$
λ = wavelength

17.8 - Beats

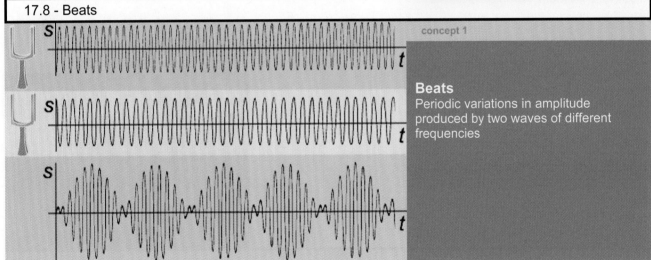

concept 1

Beats
Periodic variations in amplitude produced by two waves of different frequencies

Beats: The pattern of loud/soft sounds caused by two sound sources with similar but not identical frequencies.

So far in this chapter, we have studied combinations of traveling waves with the same amplitude, frequency and wavelength. You may wonder what happens if waves that have different properties are combined, and in this section, we consider such a situation.

To be specific, we consider two traveling waves with the same amplitude but slightly different frequencies, using sound waves as our example. We examine the waves and their combination at a fixed x position. You see the graphs above of two such waves over time **at a particular position**. Note that in this case the graphs that you see are displaying the displacement over time of a particle at a fixed position in a medium carrying longitudinal waves.

The waves were created by tuning forks, and the combined wave is shown below them. When the waves combine, they produce a wave whose amplitude is not constant, but instead varies in a repetitive pattern. For sound waves, these "beats" are heard as a repeating pattern of variation in loudness in a wave of constant frequency.

Musicians sometimes use beats to tune their instruments. Sounds that are close in frequency produce audible beats, but the beats disappear when the frequencies are the same. A guitar player, for example, might tune the "A" string by playing an "A" on another string at the same time and adjusting the tension of the "A" string until there are no longer any audible beats. This occurs when the frequencies match exactly, or are close enough that the beats are so far apart in time they can no longer be heard.

We hear beats because the waves constructively and destructively interfere over time. When they constructively interfere, there is greater condensation and rarefaction of the air at our ears and we hear louder sounds. Destructive interference means a smaller change in pressure and a softer sound.

The *beat frequency* equals the number of times per second we hear a cycle of loud and soft. This is computed as shown in Equation 1, as the difference of the original frequencies. When the frequencies are the same, the beat frequency is zero, as when two strings are perfectly in tune. Humans can hear beats in sound waves at frequencies up to around 20 beats per second. Above that frequency, the beats are not distinguishable.

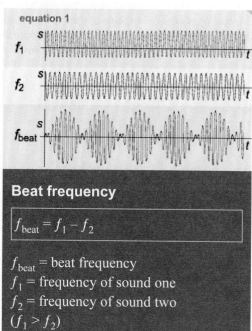

equation 1

Beat frequency

$$f_{beat} = f_1 - f_2$$

f_{beat} = beat frequency
f_1 = frequency of sound one
f_2 = frequency of sound two
$(f_1 > f_2)$

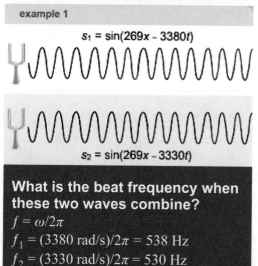

example 1

$s_1 = \sin(269x - 3380t)$

$s_2 = \sin(269x - 3330t)$

What is the beat frequency when these two waves combine?
$f = \omega/2\pi$
$f_1 = (3380 \text{ rad/s})/2\pi = 538 \text{ Hz}$
$f_2 = (3330 \text{ rad/s})/2\pi = 530 \text{ Hz}$
$f_{beat} = f_1 - f_2$
$f_{beat} = 538 \text{ Hz} - 530 \text{ Hz}$
$f_{beat} = 8 \text{ Hz}$

17.9 - Gotchas

A standing wave has its maximum displacement at an antinode. Yes, that is correct. An antinode is the opposite of a node, where no motion occurs.

The locations where peaks and troughs occur are constant in a standing wave. That is correct, and this is the distinguishing point between a standing wave and a traveling wave.

I see a standing wave on a string with two fixed ends and a single antinode. The wave has two nodes. Yes. The two fixed ends are nodes.

Two waves traveling in the same direction can cause a standing wave. No. Waves traveling in opposite directions can cause a standing wave.

300   Copyright 2000-2007 Kinetic Books Co. Chapter 17

However, a wave from a single source when it is reflected can cause a standing wave, because the reflected wave is traveling in the opposite direction.

17.10 - Summary

The principle of linear superposition says that whenever waves travel through a medium, the net displacement of the medium at any point in space and at any time is the sum of the individual wave displacements. The superposition of waves explains the phenomenon of interference.

Destructive interference occurs when two waves in the same medium cancel each other, either partially or fully. If two sinusoidal waves have the same wavelength, destructive interference will happen when the waves are close to being completely out of phase, meaning that their phase constants differ by π radians (or $180°$).

Constructive interference occurs when two waves in the same medium reinforce each other. This happens when the waves are close to being in phase for waves with the same wavelength.

Intermediate interference is a general term for a situation where the difference between the phases of two interfering waves, called the phase shift, is somewhere between 0 and π radians.

Equations

Harmonics

$$f_n = \frac{v}{\lambda_n} = n\frac{v}{2L}$$

Interference

Constructive: $\Delta p = n\lambda$

Destructive: $\Delta p = \frac{2n+1}{2}\lambda$

Beat frequency

$$f_{beat} = f_1 - f_2$$

When two identical waves traveling in opposite directions in the same medium interfere, they produce a standing wave. In standing waves, there are points called nodes that experience no displacement at all. The points that experience the maximum displacement are called antinodes. Standing waves can be either transverse, as with the oscillations of a piano string, or longitudinal, as with the sound waves in an organ pipe.

Identical waves from different sources can interfere with each other at a point in space based on the distances they travel to that point, called their path lengths. Provided they start out in phase, if the path lengths of two waves to a certain point differ by an integer number of wavelengths, they will constructively interfere at that point. If the path lengths differ by a half-integer number of wavelengths, they will exhibit completely destructive interference.

Another type of interference occurs when two waves have different frequencies. In this case, beats are produced. The waves alternate between constructive and destructive interference.

18.0 - Introduction

Thermodynamics is the study of heat ("thermo") and the movement of that heat ("dynamics") between objects. A kitchen provides an informal laboratory for the study of thermodynamics. Manufacturers offer numerous kitchen devices designed to facilitate the flow of heat: stovetops and ovens, convection ovens, toasters, refrigerators, and more. Heat flow changes the temperature of what is being cooked or cooled, and that can be monitored with thermometers.

This chapter starts with a few basic thermodynamics concepts, namely how temperature is measured, what temperature scales are, and what is meant by heat. It then begins the discussion of the relationship between heat and temperature.

Kitchen appliances are engineered using the principles of thermodynamics.

18.1 - Temperature and thermometers

Although temperature is an everyday word, like energy it is surprisingly hard to define. For now, we ask that you continue to think of temperature simply as something measured by a *thermometer*. Warmer objects have higher temperatures than cooler objects.

Traditional thermometers rely on the important principle that any two objects placed in contact with each other will reach a common temperature. For instance, when a traditional fever thermometer is placed under your tongue, after a few minutes the flow of heat causes it to reach the same temperature as your body.

While there are many different types of thermometers available, they all rely on some physical property of materials in order to measure temperature. In the "old" days, body temperature was measured with a glass thermometer filled with mercury, a material that expands significantly with temperature and whose expansion is proportional to the change in temperature.

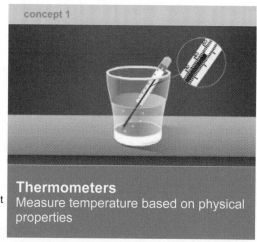

concept 1

Thermometers
Measure temperature based on physical properties

Today, a wide variety of physical properties are used to determine temperature. Some medical clinics use thermometers that measure temperature with plastic sheets containing a chemical that changes color with temperature. Battery-powered digital thermometers rely on the fact that a resistor's resistance changes with temperature. Ear thermometers use *thermopiles* that are sensitive to subtle changes in the infrared radiation emitted by your body; this radiation changes with your temperature.

18.2 - Temperature scales

In the United States, the Fahrenheit system is the most common measurement system for temperature. The units in this system are called degrees. In most of the rest of the world, however, temperatures are measured in degrees Celsius. Physicists use the Celsius scale or, quite often, another scale called the Kelvin scale. All three scales are shown on the right.

There are two things required to construct a temperature scale. One is a reference point, such as the temperature at which water freezes at standard atmospheric pressure. As shown to the right, the three scales have different values at this reference point. Water freezes at 273.15

kelvins (273.15 K), $0°$ Celsius $(0°C)$ and $32°$ Fahrenheit $(32°F)$. Notice that the standard terminology for the Kelvin scale avoids the use of "degrees." Water freezes at 273.15 kelvins, **not** 273.15 degrees Kelvin.

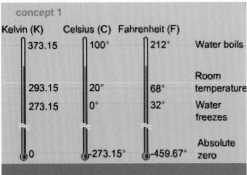

The other requirement is to pick another reference point, such as the temperature at which water boils at standard atmospheric pressure, and establish the number of degrees between these two points. This determines the magnitude of the units of the scale. The Celsius and Kelvin scales both have 100 units between the freezing and boiling points of water. This means that their units are equal: a change of 1 $C°$ equals a change of 1 K. (Changes in Celsius temperatures are indicated with $C°$ instead of $°C$.) In contrast, there are 180 degrees between these temperatures in the Fahrenheit system.

Another important concept is shown in the illustration to the right: absolute zero. At this temperature, molecules (in essence) cease moving. Reaching this temperature is not theoretically possible, but temperatures quite close to this are being achieved. Absolute zero is 0 K, or $-273.15°C$.

To standardize temperatures, scientists have agreed on a common reference point called the *triple point*. The triple point is the sole combination of pressure and temperature at which solid water (ice), liquid water, and gaseous water (water vapor) can coexist. It equals 273.16 K at a pressure of 611.73 Pa. The triple point is used to define the kelvin as an SI unit. One kelvin equals 1/273.16 of the difference between absolute zero and the triple point.

If you are a sharp-eyed reader, you may have noticed the references to both 273.16 and 273.15 in this section. The freezing point of water is typically stated as 273.15 K $(0°C)$ because this is its value at standard atmospheric pressure, but at the triple point pressure, water freezes at 273.16 K $(0.01°C)$.

18.3 - Temperature scale conversions

Since the Celsius and Kelvin scales have the same number of units between the freezing and boiling points of water, it takes just one step to convert between the two systems, as you see in the first conversion formula in Equation 1. To convert from degrees Celsius to kelvins, add 273.15. To convert from kelvins to degrees Celsius, subtract 273.15.

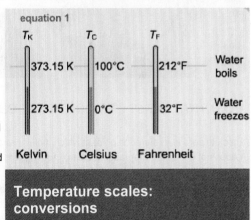

Since water freezes at $32°$ and boils at $212°$ in the Fahrenheit system, there are 180 degrees Fahrenheit between these points, compared to the 100 units in the Celsius and Kelvin systems. To convert from degrees Fahrenheit to degrees Celsius, first subtract 32 degrees (to establish how far the temperature is from the freezing point of water) and then multiply by 100/180, or 5/9, the ratio of the number of degrees between freezing and boiling on the two systems. That conversion is shown as the second equation in Equation 1. If you further needed to convert to kelvins, you would add 273.15.

To switch from Celsius to Fahrenheit, you first multiply the number of degrees Celsius by 9/5 (the reciprocal of the ratio mentioned above) and then add 32.

In Example 1, you see the conventionally normal human body temperature, $98.6°F$, converted to degrees Celsius and kelvins.

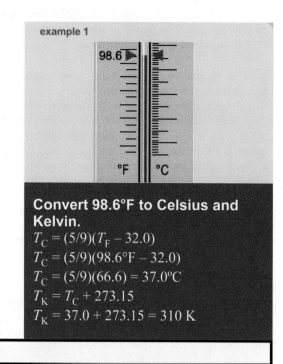

example 1

98.6 ▶

°F   °C

Convert 98.6°F to Celsius and Kelvin.

$T_C = (5/9)(T_F - 32.0)$

$T_C = (5/9)(98.6°F - 32.0)$

$T_C = (5/9)(66.6) = 37.0°C$

$T_K = T_C + 273.15$

$T_K = 37.0 + 273.15 = 310\ K$

18.4 - Absolute zero

concept 1

Absolute zero
It cannot get colder
Molecules at minimum energy state
0 K, −273.15°C

Absolute zero: As cold as it can get.

Absolute zero is a reference point at which molecules are in their minimum energy state (quantum theory dictates they still have some energy). It does not get colder than absolute zero; nothing with a temperature less than this minimum energy state can exist.

Physics theory says it is impossible for a material to be chilled to absolute zero. Instead, it is a limit that scientists strive to get closer and closer to achieving. Above, you see a photograph of scientists who chilled atoms to less than a hundred-billionth of a degree above absolute zero. At that temperature, the atoms changed into a state of matter called a Bose-Einstein condensate.

Although we exist around the relatively toasty 293 K thanks to the Sun and our atmosphere, the background temperature of the universe − the temperature far from any star − is only about 3 K. Brrrr.

18.5 - Heat

Heat: Thermal energy transferred between objects because of a difference in their temperatures.

If you hold a cold can of soda in your hand, the soda will warm up and your hand will chill. Energy flows from the object with the higher temperature – your hand – to the object with the lower temperature – the soda. This energy that moves is called heat. Ovens are designed to facilitate the flow of heat. In the diagram to the right, you see heat flowing from the oven coils through the air to the loaf of bread. As with other forms of energy, heat can be measured in joules. It is represented by the capital letter Q.

Physicists do **not** say an object has heat. Heat refers solely to the flow of energy due to temperature differences. Heat transfers *thermal energy* that is internal to objects, related to the random motion of the atoms making up the objects.

Heat is like work: It changes the energy of an object or system. It does not make sense to say "how much work a system has", nor does it make sense to say "how much heat the system has". Just as work is done by a system or on a system, heat as thermal energy can enter a system or leave a system.

Having said that heat is measured in joules, we will backtrack a little in order to explain some other commonly used units. These units measure heat by its ability to raise the temperature of water. For example, a *calorie* raises one gram of water from $14.5°C$ to $15.5°C$. The *British Thermal Unit* (BTU) measures the heat that would raise a pound of water $1°$ on the Fahrenheit scale.

The unit we use to measure one property of food – the calories you see labeled on the back of food packages – is actually a kilocalorie (good marketing!). This is sometimes spelled with a capital C, as in Calories. Food calories measure how much heat will be released when an object is burned. A Big Mac® hamburger contains 590 Calories, or 590,000 calories. This amount of energy equals about 2,500,000 J. If your body could capture all this energy, if it were 100% efficient and solely focused on the task, the energy from a Big Mac would be enough to allow you to lift a 50 kg weight one meter about 5000 times. We will skip the calculation for the french fries.

concept 1

Heat
Energy flow due to temperature difference
Not a property of an object

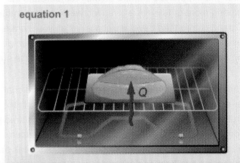

equation 1

Heat
Q represents heat
Units: joules (J)

18.6 - Internal energy

Internal energy: The energy associated with the molecules and atoms that make up a system.

In the study of mechanics, energy is an overall property of an object or system. The energy is a function of factors like how fast a car is moving, how high an object is off the ground, how fast a wheel is rotating, and so forth.

In thermodynamics, the properties of the molecules and/or atoms that make up the object or system are now the focus. They also have energy, a form of energy called internal energy. The internal energy includes the rotational, translational and vibrational energy of individual molecules and atoms. It also includes the potential energy within and between molecules.

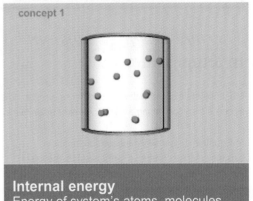

concept 1

Internal energy
Energy of system's atoms, molecules

To contrast the two forms of energy: If you lift a pot up from a stovetop, you will increase its gravitational potential energy. But in terms of internal energy, nothing has changed. The potential energy of the pot's molecules based on their relationship to each other has not changed.

However, if you turn on the burner under the cooking pot, the flow of heat will increase the kinetic energy of its molecules. The molecules will move faster as heat flows to the pot, which means the internal energy of the molecules of the pot increases.

Thermal expansion: The increase in the length or volume of a material due to a change in its temperature.

Expansion joints allow bridge sections to expand without breaking.

You buy a jar of jelly at the grocery store and store it on a pantry shelf. When it comes time to open the jar, the lid refuses to budge. Fortunately, you know that placing the jar under hot water will increase your odds of being able to twist open the lid.

By using hot water to coax a lid to turn, you are implicitly using two physics principles. First, most materials expand as their temperature increases. Second, different materials expand more or less for a given increase in temperature. The metal lid of the jar expands more than the glass container as you increase their temperatures, effectively lessening the "grip" of the lid on the glass. (The temperature of the lid is also likely to increase faster, another factor that accounts for the success of the process.)

The expansion of materials due to a temperature change can be useful at times, as the jar-opening example demonstrates. Sometimes, it poses challenging engineering problems. For example, when nuclear waste is stored in a rock mass, heat can flow from the waste to the rock, raising the rock's temperature and causing it to expand and crack. This could allow the dangerous waste to leak out. Knowing the exact rate of expansion can help engineers design storage intended to prevent cracking.

Good engineering takes expansion into account. For instance, bridges are built with expansion joints, like the one shown at the top of this page, that accommodate expansion as the temperature increases.

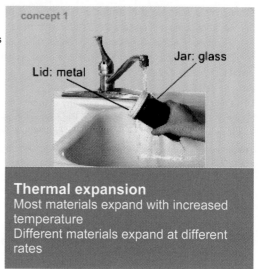

concept 1

Lid: metal

Jar: glass

Thermal expansion
Most materials expand with increased temperature
Different materials expand at different rates

Thermal linear expansion: Change in the length of a material due to a change in temperature.

Most objects expand with increased temperature; how much they expand varies by material. In this section, we discuss how much they expand in one dimension, along a line. Their expansion is measured as a fraction of their initial length.

In Equation 1, you see the equation for linear expansion. The change in length equals the initial length, times a constant α (Greek letter alpha), times the change in temperature. The constant α is called the *coefficient of linear expansion* and depends on the material. A table of coefficients of linear expansion for some materials is shown above. These coefficients are valid for temperatures around $25°C$.

Differing coefficients of linear expansion can be taken advantage of to build useful mechanisms. A *bimetallic strip*, shown to the right, consists of two metals with different coefficients of linear expansion. As the strip increases in temperature, the two materials expand at different rates, causing the strip to

Coefficient of linear expansion (1/C°)	
Carbon steel	1.17×10^{-5}
Iron	1.18×10^{-5}
Copper	1.65×10^{-5}
Silver	1.89×10^{-5}
Aluminum	2.31×10^{-5}
Magnesium	2.48×10^{-5}
Lead	2.89×10^{-5}
	at temperatures near 25°C

bend. Since the amount of bending is a function of the temperature, such a strip can be used in a thermometer to indicate temperature. It can also be used as a thermostat to control appliances, such as coffee pots and toasters. In these appliances, the bending of the strip interrupts a circuit and turns off the power when the appliance has reached a specified temperature.

Significant changes in temperature cause fairly minor changes in length. For instance, in Example 1, we calculate the expansion of a 0.50 meter copper rod when its temperature is increased $80 \ C°$. The increase in length is just $6.6×10^{-4}$ meters, less than a millimeter.

Some materials, like carbon fiber, have negative coefficients of expansion, which means they shrink when their temperature increases. By blending materials with both positive and negative coefficients, engineers design systems that change shape very little with changes in temperature. The Boeing Company pioneered the use of negative coefficient materials in airplanes and satellites.

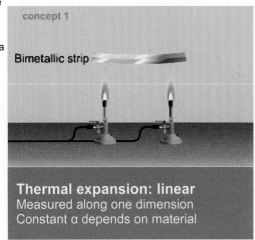

concept 1

Bimetallic strip

Thermal expansion: linear
Measured along one dimension
Constant α depends on material

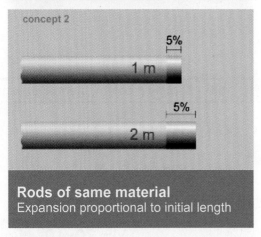

concept 2

5%

1 m

5%

2 m

Rods of same material
Expansion proportional to initial length

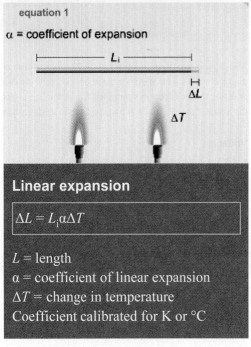

equation 1

α = coefficient of expansion

L_i

ΔL

ΔT

Linear expansion

$$\Delta L = L_i \alpha \Delta T$$

L = length
α = coefficient of linear expansion
ΔT = change in temperature
Coefficient calibrated for K or °C

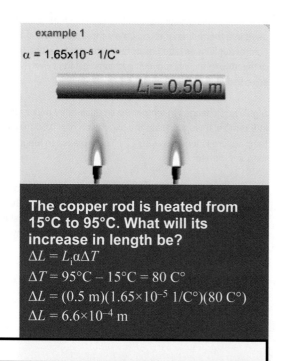

example 1

$\alpha = 1.65 \times 10^{-5}\ 1/C°$

$L_i = 0.50\ m$

The copper rod is heated from 15°C to 95°C. What will its increase in length be?

$\Delta L = L_i \alpha \Delta T$

$\Delta T = 95°C - 15°C = 80\ C°$

$\Delta L = (0.5\ m)(1.65 \times 10^{-5}\ 1/C°)(80\ C°)$

$\Delta L = 6.6 \times 10^{-4}\ m$

18.9 - Sample problem: thermal expansion and stress

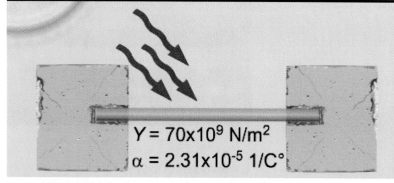

$Y = 70 \times 10^9\ N/m^2$

$\alpha = 2.31 \times 10^{-5}\ 1/C°$

What stress does the aluminum rod exert when its temperature rises 20 K?

Above, you see an aluminum rod heated by the Sun and held in place with concrete blocks. Since the rod increases in temperature, its length also increases. This exerts a force on the concrete blocks. Stress is force per unit area, and an equation for tensile stress was presented in another chapter. Young's modulus for aluminum is given; it relates the fractional increase in length (the strain) to stress. You are asked to find the stress that results from the increase in temperature.

Variables

thermal expansion coefficient	$\alpha = 2.31 \times 10^{-5}\ 1/C°$
Young's modulus	$Y = 70 \times 10^9\ N/m^2$
temperature change	$\Delta T = 20\ K$
initial length	L_i
change in length	ΔL
tensile stress	F/A

You may notice that the initial length of the rod is not known. It is not needed to answer the question.

What is the strategy?

1. Combine the equations for thermal expansion and tensile stress to write an equation to calculate tensile stress from the temperature change.
2. Use the equation to compute the stress in this case.

Physics principles and equations

We will use the equations for thermal expansion and tensile stress. Tensile stress is measured as force per unit area, or F/A.

$$\Delta L = L_i \alpha \Delta T$$

$$F/A = Y(\Delta L / L_i)$$

Step-by-step solution

We start by substituting the expression for the change in length from the thermal expansion equation into the tensile stress equation, and then do some algebraic simplification.

Step	Reason
1. $F/A = Y(\Delta L / L_i)$	tensile stress equation
2. $\Delta L = L_i \alpha \Delta T$	thermal expansion equation
3. $F/A = Y\dfrac{L_i \alpha \Delta T}{L_i}$	Substitute equation 2 into equation 1
4. $F/A = Y\alpha \Delta T$	L_i cancels out

The equation we just found does not depend on the initial length. We know all the values needed to calculate the tensile stress in the aluminum rod.

Step	Reason
5. $F/A = (70 \times 10^9 \text{ N/m}^2)(2.31 \times 10^{-5} \text{ 1/C}^\circ)(20 \text{ K})$	enter values
6. $F/A = 3.2 \times 10^7 \text{ N/m}^2$	multiply

An aluminum rod with a radius of 0.025 meters (about one inch) exerts more than 60,000 newtons of force (equivalent to the weight of a large elephant) against perfectly rigid supports when its temperature increases 20 C°! In this problem, we have ignored the expansion of the concrete in which the aluminum is embedded.

18.10 - Thermal expansion of water

Water exhibits particularly interesting expansion properties when it nears its freezing point. Above 4°C, water expands with temperature, as most liquids do. However, water also expands as it **cools** from 4°C to 0°C, a significant and unusual phenomenon. Below 0° water once again contracts as it cools. The consequence is that liquid water is most dense at a temperature of around 4°C.

This pattern of expansion means that lakes and other bodies of water freeze from the top down. Why? In colder climates, as the autumn or winter seasons approach and the air temperature drops to near freezing or below, the water in a lake cools. When the water is cold but still above 4°C, it contracts when it chills. Since it becomes denser, it sinks. This brings warmer water to the surface, which cools in turn.

Eventually, the entire lake reaches 4°C. But when the top layer then becomes colder still, it no longer sinks. Below 4°C, the water expands, becoming less dense. It floats atop the warmer water.

As the cold water at the top of the lake further cools and freezes, it forms a floating layer of ice that insulates the water below. Water is also atypical in that its solid form, ice, is less dense than its liquid form and floats on top of it. Fish and other aquatic life can live in the relatively warm (and liquid) water below, protected by a shield of ice.

If water always expanded with increasing temperature for all temperatures above 0°C, and contracted with decreasing temperature, the coldest water would sink to the bottom where it might never warm up. Water's negative coefficient of expansion in the temperature range from 0°C to 4°C is crucial to life on Earth. If ice did not float, oceans and lakes would freeze from the bottom to the top. This would increase the likelihood that they would freeze entirely, since they would not have a top layer of ice to insulate the liquid water below and their frozen depths would not be exposed to warm air during the spring and summer.

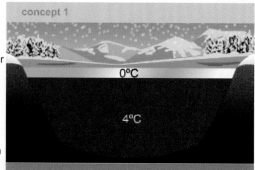

Thermal expansion of water
Water contracts and sinks as it cools, until 4°C
From 4°C to 0°C, water expands and stays on top
Then ice forms on top and floats

18.11 - Thermal expansion: volume

Thermal volume expansion:
Change in volume due to a change in temperature.

The equation for thermal linear expansion is used to calculate the thermally induced change in the size of an object in just one dimension. Thermal expansion or contraction also changes the volume of a material, and for liquids (and many solids) it is more useful to

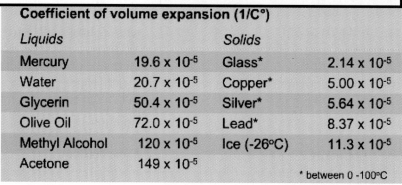

Coefficient of volume expansion (1/C°)			
Liquids		*Solids*	
Mercury	19.6×10^{-5}	Glass*	2.14×10^{-5}
Water	20.7×10^{-5}	Copper*	5.00×10^{-5}
Glycerin	50.4×10^{-5}	Silver*	5.64×10^{-5}
Olive Oil	72.0×10^{-5}	Lead*	8.37×10^{-5}
Methyl Alcohol	120×10^{-5}	Ice (-26°C)	11.3×10^{-5}
Acetone	149×10^{-5}		

* between 0 -100°C

determine the change in volume rather than expansion along one dimension. The expansion in volume can be significant. Automobile cooling systems have tanks that capture excess coolant when the heated fluid expands so much it exceeds the radiator's capacity. A radiator and its overflow tank are shown in Concept 1 on the right.

The formula in Equation 1 resembles that for linear expansion: The increase is proportional to the initial volume, a constant, and the change in temperature. The constant β is called the *coefficient of volume expansion*.

Above, you see a table of coefficients of volume expansion for some liquids and solids. The coefficients for liquids are valid for temperatures at which these substances remain liquid.

For solid materials like copper and lead, the coefficient of volume expansion β is about three times the coefficient of linear expansion α, because the solid expands linearly in three dimensions.

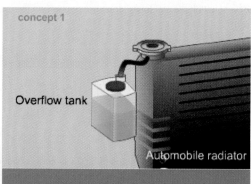

Overflow tank

Automobile radiator

Thermal expansion: volume
Volume increases with temperature
Constant β varies by material
Increase is proportional to initial volume

equation 1

Thermal expansion: volume

$$\Delta V = V_i \beta \Delta T$$

V = volume
β = coefficient of volume expansion
ΔT = change in temperature
Coefficient calibrated for K or °C

equation 2

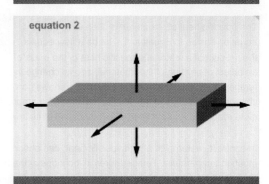

For solids
$\beta \approx 3\alpha$
β = coefficient of volume expansion
α = coefficient of linear expansion

example 1

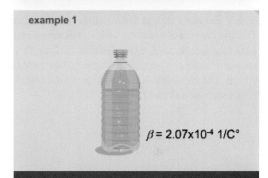

$\beta = 2.07 \times 10^{-4}\ 1/C°$

The temperature of 2.0 L of water increases from 5.0° C to 25° C. How much does its volume increase?

$\Delta V = V_i \beta \Delta T$

$\Delta T = 25°C - 5.0°C = 20\ C°$

$\Delta V = (2.0\ L)(2.07 \times 10^{-4}\ 1/C°)(20\ C°)$

$\Delta V = 0.0083\ L$

18.12 - Specific heat

Specific heat: A proportionality constant that relates the amount of heat flow per kilogram to a material's change in temperature.

Specific heat is a property of a material; it is a proportionality constant that states a relationship between the heat flow per kilogram of a material and its change in temperature.

A material's specific heat is determined by how much heat is required to increase the temperature of one kilogram of the material by one kelvin. A material with a greater specific heat requires more heat per kilogram to increase its temperature a given amount than one with a lesser specific heat. In spite of its name, specific heat is not an amount of heat, but a constant relating heat, mass, and temperature change.

The specific heat of a material is often used in the equation shown in Equation 1. The heat flow equals the product of a material's specific heat c, the mass of an object consisting of that material, and its change in temperature. The illustration in Equation 1 shows how specific heat relates heat flow to change in temperature. As you can see from the graph, lead increases in temperature quite readily when heat flows into it, because of its low specific heat.

In contrast, water, with a high specific heat, can absorb a lot of energy without changing much in temperature. Temperatures in locations at the seaside, or having humid atmospheres, tend to change very slowly because it takes a lot of heat flow into or out of the water to accomplish a small change in temperature. Summer in the desert southwest of the United States is famous for its blazing hot days and chilly nights, while on the east coast of the country the sweltering heat of the day persists long into the night. Materials with large specific heats are sometimes informally called "heat sinks" because of their ability to store large amounts of internal energy without much temperature change.

Above, you see a table of some specific heats, measured in joules per kilogram·kelvin. The specific heat of a material varies as its temperature and pressure change. The table lists specific heats for materials at $25°C$ to $30°C$ (except for ice) and 10^5 Pa pressure, about one atmosphere. Specific heats vary somewhat with temperature, but you can use these values over a range of temperatures you might encounter in a physics lab (or a kitchen).

Specific heat (J/kg·K)	
Lead	129
Silver	235
Copper	385
Iron	449
Carbon	709
Aluminum	897
Air (27°C)	1007
Ice (0°C)	2110
Water (30°C)	4178

at 10^5 Pa, $25°C$

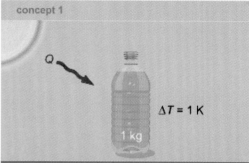

concept 1

$\Delta T = 1$ K

1 kg

Specific heat of a material
Relates heat and temperature change, per kilogram

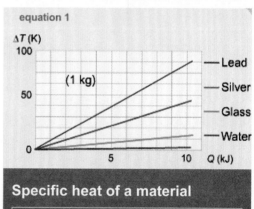

equation 1

ΔT (K)

(1 kg)

— Lead
— Silver
— Glass
— Water

Q (kJ)

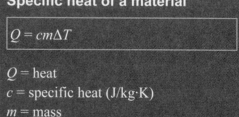

Specific heat of a material

$$Q = cm\Delta T$$

Q = heat
c = specific heat (J/kg·K)
m = mass
ΔT = temperature change in C° or K

example 1

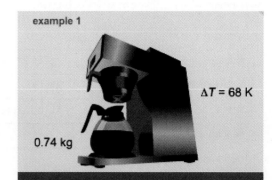

$\Delta T = 68$ K

0.74 kg

How much heat is required to increase the coffee's temperature 68 K?

$Q = cm\Delta T$

$Q = (4178 \text{ J/kg}\cdot\text{K})(0.74 \text{ kg})(68 \text{ K})$

$Q = 210{,}000 \text{ J}$

18.13 - Sample problem: a calorimeter

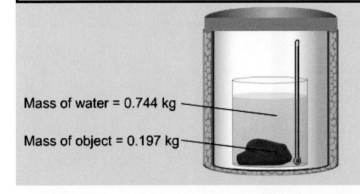

Mass of water = 0.744 kg

Mass of object = 0.197 kg

A calorimeter is used to measure the specific heat of an object. The water bath has an initial temperature of 23.2°C. An object with a temperature of 67.8°C is placed in the beaker. After thermal equilibrium is reestablished, the water bath's temperature is 25.6°C. What is the specific heat of the object?

In a calorimeter, a water bath is placed in a well-insulated container. The temperature of the water bath is recorded, and an object of known mass and temperature placed in it. After thermal equilibrium is reestablished, the temperature is measured again. From this information, the specific heat of the object can be calculated. (We ignore the air in this calculation.)

The use of a calorimeter depends on the conservation of energy. In the calorimeter, heat flows from the object to the water bath (or vice-versa if the object is colder than the water). Because the calorimeter is well insulated, negligible heat flows in or out of it. The conservation of energy allows us to say that the heat lost by the object equals the heat gained by the water bath.

The water bath consists of the water and the beaker containing it. If the mass of the water is much greater that the mass of the beaker, relatively little heat will be transferred to the beaker and it can be ignored in the calculation. We do that here.

Variables

	water	object
mass	$m_w = 0.744$ kg	$m_o = 0.197$ kg
initial temperature	$T_w = 23.2°C$	$T_o = 67.8°C$
specific heat	$c_w = 4178$ J/kg·K	c_o
heat transferred to water	Q_w	
heat transferred from object	Q_o	
final temperature	$T_f = 25.6°C$	

What is the strategy?

1. Use conservation of energy to state that the heat lost by the object equals the heat gained by the water bath. Apply the specific heat equation to write the conservation of energy equation in terms of the masses, temperatures, and specific heats.

2. Solve for the unknown specific heat, substitute the known values, and evaluate.

Physics principles and equations

By the conservation of energy, the heat gained by the water bath (beaker plus water) equals the heat lost by the object. The sum of the heat transfers is zero.

$$Q_w + Q_o = 0$$

We use the equation below to relate the heat flow to specific heat.

$$Q = cm\Delta T$$

Step-by-step solution

We start with an equation stating the conservation of energy for this experiment. Then, the heat values in the equation are written with expressions involving specific heat.

Step	Reason
1. $Q_w + Q_o = 0$ $Q_w = -Q_o$	conservation of energy
2. $Q_o = c_o m_o \Delta T$	specific heat equation
3. $Q_o = c_o m_o (T_f - T_o)$	initial and final temperatures for object
4. $Q_w = c_w m_w (T_f - T_w)$	specific heat equation
5. $c_w m_w (T_f - T_w) = - c_o m_o (T_f - T_o)$	substitute equations 3 and 4 into equation 1

Copyright 2000-2007 Kinetic Books Co. Chapter 18

Now we solve the equation for the unknown specific heat of the object and evaluate.

Step		Reason
6.	$c_o = -\dfrac{c_w m_w (T_f - T_w)}{m_o (T_f - T_o)}$	solve for specific heat of object
7.	$c_o = -\dfrac{(4178 \ \text{J/kg} \cdot \text{K})(0.744 \ \text{kg})(25.6 \,°\text{C} - 23.2 \,°\text{C})}{(0.197 \ \text{kg})(25.6 \,°\text{C} - 67.8 \,°\text{C})}$	substitute
8.	$c_o = 897$ J/kg·K	evaluate

Based on the values in the table of specific heats, it appears that the material may consist of aluminum.

18.14 - Phase changes

Phase change: Transformation between solid and liquid, liquid and gas, or solid and gas.

When you pop some ice cubes into a drink, they will melt. Heat flows from the warmer drink to the cooler ice cubes. Let's say the ice cubes start at $-10°\text{C}$, cooler than the freezing point of water, and they are dropped into a pot of hot coffee. Initially, heat flowing to the ice cubes raises their temperature. But at $0°\text{C}$, heat will flow to the ice cubes from the still warm coffee without the cubes changing temperature. That is, it takes energy to liberate the water molecules from the crystal structure of the ice and allow them to move freely at the same temperature through the coffee. This occurs as the ice melts, changing phase from a solid to a liquid. Phase changes between solid, liquid and gas do not change an object's temperature, but they do require heat transfer.

Phase changes occur as heat flows into or out of a substance. An ice cube melts in hot coffee, but the icemaker in a freezer causes water to change from a liquid to ice. In a freezer, heat is transferred from the liquid water to the cooler freezer.

concept 1

Requires energy

0°C   0°C
Releases energy

Phase change
Transformation between states
Consumes energy or releases energy
Temperature stays constant

In days of yore, refrigerators were called "iceboxes" because ice was used to cool the contents of the box. Heat would flow from the warmer air to the cooler ice, cooling the air. As the ice warmed and then melted, or changed phase, it would be replaced with a new block. Modern refrigerators continue to use phase changes (between liquid and gas), but they employ substances other than water.

The temperature at which a substance changes phase depends on the substance. For instance, water melts at $0°\text{C}$ at atmospheric pressure, but iron melts at $1538°\text{C}$.

Some substances can "skip" the liquid state by transforming directly from a solid to a gas or vice-versa. This is called *sublimation*. Mothballs sublimate: They transform from a solid directly into a gas. "Dry" ice (solid carbon dioxide) is another solid that sublimates directly into gas at atmospheric pressure. Frost in your freezer is an example of sublimation in the reverse direction. In this case, gaseous water vapor changes directly into solid ice.

Latent heat: Energy required per kilogram to cause a phase change in a given material.

Heat flow can cause a substance to change phases by converting it between a solid and a liquid, or a liquid and a gas.

Latent heat describes how much energy per kilogram is required for a given substance to change phase. It is a proportionality constant, expressing the relationship between heat and mass as shown in Equation 1. The constant depends on the material and on the phase change. Different amounts of energy are required to transform a material between its liquid and solid states than between its liquid and gaseous states.

	Melting point (°C)	Latent heat of fusion (J/kg)	Boiling point (°C)	Latent heat of vaporization (J/kg)
Aluminum	660	3.97×10^5	2519	1.09×10^7
Carbon	4489	9.74×10^6		
Copper	1085	2.09×10^5		
Iron	1538	2.47×10^5		
Lead	327	2.30×10^4	1749	8.66×10^5
Mercury	-39	1.14×10^4	357	2.95×10^5
Nitrogen	-210	2.53×10^4	-196	1.99×10^5
Table salt	801	3.78×10^5		
Water	0	3.34×10^5	100	2.26×10^6

at standard pressure

Latent heats of fusion and vaporization.

The *latent heat of vaporization* is the amount of heat per kilogram consumed when a given substance transforms from a liquid into a gas, or released when the substance transforms from a gas back to a liquid. The *latent heat of fusion* is the heat flow per kilogram during a change in phase between a solid and a liquid.

The table above shows the latent heats of fusion and vaporization for various substances. For instance, you need 3.34×10^5 J of energy to convert a kilogram of ice (at $0°C$) to liquid water. Continued flow of heat into the water will raise its temperature until it reaches $100°C$. At this temperature, it will take 2.26×10^6 joules of heat to turn it into a gas, about seven times as much as it took to convert it to a liquid.

Salt causes ice to melt, a phenomenon called "freezing point depression." When you add rock salt to the crushed ice in a hand-cranked ice cream freezer, you force the ice to melt. Heat flows from the resulting saltwater solution into the ice as it changes phase from solid to liquid, resulting in a slurry having a temperature far colder than $0°C$. Heat then flows from the ice cream solution into this mixture, and the ice cream freezes.

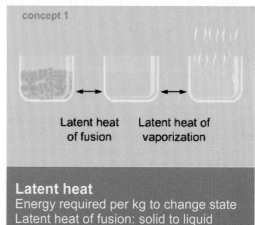

concept 1

Latent heat
of fusion

Latent heat of
vaporization

Latent heat
Energy required per kg to change state
Latent heat of fusion: solid to liquid
Latent heat of vaporization: liquid to gas
Amount same in either "direction"

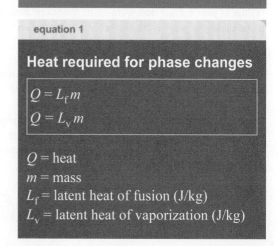

equation 1

Heat required for phase changes

$$Q = L_f m$$
$$Q = L_v m$$

Q = heat
m = mass
L_f = latent heat of fusion (J/kg)
L_v = latent heat of vaporization (J/kg)

example 1

$L_f = 3.34 \times 10^5$ $c = 4178 \text{ J/kg·K}$

A glass contains 0.0370 kg of ice at 0°C. How much heat transfers to the ice as it melts without changing temperature?

$Q = L_f m$

$Q = (3.34 \times 10^5 \text{ J/kg})(0.0370 \text{ kg})$

$Q = 1.23 \times 10^4 \text{ J}$

18.16 - Sample problem: watching ice melt

The glass contains 0.160 kg of water at 30.0°C and 0.0370 kg of ice at 0.00°C. What is the resulting temperature of the water at thermal equilibrium after the ice melts?

In the insulated container, the only source of the heat to melt the ice is the surrounding water. The water's temperature will decrease as the ice melts. The ice will melt while staying at 0°C. There is a tricky part to solving this problem: When the ice melts it turns into water, and this extra water must be accounted for when calculating the final temperature.

Variables

It is important to distinguish between the two masses of water in the final mixture: the mass that was initially liquid, and the mass that was initially solid ice. We use the subscripts L and S to distinguish these masses of water.

In the section on latent heat, we calculated the heat transferred to the same amount of ice as it melted to be 1.23×10^4 J. Here, we need the heat transferred **from** the water, not **to** the ice. Since the water loses heat, we state this as -1.23×10^4 J, with a negative sign.

mass of liquid water	$m_L = 0.160$ kg
mass of solid ice	$m_S = 0.0370$ kg
heat transferred from water to melt ice	$Q = -1.23 \times 10^4$ J
initial temperature of liquid water	$T_{Li} = 30.0°C$
initial temperature of solid ice	$T_{Si} = 0.00°C$
temperature of liquid water after ice melts	T_{Lf}
temperature of ice-melt	$T_{Sf} = 0.00°C$
final temperature of liquid water plus melted ice	T
heat transferred from liquid water for thermal equilibrium	Q_L
heat transferred to melted ice for thermal equilibrium	Q_S
specific heat of water	$c = 4178$ J/kg·K

What is the strategy?

1. Calculate the temperature of the water after it loses heat to melt the ice, using the specific heat of water.
2. As the water reaches thermal equilibrium, heat transfers **from** the originally liquid water, **to** the melted ice. These are the only heat transfers in the system, so they sum to zero. Use this fact and the specific heat equation to calculate the temperature of the total mass of water at the end.

Physics principles and equations

The specific heat equation

$$Q = cm\Delta T$$

As the two masses of water reach thermal equilibrium, the heat transferred from the originally liquid water plus the heat transferred to the melted ice must sum to zero.

$$Q_L + Q_S = 0$$

Step-by-step solution

First we calculate the temperature of the liquid water after it gives up heat to melt the ice. We use the specific heat of water, 4178 J/kg·K.

Step	Reason
1. $Q = cm\Delta T$	specific heat equation
2. -1.23×10^4 J $= (4178$ J/kg ·K)$(0.160$ kg)ΔT	substitute values
3. $\Delta T = -18.4$ K $= -18.4$ C°	solve
4. $T_{Lf} = T_{Li} + \Delta T$ $T_{Lf} = 30.0°C + (-18.4°C)$ $T_{Lf} = 21.6°C$	calculate water temperature

Copyright 2000-2007 Kinetic Books Co. Chapter 18

Now we use the fact that the heat transfers sum to zero as the two masses of water reach thermal equilibrium to calculate the final temperature of the total mass of water.

Step	Reason
5. $Q_L + Q_S = 0$	equation above
6. $cm_L(T - T_{Lf}) + cm_S(T - T_{Sf}) = 0$	specific heat equation
7. $T = \dfrac{m_L T_{Lf} + m_S T_{Sf}}{m_L + m_S}$	solve for T
8. $T = \dfrac{(0.160 \text{ kg})(21.6\,^{\circ}\text{C}) + (0.0370 \text{ kg})(0.00\,^{\circ}\text{C})}{0.160 \text{ kg} + 0.0370 \text{ kg}}$	substitute values
9. $T = 17.5°C$	evaluate

18.17 - Conduction

Conduction: The flow of thermal energy directly through a material without motion of the material itself.

concept 1

Conduction
Heat flow within object
· Does not involve "bulk" motion

When a frying pan is placed on a burner, heat flows from the burner to the pan. The heat then spreads through the pan, soon reaching the handle even though the handle is not in direct contact with the burner. This process illustrates the flow of thermal energy via conduction.

Conduction is the direct flow of thermal energy without a net motion of the materials involved. The heat flows from the bottom of the pan to its handle. Heat also flows by conduction where the burner and the bottom of the pan are in direct contact.

Conduction results from interactions at the atomic level of particles in an object: molecules, atoms and, in metals, electrons. Particles with greater average energy collide with nearby lower-average-energy particles, increasing their energy. Heat spreads as particles collide with their neighbors, and those neighbors collide with their neighbors, and so on. In this way, heat flows throughout the object. Although motion is involved at this level, the pan itself does not move, and this is part of the definition of conduction: The flow of thermal energy within an object that does not involve motion.

Different materials conduct heat at different rates. This is the topic of the next section.

	Thermal conductivity	Thermal resistance (for 1 inch)	
	k (W/m·K)	RSI-value (m²·K/W)	R-value (ft²·F°·h/Btu)
Air, sea level (15° C)	0.025	1.00	5.70
Fiberglass (50° C)	0.04	0.64	3.61
Urethane foam	0.06	0.42	2.40
Plywood	0.11	0.23	1.31
Wood (fir)	0.14	0.18	1.03
Water	0.598	0.04	0.24
Concrete (0° C)	0.8	0.03	0.18
Window glass (0° C)	0.95	0.03	0.15
Ice (0° C)	2.14	0.01	0.07
values approximate for building materials			at 10⁵ Pa, 20° C

Values for k and R.

For appliances that heat or chill (such as ovens or refrigerators), and indeed for an entire house or apartment, thermal conduction is the dominant form of **unintended** heat transfer. Since this transfer of heat is costly and wasteful, a good amount of effort is spent reducing it. In this section, we focus on building materials that are designed to minimize this heat transfer, keeping the interior of a house cool during the summer and warm during the winter.

The *thermal conductivity* of a material specifies how quickly heat transfers through it. Above, you see a table of thermal conductivity values for materials such as wood, insulating foam, glass, and some metals. The letter k represents the thermal conductivity of a material. Materials with small values for k are used as insulators to reduce the transfer of heat.

The units for thermal conductivity are joules per second-meter-Kelvin. Since watts are joules per second, this is the same as watts per meter-Kelvin, and these are the units used in the table above.

P_c represents the rate of heat transfer through conduction. As shown in Equation 1, P_c is defined as the heat transferred divided by the elapsed time. It is calculated for a slab of material like a glass window pane using the equation shown in Equation 2. The rate of heat transfer increases with the thermal conductivity k of the material that makes up the slab, the area of the slab, and the temperature difference between its two sides. It decreases with the thickness of the material. The equation also can be used to explain why the units for k have meters in the denominator, not "meters squared." Because there is a length term (thickness) in the denominator of the heat-transfer equation, a length term cancels out of the units.

The insulating effectiveness of building materials is usually specified by an R-value. A material with a high R-value is a good insulator. For a slab of material of a given thickness, the *thermal resistance R* is defined, as you see in Equation 3, as the thickness of the slab divided by its thermal conductivity. This is often called the R-value in the building trade. The SI units for R are square meters·kelvin per watt, and the building material ratings are then often called RSI-values. We show metric values with that name in the table above.

In North America, R-values based on the British measurement system are commonly used for building materials. These R-values have units of square feet·Fahrenheit degrees·hours per British thermal unit. We list them also in the table above. The thickness of the material for both RSI- and R-values is one inch, which is typical for building materials.

The term k in the equation in Equation 2 can be replaced with an expression involving R. This yields another equation, also shown in Equation 3, for the rate of heat transfer.

Considering these equations and studying the table above can help you understand why certain materials are chosen in construction. First, increasing the thickness of a material increases its R-value, so you see thicker insulating material in a colder environment where the temperature difference between inside and outside is greater.

Second, some materials have high k (low R) values, making them unlikely choices for insulators. For instance, building a house out of copper would lead to high heating costs (not to mention building costs). Building materials such as polyurethane foam are

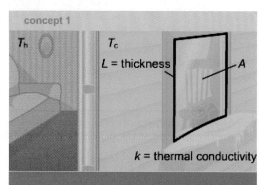

concept 1

T_h T_c

L = thickness A

k = thermal conductivity

Heat conduction
Rate of heat transfer depends on:
· thermal conductivity

· area

· temperature difference

· thickness

equation 1

Rate of heat transfer, definition

$$P_c = Q/t$$

P_c = rate of heat transfer (J/s)
Q = heat transferred
t = time

equation 2

Rate of heat transfer, calculated

$$P_c = \frac{kA\Delta T}{L}$$

effective insulators and can be combined with other reasonably good insulators such as wood for even greater energy efficiency.

Third, materials can be combined. Double-paned windows trap a quantity of an inert gas like argon between two layers of glass. Argon has a high R value and considerably reduces the rate of heat transfer through the window.

k = thermal conductivity
A = area
ΔT = temperature difference
L = thickness
k units: J/s·m·K = W/m·K

equation 3

Thermal resistance

$$R = L/k$$

$$P_c = \frac{A\Delta T}{R}$$

R = thermal resistance
R units (SI): $m^2 \cdot K/W$
R units (British): $ft^2 \cdot F° \cdot h/Btu$

example 1

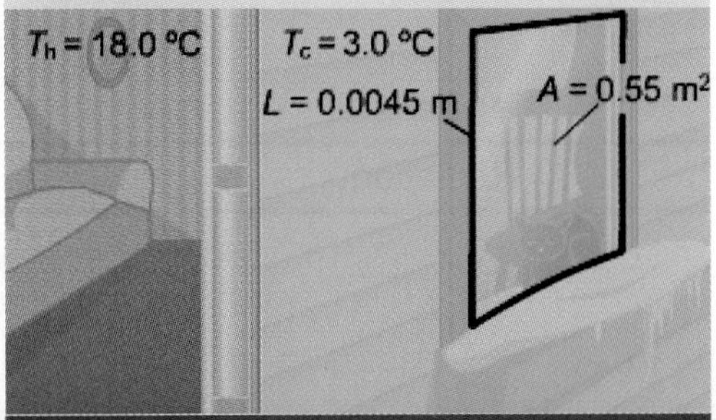

$T_h = 18.0\ °C$ $T_c = 3.0\ °C$
$L = 0.0045$ m $A = 0.55\ m^2$

Heat transfers through the window at a rate of 1700 J/s. What is its thermal conductivity constant?

$$P_c = \frac{kA\Delta T}{L}$$

$$k = \frac{P_c L}{A\Delta T}$$

$$k = \frac{(1700\ \text{J/s})(0.0045\ \text{m})}{(0.55\ m^2)(18.0\,°C - 3.0\,°C)}$$

$$k = 0.93\ \text{W/m·K}$$

Convection: Heat transfer through a gas or liquid caused by movement of the fluid.

Gases and liquids usually decrease in density when they are heated (liquid water near $0°C$ is a notable exception). When part of a body of liquid or gas is heated, the warmed component rises because of its decreased density, while the cooler part sinks. This occurs in homes, where heat sources near the floor heat the nearby air, which rises and moves throughout the room. The warmer air displaces cooler air near the ceiling, causing it to move near the heat source, where it is heated in turn. This transfer of heat by the movement of a gas or liquid is called *convection*.

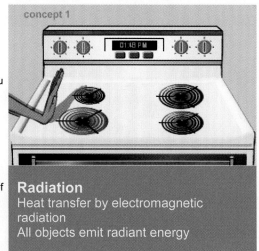

concept 1

Warmer air

Cooler air

Convection
Heat transfer due to movement in gases and liquids

All kitchen ovens, like the one shown in Concept 1, rely largely on convection for baking. The heating element at the bottom of the oven warms the air next to it, causing it to rise. The heated air then reaches the food in the oven to warm it, while the cooler air sinks to the bottom of the oven. So-called "convection ovens" speed this process with fans that cause the air to circulate more quickly.

Convection occurs in liquids as well as in gases. If you stir spaghetti sauce as it heats, you are accelerating the process of convection. Again, your goal is to uniformly distribute the thermal energy.

If you see a hawk soaring upward without flapping its wings, it may be riding what is called a "thermal." As the Sun warms the ground, the nearby air also becomes warmer. In the process, it becomes less dense, and is forced upward by air that is cooler and denser. A bird can ride this upward draft.

Radiation: Heat transfer by electromagnetic waves.

If you place your hand near a red-hot heating element and feel your hand warm up, you are experiencing thermal radiation: the transfer of energy by electromagnetic waves. You correctly think of objects like the heating element as radiating heat; in fact, every object with a temperature above absolute zero radiates energy.

Radiation consists of electromagnetic waves, which are made up of electric and magnetic fields. Radiation needs no medium in which to travel; it can move through a vacuum. The wavelength of radiation varies. For instance, red light has a wavelength of about 700 nm, and blue light a wavelength of about 500 nm. Infrared and ultraviolet radiation are two forms of radiation whose wavelengths are, respectively, longer and shorter than those of visible light.

concept 1

01:48 PM

Radiation
Heat transfer by electromagnetic radiation
All objects emit radiant energy

All objects radiate electromagnetic radiation of different wavelengths. For instance, you see the red-hot stove coil because it emits some visible light. The coil also emits infrared radiation that you cannot see but do feel as heat flowing to your hand, and it emits a minimal amount of ultraviolet radiation too.

Although any particular object radiates a range of wavelengths, there is a peak in that range, a wavelength at which the power output is the greatest. This peak moves to shorter wavelengths as the temperature of the object increases. Understanding the exact form of the spectrum of thermal radiation wavelengths requires concepts from quantum physics, and its derivation was one of the early triumphs and verifications of quantum theory.

Bodies with temperatures near the temperature of the surface of the Earth emit mostly infrared radiation. In the photograph in Concept 2, called an *infrared thermograph*, you see the radiation emitted by a horse. Since areas of inflammation in the body are unusually warm, and emit extra thermal radiation, veterinarians can use photographs like this to diagnose an animal's ailments. They are created by a digital or film camera that assigns different (visible) colors to different intensities of (invisible) infrared radiation in a process called false color reproduction.

Sunlight is a form of radiation and is crucial to life on Earth. The Sun emits massive amounts of energy in the form of radiation: 3.9×10^{26} joules every second. Some of that strikes the Earth, where it warms the planet and supplies the energy that plants use in photosynthesis.

The amount of power radiated by a body is proportional to the fourth power of its absolute temperature, its surface area, and a factor called its emissivity. The Sun emits tremendous amounts of radiation energy because it is quite hot (about 6000 K) and vast (with a surface area of about 6×10^{18} m^2).Only a small portion of the total power emitted by the Sun reaches the Earth. Even this fraction is an enormous amount: 1.8×10^{17} watts, about 100 times what human civilization consumes. The average solar power striking the Earth's atmosphere in regions directly facing the Sun is about 1370 watts per square meter. This value is called the *solar constant*.

Not all parts of the Earth directly face the Sun, and some radiation is reflected or scattered by the Earth's atmosphere before it reaches the surface. Different regions on Earth receive different average amounts of power per square meter: Measurements show that on average about 240 W/m^2 (watts per square meter) reaches the Earth's surface. North America is estimated to receive radiation of 150 W/m^2, on the average.

Given the dimensions of an average American house, this amount of radiation supplies about four times as much power as the household consumes. Using this clean "renewable resource" constructively for human purposes challenges both engineers and physicists. It also provides a significant opportunity to conserve non-renewable energy resources that would otherwise be used to heat, cool, and light our houses.

Efforts have been underway to take advantage of this form of energy for years. *Photovoltaic cells* convert solar energy directly into electricity.

The energy in sunlight can also be used without transforming it into electricity. The heat of sunlight can be used to heat both water and the interior of a house. Devices called *solar collectors* are becoming increasingly common. They are typically black; you see one in Concept 4. Solar collectors heat water for uses ranging from hot showers to warm swimming pools. Typically, the collectors contain tubes or rods that hold water, and after it is heated the water is circulated to the desired locations in the building.

Current solar collectors come in a variety of shapes and sizes. The engineers designing them have two main challenges. One is to maximize the amount of solar radiation that strikes the collector. Some collectors, particularly those designed for industrial or research purposes, use mirrors to focus sunlight onto the water tubes, increasing the amount of solar radiation that reaches the tubes.

The second engineering challenge is to efficiently transfer the heat energy of sunlight to the water inside the collector tubes and then circulate the heat out of the collector. There are many designs intended to maximize the efficiency of this process.

Residential systems can capture usable amounts of energy. One current system is capable of capturing 1000 Btu (British thermal units) per square foot of collector per day. A typical residential gas or oil furnace can supply on the order of 1.2 million Btu a day, which means a 10-by-20 foot solar panel supplies about one-sixth of the energy of a typical home furnace.

If you are interested in solar collectors, you can view a web site with information on them. You will study the physics of electromagnetic radiation in detail in a later chapter.

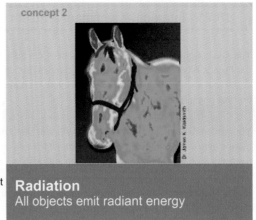

concept 2

Radiation
All objects emit radiant energy

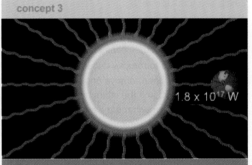

concept 3

1.8 x 10^{17} W

Sun and Earth
Sun emits enormous amounts of radiant energy
Some strikes the Earth's atmosphere

concept 4

Solar collector
Uses solar energy that reaches the Earth

18.21 - Interactive summary problem: pop the cork

You just bought a bottle of Pierrot, the water from ancient limestone caves deep in the French Alps, filtered by pure quartz crystals. But you did not realize the bottle came with a cork, and you have no corkscrew. Fortunately, your knowledge of thermal physics comes in handy.

interactive 1

Freeze the bottle to pop the cork

You remember that the density of ice is 9% less than the density of water. This means that water expands quite a bit when it freezes into ice. If you let the water in the bottle freeze, the expansion of the ice will push the cork out.

If 89.0% of the water freezes, the expanding ice will just push the cork out. But if more than 89.0% of the water freezes, the ice will expand too much and the bottle will break. You want to remove just enough heat from the water so that exactly 89.0% of it turns to ice.

In the interactive simulation on the right, you control the amount of heat removed from the water. The bottle contains 0.750 kg of water and its temperature is now $15.0°C$. You need to remove enough heat to reduce the temperature of all the water to $0°C$, and then remove enough additional heat to freeze 89.0% of it. To do these calculations, you will need to use the specific heat of water, 4178 J/kg·K, and the latent heat of fusion of water, 3.34×10^5 J/kg. We ignore the glass bottle itself in these calculations. Heat is removed from the bottle, but much more heat (about 50 times more) is removed from the water. Also, while the volume of the glass bottle decreases slightly as it cools, the expansion of the ice is much greater. Similarly, the small air space at the top of the bottle has little effect.

Set the amount of heat to be removed from the water, then press GO. If you are right, the ice will push the cork out. Press RESET to try again.

If you have trouble calculating the correct amount of heat transfer, review the sections in this chapter on specific heat and latent heat, and the sample problem that combines the two concepts.

18.22 - Gotchas

Heat is the same as temperature. No, heat is a flow of energy. Temperature is a property of an object. The flow of heat will change the temperature of an object, and a thermometer measures the object's temperature.

The Fahrenheit temperature system is the wave of the future. If you think so, can I interest you in buying a record player?

Two rods of the same material experience the same increase in temperature, which means they must have expanded by the same amount of length. Only if they were the same initial length. Their percentage increase would be the same in any case.

You throw a football upward. You have not increased the internal energy of the air within the football. Correct: You have not increased the internal energy of the molecules inside the football. (You have increased its translational kinetic energy and its rotational kinetic energy and its gravitational PE by throwing it upward, but not its internal energy.)

Temperature can be thought of simply as what thermometers measure. Thermometers rely on physical properties that vary with temperature in a reliable, reproducible way.

Different scales are used to measure temperature. The Fahrenheit scale is commonly used to measure temperature in the United States, but the Celsius scale is used in most of the rest of the world, and the Kelvin scale is used in science. Reference points such as the freezing and boiling points of water define a temperature scale and how to convert between scales. Another important (though ultimately unreachable) temperature point is absolute zero, where molecules are at their minimum energy state. This is 0 K on the Kelvin scale, or $-273.15°C$.

Heat is the flow of energy between objects resulting from a difference in temperature. Like work, heat changes the energy of an object, but we cannot say that an object *has* a certain amount of heat, any more than we could say it contains a certain amount of work. Heat can change the internal energy of a system. Heat is commonly measured in joules, or sometimes in calories or British Thermal Units. A food Calorie is actually a kilocalorie, or 1000 calories.

Objects change in length and volume when their temperature changes, in a process called thermal expansion. The change in length of an object depends on the coefficient of linear expansion of the material from which it is made, which is represented by the symbol α. Its change in volume depends on the coefficient of volume expansion, represented by β. Water has the unusual property that it expands with decreasing temperature from $4°C$ to $0°C$; this is why ice floats.

Specific heat is a property of a material, not an object, that relates the amount of heat to the change in temperature for a unit of mass of the material.

The transformation of an object from one state (solid, liquid, or gas) to another is a phase change. Phase changes require heat to be either added or taken away. The latent heat of a material is the energy consumed or released per kilogram during a particular phase change. The latent heat of fusion is the heat flow during a change between solid and liquid; the latent heat of vaporization is the heat flow during a change between liquid and gas.

Ways in which heat is transferred include conduction, convection, and radiation. Conduction is the flow of thermal energy directly through a material without motion of the material itself. Thermal resistance, sometimes called the R-value, determines the rate of heat transfer by conduction. Convection transfers heat by the bulk movement of molecules in a gas or liquid. Radiation transfers energy by means of electromagnetic waves. Every object emits electromagnetic radiation.

Equations

$$T_K = T_C + 273.15$$

$$T_C = (5/9)(T_F - 32)$$

Thermal expansion

$$\Delta L = L_i \alpha \Delta T$$

$$\Delta V = V_i \beta \Delta T$$

Specific heat

$$Q = cm\Delta T$$

Latent heat

$$Q = L_f m$$

$$Q = L_v m$$

Thermal conduction

$$P_c = Q/t$$

$$R = L/k$$

$$P_c = \frac{kA\Delta T}{L} = \frac{A\Delta T}{R}$$

$$P_c = \frac{A\Delta T}{R_{comp}}$$

chapter
19 Kinetic Theory of Gases
physics
□ Conceptual
kinetic
BOOKS

19.0 - Introduction

We live in a vast ocean of gas called the atmosphere. Deeper than the seas, it provides the oxygen we breathe, guards us against harmful radiation from space, helps to regulate the temperature, and makes flight possible.

In addition to supporting life, gases are used in many engines, and this is an important topic of study in physics. Transferring heat to a gas can cause it to expand. As the gas expands, it is able to do useful work. To understand how engines work, it is necessary to understand the behavior of gases.

In this chapter and elsewhere in this textbook, we focus on ideal gases. An ideal gas can be modeled as a number of small, hard spheres (atoms or molecules) moving rapidly around a container and colliding with each other and the container walls in perfectly elastic collisions. This aspect of the study of gases, which focuses on the motion of gas particles, is called the *kinetic theory of gases*.

interactive 1

Experiment with a molecular model of a gas

To begin your study of gases, try the simulation to the right. In the container, each particle represents a gas atom or molecule. A gauge in the simulation provides a readout of the gas pressure inside the container. The pressure is a function of various factors including the volume of the container and the speed and the number of the particles.

The pressure measured in the simulation is caused by the collisions of the particles with the walls of the container. Each time a particle strikes a wall of the container, it exerts a force on the wall and the wall exerts an equal amount of force on the particle. The greater the speed with which the particle strikes the wall, the greater the force the particle exerts on the wall.

As detailed below, you can change three properties of the gas. The changes you make will be reflected solely in changes in the pressure of the gas. Other properties of the gas could also change, but in this simulation we hold those other properties constant.

Clicking the up and down arrows for volume causes an external mechanism to raise or lower the container's lid. As the volume changes, the gas particles continue to move at the same average speed. How do you think gas pressure will relate to the volume of the container? Will decreasing the volume increase or decrease the pressure? Try it. Does the simulation help you see why there is a relationship between volume and pressure? Consider how it alters the frequency of the collisions.

You can also vary the temperature of the gas. The volume will not change as you do this, since the lid's position remains fixed. If you increase the temperature of the gas, you increase the average speed of the particles in the gas, and if you decrease the temperature, you decrease their average speed. Considering how the force and frequency of the collisions affects pressure, what do you think is the relationship between temperature and pressure when the volume is constant? Again, run the simulation to confirm your hypothesis.

The final controller allows you to add or subtract particles from the chamber. The particles you add will move at the same average speed as the gas particles already there. Do you think adding particles will result in more or less pressure? To test your conclusion, run the simulation to add particles and observe the resulting pressure.

When you have finished answering the questions above, you have experimented with some of the essential properties of a gas. The simulation should enable you to see relationships between gas pressure and the volume, temperature, and quantity of a gas.

19.1 - Ideal gas

Ideal gas: A gas that can be modeled as a set of particles having random elastic collisions. The collisions are the only interactions between the particles.

The concept of an ideal gas is used frequently in physics, both in the study of gases and later in the field of thermodynamics, where ideal gases play an important role. Real gases tend to behave like ideal gases at low enough densities (where quantum mechanical effects are not important). This makes ideal gases a good model for analyzing gas behavior. Here, we summarize the major properties defining an ideal gas.

Some gases, like carbon dioxide (CO_2) and oxygen (O_2), are composed of atoms bonded together in molecules. Other gases, like neon (Ne) and helium (He), are made up of particles that are individual atoms. For the sake of brevity, we will simply say that gases contain molecules (or particles), rather than repeatedly writing "atoms or molecules." When we analyze a gas, it is one made up of a single substance, such as oxygen or carbon dioxide.

An ideal gas consists of a large number of molecules. They are separated on average by distances that are large relative to the size of a molecule. They move at high speeds and collide frequently.

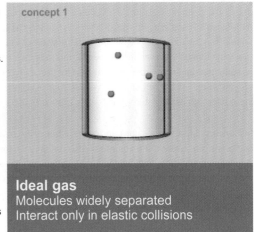

Ideal gas
Molecules widely separated
Interact only in elastic collisions

Using descriptions like "large" and "frequently" does not convey the nature of gases as well as specific numbers. Consider nitrogen molecules (N_2), the most common molecule in our atmosphere. In one cubic meter of nitrogen molecules at $0°C$ and one atmosphere of pressure, there are 2.69×10^{25} molecules. They occupy just 0.07% of the space and move at an average speed of 454 m/s. The molecules run into one another a lot: There are 9.9×10^{34} collisions each second between molecules in that space. The condition of $0°C$ (273 K) at one atmosphere is called *standard temperature and pressure* and is often used in calculations involving gases.

The molecules collide elastically with both each other and the container walls. The molecules only exert forces on one another when they collide. Forces that they exert on one another at other distances are negligible.

Each molecule can be considered as a small, hard sphere. In elastic collisions, both kinetic energy and momentum are conserved. The velocities of the molecules change after a collision, but the total momentum and kinetic energy of the molecules remain the same.

The walls of the container are rigid. When a molecule collides with a wall, its speed does not change although its velocity does (because its direction changes). Newtonian physics can be used to analyze the collisions of the molecules with each other and with the walls of the container.

19.2 - Gas pressure

Gas molecules not only collide with each other, but also with the walls of any container. During these collisions, the molecules exert a force on the walls. Dividing the total amount of force caused by these collisions by the surface area of the walls yields the absolute pressure exerted by the gas.

In this section, we consider three factors that qualitatively influence gas pressure. If you tried the simulation in the introduction section, some of this discussion should be familiar to you. In this section, we show two containers of gas. For visual clarity, we show only a small fraction of the actual number of particles in the containers. Each particle in the simulation represents about 3.4×10^{18} molecules. We have done the calculations assuming that these are nitrogen molecules in a container about 10^{-2} m wide. In the container on the left in each diagram, the pressure is one atmosphere and the temperature is $0°C$. We vary one property at a time in each illustration.

Collisions (10^{23}/s)	**3.53**	Collisions (10^{23}/s)	**4.59**
Force/collision (10^{-22} N)	**2.44**	Force/collision (10^{-22} N)	**2.44**
Fewer molecules		**More molecules**

Pressure increases with
Number of molecules

Consider two containers of equal volume containing different numbers of gas particles moving at the same speed. This is shown in Concept 1. The pressure will be greater in the container on the right (the one that contains more molecules). Why? With everything else equal, the collisions are more frequent in the container with the greater number of molecules, which means the molecules collectively exert more outward force on the walls of the container. Greater average force on the same amount of surface area means the pressure is greater.

The relationship between molecular speed and pressure is shown in Concept 2. Now each container contains the same number of molecules, but the container on the right has faster moving molecules (at a greater temperature) and, thus, greater pressure. Why does pressure increase with the speed of the molecules? There are two reasons why this is the case. First, when molecules move faster, they collide more frequently with the walls of the container. Second, when a molecule strikes the wall and rebounds, the molecule exerts more force at greater speeds than at slower speeds. (Imagine the force involved in a tennis ball rebounding off you when it is thrown at 1 m/s versus 20 m/s.) Since the average speed of molecules increases with temperature, this means pressure also increases with temperature.

In Concept 3 the temperature and the number of molecules are the same for each container. We change the volume of the container on the right. The pressure **decreases** when the container volume **increases**; pressure is inversely proportional to volume. In a larger container, the molecules collide less frequently with the walls. The surface area of the container also increases, so pressure (force divided by area) decreases for that reason, too.

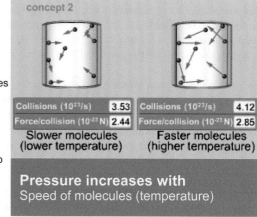

Pressure increases with
Speed of molecules (temperature)

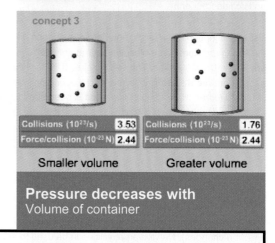

Pressure decreases with
Volume of container

19.3 - Boyle's and Charles' gas laws

In this section we take a macroscopic view of ideal gases to discuss their overall properties. Several laws state the relationship among macroscopic properties such as pressure, volume, temperature, and the amount of gas (number of molecules). We start here with Boyle's and Charles' laws.

Boyle's law is named for Irish scientist Robert Boyle, who in 1662 discovered that the absolute pressure of a fixed amount of gas **at a constant temperature** is inversely proportional to its volume. To put it another way, if you decrease the volume of a gas, its pressure increases proportionally. Boyle's law is stated in Equation 1: The product of the initial pressure and volume of a gas equals the product of its final pressure and volume.

Jacques Charles, a Frenchman who worked a century later than Boyle, also studied gases. One way to state Charles' law is that for a fixed amount of gas **at a constant pressure**, the ratio of its volume to its absolute temperature remains constant. You see this in Equation 2 using the initial and final volumes and temperatures of a gas.

These gas laws are empirical; that is, they are determined to be true through experiment and measurement rather than being derived from other laws.

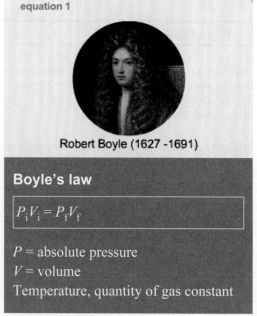

Robert Boyle (1627 -1691)

Boyle's law

$$P_i V_i = P_f V_f$$

P = absolute pressure
V = volume
Temperature, quantity of gas constant

equation 2

Jacques Charles (1746 - 1823)

Charles' law

$$\frac{V_i}{T_i} = \frac{V_f}{T_f}$$

V = volume
T = Kelvin temperature
Pressure, quantity of gas constant

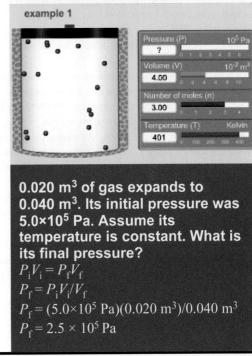

example 1

Pressure (P) 10^5 Pa
?
0 1 2 3 4 5 6

Volume (V) 10^{-2} m^3
4.00
0 2 4 6 8 10

Number of moles (n)
3.00
0 1 2 3 4

Temperature (T)   Kelvin
401
0 100 200 300 400

0.020 m^3 of gas expands to 0.040 m^3. Its initial pressure was 5.0×10^5 Pa. Assume its temperature is constant. What is its final pressure?

$P_i V_i = P_f V_f$

$P_f = P_i V_i / V_f$

$P_f = (5.0 \times 10^5 \text{ Pa})(0.020 \text{ m}^3)/0.040 \text{ m}^3$

$P_f = 2.5 \times 10^5 \text{ Pa}$

19.4 - Avogadro's number and moles

Avogadro's number: 6.022×10^{23}.

Mole: The amount of a substance that contains Avogadro's number of particles.

The concept of moles is used in the study of gases. You might find that this section reviews what you learned in a chemistry class, where this concept also figures prominently.

Physicists often need to deal with large quantities of molecules when they analyze gases. For instance, one cubic meter of air at sea level contains about $3×10^{25}$ molecules. In addition, scientists may need to quantify a given amount of gas by its number of molecules rather than its mass. To do so, they use moles and Avogadro's number.

One mole is defined as the amount of a substance containing the same number of particles as there are atoms in 12 grams of carbon-12. Carbon-12 is one form, or isotope, of carbon, having six protons and six neutrons in its nucleus. Scientists have determined that there are, to six significant figures, $6.022\ 14×10^{23}$ atoms in 12 grams of carbon-12, and have named this value Avogadro's number (after the 19th century Italian physicist Amedeo Avogadro). Avogadro's number is indicated by N_A.

A mole contains about $6.022×10^{23}$ particles of a substance. The abbreviation for mole is "mol". The concept of the mole is important enough that the mole is one of the seven fundamental units of the *Système Internationale*.

Avogadro's number specifies the number of particles per mole of a substance. It can be applied to any kind of object. For example, if you had Avogadro's number of golf balls, or one mole, you would have $6.022×10^{23}$ balls (and their mass would be $2.8×10^{22}$ kg).

Of course, moles are more typically used to specify the number of molecules in a quantity of gas. Moles are used to focus on the number of molecules, not their mass. For example, a mole of hydrogen atoms contains the same number of atoms as a mole of lead, even though one mole of lead atoms weighs 207 times more than the hydrogen atoms. If you have studied chemistry, you may be familiar with combining substances in terms of their molar amounts to achieve the correct ratio of molecules.

The following discussion will prove useful if you need to use atomic mass units. The *atomic mass scale* relates moles and the mass of individual molecules. The *atomic mass unit*, symbolized by u, is based on carbon-12. By definition, one atom of carbon-12 has a mass of exactly 12 atomic mass units, or 12 u. One atomic mass unit equals $1.660\ 54×10^{-27}$ kg. Since Carbon-12 contains six protons and six neutrons, which have about the same mass and make up almost all the mass of the atom, the mass of a proton or neutron is approximately one atomic mass unit.

A particle with an atomic mass of 24 u is twice as massive as a carbon-12 atom. This means a mole of the 24 u substance will have twice as much mass as a mole of Carbon-12.

The mass per mole of a substance is called its *molar mass*. When measured in grams (or, to be precise, g/mol) the molar mass of a particular substance has the same numerical value as the atomic mass of the substance. Why? The atomic mass of an atom of carbon-12 is 12 u by definition, and a mole of carbon-12 atoms is exactly 12 grams, by the definition of Avogadro's number.

Consider a substance with an atomic mass of 36 u. Each particle will be three times as massive as an atom of carbon-12. One mole of the substance has the same number of particles as one mole of carbon-12. This means a mole of this substance would have a mass that is three times the mass of a mole of carbon-12, or 36 grams. In physics, the molar mass is usually stated in kg/mol instead of g/mol.

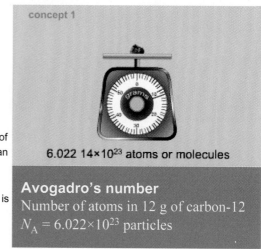

concept 1

$6.022\ 14×10^{23}$ atoms or molecules

Avogadro's number
Number of atoms in 12 g of carbon-12
$N_A = 6.022×10^{23}$ particles

concept 2

60 carats   12 grams   1 mole of carbon atoms

Mole
Contains Avogadro's number of particles

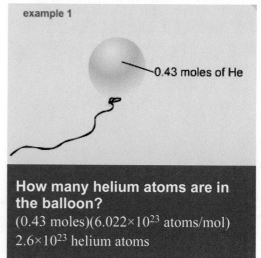

example 1

0.43 moles of He

How many helium atoms are in the balloon?
$(0.43\ \text{moles})(6.022×10^{23}\ \text{atoms/mol})$
$2.6×10^{23}$ helium atoms

Ideal gas law: The product of a gas's pressure and volume is proportional to the amount of gas and its temperature.

The ideal gas law shown in Equation 1 is an empirical law that describes the relationship of pressure, volume, amount of gas, and temperature in an ideal gas. It states that the pressure of an amount of an ideal gas times its volume is proportional to the amount of gas times its temperature. The pressure is the absolute, not gauge, pressure. (Absolute pressure equals gauge pressure plus atmospheric pressure.) The small n in the equation is the number of molecules, measured in moles. The temperature is measured in kelvins. R is a constant called the *universal gas constant*. Its value is 8.314 51 J/mol·K.

Everyday observations confirm the main precepts of the ideal gas law. When you inflate a bicycle tire, you increase the amount of gas in the tire, which increases both its pressure and volume. Once it is inflated and its volume is held nearly constant by the tire, an increase in temperature increases the pressure of the gas within. A hot day or the rolling friction from riding increases its temperature. You are told to check the pressure of a tire when it is "cold" since the correct pressure for a tire is established for $20°C$ or so. Checking tire pressure when the tire is hot may cause you to deflate the tire unnecessarily.

Sometimes, it is useful to be able to apply the ideal gas law when the number of particles N is known, rather than the number of moles. Since the number of particles is the number of moles times Avogadro's number, we can rewrite the ideal gas law as shown in Equation 2. The constant k here is called *Boltzmann's constant*, which equals the gas constant R divided by Avogadro's number N_A. Its value is $1.380\ 66 \times 10^{-23}$ J/K. While the first statement of the ideal gas law relates P, V and T to the **macro**scopic properties R and n of a gas, the second relates them to the **micro**scopic properties k and N.

If this is the ideal gas law, are there non-ideal gases? Yes, there are. For instance, water vapor (steam) is a non-ideal gas. The ideal gas law provides accurate results when gas molecules bounce into each other with perfectly elastic collisions. If the molecules also interact in other ways, as they do with steam, the law becomes a less accurate predictor of the relationship between pressure, volume, temperature, and the amount of gas. In the case of water vapor, *steam tables* are used to relate these values.

In Example 1, the volume of one mole of gas at standard pressure and temperature is calculated. The volume is 2.25×10^{-2} m³ (22.5 liters, or about six gallons). One mole of any ideal gas occupies this same volume under these conditions. In 1811, Avogadro first proposed that equal volumes of all gases at the same pressure and temperature contained the same number of molecules.

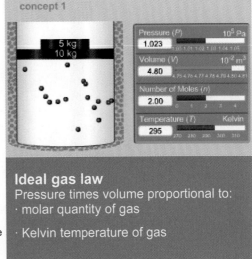

concept 1

Ideal gas law
Pressure times volume proportional to:
· molar quantity of gas
· Kelvin temperature of gas

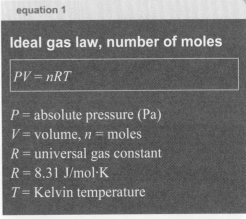

equation 1

Ideal gas law, number of moles

$$PV = nRT$$

P = absolute pressure (Pa)
V = volume, n = moles
R = universal gas constant
R = 8.31 J/mol·K
T = Kelvin temperature

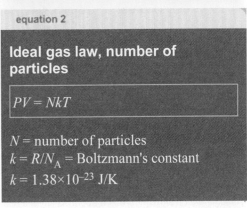

equation 2

Ideal gas law, number of particles

$$PV = NkT$$

N = number of particles
$k = R/N_A$ = Boltzmann's constant
$k = 1.38 \times 10^{-23}$ J/K

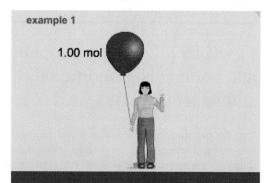

example 1

1.00 mol

What is the volume of one mole of gas at standard temperature and pressure? Standard temperature is 273 K and standard pressure is 1.01×10^5 Pa.

$$PV = nRT$$

$$V = \frac{nRT}{P}$$

$$V = \frac{(1.00 \text{ mol})(8.31 \text{ J/mol} \cdot \text{K})(273 \text{ K})}{1.01 \times 10^5 \text{ Pa}}$$

$$V = 2.25 \times 10^{-2} \text{ m}^3$$

19.6 - Sample problem: tank of air

The emergency scuba tank is filled with 8.50×10^{-2} m^3 of air at atmospheric pressure and 21.0°C. Immediately after the tank is filled, the absolute pressure is 1.53×10^7 Pa and the volume is 8.37×10^{-4} m^3. What is the temperature of the air in the tank at that time?

Scuba divers may carry small tanks like the one shown above to give them air in case of an emergency. Air that is at atmospheric pressure, 1.01×10^5 Pa, is pumped into the tank. The process of filling the tank increases the temperature and pressure of the air. The temperature will decrease as heat flows from the warmer tank to its cooler surroundings, but we assume the compression process occurs quickly enough for heat flow to be negligible. A value for atmospheric pressure is stated below.

Scuba diving equipment manufacturers use an estimated breath size of 1.6 liters, so this tank would hold a little over 50 typical breaths. Assuming a diver might breathe about 15 times a minute, an average under normal conditions, the emergency tank would give her around three minutes of air. However, she might be breathing a little more rapidly if she needs to use the tank!

Variables

initial volume of air	$V_i = 8.50 \times 10^{-2} \text{ m}^3$
initial pressure	$P_i = 1.01 \times 10^5 \text{ Pa}$
initial temperature	$T_i = 21.0°C$
final volume of air	$V_f = 8.37 \times 10^{-4} \text{ m}^3$
final pressure	$P_f = 1.53 \times 10^7 \text{ Pa}$
final temperature	T_f
moles of air	n

What is the strategy?

1. Model the air as an ideal gas. State the ideal gas law, and isolate the parameters that are constant, R and the amount n of gas, on one side of the equation.

2. Since the values mentioned above are constant, for both the initial and final states of the gas the "other" sides of the equations are equal to one another. Set them equal to each other in an equation.

3. Solve for the final temperature and evaluate.

Physics principles and equations

The ideal gas law

$$PV = nRT$$

The temperature is given in Celsius and will need to be converted to Kelvin to apply the ideal gas law.

Step-by-step solution

We start by using the ideal gas law to write an equation relating the initial and final conditions of the gas.

Step	Reason
1. $\quad P_i V_i = nRT_i$	ideal gas law, initial condition
2. $\quad \dfrac{P_i V_i}{T_i} = nR$	divide by temperature
3. $\quad \dfrac{P_f V_f}{T_f} = nR$	ideal gas law, final condition
4. $\quad \dfrac{P_i V_i}{T_i} = \dfrac{P_f V_f}{T_f}$	from steps 2 and 3

We can solve for the final temperature because all the other values are known. The initial temperature was stated in Celsius, but the ideal gas law requires that kelvins be used, so we add 273 to the Celsius temperature to convert.

Step		Reason
5.	$T_f = \dfrac{P_f V_f T_i}{P_i V_i}$	solve for T_f
6.	$T_f = \dfrac{(1.53 \times 10^7\,\text{Pa})(8.37 \times 10^{-4}\,\text{m}^3)(21.0 + 273\,\text{K})}{(1.01 \times 10^5\,\text{Pa})(8.50 \times 10^{-2}\,\text{m}^3)}$	substitute values
7.	$T_f = 439\,\text{K}$	evaluate
8.	$T_f = (439 - 273) = 166°\text{C}$	convert to Celsius

This is very hot! When tanks like this are filled, they are usually held under cold water to increase the heat flow out of the tank and reduce their temperature increase.

19.7 - Interactive problem: pressure of an ideal gas

In this simulation, a small chamber contains an ideal gas consisting of 26 gas particles held at a constant temperature of 400 K. The gas has a pressure of 897 Pa. The chamber volume is currently set at $1.6 \times 10^{-22}\,\text{m}^3$.

You can change the volume of the chamber, within a range of $0.5 \times 10^{-22}\,\text{m}^3$ to $2.5 \times 10^{-22}\,\text{m}^3$. You also can vary the number of gas particles, from 10 to 30. Your task is to set the number of particles and the volume of gas so that the gas pressure is reduced to 552 Pa. The temperature of the gas in this simulation remains fixed at 400 K.

When you launch the simulation, you will see the gas particles moving around as determined by the settings stated above. After running for a few moments, the simulation will pause so that you can enter your values. Determine how to alter the volume and the number of molecules to achieve the target pressure of 552 Pa. Specify these values using the up and down arrows in the control panel and press GO to apply the new settings to the gas.

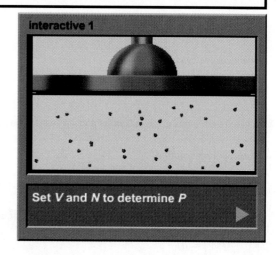

A text message will tell you whether the gas reached the correct pressure. You can also note the pressure in the pressure gauge in the simulation.

If you get the wrong answer, you can try again. Press RESET to return the gas to its initial conditions, specify new values, and press GO again.

If you have trouble with this simulation, review the section on the ideal gas law.

19.8 - Interactive checkpoint: volume of an ideal gas

A quantity of an ideal gas occupies a volume of 2.18 m² at 288 K, with an absolute pressure of 1.45×10⁵ Pa. If its temperature increases to 298 K and its pressure increases to 2.15×10⁵ Pa, what is the volume?

Answer:

$V_f =$ [＿＿＿＿] m³

19.9 - Kinetic energy and temperature

In this chapter, we have shown that by varying the speed of its molecules, we can affect the pressure of a gas. We also have mentioned that the molecules' speed increases with temperature. Now we will get more specific about this relationship.

Rather than showing a relationship between speed and temperature, it proves more productive to show a relationship between translational molecular kinetic energy and temperature. To put it another way, we find it more useful to discuss the relationship between the molecular speed squared and temperature.

The molecules that compose a gas move at a variety of speeds. As the temperature of a gas increases, the average speed of its molecules increases, as does the molecules' average kinetic energy. The kinetic theory of gases links the temperature of a gas to the **average** kinetic energy of the molecules that make up the gas.

The relationship is quantified in Equation 1. The average translational kinetic energy of a particle in an ideal gas equals $(3/2)kT$, with k being Boltzmann's constant and T the Kelvin temperature.

The equation for the kinetic energy of a particle has an interesting implication: The kinetic energy of gas molecules is solely a function of temperature. It is independent of other factors, such as pressure or volume. As the graph in Equation 1 illustrates, when the temperature of a gas increases, the kinetic energy of the molecules that make it up increases linearly.

Now we move from considering the kinetic energy of a particle to the kinetic energy of an amount of an ideal monatomic gas. A monatomic gas is one whose particles are single atoms. The internal kinetic energy of a monatomic gas is the sum of the individual kinetic energies of all the atoms.

You see the equation for the internal energy of an ideal monatomic gas in Equation 2. It can be derived from the first equation by multiplying by the number of atoms. The kinetic energy of one molecule is $(3/2)kT$, as described above. For n moles of gas, there are nN_A atoms, so the total energy is $(nN_A)(3/2)\,kT$. Since k equals R/N_A, the internal energy of n moles of monatomic gas equals $(3/2)nRT$.

This energy makes up all the internal energy of an ideal monatomic gas, because the

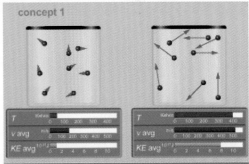

concept 1

Kinetic energy of ideal gases
As temperature of gas increases:
· average molecular speed increases
· average translational *KE* of molecule increases

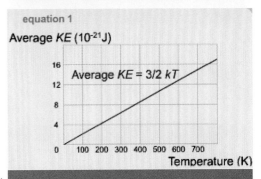

equation 1

Average *KE* (10⁻²¹J)

Average *KE* = 3/2 *kT*

Temperature (K)

Average *KE* of molecule, ideal gas

only form of energy of this type of gas is translational (linear) kinetic energy. There is no potential energy in any ideal gas. Since there are no forces between the molecules, there can be no energy due to position or configuration. The nature of monatomic molecules (single atoms) means they have neither rotational nor vibrational energy.

Although we have focused on ideal monatomic gases, the internal energy and temperature of ideal diatomic and polyatomic gases are also linearly related.

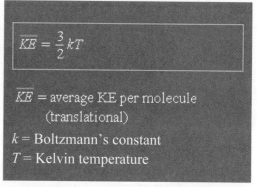

$$\overline{KE} = \frac{3}{2}kT$$

$\overline{KE}$ = average KE per molecule (translational)
k = Boltzmann's constant
T = Kelvin temperature

equation 2

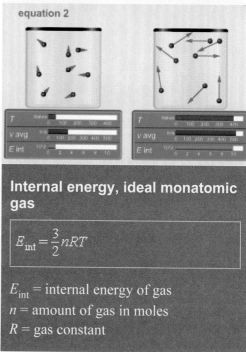

Internal energy, ideal monatomic gas

$$E_{\text{int}} = \frac{3}{2}nRT$$

E_{int} = internal energy of gas
n = amount of gas in moles
R = gas constant

example 1

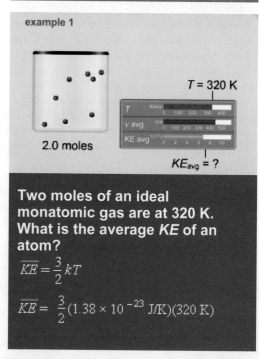

$T = 320$ K

2.0 moles

$KE_{\text{avg}} = ?$

Two moles of an ideal monatomic gas are at 320 K. What is the average *KE* of an atom?

$$\overline{KE} = \frac{3}{2}kT$$

$$\overline{KE} = \frac{3}{2}(1.38 \times 10^{-23}\ \text{J/K})(320\ \text{K})$$

$$\overline{KE} = 6.6 \times 10^{-21} \text{ J}$$

example 2

What is the total internal energy of the gas?

$$E_{\text{int}} = \frac{3}{2} nRT$$

$$E_{\text{int}} = \frac{3}{2} (2.0 \text{ mol})(8.31)(320 \text{ K})$$

$$E_{\text{int}} = 8.0 \times 10^3 \text{ J}$$

19.10 - Gotchas

Using the wrong temperature scale. Make sure you use Kelvin, not Celsius (and certainly not Fahrenheit!), when applying the equations in this chapter.

19.11 - Summary

In this chapter, you studied ideal gases, ones where the particles (atoms or molecules) can be modeled as interacting with each other and the walls of their container only in elastic collisions.

Avogadro's number is 6.022×10^{23}. It is a dimensionless number used to specify a quantity of matter. A mole contains Avogadro's number of particles.

The pressure of a gas increases with the number of molecules of the gas and its temperature, and decreases as its volume increases. The ideal gas law expresses this relationship in an equation. The ideal gas law can be stated in terms of the number of moles of a gas, or the number of particles.

The average kinetic energy of a gas molecule and the internal energy of a given quantity of gas can be calculated from its absolute temperature.

Equations

Boyle's law
$$P_i V_i = P_f V_f$$

Charles' law
$$\frac{V_i}{T_i} = \frac{V_f}{T_f}$$

Ideal gas law
$$PV = nRT = NkT$$

Energy and temperature
$$\overline{KE} = \frac{3}{2} kT$$

20.0 - Introduction

The desire to build more powerful and efficient engines led engineers and scientists to embark on pioneering research into the relationship of heat, energy and work. The engines that powered the Industrial Revolution primarily used energy provided by burning coal.

Much has changed since the first engines were used to drain marshes and pump water from the coalmines of Great Britain. New sources of energy, from gasoline for automobiles to nuclear fuel for electric power generators, are used to power engines. Engines are now used in applications undreamt of by their first designers, for whom the horseless carriage and nuclear fission would have been science-fictional fantasies.

Despite the changes, much of the fundamental science developed in the 19th century is still used to analyze engines. The goal of an engine, to get useful work out of a heat source, has not changed. Although the technology has advanced and made engines more efficient, the physics of heat engines as established by 19th century engineers and scientists applies equally well to the steam locomotives of their era and to modern electrical power plants powered by nuclear fission.

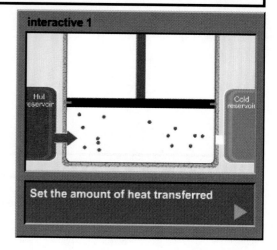

This chapter focuses on two topics, using the engine as the basis of much of the discussion. One topic is the first law of thermodynamics, the relationship between the energy supplied to an engine and how much work it does. The other topic is the role of gases in the functioning of an engine. Many engines use a gas to function; applying some basic principles of how gases behave proves very useful in understanding the functioning of engines.

The simulation on the right will get you started on your study of engines. Here you see a heat engine, a device that uses heat as its energy source to do work. There is gas (represented by some bouncing molecules) in the central chamber of the engine, a piston on top, and a "hot reservoir" on the left from which heat can be allowed to transfer into the gas. In this case, we consider the cylinder, the gas and the piston to be the system. The reservoirs on the sides allow heat to flow in and out of the system. When heat flows into the engine's gas, its temperature will rise (reflecting an increase in its internal energy), and if the piston is free to move, the gas will expand, pushing it up.

In this simulation, you will see what occurs during two distinct engine processes. In the first process, the piston is locked in place while heat is transferred to the gas. You control the amount of heat that is transferred. The internal energy of the gas is displayed in an output gauge. In the first step, you should ask yourself: What is the relationship between the amount of heat transferred to the gas and the change in the internal energy of the gas? Consider the principle of conservation of energy when you ponder your response to this question, and then test your hypothesis.

In the second process, no heat is allowed to flow in or out of the engine, but when you press GO, the piston will be unlocked so it can move. A gauge will show you how much work the gas does as it expands or contracts, changing the piston's position. At the end of this process, note how much work the gas did and again its change in internal energy. How do the values for the work and change in internal energy relate during this process?

One last calculation (there are a few here, but you will have taught yourself the first law of thermodynamics when you complete this exercise): How does the amount of heat you initially transferred to the gas relate to its change in internal energy and the work it does? Write down these three values and see if you note a fundamental mathematical relationship. You can also apply the physics you learned earlier; consider the principle of conservation of energy and the work-energy theorem. (The work-energy theorem in its most general form says that the work done by an external force on a system equals its change in total energy, which includes thermal energy as well as mechanical energy.)

If these are too many questions, read on. The first law of thermodynamics begins this chapter.

First law of thermodynamics: The net heat transferred to a system equals the change in internal energy of the system plus the work done by the system.

The first law states that the net heat transferred into or out of a system equals the change in the internal energy of the system plus any work the system does. It is written as an equation in Equation 1, with Q representing the net heat transferred to the system. You saw this law at work in the simulation in the introduction to this chapter. First, heat was transferred to the gas in the engine, increasing the internal energy of the system. The increase in the temperature of the gas in the engine reflected the increase in internal energy. When you pressed GO again, the piston rose. The engine did work, and its internal energy decreased. The amount of work done by the engine equaled the magnitude of its change in internal energy as the piston rose.

We use the simple engine in Concept 1 to discuss the first law in more depth. Heat flows from the flame into the container, causing the internal energy of the gas it contains to increase. As the gas's internal energy increases, its temperature and the average speed of its molecules increases. As the gas's temperature increases, its pressure increases and it may expand. The gas does positive work when it expands, applying a force to the moving lid in the direction of its displacement.

It is important to define what we mean by "system." Here we define the system as the engine that includes the container, with its moveable lid, and the gas. When heat flows into the engine, the gas's temperature changes, but the container's temperature is assumed to stay the same. A rod is attached to the lid. The pressure of the gas pushes against the lid, and this can force both the rod and the lid upwards. The rod might be attached to the rest of the engine, such as the drive assembly of an automobile. When the gas expands, it does work on the rod.

The first law is mandated by the principle of conservation of energy. Conservation of energy applies to isolated systems, and the system of the engine is not isolated. But the engine is part of some larger system that is isolated. Heat energy flows into the engine. This energy must be conserved: Energy can be neither created nor destroyed in the process. That means the heat flow increases the internal energy of the gas. This energy, however, can do work, increasing the energy of some object outside of the engine. Work done by the gas reduces its internal energy.

The work done by the gas equals the force it exerts times how far the lid moves. That force equals the pressure times the surface area of the lid. Calculating the work done by the gas is easier when the pressure is constant than when the gas pressure varies.

Although it is not the typical way to analyze engines, you could think of the process entirely in terms of energy. Let's further simplify the engine, ignoring the rod and any forces acting on the lid other than gravity and the gas pressure from inside the engine. Heat flows in, raising the gas's internal energy and, if the lid rises, increasing the potential energy of the disk on top (by $mg\Delta y$). The sum of the increase in the gas's internal energy and the increase in potential energy of the disk equals the amount of net heat flow.

The first law applies to any engine process, for any initial and final state of the gas plus any work done. For instance, in the simulation in the introduction, heat was added and then the piston was allowed to move, but this could have happened simultaneously, or it could have happened in a series of steps.

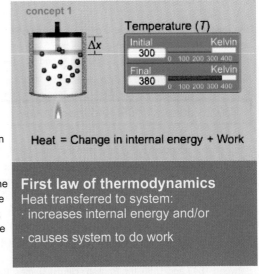

concept 1

Temperature (*T*)

		Kelvin
Initial	300	0 100 200 300 400
Final	380	0 100 200 300 400

Heat = Change in internal energy + Work

First law of thermodynamics
Heat transferred to system:
· increases internal energy and/or
· causes system to do work

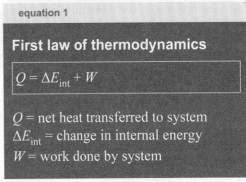

equation 1

First law of thermodynamics

$$Q = \Delta E_{int} + W$$

Q = net heat transferred to system
ΔE_{int} = change in internal energy
W = work done by system

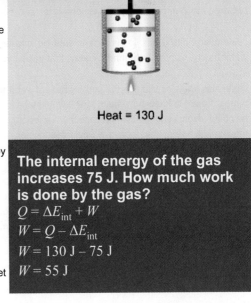

example 1

Heat = 130 J

The internal energy of the gas increases 75 J. How much work is done by the gas?

$Q = \Delta E_{int} + W$
$W = Q - \Delta E_{int}$
$W = 130\ J - 75\ J$
$W = 55\ J$

Mathematical signs are important here. A net flow of heat **into** the engine means Q is positive; a net flow of heat **out** of the engine means Q is negative. Work done by the gas raising the lid is positive, since the force is in the direction of the displacement. When the lid moves down, the work done by the gas is negative.

The relationship between heat, work and internal energy is illustrated in the example problem to the right. If 130 J of heat is transferred to an engine and its internal energy increases by 75 J, the first law of thermodynamics dictates that it must do 55 J of work. The change in internal energy and the work done by the gas must add up to equal the net heat transferred.

20.2 - James Joule and the first law

Although it is accepted today as one of the fundamental tenets of science, the proponents of the first law of thermodynamics faced a skeptical scientific community. Most scientists did not view heat as another form of energy. The prevalent theory in the early 1800s was the *caloric theory*, which proposed that a *caloric fluid* was added to matter as it was heated. This addition of fluid explained why a metal rod expanded when it was heated: It expanded because it contained more caloric fluid. One legacy of this belief is that heat still has its own units, the *calorie* and the *British thermal unit* (Btu).

Between 1843 and 1850, the English scientist James Joule performed a series of experiments that showed that heat was another form of energy. He used equipment similar to the apparatus shown in Concept 1. Rather than using heat to raise the temperature, Joule used mechanical energy. As the diagram illustrates, a falling weight causes the paddles to rotate, and the work of the paddles on the water causes its temperature to increase.

Joule applied the work-energy theorem to conclude that the work done by the paddles equaled the amount of change in the potential energy of the weight. By measuring the change in height and the mass of the weight, he could quantify the change in its PE and so the work done by the paddles. He also measured the increase in the temperature of the water.

concept 1

72° F

mg

Heat as energy
Joule showed heat is a form of energy
Change of *PE* proportional to:
· water temperature increase
· heat required for same increase

Joule performed his experiment repeatedly. He showed beyond doubt that the change in the potential energy of the weight, which equaled the amount of work done by the paddles, was always proportional to the increase in the temperature of the water. This proved a relationship between mechanical energy and temperature.

Joule used British units. In his experiments, he calculated that 772.5 foot-pounds of work would increase the temperature of one pound of water by one degree Fahrenheit. Today, that value has been refined to 778 foot-pounds. Joule's measurement was impressively accurate.

Joule also knew how to use the specific heat of water to relate an amount of heat transferred to a quantity of water to its increase in temperature. He knew how much heat it would take to raise the temperature of a given amount of water by one degree, and with his apparatus, he could also calculate how much mechanical energy it would take to do the same. He showed that one calorie of heat equals an amount of mechanical energy that today we would describe as 4.19 J. (Since scientists today know heat is just one form of energy, they do not use the calorie unit as often, but instead use the joule as the unit for all forms of energy, as well as for work.)

Modern scientists still differentiate between heat (the transfer of energy) and the internal energy of an object. Heat changes the internal energy of an object or system, just as work does. Work and heat are two ways to change some form or forms of an object's energy. They reflect a process. It does not make sense to refer to "the work of an object" or "the heat of an object." Rather, it is correct to state how much work is done on or by an object, or how much heat is transferred into or out of the object. The result is a change in the object's energy.

20.3 - Heat engines

A heat engine uses the energy of heat to do work. Many engines have been designed to take advantage of heat energy. To cite two: A steam engine in an old locomotive and the internal combustion engine in a modern automobile both use heat as the source of energy for the work they do.

A heat engine is shown on the right. It is the container with a lid and piston on top, between a hot reservoir on the left and a cold reservoir on the right. In the engines we will consider, the container encloses a gas. The gas is cooler than the hot reservoir but warmer than the cold reservoir. Heat flows spontaneously from the hot reservoir into the gas in the engine, where the energy can be used to do work. Heat will also flow spontaneously from the gas to the cold reservoir. Otherwise, the container is insulated and no heat flows through any other mechanism into or out of the engine.

The reservoirs are large enough that they can supply or absorb as much heat as we like. We control the flow of heat between a reservoir and the container by opening a hole in the insulating wall to allow heat to flow, and closing it to stop the flow. The reservoirs are **not** part of the system we consider when applying the first law of thermodynamics.

The amount of gas in the engine stays constant. The temperature and pressure are assumed to be the same everywhere in the gas at any moment. When we analyze a heat engine, we will assume it is ideal: that there is no friction to reduce its efficiency and that heat flows uniformly and instantly through the system.

The engine goes through a sequence of processes that collectively are called an *engine cycle*. (One process or step in an engine cycle is sometimes called a *stroke*.) At the end of each cycle, the engine returns to its initial state. For instance, during one process, heat might flow into the engine from the hot reservoir so the piston rises. During another process, heat might flow out to the cold reservoir as the piston falls. No matter what the processes, at the end of an engine cycle, the engine returns to its initial configuration: The piston is in its initial position and the gas is back to its initial volume, pressure and temperature.

Since the gas returns to its initial state, its internal energy does not change during a complete engine cycle. This means we can concentrate on the two other quantities in the first law, namely heat and work. To apply the first law and other equations, we consider the work done **by** the gas. The gas does positive work as it lifts the piston. If the piston moves down and compresses the gas during another part of the cycle, the gas does negative work.

The distance the piston moves up or down might be the same. However, the amount of work that occurs will typically differ, since the purpose of the engine is to do net positive work on the piston during a complete engine cycle. The gas applies more force when it expands (to move a crankshaft, for example) than when it contracts, so the **net** work done by the engine in a cycle is positive. The net transfer of heat into the engine during a complete engine cycle equals the net work it does. The net transfer of heat equals the heat in from the hot reservoir minus the heat out to the cold reservoir.

You see this stated as an equation to the right. The net work done by the engine during a cycle equals the heat transferred into the engine from the hot reservoir minus the heat that flows out to the cold reservoir. Heat that flows into the engine from the hot reservoir is called Q_h, and heat that flows out to the cold reservoir is called Q_c. We treat both Q_h and Q_c as positive quantities. This means the **net** flow of heat equals $Q_h - Q_c$. If heat flows only out of the engine during a process in an engine cycle, then the net heat flow for that process is negative.

This equation is a special case of the first law of thermodynamics. The law states that the net heat flow equals the work done plus any change in internal energy. Since the internal energy is not changed after a complete engine cycle (the engine returns to its initial state), the net work done by the engine equals the net flow of heat.

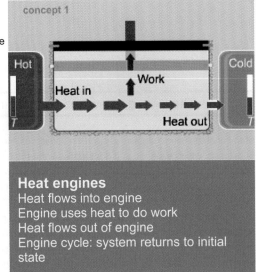

Heat engines
Heat flows into engine
Engine uses heat to do work
Heat flows out of engine
Engine cycle: system returns to initial state

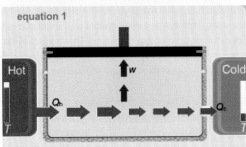

For a complete engine cycle

$$W = Q_h - Q_c$$

W = net work done by engine
Q_h = heat in
Q_c = heat out
Internal energy returns to initial value

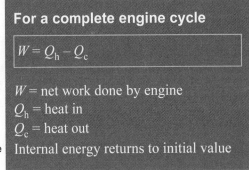

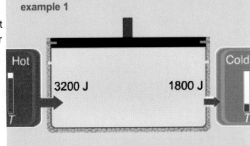

During an engine cycle, the heat transfers are as shown. What is the net work done by the

engine?

$W = Q_h - Q_c$

$W = 3200 \text{ J} - 1800 \text{ J}$

$W = 1400 \text{ J}$

20.4 - The ideal gas law and heat engines

Many engines use a gas as their *working substance*. Heat is transferred to the working substance, which expands and does work. Water (both in liquid and gaseous form) is another common working substance. However, water vapor is far from an ideal gas, and in this textbook, we focus on an ideal gas as the working substance.

In addition to the first law of thermodynamics, the ideal gas law is very useful in analyzing the processes in an engine cycle. Here, we want to briefly review this law, and show how it is used in analyzing heat engines. The ideal gas law relates pressure, volume, temperature and the amount of gas. You see the law stated in Equation 1.

In the heat engines we consider, the quantity of gas enclosed by the container is constant. This leaves three variable properties of a gas in the ideal gas law: the gas's pressure, volume and temperature. The product of the pressure and volume is proportional to the temperature. If the temperature of the gas increases, for instance, then the product of its pressure and volume must increase, as well.

The first law of thermodynamics states that when heat flows into an engine, the heat energy increases the gas's internal energy and/or causes it to do work. A change in internal energy will be reflected in the gas's temperature; greater internal energy means a higher temperature. This means the volume or the pressure of the gas will increase, or both.

To apply these two principles, consider Example 1. The piston is locked in place so that the gas can do no work. This means that the heat transferred to the engine solely increases the internal energy of the gas. That increase in internal energy is reflected by an increase in temperature. Since the piston is locked, the volume of the gas is constant and the ideal gas law enables us to conclude that its pressure must increase proportionally to the temperature increase.

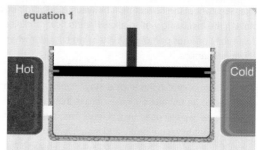

equation 1

Ideal gas law

$$PV = nRT$$

When n is constant:

$$PV \propto T$$

P = pressure, V = volume
n = number of moles of gas
R = gas constant
T = temperature (K)

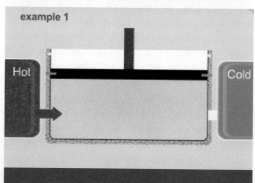

example 1

The engine piston is locked in position and heat flows into the gas. What happens to the pressure, volume, and temperature?

Volume constant (piston locked)

Temperature increases

Pressure increases proportionally

In this section, we will review an engine cycle. It involves the three processes described below. To understand these processes, watch the gauges that display the pressure, volume, molar quantity and temperature of the gas. We assume that the pressure and temperature are uniform throughout the gas.

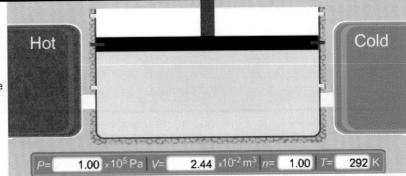

We start with one mole of gas with a volume of 2.44×10^{-2} m^3 at 292 K and a pressure of 1.00×10^5 Pa. The piston is locked and no heat is allowed to flow in or out. This state of the engine is depicted in the illustration at the top of the page.

$P=$ | 1.00 $\times 10^5$ Pa | $V=$ | 2.44 $\times 10^{-2}$ m^3 | $n=$ | 1.00 | $T=$ | 292 K

Initial state of heat engine.

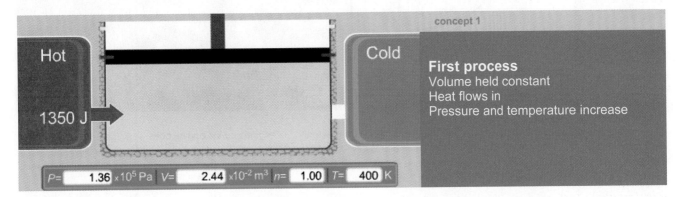

concept 1

First process
Volume held constant
Heat flows in
Pressure and temperature increase

$P=$ | 1.36 $\times 10^5$ Pa | $V=$ | 2.44 $\times 10^{-2}$ m^3 | $n=$ | 1.00 | $T=$ | 400 K

First process. Now, 1350 joules of heat are allowed to flow into the gas. The energy inflow increases the internal energy of the gas, which is reflected by its increased temperature. Since the piston is locked, the gas's volume cannot change. This means its pressure must increase. You see this directly above. Its pressure has increased from 1.00 to 1.36×10^5 Pa and its temperature has increased from 292 to 400 K.

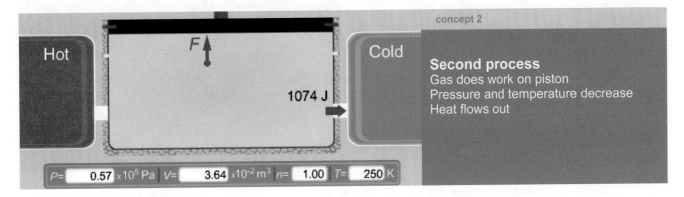

concept 2

Second process
Gas does work on piston
Pressure and temperature decrease
Heat flows out

$P=$ | 0.57 $\times 10^5$ Pa | $V=$ | 3.64 $\times 10^{-2}$ m^3 | $n=$ | 1.00 | $T=$ | 250 K

Second process. Now, we release the lock on the piston. This allows the gas to expand, doing work by moving the piston. The internal energy of the gas and its temperature decrease. A hole in the insulating wall opens to the cold reservoir, and 1074 J of heat also flow out of the engine. As you can see above, the gas's temperature and pressure are now less than they were when the cycle started.

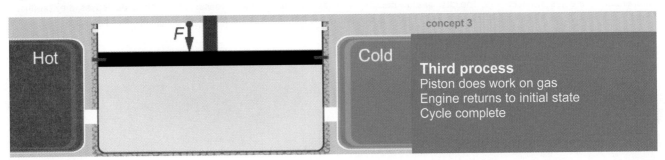

concept 3

Third process
Piston does work on gas
Engine returns to initial state
Cycle complete

Third process. The insulating walls to the reservoirs are again closed, so no heat flows. The piston pushes down, returning the gas to its initial volume. This is a lesser amount of work than was done when the piston moved up, because the gas pressure is always less during this process than during the expansion process. This work done on the gas increases its temperature to its initial value. The pressure returns to its initial state.

This is one of many possible engine cycles. We will examine some specific engine cycles in more detail later. For now, we focus on the thermodynamic processes that can make up part of an engine cycle.

20.6 - Pressure-volume graphs and heat engines

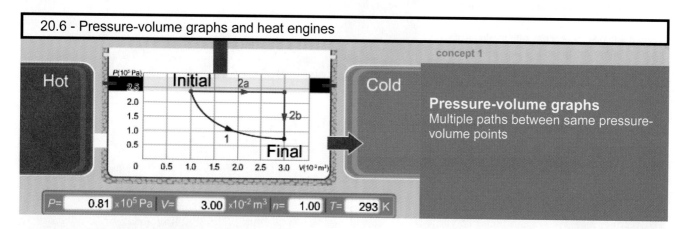

Pressure-volume graphs
Multiple paths between same pressure-volume points

$P=$ 0.81 $\times10^5$ Pa $V=$ 3.00 $\times10^{-2}$ m^3 $n=$ 1.00 $T=$ 293 K

In an engine, the pressure and volume of the gas change as heat is transferred to the engine and the engine does work. These changes can be tracked with what is called a pressure-volume graph. In a pressure-volume graph, pressure is plotted on the vertical axis and volume on the horizontal axis. You see two engine processes diagramed above, one in blue and the other in red. They illustrate how two different processes can cause a gas to move between the same initial and final states.

We will now describe these processes step-by-step. The gas starts at 2.43×10^5 Pa of pressure, 1.00×10^{-2} cubic meters of volume, and a temperature of 293 K.

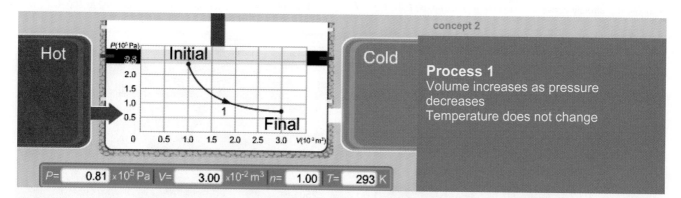

Process 1
Volume increases as pressure decreases
Temperature does not change

$P=$ 0.81 $\times10^5$ Pa $V=$ 3.00 $\times10^{-2}$ m^3 $n=$ 1.00 $T=$ 293 K

Process 1. The gas's pressure is then reduced as its volume is increased in the process labeled 1, which is immediately above. The gauges and piston position in Concept 2 show the state of the engine at the end of the process. The temperature does not change during this process.

During the first process, the amount of heat added to the engine equals the work done on the piston because the internal energy and temperature of the gas do not change. The ideal gas law must be obeyed, so as the volume increases, the pressure decreases; their product remains constant at each point along the path. Path 1 reflects one path by which the gas can change from its initial to its final state.

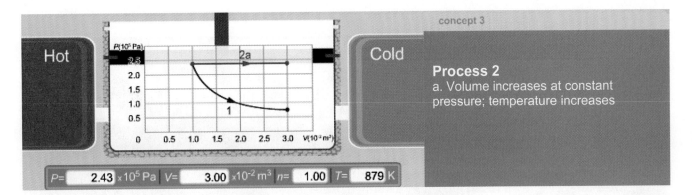

concept 3

Process 2
a. Volume increases at constant pressure; temperature increases

P= 2.43 ×10⁵ Pa | V= 3.00 ×10⁻² m³ | n= 1.00 | T= 879 K

Process 2, step a. Now we show a different process by which the gas can be caused to move between the same two states. To make the comparison clearer, we continue to show path 1 on the graph. The second process starts with the same pressure, volume and temperature as before. This process has two distinct steps. In the first step, labeled 2a in the graph above, heat energy flows into the gas from the hot reservoir as before. This increases the internal energy of the gas (as indicated by the increase in temperature). The graph is horizontal, indicating a constant pressure. We could maintain the pressure by having the gas press against a constant weight.

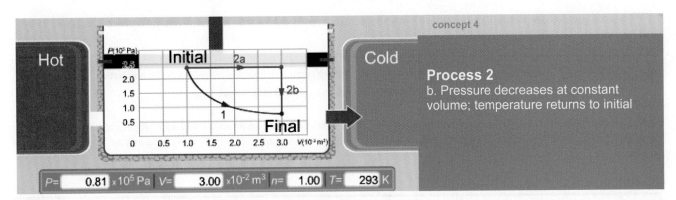

concept 4

Process 2
b. Pressure decreases at constant volume; temperature returns to initial

P= 0.81 ×10⁵ Pa | V= 3.00 ×10⁻² m³ | n= 1.00 | T= 293 K

Process 2, step b. Next, since we have the same volume that was reached by the path 1 process, we lock the piston into place, keeping the volume constant. The pressure is too high, so we allow heat to flow out to the cold reservoir. This decreases the temperature of the gas, and at this fixed volume, this means the pressure must decrease proportionally. You see this step labeled 2b in the graph above.

This two-step process arrives at the same final pressure-volume point as the first process, but in a different way. In the first, the gas's temperature remained constant while its pressure and volume constantly changed. In the second, first the volume was changed at constant pressure, and then the pressure was changed at constant volume. The temperature changed during both of the steps of process 2.

The difference in the paths reflects an important point: Gases can change from one combination of pressure and volume to another by experiencing different histories.

Both the processes sketched above obey the first law of thermodynamics and the ideal gas law. The first law is obeyed because there is the same **net** flow of heat into the engine in both cases. In process 1, all the heat is used for work, and the gas's internal energy stays the same. (To make the engine realistic, some heat should flow to the cold reservoir, since no engine is 100% efficient.) In process 2, more heat is added during step 2a than in process 1, since in this step the gas does the same amount of work as in all of process 1 **and** its internal energy increases. Heat flows out of the engine during step 2b, making the net heat into the engine the same for processes 1 and 2.

The ideal gas law is also obeyed. The product of the pressure and volume is always proportional to its temperature. For instance, on path 2b, as the gas's temperature decreases, its pressure decreases proportionally.

20.7 - Classifying thermal processes

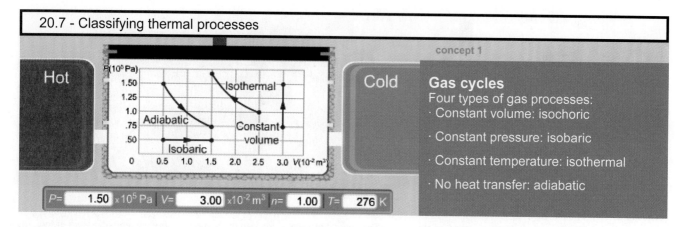

As a heat engine operates, the gas expands or contracts and its pressure changes. A gas can move from one pressure-volume state to another by different thermal processes. Four thermal processes are commonly studied and used in engines. These processes are characterized as follows.

1. Does the gas's volume remain constant? When it stays the same, the process is called a **constant-volume** process. This is also called an *isochoric process*.
2. Is the gas's pressure constant? If so, the process is called **isobaric**.
3. Does any heat flow in or out of the engine during the process? If there is **no** heat flow, the process is called **adiabatic**.
4. Does the temperature of the gas stay the same? If it does, the process is called **isothermal**.

Above, we show each of these processes on a pressure-volume graph. Although we use an arrow to show each process occurring in a particular direction, the arrows could be reversed without changing the types of the processes. Any of these processes can occur in either direction.

20.8 - Gotchas

A gas is hotter after an engine cycle is complete. No, the definition of an engine cycle is that the engine returns to its initial state.

Adding heat to an engine immediately causes it to do work. Although that is likely the purpose of the heat transfer, the heat can also increase the internal energy of the engine. It may be later in the cycle that the engine uses the energy to do work.

Doing work on an engine can cause the temperature of its gas to increase. This is true. It can also cause heat to flow out of the engine as well.

The first law of thermodynamics is the same as the principle of conservation of energy. Essentially, this is true. The first law explicitly factors in work, a way to add or subtract energy from a system. However, both physics principles are statements of conservation. Energy cannot magically appear or disappear; it can always be accounted for.

James Joule demonstrated a fundamental relationship between heat, temperature and work. Yes. He showed how both work and heat could increase the temperature (and energy) of a substance.

The first law of thermodynamics relates heat, work, and internal energy, and is a re-statement of the law of conservation of energy. It states that the net heat transferred to a system equals its change in internal energy plus the work done by the system.

Equations

First law of thermodynamics

$$Q = \Delta E_{int} + W$$

Engine cycle

$$W = Q_h - Q_c$$

A heat engine uses thermal energy to do useful work. An engine contains a working substance, usually a gas, that goes through a series of thermal processes. During a thermal process, heat can be transferred to the gas from a hot reservoir, or can flow out to a cold reservoir, or it could be that no heat exchange takes place. In an analogous way, during the process, energy transfers can also take place via work: work can be done on the system, work can be done by the system on its surroundings, or no work might be done by the system. An engine cycle is a series of processes that returns the gas to its original temperature, pressure, and volume. During a cycle, because the gas has returned to its original state and the change in its internal energy is zero, the net work done equals the difference between the heat transferred into the engine and the heat transferred out.

When the amount of gas is constant, the ideal gas law states that the product of pressure and volume is proportional to the temperature of the gas.

Four thermal processes that occur frequently in engines are constant-volume, isobaric, adiabatic and isothermal.

21.0 - Introduction

Physics often seems to be about possibilities, but it is also about limits. You can think of the first law of thermodynamics as stating a limit: An engine cannot do more work during an engine cycle than the heat added to it. If it did, it would defy the principle of conservation of energy. If such an engine existed, it would be a source of "free energy." Alas, no such engine exists.

If an engine cannot perform an amount of work greater than the energy added to it, can an engine just "break even"? This is not an idle question: The efficiency of an engine, how much work it does per amount of energy added, is a crucial measure of an engine's utility.

Automobiles, for instance, can take advantage of about one-fourth of the energy produced by the combustion of gasoline to do useful work, making them about 25% efficient.

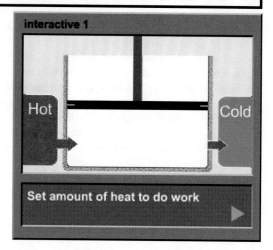

interactive 1

Set amount of heat to do work

The second law of thermodynamics establishes the theoretical limit of efficiency: It states that no heat engine can be 100% efficient; that is, no engine can convert all of the heat supplied to it into an equal amount of work. In theory, engines could be built with efficiencies of 99.9%, but never 100%. This limit cannot be reached with any conceivable improvements in engineering; it is a theoretical limit that in principle can never be realized. The second law of thermodynamics and the topic of efficiency are two areas of focus for this chapter.

The concept of entropy provides another way to study thermal processes. In general terms, entropy is a measure of how ordered a system is, and is another useful tool for understanding the efficiency and limits of engines.

The simulation on the right lets you explore the relationship between heat, work and efficiency in an engine cycle. During the engine cycle, the engine will do work and return to its initial condition at the end of the cycle. The heat engine will perform one cycle when you press GO. You can set the amount of heat transferred from the hot reservoir to the engine during the cycle, and the amount of heat the engine expels to the cold reservoir. At the end of the cycle, the work done by the engine and the engine's efficiency are calculated and displayed.

You can add from 50 to 500 joules of heat. These are small amounts of heat, appropriate for a toy or model engine. More than 500 joules will exceed the safety limits of the engine.

We want you to observe two principles at work in this process. First, apply what you learned about the first law of thermodynamics to this engine. What relationship do you expect between the net heat transferred to the engine and the net work done by the engine? (The engine does positive work on the piston as the system expands and raises the piston, and a smaller amount of negative work as the piston falls.) Make a hypothesis and then test it with the simulation.

Second, you will encounter the second law of thermodynamics: No engine is 100% efficient. The energy that flows out of the engine in the form of heat to the cold reservoir cannot be used to do useful work. The greater the heat that flows out to the cold reservoir, the less efficient the engine. In the interest of realism, the simulation requires a realistic amount of heat to flow to the cold reservoir.

Even the most efficient practical engines, like those in electric generation plants, run at less than 60% efficiency. See how efficient you can make the simulation engine; it can be much more efficient than the average engine. But, try as you might, you will find that reaching 100% efficiency is a goal you cannot achieve.

Efficiency: The ratio of the net work done by an engine during a cycle to the heat energy supplied to the engine.

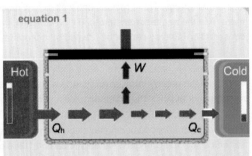

equation 1

Engine design has been refined for hundreds of years, as engineers have sought to increase the power and reliability of engines while decreasing their size. Equally importantly, they have sought to increase the efficiency of engines, the amount of useful work an engine does divided by the amount of thermal energy supplied to it.

The first formula in Equation 1 states the definition of the efficiency of a heat engine. The efficiency equals the net work W done by the engine divided by the heat Q_h transferred to the system from the hot reservoir. This ratio is often stated as a percentage. A typical internal combustion automobile engine has an efficiency of about 25%, while the diesel and coal powered engines in electrical plants have efficiencies ranging from 40% to 60%. These numbers are for the engines alone. The overall systems – the entire car, the whole electrical plant – run at lower total efficiencies due to inefficiencies outside the engines.

The second formula for engine efficiency shown in Equation 1 provides a way to calculate engine efficiency from the heat Q_h added to the engine, and the heat Q_c that flows out.

Engine efficiency

$$e = W/Q_h$$

$$e = 1 - \frac{Q_c}{Q_h}$$

e = engine efficiency
W = net work during engine cycle
Q_h = heat in during cycle
Q_c = heat out during cycle

The second equation for engine efficiency is derived below from the definition (the first equation). The derivation uses the first law of thermodynamics: The net heat flow equals the work done by the engine plus its change in internal energy. Since the internal energy of an engine is the same at the beginning and end of a cycle, the net heat flow equals the work done by the engine.

Step	Reason
1. $e = W/Q_h$	definition of efficiency
2. $W = Q_h - Q_c$	first law of thermodynamics
3. $e = \dfrac{Q_h - Q_c}{Q_h}$	substitute equation 2 into equation 1
4. $e = 1 - \dfrac{Q_c}{Q_h}$	divide

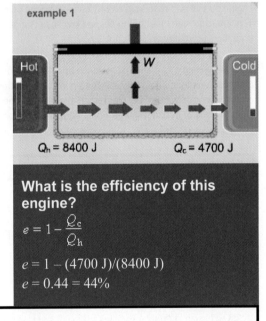

example 1

$Q_h = 8400$ J $Q_c = 4700$ J

What is the efficiency of this engine?

$$e = 1 - \frac{Q_c}{Q_h}$$

$$e = 1 - (4700 \text{ J})/(8400 \text{ J})$$

$$e = 0.44 = 44\%$$

Second law of thermodynamics: No heat engine can transform 100% of the energy supplied to it into work during a cycle.

There are several equivalent ways to express the second law of thermodynamics. The definition above states the law in a form that is one of its important consequences: There is a limit to the amount of work that can be done by a heat engine supplied with a certain amount of energy during a cycle. This is called the *Kelvin-Planck* statement of the second law.

To take a step back for a moment: The first law of thermodynamics states that the net heat transferred to a system equals the net work done by the system plus the change in its internal energy. That provides one limit to how much work an engine can do: no more than the net heat transferred to it. In essence, the first law is about energy conservation. Energy cannot be created by a process; it must stay constant.

The second law is a little more dire: It says that during an engine cycle, engines do **less** work than the energy transferred into them. In principle, the work could equal 99.9% of the energy that flows into an engine, but it can never equal 100%.

This law is not about designing an efficient engine. It is instead a physical law that limits the efficiency of any engine. No engine can be 100% efficient.

Another way to state the second law, called the *Clausius statement*, is: There can be no process whose sole final result is the transfer of heat from a cooler object to a warmer object. Heat flows spontaneously from an object at a higher temperature to an object at a lower temperature. Heat will **not** flow in the other direction unless compelled to do so. This direction of heat flow agrees with your everyday experience. If you place a quart of ice cream in a hot car, you expect the ice cream to get warmer, not colder. Energy flows from the hotter air to the cooler ice cream.

Stating the law in this fashion may help you to understand why no engine can be 100% efficient. The illustrations at the right show a conceptual diagram of a heat engine. Heat is allowed to flow into the engine from the hot reservoir. Some heat also flows out to the cold reservoir. The maximum amount of work the engine can do during a cycle is the net flow of the heat, the heat in minus the heat out.

An enterprising engineer might think she could "recycle" the heat absorbed from the engine by the cold reservoir, say by connecting the cold reservoir to the hot reservoir. The Clausius statement of the second law says that heat will not flow spontaneously from the cold reservoir to the hot.

To solve this problem, she might attach another engine to force heat to flow from the cold reservoir to the hot. This is indeed possible: Air conditioners and refrigerators cause heat to flow from a cooler region to a warmer one. However, this heat flow is not spontaneous or free; it requires work and comes at a price, as the electrical bills for air conditioners and refrigerators indicate.

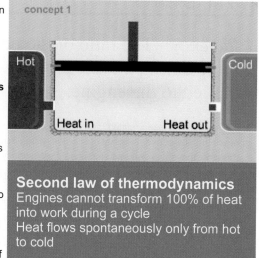

Second law of thermodynamics
Engines cannot transform 100% of heat into work during a cycle
Heat flows spontaneously only from hot to cold

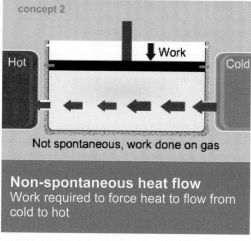

Not spontaneous, work done on gas

Non-spontaneous heat flow
Work required to force heat to flow from cold to hot

21.3 - Reversible and irreversible processes

Reversible process: A process in which a system can be returned to its initial state without the addition of energy.

Irreversible process: Energy must be added to a system to return it to its initial state after an irreversible process occurs.

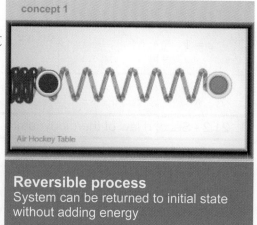

Air Hockey Table

Reversible process
System can be returned to initial state without adding energy

Some of the crucial underpinnings of the theories concerning engine efficiency rely on the concepts of reversible and irreversible processes. In general, a process is a series of steps that move a system from one state to another. When a system undergoes a reversible process, it can be returned to its initial state without the addition of energy.

Every real process is irreversible, although some are close to being reversible. Consider, for example, a puck attached to a spring on an air hockey table, as shown in Concept 1. Imagine the spring is initially compressed and the puck is held in place. When the puck is released, the compressed spring will push the puck to the right until it pauses momentarily. This is a process: The spring pushing the puck until it pauses. In an ideal system (no friction, no air resistance), the puck will return to its initial position as the spring contracts with no additional energy required. The process of spring expansion can be thought of as reversible.

In contrast, if you drop an egg and it breaks, several changes take place that cannot be easily reversed (that is quite an understatement). For example, the breaking of the egg creates sound energy through vibrations in the air. This reduces the energy of the egg. You do not expect to be able to put it back together again without extraordinary effort. This is an irreversible process. It would take an extreme amount of time and effort (Humpty Dumpty inevitably comes to mind) to return the egg to its initial state.

concept 2

Irreversible process
Cannot be reversed without adding energy
Video runs only "one way"

One way to think about reversibility is to imagine videotaping a process. If you can easily decide whether the tape is being played forward or backward, the process is irreversible. If you watched a videotape of an egg shattering, you would know the direction the tape is being played. On the other hand, with the puck and the spring, you would not be able to discern easily if the tape were being played forward or backwards. (If you watched it for several cycles of motion, however, you would note that the extreme positions of the puck were less far from equilibrium as the system lost energy to dissipative forces like air resistance and friction.)

These principles can be stated in terms of a system and its environment. With an irreversible process, a system can be returned to its initial state but its environment must change. This is particularly applicable to heat engines, where the "environment" may be modeled as hot and cold reservoirs. The engine mechanism, the gas and the piston, can be returned to their initial state, but their environment changes. The hot reservoir becomes a little less hot and the cold reservoir becomes warmer each time the engine completes a cycle.

21.4 - Entropy

Entropy: A property of a system. When heat is transferred to a system, its entropy increases.

Entropy is a concept used to describe the state of a system, and it is a property of a system, just like pressure, volume, temperature or internal energy. Some properties may be directly measured or read from a gauge. A thermometer will tell you an object's temperature and a meter stick will tell you its length. For other properties, such as kinetic energy, there are no direct measures; there are no "KE gauges." A property like kinetic energy must be computed from factors that can be measured, mass and speed.

concept 1

Entropy
Property of objects, systems
Increases as heat is transferred to object

Similarly, there are no direct "entropy gauges" available to scientists or students. In this section, we focus on the relationship of entropy, temperature and heat without concerning ourselves too much about exactly what is meant by "entropy." In other words, we will start our discussion of entropy by considering some properties that can be observed and are familiar to you, and focus on entropy itself once this groundwork has been laid. In fact, the concept of entropy was historically developed in a process like this. It arose out of the quest to understand the relationship between temperature and heat.

When heat flows into a system, its entropy increases. When heat flows out of a system, its entropy decreases. The change in entropy equals the heat divided by the temperature at which the heat flow occurs.

We express this as a formula in Equation 1. To apply this equation, the process must be reversible and the temperature measured in kelvins. Since absorbing or expelling heat will change the temperature of the system, this change in entropy must be measured for a small amount of heat, or the system must be large enough that it can expel or absorb a fair amount of heat with only a negligible change in temperature. The units for entropy are joules/kelvin.

This equation is useful for two reasons. First, it provides the tool for computing a change in entropy. Second, it (finally!) provides a definition of temperature more formal than just "something measured by a thermometer": Temperature is the slope of an entropy-heat curve. (Solving the equation on the right for temperature shows why this is the case.)

The entropy of a system, like any property, depends only on the system's state, not how the system arrived there. There are many processes that change a system from a particular initial state to a particular final state. The system's resulting change in entropy is the same for any of these processes. (This is analogous to gravitational potential energy, where only the initial and final positions of an object matter, not the path it took between them.)

At the right, you see a graph of temperature plotted against entropy. As heat flows into an object, its temperature increases, as does its entropy. The area under the curve, positive or negative, equals the amount of heat transferred.

The curve is not a straight line. The horizontal section occurs at a first-order phase transition, where heat added causes the substance to change from solid to liquid, or liquid to gas. At phase transitions, adding heat increases the entropy, but not the temperature.

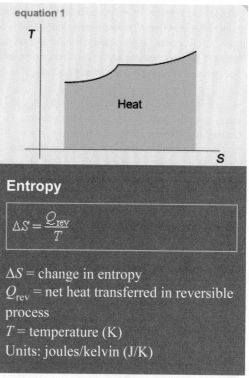

equation 1

Entropy

$$\Delta S = \frac{Q_{rev}}{T}$$

ΔS = change in entropy
Q_{rev} = net heat transferred in reversible process
T = temperature (K)
Units: joules/kelvin (J/K)

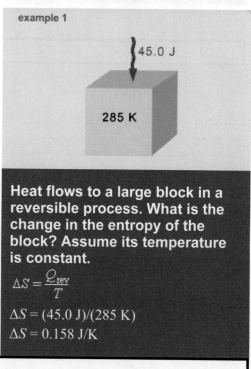

example 1

45.0 J

285 K

Heat flows to a large block in a reversible process. What is the change in the entropy of the block? Assume its temperature is constant.

$$\Delta S = \frac{Q_{rev}}{T}$$

$\Delta S = (45.0 \text{ J})/(285 \text{ K})$
$\Delta S = 0.158 \text{ J/K}$

21.5 - Second law of thermodynamics: entropy

Second law of thermodynamics: Entropy increases, or at best remains constant, in any isolated system.

If nature abhors a vacuum, as the saying goes, then it revels in messes. The universe tends toward increasing disorder. So if your life feels like it is becoming increasingly chaotic, well, you are just going with the flow.

A common non-physicist's statement of the second law is "systems tend toward disorder," a paraphrase of the definition above, which is the second law stated in terms of entropy. Entropy is considered as a measure of a system's disorder. The disorder of a system either stays constant, or increases. Your room never spontaneously becomes more orderly.

You might think that the second law is violated because you can reduce the entropy of an object by cooling it. For instance, you can place a hot drink inside a refrigerator and cool the drink.

However, the second law applies to isolated systems and the refrigerator does not function as an isolated system. If you place your hand by the back of a refrigerator, you will realize that refrigerators emit heat. This heat increases the entropy of the surrounding atmosphere. When we correctly apply the second law to the isolated system of the refrigerator and surrounding atmosphere, we find that entropy stays constant, or increases.

A series of reversible processes can, in theory, leave the entropy of a system unchanged. In practice, however, no process is perfectly reversible, and the entropy of an isolated system increases as processes occur.

Above, we asserted that the heat flow out of a refrigerator would increase the entropy of a system. We will show how this is true, using a particular instance.

We rely on the formulation of the second law that states that heat flows spontaneously only from a hotter object to a colder one. Also recall that the entropy change equals the heat flow divided by the temperature at which the heat flow occurs. The colder the temperature, the larger the increase in entropy.

In Example 1 on the right, 1100 J of heat flows from an object at 250 K to an object at 130 K. To calculate the system's entropy change, we consider the two blocks separately. For the warmer object, we divide the heat by the temperature of the warmer object. Since heat flows out of the warmer object, that heat flow is negative. The change in entropy of the hotter object is −4.4 J/K. Since heat flows into the cooler object, that heat flow is positive. Doing similar calculations for the cooler object, but dividing by the cooler object's lower temperature, we determine that its entropy change is +8.5 J/K. The net change in entropy for the system is 4.1 J/K. The positive sign for the change in entropy tells us that the entropy increases and the second law is obeyed.

This example helps to illustrate why entropy increases with spontaneous heat flow. Heat flows from hot to cold, and as the example illustrates, the reduction of entropy in the hotter object is more than matched by the increase in entropy of the cooler object. This must always be the case since the change in entropy equals the heat divided by the temperature, so a hotter object "expels" less entropy than the colder object "absorbs." In our example, we treated the two objects as being at constant temperatures, but even if their temperatures changed, the spontaneous flow of heat would still cause the entropy of the system to increase.

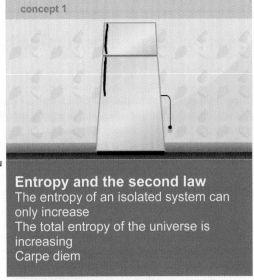

Entropy and the second law
The entropy of an isolated system can only increase
The total entropy of the universe is increasing
Carpe diem

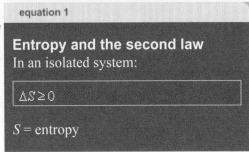

equation 1

Entropy and the second law
In an isolated system:

$$\Delta S \geq 0$$

S = entropy

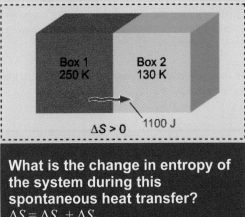

example 1

Box 1
250 K

Box 2
130 K

$\Delta S > 0$ 1100 J

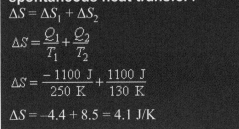

What is the change in entropy of the system during this spontaneous heat transfer?
$$\Delta S = \Delta S_1 + \Delta S_2$$

$$\Delta S = \frac{Q_1}{T_1} + \frac{Q_2}{T_2}$$

$$\Delta S = \frac{-1100 \text{ J}}{250 \text{ K}} + \frac{1100 \text{ J}}{130 \text{ K}}$$

$$\Delta S = -4.4 + 8.5 = 4.1 \text{ J/K}$$

Entropy: Sometimes defined as a measure of the disorder of a system.

The concept of entropy as disorder has entered popular culture thoroughly enough that this section both uses, and critiques, this popular definition. Entropy often is described as measuring the order, or really the disorder of a system. A system that has more disorder has more entropy. For instance, when a new deck of playing cards is shuffled, it goes from being well ordered (the cards are arranged by suit and number) to disordered (the cards can be in many possible arrangements). The deck's entropy has increased.

In thermodynamics, entropy is more often discussed in terms of heat and temperature. The entropy of an object increases as its temperature increases. For instance, when ice is heated so that it melts, and then the liquid is further heated until it turns into steam, the water's entropy increases. On the other hand, in ice the water molecules are "ordered" because of their crystalline structure. In a gas, the molecules have no defined positions, they move randomly, and a particular water molecule may wander far from its initial position. Transferring thermal energy into the system increases its temperature, and its "disorder" increases as its temperature increases.

In some respects these examples work well, providing a visual sense or metaphor to the abstraction of entropy. On the other hand, they are not particularly rigorous, and they do not necessarily link the underlying reality of entropy – its relation to heat – to what we actually see.

For instance, what we perceive as more "ordered" might in fact have greater entropy. Consider the example of ice cubes and liquid water. What looks more "orderly": a glass containing jagged irregular chunks of ice, or the same glass filled with an equivalent amount of liquid water? The glass of water "looks" more orderly, but considering water at the molecular level, the ice is more orderly.

Something is also missing if entropy is only considered to be the "disorder" of a system. Consider an unusual trick deck of cards in which every card is the two of spades. You can shuffle all you like without creating a more "disordered" deck. Entropy as disorder depends on the number of different ways the elements of a system can be arranged. For instance, you can create more disorder by shuffling a standard 52-card deck than one that consists of, say, only 13 cards since the 52-card deck can be arranged in many more ways (8.07×10^{67}) than can the 13-card one (only 6.23×10^{9}).

In summary, considering entropy as disorder, and increasing entropy as increasing disorder, can be a useful metaphor at times, but it also has its limits and potential traps.

concept 1

Temperature increase

Low entropy | Low entropy

Entropy and disorder
"Popular" definition of entropy: measure of disorder
As temperature increases, so does disorder

21.7 - Maximum engine efficiency and reservoir temperatures

Heat engines are everywhere in the modern world. They convert heat into useful work. These engines always consist of a "hot" source reservoir from which thermal energy is taken – for example, the coal burning firebox in an old-fashioned train engine – and a "cold" exhaust reservoir where thermal energy is expelled. In the case of a train's steam engine, that cold reservoir is the atmosphere.

Higher efficiency – turning more of the heat into work – is what heat engine designers strive for. This results in less fuel consumption, which saves money, extends natural resources and reduces pollution.

We can state an inequality, shown on the right, expressing the maximum efficiency of any engine as determined by the temperatures of its hot and cold reservoirs. In this section, we derive this inequality. To do so, we consider the engine, including its reservoirs, as an isolated system, and assume the reservoirs are large enough that the heat flow does not appreciably change their temperatures.

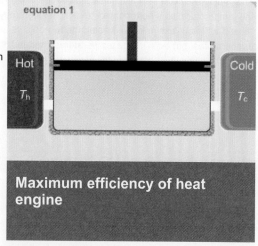

equation 1

Hot T_h | Cold T_c

Maximum efficiency of heat engine

During an engine cycle, the entropy of the hot reservoir decreases as heat flows out of it and the entropy of the cold reservoir increases as heat flows into it. The entropy of the gas does not change after the completion of a cycle because the engine returns to its initial state.

The second law of thermodynamics dictates that the entropy of an isolated system must increase or stay the same during any process, including a complete engine cycle. This means the decrease in entropy of the hot reservoir must be matched or exceeded by the increase in entropy of the cold reservoir. The net entropy increases.

$$e \leq 1 - \frac{T_c}{T_h}$$

e = efficiency
T_c = temperature of cold reservoir (K)
T_h = temperature of hot reservoir (K)

Variables

engine efficiency	e	
net change in entropy	ΔS	

	hot reservoir	cold reservoir
temperature	T_h	T_c
heat transferred	Q^h	Q_c
change in entropy	ΔS_h	ΔS_c

What is the strategy?

1. Calculate the change in entropy for the hot and cold reservoirs. The net change in entropy, which cannot be negative, is the sum of these two quantities. Write this as an inequality, and then rearrange the inequality so the ratio of reservoir temperatures is on one side.

2. Apply the definition of engine efficiency to the inequality.

Physics principles and equations

The definition of entropy

$$\Delta S = \frac{Q_{rev}}{T}$$

The entropy statement of the second law

$$\Delta S \geq 0$$

An equation for engine efficiency

$$e = 1 - \frac{Q_c}{Q_h}$$

Step-by-step derivation

We start with the entropy inequality, and use that to write an inequality with the ratio of reservoir temperatures on one side.

Step	Reason
1. $\Delta S \geq 0$ $\Delta S_c + \Delta S_h \geq 0$	entropy never decreases
2. $\Delta S_c = \dfrac{Q_c}{T_c}$	definition of entropy, cold reservoir
3. $\Delta S_h = -\dfrac{Q_h}{T_h}$	definition of entropy, hot reservoir
4. $\dfrac{Q_c}{T_c} - \dfrac{Q_h}{T_h} \geq 0$	substitute equations 2 and 3 into inequality 1
5. $\dfrac{Q_c}{Q_h} - \dfrac{T_c}{T_h} \geq 0$	multiply by T_c/Q_h

The inequality in step 4 is a concise statement of the entropy changes during an engine cycle: The increase in entropy of the cold reservoir outweighs the decrease in entropy of the hot reservoir.

Now we use the equation for engine efficiency to prove the inequality that describes the maximum engine efficiency.

Step	Reason
6. $e = 1 - \dfrac{Q_c}{Q_h}$	equation stated above
7. $e \leq 1 - \dfrac{Q_c}{Q_h} + \left[\dfrac{Q_c}{Q_h} - \dfrac{T_c}{T_h}\right]$	add inequality 5 to equation 6
8. $e \leq 1 - \dfrac{T_c}{T_h}$	Simplify

The inequality derived in step 8 shows the maximum possible efficiency for an engine with given hot and cold reservoir temperatures. The efficiency limit $1 - T_c/T_h$ is maximized when the cold reservoir is as cold as possible, and the hot reservoir is as hot as possible. For instance, an engine that has a cold reservoir of 300 K and a hot reservoir of 1000 K has an efficiency limit of 1 − 0.3, or 70%. One appeal of diesel engines is that they run "hotter" than gasoline engines, which is a reason why diesel engines are more fuel-efficient.

There are practical limits to engine efficiency. Reservoirs at 10 K and 10,000 K could make for an extremely efficient engine in principle, but it is not possible to build a cost-efficient engine that would maintain reservoirs at these temperatures. Factors other than efficiency, such as cost and the ability to supply power, also affect the design of engines.

21.8 - Carnot cycle and efficiency

Sadi Carnot devised a theoretical engine cycle that is often discussed in thermodynamics. The details of its working are less important than the conclusions that he drew from it.

Carnot proved that any fully reversible engine, like his, was the most efficient possible. In his argument, this French scientist showed that a more efficient engine cycle would violate the second law of thermodynamics, which meant it was not possible to construct such an engine. In an irreversible process, energy is lost from the system to its environment in unrecoverable ways, such as through friction or sound energy. All real engines operate irreversibly and are less efficient than a Carnot engine.

Earlier, we showed that the maximum efficiency of a heat engine was **less than or equal** to one minus the ratio of the temperature of the reservoirs. The closer an engine cycle comes to having no increase in entropy, the closer its efficiency will be to this limit.

The Carnot cycle attains the theoretical maximum efficiency for any engine functioning with reservoirs at two particular temperatures. It can be shown that the efficiency of this cycle **equals** one minus the ratio of the temperature of the cold reservoir to the hot reservoir. This important conclusion is shown in Equation 1.

Even the ideal Carnot engine is not 100% efficient. To make a Carnot engine operate at 100% efficiency, its cold reservoir would have to be at absolute zero (which is theoretically impossible), or its hot reservoir would have to be infinitely hot.

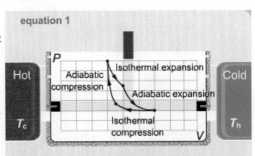

equation 1

Carnot engine efficiency

$$e_{ce} = 1 - \frac{T_c}{T_h}$$

e_{ce} = efficiency of Carnot engine
T_c = temperature of cold reservoir (K)
T_h = temperature of hot reservoir (K)

21.9 - Otto cycle: internal combustion engine

The internal combustion engine shown above is used in automobiles and is probably familiar to you. In this section, we describe the operation and engine cycle of this engine, and present an equation for its efficiency. The cycle is called the Otto cycle, after the German inventor of the "four-stroke" internal combustion engine, Nikolaus August Otto. A "stroke" is a movement in or out of a piston. In the complete Otto cycle, a piston moves in and out twice, making four strokes.

Internal combustion engine.

In an internal combustion engine, there is no heat reservoir in the usual sense. Instead of heat flowing into the engine, the working gas itself is the source of energy. It is a mixture of air and gasoline vapor that is ignited inside a cylinder (hence the term "internal combustion"), and expands to drive a piston that does work. The thermal energy that is used to do work is created by burning the gasoline mixture. You see the cylinder and piston in the illustrations below.

The four steps of the basic thermodynamic cycle together require two strokes of the piston. The steps occur rapidly. Two additional strokes drive the combustion products out of the cylinder and replace the air and gasoline mixture for the next cycle. For simplicity, we combine these two strokes into one "exhaust" step.

Here are the steps in the Otto cycle.

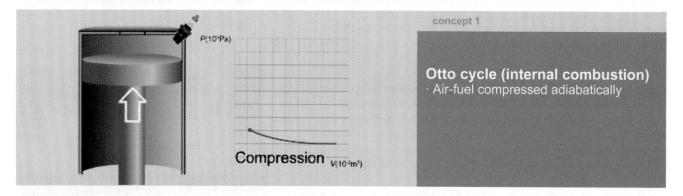

First: The piston compresses a mixture of air and gasoline vapor inside the cylinder adiabatically.

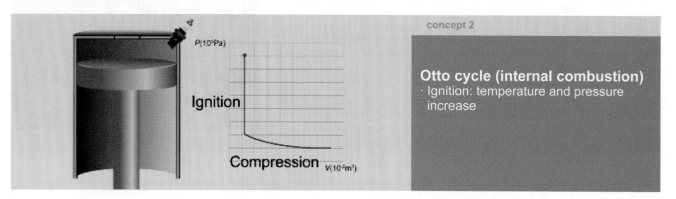

Second: A spark plug ignites the mixture. This is a constant-volume process: The temperature and pressure of the mixture both increase, but the volume stays the same.

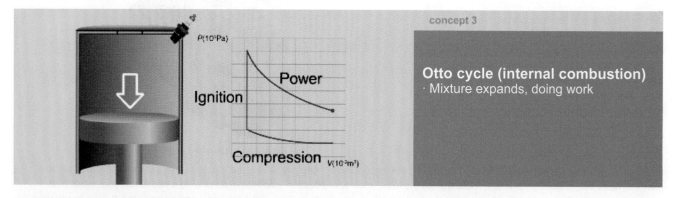

Third: The gas expands adiabatically, moving the piston to do work.

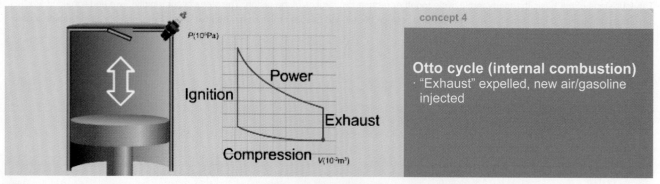

Fourth: Finally, there is an "exhaust" step involving both an up and a down stroke of the piston where the combusted mixture in the cylinder is replaced through some valves by a fresh mixture of air and gasoline at lower pressure and temperature. The piston moves in and out, but it returns to its original position so this is considered a constant-volume process, as shown on the pressure-volume graph. The cycle then begins again.

The theoretical efficiency of the engine can be computed as shown in Equation 1 on the right. V_{max} is the volume of the cylinder when the piston is "out". That is the maximum volume, and V_{min} is the minimum volume. The ratio of the molar specific heats for the air-fuel mixture C_p/C_V is indicated by γ (the Greek letter gamma). The ratio V_{max}/V_{min} is called the *compression ratio* of the engine. The higher the compression ratio, the more efficient the engine.

In Example 1 on the right, you see an example problem that computes the theoretical efficiency of a typical car engine. The actual efficiency of real car engines ranges from 20-26%, less than the equation predicts, due to the heat expelled from the engine and other factors.

You may be familiar with *octane ratings* for gasoline. Typical octane ratings, as seen on the pumps at gas stations, are in the range of 85 to 95. The octane rating of a gasoline indicates the tendency of the gasoline-air mixture to self ignite when it is compressed. The higher the octane rating, the more compression the mixture can withstand before combusting spontaneously. High compression gasoline engines require high octane fuel to prevent "knocking" that occurs when the fuel mixture in the cylinder ignites before the compression cycle is complete, creating a shockwave that collides with the piston.

A diesel engine operates in a similar fashion to a gasoline engine, but does not require a spark plug. Instead, air alone is compressed in the cylinder, causing it to reach very a high temperature. Then, fuel is injected into the cylinder, where it is ignited due to the high temperature. To create the high temperature needed to ignite the fuel, diesel engines have higher compression ratios than typical gasoline engines. This means they are more efficient than gasoline engines.

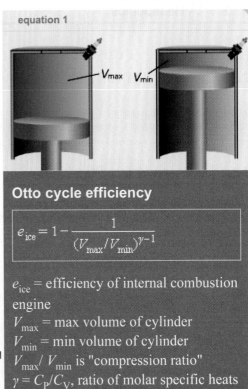

equation 1

Otto cycle efficiency

$$e_{ice} = 1 - \frac{1}{(V_{max}/V_{min})^{\gamma-1}}$$

e_{ice} = efficiency of internal combustion engine
V_{max} = max volume of cylinder
V_{min} = min volume of cylinder
V_{max}/V_{min} is "compression ratio"
$\gamma = C_p/C_V$, ratio of molar specific heats

example 1

The car engine has a compression ratio of 8.0. The molar specific heat ratio γ is 1.4. What is the theoretical engine efficiency?

$$e_{ice} = 1 - \frac{1}{(V_{max}/V_{min})^{\gamma-1}}$$

$$e_{ice} = 1 - \frac{1}{(8.0)^{1.4-1}}$$

$$e_{ice} = 0.56 = 56\%$$

Heat pump: A device that transfers heat from a colder environment to a warmer one.

It may sound a bit odd to speak of transferring heat from a colder environment (say the outdoors in the winter) to a warmer one (the interior of a building), but that is what heat pumps do: They pump heat opposite to the direction it would normally flow.

Because heat pumps are more energy-efficient than typical furnaces, they are becoming increasingly popular. An additional and very attractive benefit of heat pumps is that in the summertime, they can be run in reverse to pump heat out of the cool house into the warm outdoors, so the same appliance does double duty as a furnace and as an air conditioner.

A heat pump can be thought of as a heat engine run in reverse. With a heat engine, heat flows from the hot reservoir to the engine and then to the cold reservoir, and work is done **by** the engine. With the pump, heat flows the opposite direction, from the cold reservoir to the hot, and work must be done **on** the engine to accomplish this, since heat does not flow spontaneously from cold to hot.

As mentioned above, a heat pump is in some ways analogous to an air conditioner (or a refrigerator). In both cases, work is performed on the device, and it is used to transfer heat in the direction opposite to the direction in which it spontaneously flows. However, there is a difference between the two appliances. A heat pump moves heat from the cold outdoors to a warmer indoors, with the purpose of further increasing the temperature of the indoors. An air conditioner moves heat from indoors to outdoors, with the purpose of further cooling the interior.

Efficiency is analyzed somewhat differently with heat pumps than it is with heat engines. Recall that the maximum efficiency of a heat engine is determined by the ratio of the cold and hot reservoir temperatures ($e = 1 - T_c/T_h$). When the temperature difference is large, the ratio is small and the engine can be more efficient. In contrast, as you can see from Equation 2, heat pumps work best when there is little temperature difference. The greater the difference, the harder the pump has to work to transfer energy from the cold to the hot reservoir. For this reason, heat pumps are rated by the *coefficient of performance* (*COP*). You see the definition of the coefficient of performance in Equation 1 on the right: It is the heat transferred to the hot reservoir divided by the work done **on** the gas. Both the heat transfer and the work done on the engine are treated as positive quantities.

One way to think of the efficiency of a heat engine is as the ratio of "what you want" (work done) to "what you pay" (heat added). This applies to the *COP* as well. The *COP* for a heat pump equals the ratio of "what you want" (heat flow) to "what you pay" (the work done on the gas). The larger the *COP*, the more heat is transferred to the hot reservoir per unit of work done.

The maximum *COP* for a heat pump is determined, as for a heat engine, by the temperatures of the hot and cold reservoirs. An inequality that limits the maximum *COP* is shown in Equation 2 on the right. The right side of the inequality is the ratio of the hot reservoir temperature to the difference of the hot and cold temperatures. A Carnot engine operating "in reverse" as a heat pump achieves the maximum *COP*. That is, the equality holds.

In Example 1, the maximum *COP* is calculated for a heat pump operating to warm a house, with an indoor temperature of $21°C$ (about $70°F$) and an outdoor temperature of $13°C$ (about $55°F$). The theoretical maximum *COP* is 37; the actual operating *COP* would be less. Typical *COP*s for heat pumps range from about five to 10. A heat pump with a *COP* of five would transfer five joules of thermal energy for every joule

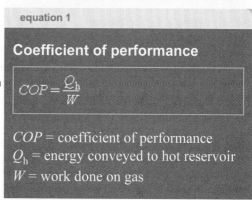

concept 1

Heat pump
Work moves heat from cold to hot reservoir

equation 1

Coefficient of performance

$$COP = \frac{Q_h}{W}$$

COP = coefficient of performance
Q_h = energy conveyed to hot reservoir
W = work done on gas

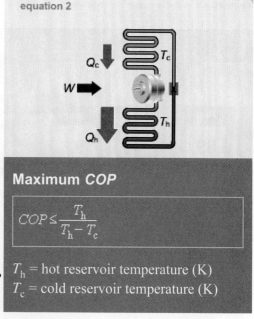

equation 2

Maximum *COP*

$$COP \leq \frac{T_h}{T_h - T_c}$$

T_h = hot reservoir temperature (K)
T_c = cold reservoir temperature (K)

of work supplied.

A refrigerator acts something like a heat pump, but its purpose is to cool the cold reservoir, the refrigerator's interior. The coefficient of performance of refrigerators is sometimes measured as Q_c/W. Again, this is the ratio of "what you want" (cooling the cold reservoir) to "what you pay" (work done). For refrigerators, COP values from four to six are typical.

example 1

21°C   13°C

What is the maximum _COP_ of a heat pump operating between these indoor and outdoor temperatures?

$$COP_{max} = \frac{T_h}{T_h - T_c}$$

$$T_h = 21 + 273.15\ \text{K} = 294\ \text{K}$$

$$T_c = 13 + 273.15\ \text{K} = 286\ \text{K}$$

$$COP_{max} = \frac{294\ \text{K}}{294\ \text{K} - 286\ \text{K}}$$

$$COP_{max} = 37$$

21.11 - Sample problem: heat pump in action

19.0°C   15.0°C

For these temperatures, what is the maximum _COP_ for a heat pump? If the _COP_ of a heat pump is 5.48, and 1250 J of work is done on it, how much heat energy could it maximally transfer inside from the outdoors?

If you heat a house using an electric furnace, the electric energy supplied to the furnace is converted into thermal energy and transferred to the air inside the house, increasing its temperature. If the furnace is supplied with 1250 joules of electrical energy, it can increase the energy of the air by at most 1250 J. It will be interesting to contrast this value with the amount of heat that a heat pump can cause to flow into the house using the same amount of energy.

Variables

temperature of cold reservoir	$T_c = 15.0°C$
temperature of hot reservoir	$T_h = 19.0°C$
work done on heat pump	$W = 1250\ \text{J}$
maximum COP of pump	COP_{max}
actual COP of pump	$COP = 5.48$
heat flowing to interior	Q_h

What is the strategy?

1. Calculate the maximum coefficient of performance of the heat pump

2. Use the definition of coefficient of performance with the actual COP to calculate the maximum amount of heat transferred to the interior.

Physics principles and equations

This inequality specifies the maximum possible COP of a heat pump with given temperature reservoirs:

$$COP \le \frac{T_h}{T_h - T_c}$$

(Be sure to use Kelvin temperatures.)

The definition of COP

$$COP = Q_h / W$$

Step-by-step derivation

We first calculate the maximum possible coefficient of performance for the heat pump.

Step		Reason
1.	$COP_{max} = \dfrac{T_h}{T_h - T_c}$	maximum COP
2.	$COP_{max} = \dfrac{(19.0 + 273.15)\ \text{K}}{(19.0 + 273.15)\ \text{K} - (15.0 + 273.15)\ \text{K}}$	substitute values
3.	$COP_{max} = 73.0$	evaluate

The maximum possible COP is over ten times higher than the actual (and more realistic) COP of 5.48 as stated in the problem. We now calculate the heat transferred into the house, using this actual value for the coefficient of performance.

Step	Reason
4. $COP = Q_h / W$	definition of COP
5. $Q_h = (COP)W$	solve for Q_h
6. $Q_h = (5.48)(1250\ \text{J})$	substitute values
7. $Q_h = 6850\ \text{J}$	evaluate

The heat pump transfers significantly more heat than the furnace would. As you might expect, this does not violate the principle of conservation of energy. The device "pumps" thermal energy from outdoors to indoors, further cooling the outdoors in order to warm the indoors.

21.12 - Interactive summary problem: efficiency of an automobile engine

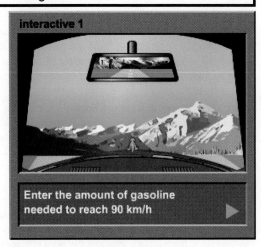

interactive 1

In the simulation to the right, you get to put an engine to work in a common situation. You are the driver of a car. You specify how much gasoline you want the engine to consume. When you press GO, the car will accelerate at full engine power until the gasoline is gone, at which point the simulation will stop and your calculations will be evaluated.

Your goal is to specify the amount of gasoline that will allow you to reach a speed of 90.0 km/h. Here, we will consider the engine as supplying an external force doing work on the car. The engine must do $9.35×10^5$ J of work to accelerate the car to 90.0 km/h. This figure is a good approximation of the amount of work a real engine must do to both increase the car's kinetic energy to the desired amount and overcome forces such as air resistance, friction, and so forth.

To decide how much gasoline you need, you must first calculate the efficiency of the engine. You can do this by adding any amount of gasoline and pressing GO to see the resulting heat added and heat expelled while the engine runs. Use these values to calculate the engine's efficiency. Next, calculate how much heat needs to be added to the engine for it to perform the desired amount of work. The gasoline is the source of the added heat. To find out how much gasoline to add, you need to know that one liter of gasoline generates $1.30×10^8$ J of heat when combusted in the engine.

The correct amount of gasoline will be under a tenth of a liter. Calculate the amount of gasoline needed to reach 90.0 km/h to three significant digits (to a ten-thousandth of a liter), enter this value, and press GO to see the results. Press RESET to try again.

If you want, you could calculate the kinetic energy of the car at the final speed and determine what percent of the work goes to overcoming resistive forces versus increasing the KE of the car. (The mass of the car is 1280 kg.)

If you have trouble getting the right answer, see the section on engine efficiency.

21.13 - Gotchas

Using Celsius temperatures. All the equations in this chapter that contain a temperature factor require the temperature to be in Kelvin.

My friend has an engine that is 101% efficient. This is not possible: It contradicts the second law of thermodynamics. It also contradicts the first law. Making that claim probably breaks some FTC regulations too.

If I clean my room, it will become more ordered and I will be breaking the second law of thermodynamics. Not to dissuade you from cleanliness, but you are not breaking the law. Your room is not an isolated system; other parts of the system (like the molecules within your body) have become more disordered.

The efficiency of a heat engine is the ratio of the net work it does divided by heat added during an engine cycle. There are several equivalent statements of the second law of thermodynamics. One states that no heat engine can transform 100% of the thermal energy supplied to it during a cycle into work.

Entropy is a property of a system. Entropy increases as heat is transferred into the system. The change in entropy can be calculated as the heat transferred during a reversible process (one in which the system can be returned to its initial state without additional energy) divided by the temperature. Another way to state the second law is that in any isolated system – such as the universe – entropy never decreases.

The maximum efficiency possible for any heat engine depends on the ratio of the temperatures of the cold and hot reservoirs. The greater the difference in temperatures, the lower the ratio and the more efficient the engine can be. A Carnot engine is a theoretical engine that achieves this maximum efficiency.

The internal combustion engine in most automobiles utilizes the Otto cycle. The efficiency of the internal combustion engine depends on the compression ratio, the ratio of the maximum to minimum gas volume in the engine.

Heat pumps can be used instead of furnaces to warm buildings. Unlike a heat engine, a heat pump uses work to transfer heat from the cool reservoir (outdoors) to the hot reservoir (the building interior). Just as we rated heat engines by their efficiency, for a heat pump the analogous quantity is its coefficient of performance. A heat pump's coefficient of performance increases when the difference in temperature between the hot and cold reservoirs decreases.

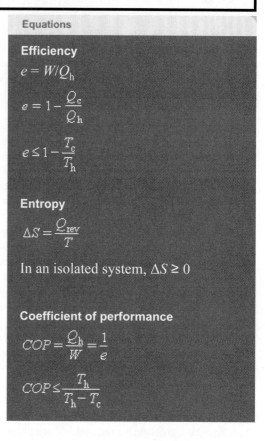

Equations

Efficiency

$$e = W/Q_h$$

$$e = 1 - \frac{Q_c}{Q_h}$$

$$e \leq 1 - \frac{T_c}{T_h}$$

Entropy

$$\Delta S = \frac{Q_{rev}}{T}$$

In an isolated system, $\Delta S \geq 0$

Coefficient of performance

$$COP = \frac{Q_h}{W} = \frac{1}{e}$$

$$COP \leq \frac{T_h}{T_h - T_c}$$

22.0 - Introduction

In this chapter, we begin the study of electricity and magnetism by discussing electric charge and the electrostatic force. Although you cannot see the individual charged particles, such as electrons and protons, that cause this force, you certainly see its effects. Phenomena ranging from the annoying static cling in freshly laundered clothing to the operation of laser printers are based on the electrostatic force. In the sections that follow, we will cover the fundamentals of electric charge: what it means to say that an object is charged and the nature of the forces created by charged objects.

We start with two simulations, shown to the right. The first allows you to experiment with positively and negatively charged particles and see the forces they exert on one another. The positively charged particles in this simulation have the same charge as protons, and the negatively charged particles have the same charge as electrons.

After you launch this simulation, drag particles from the control panel onto the screen above it. Once there, they will exert forces on each other. The amount and direction of each force will be shown on the screen. You can drag particles closer together or farther apart to see how the force they exert on one another relates to the distance between them (the heavier grid lines are exactly one meter apart). If you press GO, the particles, which all have equal mass, will be free to accelerate in response to the forces they exert on each other. *Electrostatics* is the study of electric charges at rest, so the simulation is also providing you with an extremely informal introduction to the topic of *electrodynamics*, the study of charges in motion.

As you use the simulation, take note of the direction of the forces between, say, two negative or positive particles or between a positive and a negative particle. You can also place two particles with the same charge next to each other, and see how the force on a third particle changes. How the electric force changes with both the distance between the charged particles – frequently just called "charges" – and the amount of charge is a fundamental focus of this chapter.

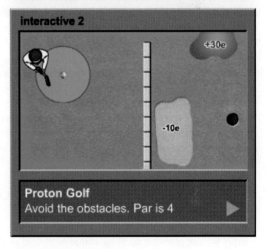

interactive 1

$F = 4.58 \times 10^{-28}$ N

$F = 4.58 \times 10^{-28}$ N

Free play with charges
Observe the force between particles

interactive 2

+30e

-10e

Proton Golf
Avoid the obstacles. Par is 4

In the second simulation, you can play "proton golf". The ball is positively charged, and you add protons to the putter to make it positively charged as well. The protons in the putter exert a force, called the electrostatic force, on the ball even when the two are not touching. You can control both the location of the putter, by dragging it, and how many protons it contains, by clicking the up- and down-arrows in the console. The moment you load protons into the putter they exert a force on the ball, but the ball is locked in place until you press PUTT. The grass of the green supplies a frictional force that will cause the ball to stop rolling.

Your mission, as always in golf, is to sink the ball in the hole – in four or less shots, if you can! The important thing (in addition to having fun) is to observe how the electrostatic force relates to the amount of charge and to distance. Be warned, though: Obstacles do exist! A clump of protons acts as a hill that causes the ball to roll away from it, while a clump of electrons is a sand trap that will attract the ball. Fore!

Electric charge: A property of the particles that make up matter. It causes attraction and repulsion.

This woman's hair is electrically charged. As you will see, the strands of her hair repel each other because each one of them carries a negative charge.

Electric charge is a property of matter that can cause attraction and repulsion. In this section, we focus on electrons and protons, and the role they play in causing an object to have an electric charge.

An electron is defined as having a **negative** charge and a proton is defined as having a **positive** charge. Charge is a scalar, not a vector. A negative charge is not less than zero, just the opposite of positive. In this book we will represent negative charges as black and positive charges as red.

The amount of charge of an electron or proton is written as e and is called the *elementary charge*. An electron has a negative charge of $-e$ and a proton has a positive charge of $+e$. This amount of charge is the smallest amount that has been isolated. (Subatomic particles called *quarks* have charges of $+2e/3$ or $-e/3$ but they have not been isolated.)

The SI unit for charge is the *coulomb*. An electron or a proton has a charge of magnitude $e = 1.602\ 18 \times 10^{-19}$ coulombs. This means approximately 6,250,000,000,000,000,000 electrons or protons are required for a coulomb of charge to be present. This is a vast number! However, numbers like this are often present in nature: A bolt of lightning typically contains about 25 C of charge. To provide you with another idea of the magnitude of a coulomb, approximately 0.8 C of charge flows through a 100 watt light bulb every second.

Some scientists, chemists in particular, use another unit, the *esu* or *electrostatic unit*. One esu equals $3.335\ 64 \times 10^{-10}$ C.

A small amount of matter contains a large number of electrons and protons. For instance, a one-kilogram sample of copper contains about 2.75×10^{26} protons. When an object has the same number of electrons and protons, it has no net charge and is said to be *electrically neutral*.

The addition or removal of electrons from an object causes it to become charged. A negatively charged object has more electrons than protons and a positively charged object has more protons than electrons. If the kilogram of copper has a charge of +0.1 C, which is a relatively large amount of charge, this means that about 0.000 002 % of its electrons have been removed.

concept 1

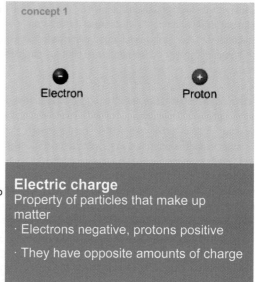

Electron　　　　Proton

Electric charge
Property of particles that make up matter
· Electrons negative, protons positive

· They have opposite amounts of charge

equation 1

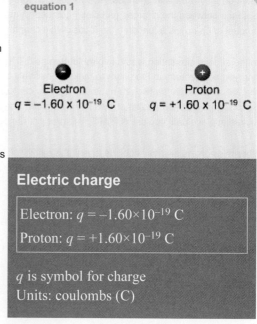

Electron　　　　　　Proton
$q = -1.60 \times 10^{-19}$ C　　$q = +1.60 \times 10^{-19}$ C

Electric charge

Electron: $q = -1.60 \times 10^{-19}$ C

Proton: $q = +1.60 \times 10^{-19}$ C

q is symbol for charge
Units: coulombs (C)

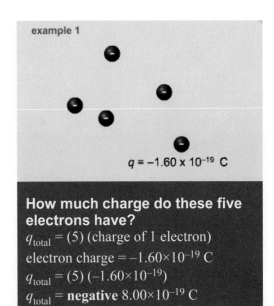

example 1

$q = -1.60 \times 10^{-19}$ C

How much charge do these five electrons have?

$q_{total} = (5)$ (charge of 1 electron)

electron charge $= -1.60 \times 10^{-19}$ C

$q_{total} = (5) (-1.60 \times 10^{-19})$

$q_{total} =$ **negative** 8.00×10^{-19} C

22.2 - Creating charged objects

How does an object become electrically charged?
The answer is that the addition or removal of
electrons creates negatively and positively charged
objects. Except under extreme conditions, protons
stay in place and electrons move.

A piece of silk and a glass rod can be used to
demonstrate one manner in which objects can
become charged. We will assume these two objects
start out electrically neutral. In other words, the silk
has equal numbers of protons and electrons, as does
the glass.

A charged comb induces electric charges in the paper dots which
cause them to stick together. This phenomenon is called static cling.

You can transfer electrons from the glass to the silk by rubbing the two materials
together. This close contact results in a net flow of electrons from the glass to the silk
and causes the silk to become negatively charged. It now contains more electrons than
protons. In turn, the glass becomes positively charged, since it now has fewer electrons
than protons.

You may wonder why rubbing silk and glass together causes them to become charged.
The electrons move because the silk molecules have a greater affinity for electrons than
do the glass molecules. Rubbing the two materials together facilitates the transfer of
electrons by providing a greater level of contact between their molecules.

The charging process can be reversed. When free to move, electrons will flow from a
negatively charged object to a positively charged one, reducing or ending a charge
imbalance. Lightning provides a dramatic example of such movement, a grand display
of excess electrons moving to a region that is less negatively charged. With lightning,
the electrons may be moving to a positively charged region of a cloud, or to an
electrically neutral region such as the surface of the Earth. Charges take advantage of
any opportunity to reduce an imbalance.

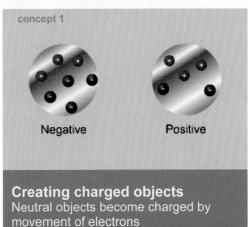

concept 1

Negative   Positive

Creating charged objects
Neutral objects become charged by
movement of electrons
Excess electrons: negatively charged
Excess protons: positively charged

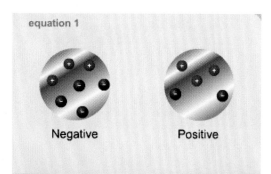

Negative   Positive

Creating charged objects

$$q = \pm Ne$$

q = charge
N = number of excess charges
· protons positive, electrons negative
e = elementary charge

example 1

What is the net charge on the disk?

N = 7 protons − 2 electrons
N = 5 protons
$q = +Ne$
$q = (5)(1.60\times10^{-19})$
$q = 8.00\times10^{-19}$ C

368   Copyright 2000-2007 Kinetic Books Co. Chapter 22

Conservation of charge: The net charge of an isolated system of objects remains constant.

Electric charge is conserved. The net charge of an isolated system may be positive, negative or neutral. Charge can move between objects in the system, but the net charge of the system remains unchanged.

Although lightning transfers a very large amount of charge from a cloud to the ground, the total charge remains constant.

To illustrate this principle, we again use the example of a silk cloth and a glass rod to demonstrate how two different objects can become charged while, at the same time, overall charge is conserved. Let's assume that the cloth and the rod are both neutral to begin with. They each become charged when rubbed together, but their combined charge is unchanged: It remains zero, or neutral. It is true that electrons have moved between the rod and the cloth, but to the extent that one object is negative, the other is positive. The cloth and the rod constitute an isolated system because all the charge moves solely between them and no charge leaves them. If charge flowed to a person holding these objects, that person would become part of the system as well, and charge would still be conserved.

Early on, scientists such as Benjamin Franklin (yes, *that* Ben Franklin) suggested this conservation principle based on experimental data and intuition, but he and his colleagues were unable to show why it was so. The discovery of electrons showed why the conjecture was true: It was the movement of electrons that created the charged objects that Franklin observed. Under ordinary circumstances, these particles are neither created nor destroyed, and Franklin observed the results of electrons flowing from one object to another.

An object is charged when it has an imbalance of electrons and protons. Charge is said to be *quantized*: It is always observed as an integer multiple of e, the magnitude of the charge of an electron or a proton.

In extreme circumstances, charged particles can be destroyed. For example, when a positron (an exotic particle that is the mirror image of an electron, identical in mass but opposite in charge) collides with an electron, the two will annihilate each other and produce gamma rays, a kind of high-energy radiation. Does this scenario violate the conservation of charge? No, because gamma rays have no net charge. Before the collision, the system of one electron and one positron has no net charge. After the collision, the system consists of neutral gamma radiation, so charge is conserved.

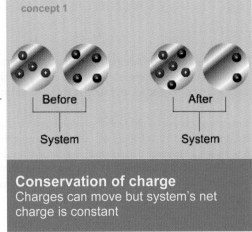

concept 1

Before | After

System | System

Conservation of charge
Charges can move but system's net charge is constant

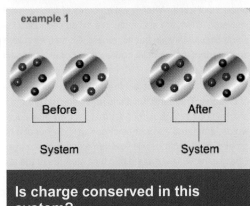

example 1

Before | After

System | System

Is charge conserved in this system?
Before: 2 excess protons
After: 2 excess protons
Net charge before = net charge after
Charge conserved!

Conductor: An object or material in which charge can flow relatively freely.

Insulator: An object or material in which charge does not flow freely.

Ground: Charge flows from a charged object to a ground, leaving the object neutral.

The lightning rod mounted atop this cupola intercepts lightning and protects a building during electrical storms.

You can easily find conductors and insulators (also called *nonconductors*) in your home or classroom. If you examine an electrical cord, you will find that it consists of a conducting core of copper wire surrounded by an insulator such as vinyl plastic.

Charge can be moved relatively easily through a conductor such as copper using a device like a battery. A battery will cause electrons to flow through a copper wire like the one shown in Concept 1. In contrast, it is difficult to cause electrons to flow in insulators like rubber or many plastics. This difference explains the design of electrical cords: Often, they are made of copper wire wrapped with a flexible vinyl insulator so that electrons flowing through the wire remain within the cord.

Insulators do not allow charges to flow when they are subjected to only moderate amounts of force. When great amounts of force are applied, charge can flow through an insulator. There are also materials called semiconductors that enable charge to flow in some circumstances, but not others. Given their role in devices like transistors, they are an important topic, but lie outside the scope of this section.

A ground is a neutral object that can accept or supply an essentially unlimited number of charges. The Earth functions as an electric ground. If you touch a conducting, charged object to the ground, the object will also become electrically neutral − in other words, grounded. Excess electrons will flow out of a negatively charged object to the ground, and electrons will flow into a positively charged object from the ground. Charges move to a ground because charges of the same sign move as far away from each other as possible due to their mutual repulsion. The ground distributes the excess charge far enough away that it ceases to affect the object.

Protecting houses from lightning presents engineers with the need to use conductors and grounds. A building is not usually a conductor, but lightning can transform a house into a reluctant conductor, with disastrous, highly flammable results. A lightning rod is a conductor that protects houses and other structures by providing an easier, alternate route to the ground. A conducting wire connects the rod to the Earth. The shape of the rod also increases the likelihood that it will be the preferred target for lightning.

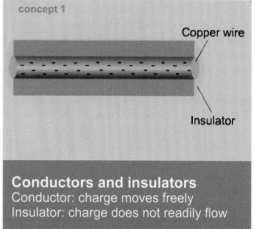

concept 1

Copper wire

Insulator

Conductors and insulators
Conductor: charge moves freely
Insulator: charge does not readily flow

concept 2

Ground
Makes conductors electrically neutral

These interactive simulations are versions of a classic game. In the original version of this game, you are given glasses, some filled with water and others empty. You are shown or told a final configuration of glasses and water. Your challenge is to start with the initial configuration, and by pouring water from one glass to another in a sequence of steps, end with the specified final configuration. For instance, a simple challenge would be to start with an empty glass, a half-full glass, and a quarter-full glass, and end up with a three-quarters-full glass. By pouring the half-full glass into the quarter-full glass, you achieve that goal.

In the simulations to the right, the same overall idea applies to electric charge. You are supplied with a configuration of charges on rods. Some of the rods have no charge, some have positive charge, and some are negatively charged. All the rods are the same size and are made of identical conducting material. In this game, charge flows between rods instead of water flowing between glasses. Charge flows until equilibrium is reached. For example, if you touch a rod with +4.000 microcoulombs of charge to a rod with no charge, both rods end up with +2.000 microcoulombs of charge.

To play the game, click on any rod and drag it to another rod. When you release the mouse button, charge will transfer between the rods.

In the topmost game to the right, you are given a rod with a charge of positive 10.000 μC, a rod with a charge of −3.000 μC, and several neutral rods. Your goal is to produce a rod with a charge of +1.000 μC. This can be done in two moves. The second game requires a greater number of moves and more planning. You can see the initial configuration to the right. The challenge again is to create a rod with +1.000 μC of charge. However skilled you are at these two games, the main point is to observe how charge is conserved.

Keep in mind that you do not have to be good at the games to practice the physics you are learning in this chapter. Give it a try! Whether you get the minimum number of moves or not, the simulations offer a chance to employ the principle of conservation of charge.

If you have any questions about the conservation of charge or about grounds, review the preceding sections on these topics.

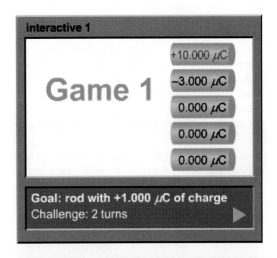

interactive 1

Game 1

+10.000 μC
−3.000 μC
0.000 μC
0.000 μC
0.000 μC

Goal: rod with +1.000 μC of charge
Challenge: 2 turns

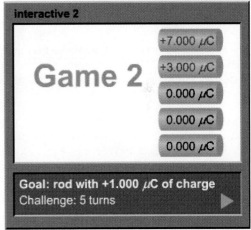

interactive 2

Game 2

+7.000 μC
+3.000 μC
0.000 μC
0.000 μC
0.000 μC

Goal: rod with +1.000 μC of charge
Challenge: 5 turns

22.6 - Electrostatic force

Electrostatic force: Attraction or repulsion due to electric charge.

Electrostatics is the study of electric forces between charges at rest. If you have ever visited a science museum, you may have seen people press their hands against an electrically charged device surmounted by a shiny metallic sphere, and then watched in amazement as their hair stands on end. This device, called a *Van de Graaff generator*, amusingly illustrates how electric charge creates a repulsive force. In the photograph above you see the spectacular display that can be created by such forces in a large Van de Graaff generator, as its huge electrostatic accumulation discharges through the atmosphere. The Boston Museum of Science states that it is home to the largest Van de Graaff generator in the world.

This Van de Graaff generator builds up an enormous electrostatic charge that escapes into the surrounding air.

Clothes dryers provide a more mundane example of electrostatic forces at work. When your socks stick to your pants and then crackle as you pull them apart, you are witnessing the static cling caused by electrostatic forces. In this case, electrostatic force is causing oppositely charged pieces of clothing to attract each other. As the clothing is pulled apart, electric charges arc between the clothing items in an attempt to reach a more balanced state. (Imagine: When you fold your laundry, you can both please your parents and review your physics studies. What a deal!) The electric charge responsible for that annoying cling in a sock is typically in the range of a few microcoulombs.

When objects have opposite charges, like laundry items or a glass rod and a silk cloth, they attract. When objects like the two balloons you see to the right have the same charge, either positive or negative, they repel each other. The old cliché – opposites attract and likes repel – proves true in physics. When dealing with issues of attraction and repulsion, it really is important to know your sign.

Two charged objects exert equal but opposite forces on each other. In other words, if they attract, they pull toward each other with the same force. If they repel, they push against each other with equal force.

The forces act along a straight line between the centers of the two charges. For instance, if they attract, each force points directly toward the other charge, as illustrated in Concept 2. If they repel, each force points directly away from the other charge.

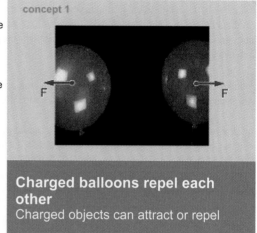

concept 1

Charged balloons repel each other
Charged objects can attract or repel

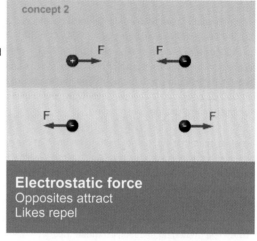

concept 2

Electrostatic force
Opposites attract
Likes repel

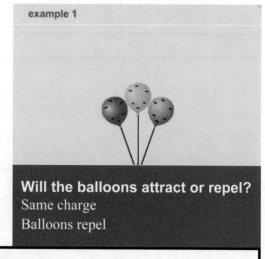

example 1

Will the balloons attract or repel?
Same charge
Balloons repel

22.7 - Inducing an electric charge

Inducing an electric charge: Creating a charged object or region of an object without direct contact.

Objects can become electrically charged when they are put into contact with each other, for example, by rubbing glass and silk together, or by touching a charged rod to a neutral one. In this process electrons flow from one object to the other.

Objects can also become charged without touching. Like gravity, electrostatic forces act at a distance, so charges cause other charges to move without direct contact. When a charged object, like the nonconducting sphere shown in Concept 1, is placed near a neutral object in which electrons are free to move, such as the joined pair of conducting metal rods to its right, the charged object causes electrons to move in the neutral object. Charges in the rods, initially evenly distributed throughout the pair, end up in the asymmetrical configuration you see in Concept 1. The rod pair as a whole is still electrically neutral.

To explain how charged objects can be created without direct contact, we use the sphere and the pair of neutral rods just discussed. First, the negatively charged sphere approaches the rods. As the sphere repels electrons in the rods, the closer end of the rod combination becomes positively charged. As a result of the movement of electrons, the far end of the rod combination becomes negatively charged. Two regions of charge have been induced without contact by a charged object.

Next, the rods are separated. The closer one will remain positive and the farther one will remain negative, even after the charged sphere has moved away. This example shows how two objects can become charged without coming into direct contact with a third charged object.

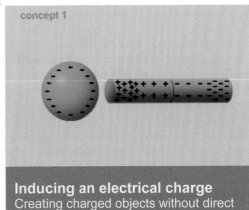

Inducing an electrical charge
Creating charged objects without direct contact
· Charge on ball moves electrons in rod pair to create positive, negative regions

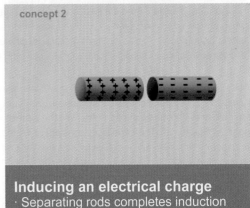

Inducing an electrical charge
· Separating rods completes induction

22.8 - Coulomb's law: calculating electrostatic forces

Coulomb's law: The electrostatic force a charged particle exerts on another is proportional to the product of the charges and inversely proportional to the square of the distance between them.

Named for Charles Augustin de Coulomb, the eighteenth century French physicist who formulated it, this law quantifies the amount of force between charged particles. His law is shown in Equation 1 to the right.

The force is measured in newtons. The constant k in the equation has been experimentally determined. It equals $8.987\ 55 \times 10^9$ N·m²/C².

The charges are shown with absolute value signs around them, so that two positive values are multiplied together to calculate the **amount** of the force. To determine the

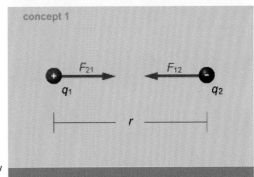

Coulomb's law
Electrostatic force
· Proportional to product of charges

· Inversely proportional to distance squared

direction, the rule "opposites attract, likes repel" is used. Two opposite charges attract, so both forces pull the charges together. Two like charges repel, so both forces push the charges away from each other. Recalling Newton's third law helps to insure the correct result: The forces are always equal but opposite to each other.

Coulomb's law means that larger quantities of charge create more force and that the force weakens with the square of the distance.

Electrostatic forces can be added; they obey the principle of superposition. For example, if there are three charges, the force exerted by two of the charges on the third equals the vector sum of the forces exerted by each charge. This is similar to other forces you have studied; if two people are pushing a car, the net force equals the vector sum of the individual forces exerted by each person.

In Coulomb's law, r is the distance between two *point charges*, two infinitesimal sites of charge. If charges are symmetrically distributed on each of two spheres, a principle called the shell theorem can be used to show that all the charge on each sphere acts as though it were located at the sphere's center. In this case, the distance r is the distance between the centers of the spheres.

If you have studied gravity, you may notice that Coulomb's law is similar to the equation for calculating gravitational force. Both are *inverse square laws*: The forces are inversely proportional to the distance squared. With Coulomb's law, the force is proportional to the product of the charges; with gravity, the force is proportional to the product of the masses. Both are field forces, acting at a distance. Similarities like these cause physicists to search for one unified explanation of gravitational and electrostatic forces. Do remember, however, there is a crucial difference between the two forces: Masses always attract, while electric charges can both attract and repel.

Sometimes Coulomb's law is expressed in another fashion, using the *permittivity constant ε_0*. This traditional way of expressing the law can be particularly helpful in your later studies. The equation expressed with the permittivity constant is also shown to the right, as Equation 2. The permittivity constant is related to Coulomb's constant by the equation $\varepsilon_0 = 1/4\pi k$, and it equals 8.854 19×10⁻¹² C²/N·m².

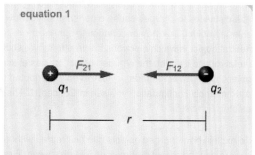

equation 1

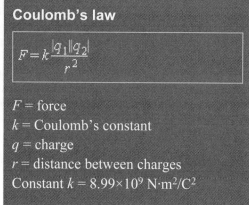

Coulomb's law

$$F = k\frac{|q_1||q_2|}{r^2}$$

F = force
k = Coulomb's constant
q = charge
r = distance between charges
Constant $k = 8.99\times10^9$ N·m²/C²

equation 2

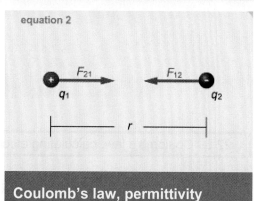

Coulomb's law, permittivity constant

$$F = \frac{1}{4\pi\varepsilon_0}\frac{|q_1||q_2|}{r^2}$$

ε_0 = permittivity constant
Constant $\varepsilon_0 = 8.85\times10^{-12}$ C²/N·m²

example 1

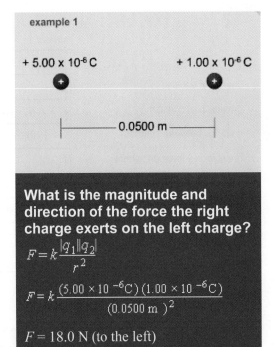

+ 5.00 x 10⁻⁶ C   + 1.00 x 10⁻⁶ C

0.0500 m

What is the magnitude and direction of the force the right charge exerts on the left charge?

$$F = k\frac{|q_1||q_2|}{r^2}$$

$$F = k\frac{(5.00 \times 10^{-6}\,\text{C})(1.00 \times 10^{-6}\,\text{C})}{(0.0500\,\text{m})^2}$$

$$F = 18.0\,\text{N (to the left)}$$

22.9 - Sample problem: electric vs. gravitational force

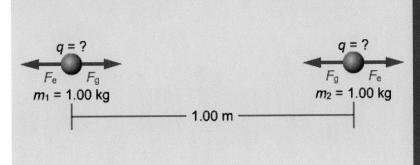

$q = ?$

F_e F_g

$m_1 = 1.00$ kg

$q = ?$

F_g F_e

$m_2 = 1.00$ kg

1.00 m

How many excess electrons must be added to each neutral lead sphere to balance the force of gravity between them?

The two balls above are floating in deep space, with the only significant gravitational forces acting upon them being the ones they exert upon one another. If they were electrically neutral, they would drift slowly together due to these forces and, after about an hour, come to rest against each other.

You are asked to determine how many electrons should be added to each sphere so that the electrostatic force exactly counteracts the gravitational force. You add the same number of electrons to each sphere, and disregard the change in mass of the spheres due to the added electrons. It is negligible.

Variables

	sphere 1	sphere 2
mass of sphere	$m_1 = 1.00$ kg	$m_2 = 1.00$ kg
charge of sphere	q_1	q_2
gravitational constant	$G = 6.67 \times 10^{-11}$ N·m²/kg²	
distance between spheres	$r = 1.00$ m	
gravitational force on sphere	F_g	
electric force on sphere	F_e	
Coulomb's constant	$k = 8.99 \times 10^9$ N·m²/C²	
number of excess electrons	N	
elementary charge	$e = 1.60 \times 10^{-19}$ C	

What is the strategy?

1. Calculate the gravitational attraction between the lead spheres.
2. Set the gravitational force equal to the repulsive electrostatic force between them and solve for the charge. The amount of charge on each sphere is the same.
3. Convert the charge from coulombs to the equivalent number of excess electrons.

Physics principles and equations

We will use Newton's law of gravitation

$$F_g = G\frac{m_1 m_2}{r^2}$$

together with Coulomb's law

$$F_e = k\frac{|q_1||q_2|}{r^2}$$

The charge due to N excess electrons is

$$q = -Ne$$

Step-by-step solution

In the first steps, we calculate the charge q needed on the spheres to balance their gravitational attraction.

Step	Reason
1. $F_g = G\dfrac{m_1 m_2}{r^2}$	Newton's law of gravitation
2. $F_g = G\dfrac{(1.00\ \text{kg})(1.00\ \text{kg})}{(1.00\ \text{m})^2}$ $F_g = 6.67 \times 10^{-11}\ \text{N}$	evaluate
3. $F_g = F_e = k\dfrac{\lvert q \rvert^2}{r^2}$	set forces equal and use Coulomb's law
4. $q = \pm\sqrt{\dfrac{F_g r^2}{k}}$	solve for q
5. $q = -\sqrt{\dfrac{(6.67 \times 10^{-11}\ \text{N})(1\ \text{m})^2}{8.99 \times 10^9\ \text{N}\cdot\text{m}^2/\text{C}^2}}$ $q = -8.61 \times 10^{-11}\ \text{C}$	note electron charge negative and evaluate

In the following steps we find the number of excess electrons.

Step	Reason
6. $q = -Ne$	equation for charge
7. $N = -\dfrac{q}{e}$	solve for N
8. $N = -\dfrac{-8.61 \times 10^{-11}\ \text{C}}{1.60 \times 10^{-19}\ \text{C}}$ $N = 5.38 \times 10^8\ \text{electrons}$	evaluate

Step 5 shows that a miniscule amount of charge – about a ten-thousandth of the charge you transfer to a balloon when you rub it on your shirt – is enough to balance the gravitational attraction between two one-kilogram masses separated by one meter. If you were concerned about whether adding the excess electrons would alter the mass of each sphere enough to require recalculating their gravitational attraction, you can compute that they add an insignificant mass, about 5×10^{-22} kg, to each sphere.

As an additional exercise, you can use Avogadro's number, and the atomic weight and atomic number of lead, to find the total number of electrons in an uncharged kilogram of lead. This calculation is not shown, but the total number is 2.39×10^{26} electrons. This means that the excess electrons constitute about 10^{-16} percent of the electrons in the sphere.

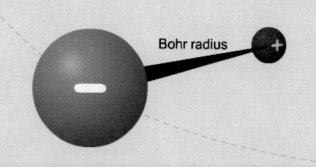

Bohr radius

Compute the ratio of the electric to the gravitational force between the proton and electron in a hydrogen atom. Use the average distance between the two, which is called the Bohr radius and equals 5.29×10^{-11} m.

Answer:

$F_E / F_G =$ [_____]

22.11 - Superposition of electrostatic forces

Electrostatic forces obey the *principle of superposition*. The forces caused by multiple charges can be added as vectors. For instance, consider the charges shown in Concept 1. To calculate the net force exerted by the other charges on the charge labeled q_1, the forces exerted by q_2 and q_3 on q_1 are individually calculated and then those two forces are added as vectors. In the next section, we solve a sample problem involving charges that requires the use of this principle.

You must be careful about the directions of electrostatic forces, especially when combining forces that may point in opposite directions. The location and signs of the charges determine the direction of the forces.

For example, consider another set of charges, q_4, q_5, and q_6, with all the charges on a line, and q_6 the rightmost charge. Let's say charges q_4 and q_5 have opposite signs. Since both are on the same side of q_6, the forces they exert upon it will act in opposite directions. There will be cancellation and the net force will be less than the sum of the magnitudes of the individual forces. There is no "rocket science" here. Just be careful to consider the direction of forces before combining them.

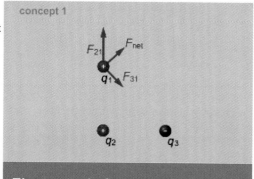

concept 1

Electrostatic forces: vectors
Electrostatic forces are vector quantities
Net force = vector sum

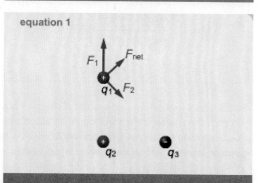

equation 1

Electrostatic forces: vectors
Forces $\mathbf{F}_1$, $\mathbf{F}_2$, ..., $\mathbf{F}_n$

$$\mathbf{F}_{net} = \sum_{m=1}^{n} \mathbf{F}_m = \mathbf{F}_1 + \mathbf{F}_2 + ... + \mathbf{F}_n$$

22.12 - Physics at work: laser printers

When you print a document created on your computer, you may use a laser printer. Laser printers use the electrostatic force as a crucial part of the process of transferring an image from the computer to a sheet of paper. The process is known as *xerography* or *electrophotography*.

A key component of the laser printer is a rotating metal cylinder or drum. This drum is coated with a light-sensitive material called an organic photoconductor, a carbon-based compound whose electric properties change when it is exposed to light. In the dark it is an insulator, and electric charges cannot move through it. When it is exposed to light, it becomes a conductor and charges can flow freely. The organic photoconductor layer is on the outside surface of the drum. Inside it is a hollow metal cylinder connected to a ground, which allows any charge trapped in a portion of the photoconductor to drain away if that portion becomes conductive.

The printing process begins with a charging step, shown on the right, where the drum is given a uniform negative charge by bringing it into contact with a charged roller. Since the drum is shielded from light in the interior of the printer, the photoconductive layer acts as an insulator, trapping negative charges on its surface.

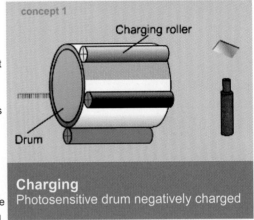

Charging
Photosensitive drum negatively charged

In the imaging step, shown next on the right, a laser controlled by signals from the computer directs light at the surface of the drum in a pattern corresponding to the image to be printed. Areas of the drum exposed to the laser light become conductive, allowing charge to escape from the drum surface to the ground. In this way the laser draws an electrostatic image of the document on the surface of the drum. Areas of the drum struck by the laser will be electrically neutral while the unexposed areas will retain their negative charge.

It is interesting to note that the laser itself is stationary. Its beam is projected onto the drum by a series of movable lenses and mirrors controlled by the printer's microprocessor, using data from your computer.

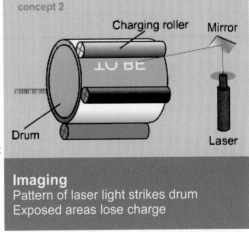

Imaging
Pattern of laser light strikes drum
Exposed areas lose charge

The next step is the development step. As the drum continues to rotate, it is brought close to a container or roller furnished with a toner, consisting of fine particles of ink that have a negative charge. The printer uses small pulses of electricity to eject the toner onto the drum surface. The negatively charged toner particles are repelled from the negatively charged unlit regions of the drum but cling to the neutral areas that were struck by the laser. The drum surface now holds toner particles in the pattern of the image to be printed.

Then the image is transferred to paper. A sheet of paper is given a positive charge and pressed against the drum. The negatively charged toner on the drum is attracted to the positively charged paper. The toner is permanently fused to the paper by a heated roller that melts the ink particles into the paper fiber. A final step, not shown on the right, prepares the drum for the next image by flashing it with light, causing the complete discharge of all charged areas on the drum.

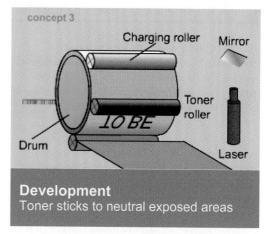

Development
Toner sticks to neutral exposed areas

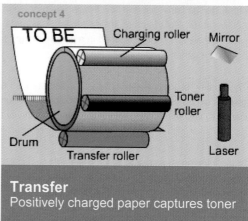

Transfer
Positively charged paper captures toner

22.13 - Interactive summary problem: proton golf

Above and to the right, you see the 24th century version of golf. Protons in the putter cause the proton golf ball to move away. Coulomb's law is well known, well loved and well used.

To sink the putt in the first game, your putter must supply an initial force of 1.96×10^{-25} newtons. This will cause the ball to be rolling slowly as it reaches the hole, overcoming the force of friction due to the grass. If you apply too much force, the ball will fly over the hole. The ball is free to move when you press PUTT. In this game, you cannot move the putter, and you get only one stroke, but you can play again by pressing RESET.

Proton Golf Association members at play in the year 2316.

The ball is initially 0.200 meters away from the putter and has a charge of $+e$. What should the charge be in the putter? You set the amount of charge by specifying the number of protons.

After you calculate your answer, click on Interactive 1 to launch the simulation. You use the up and down arrows to set the number of protons in the putter. Select your value, press PUTT and the golf ball will roll toward the hole. If you need to review how to calculate the repulsive force between two positive charges, see the section on Coulomb's law.

The second game is like the game of golf you played at the beginning of this chapter. You can change both the charge and the position of the putter. You will almost certainly need several strokes to sink the ball. The challenge of the game is to do so in as few strokes as you can. Again, the grass supplies a force of friction that must be overcome. You may feel that you are now more familiar with charges and the way they behave. Grab your prodigious proton putter and give it another try!

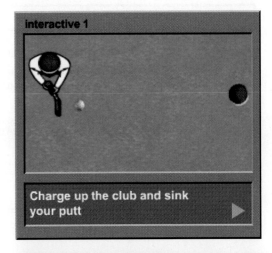

interactive 1

Charge up the club and sink your putt

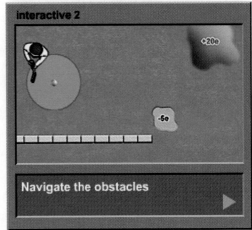

interactive 2

Navigate the obstacles

22.14 - Gotchas

A neutral object that gains electrons is negatively charged. Yes, a neutral object that **gains** electrons becomes **negative**; a neutral object that **loses** electrons becomes **positive**.

An object has a net charge of negative 10 coulombs. How many electrons does it contain? Do not bother trying to calculate a value. You could calculate how many **excess** electrons the object contains − how many more electrons than protons − with the given information. But unless someone tells you how many electrons the object contained when it was neutral, you cannot answer the question. The point here is: Charge refers to the number of excess electrons. A neutral object has electrons, too, but they are balanced by an equal number of protons.

You use the number of excess protons and electrons in Coulomb's law. No, the charges q_1 and q_2 in Coulomb's law are measured in (what else?) coulombs. If you are given the number of excess electrons or protons in a problem, you must determine the electric charge in coulombs.

I calculated a negative force from Coulomb's law. Then you erred. The **amount** (magnitude) of the force is calculated by multiplying the absolute values of the charges, so it will always be positive. The **direction** of the force will vary by sign: attraction when the signs are opposite, repulsion when they are the same.

22.15 - Summary

Electric charge is a property of matter. It occurs in positive and negative forms. One unit of charge is e. A proton has a charge of $+e$ and an electron has a charge of $-e$. Charge, represented by q, is measured in coulombs (C). The elementary charge e equals $1.602\ 18 \times 10^{-19}$ C.

An ordinary object is charged when it has an imbalance of protons and electrons.

Equations

Coulomb's law

$$F = k\frac{|q_1||q_2|}{r^2}$$

Charge is always conserved. Though charges may be transferred from object to object, charge cannot be created or destroyed, and the net charge of an isolated system will remain the same.

Electrons flow more freely in some objects than in others. Conductors allow electrons to move relatively easily, while insulators do not. A ground can drain away any excess charge from a conducting object. The most common ground is literally the ground: Earth.

Charged particles exert an electrostatic force on each other. Unlike gravity, which is always attractive, the electrostatic force can be either attractive or repulsive. Opposite charges attract each other, while like charges repel.

Coulomb's Law describes the amount of the electrostatic force between two point charges. It is proportional to the product of the charges' magnitudes and inversely proportional to the square of the distance between them.

23.0 - Introduction

An electric charge can exert force on another charge at a distance. No direct contact between the charges is required. The fact that the electrostatic, gravitational, and magnetic forces act at a distance puzzled early scientists who studied them. They speculated about the mechanism that would allow one body to push or pull on another without touching it. To explain how this could occur, the British scientist Michael Faraday (1791-1867) pioneered the concept of fields. As time has passed, this concept has assumed an increasingly important role in physics.

Today, physicists say that an electric field surrounds an electric charge, and that the electric field of one charge exerts a force on another charge. Investigating the fundamentals of fields is the central topic of this chapter.

To begin your study of fields, try the simulation to the right. Here, the charged particle you see is creating an electric field, represented by the symbol $\mathbf{E}$. The field is invisible but you can observe it using a field meter.

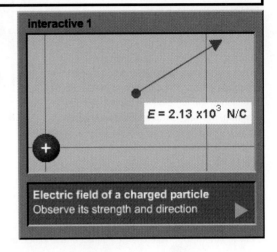

interactive 1

$E = 2.13 \times 10^3 \ \text{N/C}$

Electric field of a charged particle
Observe its strength and direction

In essence, the field supplies a "road map" to calculate the force that will be exerted on any second charge that enters the region surrounding the charged particle you see. The stronger the field at a point in space, the greater the force that will be exerted on a given second charge when it is placed there. The field points in the same direction as the force that would be exerted on a positive test charge.

Locate your mouse pointer anywhere on the screen. When you click, you will see an electric field vector that points in the direction of the field, and a readout that tells you the strength of the electric field at that point.

The initial charge of the visible particle is 1.00 nC, but you can use the controller in the simulation to change this to other values, both positive and negative.

Initially, keep this particle's charge constant in the simulation, and try to answer the following questions: How does the field strength vary with the distance from the charge? Does it seem to increase linearly as you move closer, or do you see great increases in the field at points near the charge? You should see similarities between the electric field and the force that would be exerted on a second, positive charge.

Next, try changing the charge of the visible particle in the simulation. Does the amount of its charge affect its field strength at a given point? In what direction does the field of the charged particle point when it is positive? Does the field point in the same direction if you give the source particle a negative charge?

Using the simulation, you can experiment with some of the fundamentals of electric fields. In the rest of this chapter, you will continue your exploration of this topic.

23.1 - Electric fields

Electric field: An electric field describes the nature of the electric force that a charge will encounter at a given location. Fields provide the model for forces acting at a distance.

Electrically charged objects exert forces on other charged objects at a distance: The forces occur without direct contact. Charged objects exert forces on each other analogous to the gravitational forces exerted by the Earth and the Moon on one another. Electric, gravitational and magnetic forces all act at a distance. To describe their behavior, scientists have developed the concept of fields, which have become a fundamental tool for explaining the nature of the universe.

Charges establish electric fields around themselves. A small, positive *test charge* is often used to establish the nature of an electric field. A test charge is assumed to be weak enough that it does not alter the field being analyzed. In diagrams, we represent a test charge as a white sphere with a red plus sign.

You see in Concept 1 a test charge placed in a field, which in this case is generated by a negatively charged particle. The direction of the field is the direction of the force on the test charge. In the diagram, the field is represented as a vector and labeled with E, the symbol for an electric field. This field exists at every point whether or not a test charge is present.

The muscles and heartbeats of fish generate telltale electric fields, perceptible to organs in the wide head of this hammerhead shark.

As we explain the nature of electric fields, we first review the fundamentals of the electrostatic force. Coulomb's law states that the force between two charges is proportional to their magnitudes and inversely proportional to the square of the distance between them. Opposite charges attract one another, and like charges repel.

The strength of the field equals the amount of force divided by the magnitude of the test charge. The equation for calculating the field in this fashion is shown in Equation 1. Since an electric field is used to describe the nature of the force that a test charge experiences at a point in space, the field has a specific direction and magnitude at each point. It is a vector quantity.

The strength of the field is independent of the test charge. Dividing out the charge cancels its effect in determining strength. For example, if the test charge were doubled in strength, then Coulomb's law states that the force would be twice as large, but after dividing by the doubled charge, the field strength is the same. Electric fields are measured in newtons per coulomb; there is no special name for this combination of units.

The stronger the field at a given point, the greater the force it will exert on any charge at that point. You can perhaps envision this by considering the nature of the gravitational field surrounding the Earth. The gravitational field is stronger near the surface of the Earth than it is at locations farther away. An object with a particular mass will experience more gravitational force closer to the Earth, where the field is stronger, than farther away, where the field is weaker. The gravitational field is stronger on the surface of Jupiter than it is on the Earth's surface. The stronger field means you weigh more on Jupiter because there is more gravitational force pulling on you.

In this section, we implicitly focused on fields produced by a single electric charge. This is an important case, and provides a concrete example of how fields arise. However, as you advance in your studies, you will often study fields and their effects by themselves, with less focus on their sources.

In the industrialized world, you are constantly surrounded by electric fields. You may experience electric fields ranging in strength from nearly zero up to 10 N/C due to electrical appliances and wiring as you walk around your house. Outside your house you may experience significantly greater electric fields. The field at ground level directly beneath a power transmission line is about 2000 N/C. This is enough to cause a fluorescent tube to light up if you hold it vertically in the field. Within atoms, electric fields are extremely large. The electric field due to a proton at the distance typical of an electron in a hydrogen atom is 5×10^{11} N/C.

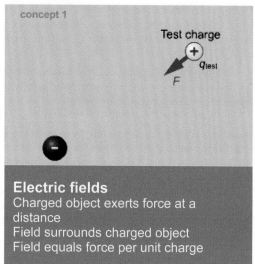

concept 1

Test charge

q_{test}

F

Electric fields
Charged object exerts force at a distance
Field surrounds charged object
Field equals force per unit charge

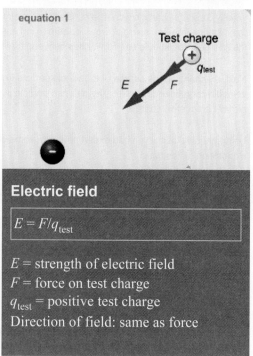

equation 1

Test charge

q_{test}

E F

Electric field

$E = F/q_{\text{test}}$

E = strength of electric field
F = force on test charge
q_{test} = positive test charge
Direction of field: same as force

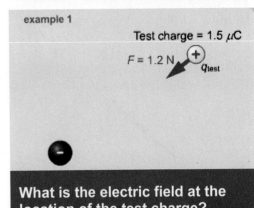

example 1

Test charge = 1.5 μC

$F = 1.2$ N q_{test}

What is the electric field at the location of the test charge?

$E = F/q_{test}$

$E = (1.2 \text{ N}) / (1.5 \times 10^{-6} \text{ C})$

$E = 8.0 \times 10^5 \text{ N/C}$

(same direction as force)

23.2 - Electric fields and Coulomb's law

You can use Coulomb's law to calculate the strength of the field around a point charge. First, calculate the amount of force exerted by that charge on a (positive) test charge using Coulomb's law. Then divide by the amount of the test charge, because the strength of an electric field equals the amount of force divided by the charge used to measure the force.

We derive the equation for the field caused by a point charge as shown in Equation 1. We state the definition of the electric field, and then expand the expression for the force, using Coulomb's law. The quantity q_{test} appears in both the numerator and the denominator of the resulting fraction, so it cancels out. As the equation states, the strength of the field is proportional to the absolute value of q, the charge causing it, divided by the square of the distance from this charge.

An example problem is shown on the right, as well: You are asked to calculate the field strength at a point 0.110 m away from a charge of positive 10.5 C.

Remember: Even after you calculate the strength of the field, your task is not finished, because an electric field has both magnitude and direction. You must specify the field's direction, as we do in the example problem.

equation 1

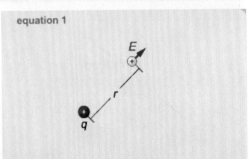

Electric field, point charge

$$E = \frac{F}{q_{test}} = \frac{k|q||q_{test}|/r^2}{q_{test}} = \frac{k|q|}{r^2}$$

E = electric field

F = force

q = charge, q_{test} = test charge

k = Coulomb's constant

r = distance between charges

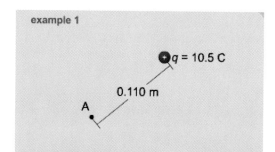

example 1

$q = 10.5$ C

0.110 m

A

What are the magnitude and direction of the electric field at point A?

$$E = \frac{k|q|}{r^2}$$

$$E = \frac{(8.99 \times 10^9 \ \mathrm{Nm^2/C^2})|10.5 \ \mathrm{C}|}{(0.110 \ \mathrm{m})^2}$$

$E = 7.80 \times 10^{12}$ N/C (away from charge)

23.3 - Interactive checkpoint: electric field

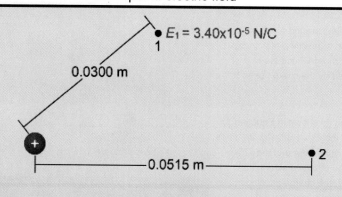

$E_1 = 3.40 \times 10^{-5}$ N/C

1

0.0300 m

+

0.0515 m

2

A point charge rests in an otherwise charge-free region. Locations 1 and 2 are 0.0300 m and 0.0515 m from the charge, respectively. If the electric field at location 1 is 3.40×10^{-5} N/C, what is the electric field at location 2?

Answer:

$E_2 = $ [　　　　　] N/C

23.4 - Electric field diagrams

Electric field diagrams are used to illustrate the nature of an electric field. An electric field diagram consists of electric field lines, as you see illustrated in Concept 1.

The left-side diagram in Concept 1 shows the electric **force** acting on several test charges at various points around a central positive charge. The vectors representing the force on each test charge point away from the positive charge, indicating the direction of the force. The length of each vector is proportional to the amount of force on each charge.

The *field diagram,* shown to the right of the force diagram, is a common and efficient way to present similar information. The field lines have arrows pointing in the direction of the field vector at each point, which is the same as the direction of the force that the field would exert on a positive test charge at that point. However, the field lines do not use length to represent magnitude. Rather, field strength is indicated by how close the lines are to one another. Field strength is roughly proportional to the density of the lines.

The illustration for Concept 2 shows how you can determine relative field strength from a field diagram. We have drawn two boxes at different distances from a negative charge. The field lines are closer together in the near box than they are in the far box, which means that the field is stronger in the region defined by the box closer to the negative charge.

concept 1

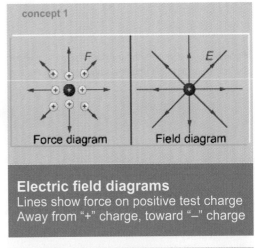

Force diagram   Field diagram

Electric field diagrams
Lines show force on positive test charge
Away from "+" charge, toward "−" charge

concept 2

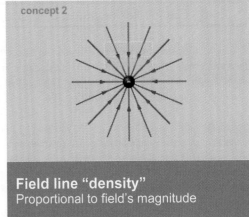

Field line "density"
Proportional to field's magnitude

23.5 - Interactive problem: fields and forces

On the right are two simulations that allow you to explore electric field diagrams, and the relationship between electric fields and the electrostatic force.

In the first simulation, you explore the relationship between force and a field that is created by two unequal charges: a charge of +90.0 nC and a charge of −45.0 nC. In this simulation your task is to drag a positive test charge (+1.00 nC) into the field and observe the direction and magnitude of the force that the field exerts on it.

After experimenting with this simulation, consider the answers to three questions. First, is the force on the test charge greater where the field lines are closer together, or where they are farther apart? Second, what is the relationship between the direction of the force and the field lines? Hint: The word "tangent" must appear in your answer. Third, what...is the air-speed velocity of an unladen swallow? (Just kidding...But Monty Python fans know the consequences of a wrong answer.)

interactive 1

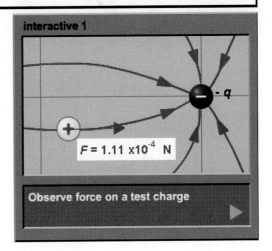

$F = 1.11 \times 10^{-4}$ N

Observe force on a test charge ▶

The *uniform field* in the second simulation is not caused by a single charge, or even by a small number of charges. The strength and direction of such a field are the same at all points. The field in this simulation points to the right, and its strength everywhere is 100 N/C.

In the simulation, you are given three small charges, having values $-q$, $+q$, and $+2q$. The negative charge is not, strictly speaking, a test charge, since test charges have to be positive. However, all three are so small that they do not interact with each other when they are placed in the uniform field.

Drag the three charges into the field, and observe the direction and magnitude of the force it causes on each one. How does the direction of the force exerted by the field differ for a positive and a negative charge? Does it exert a greater force on the $+2q$ charge or on the $+q$ charge? If so, by what factor is the force greater?

If you have trouble with the questions posed by either of these simulations, review the introduction to electric fields and electric field diagrams in previous sections.

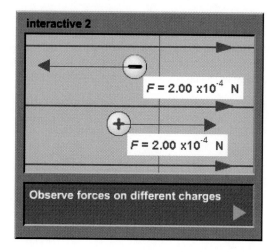

interactive 2

$F = 2.00 \times 10^{-4}$ N

$F = 2.00 \times 10^{-4}$ N

Observe forces on different charges

23.6 - Electric fields caused by multiple charges

The individual fields from multiple charges can be combined to determine the overall field they create. The net electric field at any point is the vector sum of the individual fields due to each of the source charges. This additive property of electric fields is an example of the *principle of superposition*.

To calculate the overall field at a point, you start by calculating the field vector generated by each charge at that point. You then add the vectors together. The result is the net electric field at that point due to all the charges. In the illustration of Concept 1 you see a diagram of the combined field generated by two equal, positive charges. We also show the combined electric field vectors at several points in the field. In the upper right corner of the diagram, you can see that such a vector is tangent to a curving field line.

This method of combining fields is illustrated in detail in Concept 2 for one of the combined field vectors. The individual field vectors caused by the two identical positive charges at a location in space are depicted. We also draw the net field as the vector sum of the two individual fields. At the location shown, the x components of the contributing fields cancel out since they point in opposite directions and are of equal magnitudes. The y components of these two fields point in the same direction. The result is a combined field that points in the y direction, away from the two positive charges.

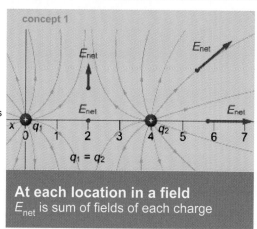

concept 1

E_{net}

E_{net}

E_{net}

E_{net}

q_1

q_2

$q_1 = q_2$

At each location in a field
E_{net} is sum of fields of each charge

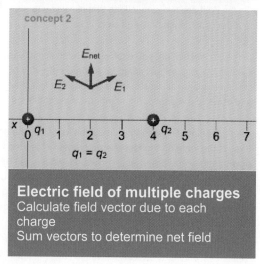

concept 2

E_{net}

E_2

E_1

q_1

q_2

$q_1 = q_2$

Electric field of multiple charges
Calculate field vector due to each charge
Sum vectors to determine net field

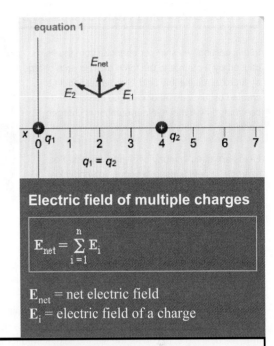

equation 1

$q_1 = q_2$

Electric field of multiple charges

$$\mathbf{E}_{net} = \sum_{i=1}^{n} \mathbf{E}_i$$

$\mathbf{E}_{net}$ = net electric field
$\mathbf{E}_i$ = electric field of a charge

23.7 - Drawing field diagrams for multiple charges

Drawing the field diagram of a field generated by multiple charges requires the application of three rules. To explain them, we use the configuration of two charges shown in Concept 1. The negative charge is twice as strong as the positive charge.

Rule 1: The number of field lines in a diagram that emanate from a positive charge, or terminate at a negative charge, is proportional to the magnitude of the charge. In the diagram to the right, 8 lines emanate from q, and 16 terminate at $-2q$.

Rule 2: Other field lines may start from or extend to infinity. The "other" eight field lines that terminate at the negative charge, the ones that do not emanate from the positive charge, start at infinity. In other words, they enter from "outside" the diagram. If the positive charge were $+4q$, there would be more field lines emanating from it than terminating at the negative charge. The "extra" field lines would extend to infinity.

Rule 3: Field lines never cross. A positive test charge located at such an intersection would be "confused" as to what force it experienced, since the field would point in two directions. This rule reflects an important point: At any location, a field has a single direction and magnitude. This point is emphasized in the Concept 2 illustration.

These rules enable you to draw a correct field diagram. They provide a starting point for drawing a field diagram like the one shown in Concept 1. Considering the nature of the force experienced by a positive charge at various locations is required to flesh out the diagram.

A last point to keep in mind: Electric field diagrams are commonly drawn in two dimensions, but electric fields exist in three dimensions. You usually see field diagrams on flat surfaces, like a computer monitor, a piece of paper or a blackboard. However, the field exists above and below the surface of the diagram as well.

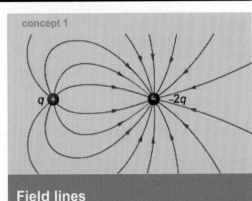

concept 1

Field lines
Incident lines proportional to charge
Start at "+" charges, end at "-" charges
Excess lines start or end at infinity

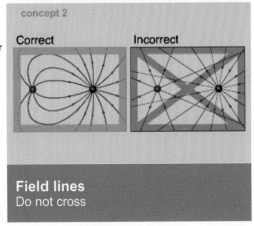

concept 2

Correct   Incorrect

Field lines
Do not cross

In this section, we shift our attention from the field caused **by** a charge to the force exerted **on** a charge by an external electric field. Such a field could be created by just one other charged particle, or it could be created by a much larger number of charged particles.

Fields are used in many everyday devices. For example, a field is used in some high-end inkjet printers to control the direction of charged ink droplets as they fly toward a sheet of paper. A charged camera flash can store energy in a field created by more than a trillion excess electrons. Given this huge

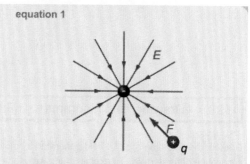

Polluting smokestacks. *Electrostatic precipitators* **could electrically charge this particulate matter and use electric fields to remove it from the effluent.**

number, determining the overall field by summing the individual fields created by each electron would be a bit tedious. Instead, placing a test charge in the field and observing the force that the field exerts on it can determine the nature of the field.

When a charged particle is in an electric field, the equation in Equation 1 can be used to describe the amount of force that the field exerts on the particle. This equation comes from the defining equation for the electric field, solved for the force.

A point charge creates a field that diminishes with the distance from the charge. This means the force it exerts on a test charge will vary by location. However, engineers are clever enough to create nearly *uniform fields*, fields whose strength and direction is the same at all locations within the field. For instance, there is a nearly uniform field in the center of the region between two large, oppositely charged flat plates separated by a small distance. In Example 1, you are asked to determine the force exerted on an electron by such a field.

Newton's second law enables you to determine the acceleration of the electron in this electric field and we do so in Example 2. The force exerted by the field is divided by the mass of an electron to determine the acceleration. The result is a large acceleration, having a magnitude of approximately 350,000 m/s^2.

equation 1

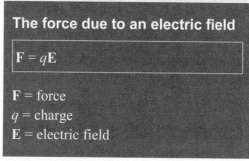

The force due to an electric field

$$\mathbf{F} = q\mathbf{E}$$

$\mathbf{F}$ = force
q = charge
$\mathbf{E}$ = electric field

This acceleration is caused by a relatively weak field (it is well below the maximum allowed for human exposure by government safety standards). At the acceleration stated, the speed of the electron would quickly approach that of light, and the acceleration would have to diminish due to the relativistic effects predicted by Albert Einstein.

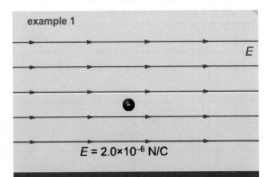

example 1

$E = 2.0 \times 10^{-6}$ N/C

What is the force on the electron?

$\mathbf{F} = q\mathbf{E}$

$F = (-1.6 \times 10^{-19} \text{ C})(2.0 \times 10^{-6} \text{ N/C})$

$F = -3.2 \times 10^{-25}$ N (opposite to field)

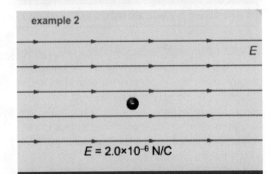

example 2

$E = 2.0 \times 10^{-6}$ N/C

What is the acceleration of the electron? Its mass is 9.1×10^{-31} kg.

$a = F/m$

$m = m_e = 9.1 \times 10^{-31}$ kg

$a = (-3.2 \times 10^{-25} \text{ N})/(9.1 \times 10^{-31} \text{ kg})$

$a = -3.5 \times 10^5$ m/s^2 (opposite to field)

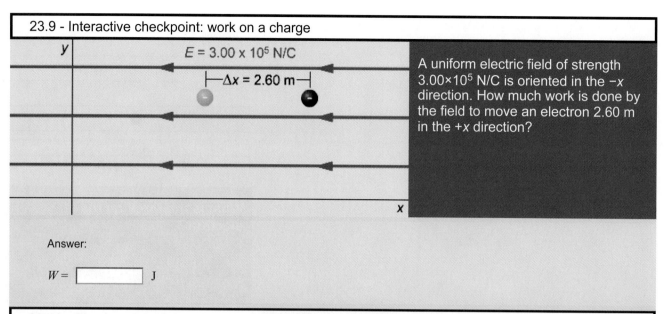

23.9 - Interactive checkpoint: work on a charge

$E = 3.00 \times 10^5$ N/C

$\Delta x = 2.60$ m

A uniform electric field of strength 3.00×10^5 N/C is oriented in the $-x$ direction. How much work is done by the field to move an electron 2.60 m in the $+x$ direction?

Answer:

$W =$ [   ] J

23.10 - Physics at work: spacecraft powered by electric fields

In 1998, NASA began testing in space a new type of rocket drive: the ion propulsion system. A conceptual diagram (not drawn to scale) of this drive is shown in Concept 1. Traditional rocket engines use chemical reactions to expel rocket fuel exhaust from the engine at high speed. If you have seen video footage of the rockets that carried astronauts to the Moon, you have seen a traditional rocket engine.

In contrast, the ion drive uses an electric field to accelerate charged gas particles, or ions. It accelerates these particles to extremely high velocities, velocities much greater than those achieved by chemical rocket exhausts. Why are higher velocities of interest? Recall the law of conservation of momentum. In this case, the "forward" momentum of the rest of the rocket must match the "backward" momentum of the rocket exhaust. Momentum is the product of mass and velocity. Since the ion drive accelerates particles to greater velocities than those of chemical drives, less fuel mass is necessary than with chemical systems to produce the same amount of momentum.

Less massive space probes are important because they require less energy to launch into space. In practice, a space probe is still launched by a powerful chemical rocket engine, but once it is relatively free of the Earth's gravity, the probe relies on a less massive ion propulsion system to maneuver. (Ion systems supply less than one newton of force, a small fraction of the force required to launch a rocket from the Earth's surface.) The system's lesser mass also means it accelerates more for a given force.

The first step in the operation of this engine system is to bombard xenon gas with electrons. These fast electrons "knock off" an electron from each xenon atom, turning it into a positive ion. The ions are then inserted into an electric field created by two charged plates. The plates are less than a meter in diameter and are placed close together. The electric field between the plates accelerates the ions to a velocity of about 30,000 m/s (70,000 mi/h). The ions escape through small holes in the rear plate. (To prevent the ions from being attracted back into the engine, a beam of electrons is fired into the ion exhaust to neutralize it.)

NASA's *Deep Space 1* ion drive undergoing testing at the Jet Propulsion Laboratory.

concept 1

Ionization chamber E

Propellant injection

Xe

Electron gun

$v = 30,000$ m/s

Plates

An electric-field rocket engine
Electron bombardment ionizes xenon gas
Field accelerates ions to 30,000 m/s
Low mass, high velocity system

NASA tested this engine system on the Deep Space 1 mission. Deep Space 1 was shut down on December 18, 2001, after successfully validating the performance of the ion propulsion system. The drive had provided more than 16,000 hours of thrust, using only 72 kg of xenon gas. This was less than 10% of the overall mass of the spacecraft. An equivalent chemical rocket drive would have needed 720 kg of fuel to generate the same amount of propulsion. This is equivalent to the difference between launching a person and launching a small car.

The ion propulsion system is now in use in satellites that orbit the Earth, where it is used to "tune" their orbits. Photovoltaic panels supply the energy required to ionize the gas and charge the plates.

23.11 - Conductors in electrostatic equilibrium

Electrostatic equilibrium: In an isolated conductor, excess charges quickly achieve a state where there is no net motion of charge.

An isolated, charged conducting object has several interesting and perhaps unexpected properties. (By isolated, we mean the object is attached neither to a source of what is called a potential difference, such as a battery, nor to a ground.) The excess charge on such an object will rapidly reach a state called electrostatic equilibrium, which means there is no further net motion of the charge. In other words, any excess charges in the object can be treated as stationary. Many experiments have confirmed the existence of electrostatic equilibrium and the properties of conductors described below.

Charge resides on the surface of the inner metallic sphere in this toy. An electric field extends radially outward, made visible by ionized gas.

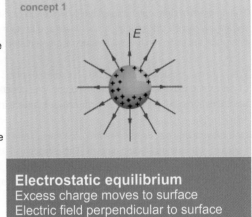

concept 1

Electrostatic equilibrium
Excess charge moves to surface
Electric field perpendicular to surface
No field inside material of conductor

What are some properties of a charged conductor in electrostatic equilibrium? First, it creates an electric field that, just outside the conductor's surface, is perpendicular to the surface. You see this in the diagram for Concept 1, which shows a solid conducting sphere.

Why is the field perpendicular? This question can be answered by asking another question: What if the field were **not** perpendicular? If there were a component of the field parallel to the surface, this would mean a charged particle there would have a force exerted on it by the field, parallel to the surface. This force would cause the particle to move along the surface, and this motion would contradict the assumption of electrostatic equilibrium.

Second, all excess charge resides on the surface of a conducting object. One way to explain this property is to note that such a configuration allows like charges to maximize their distance from one another. If a charge remained in the middle of the conductor, it would not be maximizing its distance from its fellows.

Third, there is no electric field within the bulk of a conductor. Again, consider the conducting sphere in Concept 1. If there were a field within the sphere, it would cause movement of excess charges there, meaning the sphere would not be in electrostatic equilibrium.

In Concept 2, we show what occurs when a hollow conductor is placed in an external field. In this case, two charged plates cause the field. If the sphere were not present, the electric field would be uniform, and a field diagram would represent the field with equally spaced, horizontal lines.

When the sphere is placed in the field caused by the plates, an asymmetrical distribution of charge is induced on the outside of the sphere. You can see the charge distribution and how the sphere alters the external field in the diagram.

There is another important point illustrated in the diagram: There is no field within the hollow conductor. This effect is quite useful because it means a conducting shell will insulate its contents from electric fields. When you see electric or electronic circuits placed within a protective metal box, one reason is to shield them from nearby electric fields that might distort the circuitry's operation. The shielding effect occurs only with conductors. It cannot occur with insulators because charge is not free to move within such substances.

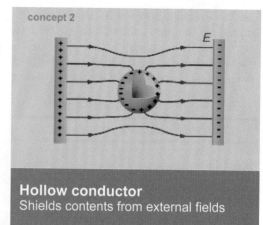

concept 2

Hollow conductor
Shields contents from external fields

23.12 - Electric dipoles

Electric dipole: Two point charges with equal strength but opposite signs separated by a fixed distance.

A configuration of two charges that are equal in strength but opposite in sign is important enough to merit its own name: the electric dipole. The two charges are at a fixed distance from each other.

The world's oceans contain about 7.8x10^{46} electric dipoles: water molecules.

The diagram in Concept 1 shows the basics of an electric dipole. The equal and opposite charges have magnitude q and are separated by the distance d. An electric dipole can be described by its electric dipole moment $\mathbf{p} = q\mathbf{d}$, where $\mathbf{d}$ is the displacement vector from the negative charge to the positive charge. The dipole moment vector points in the same direction as the displacement vector.

When an electric dipole is placed in an external electric field, the positive end experiences a force in the direction of the external field, and the negative end experiences a force in the opposite direction. As the diagram in Concept 2 shows, if the dipole moment is not aligned with the field, the dipole will experience a torque that rotates it into the direction of alignment with the external electric field.

One reason why electric dipoles are important is that the individual molecules in what is arguably the most vital substance for human existence – water – behave as electric dipoles. The oxygen side of a water molecule tends to be negatively charged, while the hydrogen side tends to have an equal but opposite positive charge. The result is a dipole. The fact that water molecules are dipoles accounts for many of water's crucial properties. The illustration below shows a conceptual model of a water molecule together with its electric dipole moment.

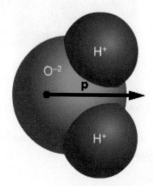

A convenient device, the microwave oven, takes advantage of the dipole nature of water molecules. The oven uses an oscillating electric field to cause water molecules to rotate back and forth, increasing their energy and the thermal energy of the food that contains them.

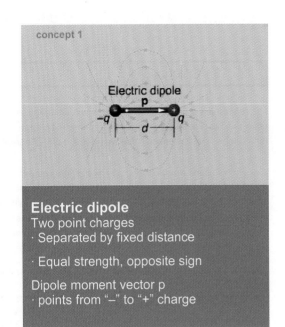

Electric dipole

Two point charges
· Separated by fixed distance

· Equal strength, opposite sign

Dipole moment vector p
· points from "–" to "+" charge

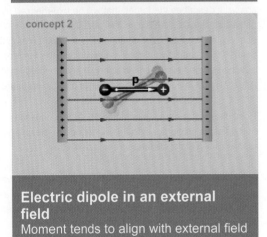

Electric dipole in an external field

Moment tends to align with external field

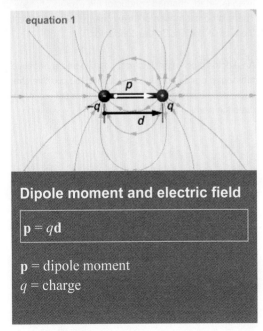

Dipole moment and electric field

$$\mathbf{p} = q\mathbf{d}$$

$\mathbf{p}$ = dipole moment
q = charge

23.13 - Gotchas

I increased the amount of the charge of a test charge, and the force exerted on it changed. This means the field I was assessing must have changed. No. Fields are independent of the test charge. The force increased, in proportion to the test charge, but the original field strength did not change. The increased force was a result of the increased magnitude of the test charge.

Electric field lines are the same as electric field vectors. No. The direction of the field is tangent to the field lines at any point. In a field diagram for a point charge, the lines are straight so they do point in the direction of the field. But in many fields the field lines are curved, and the field vector at any location on a field line is tangent to but distinct from it. Also, field lines and vectors use different conventions for representing field strength. With vectors, the length is proportional to the strength of the field. In a field diagram, the field lines are closer together in a region with greater field strength. Although a field diagram is used to represent an electric field, field lines and field vectors are not the same thing.

23.14 - Summary

An electric field is a vector quantity defined throughout a region of three-dimensional space. It describes the forces that will be experienced by an electric charge if it is placed at various locations in the field. If a positive charge is introduced, the force on it equals the field strength times its own charge magnitude, in the direction of the field. When a negative charge is introduced, the force on it is opposite to the direction of the field. The field strength is measured in newtons per coulomb (N/C). A test charge is a small positive charge used to measure a field.

Point charges generate electric fields. At any distance from the charge, the strength of the field is proportional to the magnitude of the charge and inversely proportional to the square of the distance from the charge.

An electric field diagram is a convenient means of representing the direction and strength of an electric field in a region. The direction of a field line represents the local direction of the electric field. The strength of the field at a particular location is indicated by the proximity of the field lines to each other around that location.

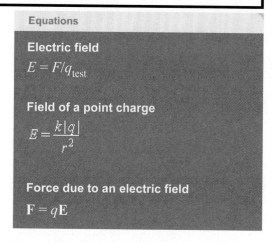

Equations

Electric field

$$E = F/q_{\text{test}}$$

Field of a point charge

$$E = \frac{k|q|}{r^2}$$

Force due to an electric field

$$\mathbf{F} = q\mathbf{E}$$

In an isolated, charged conductor the excess charges distribute themselves on the conductor's surface in a state of electrostatic equilibrium. There is no net motion of these charges. The electric field extends perpendicularly outward from all points on the conductor's surface, and there is no field inside the conductor.

An electric dipole consists of a positive and a negative charge of equal magnitude, separated by a fixed distance. A vector called the dipole moment **p** points from the negative to the positive charge. Its magnitude is equal to the magnitude of either dipole charge times the distance between the charges. When the dipole is placed in an external electric field, the dipole moment experiences a torque tending to align it in a direction parallel to the field.

24.0 - Introduction

In this chapter, we discuss electric potential energy and electric potential. Understanding these topics will be crucial to your understanding of how electric circuits and components work. For instance, when you turn on a flashlight, you are allowing an electric potential difference to drive a current that causes the light bulb to glow.

In the sections that follow, you will learn how electric charges and fields can create electric potential energy, electric potential, and electric potential differences. You may be unfamiliar with the term electric potential difference, but you likely know its units, volts, and you have probably heard the informal term "voltage" used for it.

The simulations to the right allow you to experiment with electric potential energy. Just as a configuration of masses, such as a barbell held above the Earth's surface, possesses gravitational potential energy, so too does a configuration of electrically charged particles possess electric potential energy.

The first simulation contains a stationary positive charge (red) and a positive test charge (white) that you drag around with your mouse. As you move the test charge from place to place, you can change the electric potential energy of the system of two charges. The potential energy, which depends on the distance r between the charges and their strengths, is displayed in the control panel. A graph of the PE is drawn on the right side of the simulation as you move the test charge around. A grid in the background of the simulation allows you to estimate the distance in millimeters between the two charges.

As you move the test charge, consider the following questions: What is the sign of the PE? When is the potential energy the greatest? The least? The graph shows PE as a function of the distance r between the charges.

As with gravitational potential energy, a configuration having zero potential energy must be defined. In the first two interactives, the potential energy is defined to be zero when an infinite distance separates the two charges.

Interactive 2 is the same as Interactive 1 except that the stationary charge is negative instead of positive. Experiment with this configuration by moving the positive test charge around. What is the sign of the PE now? As the distance increases, does the PE increase or decrease? Can you move the charge in a way such that the PE does not change?

In the Interactive 3 simulation, you see a test charge that you can move between two oppositely charged plates. The electric field is uniform between the plates. In this simulation, the x axis of the graph tells the distance of the test charge from the negative plate. How does the PE change as you move the test charge away from the negative plate and toward the positive plate?

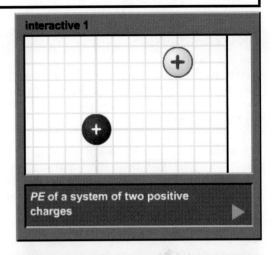

interactive 1

PE of a system of two positive charges

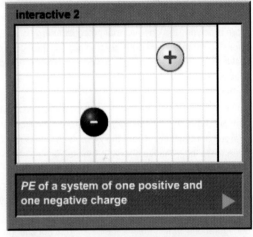

interactive 2

PE of a system of one positive and one negative charge

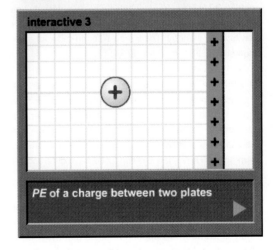

interactive 3

PE of a charge between two plates

Electric potential energy: Potential energy determined by the configuration of electric charges.

This Honda FCX automobile can cruise up to 350 km by using the electric potential energy stored in its capacitors as a configuration of electric charge.

Electric potential energy, PE_e, is the measure of the energy stored due to the configuration of a system of charges. It reflects the positions (not the motion) of the charges in the system.

The release of electric potential energy can be highly visible. In a thunderstorm, clouds often accumulate a tremendous number of charged particles in a configuration that stores huge amounts of electric potential energy. Part of this energy can be released in the form of a lightning strike, a particularly dramatic example of the effects of discharging PE_e.

Recalling the fundamentals of gravitational potential energy may help you to understand electric potential energy because the two are analogous. For example, the distance of an apple above the Earth's surface directly affects its gravitational potential energy, or more precisely, the gravitational potential energy of the Earth/apple system. Lifting the apple higher requires work – a force applied through a distance – and increases the gravitational potential energy. Lowering the apple reduces the potential energy of the system.

To apply these concepts to electric potential energy, consider the initial and final configurations of opposite charges shown in the illustration of Concept 1. Initially, the charges are touching. Then, the positive charge is moved to the right by an external force while the negative charge on the left is held stationary. The work done on the system by the force increases its potential energy.

In this chapter, since we are discussing potential energy in the context of electro**statics**, we focus on stationary charges. The charges are stationary in their initial and final configurations, which means their KE does not change. Any work done on the charges contributes only to changing their PE_e. We state that as the first equation in Equation 1: Work done on the charges equals the change of PE_e. You can think of a direct gravitational analogy: The work you do to raise an apple from one stationary position to another equals its increase in PE.

Two charges with opposite signs attract each other, just as two masses do. Separate two such charges, or two masses, and you increase their PE_e. However, like charges repel each other. It takes work to move them closer together, and this means their PE_e increases as they approach each other. The simulations you used in the introduction to this chapter are designed to emphasize these points, and this may be a good time to try them again. They show the similarities and differences in the PE_e of similar configurations of like or opposite charges.

So far, we have been discussing work done **on** a system of charges by an external force. On the other hand, the fields of the particles themselves can do work on each other, similar to what happens when an apple falls to the Earth under the pull of gravity. This is referred to as work being done **by** the system. You see an example of this in the illustration of Equation 1: After positive work done on the system separates the charges and increases its potential energy, positive work done by the system pulls them back together and **decreases** its potential energy again. This is directly analogous to the

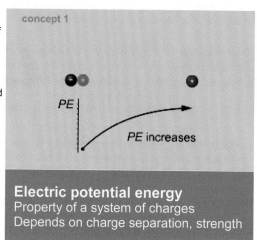

concept 1

PE

PE increases

Electric potential energy
Property of a system of charges
Depends on charge separation, strength

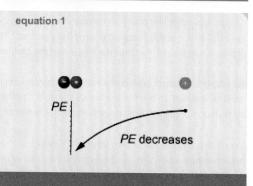

equation 1

PE

PE decreases

Changes in energy

$\Delta PE_e = W$ (work done **on** system)

PE_e = electric potential energy
W = work

$\Delta PE_e = -W$ (work done **by** system)

Charges are stationary at end points

relationship of work and gravitational potential energy: The gravitational potential energy of a system decreases when two objects approach, as when an apple falls to the Earth. We state this relationship between ΔPE_e and work as the second equation in Equation 1: The change in PE_e equals the opposite of the work done **by** the system.

In either case − work done on the system or by the system − the work equals a force applied through a displacement. The electrostatic force increases with the strength of the charges, and it decreases with distance. Be careful when you are asked to find the work done in changing the separation between two charges. The amount of force constantly varies with distance, a fact you must account for when you calculate the work. Calculus proves a useful tool for this, since it provides a technique for calculating work as the force varies over each small increment of displacement.

The electrostatic force is conservative, and the work done by an electric field on charges is path independent. This means that the work done by the field as a charged particle moves from one stationary position to another does not depend on the particle's path between the positions. For example, in the illustration of Concept 1, a horizontal force was exerted to push one particle directly away from the other to increase the system's potential energy. If the two particles had been moved from their indicated starting positions to their end positions by other paths (perhaps involving extravagant zigzags and loops), the net work done and the final potential energy would have been the same. The conservative nature of the electrostatic force means that the potential energy depends solely on the configuration, not on how it was arrived at.

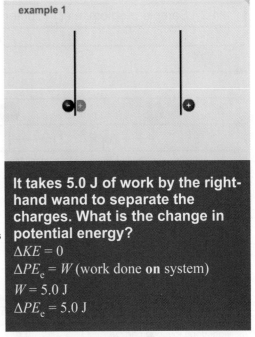

example 1

It takes 5.0 J of work by the right-hand wand to separate the charges. What is the change in potential energy?

$\Delta KE = 0$

$\Delta PE_e = W$ (work done **on** system)

$W = 5.0$ J

$\Delta PE_e = 5.0$ J

We conclude this section with a review of the relationship of the signs of work and potential energy, since they can be confusing. In terms of work done **on** the system, **separating** two charges with **opposite** signs takes positive work (force in the direction of displacement) and increases their potential energy. **Pushing together** two **like** charges also takes positive work, and also increases their potential energy. Checking a computationally based answer against some of your own physics intuition may help make this clear. For instance, if you have to pull apart opposite charges, it should seem that you are doing work on the system, increasing its energy, and in fact you are.

The proper treatment of signs is summarized in the table below.

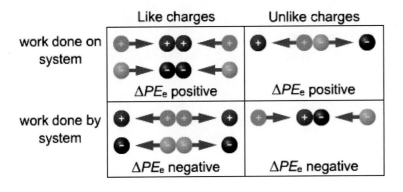

24.2 - Sample problem: electric potential energy

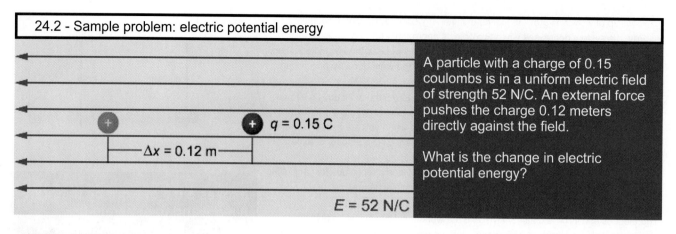

A particle with a charge of 0.15 coulombs is in a uniform electric field of strength 52 N/C. An external force pushes the charge 0.12 meters directly against the field.

What is the change in electric potential energy?

In this problem, work is done **on** the system consisting of the charged particle q and the uniform electric field E. The particle is stationary both before and after it is moved.

Variables

change in electric potential energy	ΔPE_e
work done to move particle	W
change in particle's kinetic energy	$\Delta KE = 0 \text{ J}$
force moving particle	F
charge of particle	$q = 0.15 \text{ C}$
strength of electric field	$E = 52 \text{ N/C}$
distance particle moves	$\Delta x = 0.12 \text{ m}$

What is the strategy?

1. Calculate the work done in moving the particle from its initial to its final position.
2. Since there is no change in kinetic energy, the change in potential energy equals the work done on the system. Using the given values, calculate this change.

Physics principles and equations

The work done to move the particle against the field is

$$W = F\Delta x$$

The force required to move the particle against the field is

$$F = qE$$

Since the charged particle is stationary before and after it is moved by the external force, $\Delta KE = 0$. This allows us to apply the equation relating the change in potential energy to work done on the system,

$$\Delta PE_e = W$$

Step-by-step solution

We calculate the work done to move the charge q through the displacement Δx.

Step	Reason
1. $W = F\Delta x$	definition of work
2. $F = qE$	definition of field
3. $W = qE\Delta x$	substitute equation 2 into equation 1

Since $\Delta KE = 0$, we may state that ΔPE_e equals the work done on the system, and evaluate the result.

Step	Reason
4. $\Delta KE = 0$	particle stationary before and after
5. $\Delta PE_e = W$	work done on system
6. $\Delta PE_e = qE\Delta x$	substitute equation 3 into equation 5
7. $\Delta PE_e = (0.15 \text{ C})(52 \text{ N/C})(0.12 \text{ m})$ $\Delta PE_e = 0.94 \text{ J}$	evaluate

The solution shows that the system has a greater potential energy when q is in its final position. The external force did positive work on the system, increasing its PE.

24.3 - Electric potential energy and work

For a given configuration of a system to have a certain "absolute" amount of potential energy, a reference configuration with zero potential energy must be established. Changes from that zero point will then be the measure of the potential energy of the system.

With gravitational potential energy, an infinite separation between two masses is often defined as the configuration that has zero potential energy. This convention is frequently used for orbiting bodies. It is also common to use the convention that an object at the Earth's surface represents a configuration with zero gravitational potential energy.

When analyzing electric potential energy, physicists usually state that a system of two charges has zero electric potential energy when an infinite distance separates them. The relationship between ΔPE_e and work that was introduced previously can be combined with this reference value to define a relationship between absolute PE_e and work, shown in Equation 1 on the right.

The relationship between the work W_∞ done **by** a system of two charges as one of them moves in from an infinite separation, and the PE_e of the system, is $PE_e = -W_\infty$. Why

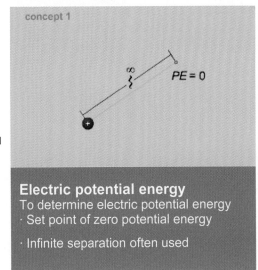

concept 1

$PE = 0$

Electric potential energy
To determine electric potential energy
· Set point of zero potential energy

· Infinite separation often used

does this equation hold true? We already know that $\Delta PE_e = -W$, and when the initial PE_e is zero, then the change in potential energy is just the potential energy of the system in its final configuration.

In Equation 2, we show you how to calculate the work done by the system as the separation between charges changes. This equation can be derived using calculus. Note that the signs of the charges **do** matter in the formula. If they are opposite, applying the equation confirms that the system (the field) does positive work as the particles approach one another. Conversely, the work done by the field is negative if two like charges are moved closer to one another, as illustrated in the diagram.

In Equation 3, we combine the work and potential energy equations using an infinite separation to define zero potential energy. Since zero is the result of dividing by infinity, the $1/r_i$ term "disappears" and only the fraction $-1/r_f$ remains in the final factor of the work formula. Its negative sign cancels the one in the potential energy equation $PE_e = -W_\infty$, to yield the equation you see as Equation 3.

Note an implication of this equation: When the signs of the two charges are opposite, the potential energy of the pair is negative. When they are the same, the potential energy is positive.

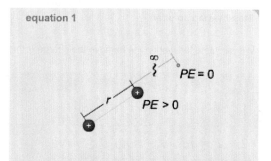

equation 1

Electric potential energy and work

$$PE_e = -W_\infty$$

PE_e = electrical potential energy
W_∞ = work done **by** system as charge moves in from infinity

equation 2

Work by field

$$W = kq_1q_2\left(\frac{1}{r_i} - \frac{1}{r_f}\right)$$

W = work done **by** field
k = Coulomb's constant
q = electric charge
r_i = initial separation
r_f = final separation

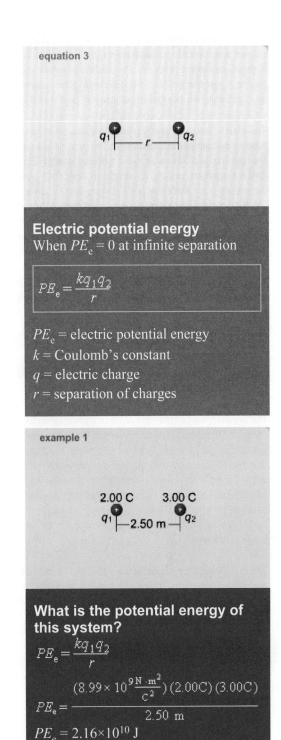

equation 3

Electric potential energy

When $PE_e = 0$ at infinite separation

$$PE_e = \frac{kq_1q_2}{r}$$

PE_e = electric potential energy
k = Coulomb's constant
q = electric charge
r = separation of charges

example 1

2.00 C   3.00 C

q_1 —2.50 m— q_2

What is the potential energy of this system?

$$PE_e = \frac{kq_1q_2}{r}$$

$$PE_e = \frac{(8.99 \times 10^9 \frac{\text{N} \cdot \text{m}^2}{\text{C}^2})(2.00\text{C})(3.00\text{C})}{2.50 \text{ m}}$$

$$PE_e = 2.16 \times 10^{10} \text{ J}$$

24.4 - Electric potential

Electric potential: The electric potential energy of a test charge at a given point in a field, divided by the test charge.

The electric potential of a location in an electric field is the measure of how much electric potential energy will be generated by placing a charge at that point. It is analogous to the concept of electric field. Just as the concept of electric field provides a way to determine how much electric force any charge will encounter at a given location, the concept of electric potential is used to determine how much potential energy placing the charge in a field will generate.

The term "electric potential" may seem confusing, since we are already using the related term "electric potential energy." The formula in Equation 1 provides a direct way to calculate electric potential. The electric potential at a point in a field is calculated by placing a test charge in a field, determining the potential energy of the system created by introducing the charge at that location, and then dividing by the test charge.

The electric potential at any point is unique, which means it has only one value. This reflects the fact that the electrostatic force is conservative, and any configuration of charges has just one value for its potential energy. Electric potential has no direction, only a magnitude, making it a scalar. In Concept 1, you see a graph of the electric potential around a positive point charge, and in Concept 2, you see the graph of the electric potential around a negative point charge. Note how the electric potential increases near the positive point charge, and becomes increasingly negative near the negative point charge. This reflects how the PE_e of a positive test charge will increase near a positive charge, and take on larger negative values near a negative charge.

The graphs on the right provide metaphors for electric potential. The positive charge creates a potential peak, a mountain to be scaled, while the negative charge creates a potential well, a hole to be climbed out of.

You should remember that, just like electric fields, real potential peaks and wells exist around charges in three-dimensional space. They would require four dimensions to properly graph! The three-dimensional graphs in Concepts 1 and 2 only show the electric potential at locations lying in a plane around a point charge.

The equation for calculating the electric potential at locations around a point charge is shown in Equation 2. The equation can be derived from the equation for the PE_e of a pair of charges. The PE_e created by placing a test charge in the field is calculated, and then the PE_e is divided by the test charge, which means the test charge factor cancels out of the equation. Like the equation for potential energy from which it comes, this equation assumes there is zero potential energy when there is an infinite separation between the charges. This is the same as stating that the electric potential infinitely far away from a point charge is zero, as suggested by the graphs of the potential peak and the potential well.

The unit of electric potential is the *volt*. A volt is defined as one joule per coulomb, or energy per unit charge. It is named after Alessandro Volta (1745-1827), the Italian inventor of the system that underlies the design of most batteries.

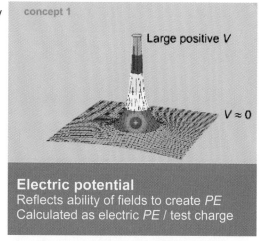

concept 1

Large positive V

$V \approx 0$

Electric potential
Reflects ability of fields to create *PE*
Calculated as electric *PE* / test charge

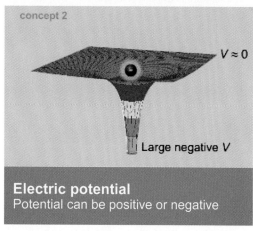

concept 2

$V \approx 0$

Large negative V

Electric potential
Potential can be positive or negative

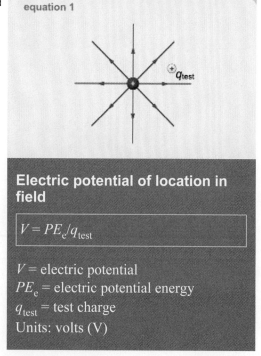

equation 1

q_{test}

Electric potential of location in field

$$V = PE_e / q_{test}$$

V = electric potential
PE_e = electric potential energy
q_{test} = test charge
Units: volts (V)

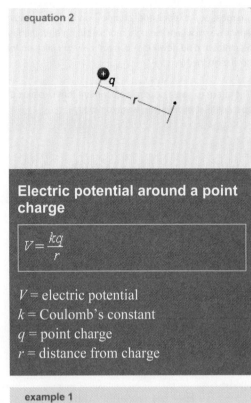

equation 2

Electric potential around a point charge

$$V = \frac{kq}{r}$$

V = electric potential
k = Coulomb's constant
q = point charge
r = distance from charge

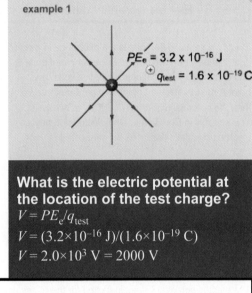

example 1

$PE_e = 3.2 \times 10^{-16}$ J
$q_{test} = 1.6 \times 10^{-19}$ C

What is the electric potential at the location of the test charge?

$V = PE_e/q_{test}$
$V = (3.2 \times 10^{-16}$ J$)/(1.6 \times 10^{-19}$ C$)$
$V = 2.0 \times 10^3$ V $= 2000$ V

24.5 - Spreadsheet: electric potential graphs

At the right, you see a three-dimensional graph of the electric potential for the points in a plane surrounding three charges. The graph was generated by a spreadsheet that you can access from this textbook if you are using a computer that can open Microsoft® Excel files. The electric potential at any point in the horizontal plane is indicated by the graph's distance above or below zero. Two positive charges of different magnitudes cause the "peaks" you see at the right, while the "well" is caused by a negative charge. The electric potential takes on extremely large positive or negative values at locations very near the positive or negative charges. We do not show the most extreme values because it would require a drastic change to the vertical scale of the graph.

The graph may remind you of very mountainous terrain. It serves as a map of electric potential, showing the locations of peaks, plains and wells. The electric PE of a test charge will increase as it "climbs up" the side of any peak. It requires positive work on the test charge to cause it to approach the underlying charge generating the peak. On the other hand, the PE of a test charge that is free to move will naturally "fall into" a well, as the test charge is attracted by the underlying negative charge.

Click here to launch the spreadsheet. You can change the amounts and locations of the charges, or add additional charges, and see the results. If the file does not open, on Windows click with the right mouse button and choose the save option. On the Macintosh, hold down the "control" key and click on the link, then choose the option to download the file.

Click here to see a separate document that explains the programming of the spreadsheet in case you want to modify it.

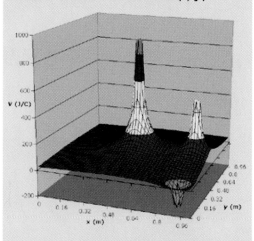

Graphing Electric Potential

Charge Locations and Magnitudes

	x(m)	y(m)	Charge(μC)	Charge(C)
Charge 1	0.5	0.5	0.002	2.00E-09
Charge 2	0.9	0.1	-0.0005	-5.00E-10
Charge 3	0.9	0.5	0.001	1.00E-09

Electric Potential V vs. Location (x, y)

24.6 - Electric potential difference

Electric potential difference is the difference in electric potential between two points. For example, if point B has an electric potential of positive five volts, and point A has an electric potential of positive three volts, then the potential difference $V_B - V_A$ is two volts. You see this in Equation 1. Like electric potentials, electric potential differences are measured in volts.

In the three illustrations to the right, you see two plates. They are both charged: The plate on the left (plate A) is negatively charged, and the plate on the right (plate B) is positively charged. In the example problem, we chose to make the electric potential of plate A negative 0.5 V and of plate B positive 1.0 V. The potential difference between the plates is 1.5 V.

The potential difference between the terminals of the car battery is 12 V. Between two contacts of a household outlet, ΔV averages 120 V.

The electric potential values just cited for the plates depend on some choice of a reference point for zero potential. Often, in practical applications, the ground (the electrically neutral Earth) is defined as having zero electric potential, and all values are measured relative to this value. In an interactive problem in the introduction to this chapter, the midpoint between the plates was selected as the location of zero potential.

Also at the right, you see a common source of electric potential difference: a battery. Its two terminals have different electric potentials. Batteries are often described by the potential difference between their terminals. For instance, the potential difference between the terminals of a D cell is 1.5 V. This is often referred to as the battery's voltage. In the configuration at the right, the potential difference between the battery's terminals caused electrons to flow to plate A and away from plate B, thereby charging the plates.

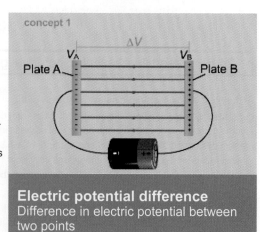

concept 1

Plate A — V_A ΔV V_B — Plate B

Electric potential difference
Difference in electric potential between two points

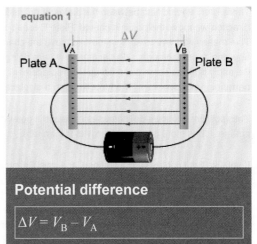

equation 1

Potential difference

$$\Delta V = V_{\mathrm{B}} - V_{\mathrm{A}}$$

ΔV = electric potential difference
V_{B} = potential at point B
V_{A} = potential at point A
Units: volts (V)

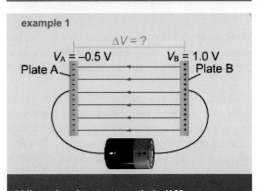

example 1

What is the potential difference between the plates?

$$\Delta V = V_{\mathrm{B}} - V_{\mathrm{A}}$$
$$\Delta V = 1.0 \text{ V} - (-0.5 \text{ V})$$
$$\Delta V = 1.5 \text{ V}$$

24.7 - Potential difference, electric potential energy and work

At the right, you see two charged conducting plates. Plate A on the left is negatively charged, and plate B on the right is positively charged. The electric potential of plate A is −6.0 V, and that of plate B is +3.0 V. In this section, we will use this configuration to summarize the relationship of electric potential difference, electric potential energy and work.

The potential difference between the plates is +9.0 V (+3.0 V minus −6.0 V). How does this relate to potential energy and work? Consider a positive test charge with a charge of one microcoulomb that we cause to move between the plates. The charge is initially stationary at plate A. We move it to the positive plate B, and hold it still against this plate. The work we do changes only the charge's PE_{e}: It is stationary at its initial and final positions, so it has zero KE at both plates. The movement of the charge between the two plates is indicated in Concept 1.

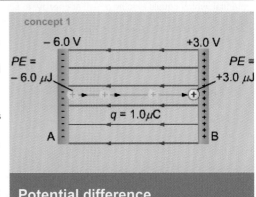

concept 1

Potential difference
Change in energy per unit charge

There is an electric field between the plates. It points from B to A, opposite to the direction we move the positive charge. Plate B repels the charge and plate A attracts it. This means we have to apply a force to move the charge from A to B. Since we are applying a force through a displacement, we are doing work on the system. The force we apply is in the same direction as the displacement of the test charge, so we are performing positive work. The force through a displacement is shown in Concept 2.

The (positive) work we do increases the electric potential energy of the positive test charge. It has more potential energy at B than at A.

If you like, you can use a gravitational analogy. Consider the work required to roll a ball from an area of low gravitational potential, a valley, up an inclined ramp to an area of high gravitational potential, a mountaintop. Moving the ball uphill requires work, and the positive work done on the ball increases its potential energy. This resembles the positive test charge's trip from plate A to plate B. Conversely, if the ball rolls back down the hill (or the test charge is allowed to coast back to plate A), its potential energy decreases.

Now we discuss the same points, using equations. Electric potential can be calculated as the electric potential energy created by placing a test charge in a field, divided by the test charge. The electric potential **difference** is the **change** (difference) in electric potential energy divided by the test charge. These two equations are shown in Concept 1.

What causes this change in potential energy? The work done **on** the system. Taking the previous equation and replacing ΔPE with work W, we find that the electric potential difference is W/q, or work per unit charge. This is shown in Concept 2.

In all this discussion, a positive test charge has been used. This is the standard way to determine the electric potential. However, negative charges (like electrons) can move, too. When free to move, a negative charge will naturally move to an area of higher potential (the positive plate in this example). This will decrease the system's potential energy. With positive work, it can be forced to return to the negative plate, and this will increase the potential energy of the system. (As a form of shorthand, you may sometimes see this referred to as the PE of the charge, but it is important to remember that the charge only has PE because of the field caused by other charges.)

The *electron volt*, a common unit of energy in many areas of physics study, is based on the relationship of energy, charge and potential difference. One electron volt (eV) equals the change in the potential energy of an elementary charge (1.60×10^{-19} C) when it moves through a potential difference of one volt. We can use a rearrangement of the second equation in Concept 1, $\Delta PE_e = q\Delta V$, to calculate that an electron volt equals $1.602\ 18 \times 10^{-19}$ J. Note that the electron volt equals charge multiplied by electric potential, which equals electric potential **energy**. In spite of its name this unit refers to electric potential energy, not electric potential as volts do.

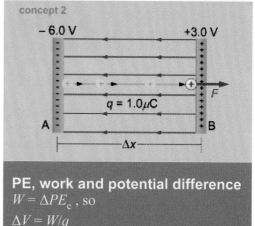

$V = PE_e/q$, and
$\Delta V = \Delta PE_e/q$

concept 2

−6.0 V   +3.0 V

$q = 1.0\mu C$

A   B

Δx

PE, work and potential difference
$W = \Delta PE_e$, so
$\Delta V = W/q$

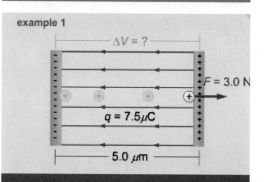

example 1

$\Delta V = ?$

$F = 3.0$ N

$q = 7.5\mu C$

5.0 μm

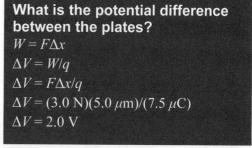

What is the potential difference between the plates?
$W = F\Delta x$
$\Delta V = W/q$
$\Delta V = F\Delta x/q$
$\Delta V = (3.0 \text{ N})(5.0\ \mu\text{m})/(7.5\ \mu\text{C})$
$\Delta V = 2.0$ V

24.8 - Interactive checkpoint: lead acid cell

A typical car battery consists of six lead-acid cells. Each cell has a potential difference of 2.05 V across it. The negative electrode is at a potential of −1.685 V, while the positive electrode is at a potential of +0.365 V. What is the change in electric potential energy for one electron that is moved from the positive to the negative electrode of one of the cells?

Answer:

$\Delta PE_e = $ [   ] J

24.9 - A comparison of electric and gravitational fields

In this section, we compare the uniform electric field produced by a large negatively charged plate with the gravitational field created by the Earth. The goal is to use the gravitational field − one you experience all the time − to help you better understand the electric field.

In the gravitational field, the test objects in the illustrations to the right are people: Individuals of varying masses can walk up or down the stairs of a building to change their height above the Earth's surface. In the electric field, the test objects are positive test charges that can be farther from or closer to the charged plate. Their distance from the plate is indicated by d. In this discussion, the surface of the plate, and the Earth, are assumed to be points of zero potential energy.

Points in space around Jupiter have more potential in its gravitational field than would points the same distance from the Earth in its gravitational field.

Let's now use the analogy. First, consider two people on the stairs. One person has a mass of 50 kg, the other 100 kg. Say they are both on the 12th floor of a building. Each person's potential energy is a function of his mass and height above the ground, and the acceleration due to Earth's gravitational field. Specific examples of this are illustrated in the Concept 2 diagram to the right: A 100 kg person on the 12th floor has twice as much gravitational potential energy as a 50 kg person on the same floor.

An analogous situation exists for a positive test charge above the center of the large negatively charged plate. The plate attracts the charge because it creates a field with the same downward orientation as the gravitational field. The electric potential energy of the charge is a function of its magnitude, its distance from the plate, and the strength of the field. In the Concept 2 diagram, two charges of different magnitudes are the same distance from the plate. The stronger charge will have more electric potential energy, just as the more massive person at a given height has more gravitational potential energy.

Now we will observe how position relates to potential energy. This is shown in the

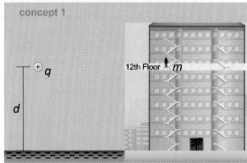

Electric and gravitational fields
Compare electric and gravitational effects
· Use charged plate, tall building
· Consider distance
· Use test object's charge or mass

Concept 3 diagram. The same person is shown on the 12th and 6th floors. (To simplify the discussion, we use the European convention that the ground level is the "zeroth" floor, not the first, so that the 12th floor is twice as far above the ground as the 6th.) The person's gravitational potential energy is twice as much on the 12th floor as on the 6th floor. We also show two test charges of the same magnitude at different distances from the plate. The test charge at twice the distance from the plate has twice the potential energy.

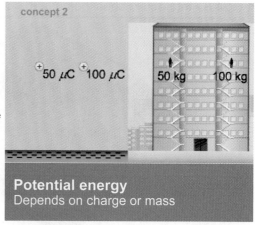

Potential energy
Depends on charge or mass

Finally let's consider the role of the field. Potential energy is a function of the strength of the field-producing object. For example, if we moved the building to Jupiter, the same people on the same floors would have greater gravitational potential energy than they do on Earth. Jupiter's stronger gravitational field would account for the greater gravitational PE. If the plate had more charge and therefore a stronger field, test charges at the same positions would have greater electric potential energy. With a mass like Earth or with an electrically charged plate, you can think of fields as surrounding these entities, waiting to exert forces on nearby objects.

In both fields, the **work** done on an object equals its change in potential energy. For instance, if an elevator picks up a person at the 6th and drops him off at the 12th floor, the work done by the elevator equals the change in his potential energy. Similarly, if you exert a force to move a test charge farther from the plate, the work you do equals the change in the system's potential energy. (The person and charge are both stationary at the beginning and end of their journeys, so the work only changes their PE_e. Their KE at the beginning and end is zero.)

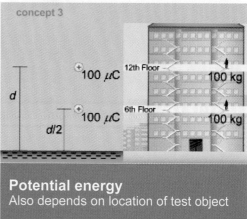

Potential energy
Also depends on location of test object

Now consider the concept of gravitational potential. As illustrated in the Concept 4 diagram, gravitational potential depends only on height above the Earth's surface. The gravitational potential is twice as great on the 12th floor as it is on the 6th floor.

We can also compare positions 12 floors above the ground on Jupiter and on the Earth, two planets of different masses. The gravitational potential 12 floors above the ground is greater on Jupiter than it is on the Earth. To put it another way, any object you place on the 12th floor on Jupiter will have more potential energy than the same object would on the 12th floor on the Earth. This is because Jupiter's gravitational field is stronger than the Earth's. The important distinction between potential energy and potential is that the potential is independent of the test object. Jupiter's mass generates more gravitational potential at a given height above its surface than the Earth's mass does.

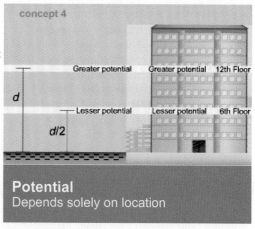

Potential
Depends solely on location

The concept of gravitational potential is analogous to electric potential. You see this also in the Concept 4 diagram. A location one centimeter above the plate has twice the electric potential of a location only half a centimeter above the plate. The distance above the plate determines the electric potential. It is independent of the strength of the test charge. Any charge, regardless of its magnitude, placed in an area of greater electric potential will create a system with more electric potential energy than when it is placed in an area of lower electric potential.

On the other hand, a location one centimeter from a highly charged plate with a stronger electric field has more potential than a location the same distance from a less charged plate. Again, this idea directly parallels the idea of gravitational potential. The statement for charged plates is true no matter what test charge you might use to assess the electric potential.

For the last idea, turn your attention to the illustration for the Concept 5 diagram. If you want to calculate the potential **difference** between the 6th and 7th floors, subtract the value of the potential at the 6th floor from its value at the 7th floor. Since we can treat the Earth's gravitational field as essentially uniform near its surface, the gravitational potential difference between the 6th and 7th floors is the same as it is between the 12th and 13th floors.

You should think of electric potential difference in a similar way. If you know the electric potentials at two points, you can subtract them to calculate the potential difference. With electric potential difference, the actual potentials at the points do not matter, only the change in potential between two points. The concept of electric potential difference is used frequently in everyday devices. For instance, if you are told you have a nine-volt battery, you are being told the difference between the terminals, **not** the electric potential of either terminal. This is analogous to how you might think if you were told to run up the stairs of a skyscraper. It does not matter whether you run from the 5th floor to the 15th, or from the 18th to the 28th. In either case, you have to run up 10 flights of stairs.

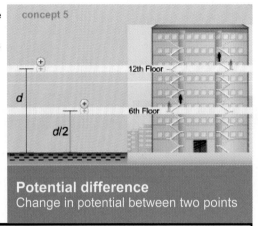

concept 5

Potential difference
Change in potential between two points

24.10 - Equipotential surfaces

Equipotential surface: A surface with the same electric potential everywhere.

As its name indicates, an equipotential surface is one along which the electric potential of a field is everywhere the same. The boundary of a sphere centered about a point charge q is an equipotential surface. All the points on this surface are the same distance r from q. This means the electric potential, which in this case can be calculated with the formula kq/r, is the same at all points on the surface.

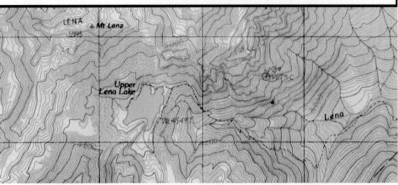

The mountainous contour map above displays curves of constant altitude. Its "equi-altitude" curves are like equipotential surfaces in an electric field.

Such an equipotential surface is shown in the first diagram to the right. In the illustration, we represent the equipotential surface around q with a circle instead of a sphere for the sake of visual clarity.

No work is needed to move a charge from one resting place to another along an equipotential surface, because the potential energy neither increases nor decreases as the charge moves. If work were needed to change the charge's position, its electric potential energy would change, which means it would be in a location with a different electric potential.

The second diagram shows a particular example of a relationship that holds true in general: Electric field lines that intersect an equipotential surface are always perpendicular to the surface where they intersect it.

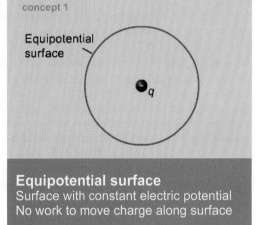

concept 1

Equipotential surface

q

Equipotential surface
Surface with constant electric potential
No work to move charge along surface

This is true because any motion of a charged particle from one place to another along such a surface must be in a direction perpendicular to the force exerted by the field. Work equals the component of the force parallel to the motion, multiplied by the displacement. No parallel component means no work occurs. In turn, no work means no change in potential energy, and no change in potential energy means no change in potential.

You can explore equipotential surfaces in the simulations in the introduction to this chapter. If you move a test charge along an equipotential surface, you will see that its electric potential energy stays the same.

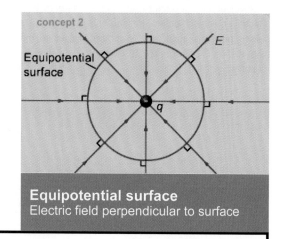

concept 2

Equipotential surface

Equipotential surface
Electric field perpendicular to surface

24.11 - Electric potential and a uniform electric field

The concepts of electric potential and electric field are linked. In Concept 1, you see their relationship illustrated in the context of a uniform electric field. Plate A is negatively charged and plate B is positively charged. Assume that the plates are large enough compared to their spacing that the **electric field** between them is of uniform strength and direction, pointing from plate B toward plate A.

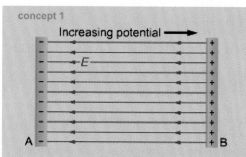

concept 1

Increasing potential ⟶

A   B

Displacement parallel to uniform field
Potential *V* changes at constant rate
Field directed from higher to lower *V*

The **electric potential** between the plates increases in the opposite direction, from plate A to plate B. Since it takes positive work to push a test charge against the field from left to right, the potential energy of the charge increases as it moves from plate A to plate B. Since the strength of the field is everywhere the same, the electric potential increases at a constant rate as the charge moves from left to right. The potential's change per unit displacement parallel to the field is constant.

Another way of expressing the opposite orientations of the field and the direction of increasing potential is to say that the field is always directed from regions of higher potential to regions of lower potential.

We state the proportionality between the change of potential and the displacement as the first equation in Equation 1, and derive it below. The variable Δs measures a displacement parallel to the field lines. The negative sign in the equation reflects the fact that the potential difference is negative for a displacement $\Delta \mathbf{s}$ in the same direction as the field. Movement perpendicular to the field lines results in no change in electric potential. Again, we stress that the field must be uniform.

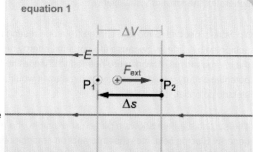

equation 1

ΔV

P_1 F_{ext} P_2

Δs

Potential difference in uniform field

$$\Delta V = -E\Delta s$$
$$E = -\frac{\Delta V}{\Delta s}$$

ΔV = potential difference
E = electric field strength

In many applications later in this book, we will only be interested in the magnitude of the potential difference between two points in a uniform field that are separated by a distance d parallel to the field, and we will write $\Delta V = Ed$.

The second equation in Equation 1 is just the first equation, solved for the electric field. It proves to be a very useful formulation. It shows how the electric field strength can be determined when the potential difference between two points in the field is known. This form of the equation is applied in the example problem below.

Derivation. We will show that for a uniform electric field **E**, and a displacement $\Delta \mathbf{s}$ measured in the direction of the field, the potential difference between two points separated by Δs is given by the equation $\Delta V = -E\Delta s$. This is shown in the illustration of Equation 1.

Variables

uniform electric field	$\mathbf{E}$
two points in field	P_1, P_2
test charge	q_{test}
force	$\mathbf{F}$
work	W
distance parallel to field	Δs
potential difference between points	ΔV

We use the subscripts $_{field}$ and $_{ext}$ in the steps below to distinguish the forces exerted and the work done by the field and by an external force that moves a test charge against the field.

Strategy

1. Calculate the work done by an external force to move a test charge against the constant force of the field.
2. State the work done on the field in a different way, using the relationship of potential difference, work done on the field, and charge.
3. Set the two expressions for work equal to each other and simplify to get the desired equation.

Physics principles and equations

The work done to move a test charge from point P_1 to point P_2, opposite to the direction of $\Delta\mathbf{s}$, is $\mathbf{F}\cdot(-\Delta\mathbf{s})$. Since $\mathbf{F}$ is constant and parallel to the displacement between the points, this dot product can be written as the scalar product $F\Delta s \cos 0°$, or just

$$W = F\Delta s$$

The force exerted on the test charge by the electric field is

$$F = qE$$

A relationship stated and derived earlier for the relationship between potential difference and work done **on** a system is

$$\Delta V = W/q$$

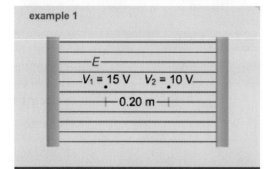

Δs = displacement parallel to field

example 1

What are the magnitude and direction of this uniform electric field?

Field is directed to the right

$\Delta\mathbf{s}$ directed from left to right

$\Delta V = 10\text{ V} - 15\text{ V} = -5.0\text{ V}$

$$E = -\frac{\Delta V}{\Delta s}$$

$E = -(-5.0\text{ V})/(0.20\text{ m}) = 25\text{ N/C}$

$\mathbf{E} = 25\text{ N/C to the right}$

Step-by-step derivation

We find two expressions for the work W and set them equal to each other. We derive this using a positive charge being pushed against the field. The work done by the external force is positive in this case; work done by the field is negative.

Step	Reason
1. $W = F\Delta s$	definition of work
2. $F_{field} = q_{test}E$	electric field force on test charge
3. $F_{ext} = -q_{test}E$	external force on test charge
4. $W_{ext} = -q_{test}E\Delta s$	substitute equation 3 into equation 1
5. $W_{ext} = q_{test}\Delta V$	potential difference and work
6. $\Delta V = -E\Delta s$	equate steps 4 and 5 and simplify

Although we derived Equation 1 for the case of a positive charge being moved against a uniform field, the equation is equally true for negative charges, and for charges moving in either direction.

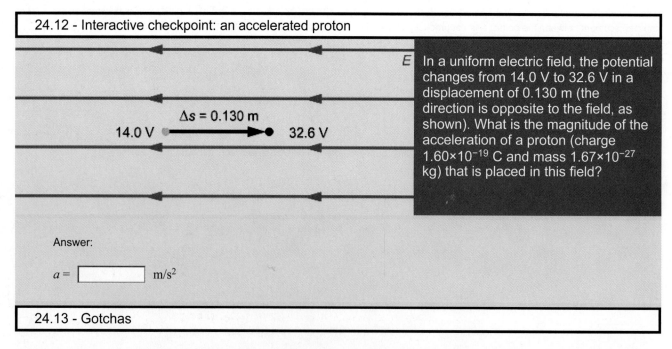

24.12 - Interactive checkpoint: an accelerated proton

$\Delta s = 0.130$ m

14.0 V   32.6 V

E

In a uniform electric field, the potential changes from 14.0 V to 32.6 V in a displacement of 0.130 m (the direction is opposite to the field, as shown). What is the magnitude of the acceleration of a proton (charge 1.60×10^{-19} C and mass 1.67×10^{-27} kg) that is placed in this field?

Answer:

$a = $ [   ] m/s^2

24.13 - Gotchas

Electric potential energy and electric potential are the same. No, they are not even measured in the same units. Potential energy is a property of a specific configuration of charges, while electric potential is a property of a point in space. Electric potential is measured by assessing the potential energy with a test charge, and then dividing by the magnitude of that charge.

*I quadrupled the strength of a **test** charge, but I think the electric potential at the location is unchanged.* You are correct. Like an electric field, electric potential is independent of the test charge.

There is electric potential surrounding a single charge. Yes, there is. There is a field. Add a second charge, and you will have created a system with electric potential energy.

Where does an electron go when it is free to move: to a location of higher or lower potential? Toward a location of higher potential. Electrons tend to move toward positive charges and away from negative charges, which means they move toward regions of higher electric potential, minimizing the electric potential energy. A positive test charge (or proton) would do the opposite, moving toward a region of lower potential, which also minimizes the electric potential energy.

I calculated a negative potential difference between two points. Is that possible? Quite possible. If point A has an electric potential of 9.0 volts, and point B an electric potential of 6.0 volts, the difference $V_B - V_A$ is −3.0 volts. It is perhaps an unstated convention that when calculating a potential difference, V_A is subtracted from V_B.

24.14 - Summary

Electric potential energy is conceptually similar to gravitational potential energy. It is determined by the configuration of a system of charges. As with gravitational potential energy, external positive work that is done **on** a system results in a positive change in the sum of the system's PE and KE. On the other hand, positive work done **by** the system on something outside the system results in a negative change in the sum of the system's PE and KE.

Since in this chapter we often assume that charges move from one stationary configuration to another, there is no change in KE due to work, and positive work done **on** a system increases its PE. Negative work done on a system, as when two opposite charges are moved closer together, decreases its PE.

Electric potential is a scalar quantity defined throughout an electric field in a region of three-dimensional space. It describes the electric potential energy that will be possessed by an electric test charge – or more properly by the system of charges – when the test charge is placed at various locations in the field. When a test charge is introduced, its electric potential energy equals the electric potential at its location, times its own charge value. The potential is measured in joules per coulomb, or volts (V), where 1 V = 1 J/C.

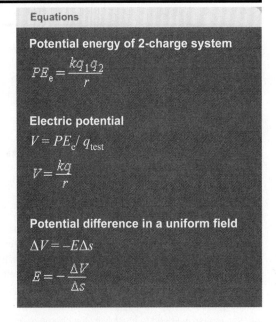

Equations

Potential energy of 2-charge system

$$PE_e = \frac{kq_1q_2}{r}$$

Electric potential

$$V = PE_e / q_{test}$$

$$V = \frac{kq}{r}$$

Potential difference in a uniform field

$$\Delta V = -E\Delta s$$

$$E = -\frac{\Delta V}{\Delta s}$$

Electric potential difference is more commonly measured and used than the electric potential itself. It is the difference in electric potential between two points. Batteries are categorized by the potential difference between their terminals, which is 1.5 V for commonly sold small batteries.

The electric potential difference between two points also equals the work required to move a test charge from one point to the other, divided by the value of the charge.

An equipotential surface in a field is a surface that has the same electric potential at all points. Because there is no potential difference between any two points in the surface, no work is required to move a charge along the surface. The electric field is perpendicular to such a surface at every point on the surface.

25.0 - Introduction

We began our study of electricity and magnetism with electrostatics, which focuses on the forces and fields created by stationary charges.

Now we will concentrate on charges that are in motion, a branch of physics called electrodynamics. We will discuss the flow of charge (electric current), resistance to current, and the relationship among potential difference, resistance, and current.

In this chapter, we focus primarily on the fundamentals of these topics rather than their applications. We will not concern ourselves too much about the source of the potential difference, nor worry too about where the current may be flowing or why one would want it to flow. Once we have discussed the essentials, we can apply these concepts to electric circuits, and consider typical sources of potential difference, such as batteries, and common sources of resistance such as resistors and light bulbs.

25.1 - Electric current

Electric current: Amount of net charge passing through a surface per second.

Current is the rate at which net charge passes through a hypothetical surface, the number of coulombs of charge per second. As a practical matter, currents are often measured as they pass through a wire, so we use this configuration to explain currents in the illustrations to the right. In this section, we focus solely on the current, not its cause.

To measure the amount of current, we can place an imaginary surface across the wire shown in Concept 1 and count the net number of electrons moving through it each second. The electrons we show are the *charge carriers*, the charges that make up the current. In this example, they are moving from right to left.

Counting the electrons as they pass by is a useful start, but electric current is charge per second, so we need to multiply by the charge of an electron. An electron has a charge of -1.6×10^{-19} C, so if there are five electrons flowing by every second, the electric current is 8.0×10^{-19} coulombs per second. For reasons discussed below, the flow of current here is considered positive.

The equation in Equation 1 states that current is the net charge passing through a surface divided by time. The *ampere* (A) is the unit for electric current. It is named after the French scientist André-Marie Ampère. One ampere equals one coulomb per second. A coulomb of charge is equivalent to 6.2×10^{18} electrons, so one ampere equals that number of electrons passing through every second. The letter I represents current.

Using water as an analogy may help you understand electric currents. The rate of water flow is measured in several settings. You may have seen water flow ratings for shower heads. Newer shower heads allow a water flow of nine liters per minute, about half the rate of flow of older models. Boaters also keep a close eye on water flow. For a particular river, a rafter might measure how much water is flowing, in cubic feet per second, to judge whether it is safe to run the rapids.

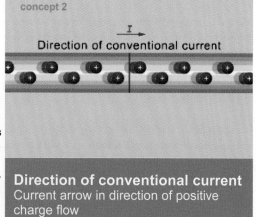

concept 1

Electric current
Rate of net flow of charge
Typically composed of moving electrons

concept 2

I
Direction of conventional current

Direction of conventional current
Current arrow in direction of positive charge flow

Similarly, the rate of flow of electrons can be measured. Many electrons move in the currents used in household devices. About 2.5×10^{18} electrons pass through the light bulb in a typical household flashlight every second, which is 0.4 amperes.

Current is a scalar quantity. It states the rate of flow of charge, not the direction of the flow of charge. Again, think of water. Liters per second tells you how much water is flowing, but not in which direction. Often, it is important to know the direction of an electric current: which way the charge is flowing. Confusingly, the arrow used to indicate a current's direction points opposite the way you might expect. It does not point in the direction that electrons flow. Instead, it points the way positive charges would be flowing if they were the charges moving in an electric current. This is shown in Concept 2. The arrow indicates the direction of what is called *conventional current*, the direction in which positive charge carriers creating the current would move. The flow of electrons discussed above would be described as a positive current flowing to the right, not a negative current flowing to the left.

Why is typical electric current shown as though positive charge carriers flow, even if they do not? Scientists began studying electric currents before they knew about electrons and protons. One of the early explorers of electricity, Benjamin Franklin, established the convention that the current points in the direction of positive charge flow. More than a hundred years later, when the scientist Edwin Hall determined that current is actually the movement of negative charge carriers (electrons), the positive charge flow convention had already been established, and it remains in place to this day.

In basic configurations like the segment of conducting wire shown to the right, electric current is stated as a positive quantity and its direction is indicated with an arrow. In other circumstances, such as alternating current circuits where the direction of current flow changes constantly, signs can be used to indicate the direction of current.

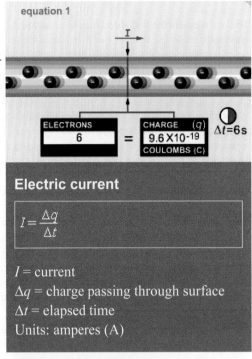

Electric current

$$I = \frac{\Delta q}{\Delta t}$$

I = current
Δq = charge passing through surface
Δt = elapsed time
Units: amperes (A)

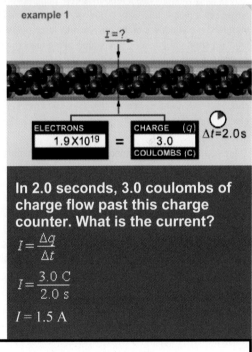

In 2.0 seconds, 3.0 coulombs of charge flow past this charge counter. What is the current?

$$I = \frac{\Delta q}{\Delta t}$$

$$I = \frac{3.0 \ \text{C}}{2.0 \ \text{s}}$$

$$I = 1.5 \ \text{A}$$

25.2 - Drift speed

Drift speed: Average speed of charge carriers that make up a current.

Whether or not there is an electric current in a wire, the electrons in the wire move randomly at high speed, on the order of a million meters per second, due to their thermal energy. This random motion does not create a current because it causes no **net** motion of charge over time.

When there is an electric current, there is a net motion of charge. The average speed at which charge moves in a current is called its drift speed. To illustrate this concept, we use the simplified diagram of the wiring in a car shown in Concept 1. In the diagram, a battery is shown; the potential difference between its terminals causes electrons to move counterclockwise along the wire. The average speed at which they move along the wire is the drift speed.

The magnitude of the drift speed may surprise you; it is on the order of 10^{-4} m/s. That is less than a meter per hour, slower than a snail slimes across the ground. This may seem surprising because when you flip the car's headlight switch, the lights illuminate almost instantaneously. It may seem as if electrons are flowing from near the battery to the headlights at an incredible speed.

Why do the lights go on so quickly? When the switch is flipped, the electric field created by the car's battery travels through the wires at nearly the speed of light, 3.00×10^8 m/s. It causes electrons everywhere in the wire, including those in the filaments of the headlights, to start to move almost immediately. It is like when you turn on a water faucet: water flows out very quickly. You receive water near the faucet; you do not have to wait for water to flow all the way from the reservoir to your tap.

Why do the electrons move along the wire so slowly? If the electrons were in a vacuum, the electric field would accelerate them until they moved at near the speed of light, since there would be no force opposing their motion. But in a wire, the electrons collide with the atoms that make up the wire. The combination of the collisions and the electric field cause them to move in the erratic zigzag pattern you see in Concept 2. (We overstate the curved element of their paths to emphasize the effect of the field on their motion.)

The motion of these electrons is like that of a ball in play in a pinball machine. The ball moves fairly randomly as it rebounds from bumpers and other obstacles. However, the surface of a pinball table slants downward, so despite the erratic motion caused by the bumpers, a component of the gravitational force pulls the ball down toward you over time. (In short, the maker of the pinball game uses gravity to ensure that the ball "drifts" downward and "drains".)

There is no simple relationship between drift speed and the amount of current in various conductors. A great number of charge carriers moving slowly can result in a larger electric current than a smaller number of charge carriers flowing quickly.

There is a final point to be made about the erratic motion of electrons in the current. Energy transfers from the electrons to the atoms during the collisions. The collisions increase the random (thermal) motion of the atoms. This explains why the temperature of the filaments in the car headlights increases when a current flows through them: Energy is being transferred from the electrons in the current to the atoms that make up the filaments. The filaments become hot and emit light. The other parts of the wiring increase in temperature as well, but the system is designed to maximize the temperature increase in the filaments and minimize it elsewhere.

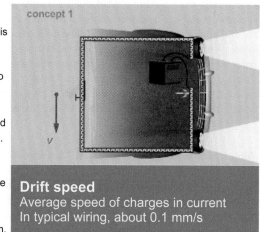

Drift speed
Average speed of charges in current
In typical wiring, about 0.1 mm/s

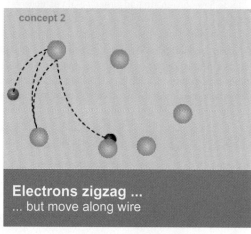

Electrons zigzag ...
... but move along wire

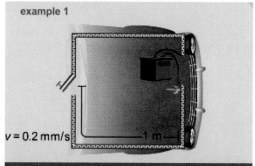

example 1

$v = 0.2$ mm/s

If the switch is 1.0 meter away from the headlights, and charge carriers move at the speed shown above, how long will it take for the headlights to light once the switch is thrown?
Nearly instantaneous
· Field acts along entire wire very quickly

Resistance: The ratio of the potential difference across a conductor to the current through it.

Resistor: An electrical component often used to control the amount of current flow.

Resistors wired into a computer circuit board. Each resistor has a color code that indicates its resistance in ohms.

Resistance is defined as the potential difference across two points on a conductor divided by the current flowing through the conductor. At the right, we use a common electrical component called a resistor to illustrate this concept. There is a potential difference across the resistor and current flowing through it. Divide the potential difference by the current and you have calculated the resistance of this resistor.

The resistance of a resistor such as those shown above or to the right is constant. The resistor is made of *ohmic* materials, which are empirically known to obey Ohm's law. Increase the potential difference and the current increases proportionally. The resistance does not change. The linear relationship between potential difference and current is shown as the first equation in Equation 1.

Since resistance equals potential difference divided by current, its unit, the ohm, is volts per ampere. Resistance is represented by Ω, the Greek letter omega.

Resistors are not the only components that resist the flow of current. The filament in a light bulb or the coils of an electric hot plate both function as resistors. The term "resistor" broadly refers to any element that is a source of resistance.

Again, water is a good analogy. The potential difference driving current in a wire resembles the pressure exerted on water in a pipe. Increase the pressure, and the water flow increases. Different pipes have different amounts of resistance. For instance, one with a rough interior wall would have greater resistance to water flow than one with a smooth wall.

Materials that do not obey Ohm's law are called *non-ohmic*. Many components used in modern circuitry are made of non-ohmic materials. For instance, a diode has little resistance to current flow in one direction, and great resistance to current flow in the other.

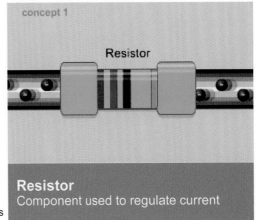

concept 1

Resistor

Resistor
Component used to regulate current

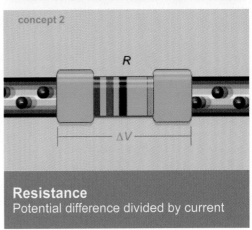

concept 2

R

ΔV

Resistance
Potential difference divided by current

Georg Ohm published his major work, including what we now know as Ohm's law, in 1827. His theories were greeted with skepticism and his career was slow to progress. Why it took so long for his work to be appreciated is hard to say. Perhaps it is because the law is empirical as opposed to a fundamental law of nature. It is fair to note that many major leaps forward in physics were met with skepticism and opposition.

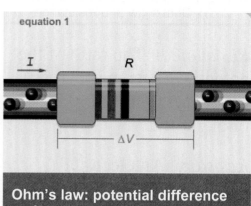

equation 1

Ohm's law: potential difference and current

$$\Delta V = IR$$
$$R = \frac{\Delta V}{I}$$

ΔV = potential difference
I = current
R = resistance
Units of resistance: ohms (Ω),
volts/ampere

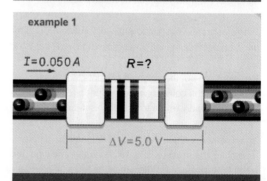

example 1

What is the resistance of this resistor?

$$R = \frac{\Delta V}{I}$$
$$R = \frac{5.0 \text{ V}}{0.050 \text{ A}}$$
$$R = 100 \ \Omega$$

25.4 - Interactive problem: Ohm's law

The interactive problem on the right shows a tanning bed, an electrical appliance through which current can flow.

Your challenge is to configure the tanning bed so that 2.4 amperes of current flow through it. If you accomplish this goal, Joe Pasty will get a perfect tan. Anything less and he will remain pasty. Anything more and it will be red and toasty for Joe.

In the simulation, the potential difference applied to the lamps of the tanning bed is 240 volts. (Assume that this potential difference is

Copyright 2000-2007 Kinetic Books Co. Chapter 25

unchanging.)

You can control the tanning bed's resistance using the up and down buttons in the control panel. The resistance can vary from 10 to 200 ohms.

Use Ohm's law to calculate the tanning bed resistance that will result in 2.4 amperes of current flowing through the device. Set the resistance to the nearest 10 ohms, then press GO to see if you were correct. A gauge located on the tanning bed will display the amount of current flowing through the device.

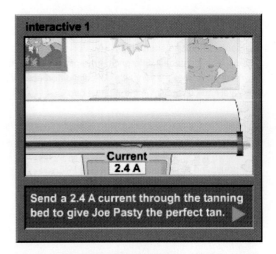

interactive 1

Current
2.4 A

Send a 2.4 A current through the tanning bed to give Joe Pasty the perfect tan.

25.5 - Resistivity

Resistivity is used to quantify how much a material resists the flow of current. It is represented by the Greek letter ρ (rho). A material considered a good conductor, such as copper, has low resistivity. Materials used as insulators, such as glass or rubber, have high resistivity.

Resistivity is the inverse of conductivity (which quantifies how well a material conducts current). Current does not readily flow through materials with very high resistivity. As the table in Concept 2 shows, there is an enormous range in the resistivity of materials.

The table includes nichrome, an alloy of nickel and chromium. Due to its high resistivity, Nichrome is commonly used in hot plates, toasters and other electrical appliances that generate intense heat. Its large amount of resistivity causes electrons in the current to lose energy to the nichrome atoms, increasing their thermal energy.

Extension cords, designed to allow current to flow safely from one point to another, take advantage of the relative resistivities of materials. The cords typically are composed of copper wire, a material with low resistivity, surrounded by rubber or vinyl, materials with high resistivity. Electrical current flows readily through the copper, but not through the material that surrounds it.

Resistivity is a property of a material. Its units are the ohm·meter ($\Omega\cdot$m). In contrast, resistance is the property of a component like a resistor or the filament in a light bulb. Resistivity is one factor that determines a resistor's resistance; the other factor is the geometry of the resistor. The longer a resistor, the greater its resistance; the wider it is (the greater its cross sectional area), the less its resistance. Again, water can be used to provide an analogy: a long, thin pipe resists the flow of water more than a short, fat one.

The equation used to calculate resistance as a function of a resistor's geometry and composition is shown in Equation 1.

The problem in Example 1 asks you to compute the amount of resistance found in a segment of copper wire. The resistance of resistors that are sold in electronics shops runs from the tens of ohms to the thousands of ohms and beyond. When electric circuits are analyzed, the resistance of wire is often ignored because it is relatively insignificant.

The low resistivity of wire, along with Ohm's law, helps to answer a question physicists like to pose: Why can a bird safely stand on an unshielded high voltage line? Why does the bird not get injured as current flows up one of its feet, through its body, and down the other foot?

concept 1

Rubber Eraser

Copper
good conductor,
low resistivity

Rubber
poor conductor,
high resistivity

Resistivity
Inverse of conductivity
· Conductors have low resistivity

· Insulators have high resistivity

concept 2

RESISTIVITIES ($\Omega\cdot$ m), at 20° C

Conductors		Semi-conductors	
Silver	1.6×10^{-8}	Carbon	3.5×10^{-5}
Copper	1.7×10^{-8}	Silicon	2.5×10^{3}
Aluminum	2.7×10^{-8}		
Iron	9.6×10^{-8}	Insulators	
Platinum	10.5×10^{-8}	Glass	$10^{10} - 10^{14}$
Nichrome	107.5×10^{-8}	Rubber	1.0×10^{13}

Table of resistivities, ρ

The answer is that the potential difference is very small across the segment of wire involved because the wire's resistance is quite low. Its resistance is low because the segment is wide and short and is made of a material with low resistivity. Ohm's law states that the potential difference is the product of the current and the resistance. With low resistance, there is very little potential difference. With very little potential difference, effectively no current flows through the bird.

Do NOT test this out yourself. High voltage lines are enormously dangerous. If you touch such a line while standing on the ground, you are providing a path for current to flow from the wire to the Earth. The potential difference between these points is enormous, and the resulting current could kill you.

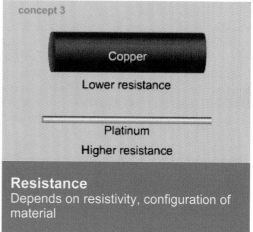

concept 3

Copper
Lower resistance

Platinum
Higher resistance

Resistance
Depends on resistivity, configuration of material

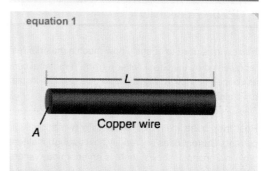

equation 1

L

A

Copper wire

Resistance

$$R = \rho \frac{L}{A}$$

R = resistance of component
ρ = resistivity of material
L = length of component
A = cross-sectional area
Units of resistivity: $\Omega \cdot m$ (ohm-meters)

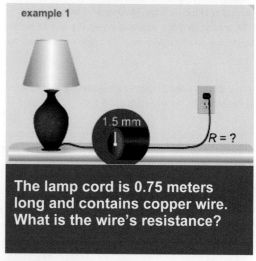

example 1

1.5 mm

$R = ?$

The lamp cord is 0.75 meters long and contains copper wire. What is the wire's resistance?

Copyright 2000-2007 Kinetic Books Co. Chapter 25

$$R = \rho \frac{L}{A} = \rho \frac{L}{\pi r^2}$$

$$R = (1.7 \times 10^{-8} \ \Omega \cdot m) \frac{(0.75 \ m)}{\pi (0.0015 \ m)^2}$$

$$R = 0.0018 \ \Omega$$

25.6 - Resistivity and temperature

The resistance of many conductors increases with temperature. As the temperature of the metal coils of the hot plate shown on the right increases, so do the resistivity of the metal and resistance of the coils. Other materials, such as semiconductors, have decreasing resistivity with temperature.

Equation 1 shows two equations that reflect the relationship of resistivity and resistance to temperature. Both include the *temperature coefficient of resistivity*, represented by α (the Greek letter alpha). A table of these coefficients is shown in Concept 2 for some materials. These coefficients are empirically determined and apply over a specific range of temperatures. To apply the resistivity equation, the material's resistivity must be known at one temperature, T_1. Its temperature coefficient of resistivity must also be known for the temperature T_1. These values are used to calculate the resistivity at another temperature.

The second equation is used to determine the change in resistance of a resistor. If the resistance of a resistor is known at one temperature, the equation can be used to calculate its resistance at another temperature. This equation can be derived from the first.

In Example 1, we use this equation to calculate the change in resistance of a nichrome coil in a hot plate that is heated from $25°C$ to $375°C$.

concept 1

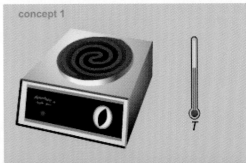

In many materials:
Resistivity and resistance vary linearly with temperature

concept 2

	Temperature coefficient of resistivity, α, at 20°C ($°C^{-1}$)
Brass	0.0015
Copper (drawn)	0.00393
Iron (electrolytic)	0.0064
Platinum silver	0.00031
Silver	0.0038
Tungsten	0.005
Carbon	negative*
Germanium	negative*
Silicon	negative*

*Dependent upon purity of sample

Temperature coefficient of resistivity, α
Positive α indicates resistivity increases with temperature
Negative α indicates resistivity decreases with temperature

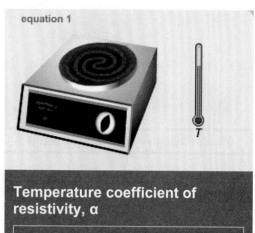

equation 1

Temperature coefficient of resistivity, α

$$\rho_2 = \rho_1[1 + \alpha(T_2 - T_1)]$$
$$R_2 = R_1[1 + \alpha(T_2 - T_1)]$$

ρ = resistivity
α = temperature coeff. of resistivity
T = temperature
R = resistance

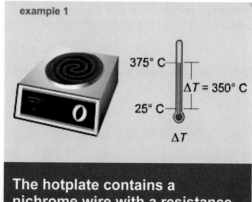

example 1

375° C
ΔT = 350° C
25° C
ΔT

The hotplate contains a nichrome wire with a resistance of 15 Ω at 25°C. What is its resistance at 375°C? For this nichrome alloy, α = 4.0×10⁻⁴ °C⁻¹ at 25°C.

$$R_2 = R_1[1 + \alpha(T_2 - T_1)]$$
$$R_2 = R_1[1 + (4.0\times10^{-4}\ °\text{C}^{-1})(T_2 - T_1)]$$
$$R_2 = 15\ \Omega\ [1 + (4.0\times10^{-4})(350)]$$
$$R_2 = 17\ \Omega$$

25.7 - Electric power

Power is defined as work per unit time. Power also can be stated as the amount of energy transfer per unit time, and this is often a useful formulation when considering electric circuits.

Electrical devices are often rated on how much energy they use per second. A 100-watt light bulb requires an average of 100 joules every second. As it operates, the light bulb's filament warms up and emits heat. This flow of heat from a resistor is called *joule heating*.

Power can also be calculated as the product of current flowing through a resistor and the potential difference across it. This is the equation in the first line in Equation 1. Ohm's law can be used to then restate this equation in terms of resistance and current, or in terms of potential difference and resistance. We show these equations in the second line in Equation 1.

In the example problem, we simplify things by using an average or constant value for current and potential difference − likely this burner is powered with an alternating current where these values vary. Alternating current (AC) is a topic later in the textbook.

Below we derive the first equation, $P = I\Delta V$. Before deriving it, we review why a resistor consumes power. The essential component of many household devices − toasters, light bulbs, electric burners − is a resistor.

As electrons move through any resistor, they collide with the atoms that make up the resistor. The electrons lose energy in these collisions and the atoms gain it, which increases the temperature of the resistor. More current through a given resistor means more collisions, and a warmer resistor. This analysis confirms one aspect of the power equation: Power increases with the amount of current.

To derive the power equation, we will consider the work done on the electron by the electric field. We will state the work in terms of the potential difference: It equals the charge times the potential difference. We will use that equation to derive the power equation.

Variables

work	W
total charge moving across resistor	q
potential difference across resistor	ΔV
time interval	Δt
power consumed by resistor	P
current passing through resistor	I

Strategy

1. State the equation that relates work, charge and potential difference.
2. Divide by the time interval Δt to calculate the work per unit time, which is power.

Equations

Here, work is related to charge and potential difference by

$$W = \Delta PE = q\Delta V$$

We will also use the definitions of power and current.

$$P = \frac{W}{\Delta t}, \quad I = \frac{q}{\Delta t}$$

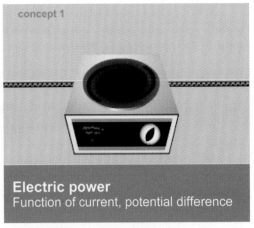

concept 1

Electric power
Function of current, potential difference

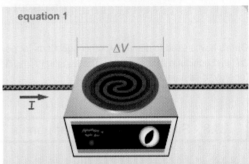

equation 1

Electric power

$$P = I\Delta V$$
$$P = I^2 R = \Delta V^2/R$$

P = power
I = current
ΔV = potential difference
R = resistance

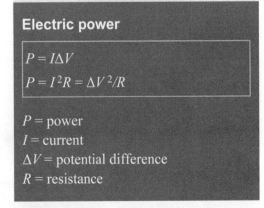

example 1

$\Delta V = 120$ V

$I = 8.00$ A

How much power is being supplied to this hot plate?
$$P = I\Delta V$$
$$P = (8.00 \text{ A})(120 \text{ V})$$

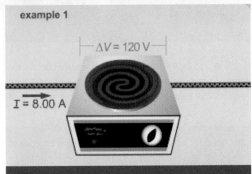

Step-by-step derivation

We state the relationship between work and potential difference, then divide by the time interval Δt. This converts work to power and total charge to current, resulting in the first formulation of the power equation.

$$P = 960 \text{ W}$$

Step	Reason
1. $W = q\Delta V$	work and potential difference
2. $\dfrac{W}{\Delta t} = \dfrac{q\Delta V}{\Delta t}$	divide by Δt
3. $P = I\Delta V$	definitions of power and current

Ohm's law is used to derive the other equations for power in the second line of Equation 1. For instance, $\Delta V = IR$, so we can substitute for ΔV and conclude that $P = I^2R$. The equation $P = I\Delta V$ holds true for all electrical devices, while the other equations apply solely to power (energy) dissipated as heat by resistors.

25.8 - Sample problem: solar panels

This public school uses solar power. Using information supplied below, determine how many watt-hours of electricity the solar panels will provide during their lifetime.

What will the cost per kW·h of the solar panel system be over its lifetime? Suppose the cost of traditional energy will average $0.11 per kilowatt-hour over the next 25 years. Will the school save money?

A school in Los Angeles is deciding whether or not to install solar panels on its roof. The photovoltaic system under consideration provides 680 watts of power under direct sunlight, costs $3500, and is expected to last 25 years, according to the experts at Stewart Solar Systems. In Los Angeles the average *insolation*, or equivalent hours of direct sunlight reaching the Earth's surface, is 5.62 hours per day.

(a) How many watt-hours of electricity will the solar panels provide during their lifetime? (A watt-hour is a unit of energy just like the Joule; it is calculated by multiplying the power and the amount of time that power is produced.)

(b) Suppose the cost of electricity coming from the local utility company is predicted to average $0.11 per kilowatt-hour (kW·h) over the next 25 years. What is the cost per kW·h of the solar panel system over its lifetime? Should the school buy the solar panels?

Variables

generation power of solar panel system	$P = 680$ W
lifetime of system	$t = 25$ y
average equivalent hours of sunlight per day	$s = 5.62$ h/d
equivalent hours of sunlight over system lifetime	S
energy produced over system lifetime	E
price of utility electricity per kW·h	$p = \$0.11$
one-time cost of solar panel system	$C = \$3500$
cost of solar panel system per kW·h	c

What is the strategy?

1. Find the total number of hours of direct sunlight the solar panels will receive over their lifetime.
2. Calculate the number of watt-hours the solar panels will produce over their lifetime. Convert to kW·h.
3. Calculate the price per kW·h from the solar panels and compare it with the utility company's price.

Physics principles and equations

Power stated as energy used over a period of time

$$P = \Delta E / \Delta t$$

Step-by-step solution

First, find the total amount of energy the solar panels will produce over their lifetime.

Step	Reason
1. $S = st$	hours of sunlight over lifetime
2. $S = (5.62$ h/d$)(25$ y$)(365$ d/y$)$ $S = 51{,}283$ h	enter values
3. $E = PS$	energy produced over lifetime
4. $E = (680$ W$)(51{,}283$ h$) = 3.49 \times 10^{7}$ W·h	enter values

For part (b), calculate the cost per $kW \cdot h$.

Step	Reason
5. $E = (3.49 \times 10^7 \text{ W·h})/(1000 \text{ kW/W})$ $E = 3.49 \times 10^4 \text{ kW·h}$	convert to $kW \cdot h$
6. $c = C/E$	cost per $kW \cdot h$
7. $c = (\$3500)/(3.49 \times 10^4 \text{ kW·h})$ $c = \$0.10/\text{ kW·h}$	enter values

This is **less** than the predicted cost of electricity from the utility company, so the school will save money in electricity costs if they install the solar panels. Even better, by using renewable energy they will contribute to a less polluted future.

On the web, you can find out more about solar energy and find out the average insolation anywhere in the world.

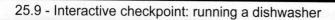

25.9 - Interactive checkpoint: running a dishwasher

Suppose you measure the current flow to a dishwasher and find that the average current is 9.50 A over the 45.0-minute dishwasher cycle. The dishwasher is powered by a potential difference of 120 V. If electricity costs $0.0900 per kilowatt-hour, what is the cost of running one dishwasher load?

Answer:

$p = \$$ [_____] per dishwasher cycle

25.10 - Sample problem: using a hair dryer

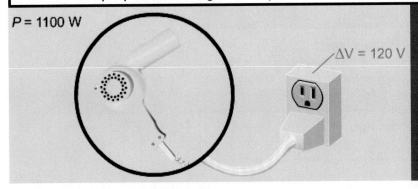

$P = 1100$ W

$\Delta V = 120$ V

The label on an electric blow dryer says it uses 1100 W and is designed for 120 V outlets. How much current flows through the hair dryer? What is its resistance?

Here, you will treat the hair dryer as though it were a direct current (DC) appliance.

Variables

power rating	$P = 1100$ W
potential difference	$\Delta V = 120$ V
current	I
resistance	R

What is the strategy?

1. Use the equation for power as a function of current and voltage to find the current through the hair dryer.
2. Use Ohm's law to find the hair dryer's resistance.

Physics principles and equations

Power in an electric circuit

$$P = I\Delta V$$

Ohm's law

$$\Delta V = IR$$

Step-by-step solution

We use the power equation to find the current through the hair dryer.

Step	Reason
1. $P = I\Delta V$	power equation
2. $I = \dfrac{P}{\Delta V}$	solve for I
3. $I = (1100 \text{ W})/(120 \text{ V}) = 9.2$ A	evaluate

Now we can use the current to find the resistance of the hair dryer.

Step	Reason
4. $\Delta V = IR$	Ohm's law
5. $R = \dfrac{\Delta V}{I}$	solve for R
6. $R = \dfrac{120\text{ V}}{9.2\text{ A}} = 13\ \Omega$	evaluate

25.11 - Sample problem: power transmission

A power plant provides 450 MW of power through transmission lines at a potential difference of 500 kV. What current flows through the lines?

For a city 300 km away from the power plant the total resistance in the transmission lines is 60 ohms. What fraction of the generated power is dissipated as "line loss"?

If the generated power is transmitted at a potential difference of 175 kV instead, what fraction is dissipated?

Variables

generated power	$P = 450 \times 10^6$ W
transmission line potential difference	ΔV
resistance	$R = 60\ \Omega$
dissipated power	P_{D}

What is the strategy?

1. Find the current in the wire using the equation for power in terms of the potential difference and the current.
2. Calculate the power dissipated by the power lines using the equation for power dissipated by a resistor.
3. Divide the dissipated power by the generated power to find the fraction of the power dissipated by the lines.
4. Repeat this calculation for the last question asked above.

Physics principles and equations

Power as a function of potential difference and current

$$P = I\Delta V$$

Power dissipated by a resistor

$$P = I^2 R$$

Power in an electric circuit

$$P = (\Delta V)^2 / R$$

Step-by-step solution

First we calculate the current in the transmission lines when the potential difference is 500 kV. We do this using the power for the power plant and the potential difference across the wires, which are both stated above.

Step	Reason
1. $\quad P = I \Delta V$	power equation
2. $\quad I = \dfrac{P}{\Delta V}$	solve for I
3. $\quad I = \dfrac{(450 \times 10^6 \text{ W})}{(500 \times 10^3 \text{ V})}$ $\quad I = 900 \text{ A}$	evaluate

First, we find the power dissipated as heat by the wire. Then we divide that by the amount of power generated by the plant to determine what fraction is wasted.

Step	Reason
4. $\quad P_D = I^2 R$	power dissipated by a resistor
5. $\quad P_D = (900 \text{ A})^2 (60 \ \Omega)$ $\quad P_D = 48.6 \times 10^6 \text{ W}$	evaluate
6. $\quad \dfrac{P_D}{P} = \dfrac{48.6 \times 10^6 \text{ W}}{450 \times 10^6 \text{ W}}$ $\quad \dfrac{P_D}{P} = 0.108$	divide by generated power

For the second case we repeat the same calculations with a lesser potential difference.

Step	Reason
7. $$I = \frac{450 \times 10^6 \text{ W}}{175 \times 10^3 \text{ V}}$$ $$I = 2570 \text{ A}$$	evaluate equation in step 2
8. $$P_D = (2570 \text{ A})^2 (60 \ \Omega)$$ $$P_D = 397 \times 10^6 \text{ W}$$	power dissipated by resistor
9. $$\frac{P_D}{P} = \frac{397 \times 10^3 \text{ W}}{450 \times 10^3 \text{ W}}$$ $$\frac{P_D}{P} = 0.882$$	evaluate

The differing rates of power consumption explain why power companies transmit power at high potential differences. The potential difference is lowered at transformers near the consumer. (Transformers are discussed further in the chapter on electromagnetic induction.) The potential difference is lowered to 120 V, the standard potential difference of a power outlet in a house, just before it enters the house or building using the power.

25.12 - Gotchas

Do conventional current arrows reflect the flow of negative or positive charge? Positive charge. Although in a typical current found in household appliances and such, it is negatively charged electrons that flow, the convention is that the arrow indicates the direction of positive charge flow. If electrons flow to the left, the conventional current arrow points to the right.

Current decreases when passing through a resistor and then increases again upon exiting. No. The current before, in and after the resistor is the same.

A wire with a current has a net electrostatic charge. No. Although there is a net charge flowing by any given point, the overall wire is neutral.

A person walks by. The person contains electrons. Therefore, there is a current. No, the person is electrically neutral. Current is the flow of net charge. In this case, there is no movement of **net** charge and therefore no current. If the person were electrically charged, there would be a current as the person passed by.

Electric current is the rate at which charge flows through a conductor. The symbol for current is I and it is measured in amperes (A), where 1 A = 1 C/s.

Current usually consists of moving electrons, which have negative charge. However, current is almost always represented in descriptions and diagrams as conventional current, which is a flow of positive charges that would constitute the same current, so the direction of conventional current is opposite to the actual movement of electrons. Even though drawings often show the direction of current with an arrow, current is a scalar.

Individual electrons in a wire travel much more slowly than the electric field that propels them. Collisions with the atoms that make up the wire prevent the electrons' continued acceleration, and cause them to follow a meandering zigzag path. The drift speed is the average net speed of electrons along the wire. In household wiring, it is about the speed of a snail.

Equations

Definition of current

$$I = \frac{\Delta q}{\Delta t}$$

Ohm's law

$$\Delta V = IR$$

Electric power equations

$$P = I\Delta V$$

$$P = I^2 R = \Delta V^2 / R$$

Ohm's law states the relationship between potential difference, current and resistance. A resistor is an electrical component that can be used to regulate current. A particular resistor is characterized by its resistance. Resistance is measured in ohms (Ω). 1 Ω = 1 V/A.

Resistivity is a measure of how much the material resists current. For a simple wire made of a single material, the resistance is the resistivity of the material times the wire's length, divided by its cross-sectional area.

The temperature of a material can affect its resistivity.

Energy is dissipated, often as heat, when an electric current passes through a resistance. Electric power measures the amount of energy consumed per unit time. It is equal to the current through a circuit element times the potential difference across it. Sometimes, as when a battery is being charged, the energy consumed is stored rather than dissipated. For resistors that obey Ohm's Law, the two equations shown in the last line on the right may also be used to calculate power.

26.0 - Introduction

Capacitors store charge, and in doing so, they store energy. They are used to store energy in devices ranging from camera flashes to defibrillators, the systems used to "shock" the human heart back into its proper rhythm.

Capacitors are employed for other purposes as well. Because it takes a fixed amount of time to charge or discharge a given capacitor, capacitors are used in circuits where timing is essential, such as the tuner of a radio.

The "capacitor tree" (left) at the Fermilab National Accelerator Laboratory stored huge amounts of energy for high-energy accelerator experiments.

At the right, you see the design of a basic capacitor. It consists of two conducting plates separated by air. There is a wire connected to each plate, and these wires are attached to a source of potential difference that has caused the plates to become charged. The amounts of charge on the plates are equal in magnitude but opposite in sign.

You can launch the simulation and try an experiment that demonstrates one of the capacitor's fundamental properties. In the simulation, you can change the potential difference across the plates with the ΔV controller next to the capacitor. When you change the potential difference, note what happens to the amount of charge stored by the capacitor. The approximate charge is displayed visually on the capacitor plates; for a more precise value you can rely on the charge readout gauge displayed below. Is the charge proportional to the potential difference?

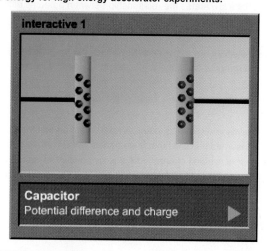

interactive 1

Capacitor
Potential difference and charge

26.1 - Capacitors

Capacitor: A device with two conducting plates that can hold equal but opposite amounts of charge.

Capacitance: The ratio of the charge on one of the capacitor's plates to the potential difference between the plates.

Various capacitors

The simplest capacitors consist of two parallel metal plates separated by a narrow gap. We use this configuration, a parallel-plate capacitor, for the definitions above. A battery (or other source of potential difference) causes the plates to become electrically charged: The plates contain equal but opposite amounts of charge. An insulator, which can be as simple as an air gap, separates the plates.

The capacitance of a capacitor tells how much charge it can store for a given potential difference between the plates; specifically, it equals the value of the positive charge on one plate in coulombs, divided by the potential difference in volts, a relationship shown in Equation 1. The amount of charge on **one** plate is represented by the letter q. The potential difference is also measured as a positive value, so charge, potential difference and capacitance are all positive values.

The geometry of a capacitor and the nature of its insulator are the two factors that determine its capacitance. Capacitors with larger plates, or with plates separated by a narrower distance, have greater capacitance.

The other factor that can affect capacitance is the nature of the insulator between the plates. This insulator is called a *dielectric*. Air is one dielectric, but other dielectrics can be used to increase the capacitance.

The unit of measure of capacitance is the farad (F), named after the physicist Michael Faraday. A one-farad capacitor has a great deal of capacitance. It can store a lot of charge. Many commonly encountered capacitors have capacitances ranging from microfarads (10^{-6} F) down to picofarads (10^{-12} F). However, capacitors with greater capacitances certainly exist: car audio enthusiasts often boast systems employing one-farad capacitors.

The movement of electrons creates the charges on the two plates of a capacitor. They move away from one plate, leaving a net positive charge behind, and go toward the other plate, which takes on a negative charge. Note that the electrons do **not** move across the gap between the plates. Rather, they move along the wires whose ends you see in the illustrations.

A source of potential difference such as a battery exerts a force on the electrons, causing them to move. This force through a distance constitutes work. The amount of work done during the charging process equals the electric potential energy stored by the plates. The greater the charge on its plates, the greater the amount of energy a particular capacitor is storing.

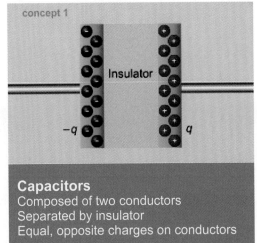

concept 1

Capacitors
Composed of two conductors
Separated by insulator
Equal, opposite charges on conductors

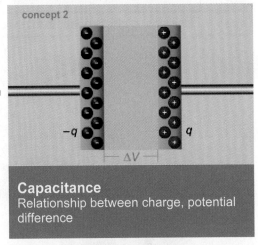

concept 2

Capacitance
Relationship between charge, potential difference

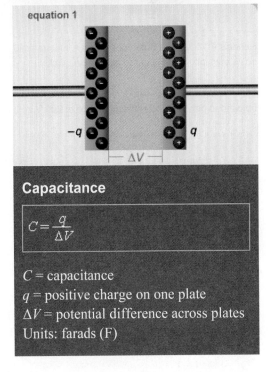

equation 1

Capacitance

$$C = \frac{q}{\Delta V}$$

C = capacitance
q = positive charge on one plate
ΔV = potential difference across plates
Units: farads (F)

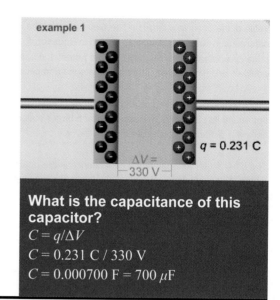

example 1

$q = 0.231$ C

$\Delta V = 330$ V

What is the capacitance of this capacitor?

$C = q/\Delta V$

$C = 0.231$ C $/ 330$ V

$C = 0.000700$ F $= 700 \ \mu F$

26.2 - Interactive checkpoint: the fuel-cell car

How much charge does an 8.00-farad ultracapacitor accumulate when it is charged with a potential difference of 200 V?

Honda's FCX fuel-cell automobile uses a custom built, 8.00-farad *ultracapacitor* that provides power in faster bursts than a fuel cell can deliver on its own, allowing the car to accelerate quickly.

The ultracapacitor is charged by both the car's fuel cell and energy recovered each time the car brakes. Together, these energy sources can be used to provide a potential difference of 200 V across the capacitor electrodes (plates).

Answer:

$q =$ [   ] C

Your computer keyboard may contain capacitors. In some types of keyboards, each key sits above its own capacitor. Although more expensive to produce than those based on other designs, capacitor based keyboards are more reliable. The bottom part of the capacitor is fixed, and the top is a movable plate. A springy insulating material separates the plates. As you press down on a key, the two plates of its capacitor are pushed closer together. Since this changes the geometry of the capacitor, it also changes the capacitance: Specifically, it increases it.

A microprocessor in the keyboard interprets the change in capacitance as a signal that the key has been pressed.

The keyboard microprocessor relays this information to the computer's central processing unit, which responds to it according to which application is running. For example, a word processor might display the keystroke as a character, while a game might interpret it as a command for a player to shoot a basketball.

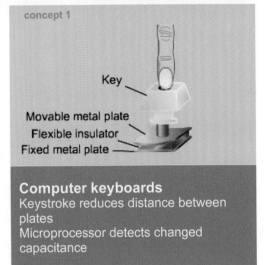

concept 1

Key

Movable metal plate
Flexible insulator
Fixed metal plate

Computer keyboards
Keystroke reduces distance between plates
Microprocessor detects changed capacitance

26.4 - Energy in capacitors

Capacitors store energy. A battery or other device performs work as its electric field pulls electrons from the positive plate of a capacitor and pushes them to the negative plate. The force of this field drives electrons away from the attractive force of the positive plate and toward the repulsive force of other electrons already on the negative plate. This work increases the electric potential energy of the capacitor.

To the right you see two equations that express the energy stored in a capacitor. The first equation is stated in terms of the charge on the capacitor; the second is stated in terms of the potential difference across the capacitor. We can derive these equations by calculating the work required to move each charge from one plate to the other.

The example problem asks you to find the amount of energy stored in a capacitor with a potential difference of 25,000 V across its plates. This is representative of the voltages found in television sets. The stored energy in a TV capacitor can give you a dangerous shock, even after the set is unplugged. This is why the back panels of televisions are labeled with warnings against attempting to disassemble them yourself. We recommend that you follow this advice!

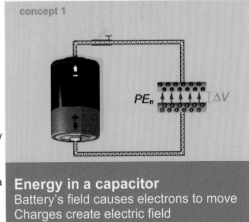

concept 1

PE_n ΔV

Energy in a capacitor
Battery's field causes electrons to move
Charges create electric field
Electric field stores energy

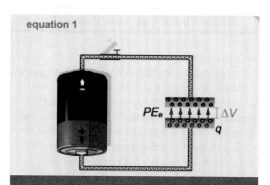

equation 1

Energy in a capacitor

$$PE_e = \frac{q^2}{2C}$$

$$PE_e = \frac{C(\Delta V)^2}{2}$$

PE_e = electric potential energy
q = charge on capacitor plate
C = capacitance
ΔV = potential difference

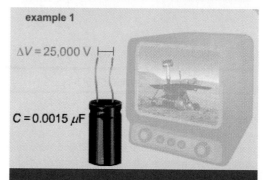

example 1

$\Delta V = 25{,}000$ V

$C = 0.0015\ \mu F$

What is the electric potential energy stored in this capacitor?

$PE_e = C(\Delta V)^2\,/2$
$PE_e = (0.0015\ \mu F)(25{,}000\ V)^2\,/2$
$PE_e = (1.5\times10^{-9}\ F)(2.5\times10^4\ V)^2\,/2$
$PE_e = 0.47$ J

26.5 - Interactive checkpoint: energy in a fuel-cell car

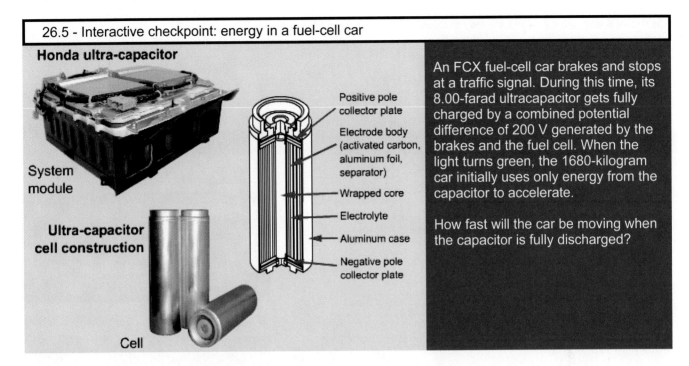

Honda ultra-capacitor

System module

Ultra-capacitor cell construction

Cell

Positive pole collector plate

Electrode body (activated carbon, aluminum foil, separator)

Wrapped core

Electrolyte

Aluminum case

Negative pole collector plate

An FCX fuel-cell car brakes and stops at a traffic signal. During this time, its 8.00-farad ultracapacitor gets fully charged by a combined potential difference of 200 V generated by the brakes and the fuel cell. When the light turns green, the 1680-kilogram car initially uses only energy from the capacitor to accelerate.

How fast will the car be moving when the capacitor is fully discharged?

In this problem, assume that road friction, air resistance, and electrical resistance use up 20.0% of the energy available, and that the rest of the electric potential energy stored in the capacitor's electric field is transformed into the kinetic energy of the car.

State your answer in miles per hour (1.00 m/s = 2.24 mph).

Answer:

$v =$ [   ] mph

26.6 - Physics in medicine: defibrillator

Although electricity can be harmful if misused, doctors have used it for medicinal purposes since the days of the ancient Greeks. For example, early physicians used discharges from the electric torpedo fish to relieve aches and pains.

Electricity continues to be used in medicine. If you have ever watched the television show *ER*, chances are you have become well acquainted with a device called a *defibrillator*. The heart relies on electrical impulses to cause its muscles to contract. When the muscle cells of the heart begin to contract out of

Cardiac defibrillator.

synchronization, or to fibrillate, a defibrillator can be used to jolt them back into a synchronous rhythm. Contrary to popular belief, defibrillators are not used to "restart" a heart that has stopped beating. You may get the impression from TV shows that doctors use defibrillators as frequently as stethoscopes, but that is just one of the exaggerations of television. However, these instruments are becoming standard equipment in ambulances and on airplanes.

A conceptual diagram of a defibrillator is shown on the right. The source of potential difference on the left charges the capacitor. When the switch on the right is closed, the capacitor rapidly discharges, sending an electrical current through the patient's heart.

The example problem shows how to calculate the average current when the discharge time, capacitance and potential difference are known.

The current is large, but it lasts for just a few milliseconds, providing a powerful but brief shock.

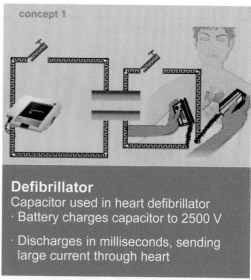

concept 1

Defibrillator
Capacitor used in heart defibrillator
· Battery charges capacitor to 2500 V

· Discharges in milliseconds, sending large current through heart

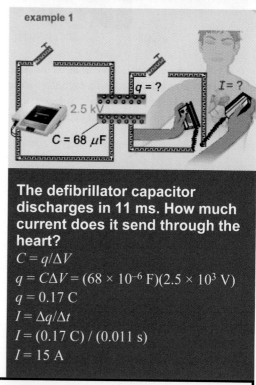

example 1

$q = ?$ $I = ?$

2.5 kV

$C = 68\ \mu F$

The defibrillator capacitor discharges in 11 ms. How much current does it send through the heart?
$C = q/\Delta V$
$q = C\Delta V = (68 \times 10^{-6}\ \text{F})(2.5 \times 10^3\ \text{V})$
$q = 0.17\ \text{C}$
$I = \Delta q/\Delta t$
$I = (0.17\ \text{C}) / (0.011\ \text{s})$
$I = 15\ \text{A}$

26.7 - An insulator (dielectric) in an electric field

The simplest capacitor is made up of two plates separated by a vacuum. In this section we will discuss what happens when an insulating material, a *dielectric*, is placed between the plates.

Like a vacuum, this insulating material is intended to prevent the flow of charge between the plates, but it has another effect, as well: It reduces the overall strength of the field between the plates, and this proves to be a desirable effect.

To understand how a dielectric reduces the net field, let's first consider what happens when an atom is placed in the electric field generated by two charged plates. It might seem that nothing would happen because the atom is electrically neutral.

However, an atom is made up of a positive nucleus surrounded by negative electrons. If the field is very strong, it can *ionize* atoms, separating electrons from the atoms. At this point, the dielectric material becomes a conductor: Current can flow between the plates, causing the capacitor to break down. Although an interesting phenomenon to witness, this outcome is not relevant to the rest of this section.

Less extreme fields can *polarize* an atom, in essence stretching it so that its electrons tend to be on one side and its positive nucleus is on the other. This turns the atom into a dipole, a body with positively and negatively charged regions.

Some kinds of molecules, such as water molecules, are always dipoles. This type of molecule (called a *polar molecule*) has regions of positive and negative charge based on its structure. When no external electric field is present, the dipoles of substances such as water are randomly aligned, and they create no net electric field.

When a substance containing dipoles is placed in the electric field between a charged capacitor's plates, the field will cause some of the dipoles to align so that their positive poles point toward the negative plate and their negative poles point toward the positive plate.

Many, but by no means all, of the dipoles that compose the substance will align in this manner with the external field. Their random thermal motion provides a constant counterbalance to the organizing tendency of the field. The effect of the alignment that does occur is to weaken the overall field between the plates. There are two ways to understand the weakening of the capacitor field in the presence of a dielectric.

First, consider the net effect of the individual fields of all the aligned dipoles. Each aligned dipole has its own electric field, oriented in the direction opposite to the field created by the plates. This is shown in Concept 1. The aligned dipoles' fields reduce the overall field between the plates because they point oppositely to the capacitor's field.

You can also look at the diagram in Concept 2 to understand why the overall field is diminished. In the bulk of the dielectric the net charge is zero. This is because every aligned positive pole there is next to an aligned negative pole on a neighboring dipole, which it balances out. However, on the far left there is an unbalanced layer of negative charge, and on the far right there is an unbalanced layer of positive charge. This means there is a layer of negative charges adjacent to the positive plate of the capacitor and a layer of positive charges adjacent to the negative plate.

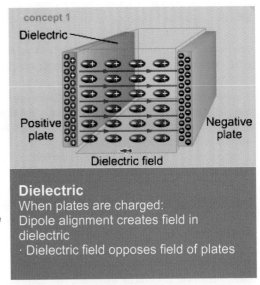

Dielectric
When plates are charged:
Dipole alignment creates field in dielectric
· Dielectric field opposes field of plates

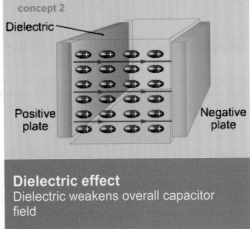

Dielectric effect
Dielectric weakens overall capacitor field

For this reason the entire dielectric material can be said to be polarized (to have positive and negative regions). This polarization decreases the net charge in close proximity to the surface of each capacitor plate. The net charge of each plate is now the charge on the plate surface minus the charge on the adjacent face of the dielectric. Less effective charge on each plate surface means the overall field between the plates is weaker.

26.8 - Dielectrics

Dielectric: An insulating substance placed between the plates of a capacitor to increase its capacitance.

Dielectric constant (κ): Measures reduction in electric field caused by a dielectric. It equals the ratio of the field in a vacuum to the field in the dielectric.

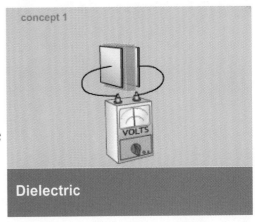

Dielectric

Dielectrics are insulating materials used in capacitors to increase their capacitance. Effective dielectrics make possible the manufacture of small, high-farad capacitors.

The materials discussed in this section are *linear dielectrics*. The dielectric field of a linear dielectric is linearly proportional to the strength of the external electric field.

The dielectric constant, represented by κ (Greek letter kappa), is a property of a material. It equals the ratio of two electric fields: the electric field inside a capacitor with a vacuum separating the plates and the field strength for the same capacitor charge with the dielectric present. This is stated in Equation 1. The greater the dielectric field within a dielectric, the more it diminishes the field caused by the plates, and the greater the value of the dielectric constant.

Dielectrics increase the capacitance of capacitors. As is stated in Equation 2, the capacitance with the dielectric present equals the capacitance without it times the dielectric constant.

The table in Equation 3 lists some dielectric constants. As you can see, the dielectric constants for vacuum and air are quite close. Strontium titanate, a substance used in commercial capacitors, has a far greater dielectric constant, especially at low temperatures, than a vacuum or air.

Dielectrics also can be classified by their *dielectric strength*. The dielectric strength characterizes the field strength at which the dielectric becomes a conductor and charge will flow through it. This is not a desirable effect, so capacitors are often labeled with their maximum safe field strength (in V/m). Like many stress properties, the dielectric strength of a material can be difficult to determine precisely, so the stated dielectric strength should be an approximate, conservative value. The dielectric strengths of selected materials are also shown in the table.

Lightning is a very visible example of the breakdown of a dielectric – air – between oppositely charged objects, such as two clouds or a cloud and the nearby surface of the Earth. When the electric field between them becomes strong enough, the separating atmosphere becomes a conductor and current flows through it as a lightning bolt.

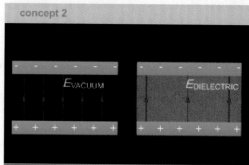

Insulator that increases capacitance

concept 2

Dielectrics and electric fields
Dielectric diminishes electric field

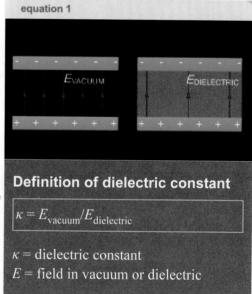

equation 1

Definition of dielectric constant

$$\kappa = E_{vacuum}/E_{dielectric}$$

κ = dielectric constant
E = field in vacuum or dielectric

equation 2

Same potential difference

Lesser charge   Greater charge

Capacitance with dielectric present

$$C_\kappa = \kappa C$$

C_κ = capacitance with dielectric

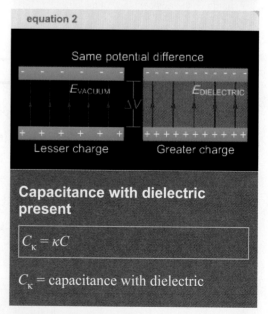

κ = dielectric constant
C = capacitance with vacuum

equation 3

	Dielectric constant	Dielectric strength (in 10^6 V/m)
Vacuum	1	n/a
Air	1.00054	3.0
Paper	1.7 to 2.6	4 to 9
Rubber	2 to 3.5	20 to 27
Glass	5.4 to 9.9	30 to 150
Water (293K)	80.20	65 to 70
Strontium titanate (298K, 78K)	332, 2080	

Table of dielectric constants

example 1

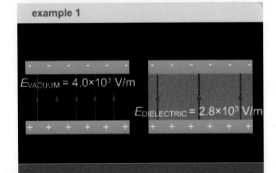

The capacitors have identical dimensions and charges. What is the dielectric constant of the dielectric on the right?

$\kappa = E_{vacuum}/E_{dielectric}$

$\kappa = (4.0 \times 10^3 \text{ V/m}) / (2.8 \times 10^3 \text{ V/m})$

$\kappa = 1.4$ (dimensionless)

A battery causes the plates of a capacitor to charge so that the potential difference between them is 9.0 V. The capacitor is then isolated so that its charge remains constant and the battery no longer acts on it.

After a dielectric (K = 16) is inserted between the plates, what is the potential difference between them?

Variables

initial potential difference	$\Delta V = 9.0 \text{ V}$
initial capacitance	C
charge on capacitor	q
dielectric constant of material	$\kappa = 16$
capacitance with dielectric present	C_κ
potential difference with dielectric present	ΔV_κ

Strategy

1. Use the definition of capacitance, and the equation for capacitance with a dielectric present, to determine the potential difference when the dielectric is present.

Physics principles and equations

The definition of capacitance is

$$C = q/\Delta V$$

The relation between capacitances with and without a dielectric present is

$$C_\kappa = \kappa C$$

Charge in any isolated system is conserved.

Step-by-step solution

We use the definition of capacitance twice; once when the dielectric is not present, and again when it is. The amount of charge remains constant since the capacitor is isolated.

Step	Reason
1. $q = C\Delta V$	definition of capacitance
2. $C_\kappa = \kappa C$	capacitance with dielectric
3. $\Delta V_\kappa = \dfrac{q}{C_\kappa}$	definition of capacitance

Now we combine the above expressions to find a relation between the potential differences with and without a dielectric present. We evaluate the resulting equation to answer the problem.

Step	Reason
4. $\Delta V_\kappa = \dfrac{C\Delta V}{\kappa C}$	substitute equations 1 and 2 into equation 3
5. $\Delta V_\kappa = \dfrac{\Delta V}{\kappa}$	simplify
6. $\Delta V_\kappa = \dfrac{9.0\ \text{V}}{16} = 0.56\ \text{V}$	evaluate

The potential difference between the plates after inserting the dielectric turns out to be the original potential difference divided by the dielectric constant. The higher the dielectric constant, the more the potential difference will be decreased after the dielectric is introduced.

This result is interesting when applied to the potential energy $PE_e = \frac{1}{2}C(\Delta V)^2$ stored by a capacitor. After you insert a dielectric, the potential energy becomes

$$PE_\kappa = \frac{1}{2}C_\kappa(\Delta V_\kappa)^2 = \frac{1}{2}(\kappa C)\left(\frac{\Delta V}{\kappa}\right)^2 = \frac{\frac{1}{2}C(\Delta V)^2}{\kappa} = \frac{PE_e}{\kappa}$$

In other words, the potential energy decreases when you insert a dielectric between the plates of a capacitor. Why? The capacitor is doing work on the dielectric as you insert it, rotating many of its small dipoles into alignment.

26.10 - Interactive checkpoint: dielectric in a capacitor

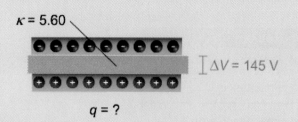

$\kappa = 5.60$

$\Delta V = 145$ V

$q = ?$

A parallel plate capacitor has a capacitance of 3.50 μF when a vacuum separates its plates. You insert an insulator with a dielectric constant of $\kappa = 5.60$ and apply a potential difference of 145 V across the plates.

How much charge builds up on a plate?

Answer:

$q =$ [   ] C

26.11 - Physics at work: commercial capacitors

Capacitors in electronic equipment, like a stereo system, that you might have at home are often made from two layers of metallic foil backed by thin sheets of a dielectric material. When these layers are rolled up, the result is a multilayer cylindrical capacitor with alternating positive and negative cylindrical conductors, separated by the dielectric material. Several capacitors of this type are shown in Concept 1.

A variable capacitor used for tuning a radio.

Higher voltage capacitors can consist of sets of thin parallel metallic plates immersed in insulating silicone oil. Other capacitors, capable of storing large amounts of charge, are made with insulators consisting of ceramic materials that can have very high dielectric constants.

A *variable capacitor*, like the one in the picture above, features interleaved metal plates. You change the capacitance by rotating the knob, increasing or decreasing how much of the area of each plate is close to the neighboring plates on either side. Devices like this can be used to change the capacitance of a circuit in a radio tuner, altering what is called the resonant frequency of the circuit and enabling it to "tune in" a radio station broadcasting at a particular frequency.

Electrolytic capacitors can operate with very high potential differences across their two conducting surfaces. An electrolyte is a nonmetallic conductor, or a substance that when dissolved in a suitable solvent becomes a conductor. In an electrolyte, current is composed of ions, not electrons.

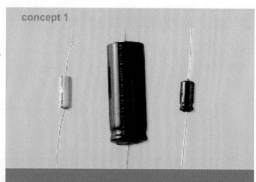

concept 1

Commercial capacitors
Rolled foil capacitors

In an electrolytic capacitor, one of the conductors is a solid or porous metal electrode, the dielectric is an insulating metal oxide coating on the surface of the electrode, and the other conductor is an electrolytic liquid or solid. Since the distance between the "plates" is the thickness of the insulating metal oxide, which is quite small, tiny electrolytic capacitors can have extremely high capacitance. The capacitors used in certain fuel-cell automobiles are a form of electrolytic capacitor.

26.12 - Gotchas

The total amount of charge on the plates of a capacitor is designated by q. No, the amount of charge on **one** plate of the capacitor is q. Each plate has the same amount of charge: positive on one plate and negative on the other. The total charge is zero.

Capacitors have a net charge. No, the two plates have equal and opposite amounts of charge, so the capacitor is electrically neutral. When you say "the capacitor has a charge" or the like, it means each plate is charged.

26.13 - Summary

A capacitor is a device with two conductors that are placed in close proximity, and which store equal but opposite amounts of charge.

Capacitors are characterized by their capacitance, represented by the symbol C, which equals the amount of charge on one conductor divided by the potential difference between the conductors. The unit of capacitance is the farad (F). 1 F = 1 C/V.

By storing charge, capacitors also store electric potential energy. A battery or other device causes charge to accumulate on the conductors of the capacitor. The opposite charges on the conductors create an electric field between them. Electric potential energy is stored in the electric field.

Between the conductors of a capacitor there may be a dielectric, an insulator that can increase the capacitance by decreasing the field strength between the conductors for a given charge. The factor characterizing the increase in capacitance (or the decrease in field strength) is called the dielectric constant, κ.

Equations

Definition of capacitance

$$C = \frac{q}{\Delta V}$$

Potential energy in a capacitor

$$PE_e = \frac{q^2}{2C}$$

$$PE_e = \frac{C(\Delta V^2)}{2}$$

Dielectric constant

$$\kappa = E_{vacuum} / E_{dielectric}$$

$$C_\kappa = \kappa C$$

□ Conceptual physics

kinetic BOOKS

27.0 - Introduction

Electric circuits include components such as batteries, resistors and capacitors. These basic elements can be combined in a myriad of ways. How these components function, by themselves and in combination, defines the fundamental operation of electric circuits. In this chapter, we examine direct current electric circuits, circuits in which the current always flows in the same direction.

In this chapter, you will learn how to analyze direct current circuits. On the right is a simulation in which you can build your own electric circuits. Initially, the circuit consists of a battery, a light bulb and wires that connect these components. The simulation also contains additional wire segments and light bulbs.

You can place light bulbs in various places in the circuit. Pay special attention to the brightness of the light bulbs: The brighter the light, the more power the circuit is supplying to it. You can also use two devices in the control panel to study the circuit. One, a voltmeter, measures the potential difference across components, while the other, an ammeter, measures the current flowing through the wire at any location in the circuit.

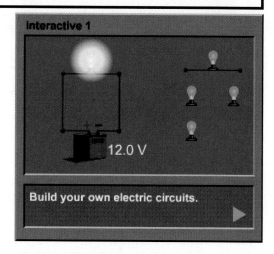

interactive 1

12.0 V

Build your own electric circuits.

In this simulation, the battery and wires effectively have zero resistance. The simulation includes a total of five light bulbs, each with a resistance of 50 ohms. You add and remove light bulbs and wires by dragging them; the components will snap into place. Only one light bulb can be placed on each wire segment.

The purpose of this simulation is for you to experiment with the electric components in a circuit. One way to start is by assessing the circuit in its initial state using the voltmeter and ammeter. How does the potential difference across the battery compare with the potential difference across the light bulb? What about the current? Is it the same everywhere or does it differ from place to place?

Now add another light bulb above the first one in the circuit: Snap in two wire segments in a vertical orientation, and then put a segment containing a light bulb between them. How does the potential difference across the battery now compare to the potential difference across each light bulb? Is the current still the same everywhere? This time you should find that the current can differ by location.

You can also use the voltmeter to confirm Ohm's law. Since you are told the bulb's resistance (50 ohms) and can measure the potential difference across it using the voltmeter, you can use the law to calculate the current flowing through the wire segment containing the bulb. You then can verify your calculation using the ammeter.

You are probably thinking that this introduction has asked you to answer a lot of questions! If you cannot answer all the questions above, that is fine. This chapter is dedicated to preparing you to address them.

27.1 - Electric circuits

In this section, we provide an overview of the components of a basic circuit. All these components merit more discussion, but here we want to provide some context on how they function together in a circuit.

A flashlight provides an example of a circuit. The flashlight we show contains two batteries, a switch, a light bulb, and some metal wires that connect these components.

In the flashlight, the batteries are the source of the energy that causes the net motion of charge in the circuit. The ends of a battery are at different electric potentials. There is a potential difference across the two terminals that are at opposite ends of the battery. A typical potential difference for a battery like those shown is 1.5 volts. The terminal with the greater electric potential is marked with a plus (+) sign, and the terminal with the lower electric potential is marked with a negative (−) sign. Putting together two batteries as shown creates a potential difference across the two batteries of approximately 3.0 volts. The batteries are used to create an electric field that causes a net flow of electrons: a current.

Current will only flow when there is a complete path: a loop, as opposed to a dead end. (Circuit comes from the Latin word *circumire*, to go around). When the switch is in the "off" position, it creates a gap in the circuit, and current cannot flow. When the switch is pushed to "on", the gap is closed and a current can flow.

We have highlighted the circuit inside a flashlight in Concept 2. Let's trace the direction of conventional current around the circuit. A positive charge starts at the positive terminal of the battery on the right, and moves through a coiled wire called the filament in the light bulb. It exits the filament and moves through the wire that contains the switch. The charge then flows through the batteries and starts its round trip over again.

There is resistance inside the batteries, in the wires and in the light bulb. The resistance inside the batteries and in the wires is minor compared to that of the filament in the light bulb, and it is often reasonable to ignore these minor resistances. The light bulb is the major source of resistance, and it supplies what is called the *load resistance* of the circuit. The resistance of this component and the potential difference across the batteries determine the amount of current in the circuit.

The flashlight creates light when current flows through the filament. Modern day filaments often are made of very thin tungsten wires. As a current passes through the filament, electrons lose energy in collisions with the atoms of the filament, and the filament's temperature increases. It becomes hot (up to $3000°C$), and energy leaves the filament in the forms of heat and light.

Although tungsten is an effective filament, when it is hot the tungsten vaporizes and the filament becomes thinner. This increases its resistance, which means it shines less brightly. Eventually, when it "burns out", it becomes so thin and brittle that it ruptures.

The flashlight contains all the essential elements of a circuit. It has a source of energy, the batteries. They create a potential difference that causes electrons to move. As the electrons move through the light bulb, they encounter resistance, which causes this resistor to dissipate energy.

The current flows only in one direction in this circuit, which makes it a *direct current* circuit. Direct current circuits are the topic of this chapter. We study these circuits primarily when the current has reached a steady state – a constant flow – not in the brief moments when the current changes, such as immediately after the flashlight is switched on or off.

Scientists and engineers use symbols to represent components in circuit diagrams, as shown in Concept 3. The thin black lines represent wires. The battery and resistance symbols are labeled in the circuit. The switch is "on", so it is in its closed position in this diagram. The red arrow indicates the direction of flow of the conventional current.

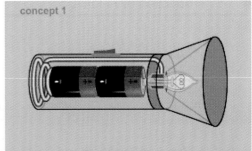

concept 1

Electric circuit
Set of electric components connected by wires

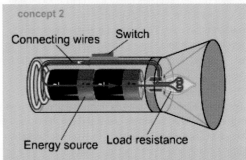

concept 2

Connecting wires   Switch

Energy source   Load resistance

Circuits usually contain:
An energy source
A load resistance
Wires connecting it all in a loop
A switch

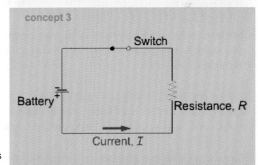

concept 3

Switch

Battery

Resistance, R

Current, I

Drawing electric circuits
Use circuit diagrams with symbols

Electromotive force (emf, ℰ): Maximum potential difference from an energy source such as a battery.

A potential difference applied across a conductor causes a current to flow. Common devices such as a flashlight need a continuing source of potential difference – an *emf* – so that current will keep flowing and the flashlight's bulb will stay illuminated.

Batteries are a common source of emf.

A battery often supplies the emf. The symbol for emf is $\mathcal{E}$. Like any potential difference, an emf is measured in volts. There are many sources of emf: electric generators, solar photovoltaic cells and so on. Even living creatures can be an emf source. Humans rely on emfs generated in the body to cause electric currents in nerves.

The term "electromotive force" is misleading because an emf is **not** a force. It is a potential difference and its unit is the volt. It is a well-established term in physics, however, and we will use it too. In any case, since we typically write it in its abbreviated form as emf, you should not too often be confused by seeing the word "force".

A battery is the typical emf source for direct current circuits. Chemical reactions within the battery cause one terminal of the battery to be positively charged, and the other to be negatively charged. These terminals are marked with plus (+) and minus (−) signs.

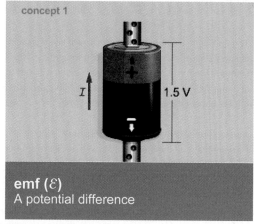

concept 1

I 1.5 V

emf ($\mathcal{E}$)
A potential difference

Batteries are classified by their emf. A typical battery used in a flashlight has an emf of 1.5 volts, while a car battery has an emf of 12 volts. If a battery has an emf of 1.5 volts, this means that the electric potential of its positive terminal is 1.5 volts higher than that of its negative terminal.

Sometimes batteries are referred to as "charge pumps." They increase the potential energy of the charge flowing through the circuit. The unit of emf, the volt, equals joules per coulomb. You can think of a nine-volt battery as doing nine joules of work on each coulomb of charge that flows through it.

Batteries also are defined by how much energy they can supply over their lifetimes. AAA and D batteries are both 1.5-volt batteries, but the larger D battery supplies more energy over its lifetime. This total available energy is measured in watt-hours. A small battery for watches will have about 0.1 watt-hours of total energy, while a car battery has a total available energy of about 500 watt-hours.

When current flows through a battery, it encounters resistance. This is called a battery's *internal resistance*. This means that when placed in a circuit, a battery's emf and the potential difference across its terminals are not the same. The emf is greater than the potential difference (unless the battery is being charged, in which case the emf can be greater). The internal battery resistance is usually minor, however. Many times in this chapter we will treat it as zero, and consider the emf and the potential difference to be the same.

27.3 - Energy and electric potential in a circuit

We will use the simple circuit shown to the right as our starting point for discussing how to analyze circuits. Specifically, it is important to correctly determine the changes in electric potential across various components in the circuit.

The circuit in Concept 1 contains a resistance-free battery and a resistor: a flashlight bulb. As the diagram reflects, the resistor has a resistance of 5.0 ohms, and the battery has an emf of 1.5 volts. We want to determine the potential difference across the resistor.

To analyze the changes in electric potential occurring around the circuit, consider some charge conducting a hypothetical journey around the circuit loop, as shown in Concept 2. Imagine 0.5 coulombs of positive charge traveling one complete loop in the direction of conventional current (clockwise in this case). What happens to the potential energy of this charge as it passes through each component – the battery and the resistor – in completing a round trip around the loop?

For starters, the potential energy must be the same at the beginning and end of the closed path, because the electrostatic force is a conservative force. Just as your gravitational PE is the same after you take a round trip walk, even if you go uphill and down on the way, so too the charge's electrostatic PE is the same when it returns to its starting point.

To determine the changes in potential energy as the charge makes its journey through each component, we will use an equation that relates the change in potential energy to charge and potential difference: $\Delta PE = q\Delta V$.

We will start with the charge at the negative terminal of the battery, and have it flow through the battery to the positive terminal. The **change** in potential energy for a positive charge traveling across the battery in this direction is positive. The battery must do work on this positive charge to move it toward the positive terminal. The charge's change in PE is the product of the charge and the potential difference, (0.5 C)(1.5 V), which equals +0.75 J. The electric potential energy of the charge increases and the chemical potential energy of the battery decreases correspondingly.

Next, the charge flows through the wire around the circuit. We assume that the wire has negligible resistance. To complete a circuit, the charge must pass through the resistor. This is the one location in this simple circuit where the charge loses energy before returning to its starting point. The resistor heats up, giving off this energy as heat. The charge's change in potential energy in the resistor must equal −0.75 joules, because the sum of the changes in potential energy around the complete loop must equal zero.

Now that we have assessed the potential energy changes around a circuit loop, we can also assess the changes in electric potential. Concept 3 shows the changes in electric potential around a complete circuit loop. The changes in electric potential can be determined using the equation $\Delta V = \Delta PE/q$.

Concept 3 again shows a clockwise path around the circuit. Moving in this direction, the electric potential increases by +1.5 V as the battery is traversed. The potential difference across the battery traveling in this direction is equal to the change in PE, +0.75 J, divided by the amount of charge, 0.5 C. Across the resistor, since the change in PE is −0.75 J in this direction, the change in potential is −1.5 V. The electric potential is greater on the "upstream" end of the resistor than on the "downstream" end. The charge moves across the resistor from a region of a higher electric potential to one of lower electric potential.

What we have shown is fundamental and important. In this two-component circuit, the change in electric potential across one component – the battery – is equal to but opposite the change in electric potential across the other component: the resistor. The changes sum to zero. We have shown this in a specific case, but the rule holds in general for any closed loop around a circuit.

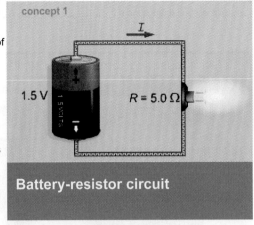

concept 1

1.5 V $R = 5.0\ \Omega$

Battery-resistor circuit

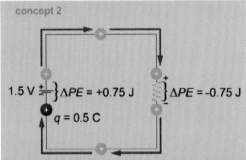

concept 2

1.5 V $\dashv\vdash$ } $\Delta PE = +0.75$ J $\Delta PE = -0.75$ J

$q = 0.5$ C

Circuit energy analysis
PE of charge is unchanged after any round-trip
· Energy increases in battery
· Energy decreases in resistor

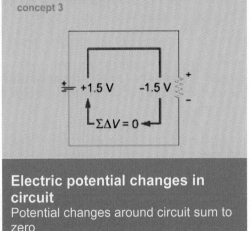

concept 3

$\dashv\vdash$ +1.5 V   −1.5 V

$\Sigma\Delta V = 0$

Electric potential changes in circuit
Potential changes around circuit sum to zero

The direction we chose to travel the circuit was arbitrary. Had we chosen to travel the circuit in a counterclockwise direction, the change in electric potential would be negative as we crossed the battery and positive as we crossed the resistor. We also chose to consider a positive charge rather than a negative one. In any case, clockwise or counterclockwise, positive or negative, the principle holds that the changes in electric potential around a complete circuit loop sum to zero.

This section can be used to illustrate a more general principle: As you traverse a circuit, you can add the potential differences across the components. For instance, if you traversed two resistors, the potential difference across the two resistors would equal the sum of each resistor's potential difference.

27.4 - Measuring current and potential difference

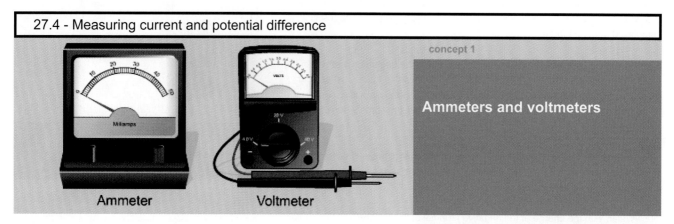

Ammeter

Voltmeter

concept 1

Ammeters and voltmeters

Ammeter: A device that measures current in a wire.

Voltmeter: A device that measures the potential difference between two points.

Ammeters and voltmeters are common tools for analyzing circuits. Both are shown above.

Ammeters measure current. An ammeter is inserted in the circuit, as shown in Concept 2, so that all the current in that part of the circuit flows through it. Because current flows through them, ammeters are built to have extremely low resistance in order to minimize their impact on the circuit. An ideal ammeter would have no resistance.

A voltmeter measures the potential difference (voltage) between two points in a circuit. In Concept 3, the potential difference across the two terminals of a battery is being measured. To use the voltmeter, a lead is placed on each side of the battery.

Voltmeters are also designed to have minimal effects on a circuit. In the case of the voltmeter, this means they are designed to have a high resistance, so little current flows through them, and the rest continues to flow through the circuit component being measured.

Ammeters and voltmeters often are combined into one instrument called a *multimeter*. A multimeter may also contain a device for measuring resistance, called an *ohmmeter*.

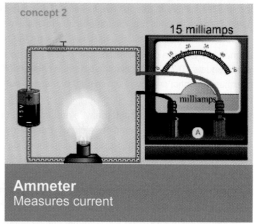

concept 2

15 milliamps

Ammeter
Measures current

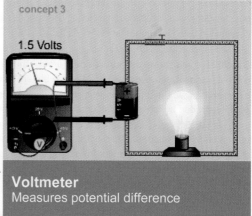

concept 3

1.5 Volts

Voltmeter
Measures potential difference

27.5 - Series wiring

Series wiring: Circuit wiring in which the components are placed one after another. All of the current flows through each component.

The diagram to the right shows an example of a series circuit. The same amount of current passes through the battery and through each light bulb. The circuit has no branches; there are no places where the current can split to follow another path. The light bulbs and the battery are said to be connected in series.

Place an ammeter anywhere in this circuit and you will measure the same value for the current. The same amount of current passes through the battery, the first light bulb, the second light bulb and the wires that connect these components.

If the current in a series circuit is interrupted anywhere, it is interrupted everywhere. Because there are no alternative routes, if the circuit is broken at any point, then there is no detour path for the current to follow.

This phenomenon is explored in more detail in Example 1. Two light bulbs are wired in series, similar to old-fashioned holiday lights. The filament of each light bulb is part of the circuit. When a light bulb burns out, its filament breaks, and there is no path for current through that bulb. The example problem asks what happens to the second light bulb in a series circuit if the first bulb burns out.

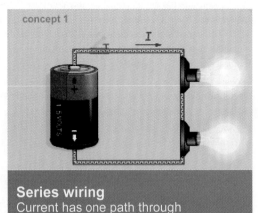

Series wiring
Current has one path through components
Current same at all points

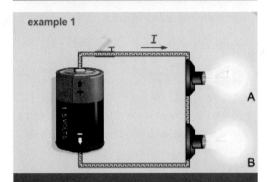

If light bulb A burns out, will light bulb B remain lit?
No – a break in a series circuit causes all current to stop

27.6 - Resistors in series

To calculate the equivalent resistance of resistors in series: Add each resistor's resistance.

Analyzing circuits with multiple components can be complex. The task can sometimes be simplified by treating several components of the same type as if they were one. You can simplify a circuit by calculating what is called the "equivalent resistance" or "equivalent capacitance" of multiple resistors or capacitors. You can then treat the components as one, using their equivalent resistance or equivalent capacitance.

Our first case for doing this is resistors in series. Once we determine their equivalent resistance, we can treat them as though they were one component, and determine how much current flows through the circuit in Example 1. In the case of resistors wired in series, the equivalent resistance is the sum of the resistances. We show this in Equation 1.

Consider the circuit shown in Example 1 that contains two resistors in series. The question asks for the amount of current in this circuit. You can determine the current using Ohm's law, $\Delta V = IR$, but what should you use for R?

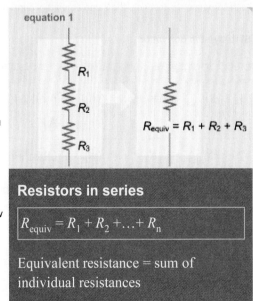

Resistors in series

$$R_{equiv} = R_1 + R_2 + \ldots + R_n$$

Equivalent resistance = sum of individual resistances

First, determine the series circuit's equivalent resistance by summing the individual resistances. The 6 Ω resistor plus the 4 Ω resistor equals an equivalent resistance of 10 Ω. The circuit in the example has a 20-volt battery. Since the two resistors create an equivalent resistance of 10 Ω, you can use Ohm's law to calculate the current through them. It equals 20 V divided by 10 Ω, or 2 A.

Derivation. Why can resistances in series be added? We now derive the series rule for resistors, for n resistors in series.

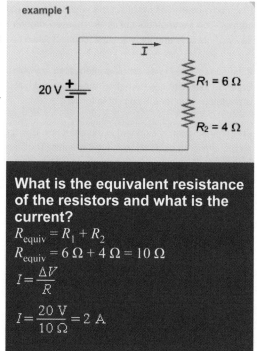

example 1

What is the equivalent resistance of the resistors and what is the current?

$$R_{equiv} = R_1 + R_2$$
$$R_{equiv} = 6\,\Omega + 4\,\Omega = 10\,\Omega$$
$$I = \frac{\Delta V}{R}$$
$$I = \frac{20\text{ V}}{10\,\Omega} = 2\text{ A}$$

Variables

potential difference across all resistors	ΔV_{total}
potential difference across i^{th} resistor	ΔV_i
current through circuit	I
current through i^{th} resistor	I_i
equivalent resistance of circuit	R_{equiv}
resistance of ith resistor	R_i

Strategy

1. Find the total potential difference across all the resistors combined.
2. Use Ohm's law to rewrite potential difference in terms of current and resistance. An algebraic simplification gives the series rule for resistors.

Physics principles and equations

With components in series, the total potential difference equals the sum of the potential differences across each component.

Ohm's law relates potential difference, current and resistance:

$$\Delta V = IR$$

With components in series, the same amount of current flows through each component.

Step-by-step derivation

Step	Reason
1. $\Delta V_{total} = \Delta V_1 + \ldots + \Delta V_n$	total ΔV is sum of series ΔV's
2. $IR_{equiv} = I_1 R_1 + \ldots + I_n R_n$	Ohm's law
3. $I = I_1 = I_2 = \ldots = I_n$	current the same
4. $R_{equiv} = R_1 + \ldots + R_n$	divide by equal current

27.7 - Interactive problem: series wiring

The circuit to the right contains two light bulbs and a 12-volt battery. One of the light bulbs, R_1, has a resistance of 75 Ω. Your task is to determine the resistance of the R_2 bulb.

You have an ammeter at your disposal. You drag this tool onto the circuit to measure the current.

Use the ammeter, Ohm's law and your knowledge of equivalent resistance in series circuits to determine the resistance of the R_2 bulb. In order to solve the problem you may want to first consider what the equivalent resistance of the two resistors must be given the reading of the ammeter and the voltage shown for the battery.

Type your answer in the space provided. Press CHECK, and a message will indicate whether your answer is correct.

You can try again by entering a new answer and pressing CHECK again.

If you have trouble solving this problem, review Ohm's law and the section on the equivalent resistance of resistors in series.

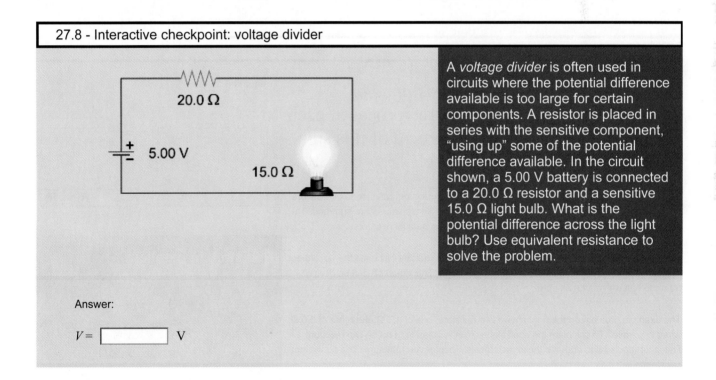

interactive 1

$R_1 = 75.0\ \Omega$ $R_2 = ?$

12.0 V

Use ammeter to determine the unknown resistance. ▶

27.8 - Interactive checkpoint: voltage divider

20.0 Ω

5.00 V

15.0 Ω

A *voltage divider* is often used in circuits where the potential difference available is too large for certain components. A resistor is placed in series with the sensitive component, "using up" some of the potential difference available. In the circuit shown, a 5.00 V battery is connected to a 20.0 Ω resistor and a sensitive 15.0 Ω light bulb. What is the potential difference across the light bulb? Use equivalent resistance to solve the problem.

Answer:

$V =$ [   ] V

27.9 - Parallel wiring

Parallel wiring: Circuit wiring that branches. The same potential difference exists across each branch.

In parallel wiring, there are junctions where multiple wires come together. A current can flow into a junction and then divide along different paths. A path between two junctions is called a *branch*.

Consider electrons just to the left of junction A in Concept 1. The electrons are moving to the right when they reach the junction. As they reach it, some turn left into the branch along the middle wire, while others continue moving straight into the branch around the outer wire loop. The two flows of electrons, the two currents, rejoin at the junction labeled B.

Because charge is conserved around a circuit, the sum of the currents flowing into a junction equals the sum of the currents flowing out. This is an important principle known as Kirchhoff's junction rule.

The potential difference is the same across the end points of parallel branches in a circuit. This is a crucial concept required for understanding the functioning of parallel circuits.

In the circuit on the right, a battery is connected in parallel with the light bulb in the branch AB, and with the light bulbs in the branch CD. The potential difference is identical across the battery and these two branches. The potential differences do not sum as in a series circuit.

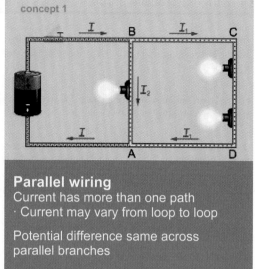

concept 1

Parallel wiring
Current has more than one path
· Current may vary from loop to loop

Potential difference same across parallel branches

In this circuit, the battery is a 1.5-volt flashlight battery. If you placed a voltmeter's leads on either side of the battery, you would read a value of 1.5 volts. You would also read the same value if you placed the leads across the middle branch or across the CD branch. The potential difference across all three branches is identical. This confirms that all three branches are in parallel.

27.10 - Resistors in parallel

To calculate the equivalent resistance of resistors in parallel: Add the reciprocal of each resistor's resistance. The reciprocal of this sum equals the equivalent resistance.

The equation on the right shows how to calculate the equivalent resistance of resistors in parallel. First, take the reciprocal of each resistance. Those values are summed. The reciprocal of that sum is the equivalent resistance of the parallel resistors.

Another equation, also shown to the right, allows you to quickly calculate the equivalent resistance when just two resistors are wired in parallel. This equation can be derived from the first with a little algebra.

The example problem on the right shows two resistors, one of 4.0 Ω, the other of 6.0 Ω, wired in parallel. To calculate the equivalent circuit resistance of these two resistors, first invert each value and add these reciprocals. Then, invert that sum. The equivalent resistance is 2.4 Ω.

We can then calculate the current in the circuit. We must specify the current's location, because the current is not the same in all parts of the circuit. In the example problem, we specify that we are calculating it near the battery.

In this circuit, there is less current in the branches containing the resistors than in the branch that contains the battery. You use Ohm's law to calculate the current in the branches with the resistors. The potential difference across each branch must be the

equation 1

$$\frac{1}{R_{equiv}} = \frac{1}{R_1} + \frac{1}{R_2}$$

Resistors in parallel

$$\frac{1}{R_{equiv}} = \frac{1}{R_1} + \frac{1}{R_2} + \ldots + \frac{1}{R_n}$$

Reciprocal of equivalent resistance = sum of reciprocals of resistances

For two resistors:

$$R_{equiv} = \frac{R_1 R_2}{R_1 + R_2}$$

same as that of the battery, 20 volts. Using Ohm's law, you determine that there is a 5.0 A current in the branch that contains the 4.0 Ω resistor. (The current equals the potential difference, 20 V, divided by the resistance, 4.0 Ω.) A similar process enables you to determine that the current in the middle branch is 3.3 A. Since charge is conserved, you add these two currents to determine that 8.3 A flows in the branch that contains the battery.

Derivation

Variables

current through circuit	I_{total}
current through i^{th} resistor	I_i
potential difference across all resistors	ΔV
potential difference across i^{th} resistor	ΔV_i
equivalent resistance of circuit	R_{equiv}
resistance of ith resistor	R_i

Strategy

1. Find the total current flowing through all the resistors combined.
2. Use Ohm's law to rewrite the current in terms of potential difference and resistance. An algebraic simplification gives the parallel rule for resistors.

Physics principles and equations

Since charge is conserved, the current flowing out of a junction equals the sum of the currents flowing into the junction.

Ohm's law

$$\Delta V = IR$$

The potential difference is the same across all parallel branches.

Step-by-step derivation

Step	Reason
1. $\quad I_{total} = I_1 + I_2 + \dots + I_n$	conservation of charge
2. $\quad \dfrac{\Delta V}{R_{equiv}} = \dfrac{\Delta V_1}{R_1} + \dfrac{\Delta V_2}{R_2} + \dots + \dfrac{\Delta V_n}{R_n}$	Ohm's law
3. $\quad \Delta V = \Delta V_1 = \Delta V_2 = \dots = \Delta V_n$	potential differences equal
4. $\quad \dfrac{1}{R_{equiv}} = \dfrac{1}{R_1} + \dfrac{1}{R_2} + \dots + \dfrac{1}{R_n}$	divide by equal potential difference

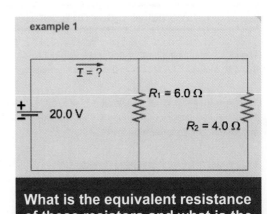

example 1

What is the equivalent resistance of these resistors and what is the current at the point shown?

$$\frac{1}{R_{equiv}} = \frac{1}{R_1} + \frac{1}{R_2}$$

$$\frac{1}{R_{equiv}} = \frac{1}{6.0\ \Omega} + \frac{1}{4.0\ \Omega} = 0.42$$

$$R_{equiv} = \frac{1}{0.42} = 2.4\ \Omega$$

$$I = \frac{\Delta V}{R}$$

$$I = \frac{20.0\ V}{2.4\ \Omega} = 8.3\ A$$

27.11 - Interactive problem: a parallel circuit

The circuit contains a battery and three light bulbs. The resistance of two of the light bulbs is known. Your task is to determine the resistance of the third light bulb.

You have an ammeter. It can be placed anywhere in the circuit to determine the current at that point. Use the ammeter, along with your knowledge of parallel circuits and Ohm's law, to determine the resistance R.

Type your answer in the space provided. Press CHECK to see if your answer is correct. You can try again by entering a new value and pressing CHECK again.

Central to solving this problem is the nature of potential difference and equivalent resistance in parallel circuits. You also need to calculate the equivalent resistance for resistors arranged in series, and apply Ohm's law. Review the sections of the textbook on these topics if you are having trouble.

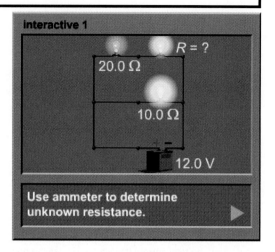

interactive 1

$R = ?$

$20.0 \, \Omega$

$10.0 \, \Omega$

$12.0 \, V$

Use ammeter to determine unknown resistance.

27.12 - Circuits with series and parallel wiring

Circuits commonly include some components that are wired in series and some that are wired in parallel. The diagrams to the right show an example of such a circuit.

You can use the current to determine what is in series and what is in parallel. If the current flows along a single path from one component to another, then the two components are in series. If the current divides, then the components are in parallel.

In the circuit on the right, for example, the two resistors on the far right wire of the circuit, labeled R_2 and R_3, are in series with one another. There is no junction between them, no place for the current to split. Since there is only a single path for the current between the resistors, the resistors are in series, as emphasized in Concept 2.

This pair of series resistors is wired in parallel with the resistor in the middle, R_1. Both branches are in parallel with the battery. Consider current that exits the battery. It encounters a junction at A where it can flow to R_1 or to the R_2R_3 combination. The current then recombines at B after flowing through those resistors. The same potential difference exists across R_1 as across the R_2R_3 combination. This means R_1 is in parallel with the R_2R_3 combination.

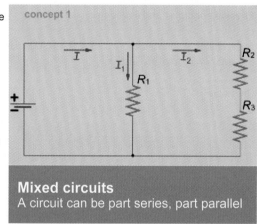

concept 1

I
I_1
I_2
R_1
R_2
R_3

Mixed circuits
A circuit can be part series, part parallel

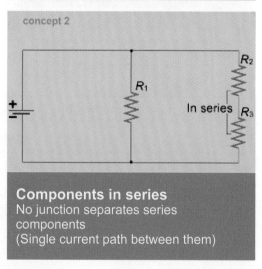

concept 2

R_1
R_2
In series R_3

Components in series
No junction separates series components
(Single current path between them)

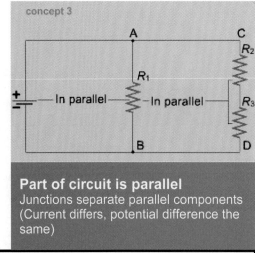

concept 3

Part of circuit is parallel
Junctions separate parallel components
(Current differs, potential difference the
same)

27.13 - Sample problem: circuits with series and parallel wiring

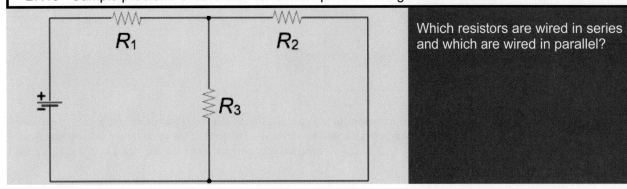

Which resistors are wired in series
and which are wired in parallel?

The diagram shows a circuit with three resistors and asks which resistors are wired in series and which are wired in parallel.

What is the strategy?

1. Use the definitions of series and parallel wiring.
2. Once two or more resistors are identified as series or parallel, simplify the circuit by determining the equivalent resistance. Then see whether the resulting equivalent resistance is in series or parallel with other resistors. Continue this process until the circuit cannot be simplified any further.

Physics principles and equations

Resistors are wired in series if there is only a single path for current to flow through them.

Branches are wired in parallel if the potential difference across them is the same.

Step 1

We start by checking for resistors in series. As the circuit is depicted above, none of these resistors are wired in series. The current running through any of the three resistors branches before reaching any of the other resistors.

Step 2

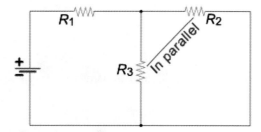

Next we check for parallel resistors. The resistors R_2 and R_3 are wired in parallel.

Step 3

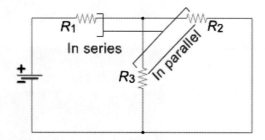

Now, we reexamine the circuit having made a parallel combination out of R_2 and R_3. The resistor R_1 is in series with the equivalent resistance of the R_2R_3 combination. This may be tricky to see, but applying the tests for series wiring confirms it. The same current flows through R_1 as flows through the equivalent combination of R_2 and R_3. Another way of saying this is that the sum of the currents going to R_2 and R_3 is equal to the current through R_1.

(Note: It is possible to create circuits that are irreducible, in which the components are neither in parallel nor in series. If you think you have simplified a circuit as much as you can, you may be right.)

27.14 - Gotchas

Components in series must have the same potential difference across them. No, they have the same amount of current flowing through them.

The potential difference across components in parallel is the same. Yes.

27.15 - Summary

An electric circuit is a set of electric components such as batteries, capacitors and resistors that are connected directly or through wires.

Current will only flow through a circuit that is closed, which means that it makes a loop. To cause current to flow continuously through a circuit, a source of emf, $\mathcal{E}$, such as a battery, must be present.

One basic type of circuit wiring is series wiring. Two circuit components are said to be in series when current must go through both components: there is only one possible path. The same amount of current flows through both components, and the sum of the potential differences across the components is the net potential difference across the combination.

Resistances in series add to give the equivalent resistance of a combination of resistors.

The other basic type of wiring is parallel wiring. Components are connected so that they have the same potential difference across them, but may have different currents through them.

The sum of the reciprocals of resistances wired in parallel equals the reciprocal of the equivalent resistance of a combination of resistors.

Equations

Resistors in series

$$R_{equiv} = R_1 + R_2 + \ldots + R_n$$

Resistors in parallel

$$\frac{1}{R_{equiv}} = \frac{1}{R_1} + \frac{1}{R_2} + \ldots + \frac{1}{R_n}$$

28.0 - Introduction

Humankind has long been familiar with magnets, objects possessing "north" and "south" poles that can attract or repel certain other objects. The ancient Greeks understood their properties, and the word "magnet" itself likely originates from the Greek region of Magnesia, where naturally occurring magnets are found. Early navigators learned to steer their ships with the aid of magnetic devices that were the forerunners of today's compasses. The natural world also takes advantage of magnetism. A notable example of this is *Aquaspirillum magnetotacticum*, a bacterium that synthesizes tiny magnets that help it determine which way to move. We are a little worried about these creatures: Since the Earth's magnetic field changes its orientation every several hundred thousand years or so, the microorganisms may find themselves unintentionally heading away from dinner one day.

Much more complex creatures, namely scientists, employ magnets as well. In the 16th and 17th centuries, they learned to create their own magnets and used them to study the Earth's magnetic field. In the 19th century, scientists began the crucial work of piecing together a more complete picture of the relationship between magnetic fields and electric currents.

Despite centuries of practical use, magnets and their fields still pose mysteries. For instance, scientists cannot definitively establish the cause of the Earth's magnetic field, and they are only able to speculate about why its direction periodically changes. In addition, physicists continue their quest for the magnetic monopole: a magnet with just one pole. As you proceed in your studies in this chapter, remember that you are in the good company of other fine minds who have found the workings of magnets to be an area of continuing fascination.

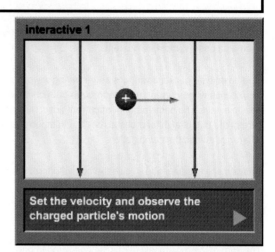

Set the velocity and observe the charged particle's motion

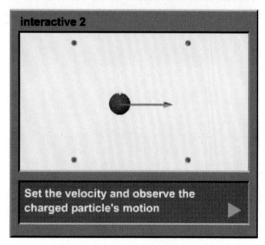

Set the velocity and observe the charged particle's motion

You can begin your exploration of magnetic fields by launching the simulations to the right that show the effect of a magnetic field on the motion of a charged particle. These two simulations are the same except for the initial viewing angle, the angle at which you view what is occurring in the simulation. In both, you control the initial velocity of a positively charged particle that moves in a magnetic field, represented by magnetic field lines. In the illustration for Interactive 1, you see that the magnetic field points straight down the screen and the initial velocity vector points to the right, perpendicular to the magnetic field. As the particle moves you will see, represented as a purple vector, the force exerted on it by the magnetic field.

Clicking on Interactive 2 launches the same simulation but with the viewing angle rotated $90°$. Here, the magnetic field points directly toward you, and you are seeing the heads of the field lines. With either simulation, you can change the viewing angle by using the slider provided, and see either of these points of view. In the simulations you will also see a magnetic field meter that is there principally to help you understand the changing perspective as you manipulate the viewing angle slider.

Launch the upper simulation and conduct some experiments. Does the moving particle travel along a straight line or a curve? To answer this question, you will need to change the viewing angle, in the process seeing why a three-dimensional view of a charged particle moving through a magnetic field is so useful.

As you study the path, answer two more questions. First, is the particle's speed changing? Second, is it accelerating? For the second question, recall that acceleration measures the change in velocity, which is a vector.

You can also consider the relationship of the directions of the various vectors you see. What is the relationship between the force and velocity vectors? Are they parallel or perpendicular? What is the angle between the force vector and the magnetic field? Again, the viewing angle slider proves a useful tool. You can only change the direction of the initial velocity when the viewing angle is set to the far right so that the magnetic field is pointing straight down the screen; this makes it easy to see the angle between the velocity vector and the magnetic field vector.

As another experiment, set the velocity to zero. Does the magnetic field exert a force on the particle? If the magnetic field exerts a force, the particle will accelerate. How does this compare to what would occur if the stationary charged particle were in an electric field? (Note: We ignore other forces, notably gravity and air resistance, in these simulations.)

We have asked a lot of questions above. Answer as many as you can now, and prepare to explore magnetism in depth in this chapter.

28.1 - Magnet fundamentals

Magnet: An object that creates a magnetic field and exerts a magnetic force. All known magnets have two poles.

This boy is holding a U magnet. The magnet suspends a few paperclips.

Just like electrical charges, magnets create fields and exert forces. All magnets are dipoles, meaning they have two poles: a north pole and a south pole. As with electrical charges, magnetic opposites attract and likes repel; a north pole attracts a south pole, and a pair of like poles, such as two south poles, repel each other.

A rectangular magnet like the one shown to the right is called a bar magnet. It has a magnetic pole at each end. If you were to bend this magnet into a "U," you would create a horseshoe magnet like the one the boy is holding in the photo above. Even though you have changed the magnet's shape, the poles remain at the two extremities.

The attraction and repulsion of magnetic poles can be demonstrated with a pair of bar magnets. If you have two such magnets, position them so that their opposite poles are adjacent. What happens? They attract each other. You can see this illustrated in Concept 1. Now place them so their like poles are next to each other; the magnets will repel each other. This is shown in Concept 2.

The strongest and most frequently found form of magnetism is called *ferromagnetism*. Only certain types of material (iron is a notable example) exhibit this form of magnetism. Everyday videotapes reveal a common application of ferromagnetism: A movie is encoded as a pattern of small magnets on the videotape, and the VCR "reads" this data. Computer hard drives function in a similar way.

You may have noticed that magnets can "stick" to surfaces that do not initially exhibit magnetism. For instance, the exterior of your refrigerator is typically not magnetic, and yet if it is made of a ferromagnetic metal, magnets will stick to it. A magnet sticks because it is able to induce a temporary magnetic field in the refrigerator's surface. The permanent and temporary magnets then attract each other.

Another way to observe this phenomenon is to attach a metal paper clip to a magnet and then attach a second clip to the first clip. The two clips will attract each other. When you remove the original magnet, however, the clips will no longer attract one another because the fields of the paper clips disappear when they are removed from the influence of the magnet's field.

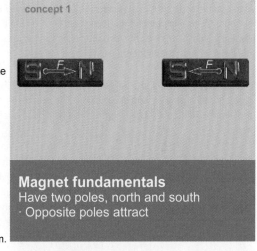

Magnet fundamentals
Have two poles, north and south
· Opposite poles attract

Magnet fundamentals
· Like poles repel

No one has created a magnet with just one pole (a monopole). Magnetic poles always come in pairs. If you take a bar magnet and cut it in half, you will create two magnets, each with a south and a north pole. Cut each of those in half and you will have four magnets, each with two poles. In principle, if you could cut the magnet into its constituent atoms, each atom would have its own magnetic field.

28.2 - Magnetic fields

Two magnets can attract or repel each other without touching: They exert a force at a distance. Magnetic fields surround magnets. Like an electric field, the magnetic field is a vector field. It has a strength and a direction at every point. The letter **B** represents the magnetic field and the unit for magnetic field strength is the *tesla* (T).

Iron filings line up with the magnetic field.

The photographs above show the alignment of iron filings gathered around the poles of two pairs of magnets held close together. The filings in both photos align with the magnetic fields between the poles. The photograph on the upper left shows the filings between a south pole and a north pole, which attract each other. The filings are connected and aligned in the same direction as the magnets because the magnetic field lines pass directly from the north pole to the south pole. In the photograph on the upper right, two south poles are repelling each other, which causes the filings to separate.

Like electric fields, magnetic fields can be diagrammed with field lines. We have superimposed a drawing of magnetic field lines on the illustrations to the right. You can see how the orientations of bits of iron filings reflect the direction of the field at a number of places around the magnet.

As the diagram shows, the field lines run outside the magnet from the north to the south pole, and they always form closed loops. As with an electric field, the closer the lines, the stronger the field. The strength of the field decreases with distance from the magnet.

The table in Equation 2 shows approximate magnetic field strengths near some magnetic objects. The magnetic fields you encounter every day are much less than one tesla. The most powerful lab magnets have field strengths of tens of teslas. However, human technology cannot create magnetic fields anywhere near the field strengths exhibited by a class of highly magnetized neutron stars called *magnetars*.

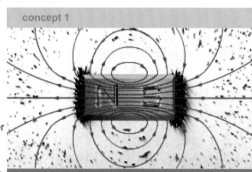

concept 1

Magnetic field
Region where magnet exerts force
External lines point from north to south

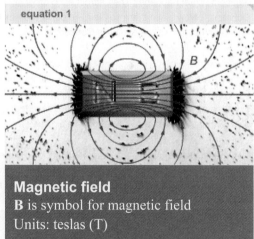

equation 1

B

Magnetic field
B is symbol for magnetic field
Units: teslas (T)

equation 2	Approximate magnetic field (T)
1 foot from hairdryer	10^{-7}
Under power distribution line	10^{-5}
Earth's surface	10^{-4}
Refrigerator magnet	10^{-2}
Medical MRI	1.5
Most powerful lab magnets	60-100
White dwarf star surface	100
Magnetar star surface	10^{11}

Magnetic field strength near magnetic objects

28.3 - Physics at work: lodestones

Lodestone: A naturally occurring magnetic rock found in various regions of the world.

The Chinese first used lodestone magnets in their navigational compasses in the twelfth century. Later explorers, including Columbus, carried lodestones to "recharge" their iron-based compasses. To do so, they would pass the needle of a compass near the lodestone to strengthen its magnetic properties.

A lodestone consists of two materials, one with a high *saturation magnitude*. Saturation magnitude is the measure of the maximum strength of the magnetic field that can be induced in a substance. Iron, for example, has a high saturation magnitude. The other material has high *coercivity*, which is the measure of how well a substance retains its magnetic field. Pure iron loses its magnetic properties relatively easily, while a substance such as magnetite does not.

The combination of these two materials results in a strong and durable magnetic source. One substance supplies the strength, the other supplies durability.

concept 1

Lodestones
Natural magnetic rock combines materials with
· Strong magnetic field
· Long-lasting magnetic field

28.4 - The Earth and magnetic fields

The Earth acts like a huge magnet with an accompanying magnetic field. Compasses take advantage of this field: Their needles are mounted so that they can rotate freely and align with it. Once a compass has established the north and south directions, other directions can be established relative to them.

The Earth's **magnetic** south pole is located near its **geographic** North Pole. This means that the north pole of the magnet in a compass points north, since the south pole of the planetary magnet attracts it. The geographic poles lie on the planet's axis of rotation.

Scientists still do not know exactly how our planet produces its magnetic field, though the prevalent theory is that Earth's magnetism arises from processes that occur in its core. Scientists have arrived at this conclusion because of the fundamental differences between the cores of the Earth and the Moon. The Earth has a molten metallic core and a magnetic field, while the Moon has a solid core and no magnetic field. Many scientists believe the large-scale liquid flow that occurs inside the Earth's core causes its

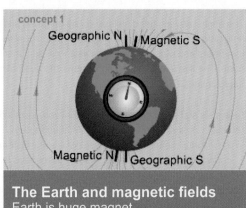

concept 1

Geographic N | Magnetic S

Magnetic N | Geographic S

The Earth and magnetic fields
Earth is huge magnet
· North Pole ≈ south pole of magnet

magnetic field.

While scientists are still puzzled by the "why" of Earth's magnetic field, they do know that the locations of its magnetic north and south poles change. The magnetic south pole is currently about 1900 km away from the geographic North Pole of the Earth. The magnetic north pole resides in the ocean south of Australia, not even in the continent of Antarctica! These positions are not fixed; shifts of several degrees in their locations have been measured over the last century. The poles do more than wander, they also reverse their orientation. The last switch occurred a few hundred thousand years ago, when magnetic north became magnetic south, and vice versa.

Scientists deduce this change in orientation by analyzing parts of the ocean floor that originate as magma (molten rock) emerging from cracks in the Earth's crust. Over a period of millions of years, vast quantities of solidified magma have been deposited on the ocean floor. As magma congeals at any point in time, the iron it contains "records" the orientation of the Earth's magnetic field. New magma flows force earlier deposits apart, which separates them and enables scientists to establish their sequence. By examining different sections of the rock, scientists can deduce the direction of the magnetic field at various times throughout Earth's history.

The current strength of Earth's magnetic field is about 5×10^{-5} teslas, and that strength is decreasing at about 0.07 percent per year. If it continues to weaken at this rate, it will be reduced to only 1 percent of its present value in 6,500 years. Since the magnetic field helps to shield our biosphere from cosmic rays and charged particles from the Sun, this could be a matter of concern.

Scientists theorize that the poles "flip" alignment after the field passes through a state with zero magnitude. Because there are no signs of massive mutations in the fossil record that date from the period of the last "flip," perhaps the results are not as severe as one might fear. No one knows exactly how long the zero-field condition exists, whether five years, 50 years, or 1000 years. As the NASA website above has stated, "Stay tuned..."

28.5 - Physics at work: compasses and the Earth

A magnetized compass needle aligns with the Earth's magnetic north and south poles. The needle's north pole, sometimes distinguished by a bright color as in the photograph above, points toward the Earth's magnetic south pole. However, the Earth's magnetic poles are not at the same locations as its geographic poles. For instance, in 1831, British explorer James Clark Ross located the magnetic south pole off the coast of Canada (remember, the magnetic south pole corresponds to the geographic North Pole). He tried to duplicate this feat for the magnetic north pole near Antarctica, but failed due to weather and ice. Nonetheless, many regions of that continent (such as the Ross Sea) are named after him.

In mountains near Seattle, Washington, the magnetic declination is about 20°.

The angle between the directions to the magnetic and geographic poles is called the magnetic *declination*. Many topographic maps provide the local angle of declination so that hikers and others can compensate for it and orient their compasses to geographic north. The first sketch on the right shows the declination for Seattle, Washington: It is approximately $20°$.

Scientists and navigators also found that compasses could be used to estimate latitude (north/south position on the planet). Although today's compasses are designed to move in a horizontal plane, the needles in some early instruments were allowed to rotate freely in all directions (like a bar magnet suspended by a string tied around its middle). When carried to a magnetic pole of the Earth, the magnetic needles of these compasses would point straight up or down; conversely, when near the equator, they would point almost horizontally. By measuring the angle of the needle from the horizontal, navigators could estimate their latitude.

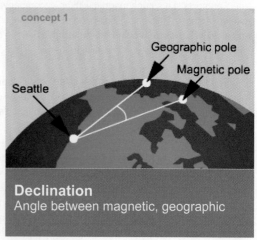

concept 1

Geographic pole

Magnetic pole

Seattle

Declination
Angle between magnetic, geographic

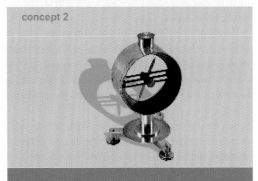

pole

concept 2

Latitude
Can be estimated with a dip needle

28.6 - Ferromagnetism

Ferromagnetism: A strong magnetic effect exhibited by the atoms of certain elements, notably iron. It is the cause of the magnetic field of commonly used magnets.

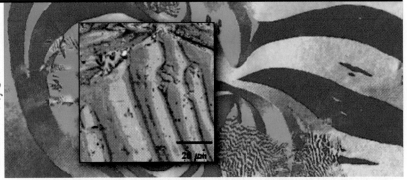

Color image: magnetic domains in an amorphous ferromagnet.
Inset: magnetic domains in heat-treated carbon steel.

Ferromagnetism is the basis of the most familiar type of magnetic devices. When you see a magnet affixed to a refrigerator door, you are witnessing the results of ferromagnetism. "Ferro" comes from the Latin word for iron, since iron is the most common element to exhibit this property. Ferromagnetism is present in the magnets that can be purchased in toy or hardware stores.

Nickel and cobalt are two other common elements with atoms that exhibit ferromagnetism, though to a lesser extent. Gadolinium and dysprosium are two exotic elements that can be used to make strong magnets that perform well at low temperatures.

In order to explain the source of ferromagnetism, we have to pay a quick visit to a concept developed in quantum theory. The classic model of atoms − electrons revolving about a central nucleus − does not suffice. Ferromagnetism is caused by a property of electrons called *spin*. For the purposes of this discussion, we say that spin is used to describe the angular momentum of an electron due its rotation, akin to the angular momentum of the Earth due to its rotation about its axis. (This is only an analogy. A more detailed, much less mechanistic description requires the context of quantum theory.) This is one form of angular momentum possessed by the electrons.

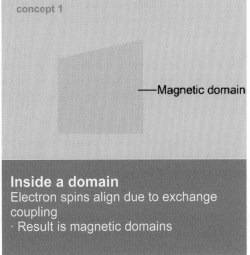

concept 1

—Magnetic domain

Inside a domain
Electron spins align due to exchange coupling
· Result is magnetic domains

They also possess *orbital angular momentum* due to their motion about the nucleus. Both contribute to the magnetic moment of the electron, but only spin is relevant to the discussion of ferromagnetism. The magnetic moment vector helps quantify how much torque a magnetic dipole will experience in a magnetic field; the larger the moment, the greater the torque. The moment points from the south pole to the north pole of the dipole.

Spin means that each electron has its own magnetic field. It can be considered as acting like a bar magnet, a dipole with north and south poles.

In many materials, the spin of each electron cancels out that of another electron in the same atom with which it is "paired," resulting in no net magnetic field. Ferromagnetism results from the net magnetic field created by unpaired electron spins. For example, each iron atom contains four electrons with uncancelled spins, giving the iron atom a net dipole moment.

In ferromagnetic materials, the spins of the electrons of one atom interact with the spins of electrons of neighboring atoms. This interaction, called *exchange coupling,* is quantum mechanical in nature. As a result of exchange coupling, the magnetic dipoles of atoms within a ferromagnetic material tend to align in the same direction.

When the magnetic dipole moments of ferromagnetic atoms align, the result is a *magnetic domain*, a region in a material where there is a net magnetic field. Magnetic domains can be seen under powerful microscopes, often with the aid of a technique called magnetic force microscopy. In the color micrograph above, domains are given false colors to be more easily seen in the image. Typical domains have a diameter about one-third that of a human hair. This can be best seen in the small inset micrograph that shows the magnetic domains in a sample of carbon steel. Even small amounts of magnetic materials contain vast numbers of domains. A domain may contain 10^{12} to 10^{15} atoms, but since a cubic centimeter of iron contains about 2.5×10^{19} atoms, there are still a large number of domains.

There is a good question here: Why are not all iron objects magnets? The reason is that although domains have magnetic fields, they point in random directions unless they have been subjected to an external magnetic field. This is shown in Concept 2. The random nature of their directions means there is no net magnetic field in the substance.

However, when the ferromagnetic material is placed in an external magnetic field, a process occurs that results in the material gaining its own overall magnetic field. This happens because the external field exerts a torque on the magnetic dipoles.

The magnetic field overcomes the tendency of the dipoles to stay aligned with their neighbors, and causes them to align with the field. Unaligned dipoles bordering domains that are aligned with the field steadily become "converted" to the new orientation. This causes the domains aligned with the external field to expand. This is shown in Concept 3, where the domains shown in Concept 2 have combined to form three domains.

Since there is a tendency for the dipoles to remain aligned, when the external magnetic field is removed, the domains (and the dipoles that make them up) remain aligned. This means the material now has its own magnetic field. In short, a magnet has been created.

An external magnetic field can cause non-ferromagnetic materials to develop their own magnetic field. These other forms of magnetism are called diamagnetism and paramagnetism. However, ferromagnets are distinct and quite useful for two reasons. First, a ferromagnet retains its magnetic field after the external field is removed. A refrigerator magnet, or the information stored on a VCR tape, both rely on the longevity of ferromagnets. The other forms of magnetism disappear after the external magnetic field is removed.

Second, the magnetic field created by ferromagnetic materials is typically orders of magnitude stronger than that found in the other forms of magnetism in most materials. This makes ferromagnets useful for a wide range of everyday applications.

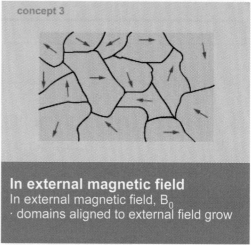

Random domains
Unaligned domains mean no net magnetic field

concept 3

In external magnetic field
In external magnetic field, B_0
· domains aligned to external field grow

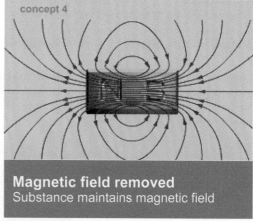

Magnetic field removed
Substance maintains magnetic field

Magnetic fields exert forces on **moving**, electrically charged particles.

This phenomenon makes for a good demonstration in a physics class. A current-carrying wire is placed near a magnet. The magnet exerts a force on the electrons moving in the wire, which causes the wire to move toward or away from the magnet. When the current is turned off, the magnetic field stops exerting a force on the wire.

The images on the screens of traditional televisions and computers are the result of electrons being accelerated by an electric field, subsequently being

TV tube. A gun (far left) accelerates electrons across a potential difference. Electromagnets (brown) steer the moving charges to light up screen pixels.

"steered" by magnetic fields, and then striking the screen to create light of different colors at specific locations. If you were to place a magnet close to such a system, you would distort the image. However, we do not recommend you do this, as it could cause expensive or irreversible damage!

Four factors determine the amount of force exerted by a magnetic field on a moving particle. They are the particle's charge and speed, the strength of the magnetic field and the angle of intersection between the particle's velocity and the magnetic field. The force is greatest when these two vectors are perpendicular, and zero when they are parallel.

When a charged particle is surrounded by an external **electric** field, the electric force on the charge is exerted along the field lines. The electric field exerts a force on the charge whether it is moving or stationary. In contrast, **magnetic** fields only exert a force on **moving** charged particles, pushing them neither in the direction of the particle's motion nor along the lines of the field. The force exerted on a moving charge by a magnetic field is perpendicular to **both** the particle's velocity and the direction of the field.

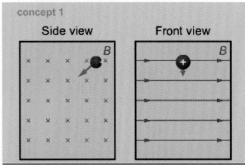

concept 1

Side view   Front view

Magnetic field, charged particle
Magnetic field exerts force on moving charge
· Force perpendicular to velocity, field

You see this illustrated to the right, and you also experienced it when you used the two simulations in the introduction to this chapter. In Concept 1, the same phenomenon is shown from two different vantage points.

In both illustrations, a positive charge is moving through a magnetic field. In the view labeled "side view," the magnetic field points away from you. This is depicted with ×'s, which represent the field lines viewed from behind. This view is used to best show the direction of the force: It is perpendicular to both the field and the velocity vectors.

In the view labeled "front view," your viewpoint has been rotated $90°$ so the field appears parallel to the screen. The force vector in the front view points toward you and is represented by a dot. You are looking at "the business end" of the vector's arrow.

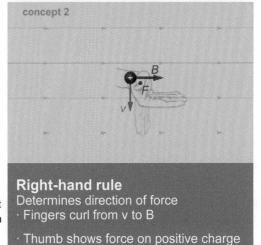

concept 2

Right-hand rule
Determines direction of force
· Fingers curl from v to B

· Thumb shows force on positive charge

A right-hand rule is used to determine the direction of the force. The front view makes it easier to see, so we use that in Concept 2. To apply the right-hand rule, the fingers of a flat hand start out pointing in the same direction as the velocity vector of the charge. Then they curl, so that the fingers point in the same direction as the magnetic field. The fingers wrap **from** the velocity vector **to** the magnetic field vector.

For a positive charge, the thumb points in the direction of the force exerted on the moving charge. The thumb points **opposite** to the direction of the force for a **negative charge**. In other words, with a negative charge, you apply the same rule, but reverse the results.

The equation to determine the force is shown to the right. The force equals the charge times the cross product of the velocity and magnetic field vectors. The cross product is calculated with the sine, as shown to the right.

To determine the amount of force, multiply the absolute value of the charge (its positive value), the charge's speed, the field strength, and the sine of the angle between the velocity and field vectors. This angle is shown in the illustration for the equation. When calculating the force magnitude, you use the smaller, positive angle between the velocity and magnetic field vectors. For instance, in the Equation 1 diagram the angle is 90°, not −90° or 270°.

As mentioned earlier, the unit for magnetic field strength is the tesla. One tesla equals one newton·second per coulomb·meter, or N·s/C·m. In other words, one coulomb of charge traveling at one meter per second through a magnetic field having a strength of one tesla experiences one newton of force. A tesla is a rather large unit (remember that one coulomb is a lot of charge), so the smaller unit *gauss* (G) is fairly common. Ten thousand gauss equals one tesla. As mentioned earlier, the Earth's magnetic field is about 5×10^{-5} T, which equals 0.5 G.

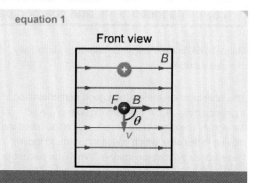

equation 1

Front view

Force on charge moving through magnetic field

$$\mathbf{F} = q\mathbf{v} \times \mathbf{B}$$
$$F = |q|vB \sin \theta$$

$\mathbf{F}$ = magnetic force on particle
q = charge
$\mathbf{v}$ = velocity
$\mathbf{B}$ = magnetic field
θ = angle between velocity and field

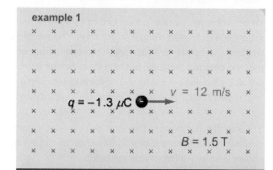

example 1

$q = -1.3\ \mu C$ $v = 12$ m/s

$B = 1.5$ T

The particle is moving to the right. What are the magnitude and direction of the force on it?

$\theta = 90°$

$F = |q|vB \sin \theta$

$F = |-1.3 \times 10^{-6} C|\left(12\ \tfrac{m}{s}\right)(1.5T)(\sin 90°)$

$F = 2.3 \times 10^{-5}$ N
directed down (opposite to thumb)

28.8 - Interactive checkpoint: a charge in a magnetic field

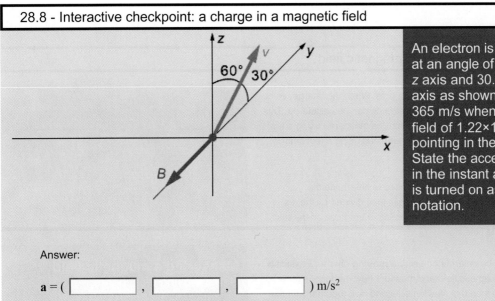

An electron is traveling in the *yz* plane at an angle of 60.0° from the positive *z* axis and 30.0° from the positive *y* axis as shown. Its speed is a constant 365 m/s when a uniform magnetic field of 1.22×10^{-3} T is turned on, pointing in the negative *y* direction. State the acceleration of the electron in the instant after the magnetic field is turned on as a vector in rectangular notation.

Answer:

$$\mathbf{a} = (\boxed{} , \boxed{} , \boxed{}) \text{ m/s}^2$$

28.9 - Interactive problem: charged particle moving in a B field

In this simulation you can change two properties of a particle: its charge and its velocity (both speed and direction). We ask you to alter the velocity of the particle in order to achieve certain forces.

In the initial view of the magnetic field it is directed straight down, and the charge starts near the middle of the screen. You can use the slider in the control panel to change the viewing angle. Press GO to start the simulation, and press RESET whenever you want to change the particle's initial velocity or charge.

You can only change the direction of the initial velocity when the viewing angle is set to the far right and the magnetic field is pointing straight down. This orientation makes the angle between the velocity vector and the magnetic field vector easy to see. You change the direction of the velocity vector by dragging it with the mouse.

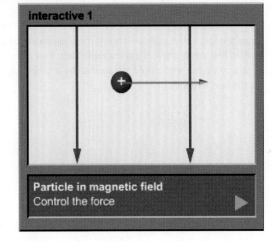

interactive 1

Particle in magnetic field
Control the force

Your first task is to set the direction of the particle's initial velocity so that no force is exerted on the charge by the field. No shortcuts! You could solve this by setting the velocity to 0 m/s, but we want you to solve the problem by setting the velocity vector's direction correctly. When the field exerts no force, both the direction and speed of the particle will remain constant.

Note that after you change the charge or the velocity vector (speed or direction), but before you press GO, the force meter tells you what the force on the particle will be, not what it is. The force is zero whenever the particle is not moving, but we thought you would appreciate seeing immediate feedback on your changes, without having to launch the particle every time.

What is the relationship between the directions of the field and the velocity vector when the force equals zero? (Note: There are actually two directions in which you can set the velocity vector to achieve this, one $180°$ opposed to the other.)

For your next challenge, set the parameters in the simulation to maximize the amount of force on the particle. As with your first task, there are two directions that result in a maximum force on the charge. You will find yourself clicking the up and down arrows on parameters like "Charge" until you reach their maximum value in the simulation. The maximum amount of force you can achieve in this simulation is 1.68×10^{-8} newtons.

For your final task, change the charge from positive to negative while keeping the initial velocity the same. What effect does this have on the magnitude and direction of the force?

If you are surprised by the results of any of these configurations, refer back to the section that discussed the effect of a magnetic field on a moving charged particle.

28.10 - Determining the strength of a magnetic field

A magnetic field exerts a force on a moving charged particle. When the charge, velocity and field are known, the direction and magnitude of that force can be calculated. This process can also be reversed: Just as an electric field can be measured using a test charge, the strength of a magnetic field can also be determined using a test charge. The process is similar, but with a couple of twists.

In an electric field, a stationary positive test charge is used to determine the electrostatic force at a given point. The amount of force is then divided by the test charge to determine the electric field strength. The direction of the force on the test charge indicates the direction of the field.

In a magnetic field, the force must be determined using a **moving** charge. Physicists fire a charged particle through a magnetic field and measure how the force exerted on it by the field alters its velocity. They then use Newton's second law, together with the observed acceleration and the mass of the particle, to calculate the force the field exerts on it.

The angle between the velocity and the magnetic field vectors must also be known to determine the field. (A compass can be used to determine the direction of the field.) Once the force and angle are known, they can be used in the equation shown on the right to find the strength of the magnetic field. This is the same equation shown earlier to determine the amount of force exerted by a given magnetic field, but here it is solved for the field strength.

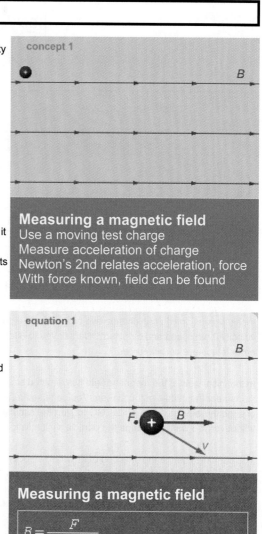

concept 1

Measuring a magnetic field
Use a moving test charge
Measure acceleration of charge
Newton's 2nd relates acceleration, force
With force known, field can be found

equation 1

Measuring a magnetic field

$$B = \frac{F}{|q|v\sin\theta}$$

B = magnetic field strength
F = force, q = charge
v = speed
θ = angle between velocity and field

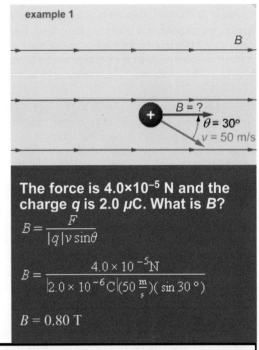

example 1

B

B = ?
$\theta = 30°$
v = 50 m/s

The force is 4.0×10⁻⁵ N and the charge _q_ is 2.0 _μ_C. What is _B_?

$$B = \frac{F}{|q|v \sin\theta}$$

$$B = \frac{4.0 \times 10^{-5}\text{N}}{|2.0 \times 10^{-6}\text{C}|(50\,\frac{\text{m}}{\text{s}})(\sin 30\,°)}$$

$$B = 0.80 \text{ T}$$

28.11 - Interactive problem: B field strength and particle motion

In this simulation, you want the magnetic field to exert a force of 1.16×10^{-8} newtons on the positively charged particle. Set the particle's speed v (the maximum possible value is 520 m/s) and the magnetic field strength B (the maximum possible value is 3.00 T) to cause the required amount of force, using the controllers provided in the control panel. You will find that you need to adjust both the speed and the field strength upward from their initial settings to achieve this force.

If you have any trouble achieving the desired force, review the discussion in the previous section on determining the strength of a magnetic field. If you have any questions about how to use the simulation, see the previous interactive problems in this chapter for complete instructions.

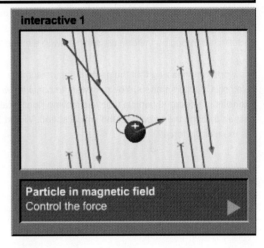

interactive 1

Particle in magnetic field
Control the force

28.12 - Physics at work: velocity selector

A velocity selector is a device that allows charged particles moving only at a specified speed to pass through it. It uses a combination of an electric field and a magnetic field to "trap" particles moving at other speeds. In addition to being a useful tool, a velocity selector provides a good way to explore the contrasting effects of electric and magnetic fields.

To the right is a conceptual diagram of a velocity selector for charged particles. Perhaps a scientist wants only electrons moving at 50,000 m/s to pass through. The electric field of the velocity selector points down, and will exert an upward force on an electron. (Remember that the force is opposite to the direction of the electric field because electrons are negatively charged.)

A magnetic field is used to counter the effect of the electric field. The magnetic field

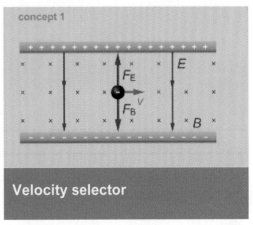

concept 1

F_E
E
v
F_B
B

Velocity selector

strength is set so that the field exerts an equal but opposite force on any electron moving at 50,000 m/s. Since the force exerted on the electron by the electric field is upward, the magnetic field force must point down. Electrons with the required speed will travel horizontally and pass through an aperture at the right end of the selector. Slower or faster ones will experience a net force and be forced up or down. (We ignore the force of gravity, whose effect would be minor for a particle moving at this speed.)

The sum of the forces on the particle is $q\mathbf{E} + (q\mathbf{v} \times \mathbf{B})$. This equation is called the *Lorentz force law*. The strength of the electric force equals $|q|E$. The strength of the magnetic force equals $|q|vB$ (since the velocity is perpendicular to the field). When the forces sum to zero, these two expressions are equal in magnitude. On the right, we solve for the speed and see that it equals the ratio of the electric to the magnetic field strength. As you can see, the charge cancels out.

Can you predict the direction in which this device's magnetic field needs to point using a right-hand rule? The electric force on the electron points up, so we want the magnetic field force to point down. Since the charge is negative, the thumb will point in the opposite direction of the force. This means you want the thumb to point up. The fingers must wrap from the velocity vector to the magnetic field vector. You can conclude that the magnetic field vector must point away from you, which is how it is depicted in the diagram.

In the setup shown here, if a negatively charged electron is moving too fast, the force exerted by the magnetic field will be greater than that exerted by the electric field, and as a result it will pull it down. If the electron is moving too slowly, the electric field will win the contest and pull it up. The example problem to the right shows how to determine the strength of the magnetic field that permits an electron moving at 53,000 m/s to pass undeflected through a uniform electric field with a magnitude of 4.0 N/C.

It is worth emphasizing that the name of the device is a *velocity* selector, not a *speed* selector. Direction matters. You may want to consider what magnetic force would be exerted on a charged particle that was moving horizontally, but from right to left as it passed through the selector at the critical speed. Would the magnetic force still cancel out the electric force?

Charges of specific speed pass through
Uses electric and magnetic fields
Electric force balances magnetic force

equation 1

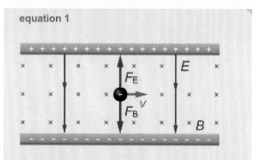

At equilibrium:
$\mathbf{F}_E + \mathbf{F}_B = 0$, so $|q|E - |q|vB = 0$, and

$$v = \frac{E}{B}$$

$\mathbf{F}_E$ = force of electric field
$\mathbf{F}_B$ = force of magnetic field
q = charge, v = speed of charge
E = electric field strength
B = magnetic field strength

example 1

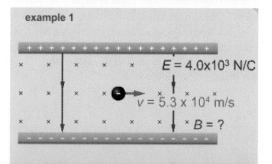

$E = 4.0 \times 10^3$ N/C
$v = 5.3 \times 10^4$ m/s
$B = ?$

This electron passes through the velocity selector with its velocity unchanged. What is B?
$v = E/B$
$B = E/v$
$B = (4.0 \times 10^3 \text{ N/C})/(5.3 \times 10^4 \text{ m/s})$
$B = 0.075$ T

28.13 - Circular motion of particles in magnetic fields

When the velocity of a charged particle is perpendicular to a uniform magnetic field, it causes the particle to move in a circular path. In this section we discuss why this occurs, and we state some properties of that motion.

At the right is a diagram showing a magnetic field (pointing directly into the screen) and a positively charged particle moving in a circular path. Its motion started when the particle was fired into the field along the surface of the page.

Why is the motion circular? First, recall that the magnetic force is always perpendicular to the velocity vector. This means it neither increases nor decreases the speed of the particle. It only changes the direction of its motion.

The force always points toward the center of the circle. You can use the right-hand rule at any point of the circle to confirm this. (The fingers wrap from **v** to **B**, so the thumb points toward the center.)

The magnitude of the force is constant. The quantities that determine the force, q, v, B, and θ, do not change as the particle moves. Even as the particle's velocity changes direction, the angle θ between the velocity and magnetic field stays constant at $90°$.

If you recall your studies of uniform circular motion and centripetal forces, this may all sound familiar. A constant force that points toward the center causes uniform circular motion. In other words, the force exerted by the magnetic field is a centripetal force.

An interesting aspect of this kind of motion is that the field does no work on the particle. One way to conclude this is by noting that the particle's energy does not change. Its speed is constant (which means its KE is constant) and its PE does not change in this uniform field. Since there is no change in energy, no work occurs. This is quite distinct from the situation of a charged particle in an electric field: Electric fields can do work on charged particles.

Now we summarize the equations on the right. In Equation 1, we take the centripetal force in uniform circular motion to be the magnetic force, and use Newton's second law to state that this must equal the mass of the particle times its centripetal acceleration v^2/r. We then solve for the radius r.

We can state other equations that further describe the motion of the particle. First, we calculate the period T of the particle's motion: The result is shown in Equation 2. We derive this equation by starting with the equation for the period of an object in circular motion (the circumference divided by the speed). Then we substitute the formula for the speed of the particle in the magnetic field (obtained by solving the radius equation in Equation 1 for v).

Notice the interesting fact that the period is not a function of the speed, but only of the mass and charge of the particle, as well as the strength of the magnetic field. A faster moving particle moves in a circle of greater circumference, but the period does not change.

We have also included in Equation 3 the equations for the frequency f and the angular frequency ω of the particle's motion. These can be derived using the relationship of period and frequency, and of frequency and angular frequency.

Without discussing it further in this section, we do note that if the velocity of the charged particle is not perpendicular to the field, but has a component parallel to the field, then it will move in helical motion. If you would like to observe helical motion, go to the simulation in the introduction to this chapter, move the particle's velocity vector to a direction that is not perpendicular to the field, press GO, and use the viewing angle slider to watch the resulting motion from various vantage points.

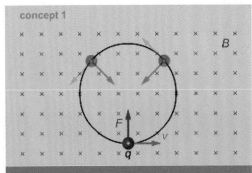

concept 1

Circular motion

Velocity perpendicular to magnetic field
· Force perpendicular to velocity

· Magnitude of force constant

· Circular motion results

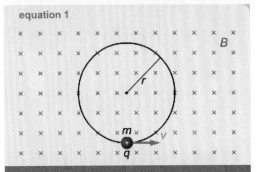

equation 1

Radius

$|q|vB = ma = m(v^2/r)$, so

$$r = \frac{mv}{|q|B}$$

r = radius, m = mass
v = speed, q = charge
B = magnetic field strength

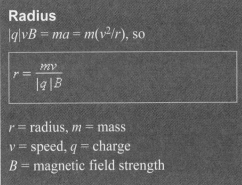

equation 2

Period

$T = \dfrac{2\pi r}{v}$, and $v = \dfrac{|q|rB}{m}$ so

$$T = \dfrac{2\pi m}{|q|B}$$

T = period

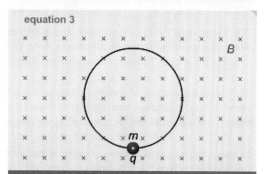

equation 3

Frequency, angular frequency

$$f = \dfrac{|q|B}{2\pi m}, \qquad \omega = \dfrac{|q|B}{m}$$

f = frequency, ω = angular frequency

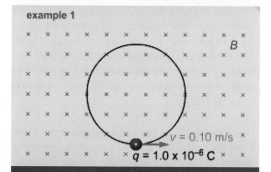

example 1

$v = 0.10$ m/s

$q = 1.0 \times 10^{-6}$ C

$m = 2.5\times10^{-7}$ kg and $B = 0.50$ T. What is the angular frequency of the particle's motion?

$$\omega = \dfrac{|q|B}{m}$$

$$\omega = \dfrac{(1.0 \times 10^{-6}\ \text{C})\,(0.50\ \text{T})}{(2.5 \times 10^{-7}\ \text{kg})}$$

$$\omega = 2.0\ \text{rad/s}$$

28.14 - Sample problem: proton in a magnetic field

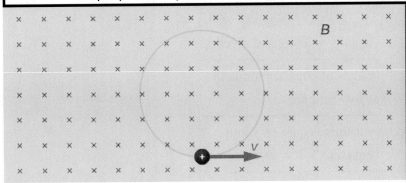

This proton is moving in a circular path in a magnetic field. Its angular velocity is 2.00×10^7 rad/s.

What is the strength of the magnetic field?

Variables

angular velocity	$\omega = 2.00 \times 10^7$ rad/s
speed	v
radius of circular path	r
magnetic field strength	B
mass of proton	$m_p = 1.67 \times 10^{-27}$ kg
charge of proton	$q = 1.60 \times 10^{-19}$ C

What is the strategy?

1. Find the speed of the circling proton in terms of the radius and angular velocity of its motion.
2. State the equation for the radius of the circular motion of a charged particle in a magnetic field. For the particle's speed, use the expression from strategy step 1.
3. Solve for the magnetic field and evaluate.

Physics principles and equations

The relationship between angular velocity and tangential speed is

$$v = r\omega$$

The radius of a particle's circular motion in a magnetic field is

$$r = \frac{mv}{|q|B}$$

Step-by-step solution

Step	Reason
1. $v = r\omega$	angular velocity and speed
2. $r = \dfrac{m_{\text{p}} v}{|q| B}$	radius of circular motion in a magnetic field
3. $r = \dfrac{m_{\text{p}} r \omega}{|q| B}$	substitute equation 1 into equation 2
4. $B = \dfrac{m_{\text{p}} \omega}{|q|}$	simplify and solve for B
5. $B = \dfrac{(1.67 \times 10^{-27}\ \text{kg})(2.00 \times 10^{7}\ \text{rad/s})}{1.60 \times 10^{-19}\ \text{C}}$ $B = 0.209\ \text{T}$	evaluate

28.15 - Physics at work: mass spectrometer

Mass spectrometers are used to determine the masses of atoms or molecules, or their relative abundance in a sample. They are used in a range of settings from surgery (to determine the mixture of gases in a patient's lungs) to space missions (to analyze the atmospheres or soils of planets and other celestial bodies). Chemists also frequently use them to analyze materials.

A conceptual diagram of a mass spectrometer is shown to the right. To use the device, the substance being analyzed is first vaporized if it is not already a gas. It is then ionized: An electron is removed from each particle so that it has a net positive charge equal to $+e$. The ionized particles are then accelerated across a potential difference between two charged plates.

The particles all have the same charge, and the experimenter keeps the potential difference between the plates, and the resulting electric field strength, at a constant value. This means the force exerted on various particles by the electric field does not change; their accelerations depend only on their masses.

Each moving, charged particle passes through an entry port into a uniform magnetic field. The field is perpendicular to the velocity of the particle, which means the particle will move in a circular path. The magnetic field is kept constant so that the radius of the path is a function of the particle's speed and mass.

Each particle traverses a circular path and the point where it strikes the sensing plate of the device is recorded. The radius of the path is one-half the distance from the entry port. The particle's mass can be determined using the equation shown to the right.

Determining the mass of a particle (Derivation). In the following derivation we assume that the ion has a charge of $+e$, so that it is accelerated from the positively charged plate to the negatively charged plate, and then curves to the right after it enters the magnetic field, which is directed out of the screen toward you.

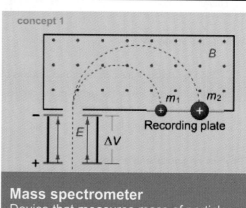

concept 1

Mass spectrometer
Device that measures mass of particles
Electric field accelerates ions
Radius measured to determine mass

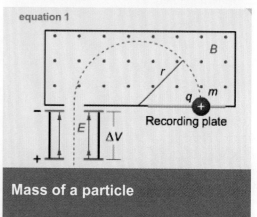

equation 1

Mass of a particle

Variables

change in kinetic energy	ΔKE
mass of ion	m
accelerated speed of ion	v
radius of circle in magnetic field	r
charge of positive ion	$q = +1.6 \times 10^{-19}$ C
magnetic field strength	B
change in potential energy	ΔPE
potential difference across plates	ΔV

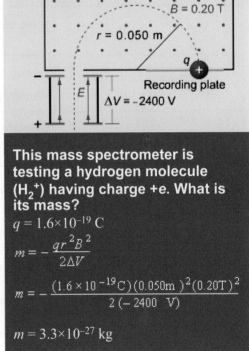

$$m = -\frac{qr^2 B^2}{2\Delta V}$$

m = mass, q = charge
r = radius
B = magnetic field strength
ΔV = potential difference

Strategy

1. Express the change in the **kinetic** energy of the ion during the acceleration phase in terms of its mass and quantities that can be controlled or measured by the experimenter. By "acceleration phase," we mean the linear acceleration in the electric field.

2. Express the change in the **potential** energy of the ion during the acceleration phase in terms of some of the same quantities, including the potential difference between the plates.

3. Use the conservation of energy to relate kinetic energy to potential energy, and solve for the unknown mass of the charged particle.

Physics principles and equations

We use the definition of kinetic energy.

$$KE = \tfrac{1}{2} mv^2$$

The radius of the circular path of a charged particle moving perpendicular to the magnetic field is

$$r = mv/qB$$

The potential difference equals the change in PE per unit charge.

$$\Delta V = \Delta PE / q$$

The principle of the conservation of energy applied to mechanical energy states that

$$\Delta KE + \Delta PE = 0$$

Since the magnetic field changes the particle's direction but not its speed, its KE is not changed by the magnetic field.

example 1

$B = 0.20$ T
$r = 0.050$ m
q
Recording plate
$\Delta V = -2400$ V
E

This mass spectrometer is testing a hydrogen molecule (H_2^+) having charge +e. What is its mass?

$$q = 1.6 \times 10^{-19} \text{ C}$$

$$m = -\frac{qr^2 B^2}{2\Delta V}$$

$$m = -\frac{(1.6 \times 10^{-19}\text{C})(0.050\text{m})^2(0.20\text{T})^2}{2(-2400 \text{ V})}$$

$$m = 3.3 \times 10^{-27} \text{ kg}$$

Step-by-step derivation

In the first stage of the derivation we write ΔKE in terms of the mass m and the speed v of an ion as it leaves the electric field and enters the magnetic field. Neither m nor v can be directly observed. We use another equation to replace v by quantities that can be controlled or observed in the laboratory.

Step	Reason
1. $\Delta KE = \frac{1}{2}mv^2$	change in KE for particle starting at rest
2. $r = \dfrac{mv}{qB}$	radius of positive ion's path in magnetic field
3. $v = \dfrac{rqB}{m}$	solve equation 2 for v
4. $\Delta KE = \frac{1}{2}m\dfrac{r^2q^2B^2}{m^2}$	substitute equation 3 into equation 1
5. $\Delta KE = \dfrac{r^2q^2B^2}{2m}$	simplify

Now we write ΔPE in terms of q and the potential difference ΔV across the accelerating plates. Finally, we write an equation for ΔKE and ΔPE based on the conservation of energy, substitute the expression found above, and solve for the unknown mass m of the charged particle.

Step	Reason
6. $\Delta PE = q\Delta V$	change in potential energy
7. $\Delta KE = -\Delta PE$	conservation of energy
8. $\dfrac{r^2q^2B^2}{2m} = -q\Delta V$	substitute equations 5 and 6 into equation 7
9. $m = -\dfrac{qr^2B^2}{2\Delta V}$	solve for m

Although we derived the mass equation for a positively charged particle, we could equally well do so for a negatively charged particle (the charged plates in the mass spectrometer would have to be reversed to accelerate it in the correct direction).

In order for a charged particle to move in a circular path in a uniform magnetic field, it must enter the field with a perpendicular velocity. But what if its velocity has a component parallel to the field?

Aurora Borealis display in the northern sky.

The result is shown to the right: It is called *helical* motion. The particle traces out circles that wind upward (or downward) in a fashion similar to the motion of a car navigating the "corkscrew" ramps found in many multistory parking garages. The particle moves both in circles and up or down at the same time. You can use the interactive simulation in a following section to observe helical motion.

To explain why helical motion occurs, we need to decompose the velocity into components perpendicular and parallel to the magnetic field. The two diagrams in Concept 1 do this. In the left-hand diagram, the magnetic field is viewed obliquely (but not fully parallel to the surface of the screen) and you can see both components of the particle's velocity.

The component $v_{perpendicular}$ is perpendicular to the magnetic field. This component accounts for the circular motion of the particle. The other component of the velocity, $v_{parallel}$, is parallel to the magnetic field. Since there is no magnetic force exerted on a charge moving parallel to a magnetic field, this velocity component does not change. It accounts for the constant upward or downward motion of the particle.

The result of the forces exerted on the particle is that the particle moves in circles in a plane perpendicular to the magnetic field and at a constant speed in a direction parallel to the magnetic field. The sum of these motions is helical motion.

As the particle moves in a helical path, the vertical spacing between the loops of the helix, known as the *pitch*, remains constant since the vertical velocity component does not change.

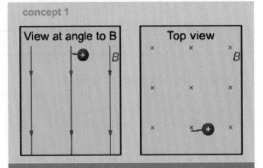

concept 1

| View at angle to B | Top view |

Helical motion
Velocity components perpendicular, parallel to field
· Perp: force causes circular motion
· Parallel: force zero, $v_{parallel}$ constant
Helical motion results

Helical motion can arise in a nonuniform magnetic field, as well. A magnetic field that is stronger at its outer edges can cause a particle to become trapped in a *magnetic bottle*. The particle moves in a helical fashion, spiraling up and down inside the "bottle." Physicists construct bottles like this as three-dimensional systems that can contain charged particles indefinitely.

The Earth creates a magnetic bottle of this type. Its magnetic field is stronger near the poles. Electrons and protons are trapped in the bottle created by the Earth. They oscillate back and forth over a short distance every few seconds, resulting in what are called the *Van Allen radiation belts*.

Such belts, as well as solar flares, are responsible for *auroras*, the glorious bands of light visible in the sky at high latitudes at certain times of the year. The auroras result from solar flares that shoot ionized particles, primarily electrons and protons, into the Earth's atmosphere. These particles get trapped in the Van Allen belts. As the particles collide with oxygen and nitrogen molecules from the atmosphere, they emit green and pink light respectively. From a great distance, you may perceive a faint aurora as white light.

28.17 - Interactive problem: helical particle motion

In this simulation you will have a chance to observe a charged particle following a helical path through a magnetic field.

If you use the initial velocity provided by the simulation, which is perpendicular to the field, the particle will move in a circle. You can cause its path to be a helix by supplying a component to its initial velocity that is parallel to the field.

To do this, first make sure the magnetic field lines are viewed as pointing straight down. Now you may drag the tip of the velocity vector arrow to set the initial speed and direction of the particle. Once you have the initial velocity you want, change the viewing angle by moving the slider provided for this purpose to a position near the middle of its range. Press GO to observe the helical motion of the particle.

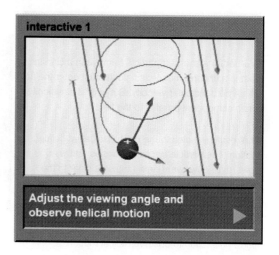

interactive 1

Adjust the viewing angle and observe helical motion

28.18 - Magnetic force on a current-carrying wire

A magnetic field exerts a force on a wire carrying a current. Since the moving charges in the wire – electrons in this case – cannot escape from it, the wire as a whole will react to the magnetic force on them, just as a large net full of helium balloons will rise due to the balloons' individual buoyancies.

At the right, we depict a configuration that shows how to determine the magnetic force exerted by a uniform magnetic field on a straight, current-carrying wire. We show only a segment of the wire, and not the entire circuit loop that allows current to flow.

The right-hand rule can be used to determine the direction of the force. Since the current shown is conventional (positive), the thumb points in the direction of the force when the fingers wrap from the direction of current flow to the magnetic field. (If the current were shown as flowing electrons, the thumb would point in the direction opposite to the current.) In this case the force points out of the screen, toward you.

To calculate the magnitude of the force exerted on a given length of wire, use the second equation shown in Equation 1. The amount of force increases with the amount of current, the length of the wire and the strength of the magnetic field. Since more current means either more electrons flowing, or the electrons moving faster, this relationship follows from the equation for force on a single charge, $F = qvB \sin \theta$ (or to state it using cross-product notation, $\mathbf{F} = q\mathbf{v} \times \mathbf{B}$). A greater length of wire will also experience more force since it contains more moving charge.

Variables

We list below the variables that are used in the derivation, but which do not already appear in Equation 1. The vector $\mathbf{L}$ appearing in the equation is the "directed length" of the wire segment. That is, $\mathbf{L}$ is parallel to the segment, in the direction of the current, and its magnitude L equals the length of the segment.

amount of free charge in wire segment	Q
velocity of a charge carrier in segment	$\mathbf{v}$
time for carrier to move through segment	Δt

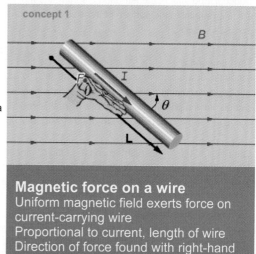

concept 1

Magnetic force on a wire
Uniform magnetic field exerts force on current-carrying wire
Proportional to current, length of wire
Direction of force found with right-hand rule

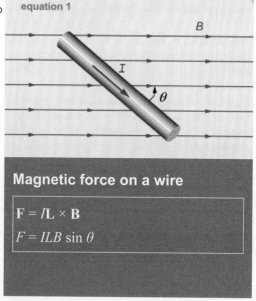

equation 1

Magnetic force on a wire

$$\mathbf{F} = I\mathbf{L} \times \mathbf{B}$$
$$F = ILB \sin \theta$$

Strategy

1. Use the definition of the current flowing through the segment to find that $I\mathbf{L} = q\mathbf{v}$.
2. Substitute this equation into the cross-product formula for the force exerted on a moving charge by a magnetic field to get Equation 1.

Physics principles and equations

The force exerted on a moving charged particle by a magnetic field is,

$$\mathbf{F} = q\mathbf{v} \times \mathbf{B}$$

Step-by-step derivation

We use the definition of the current flowing through the wire to obtain an equation relating $I\mathbf{L}$ and $q\mathbf{v}$. This enables us to make a substitution into the equation for the force exerted by a magnetic field on a moving charge.

Step	Reason
1. $I = q/\Delta t$	definition of current
2. $I\mathbf{L} = q\mathbf{L}/\Delta t$	multiply both sides by $\mathbf{L}$
3. $I\mathbf{L} = q\mathbf{v}$	$\mathbf{L}/\Delta t$ equals velocity of charge carrier
4. $\mathbf{F}_B = q\mathbf{v} \times \mathbf{B}$	equation for force on charged particle
5. $\mathbf{F}_B = I\mathbf{L} \times \mathbf{B}$	substitute equation 3 into equation 4

We state the equation proved above as a cross product. It is the same as saying the amount of force is $F_B = ILB \sin \theta$.

$\mathbf{F}$ = force, I = current
$\mathbf{L}$ = directed length of wire segment
$\mathbf{B}$ = magnetic field
θ = angle between wire and field

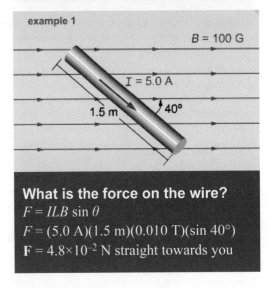

example 1

$B = 100$ G

$I = 5.0$ A

1.5 m   40°

What is the force on the wire?

$F = ILB \sin \theta$
$F = (5.0 \text{ A})(1.5 \text{ m})(0.010 \text{ T})(\sin 40°)$
$F = 4.8 \times 10^{-2}$ N straight towards you

28.19 - Physics at work: direct current electric motor

Direct current motors power a range of familiar everyday devices, from hairdryer fans to handheld electric drills. In these appliances, a few fundamental physics principles and clever engineering combine to create a motor that yields a constant amount of torque.

To understand how electric motors work, recall that a magnetic field exerts a force on a wire that is conducting electricity perpendicular to the field. When the wire is in the shape of a loop, one side of the loop will experience a force in one direction, and the other in the opposite direction. This means there will be a torque on the loop and it will rotate.

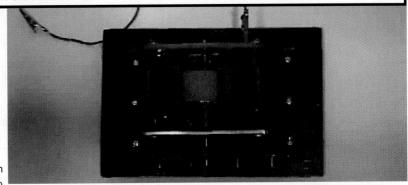

DC electric motor. The sparking copper commutator is visible between the rotors and the red plate at the top of the image.

The magnetic moment of a coil of loops is a vector, perpendicular to each loop, used to describe how much torque the coil will experience in a magnetic field. You can think of the coil as acting like a bar magnet. When the coil's moment is parallel to the field, it experiences no torque, since the "magnet" is lined up with the field. When it is perpendicular to the field, it experiences maximum torque.

At its simplest, a direct current motor consists of a current-carrying wire coil, wrapped around a metal armature, inside a uniform magnetic field. The external field creates a torque on the coil when current flows through it. That torque is used to rotate something: a fan, a drill bit, the blades of a blender and so forth.

However, a motor has two requirements that this configuration alone does not meet. First, it needs to rotate continuously in the same direction. The simple wire coil with a current will not do this: It will rotate in one direction until the field exerts no net torque on it, continue on beyond that due to its momentum, and then rotate back.

The second requirement for the motor is that it should provide a nearly constant torque. The torque on a simple coil varies as the angle of the coil in the field changes.

In Concept 1, you see a schematic diagram of a simplified direct current motor. Two permanent magnets form the circular outer edge of the motor. A magnetic field is directed from the north poles of these two magnets to the south poles. Inside these magnets is a wire coil, which is connected to a direct current, such as the current from a battery. This assembly is called a *rotor*.

The problem of rotating the rotor in a constant direction is solved with a commutator. A *commutator* consists of two sets of contacts that supply current to the coil. During one-half of a rotation, the coil is in contact with one set and the current flows in one direction. During the other half turn, the coil is in contact with the other set and the current flows in the opposite direction. In Concept 2, you can see that the current keeps reversing direction, which alters the direction of the coil's magnetic dipole moment. This reversal of current causes the rotor to keep experiencing a counterclockwise torque.

The problem of supplying constant torque is addressed with multiple rotors as you see in Concept 3. At any moment in time, current flows through two of the rotors, which are at different angles to the permanent field. Although the torque on any one rotor varies as it rotates, the sum of the torques on all three rotors stays nearly constant. This combination of current-reversing commutators with multiple rotors enables the motor to provide a steady source of torque.

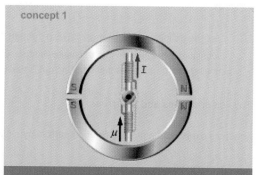

concept 1

Electric motor
Rotor: bar surrounded by wire coil
Current flows through coil
Current creates magnetic moment
External field exerts torque on coil

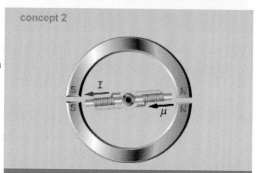

concept 2

Commutator
Changes direction of current
Reverses magnetic moment

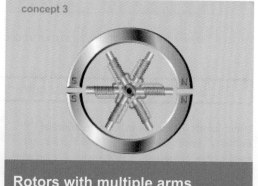

concept 3

Rotors with multiple arms
More arms = smoother torque

28.20 - The magnetic field around a wire

Currents produce magnetic fields. In this section, we analyze the orientation of the magnetic field created by a current flowing through a wire. In the Concept 1 and 2 diagrams, the electrons that make up the current are moving to the right. Conventional current flow is indicated (as always) with an arrow pointing in the opposite direction.

The Concept 1 diagram uses two compasses to show the direction of the magnetic field due to the current at two different points. Each needle points in the direction of the magnetic field at its location.

As the diagram shows, the magnetic field wraps around the current. The arrows indicate its direction. The field is strongest near the wires. As with electric field diagrams, the density of lines reflects the strength of the field. This means the lines are drawn close together near the wire.

How do you determine the direction of the magnetic field? You use the *right-hand rule for currents*. Wrap your hand around the wire so that your thumb points in the direction of the (conventional) current. Your fingers wrap around, just like the concentric circles in the diagram, and they point in the direction of the magnetic field. You see this shown in Concept 2. If the direction of the current were to reverse, your thumb would point in the opposite direction, and your fingers would wrap in the other direction. When the direction of the current changes, so does the direction of the magnetic field.

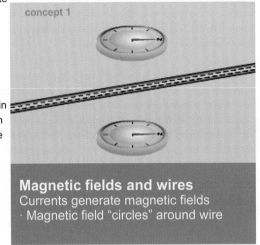

Magnetic fields and wires
Currents generate magnetic fields
· Magnetic field "circles" around wire

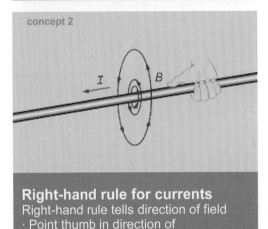

Right-hand rule for currents
Right-hand rule tells direction of field
· Point thumb in direction of conventional current
· Curled fingers show direction of magnetic field

28.21 - Two wires and their magnetic fields

To illustrate the nature of the fields and forces produced by currents, we use the example of two wires placed parallel to one other and conducting currents flowing in the same direction, as illustrated in Concept 1. The two wires attract each other.

Let's determine why they attract each other by first considering the orientation of the magnetic field created by the wire on the bottom. We use the right-hand rule for currents to determine this orientation. This is shown in Concept 1.

Next, we determine the direction of the force exerted by the magnetic field on the electrons moving in the upper wire. The direction of electron movement is shown with velocity vectors in Concept 2. The right-hand rule for a charge moving in a magnetic field is used to determine the direction of the magnetic force on the electron. To apply the rule, point your fingers in the direction of the velocity vector and wrap them in the direction of the magnetic field. As the diagram shows, when it intersects the upper wire, the field is pointing away from you. Wrapping your fingers from the velocity vector to the field vector will cause your thumb to point up. Since an electron is a negative charge, your thumb will point in the direction opposite to the magnetic force on it. The result is that the force points down, toward the lower wire.

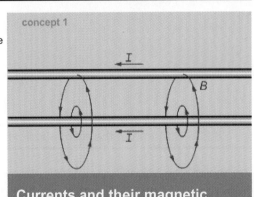

Currents and their magnetic fields
Each current creates a magnetic field
· Field intersects other wire

The right-hand rule for force can be used again to determine the force on the moving charges in the lower wire. If you apply it, you can confirm that they experience an upward force. This analysis explains why the two wires attract each other. We show the forces acting on both wires in Concept 3.

If the currents flow in opposite directions, the two wires repel each other. This scenario is illustrated in Concept 4. Here, the current in the bottom wire now flows in the opposite direction than in the prior discussion, which means its field has the opposite orientation. The force on the electrons in the upper wire now pushes them and the wire that contains them up, as the diagram reflects. The field of the upper wire pushes the electrons in the lower wire down. The two wires repel each other.

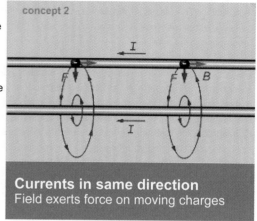

Currents in same direction
Field exerts force on moving charges

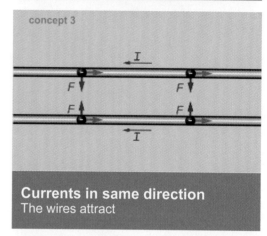

Currents in same direction
The wires attract

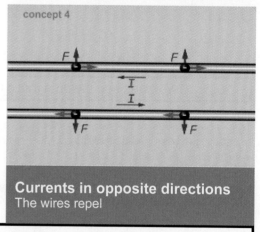

Currents in opposite directions
The wires repel

28.22 - Strength of the magnetic field around a wire

The strength of the magnetic field around a current-carrying wire can be calculated with the equation to the right. The field strength is a function of two variables: the amount of current and the distance from the wire. The field increases with current and decreases with distance. The equation includes μ_0, the *permeability constant of free space*. This constant equals $4\pi \times 10^{-7}$ N/A^2.

This equation is derived under the assumption that the wire is long and thin. It provides accurate values when the distance from the wire is significantly less than the wire length.

The direction of the magnetic field is determined using the right-hand rule for currents. To review: The conventional current runs to the right, so the thumb points to the right and the fingers wrap in the direction of the magnetic field.

To gain a sense of the strength of the magnetic field around a typical wire, you can look at the example problem to the right. Calculations show that the magnetic field strength 15.0 cm away from a current of two amperes is 0.0267 G.

The field at this distance from the wire is much less than the average magnetic field strength of the Earth, which is about 0.5 G. On the other hand, at a point 1.5 cm from the wire, the field would be 0.267 G, or about half as strong as the Earth's field.

concept 1

Magnetic field around a wire
Strength of magnetic field
· Increases with amount of current

· Decreases with distance from wire

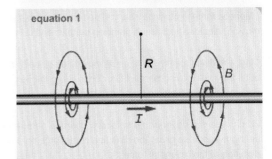

equation 1

Magnetic field around a wire

$$B = \frac{\mu_0 I}{2\pi R}$$

B = magnetic field
μ_0 = permeability of free space
I = current
R = distance from center of wire
Constant $\mu_0 = 4\pi \times 10^{-7}$ N/A^2

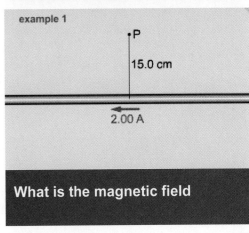

example 1

•P

15.0 cm

2.00 A

What is the magnetic field

28.23 - Gotchas

Compass needles point north because Earth's magnetic north pole is located near the geographic North Pole. No, the north end of the needle on a compass is attracted to the magnetic south pole of the Earth. Compass needles point approximately to the geographic North Pole because the magnetic south pole of the Earth is near its geographic North Pole.

Magnetic force vectors on charged particles point in the same direction as the magnetic field. No, the magnetic force vectors which act on moving, electrically charged particles are perpendicular to the magnetic field, and to the particles' velocities, as well.

Magnetic fields exert a force on all moving electrically charged particles. Almost true. The charges have to be moving for there to be a force, but if they are moving parallel to or opposite to the field, there will be no force. There must be at least some component of the velocity perpendicular to the field for a force to exist.

When I use the right-hand rule for any charged particle moving in a magnetic field, my thumb points in the direction of the magnetic force. No, the right-hand rule gives the direction of the force on a positively charged particle. For negative particles, the thumb points opposite to the direction of the magnetic force.

A magnet is an object that creates magnetic fields and can exert a magnetic force on other magnets or on moving charged particles. Magnets always have two poles, called north and south poles. As with electrical charges, opposite poles attract each other and like poles repel.

The exterior field lines of the magnetic field generated by a magnet are directed from its north pole to its south pole. The symbol for a magnetic field is **B**, a vector. Magnetic fields are measured in teslas (T). 1 T = 1 N·s / C·m. Magnetic fields – especially weaker ones – are also measured in smaller units called gauss (G). 1 G = 10^{-4} T.

The Earth has its own magnetic field, which is why compasses work on its surface. The Earth's magnetic south pole is near the geographic North Pole. Because the two do not coincide, when using a compass you need to know the declination, the angle between the magnetic and geographic poles at your location. Compasses can also help you estimate your latitude if they are allowed to orient in three dimensions.

Equations

Force on charge moving in B field

$$F = |q| v B \sin \theta$$

Motion of a charge in a B field

$$r = \frac{mv}{|q|B}$$

Magnetic force on a wire

$$F = ILB \sin \theta$$

Materials that are able to become permanent magnets, like iron, are said to exhibit ferromagnetism. Ferromagnetic materials contain small regions with their own magnetic fields called domains. Domains are in turn made up of electrons whose spins have a net alignment.

A magnetic field exerts a force on a moving charge. The force is perpendicular to both the velocity of the charge and the magnetic field. If you wrap the fingers of your right hand from the velocity vector to the magnetic field vector, your thumb points in the direction of the force on a positive charge. Your thumb is pointing in the direction opposite to the force on a negative charge.

A charged particle that is moving perpendicularly to a uniform magnetic field will move in a circular path. If it has a velocity component parallel to the field, that component will cause helical motion: The particle will move in a circular path (in two dimensions) while moving at a constant velocity in the third dimension.

A device called a mass spectrometer takes advantage of the circular motion caused by a magnetic field to separate moving particles by their mass-to-charge ratios.

Since an electric current consists of moving charges, a current-carrying wire can have a force exerted on it by a magnetic field. The strength of the force is proportional to the magnitude of the current, the length of the wire, the magnetic field strength, and the sine of the angle between the wire and the field.

An electric motor takes advantage of the torque exerted by a magnetic field on a loop of current to spin a rotor, which turns a shaft to perform useful work.

Magnetic fields exert a force on moving charges, but moving charges also create magnetic fields of their own.

A current-carrying wire creates a magnetic field that circles around the wire. The strength of the field decreases as you move farther from the wire, and increases as the current increases. The direction of the field lines is given by the right-hand rule: Your thumb points in the direction of current and your fingers wrap around the wire in the direction of the field lines.

When two current-carrying wires are placed parallel to each other, the magnetic field of each one affects the other. When the currents in the wires are in the same direction, the wires attract. When the currents are running in opposite directions, the wires repel each other.

29.0 - Introduction

It was a chance occurrence that led the British scientist Michael Faraday (1791-1867) to discover electromagnetic induction.

It was 1831. Scientists already knew that an electric current could be used to create a magnetic field. Faraday and others were trying to achieve the opposite: They wanted to use a magnetic field to create an electric current.

Faraday was conducting an experiment in which he wrapped two lengths of insulated wire around a soft iron ring. One of the lengths was part of a circuit that included a battery. The second was part of a different circuit containing an ammeter that could measure any current passing through it. The wires were insulated so that no current could flow through the iron ring between the circuits.

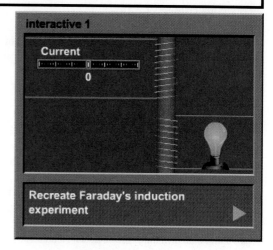

interactive 1

Current

0

Recreate Faraday's induction experiment

Faraday knew he could create a magnetic field in the iron ring by running electricity through the first coil. His goal was to use this magnetic field to create a current in the second coil. The illustration to the right shows a modern-day recreation of his experiment. The upper coil is the part of the circuit that in Faraday's experiment contained the battery; we have replaced the battery with a slider control labeled "Current" so that you can control the amount of current in this circuit. The coil of the second circuit is the lower one in the illustration; we have included a light bulb to make it easier to see when a current flows in the second circuit.

Faraday had always connected the battery before he connected the ammeter, and he detected no current in the second circuit. However, on the morning of August 29, Faraday connected the ammeter first and then connected the battery. To his delight, he detected a momentary current in the second circuit; connecting the battery after the ammeter meant that it was measuring what happened as the current changed in the upper circuit. Today, scientists would say he created a basic transformer, and they understand that it was the **change** in the magnetic field caused by the change in current in the first circuit that caused the current in the second.

Faraday rapidly pushed his work ahead. In the next few months, he discovered that by moving a wire in a magnetic field he could also generate a current in a circuit. Today, this principle is employed in the machinery that generates most of the electricity we use.

Faraday's simple lab equipment yielded powerful insights that engineers continue to utilize today. Electric generators, microphones, VCRs, and induction stoves all rely on Faraday's discovery that a current-producing emf can be induced by changing the strength of a magnetic field, or by moving a wire in a magnetic field.

In the simulation to the right, you can recreate Michael Faraday's groundbreaking experiment. The simulation contains an experimental setup similar to the one Faraday used in 1831. You use a slider to control the current in the upper circuit on the left. By setting the slider's position, you determine the amount and direction of the current. You will see the magnetic field lines created by the current of this circuit; the more intense their color, the stronger the magnetic field.

When you launch the simulation, you will see that an oscilloscope, rather than Faraday's ammeter, is attached to the bottom circuit. It displays the potential difference across the light bulb that is part of the bottom circuit.

Experiment by changing the current in the top circuit and observing what happens in the bottom circuit. By moving the slider back and forth, you can continuously change the current. Is there a current in the bottom circuit if the current in the top circuit is steady and unchanging? What if the current in the top circuit is changing? Does the rate at which the current in the top circuit changes have any effect on the potential difference you measure in the second circuit?

Motional electromagnetic induction: Moving a wire through a magnetic field induces an emf.

Michael Faraday demonstrated two ways to generate a current in a circuit: by changing the strength of a magnetic field passing through a wire coil or by moving a wire through a magnetic field. This section examines the current generated by moving a wire through a field. The phenomenon is called motional electromagnetic induction, or just motional induction.

We start our explanation of motional induction by making sure the diagram on the right is clear to you. The vertical segment of conducting wire is pushed from left to right, sliding across the horizontal wires connected to the light bulb. The wires connect to form a complete circuit. The sliding vertical wire moves through an external magnetic field, represented by ×'s, that points directly into the computer screen. The sliding wire moves perpendicularly to this magnetic field.

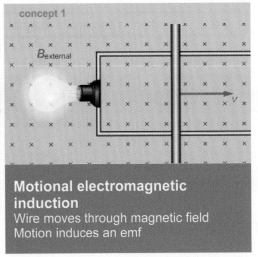

concept 1

$B_{external}$

Motional electromagnetic induction
Wire moves through magnetic field
Motion induces an emf

The result is called an induced emf ($\mathcal{E}$). You studied another source of emf, a battery, earlier. The process shown here creates an emf, "induced" by sliding the vertical segment of wire through the field. Since this segment is part of a circuit, the emf causes an induced current to flow. Remember that the units of emf are volts, the same as for potential difference. We will often measure the amount of induced emf by measuring the potential difference it causes across a component like a light bulb.

Why does current flow? It flows because the motion of the wire causes the electrons in it to be moving in a magnetic field, and the magnetic field exerts a force on the moving electrons that is directed along the wire.

In the illustration on the right, you see how the motion of the sliding wire causes the bulb to glow. You may wonder: Where does the energy to illuminate the bulb come from? The answer is that it comes from whatever is doing the work of pushing the wire through the field.

In this simulation, you can drag a wire left and right, perpendicular to a magnetic field that is pointing directly into the screen. This is the same configuration that was used to explain motional induction in the previous section. If your efforts induce an emf, current will flow and the light bulb will light.

Conduct some experiments: Drag the wire slowly, and then drag it very fast. Does the speed of the wire through the magnetic field affect the amount of potential difference across the light bulb? How do the two relate? How does changing the direction you move the wire change the current? How does it change the potential difference?

You can also use the magnetic field strength control to make the magnetic field in the simulation stronger (or weaker, or oppositely directed). Does changing the field strength change the results of your efforts?

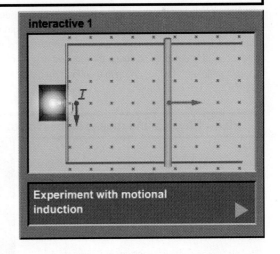

interactive 1

I

Experiment with motional induction ▶

To help you to answer these questions, the simulation has an oscilloscope that measures the potential difference across the light bulb. The oscilloscope in this simulation is functionally similar to real-world ones. You can change the output scale by clicking on its dial. Initially, it is set so that one box of the display grid equals 0.5 volts, but you can change that so one box equals 0.1 volts, 10 volts, and other values shown on the dial as well. (We chose not to show the oscilloscope's connection to the circuit in this simulation for the sake of visual simplicity.) An output gauge shows the amount of current; we show its value as positive or negative to indicate direction.

There is also a slider control that lets you change the viewing angle of the simulation. This may allow you to better see the orientation of the magnetic field, and the wire moving through it.

29.3 - Induction: a coil and a magnet

At the right, you see an apparatus often used to demonstrate induction. A bar magnet passes through a coil of wire loops and the bulb lights up.

A current flows when the magnet passes by the wire, or when the wire moves past the magnet. It does not matter which one is described as moving: The change in the magnetic field inside the coil as one moves past the other induces an emf that causes a current.

The emf induced in this demonstration will vary, based on several factors:

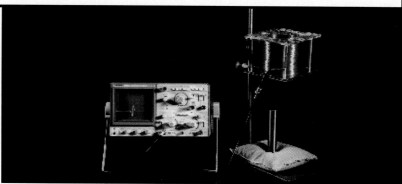

Motional induction demonstration: The magnet is dropped through the coil of wire, and the resulting induced emf is displayed on the oscilloscope.

1. The strength of the magnetic field. The stronger the field, the greater the change in field strength as the loops move by, and the greater the induced emf.

2. The speed of the wire relative to the magnetic field. The faster one passes by the other, the greater the emf.

3. The area of the loops. The greater the area enclosed by each loop, the greater the emf.

4. The number of loops of wire. Increasing the number of loops increases the total area through which the field passes. This, too, increases the induced emf.

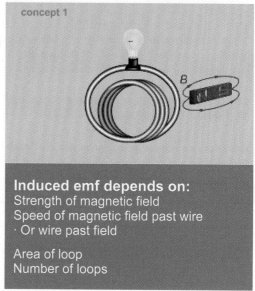

concept 1

Induced emf depends on:
Strength of magnetic field
Speed of magnetic field past wire
· Or wire past field

Area of loop
Number of loops

The list of factors above includes field strength and surface area, two of the factors that determine a quantity called magnetic field flux. We will discuss magnetic field flux shortly; it is analogous to electric field flux. Later, we will discuss how it is the rate of change of this flux that determines the amount of induced emf.

Although this is a classic way of illustrating motional induction, it is difficult to calculate the actual emf induced in this configuration. The strength and orientation of the magnetic field that intersects the coil both change as the bar magnet approaches the wire loops. It is easier to calculate the induced emf for other configurations, like a straight segment of wire moving in a uniform magnetic field.

29.4 - Physics and music: electric guitars

Electric guitars use electromagnetic induction in a component called a *pickup* to produce music. In the pickup, the vibrations of the strings are converted into an electrical signal so they can be amplified and then played over speakers.

The pickup consists of a permanent magnet surrounded by a coil of wire. You see a conceptual diagram of a pickup in the illustration to the right. Guitars typically have two or three pickups under every string, each pickup designed to be maximally sensitive to a particular frequency.

The *pickups* (raised black modules) on this electric guitar convert the vibrations of the strings into a varying electric current.

The permanent magnet in the pickup serves to magnetize the nearby guitar string. A musician plucks the string, making it vibrate. With this vibration the magnetized string moves back and forth near the coil, inducing an emf in the wire. This emf causes a current in the wire. The emf and the current oscillate at the same frequency as the string.

The signal is transmitted through a circuit to an amplification system, which increases its strength, or energy. The system then sends the signal to a loudspeaker and the audience hears the music.

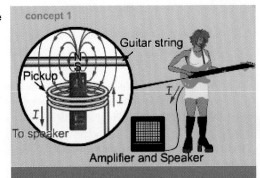

Physics and music: electric guitars
String magnetized by permanent magnet in pickup
Guitar player makes string vibrate
Motion of magnetized string induces current in coil
Current flows to amplifier/speaker

29.5 - Motional induction: calculating the potential difference

The diagram to the right shows a vertical wire segment moving through a uniform magnetic field. This field has a constant strength and points into the screen. The wire moves at a constant velocity to the right, which means its motion is perpendicular to the magnetic field. In this section, we show how to calculate the potential difference induced between the ends of the wire segment by its lateral motion.

The potential difference is caused by the force of the magnetic field on mobile electrons in the moving wire. The electrons move together with the wire as it is pushed through the field. Because charged particles experience a force when they move through a magnetic field, the mobile electrons get pushed to one end of the wire, leaving a positive charge on the other end. (Which end the electrons move to can be determined by a right-hand rule.) As more and more electrons accumulate on one end, leaving more and more positive charge on the other, there is an increasing potential difference across the wire.

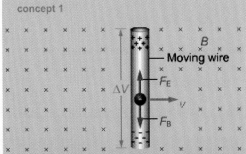

Calculating potential difference
Potential difference induced across wire moving in a magnetic field
Electric, magnetic forces act on charge
· Forces balance

The wire's motion causes the formation of two charged regions, one positive and the other negative. Now, let's consider the electron that is shown in the center of the wire in Concept 1. The motion in the magnetic field causes it to experience a downward magnetic force F_B, and the charged regions cause it to experience an upward electric force F_E. When these two forces balance, the electron experiences no net force and stays in place. The system is in equilibrium and the equation on the right can be used to determine the potential difference across the wire.

In a simulation a few sections ago you saw how, when a moving wire segment like this is part of a circuit, it becomes an emf source that can be used to illuminate a light bulb. The amount of the potential difference in this scenario equals the amount of the motional emf in the former one.

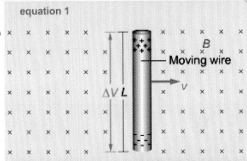

Potential difference across wire segment

To derive an expression for the equilibrium potential difference, we start with an equation stating that the magnetic force on the charged particle equals the electric force. The other variables we use are shown in Equation 1 or defined in the strategy steps below.

Strategy

1. State that the forces are in equilibrium: $F_B = F_E$.
2. Substitute expressions for F_B and F_E, the magnetic and electric forces respectively, in terms of the quantities they depend on.
3. Use the relationship between field strength, potential difference and distance in a uniform electric field to rewrite E, and then solve for the potential difference between the ends of the wire segment.

Physics principles and equations

For motion perpendicular to field:

$$\Delta V = LvB$$

ΔV = potential difference across wire
L = length of wire
v = speed
B = magnetic field strength

The strength of the force exerted by a magnetic field on a charge moving perpendicular to it is

$$F_B = qvB$$

We will also use the definition of an electric field.

$$E = \frac{F_E}{q}$$

The equation that relates potential difference to electric field strength and distance in a uniform electric field is

$$\Delta V = Ed$$

In this case, the distance d is the wire length L.

Step-by-step derivation

We employ the strategy and equations mentioned above and use algebra to solve for the potential difference.

Step	Reason
1. $F_B = F_E$	forces in equilibrium
2. $qvB = Eq$	substitute expressions for forces
3. $vB = E$	divide by q
4. $E = \dfrac{\Delta V}{L}$	solve given equation for E
5. $vB = \dfrac{\Delta V}{L}$	substitute equation 4 into equation 3
6. $\Delta V = LvB$	solve for ΔV

As the equation indicates, longer wires, higher velocities, and stronger magnetic fields lead to greater induced potential differences. This derivation considered the case of motion perpendicular to the magnetic field. If the motion were not perpendicular, we would use trigonometry to determine the component of the motion that was perpendicular to the field. In general, we would conclude that $\Delta V = LvB \sin \theta$, just as the magnetic force equals $qvB \sin \theta$.

Copyright 2000-2007 Kinetic Books Co. Chapter 29

Magnetic flux is analogous to electric flux. Specifically, magnetic flux is the product of a surface area with the component of a magnetic field passing perpendicularly through the surface, just as electric flux is the measure of how much electric field passes perpendicularly through a surface. The unit for magnetic flux is the *weber* (Wb). One weber is one tesla·m^2, the units for magnetic field strength times those for area.

With both electric and magnetic flux, the cosine of the angle between the field and the area vector is used to measure the component of the field passing perpendicularly through the surface. The area vector is normal to the surface and equal in magnitude to its area.

In Equation 1, you see the equation for magnetic flux. It states that magnetic flux equals the dot product of the magnetic field and area vectors, which is calculated as the product of the magnetic field strength, the surface area, and the cosine of the angle θ. This angle is shown in the diagram.

You will use the concept of magnetic flux, and changes in magnetic flux, to further your understanding of how changing magnetic fields induce emfs.

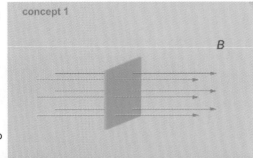

concept 1

Magnetic flux
Amount of field passing through surface
Depends on:
· Field strength at surface

· Amount of surface area

· Angle between field, area vector

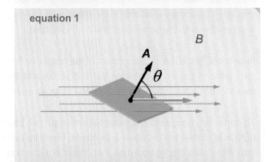

equation 1

Magnetic flux

$$\Phi_B = \mathbf{B} \cdot \mathbf{A}$$
$$\Phi_B = BA \cos \theta$$

Φ_B = magnetic flux
$\mathbf{B}$ = magnetic field, $\mathbf{A}$ = area vector
θ = angle between field, area vector
Units: webers (Wb = T·m^2)

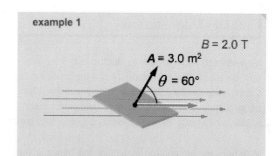

example 1

$B = 2.0$ T
$A = 3.0$ m²
$\theta = 60°$

What is the magnetic flux through this surface?

$\Phi_B = BA\cos\theta$

$\Phi_B = (2.0 \text{ T})(3.0 \text{ m}^2)(\cos 60°)$

$\Phi_B = 3.0$ Wb

29.7 - Faraday's law

Faraday discovered two ways to induce an emf. The first was by moving a wire through a magnetic field; the second was by changing the strength of the magnetic field passing through a stationary wire coil. In the latter case, the magnetic flux changed because flux is proportional to the strength of the magnetic field.

In general, since flux is the product of the magnetic field strength, the surface area, and the cosine of the angle between the field vector and the area vector, changing any of these three factors changes the flux and induces an emf.

To consider changes in magnetic field strength, we use the apparatus shown to the right. It is similar to Faraday's equipment. Two wire coils are wrapped around a piece of iron. Both coils are insulated so that no current can flow directly between them. The coil on the left is connected to a variable current source, a device that can cause a current that changes over time to flow through the coil. As the current in this coil changes, so will the magnetic field that it creates.

The iron core facilitates the transmission of the magnetic field from within the left-hand coil to within the coil on the right. We use two illustrations of the same configuration to show what occurs. In Concept 1, you see the overall configuration: the variable current source attached to a coil on the left, the changing magnetic field passing through the iron core, and the current that is induced in the coil on the right. In Equation 1, we show the view looking down the coil on the right. The increasing magnetic field points away from you down the coil in this view, resulting in a counterclockwise induced current.

Let's discuss in more detail what is happening in this system. The iron core ensures that the magnetic field passes essentially unchanged from within one coil to the other. Since the field is perpendicular to the loops of the coil on the right, the magnetic flux passing through this coil equals the product of the magnetic field strength, the surface area of a loop, and the number of loops in the coil.

The current flowing through the coil on the left creates a magnetic field. As that current changes over time, so does the magnetic field it generates, which means the magnetic flux passing through the coil on the right changes. That change in magnetic flux induces an emf in the coil on the right, which in turn causes the current in the circuit on the right.

This process is used to illustrate a general principle, called Faraday's law: A change in

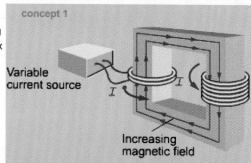

concept 1

Variable current source

I I

Increasing magnetic field

Changing magnetic flux and induced emf
Change in magnetic field strength yields change in magnetic flux
Flux change induces emf
emf drives induced current

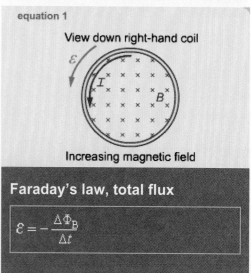

equation 1

View down right-hand coil

ε

I B

Increasing magnetic field

Faraday's law, total flux

$$\varepsilon = -\frac{\Delta \Phi_B}{\Delta t}$$

magnetic flux induces an emf. In Equation 1, you see this expressed in mathematical form. Faraday's law states that the induced emf equals the negative of the rate of change of magnetic flux.

Faraday's law is often applied to a coil having N loops, as we do in this section, and we state this version in Equation 2. In this case, the flux refers to the flux passing through each loop, and the total flux equals the flux passing through each loop times the number of loops.

The negative sign appearing in both equations indicates that the induced emf acts to "oppose" the change in magnetic flux that causes it. What this means is explained in more depth in a later section.

$\mathcal{E}$ = induced emf
Φ_B = total magnetic flux through circuit
t = time

equation 2

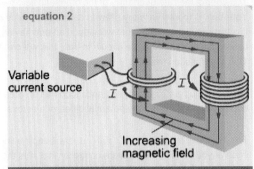

Variable current source

Increasing magnetic field

Faraday's law, coil of N loops

$$\mathcal{E} = -N\frac{\Delta\Phi_B}{\Delta t}$$

Φ_B = magnetic flux through one loop
N = number of loops

example 1

View down right-hand coil

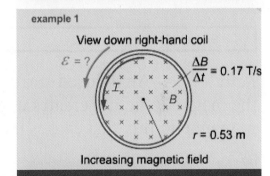

$\mathcal{E} = ?$

$\frac{\Delta B}{\Delta t} = 0.17$ T/s

$r = 0.53$ m

Increasing magnetic field

The field passes through six loops. What is the induced emf?

$$\mathcal{E} = -N\frac{\Delta\Phi_B}{\Delta t} = -N\frac{\Delta B}{\Delta t}A$$

$$A = \pi r^2 = \pi(0.53\text{ m})^2 = 0.88\text{ m}^2$$

$$\frac{\Delta\Phi_B}{\Delta t} = \frac{\Delta B}{\Delta t}A = (0.17\frac{\text{T}}{\text{s}})(0.88\text{ m}^2)$$

$$\frac{\Delta\Phi_B}{\Delta t} = 0.15\text{ V}$$

$$\mathcal{E} = -(6\text{ loops})(0.15\text{ V}) = -0.90\text{ V}$$

In this simulation, a magnetic field is passing through a solenoid. The solenoid is part of a circuit that contains a resistor. The potential difference across the resistor equals the magnitude of any emf induced in the solenoid.

You control the rate of change of the magnetic field passing through the solenoid. Your task is to use Faraday's law to calculate the time rate of change of magnetic flux through the solenoid that will induce an emf having a magnitude of 12.5 V and cause current to flow in the circuit. In turn, this will create a potential difference of 12.5 V across the resistor.

The solenoid has 20 loops, and each loop has an area of 0.0100 m². An oscilloscope measures the potential difference across the resistor.

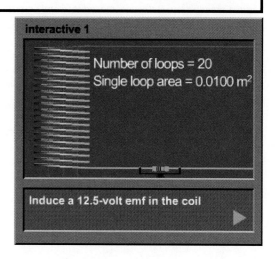

interactive 1

Number of loops = 20
Single loop area = 0.0100 m²

Induce a 12.5-volt emf in the coil

The magnetic field starts at 0.500 T and will decline linearly to 0 T during a time interval you specify. You have a controller that sets the time interval during which the change in field strength will occur to values from 5.00 to 20.00 milliseconds. The field will then continue to vary back and forth between 0 T and 0.500 T during alternating time intervals of the same length. The rate of change will alternate between positive and negative values, but it will have a constant magnitude based on the duration of the time interval you select.

Specify the time during which you want the field to decline to zero. (You change it in increments of 0.10 milliseconds.) Press GO to see if the changing field induces an emf of magnitude 12.5 volts. If not, press RESET, redo your calculations and try again.

If you have trouble answering this problem, review the section on Faraday's law. The oscilloscope displays a graph of the potential difference across the resistor, with the potential difference plotted on the vertical axis and elapsed time on the horizontal axis. By clicking on different values on the oscilloscope's control knob, you can specify what you want the vertical measure, in volts, of one grid square to be.

29.9 - Lenz's law

Lenz's law: An induced current flows so that the magnetic field it creates opposes the change in magnetic flux that causes the current.

Lenz's law, named after the Russian scientist Heinrich Lenz (1804-1865), is used to determine the orientation of the current induced by a change in magnetic flux.

The law states that the magnetic field of the induced current opposes the change in magnetic flux that causes the current. To apply the law, you first note the change in magnetic flux and then determine the orientation of the magnetic field that will oppose that change in flux. The current will flow in the direction that causes this magnetic field.

concept 1

Increasing external B field

Lenz's law
Determines direction of induced current

To illustrate this law being applied, we use the wire loop shown to the right. The external magnetic field is pointing into the page and it is **increasing** in strength. This will cause a current. But in which direction does the current flow, clockwise or counterclockwise?

To answer this question, consider the direction of the magnetic field created by the induced current. Lenz's law says this field will oppose the change that caused it. The external field is increasing, so the magnetic field of the induced current points in the direction that opposes this change. This means it will point toward you, as the diagram in Concept 2 shows. (In this diagram we have dimmed the external field to make the opposing field easier to see.)

The right-hand rule for currents dictates that the current must be flowing counterclockwise through the wire loop. If you apply the rule, your fingers inside the loop must point toward you, opposing the increase of the external magnetic flux that is pointing away from you. This means the thumb points up on the right side of the loop, as illustrated in Concept 2, and down on the left side, as you can imagine, indicating the direction of conventional current. "Up on the right" and "down on the left," means the current flows counterclockwise.

(Perhaps it is useful to state a right-hand rule for induction loops: "The thumb points in the direction of the induced magnetic field, and the fingers wrap around the loop to indicate the direction of the current.")

If the external field were decreasing, then the induced magnetic field would oppose the decrease. It would point in the same direction as the external field, and this means the current would flow clockwise.

The example problem asks you to determine the direction of the current in a loop when a decreasing external magnetic field passes through it, directed toward you. Remember: The current must flow so that it creates a magnetic field inside the loop that opposes this decrease in flux.

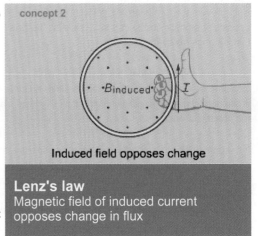

Induced field opposes change

Lenz's law
Magnetic field of induced current opposes change in flux

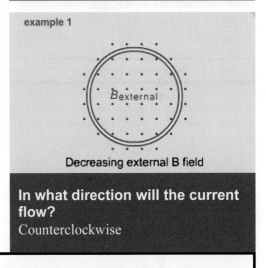

Decreasing external B field

In what direction will the current flow?
Counterclockwise

29.10 - Eddy currents

Eddy currents: Electric currents created when a solid conductor moves through a magnetic field.

We have used a relatively simple configuration to analyze the current created by moving a wire in a magnetic field. The moving wire was a straight segment, and an overall rectangular circuit contained three other straight segments.

Here, we use eddy currents to illustrate a significant point: Even when a circuit is not well defined, currents can still be caused to flow in a conductor at rest in a time-varying magnetic field or passing through a nonuniform magnetic field. For instance, the rectangular block to the right is made of a conducting material. When it moves into or out of the magnetic field shown, currents flow in it, but not in straight lines. These types of current flow are called *eddy currents*, and they flow in a complex pattern that resembles a whirlpool. The diagram in Concept 1 visually approximates the eddy currents by depicting them as circular.

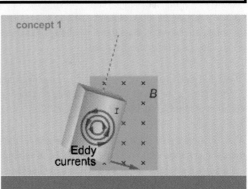

Eddy currents
Caused by changing flux in solid conductors
Eddy currents damp motion

The existence of eddy currents can be vividly demonstrated with two differing pieces of conducting material. One piece is a solid block attached to a string, swinging in and out of a magnetic field. This motion generates eddy currents in the block. The magnetic fields of the eddy currents oppose the change in flux that causes them. In essence, the block becomes an electromagnet whose motion is opposed by the external magnetic field. The opposing force quickly damps (reduces) the motion.

A second block, with slots cut through it, swings through the same field. Because the slots prevent the formation of significant large-scale eddy currents, a much weaker opposing magnetic field is created. There is less force to damp the motion, and the block swings relatively freely.

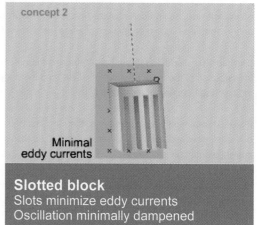

concept 2

Minimal eddy currents

Slotted block
Slots minimize eddy currents
Oscillation minimally dampened

Like any phenomenon that removes mechanical energy from a system, causing it to dissipate as heat, eddy currents can be either an undesirable source of inefficiency, or in the right circumstances, a valuable tool. One useful application of eddy currents is to the braking of trains.

If the upper half of a spinning train wheel is subjected to a strong magnetic field, each portion of the wheel will rotate into and out of this field. The changing magnetic flux in that portion of the wheel will induce eddy currents that apply a countertorque to the whole wheel, acting to slow it down. Since the magnitude of the countertorque is proportional to the angular velocity of the wheel, the braking effect diminishes as the train slows, allowing it to come to a smooth stop. Eddy-current brakes are promoted as being quieter and less prone to slippage than train brakes that rely on mechanical friction.

29.11 - Interactive problem: a generator

In this simulation your task is to establish how the angle between a magnetic field and the velocity vector of a horizontal segment of a rotating loop relates to the emf induced in the loop.

When you open the simulation by clicking on the diagram to the right, you will see a loop of wire suspended in a magnetic field. Start the loop spinning by pressing GO.

An oscilloscope displays the emf induced in the loop. For simplicity's sake, we omit showing the oscilloscope's connection to the generator circuit. We also show the current induced in the visible portion of the circuit.

A black vector represents the tangential velocity of a horizontal loop segment. You control how fast the loop rotates by setting its angular velocity. You can also change the angle at which you view the simulation. The side view of the magnetic field is particularly helpful for this exercise.

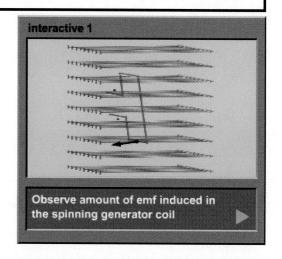

interactive 1

Observe amount of emf induced in the spinning generator coil ▶

Watch the loop spinning in the field. Observe the orientation of the velocity vector to the magnetic field lines. (The angle θ displayed in the control panel is the angle between the field and the velocity vector as viewed from behind the crank.) With what orientation of the velocity vector is the emf a maximum? A minimum? Can you explain why?

Also, observe the oscilloscope trace of the emf as the generator spins faster or slower. This always appears to be a sinusoidal wave. Does its frequency change with angular velocity? Does its amplitude? To answer the second question, consider the relationship between speed and the induced emf when a wire moves in a straight line through a magnetic field.

29.12 - An AC generator, its emf, and AC current

In this section, we consider the implications of adding an *AC (alternating current)* generator to a circuit. We start with the circuit you see on the right, one that contains only a generator and a resistor. The AC generator is represented by a blue circle with a wave inside.

At its simplest, an AC generator consists of a wire loop that rotates in a magnetic field. It generates an emf that varies sinusoidally with time.

The emf created by the generator can be described mathematically as the product of its maximum emf and a sine function, as shown in Equation 1. The factor ω in the argument of the function is the angular frequency of the current. In the United States and East Asia, alternating current has a **frequency** of 60 cycles per second (Hz), meaning the emf reaches its maximum positive value 60 times per second. The **angular frequency** is 2π times this value, about 377 rad/s.

In the United States, the maximum emf of alternating current is approximately 170 volts. Utilities strive to provide a potential difference that, calculated in a specific way, averages to 120 volts.

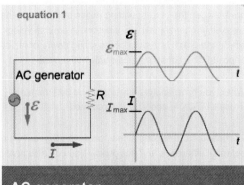

equation 1

AC generator

AC generator

$$\mathcal{E} = \mathcal{E}_{max} \sin \omega t$$
$$I_R = I_{max} \sin \omega t$$

$\mathcal{E}$ = emf
I_R = current through resistor circuit
ω = angular frequency
t = time

29.13 - Interactive problem: alternating current

In this simulation, there is a circuit that contains a signal generator and a resistor. The emf of the signal generator causes a current to flow. Your task is to use an oscilloscope to determine the maximum current I_{max}, the maximum potential difference across the resistor ΔV_{max} and the signal frequency f.

You will see sinusoidal graphs in the oscilloscope similar to those you see in illustrations in other sections of this chapter.

One probe from the oscilloscope is used to measure current. The current is the same everywhere in the circuit. The two ends of the potential difference ("voltage") probe in this exercise are placed so it measures ΔV across the resistor.

The oscilloscope displays information in the form of two graphs. In the upper graph, the current is displayed on the vertical axis and time is on the horizontal axis. In the lower graph, ΔV is displayed on the vertical axis, and time once again is on the horizontal axis.

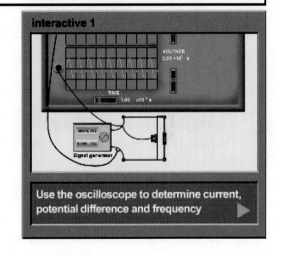

interactive 1

Use the oscilloscope to determine current, potential difference and frequency

Sliders allow you to change the scales of the graphs. The base unit is a single gray square in the oscilloscope window. For example, if you set the current slider to "8.00×10^{-2} A," then the height of a gray box represents 8.00×10^{-2} amperes. You can set the scale for the time in an analogous fashion. All this resembles the working of typical laboratory oscilloscopes.

You set the scale by trial and error. If you cannot see any signal, move the slider so the units are smaller until you can see the graph. If the waves you see are so large that you cannot see their peaks, increase the scale until their peaks "shrink" into view.

When you launch the simulation, the signal generator is on and all the probes are attached. The peak of the wave in the current display is the maximum current, I_{max}. The peak of the wave in the voltage display is ΔV_{max}.

You also have to analyze the wave to determine the frequency of the signal. To do so, identify two adjacent matching points in the wave (such as two peaks) in order to identify a cycle. The time it takes to complete this cycle is the period of the wave, and the reciprocal of the period is frequency. For instance, if the time between two peaks is 1.0×10^{-3} seconds, then the frequency is $1/(1.0\times10^{-3})$, or 1,000 hertz (Hz).

A couple of tips may help here. Since the horizontal axis measures time, you can determine the period by counting how many gray boxes there are between the corresponding points on the wave (be careful to note what the time scale is). It can be easier to use locations where the wave crosses the horizontal axis, since more precise values can be noted there. But if you use those points, remember that matching points are where the graph is in both cases going down, or in both cases going up. Two adjacent points where the wave crosses the horizontal axis, but in opposite directions, represent only half a cycle.

When you have analyzed a signal and determined I_{max}, ΔV_{max} and the signal frequency, enter these values in the boxes in the simulation. Press CHECK to see if you are correct.

To measure the second signal, press the Signal Two button on the signal generator. The signal generator will create a signal with a different potential difference and frequency. You can also analyze this signal, enter your conclusions and check them by pressing CHECK.

29.14 - Mutual induction

Mutual induction: The induction of an emf in one circuit by a changing current in another circuit.

Currents create magnetic fields. A changing current in a circuit creates a changing magnetic field. This changing magnetic field will induce an emf and a current in a nearby second circuit, in a process called mutual induction.

At the right, you see an illustration of the steps involved in mutual induction:

1. A switch is closed in the left-hand circuit. This circuit contains a battery.
2. A current in the left-hand circuit starts to flow after the switch is closed, increasing toward its steady state value.
3. The increasing current on the left generates a changing magnetic field.
4. The changing magnetic field causes a changing magnetic flux through the circuit on the right, which induces an emf in this circuit.
5. The induced emf in the right-hand circuit causes a current there, lighting the light bulb for a brief time.
6. Once the current on the left reaches its steady state, the light bulb on the right goes out, because there is no longer a changing magnetic field to induce a current there.

An important point to remember is that currents are induced by *a* **changing** magnetic field. The closing of the battery circuit starts a current that in turn creates a magnetic field where before there was none. It is this **change** in magnetic field that induces the emf and the current in the second circuit. When the current caused by the battery reaches a steady state, which occurs quite quickly, then its magnetic field will also be constant and it will cease to induce an emf or a current in the circuit on the right.

If the current on the left-hand side were an alternating instead of a direct current, it would induce an undiminished alternating current on the right-hand side. Why? The magnetic field due to the changing left-side current would constantly change in strength and orientation. The constantly changing magnetic field would continuously induce an emf and current in the circuit on the right, and the light bulb would stay lit.

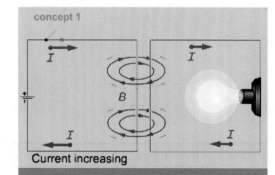

concept 1

Current increasing

Mutual induction
Changing current in one circuit creates current in other
· Changing current causes changing magnetic field
· Changing magnetic field induces current

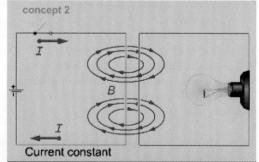

concept 2

Current constant

Mutual induction
When current is constant, no induction occurs

Copyright 2000-2007 Kinetic Books Co. Chapter 29

Transformer: A device used to increase or decrease an alternating potential difference.

Power transmission lines conduct AC current at high voltages. Transformers convert this current from one voltage to another.

The way in which electricity is transmitted and distributed requires conversions of potential differences across an enormous range of values. Long distance power transmission lines typically operate at about 350,000 V, while city power lines near a home function at 15,000 V. Before the electricity enters a house, the potential difference between a current-carrying and a "neutral" wire is further reduced to 120 V. All of these currents are alternating, and transformers are used to convert potential differences in alternating currents. (One reason why alternating current is used in power systems is the ease with which transformers can change its potential difference.)

The illustration in Concept 1 shows a transformer: two coils of wire wrapped around an iron core. The wires are insulated so that no current flows directly between them. The iron core allows a magnetic field to be efficiently transmitted from one coil to the other: Less than 5% of the energy transformed in a typical transformer is dissipated as heat. In this section, we focus on the characteristics of an ideal transformer, one in which no energy is lost.

The wire wrapped around the iron core on the left-hand side is called the *primary winding*. In our scenario, it is directly attached to an AC generator. The current passing through this coil generates a magnetic field. Since the current continually changes, so does the magnetic field it creates.

The field passes through the second coil on the right. This coil is called the *secondary winding*. The change in magnetic flux through this coil induces an emf that causes a current in the secondary circuit. The secondary circuit powers a resistive component, such as a light bulb, that is called the *load*. The transformer changes the emf from that created by the AC generator to that required by the load.

There are a different number of loops, or turns, in the primary and secondary windings. This is crucial to the operation of the transformer. The ratio of the number of primary loops to the number of secondary loops is called the *turns ratio*.

The transformer "transforms" the potential difference created by the generator: The potential difference across the secondary winding differs from that across the primary winding. In the transformer to the right, the potential difference decreases. This is a *step-down* transformer. *Step-up* transformers increase potential difference. The transformer symbol that is used in circuit diagrams is shown in Concept 2.

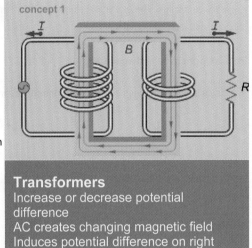

concept 1

Transformers
Increase or decrease potential difference
AC creates changing magnetic field
Induces potential difference on right

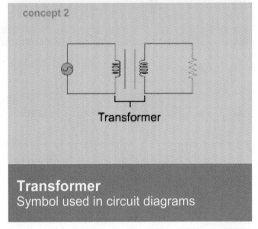

concept 2

Transformer

Transformer
Symbol used in circuit diagrams

The change in the potential differences depends on the turns ratio. The proportion in Equation 1 states that the ratio of the potential differences equals the turns ratio. To put it another way: If the number of loops on a given side is reduced, the potential difference on that side decreases.

We derive this "turns equation" below using Faraday's law. The loops in each coil are assumed to span an equal surface area, and the same amount of magnetic field passes through each one. This means the ratio of the changes in flux in the primary and secondary windings is proportional solely to the number of loops in each coil.

Variables

potential difference across primary coil	ΔV_1
potential difference across secondary coil	ΔV_2
number of loops in primary coil	N_1
number of loops in secondary coil	N_2
time interval	Δt
change in magnetic flux through one loop during Δt	$\Delta \Phi_B$

Strategy

1. State Faraday's law twice, for the emf induced across each coil by the changing magnetic flux. The emf equals the potential difference across the components.
2. Divide the two equations.

Physics principles and equations

Faraday's law stated in terms of potential difference, and for a coil of N loops, is

$$\Delta V = -N\frac{\Delta \Phi_B}{\Delta t}$$

With transformers, it is traditional to refer to potential differences rather than emfs in the primary and secondary windings.

Step-by-step derivation

We state Faraday's law for each coil, then divide the two equations and simplify the result.

Step		Reason
1.	$\Delta V_1 = -N_1\frac{\Delta \Phi_B}{\Delta t}$	Faraday's law
2.	$\Delta V_2 = -N_2\frac{\Delta \Phi_B}{\Delta t}$	Faraday's law
3.	$\dfrac{\Delta V_1}{\Delta V_2} = \dfrac{-N_1\dfrac{\Delta \Phi_B}{\Delta t}}{-N_2\dfrac{\Delta \Phi_B}{\Delta t}}$	divide
4.	$\dfrac{\Delta V_1}{\Delta V_2} = \dfrac{N_1}{N_2}$	simplify

Transformers can increase a potential difference, but by now you have learned that in physics, you do not get something without also giving something up. The principle of conservation of energy must apply to transformers. How does this precept apply? It requires that the power, or energy produced or consumed per unit time, is the same on both sides of an ideal transformer. Power equals the current times the potential

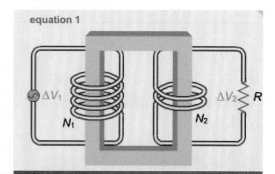

equation 1

Potential differences ratio equals turns ratio

$$\frac{\Delta V_1}{\Delta V_2} = \frac{N_1}{N_2}$$

ΔV_1 = primary potential difference
ΔV_2 = secondary potential difference
N_1 = primary number of loops
N_2 = secondary number of loops

equation 2

Currents ratio is inverse of turns ratio

$$\frac{I_2}{I_1} = \frac{N_1}{N_2}$$

I_1 = primary current
I_2 = secondary current

example 1

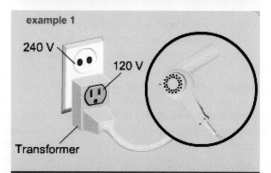

240 V
120 V
Transformer

What should the turns ratio of the transformer be?

$$\frac{\Delta V_1}{\Delta V_2} = \frac{N_1}{N_2}$$

Copyright 2000-2007 Kinetic Books Co. Chapter 29

difference. If you boost the potential difference, you decrease the current.

The ratio of the currents is the inverse of the turns ratio. This is shown in Equation 2 .

$$\frac{240 \text{ V}}{120 \text{ V}} = \frac{N_1}{N_2} = 2:1$$

The example problem asks you to analyze a type of transformer commonly sold in travel stores. This transformer steps down European voltage (240 V AC) to USA standard voltage (120 V AC), and you may need one if you intend to use any of your personal appliances on a trip abroad.

29.16 - Sample problem: primary winding in a transformer

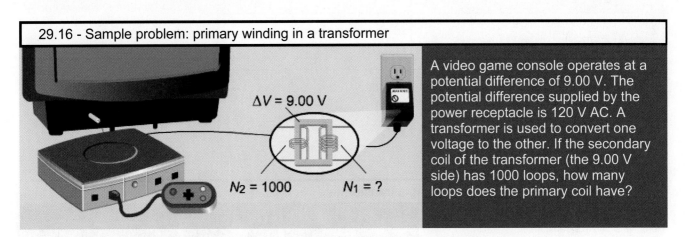

$\Delta V = 9.00 \text{ V}$

$N_2 = 1000$ $N_1 = ?$

A video game console operates at a potential difference of 9.00 V. The potential difference supplied by the power receptacle is 120 V AC. A transformer is used to convert one voltage to the other. If the secondary coil of the transformer (the 9.00 V side) has 1000 loops, how many loops does the primary coil have?

Low-voltage devices like the game console above typically run on direct current, so the power converter would not only transform the potential difference, but also convert AC to DC. Here, we only consider the AC transformer part of the power converter.

Variables

primary potential difference	$V_1 = 120 \text{ V}$
secondary potential difference	$V_2 = 9.00 \text{ V}$
primary number of loops	N_1
secondary number of loops	$N_2 = 1000$

What is the strategy?

1. State the turns ratio equation.
2. Solve for the number of primary loops and evaluate.

Physics principles and equations

The turns equation for transformers is

$$\frac{\Delta V_1}{\Delta V_2} = \frac{N_1}{N_2}$$

Step-by-step solution

We solve the turns equation for N_1, then evaluate.

Step	Reason
1. $\dfrac{\Delta V_1}{\Delta V_2} = \dfrac{N_1}{N_2}$	turns equation
2. $N_1 = \dfrac{\Delta V_1}{\Delta V_2} N_2$	solve for number of primary loops
3. $N_1 = \dfrac{120\text{V}}{9.00\text{V}}(1000)$ $N_1 = 1.33 \times 10^4$	evaluate

29.17 - Interactive problem: configuring a transformer

Here, we simulate a transformer.

An alternating potential difference across the primary winding on the top creates a magnetic field that passes through the iron core to the secondary winding on the bottom. This magnetic field induces an emf in the bottom coil. The value of the potential difference across the resistor in the bottom, secondary circuit (equal to the induced emf) is displayed on an oscilloscope. You can turn the dial on the oscilloscope to change the scale of the display. The height of a grid box equals the setting on the dial.

The large cylindrical transformers on the left of this photo convert electricity from 350,000 V to 15,000 V at an electrical substation.

Your task is to determine the maximum positive potential difference in the top, primary circuit using information you glean from the simulation. We use the word "maximum" because the potential difference of the alternating current varies sinusoidally with time.

There are ten loops in the top coil. You can vary the number of loops in the bottom coil from 20 to 50, in increments of 5. Pick a number of loops and then use the oscilloscope to determine the maximum potential difference across the resistor in the secondary circuit. You can use that value and the ratio of loops to determine the maximum potential difference in the primary circuit.

Enter this value in the box provided in the control panel and press CHECK to see if you are right. If not, redo your calculations, enter a new answer, and press CHECK again.

If you need help, review the section on transformers.

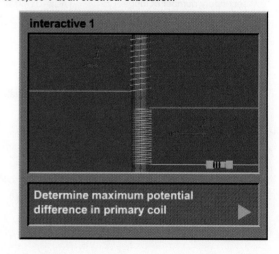

interactive 1

Determine maximum potential difference in primary coil

29.18 - Gotchas

Any magnetic field induces an emf in a loop of wire. No, a **changing** magnetic field induces an emf in such a loop. A uniform, constant magnetic field alone induces no net emf in a loop of wire. However, a potential difference can be induced across a segment of wire by moving it through a magnetic field.

Transformers change potential differences. Power is a function of potential difference, so they change power, as well. No, the current changes in inverse proportion to the potential difference, so the power stays constant.

29.19 - Summary

A changing magnetic field can generate an emf in a loop of wire. This phenomenon is called electromagnetic induction.

The motion of a coil in a nonuniform magnetic field can also induce an emf. The same effect is achieved whether you move the coil through the field, or move the field past the coil.

Magnetic flux, Φ_B is the amount of magnetic field passing perpendicularly through a surface. The amount of flux can be computed as the dot product of the field and area vectors, which is the product of the field strength, the area, and the cosine of the angle between them. The unit of magnetic flux is the weber (Wb). 1 Wb = 1 T·m2.

Faraday's law states that the induced emf in a circuit is proportional to the rate of change of magnetic flux through the circuit.

When a change in the magnetic flux due to an external magnetic field induces a current in a circuit, the induced current creates its own magnetic field. Lenz's law states that the induced magnetic field always opposes the change in flux that caused it. This helps you to deduce the direction of the induced current.

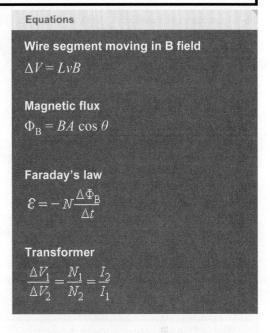

Equations

Wire segment moving in B field
$$\Delta V = LvB$$

Magnetic flux
$$\Phi_B = BA \cos \theta$$

Faraday's law
$$\mathcal{E} = -N\frac{\Delta \Phi_B}{\Delta t}$$

Transformer
$$\frac{\Delta V_1}{\Delta V_2} = \frac{N_1}{N_2} = \frac{I_2}{I_1}$$

A loop of wire rotating in a magnetic field is the basis of an electric generator. A torque causes the loop to rotate in the field, constantly moving its wires through the field and inducing an emf and an electric current in it. The induced current reverses direction every half turn of the loop, and is called an alternating current (AC). Both the induced emf and the current vary sinusoidally with time.

Currents induced in large solid pieces of conducting material are not like those induced in a wire. When a solid conductor moves through a nonuniform magnetic field, eddy currents flow through it in complex "whirlpools." Eddy currents oppose the motion of the conductor through the nonuniform field.

Mutual induction occurs when a changing current in a circuit generates a changing magnetic field, which in turn induces a current in a second nearby circuit.

A transformer is a device that increases or decreases potential difference from one alternating-current circuit to another. Both circuits contain coils wrapped around the same iron core, but with a different number of loops in each coil.

chapter

30 Electromagnetic
Radiation

□ Conceptual

physics

kinetic
BOOKS

30.0 - Introduction

Radio and television signals, x-rays, microwaves: Each is a form of electromagnetic radiation. If steam and internal combustion engines symbolize the Industrial Revolution, and microprocessors and memory chips now power the Information Revolution, it almost seems that we have neglected to recognize the "Electromagnetic Revolution." Think about it: Can you imagine life without television sets or cell phones? You may long for such a life, or wonder how people ever survived without these devices!

Electromagnetic radiation: Rainbows and radios. Sundazzled reflections. Shadowlamps and lampshadows. Red, white, and blue.

These examples are from the world of engineered electromagnetic radiation. Even if you think we might all prosper without such technologies to entertain us, do our cooking, carry our messages, and diagnose our illnesses, you would be hard-pressed to survive without light. This form of electromagnetic radiation brings the Sun's energy to the Earth, warming the planet and supplying energy to plants, and in turn to creatures like us that depend on them. There are primitive forms of life that do not depend on the Sun's energy, but without light there would be no seeing, no room with a view, no sunsets, and no Rembrandts.

Some of the electromagnetic radiation that reaches your eyes was created mere nanoseconds earlier, like the light from a lamp. Other electromagnetic radiation is still propagating at its original speed through the cosmos, ten billion years or more after its birth. An example of this is the microwave background radiation, a pervasive remnant of the creation of the universe that is widely studied by astrophysicists.

Back here on Earth, this chapter covers the fundamental physical theory of electromagnetic radiation. Much of it builds on other topics, particularly the studies of waves, electric fields and magnetic fields.

30.1 - The electromagnetic spectrum

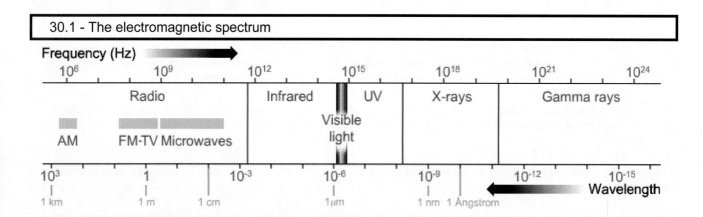

Electromagnetic spectrum: Electromagnetic radiation ordered by frequency or wavelength.

Electromagnetic radiation is a traveling wave that consists of electric and magnetic fields. Before delving into the details of such waves, we will discuss the electromagnetic spectrum, a system by which the types of electromagnetic radiation are classified.

The illustration of the electromagnetic spectrum above orders electromagnetic waves by frequency and by wavelength. In the diagram, frequency **increases** and wavelength **decreases** as you move from the left to the right. The chart's scale is based on powers of 10. Wavelengths range from more than 100 meters for AM radio signals to as small as 10^{-16} meters for gamma rays.

All electromagnetic waves travel at the same speed in a vacuum. This speed is designated by the letter c and is called the speed of light. (The letter c comes from *celeritas,* the Latin word for speed. It might be more accurate to refer to it as the speed of electromagnetic radiation.) The speed of light in a vacuum is exactly 299,792,458 m/s, and it is only slightly less in air.

The unvarying nature of this speed has an important implication: The wavelength of electromagnetic radiation is inversely proportional to its frequency. As you may recall, the speed of a wave equals the product of its frequency and wavelength. This means that if you know the wavelength of the wave, you can determine its frequency (and vice versa). For instance, an electromagnetic wave with a wavelength of 300 meters, in the middle of the AM radio band, has a frequency of 1×10^6 Hz. This equals 3×10^8 m/s, the speed of light, divided by 300 m. The frequencies of electromagnetic waves range from less than one megahertz, or 10^6 Hz, for long radio waves to over 10^{24} Hz for gamma rays.

We will now review some of the bands of electromagnetic radiation and their manifestations. The lowest frequencies are often utilized for radio signals. AM and FM *radio waves* are typically produced by transmitters that incorporate electric oscillator circuits attached to antennas. The AM and FM radio bands are shown in Concept 1. *Microwave radiation* is at the upper end of the radio band, and is used for cellular telephone transmissions as well as for heating food in microwave ovens.

Infrared radiation has a higher frequency than microwaves and is associated with heat. It is generated by the thermal vibration or rotation of atoms and molecules.

Visible light is next as we go up the frequency range. It is of paramount importance to human beings, although it occupies only a small portion of the electromagnetic spectrum. Like some other forms of electromagnetic radiation, it is created when atoms emit radiation as their electrons drop from higher to lower energy levels. Light consists of electromagnetic waves that oscillate more than 100 trillion (10^{14}) times a second. The wavelengths of the various colors of light are in the hundreds of nanometers. Red light has the lowest frequency and longest wavelength, while violet light has the highest frequency and shortest wavelength. The visible light spectrum is shown in Concept 2.

The Sun emits a broad spectrum of electromagnetic radiation, including *ultraviolet* (UV) waves, with frequencies higher than those of visible light. These waves are the main cause of sunburn: Sunscreen lotion is designed to prevent them from reaching and harming your skin. This radiation can also harm your eyes, especially if you wear plastic sunglasses that diminish the amount of visible light reaching your eyes, but do not block UV rays. Typically, you squint when your eyes are exposed to strong light, and this helps protect them. If you wear sunglasses that do not stop ultraviolet light, your pupils will dilate, allowing an extra dose of harmful ultraviolet waves to enter your eyes.

The Earth's atmosphere, specifically the layer that contains a molecular form of oxygen called *ozone*, absorbs a great deal of the Sun's ultraviolet radiation, protecting plants and animals from its harmful effects. However, substances once commonly used in refrigerators and aerosols catalyze ozone-destroying chemical reactions in the atmosphere. Fortunately, the use of such substances has been restricted, but a "hole" in the ozone, a region where the amount of ozone has been significantly depleted, has been created above Antarctica. This hole varies in size from year to year, but on average is approximately the size of North America.

X-rays, the next band of electromagnetic frequencies, are even more dangerous than UV, but they are also useful. Doctors can use them to "see" shadowy images of the inside of the human body because they travel more easily through some tissues than others. Scientists also use them to discern the detailed crystalline structure of materials and to deduce the spatial configuration of complex molecules. NASA launched the Chandra X-ray Observatory in 1999 to capture the radiation emitted from high-energy regions of the universe, such as the parts of space around exploded stars. The acceleration of high-energy electrons is one source of x-rays.

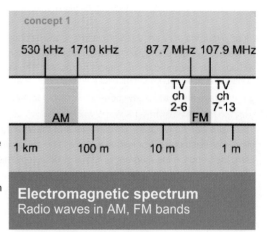

Electromagnetic spectrum
Radio waves in AM, FM bands

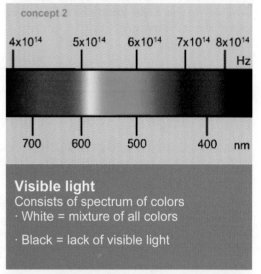

Visible light
Consists of spectrum of colors
· White = mixture of all colors
· Black = lack of visible light

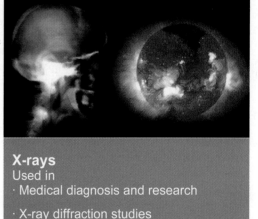

X-rays
Used in
· Medical diagnosis and research
· X-ray diffraction studies
· X-ray astronomy

Because these rays can damage or destroy living cells and tissues, human exposure to them must be strictly limited.

Finally, *gamma rays* are the highest frequency electromagnetic waves. They are emitted by atomic nuclei undergoing certain nuclear reactions, as well as by high energy astronomical objects and events. These rays may enter the Earth's atmosphere from space, but they usually collide with air molecules and do not reach the ground. Those few that do reach the Earth can cause mutations in the DNA of living cells. Gamma radiation is highly destructive, which is one reason for the thick shielding used to protect workers from nuclear materials. However, like x-rays, gamma rays also have some beneficial uses. "Gamma knife" radiosurgery uses concentrated beams of gamma rays to kill cancer cells.

The distinction between the different parts of the spectrum appears clearer in the diagram above than it is in reality; the labeled bands actually blend into each other. For instance, there is no clear-cut frequency at which the shortest "radio waves" stop and the longest "far infrared" waves start; the bands in the diagram simply provide a convenient way to classify frequency ranges. Frequency classifications do become precise when business people enter the discussion: The rights to use certain frequency ranges, such as those for radio and television stations and cell phones, are worth tens of billions of dollars.

Despite the different names − AM radio signals, visible light, x-rays, gamma rays − the phenomena organized in the chart above and illustrated to the right are all forms of electromagnetic radiation. In the same way that you think of both tiny puddle ripples and long, slow ocean swells as being water waves, so you should think about the types of electromagnetic radiation. The frequency of the wave does not alter the fundamental laws of physics that govern it.

30.2 - Electromagnetic waves

Electromagnetic wave: A wave consisting of electric and magnetic fields oscillating transversely to the direction of propagation.

Physicist James Clerk Maxwell's brilliant studies pioneered research into the nature of electromagnetic waves. He correctly concluded that oscillating electric and magnetic fields can constitute a self-propagating wave that he called electromagnetic radiation. His law of induction (a changing electric field causes a magnetic field) combined with Faraday's law (a changing magnetic field causes an electric field) supplies the basis for understanding this kind of wave.

As the diagrams to the right show, the electric and magnetic fields in an electromagnetic wave are perpendicular to each other and to the direction of propagation of the wave. These illustrations also show the amplitudes of the fields varying sinusoidally as functions of position and time. Electromagnetic waves are an example of *transverse waves*. The fields can propagate outward from a source in all directions at the speed of light; for the sake of visual clarity, we have chosen to show them moving only along the *x* axis.

The animated diagram in Concept 2 and the illustrations below are used to emphasize three points. First, the depicted wave moves away from the source. For example, if you push the "transmit" button on a walkie-talkie, a wave is initiated that travels away from the walkie-talkie.

Second, at any fixed location in the path of the wave, both fields change over time. The wave below is drawn at intervals that are fractions $T/4$ of the period T. Look at the point P below, on the light blue vertical plane. The vectors from point P represent the direction and strength of the electric and magnetic fields at this point. As you can see, the vectors, and the fields they represent, change over time at P. Concept 2 shows them varying continuously with time at the point P.

Third, the diagrams reflect an important fact: The electric and magnetic fields have the same frequency and phase. That is, they reach their peaks and troughs simultaneously.

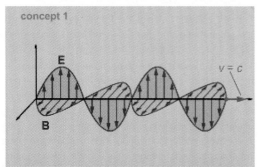

Electromagnetic waves
Consist of electric and magnetic fields
· Perpendicular to each other

Propagate as transverse waves
· Perpendicular to direction of travel

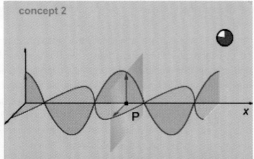

Electric, magnetic fields
Vary in strength over time at each point
Have same frequency and are in phase
Drive each other by changing strength

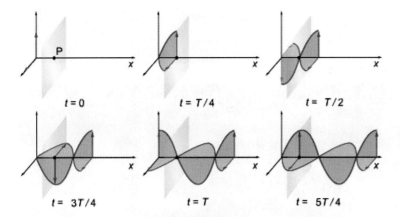

$t = 0$ $t = T/4$ $t = T/2$

$t = 3T/4$ $t = T$ $t = 5T/4$

A wave on a string provides a good starting point for understanding electromagnetic waves. Both electromagnetic radiation and a wave on a string are transverse waves. The strengths of the two fields constituting the radiation can be described using sinusoidal functions, just as we can use a sinusoidal function to calculate the transverse displacement of a particle in a string through which a wave is moving.

There is a crucial difference, though: Electromagnetic radiation consists of electric and magnetic fields, and does not require a medium like a string for its propagation. Electromagnetic waves can travel in a vacuum. If this is troubling to you, you are in good company. It took some brilliant physicists a great deal of hard work to convince the world that light and other electromagnetic waves do not require a medium of transmission.

Furthermore, when electromagnetic waves radiate in all directions from a compact source like an antenna or a lamp, the radiation emitted at a particular instant travels outward on the surface of an expanding sphere, and its strength diminishes with distance from the source. The waves cannot be truly sinusoidal, since the amplitude of a sinusoidal function never diminishes.

In the sections that follow we will analyze *plane waves*, which propagate through space, say in the positive x direction, in parallel planar wave fronts rather than expanding spherical ones. They are good approximations to physical waves over small regions that are distant from the source of the waves. Plane waves never diminish in strength; they can be accurately modeled using sinusoidal functions, and we will do so.

30.3 - Proportionality of electric and magnetic fields

Although the electric and magnetic field vectors of an electromagnetic wave point in perpendicular directions, their magnitudes are strictly proportional to each other at all positions and at all times. We graphically display the magnitudes at a particular instant on the same coordinate system in Equation 1. Their proportionality is expressed in the equation to the right, using a constant c that depends on two other fundamental physical constants.

This proportionality turned out to have important implications in the study of electromagnetic radiation. Why? Because when calculated, the value of c was very close to the measured speed of light. This crucial discovery accelerated the understanding of the relationship between electromagnetic radiation such as light or radio waves, and electric and magnetic fields.

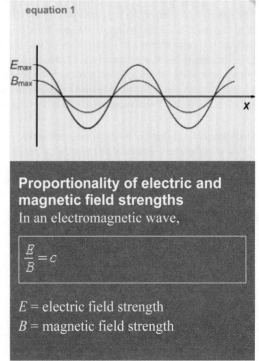

equation 1

E_{max}
B_{max}

x

Proportionality of electric and magnetic field strengths
In an electromagnetic wave,

$$\frac{E}{B} = c$$

E = electric field strength
B = magnetic field strength

30.4 - Calculating the speed of light from fundamental constants

One of the major discoveries of 19th century physics was that light is a form of electromagnetic radiation. By applying and extending their knowledge of electric and magnetic fields, physicists were able both to create electromagnetic radiation (initially radio waves) and to predict the speed of the waves.

James Maxwell published his four laws governing electromagnetic phenomena in 1864, and at the same time he predicted the existence of self-propagating electromagnetic waves. His work enabled him to calculate what the speed of these waves would have to be.

Heinrich Hertz transmitter, 1888. Transformer voltage causes a spark to jump between the postionable brass spheres, generating a radio pulse.

The angular frequency of any wave is $\omega = 2\pi f$, where f is its frequency in cycles per second. The angular wave number is $k = 2\pi/\lambda$, where λ is the wavelength. The speed of any wave is $v = \lambda f$. This means that the speed in terms of the angular frequency and wave number is $v = (2\pi/k)(\omega/2\pi)$, or ω/k.

Maxwell had already shown that the wave speed ω/k is a constant for electromagnetic waves, a constant he had designated as c and expressed in terms of μ_0 and ε_0. We state the relationship of c to these several variables and constants in Equation 1.

The fundamental constants μ_0 and ε_0 are used elsewhere in physics. For example, the permeability constant is used in equations that describe the magnetic field created by various electric current configurations. The permittivity constant is used to express one form of Coulomb's law. In other words, these constants determine the strengths of the electric and magnetic forces in the physical universe.

The example problem on the right asks you to repeat Maxwell's calculation of the value of c. The result is 2.998×10^8 m/s. In the year 1864, the speed of visible light in a vacuum had been known with fair accuracy for well over a century. The English physicist James Bradley estimated it in 1728 to be 3.1×10^8 m/s, based on his study of "stellar aberration," or the apparent change in the positions of stars as the Earth moves around the Sun. Because the calculated and observed speeds were so close, Maxwell's results provided the first evidence that light is a kind of electromagnetic wave.

Understanding that light is an electromagnetic wave, and knowing the general relationship between frequency and wavelength, sparked the discovery of additional types of electromagnetic radiation. In 1888 Heinrich Hertz created what we would now call radio receivers and transmitters, one of which you see in the illustration above. He proved the existence, and wavelike nature, of radiation having frequencies around 100 MHz.

concept 1

James Clerk Maxwell

Speed of light
Theoretical speed of radiation
= the measured speed of light
Conclusion: Light is electromagnetic radiation!

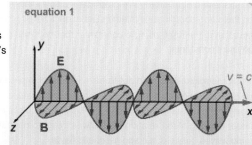

equation 1

Speed of an electromagnetic wave

$$c = \frac{\omega}{k} = \frac{1}{\sqrt{\mu_0 \varepsilon_0}}$$

c = speed of electromagnetic wave

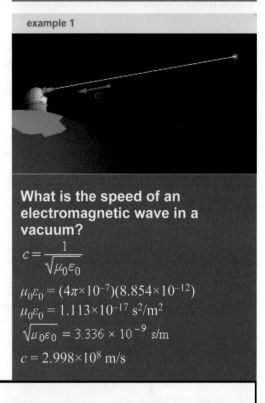

ω = angular frequency of wave
k = angular wave number of wave
μ_0 = permeability of free space
Constant $\mu_0 = 4\pi\times10^{-7}$ T·m/A
ε_0 = permittivity of free space
Constant $\varepsilon_0 = 8.854\times10^{-12}$ C²/N·m²

example 1

What is the speed of an electromagnetic wave in a vacuum?

$$c = \frac{1}{\sqrt{\mu_0\varepsilon_0}}$$

$$\mu_0\varepsilon_0 = (4\pi\times10^{-7})(8.854\times10^{-12})$$

$$\mu_0\varepsilon_0 = 1.113\times10^{-17} \text{ s}^2/\text{m}^2$$

$$\sqrt{\mu_0\varepsilon_0} = 3.336 \times 10^{-9} \text{ s/m}$$

$$c = 2.998\times10^8 \text{ m/s}$$

30.5 - Creating electromagnetic waves: antennas

Radio antennas create electromagnetic waves. A radio antenna is part of an overall system called a radio transmitter that converts the information contained in sound waves into electromagnetic waves. A radio receiver then reverses the process, converting the signals from electromagnetic waves back to sound waves.

The system depicted to the right shows the fundamentals of a radio transmitter. In the illustrations, the terminals of an AC generator are connected to two rods of conducting material: an antenna. The AC generator produces an emf $\mathcal{E}$ that

Radio-wave transmitters. A cable carries a modulated electric signal to the dipole antenna rod assembly visible at the top of each tower.

varies sinusoidally over time. The emf drives positive and negative charges to opposite ends of the antenna. The **separation** of the charges on the rods produces an electric field. The AC generator causes the amount and sign of the charge on each rod to vary over time, so that the resulting electric field varies in strength and orientation as well. (The flow of charge – that is, the current – also produces a varying magnetic field close to the antenna, part of what is called the *near field*, which we do not show here.)

The electric field produced by the antenna at each instant in time propagates outward in all directions at the speed of light. For simplicity's sake, we only show it traveling in the positive x direction in Concept 2. The electric field changes continuously with time and that change induces a magnetic field. To be precise, it induces a magnetic field proportional to the rate of change of the electric flux with respect to time, as described by Maxwell's law of induction. In turn, the changing magnetic field regenerates the electric field as the wave travels.

This coupling of changes in the magnetic and electric fields enables the electromagnetic wave to cross vast gulfs of space over immense spans of time. Electromagnetic radiation from distant stars, including light, reaches the Earth after billions of years of travel.

How does an antenna differ from other circuits you may have studied in which current flows or charge is stored? Consider a battery-resistor circuit or a battery-capacitor circuit in equilibrium; the current in the first creates a constant magnetic field, and the stored charge in the second creates a constant electric field. Both fields rapidly diminish as they extend outward in space. The crucial difference with the antenna is that not only does charge accumulate at its ends, but the AC generator continually causes the distribution of charge to change. The electric field varies sinusoidally over time, and a constantly changing electric field is the crucial element required to create continuous, self-propagating electromagnetic radiation.

Electromagnetic waves are generated when charges move at nonconstant velocities, as in an antenna. That is, they are generated by **accelerating** charges. In an antenna, the acceleration is in a straight line. Charged particles moving in uniform circular motion also emit electromagnetic radiation, called *synchrotron radiation*, due to their centripetal acceleration.

The AM and FM radio bands are located in different parts of the electromagnetic spectrum, and they are used in different ways to broadcast program content. The difference between them consists in how the information they convey is encoded. In *amplitude modulated* or *AM radio*, sound waves are encoded by varying the amplitude of a *carrier radio wave* around some reference value. Changes in amplitude convey the signal. The frequency of the carrier wave is around 1 MHz for AM radio.

In *frequency modulated* or *FM radio*, sound is encoded by slightly varying the frequency of the carrier wave around its base frequency. For FM radio, and television, the carrier wave frequency extends upward from around 100 MHz.

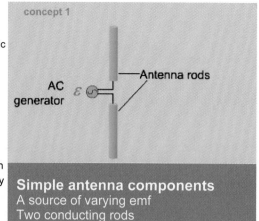

Simple antenna components
A source of varying emf
Two conducting rods

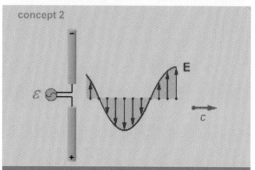

Simple antenna operation
Generates varying charge on rods
Charged rods create electric field
Electric field varies over time
Changing E-field induces B-field

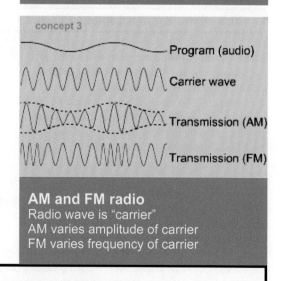

AM and FM radio
Radio wave is "carrier"
AM varies amplitude of carrier
FM varies frequency of carrier

30.6 - Earth's seasons

Almost all the energy we use on Earth originates in the Sun and arrives in the form of electromagnetic radiation. Roughly the same amount of solar power reaches the planet throughout the year, yet many places on the globe experience significant seasonal variations in the rate at which they receive this energy.

The cause of seasonal changes in the Earth's climate is the tilt of its axis, the line about which it rotates. The illustration in Concept 1 shows the position of the Earth in its orbit at different times of the year, as well as the direction in which the axis points. The axis is tilted at a $23.5°$ angle away from a line perpendicular to the Earth's orbital plane. It always points towards the same direction in space (which is why Polaris remains the North Star throughout the year).

March 21 and September 22 are known as the *equinoxes*. The name refers to the equal lengths of night and day (12 hours each) for all locations on Earth on these dates. December 21 and June 21 are the *solstices*. As the season progresses from autumn to winter, the Sun rises to a lower high point in the sky each day, and the days get shorter. On the winter solstice (meaning "sun stop"), the Sun stops getting lower and begins to rise to a higher apex each day, as it does through the rest of the winter and spring. The opposite happens after the summer solstice – the Sun once again peaks at a lower point each day. (The dates of the equinoxes and solstices vary from year to year, but are always around the 21st of the month.)

While June 21 is the summer solstice in the Northern Hemisphere, it is the winter solstice for the Southern Hemisphere. Concept 2 illustrates why this is true. It shows a Northern Hemisphere city, Beijing, and a Southern Hemisphere city, Perth, at noon on June 21.

Imagine a solar collection plate of area A lying flat on the ground, tangent to the Earth's surface in either of these cities. Light rays from the Sun arrive approximately parallel to the plane of the Earth's orbit. On June 21, the sunlight intersects the collecting plate in Beijing at a steeper angle than in Perth. Because Beijing is receiving sunlight more vertically, the energy from that light is more concentrated – Beijing is receiving more power over the area of its collecting plate.

In Perth, a smaller amount of sunlight is being spread over the same collecting area because of the oblique, slanting angle at which it hits the plate. The plate absorbs less power. It is summer in Beijing, and winter in Perth.

Six months later, on December 21, the situation will be reversed: Perth will receive directer sunlight than Beijing.

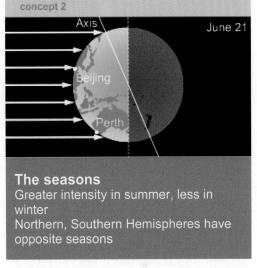

concept 1

September 22

June 21

December 21

$23.5°$

March 21

Cause of varying intensity
Earth's axis of rotation is tilted

concept 2

Axis

June 21

Beijing

Perth

The seasons
Greater intensity in summer, less in winter
Northern, Southern Hemispheres have opposite seasons

Generally speaking, locations farther than Beijing or Perth from the equator experience a greater variation in the power they receive throughout the year, and places closer to the equator experience less change. At the poles – dark six months of the year – this difference is extreme.

Some people mistakenly believe that the seasons are due to the eccentricity of the Earth's orbit – the fact that the Earth's distance from the Sun changes throughout the year. Your first clue that this belief is false is the observation that summer in the Southern Hemisphere occurs at the same time as winter in the Northern Hemisphere (you merely have to make a long-distance phone call to confirm this). In fact, during winter in the Northern Hemisphere, the Earth is actually **closer** to the Sun than in summer. The reason the eccentricity has only a slight effect is that the Earth's orbit is only slightly elliptical. The annual variation in insolation due to the eccentricity of the Earth's orbit is about 7%, in contrast to an approximately 110% increase from winter to summer (at the latitude of Beijing) due to axial tilt.

30.7 - How electromagnetic waves travel through matter

Light and other forms of electromagnetic radiation can travel through a vacuum, and it is often simplest to study them in that setting. However, radiation can also pass through matter: If you look through a glass window, you are viewing light that has passed through the Earth's atmosphere and the glass. Other forms of radiation such as radio waves pass through matter, as well.

This section focuses on how such transmission occurs. It relies on a classical model of electrons and atoms that predates quantum theory. In this model, electrons orbit an atom. They have a resonant frequency that depends on the kind of atom. On a larger scale, atoms themselves and the molecules composed of them also have resonant thermal frequencies at which they can vibrate or rotate.

We will use the example of light striking the glass in a window to discuss how substances transmit (or do not transmit) electromagnetic radiation. When an electromagnetic wave encounters a window, it collides with the molecules that make up the glass. If the frequency of the wave is near the resonant thermal frequency of the glass molecules, which is true for infrared radiation, the amplitude of the molecules' vibrations increases. They absorb the energy transported by the wave, and dissipate it throughout the glass by colliding with other molecules and heating up the window. Because it absorbs so much infrared energy, the glass is opaque to radiation of this frequency, preventing its transmission.

Scientists in the 19th century noted a phenomenon in greenhouses caused by the opaqueness of glass to infrared radiation, which they called the *greenhouse effect*. The glass in a greenhouse admits visible light from the Sun, which is then absorbed by the soil and plants inside. They reradiate the solar energy as longer infrared waves, which cannot pass back out through the glass and so help warm up the greenhouse. The same phenomenon occurs on a vaster scale in the atmosphere as gases like methane and carbon dioxide trap solar energy near the Earth's surface.

In contrast to infrared radiation, higher frequency radiation such as visible light does not resonate thermally with atoms or molecules, but may resonate with the electrons of the atoms of a substance. In glass, visible light experiences much less reduction in the amplitude of its waves than infrared radiation does, and most of its energy passes through the glass quite easily. Atoms with resonant electrons that do absorb energy from a light wave quickly pass on that energy by re-emitting it as radiation of the same frequency to other atoms, which in turn pass it on to their neighbors.

This chain of absorptions and re-emissions, called *forward scattering*, follows a path close to the light's original direction of travel. A beam of light that strikes a pane of glass will reach the "last atom" on the far side of the pane in an extremely short time. We see the light after it emerges, and think of glass as transparent.

This process does slow the transmission of the wave, which is why light travels slower in glass than it does in air or a vacuum (a fact captured numerically by the *index of refraction* of glass). For instance, light travels through a typical piece of optical glass at about 2/3 of its speed in a vacuum. Of course, 2/3 of the speed of light in a vacuum is still a rather rapid pace….

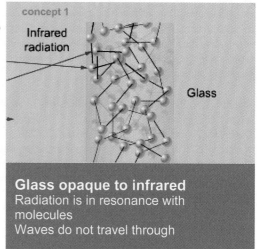

concept 1

Infrared radiation

Glass

Glass opaque to infrared
Radiation is in resonance with molecules
Waves do not travel through

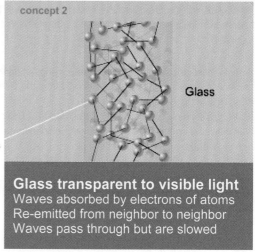

concept 2

Glass

Glass transparent to visible light
Waves absorbed by electrons of atoms
Re-emitted from neighbor to neighbor
Waves pass through but are slowed

If atoms of certain substances, such as cobalt, are added to glass, they may absorb certain frequencies of light without re-emitting them. Cobalt glass has a deep blue-violet color, which indicates that all the lower visible frequencies (from red through green) are absorbed and cannot pass through it. Substances which absorb all frequencies of visible light are called *opaque*.

Polarized wave: A transverse wave that oscillates in a single plane.

Polarized radiation: A form of radiation in which the electric field of every wave oscillates in the same plane.

Polaroid sunglasses block some light waves.

Polaroid sunglasses like the ones shown above reduce the amount of light that passes through them. How do they do it? They only let through light waves whose electric fields oscillate in a certain plane. When a source such as the Sun emits light, waves emerge whose electric fields vibrate in every plane parallel to the direction of propagation. This is shown in Concept 1. The electric field of each individual wave does oscillate consistently in its own plane, which is called the wave's plane of polarization, but the radiation as a whole does not have this property.

The electric field of any electromagnetic wave is a vector quantity. A polarizing lens or filter works by only letting through a certain **component** of the electric field of every light wave that strikes it. An ideal polarizing filter can be visualized as a set of narrow parallel slits whose direction is the filter's *transmission axis*.

When a wave passes through the filter, the component of its electric field parallel to the transmission axis is what passes through. The component perpendicular to the axis is absorbed. As a result, waves that oscillate parallel to the slits pass through unhindered, while waves that oscillate perpendicularly to them are completely absorbed. You may want to consider an analogy: a rope passing through a gap in a picket fence. If you shake the rope vertically, the wave you create passes through unhindered. If you shake the rope horizontally, the wave collides with the pickets, transfers energy to them, and does not pass through. In the case of a wave passing through at an oblique angle, the component of its transverse displacement along the "picket axis" passes through while the fence absorbs the other component.

This basic model of how polarization works is shown with an ideal polarizing filter in Concept 2. In the diagram, the transmission axis happens to be **vertical**. A "slit" allows waves oscillating in a vertical plane to pass through. For waves that oscillate in other planes, only the vertical component of the electric field of the wave can pass through. Waves with a horizontal plane of polarization cannot get through the slit at all.

Ordinary light consists of waves whose electric fields are randomly oriented in all lateral directions. This is called *unpolarized* radiation. Two common sources of unpolarized light are the Sun and incandescent light bulbs. If the radiation is created or filtered so that it has only waves oscillating in a single plane, then it is *linearly polarized*. In the illustration in Concept 2, the polarizing filter is exposed to unpolarized radiation, and it transmits linearly polarized radiation.

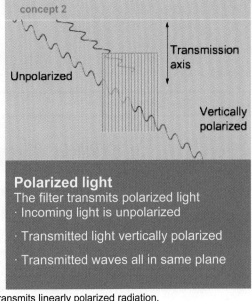

concept 1

Plane of polarization

Unpolarized light
Radiation can oscillate in many planes

concept 2

Unpolarized

Transmission axis

Vertically polarized

Polarized light
The filter transmits polarized light
· Incoming light is unpolarized
· Transmitted light vertically polarized
· Transmitted waves all in same plane

In Concept 3 you see an end-on "close up" of several light waves striking a polarizing filter that has a vertical transmission axis. The light waves are coming toward you. In each case, the vertical component of the electric field of the light is transmitted, and the filter absorbs the horizontal component. The original field is shown as a solid, dimmed vector; its components are hollowed out. The vertical component that passes through is drawn with a bright color, and the horizontal component that is blocked is dimmed and marked with a red ×. In each example illustrated, the electric field amplitude of the transmitted light, and with it the light's intensity, is reduced.

The final illustration, in Concept 4, displays an experiment with two polarizing filters. Unpolarized light is coming toward you from a distant source. It passes first through the upper filter, which allows the passage of light that is polarized at the angle shown by the "slit" lines. This polarized light continues toward you and passes through the lower filter.

The left-hand part of the illustration shows the orientation of the filters, with parallel lines indicating the transmission axis of each filter. The right-hand side shows you the amount of light that passes through the area of overlap, and how that changes with the angles between the two axes. When the axes are perpendicular, no light at all can pass through.

Radiation also can be *partially polarized*, having a few waves oscillating in all planes, but with most of its waves concentrated in a single plane. This is true of sunlight scattered by the atmosphere. As the photo above shows, the sky in certain directions is partially polarized in a vertical plane so that most of its light can pass through a pair of sunglasses whose transmission axis is vertical. Less light (but still some) passes through the rotated sunglasses. (Polarizing sunglasses are specifically intended to reduce horizontally polarized glare reflected from roadways and water, not skylight.)

Many forms of artificial electromagnetic radiation are polarized. A radio transmitter emits polarized radiation. If the rods of its antenna are vertical, then so is the electric field of every radio wave it creates. In this case, the most efficient receiving antenna is also vertically oriented; a horizontal receiving antenna would absorb radio waves much less efficiently. You may be familiar with this fact if you have ever tried to maneuver a radio antenna wire or a set of television "rabbit ears" to get the best reception. (If you do not know what "rabbit ears" are for television, well, before there was cable television, there was….)

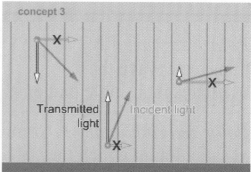

E-field component passes through filter
If transmission axis is vertical, filter …
· Transmits vertical E-field component

· Absorbs horizontal E-field component

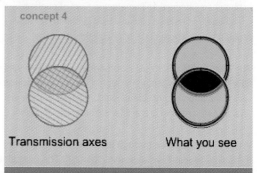

Transmission axes   **What you see**

Two Polaroid filters
Light passes through back (upper) filter
Then passes through front (lower) filter
Intensity depends on orientation of filters

30.9 - Scattering of light

Scattering: Absorption and re-emission of light by electrons, resulting in dispersion and some polarization.

The answer to a classic question – Why is the sky blue? – rests in a phenomenon called scattering. In this section, we give a classical (as opposed to quantum mechanical) explanation of how scattering occurs.

Scattered sunlight gives the sky its blue glow.

When light from the Sun strikes the electrons of various atoms in the Earth's atmosphere, the electrons can absorb the light's energy, oscillating and increasing their own energy. The electrons in turn re-emit this energy as light of the same wavelength. In effect, the oscillating electrons act like tiny antennas, emitting electromagnetic radiation in the frequency range of light.

An electron oscillates in a direction parallel to the electric field of the wave that energizes it, as shown in Concept 1. The electron then emits light polarized in a plane parallel to its vibration. We show a particular polarized wave that is re-emitted downward toward the ground, since we are concerned with what an observer on the surface of the Earth sees. Other light is scattered in other directions, including light scattered upward and light scattered forward in its original direction of travel.

Scattering explains why we see the sky: Light passing through the atmosphere is redirected due to scattering toward the surface of the Earth. In contrast, for an astronaut observer in the vacuum of space, sunlight is not scattered at all so there is no sky glow: Except for the stars, the sky appears black. To the astronaut, the disk of the Sun, a combination of all colors, looks white. We illustrate this below: The full spectrum combines to form white light.

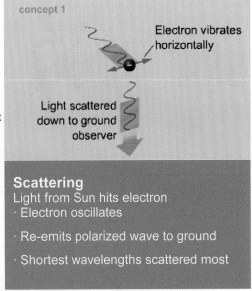

concept 1

Electron vibrates horizontally

Light scattered down to ground observer

Scattering
Light from Sun hits electron
· Electron oscillates

· Re-emits polarized wave to ground

· Shortest wavelengths scattered most

No scattered light

concept 2

View from space
No scattering: sky is black
Sun appears white

The question remains, why is our sky blue rather than some other color? Light at the blue end of the visible spectrum, which has the shortest wavelength, is 10 times more resonant with the electrons of atmospheric atoms than red light. This means blue light is scattered more than red, so that more of it is redirected toward the ground.

Scattering also explains why we see the Sun as yellow rather than white. When you look up at the disk of the Sun from the Earth's surface, the bluest portion of its light has been scattered away to the sides. The remaining part of the Sun's direct light appears somewhat yellowish.

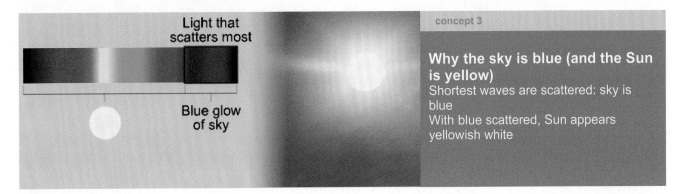

Light that scatters most

Blue glow of sky

concept 3

Why the sky is blue (and the Sun is yellow)
Shortest waves are scattered: sky is blue
With blue scattered, Sun appears yellowish white

You may also have noted how the Sun appears to change color when it sets. As the Sun's disk descends toward the horizon, its light must pass through a greater and greater thickness of atmosphere in order to reach you. Since a certain amount of sunlight is scattered aside for each kilometer of atmosphere it passes through, its position at sunset causes it to lose large amounts of light at the blue end and even toward the middle of the visible light spectrum. At sunset, practically all the shorter wavelengths of light have been scattered out of it, leaving only light at the red end of the spectrum to be viewed by you. The "missing" blue light is not really missing. People to the west of you perceive it as the daytime sky.

Light that scatters most

Blue glow of sky

Sunset
Longer wavelengths also scattered
Sun appears red

Scattering also explains why skylight is partially polarized. When the Sun is low in the sky, as depicted in Concept 1, horizontally polarized light that gets scattered down from the overhead sky is polarized in the plane of the downgoing wave you see in the illustration. Incoming sunlight that is polarized in other planes also gets scattered, but not straight down towards the ground.

You can experiment with skylight polarization yourself if you have a pair of polarizing sunglasses. In the early morning or late afternoon hold your glasses against the northern or southern sky at arm's length. Turn one of the lenses slowly, recalling that its transmission axis is vertical when the sunglasses are worn normally. You will find that the skylight is partially polarized in a plane perpendicular to the direction to the Sun.

30.10 - Physics at work: liquid crystal displays (LCDs)

Substances that change the direction of polarization of light passing through them are called optically active. In other words, an optically active substance rotates the plane of polarization of light passing through it.

The liquid crystal display (LCD) in the watch face above demonstrates *variable optical activity* at work. LCDs are found in many common devices, including calculators, cellular telephones and clocks. There are two types of LCDs: backlit and reflective. The one shown above is a reflective LCD, but we will explore both types in this section. Backlit LCDs generate light behind their displays; reflective LCDs like the one above utilize ambient light.

This digital watch displays the time with a reflective LCD.

LCDs rely on polarization. The characters of a digital watch display consist of "digit" segments: regions that can be made dark. These segments are filled with a substance called *liquid crystal* that is optically active in its natural state but becomes inactive when a potential difference is applied across it. You see this phenomenon illustrated for a backlit LCD in Concepts 1 and 2. In Concept 1, the power is off (there is no potential difference across the crystal), so the crystal is optically active and rotates the plane of polarization of the light. The thickness of the crystal is designed to rotate the light by 90°. In Concept 2 a potential difference is applied, the crystal becomes inactive, and there is no rotation of the light's plane of polarization.

The liquid crystal is sandwiched between two polarizing filters with perpendicular tranmission axes, as shown in Concept 3. In the backlit LCD shown there, a light behind the display shines through the left-hand filter. Following our usual practice we will call this filter that is closer to the light source the polarizer, and the one farther away the

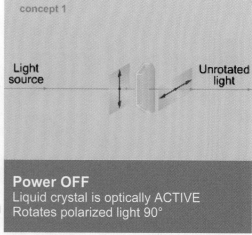

Light source

Unrotated light

Power OFF
Liquid crystal is optically ACTIVE
Rotates polarized light 90°

analyzer. The polarizer allows light with a particular plane of polarization to pass through. When the liquid crystal is "on" (optically inactive), it does not rotate the polarized light, and the analyzer prevents any of the light from passing through, creating a dark area.

When **no** potential difference is applied across the liquid crystal, it is "off" and reverts to its normal optically active state. The perpendicular orientation of the analyzer now allows the polarized light to pass through. Instead of being black, the material of the segment looks the same as the adjoining material. In order to make the transmitted light difficult to see, the display's background is colored to resemble it. This is shown in Concept 4.

If you examine the watch in the illustration above or one on your wrist, or a friend's wrist, you will see that the digits it displays are pieced together from segments that appear black when they are "turned on." When they are off, these segments are invisible to the casual glance, but they can still be made out as faint shadows if you look very carefully.

We have been describing a typical backlit LCD, which can be read in the dark. The backlighting consumes more power than any other part of the display, since the amount of power required to turn on each digit segment is negligible. Backlit LCDs are typically found in automobile dashboards, where their power usage is not a particular concern and where readability at night is important.

A reflective LCD, such as the one in the watch above, consumes less power. We show how a reflective LCD works in Concept 5; it is a bit more complicated than a backlit LCD. A mirror that can reflect ambient light coming from in front of the LCD replaces the backlight behind the polarizer. As with the backlit display, the transmission axes of the polarizer and analyzer are at right angles to each other.

Concept 5 shows what happens when a liquid crystal digit segment in this type of LCD is turned **off**. In this state, light passes through each of the analyzer, the liquid crystal segment, and the polarizer twice. Unpolarized light enters the display from the right and becomes horizontally polarized as it passes through the right-hand filter (the analyzer). It rotates $90°$ to a vertical orientation as it passes through the optically active liquid crystal component. In this orientation it can pass through the polarizer, reflect off the mirror, and come back out through the polarizer without hindrance. (A keen-eyed observer will note that the angular symmetry of reflection is apparently being violated where the light strikes the mirror: We drew the incident ray at a different angle in order to fit all the details into the diagram.)

After passing through the polarizer, the light retraces its path through the liquid crystal, again rotating and again becoming horizontally polarized. It passes back out through the analyzer without absorption, creating a region that blends into the background color of the display.

When the segment is turned on, it becomes optically inactive; optically, it can be treated as if it were no longer there. Light entering from the right gets horizontally polarized by the analyzer, and propagates to the left until it strikes the polarizer, where it is absorbed. This light never even reaches the mirror, and the segment appears dark. You see this happening in the watch above, where the dark segments spell out the time of day.

More elaborate LCDs of both types can be manufactured with "segments" having any shape, not just the parts of digits. For example, the battery and signal strength icons on a cellular telephone display, or the letters "H" and "M" on the watch above, use specially shaped segments. Some flat panel display screens use an array of thousands or even millions of tiny LCD dot-segments to produce virtually any image. With the appropriate refinements, color images can be produced.

As with polarized light from the sky, you can use a pair of Polaroid sunglasses to experiment with the polarized light emitted by a liquid crystal display. For example, you will find that a watch, viewed through the glasses, looks quite different depending on its orientation. At some angles the display looks more or less normal, while at others it becomes completely unreadable.

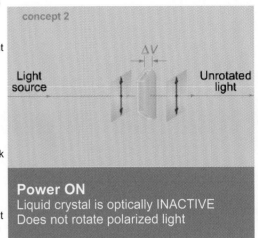

Power ON
Liquid crystal is optically INACTIVE
Does not rotate polarized light

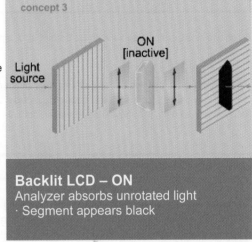

Backlit LCD – ON
Analyzer absorbs unrotated light
· Segment appears black

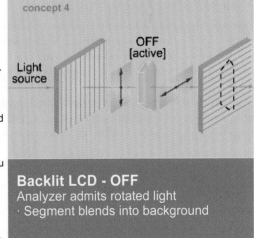

Backlit LCD - OFF
Analyzer admits rotated light
· Segment blends into background

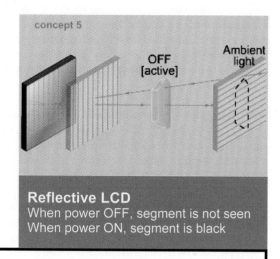

concept 5

OFF
[active]

Ambient
light

Reflective LCD
When power OFF, segment is not seen
When power ON, segment is black

30.11 - Gotchas

A light wave is a transverse wave. Yes. Both of its components, an electric and a magnetic field, oscillate perpendicularly to its direction of travel.

Radio signals and light waves are fundamentally different. Both are forms of electromagnetic radiation, so we lean toward "no" in response to this statement. The wavelength and frequency of radio transmissions and light are significantly different, and humans can see light, but not radio waves, so one could say "yes". However, both are electromagnetic waves, and both move at the speed of light.

30.12 - Summary

An electromagnetic wave is a traveling wave consisting of mutually perpendicular electric and magnetic fields that oscillate transversely to the direction of propagation. Electromagnetic radiation moves at the "speed of light," or c, which is 299,792,458 m/s in a vacuum. The value 3.00×10^8 m/s is often used.

Equations

Proportionality of fields

$$\frac{E}{B} = c = \frac{1}{\sqrt{\mu_0 \varepsilon_0}}$$

Every electromagnetic wave has a characteristic frequency and wavelength. The electromagnetic spectrum is an ordering of electromagnetic radiation in accordance with these two properties and extends far beyond the tiny gamut called visible light that we can detect with our eyes. Some other kinds of electromagnetic radiation are radio waves (AM and FM), television signals, microwaves, infrared light, ultraviolet light, x-rays, and gamma rays.

Maxwell proved that the speed of an electromagnetic wave equals the reciprocal of the square root of the product of two fundamental physical constants, the electric permittivity of free space ε_0, and the magnetic permeability of free space μ_0. This value turned out to be equal to the empirically well-measured speed of light, providing strong evidence that light is a form of electromagnetic radiation.

Linearly polarized light consists of light waves whose electric fields all oscillate in the same plane. This type of light can be created by several methods, such as by passing unpolarized light, whose electric fields oscillate in many directions, through a polarizing filter. The direction of polarization that results is called the transmission axis of the filter. As a randomly polarized wave passes through such a filter, only the component of its oscillating electric field that is aligned with the transmission axis passes through.

The scattering of light passing through a transparent substance is the absorption and re-emission of light waves of characteristic frequencies by atoms in the substance. Scattering in the atmosphere is responsible for the blue glow of the sky, the yellowish hue of the Sun, and the red color of sunsets.

Optical activity forms the technological basis of the liquid crystal displays (LCDs) used in many consumer electronic devices.

31.0 - Introduction

"Image is everything," one well-known advertisement blared for years. (An ad from another company then trumpeted the contradictory message that "image is nothing." Go figure!)

For physicists, image is as much a matter of mirrors and lenses as it is of appearance and athleticism. By arranging mirrors and lenses, they can magnify or shrink images and place them where they are needed. The design of a wide range of devices, from reading glasses and cameras to telescopes, depends on a thorough understanding of how to manipulate images created with light.

This chapter begins with a discussion of light rays and mirrors, two essential elements of your understanding of images. The simulation to the right features a concave mirror. The mirror creates images of objects. In this case, the object is a penguin. You can move the penguin left and right, and observe how its positioning changes the location and size of the image created by the mirror. The image is shown as a faded out version of the object itself. At some locations of the object, the image will be off the screen, but it will reappear when you drag the object to another location.

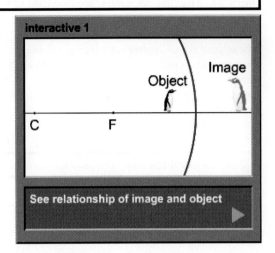

interactive 1

See relationship of image and object

As you move the object back and forth, consider the following questions. Where can you place the object so that the image and object are on the same side of the mirror? On opposite sides? Where can you place the object so that the image is smaller than the object? Larger? The variety of images produced by different types of mirrors is a major topic in this chapter.

If you press the SHOW RAYS button in the simulation, you will see three light rays that emanate from the penguin, reflect off the mirror, and converge to define the top of the image. These rays are used extensively in the study of mirrors and lenses, and this is your chance to begin to experience their properties. (The rays do not always converge perfectly; this is a realistic depiction of the way curved mirrors work.) You can turn off the rays by pressing the HIDE RAYS button.

31.1 - Light and reflection

Reflection: Light "bouncing back" from a surface.

When you look at yourself in a mirror, you are seeing a reflection of yourself. When you look at the Moon at night, you are seeing sunlight reflecting off that distant body.

Not all the light that reaches a surface reflects. In fact, you see an object like a tree as having different colors because its varied parts reflect some wavelengths of

To form a mirror image, light bounces back from the mirror's surface.

light and absorb others. Light can pass through a material, as it does with a glass window. It can also be absorbed by a material, as evidenced by how a black rock warms up during a sunny day. All this can happen simultaneously: Light will reflect off the surface of a lake (which is why you see the lake), penetrate the water (otherwise, it would be completely dark below the surface), and be absorbed by the water, warming it.

To understand reflection, it is often useful to treat light as a stream of particles that move in a straight line and change direction only when they encounter a surface. Each light "particle" acts like a ball bouncing off of a surface, and like a ball, it reflects off the surface at a rebound angle equal to its incoming angle. You see yourself in a mirror because the light bounces back to your eyes from the mirror.

The term "reflection" likely conjures up images of light and perhaps mirrors. Studying mirrors is a good way to learn about reflection because they are designed to reflect light in a way that creates a clear visual image. However, it is worth noting that reflection does not apply only to light. Some creatures use the reflection of sound (echoes) to help them perceive their surroundings and stalk their prey. For example, bats, seals and dolphins emit high frequency sound and then listen for the reflected waves. By analyzing these reflections, they can "see" with great precision.

Radar, used to track airplanes, is based on the reflection of radio waves. A sophisticated understanding of reflection can be used to design "stealth" aircraft that are difficult to detect with radar. Stealth aircraft register on radar screens as being about as large as a BB, in part because of their ability to reflect incoming waves in "random" directions.

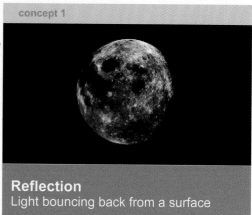

concept 1

Reflection
Light bouncing back from a surface

31.2 - Light rays

Light ray: A straight line used to represent the path of light.

Light rays are used to analyze devices such as mirrors and lenses. Light emanating from a point in a particular direction is treated as moving in a straight line. You can think of this as modeling light with a collection of laser beams, each ray moving in a straight and narrow line until it intersects a surface.

You can see an example of light rays depicted on the right, where a penguin views himself in a mirror. Several rays are shown emanating from a point on the penguin's foot. We show the full path of a single ray to illustrate how the penguin can see his foot reflected in the mirror. The light ray starts at the foot, reflects at the mirror and then reaches his eye. The arrowheads indicate the direction of the light's travel.

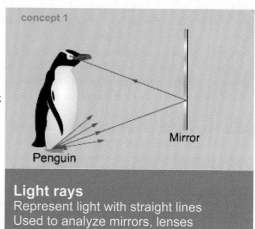

concept 1

Mirror

Penguin

Light rays
Represent light with straight lines
Used to analyze mirrors, lenses

The penguin's feet are not the source of the light. That might be the Sun or an electric lamp. But for the purposes of analyzing the mirror, we will proceed as though the light rays originate from the object whose image we intend to analyze.

Light is a complex phenomenon. Treating it as propagating in a straight line does not explain why a beam from a flashlight spreads out as it travels; other concepts are needed there. But to understand mirrors and lenses, light rays prove very useful.

31.3 - Mirror basics

At the right, you see a penguin looking at himself in a *planar mirror*. A planar mirror is a flat, smooth surface that reflects light. A typical planar mirror is manufactured by coating one side of a sheet of glass with a metallic film. It is designed to reflect as much light as possible and to create distinct images. Either by looking at yourself in a planar mirror or referring to the illustration in Concept 1, you can observe four essential properties of an image produced by this kind of mirror:

1. Your image is the same size as you are. The variable h is used to represent its height.

2. Your image appears as far behind the mirror as you are in front of it. Your distance is called the object distance, and how far the image is behind the mirror is called the image distance. The object distance, represented by d_o, is positive by convention. When an image is on the opposite side of a mirror from the object, its distance d_i from the mirror is negative by convention.

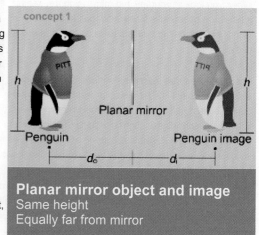

concept 1

Planar mirror

h Penguin   Penguin image h

d_o d_i

Planar mirror object and image
Same height
Equally far from mirror

3. The image has front-back reversal. If you are facing north, then your mirror image is facing south. If this reversal did not occur, you would see your back.

Image is right side up

4. The image is **not** reversed either right-left or up-down. If you look in a mirror and raise your left hand, its reflection will rise up on your left. Your head also still appears on the top of the image. The image is not inverted.

Mirrors do create the illusion of left-right reversal. For instance, if you raise your left hand, it will appear on your left but on the image's "right," because your image is facing the opposite direction than you are. This is akin to "stage left" or "stage right" directions for actors, which are based on the perception of what is left or right for the audience, not for the actors themselves as they face the audience. Their "left" and "right" are reversed because they are facing in the opposite direction than the audience, just as your mirror image is.

You cannot easily read normal writing in a mirror (unless you are as gifted as Leonardo da Vinci, who wrote in "mirror writing" so that others could not easily decipher his work). Mirror writing does have its uses: An emergency vehicle may have "ǝɔuɐludɯA" written on its front so that the text can be readily read when seen in the rearview mirror of a car.

31.4 - Virtual and real images

Image: A reproduction of an object by means of light.

Virtual image: An image on the opposite side of a mirror than the object it is created from. The image cannot be projected onto paper at its perceived location.

Kitten looking for its image behind a mirror.

Real image: An image on the same side of a mirror as the object it is created from. The image can be projected onto paper at its perceived location.

concept 1

Image
A reproduction created by light

When you look into a planar mirror, your image appears to be on the **opposite** side of the mirror, in a "looking glass" world that you cannot reach except in literature. The light of the image registered by your eyes is not actually coming from behind the mirror, even though your brain may interpret it this way.

You may be so accustomed to virtual images such as those formed by planar mirrors that you take them for granted and believe them to be as "real" as any other image. But not as real as any other **object**: A true understanding of virtual images must be learned. A kitten, when first exposed to a mirror, believes its reflected image to be another kitten and will search for the potential playmate behind the mirror. Over time, some animals (including humans, chimpanzees and dolphins) can learn how to interpret the nature of the images created by mirrors.

It will now be helpful to be more formal about some basic terminology. Objects are "in front" of a mirror: They are on its reflecting side. (In the diagrams in this book we will almost always place an object to the left of the mirror, but that certainly is not a law of physics, just a convention of sorts about which side is "in front.") If the image is on the same side of the mirror as the object, it also is in front of the mirror. If the image is on the opposite side of the mirror from the object, we say it is "behind" or in back of the mirror. A virtual image created by a mirror is behind the mirror. The distance between a virtual image and the mirror is negative.

Curved mirrors can create what is called a real image. In Concept 3, you see a diagram of a concave mirror creating a real image: an image on the same side of the mirror as the object. By convention, the distance between the mirror and the real image is positive. We stress the conventions of sign because they will prove essential when equations are used to calculate certain properties of an image, such as its position.

The terms "real" and "virtual" can be confusing. One way to decide whether an image is real or virtual is to imagine placing a piece of paper at the location of the image and then observing the results. With real images, the light passes through the location of the image; with virtual images, it does not. If you place a piece of paper "behind" a planar mirror, where the virtual image is located, you will not find an image projected there. With virtual images the brain projects the location of the image as it interprets the light it receives.

On the other hand, if you place a piece of paper at the location of a real image, you will see the image on the paper. For instance, images created by movie projectors are real, which is why you can see them on movie screens.

Concept 4 shows an optical illusion created by a popular toy. A special combination of curved mirrors creates a real image that is so solid looking you are tempted to reach out and grasp it.

concept 2

Planar mirror

Penguin

Penguin image

d_i

Virtual image
Opposite side of mirror
Negative distance

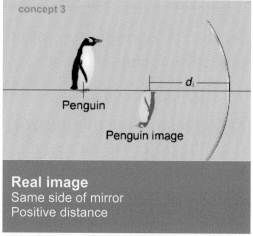

concept 3

Penguin

d_i

Penguin image

Real image
Same side of mirror
Positive distance

concept 4

An optical illusion
Real image perceived as object

Law of reflection: The angle of incidence equals the angle of reflection.

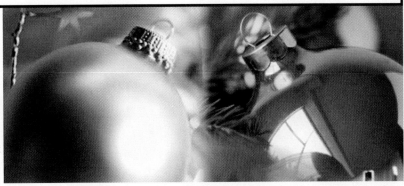
Diffuse and specular reflections from holiday ornaments.

At the right, you see a planar mirror. A light ray from the penguin's foot is reflecting off the mirror. The light ray before reflection is called the *incident ray*; the light ray that reflects off the mirror is known as the *reflected ray*. In this illustration, the rays are in the same vertical plane.

The *angle of incidence* θ_i is shown in the diagrams to the right. The angle θ_i represents the angle between a line perpendicular (normal) to the mirror's surface and the incident ray of light.

The light leaves the surface at the *angle of reflection* θ_r. This is the angle between the normal line and the reflected ray. As you can see in the diagrams, the angles of incidence and reflection are the same. This is the law of reflection: The angle of incidence equals the angle of reflection. This law is confirmed by experiments and theory.

The law of reflection applies to smooth surfaces, which exhibit *specular reflection*. The right-hand ornament in the photograph above is extremely smooth and produces a specular reflection. Rays that are parallel and close together when they strike the ornament will all be moving in a new direction after they reflect, but they will still be parallel. Specular reflection is the topic of this chapter.

If the reflecting surface is rough, *diffuse reflection* results. The left-hand ornament above provides an example of diffuse reflection. With a rough surface, neighboring incident rays will reflect in a variety of directions. Rays that are parallel and close together when they strike the surface will not be parallel after they reflect. Diffuse reflection is sometimes desirable. For instance, matte (low gloss) wall paint is designed to achieve diffuse reflection for surfaces where a shiny appearance is undesirable.

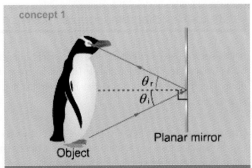
concept 1

The law of reflection
Incidence angle equals reflection angle
Angles measured between light rays and normal line

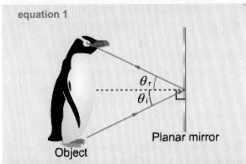
equation 1

The law of reflection

$$\theta_i = \theta_r$$

θ_i = angle of incidence
θ_r = angle of reflection

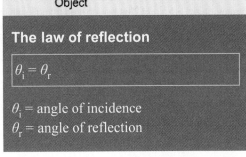

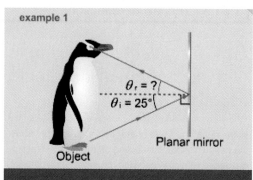

31.6 - Ray diagrams for planar mirrors

In this section, we use ray diagrams to explore some properties of an image produced by a planar mirror. To review these: The image created by a planar mirror is virtual, upright (right side up), the same distance from the mirror as the object, and the same size as the object.

Using the ray diagram in Concept 1, we first show why the image is virtual. You see two rays emanating from a point on the penguin's head. They reflect off the mirror and travel to the eye of an observer viewing the penguin's image. In this diagram, we are not concerned with what the penguin sees. We are using him as an object whose image is being viewed by an observer.

Because the observer's brain assumes that light travels in a straight line, it projects an image behind the mirror. Dashed lines, called *virtual rays*, show the paths the brain presumes are followed by rays emanating from the source of the light. The brain locates the top of the image at the point where these virtual rays converge. Since this point is behind the mirror, and no light actually comes from it, it forms part of a virtual image.

Rays also emanate from a point on the penguin's foot and reflect from a lower point on the mirror back to the observer's eye. The observer's brain locates the bottom of the image at a point where the virtual extensions of those rays intersect, a point behind the mirror and below the location of the image's head. This confirms that the image is not only virtual, but upright as well.

The diagram in Concept 2 shows that the image is the same distance behind the mirror as the object is in front. The two colored triangles share a common side (the mirror) and two pairs of equal angles, including a pair of right angles. This means the triangles are congruent, so their bottom legs must have equal lengths, and d_i and d_o must have equal magnitudes. A similar argument with two other congruent triangles demonstrates that the image has the same height as the object.

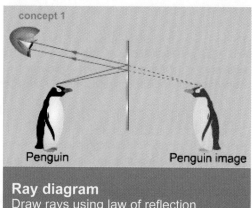

Penguin   Penguin image

Ray diagram
Draw rays using law of reflection
Find image location with virtual rays

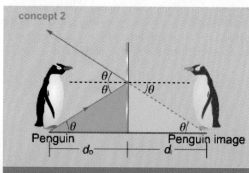

Penguin   Penguin image

To relate object, image distances
Draw a ray
Identify equal angles
Congruent triangles prove object, image distances have same magnitude

Spherical mirror: A mirror that is a portion of a sphere.

Concave mirror: A curved mirror whose reflective side is on the inside of the curve.

Convex mirror: A curved mirror whose reflective side is on the outside of the curve.

Concave and convex spherical mirrors.

Mirrors can be curved as well as flat. One type of curved mirror is a spherical mirror, which consists of a section of a sphere. To describe spherical mirrors it is common to consider a sphere with silvered reflecting surfaces. In a concave mirror, reflection occurs on the inside surface, as illustrated in Concept 2. A convex mirror is made by using a section of the exterior of the sphere, as shown in Concept 3.

If you like mnemonics, a good way to remember which type is which is to recall that a con**cave** mirror is like a **cave** whose walls curve around you. Though we concentrate on spherical mirrors here, concave and convex are terms that can apply to curved mirrors other than spherical mirrors.

The photos above show two examples of spherical mirrors and the images they create. The left-hand photo shows a concave makeup mirror. These mirrors, often found in bathrooms, are designed to magnify an image: You look in the mirror and see a larger image of yourself. Lucky you!

The photograph on the right above shows a convex safety mirror that allows drivers to see around a corner of a twisty seaside road. Security mirrors are also often convex. They provide a larger field of view than a flat mirror, enabling store personnel, for example, to survey a large area. Convex auxiliary mirrors are often affixed to the flat rearview mirrors of trucks and RVs.

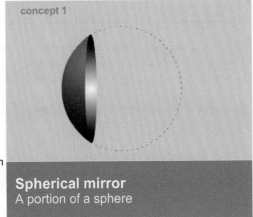

concept 1

Spherical mirror
A portion of a sphere

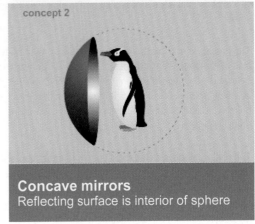

concept 2

Concave mirrors
Reflecting surface is interior of sphere

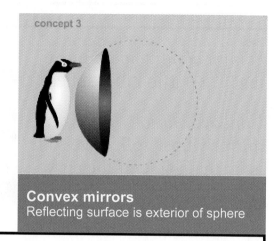

Convex mirrors
Reflecting surface is exterior of sphere

31.8 - Mirror terminology

Before we proceed to a further discussion of mirrors, we need to introduce some terminology. The diagrams to the right are used to illustrate these new terms. Many of the same terms are used to describe lenses, a topic you will study later.

The mirrors discussed in this section are spherical. The sphere's *center of curvature* is shown as point C in the diagrams.

A line passing through the center of curvature and the midpoint of a spherical mirror, like the one shown in Concept 1, is called the *principal axis* of the mirror. This line is perpendicular to the surface of the mirror where they intersect.

While planar mirrors produce only virtual images, a curved mirror can produce either a virtual or a real image, depending on the shape of the mirror and the location of the object.

The *image point* corresponding to an object on the principal axis is the location on the axis of its image. When an object is infinitely far away from the mirror, its image point defines the *focal point* of a mirror or lens. You see this point, F, in Concept 2. "Infinitely far away" means the incident light rays from the object are effectively parallel. The focal point is located on the principal axis, and it is an unchanging characteristic of a particular mirror.

The distance between the focal point and the midpoint of a mirror is its *focal length*, represented with the symbol f. By convention, concave mirrors have positive focal lengths, while convex mirrors have negative ones. You see an example of a negative focal length in Concept 3. This convention allows the use of a single equation to locate images and objects for both types of mirrors.

Our study of mirrors will focus on *paraxial rays*. Paraxial rays are incident rays that are relatively close to the principal axis. Rays that are far from the principal axis and do not converge at a single image point are called *nonparaxial rays*. Nonparaxial rays cause blurry images. This effect is called *spherical aberration*.

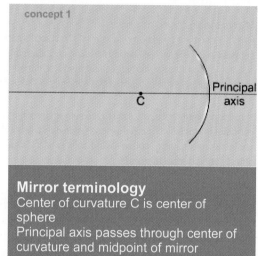

Mirror terminology
Center of curvature C is center of sphere
Principal axis passes through center of curvature and midpoint of mirror

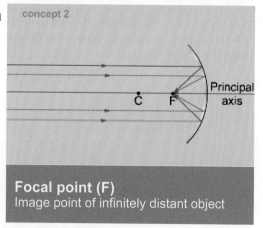

Focal point (F)
Image point of infinitely distant object

For our purposes, the base of an object is located on the principal axis. When an object's base is on the principal axis, then the base of its image will be too, though it may be inverted, like the image shown in Concept 4. The *height* of such an object or image is measured from the principal axis. Like most quantities associated with objects and images in optics, height has a sign. A positive value means the image is upright. Its top is still on top. A negative sign means an image is inverted, as you see in Concept 4. Its base still lies on the principal axis, but its top is now below the axis.

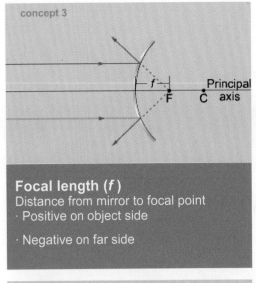

Focal length (f)
Distance from mirror to focal point
· Positive on object side

· Negative on far side

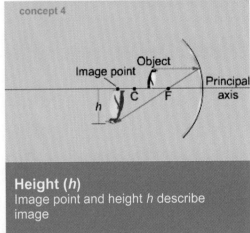

Height (h)
Image point and height h describe image

31.9 - Spherical mirrors: focal length equation

In Concept 1, you see a diagram of a concave mirror with center of curvature C and radius of curvature r. A distant object and its image are shown. (The object and image distances as well as the relative heights are not drawn to scale.) Because the object is far away, the image point is at the focal point. The focal length f is the distance from the mirror to the focal point.

How does the focal length change as the mirror radius changes? Imagine you are using a mirror to create an image of a distant object. A concave mirror with a very slight curvature would correspond to a sphere with a large radius. If you consider the law of reflection and how rays would reflect from this mirror, you will realize that the focal point (and image) would be relatively far away from it. In contrast, a sharply curving mirror would create an image quite close to the surface.

The equation shown in Equation 1 quantifies this general relationship. The magnitude of the focal length f equals one-half the radius r of the sphere. It is positive for a concave mirror, and negative for a convex mirror.

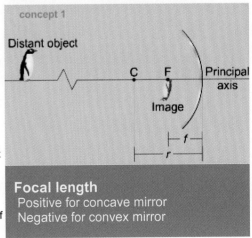

Distant object

Focal length
Positive for concave mirror
Negative for convex mirror

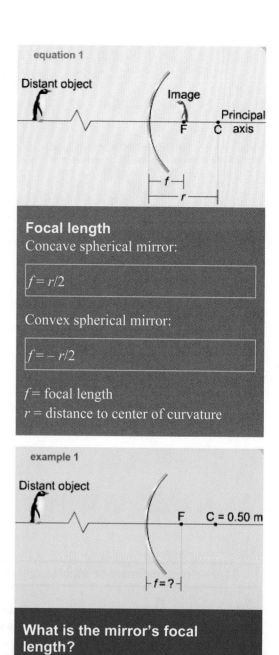

Focal length

Concave spherical mirror:

$$f = r/2$$

Convex spherical mirror:

$$f = -r/2$$

f = focal length
r = distance to center of curvature

example 1

Distant object

F   C = 0.50 m

$f = ?$

What is the mirror's focal length?

$f = -r/2$
$f = -(0.50\ \text{m})/2$
$f = -0.25\ \text{m}$

Parabolic mirrors provide a solution to the problem of spherical aberration. Spherical aberration occurs because some reflected rays do not pass precisely through the focal point of a spherical reflector. The farther the incident rays are from the mirror's principal axis, the more their reflected rays will miss the focal point. The result is a blurry image.

Spherical aberration is a serious problem for astronomers and others who need high quality images. Astronomers use telescopes to create images of distant objects. These telescopes often include very large concave mirrors to collect as much light as possible, allowing them to create images of objects that are exceedingly dim. (And by "large" we truly mean large: The diameter of a modern reflecting research telescope is in the eight to ten meter range.) If spherical mirrors were the basis of such telescopes, the images they created would be blurry due to spherical aberration.

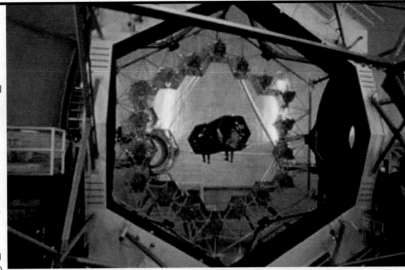

This telescope mirror is a hexagonal mosaic of smaller spherical mirror segments. Note the workman sitting at the focal point.

To produce a sharp image, some telescopes instead use a mirror that has a cross section in the shape of a parabola rather than a section of a circle. Why? Reflected rays from distant objects converge to form a sharp image, no matter how far the incident ray is from the principal axis. The parabolic design is used not just for visible light but for other forms of electromagnetic radiation, like radio waves, as well.

For instance, the *dish antennas* used for satellite television are small parabolic reflectors. These antennas do not have to be as smooth as light reflectors because the wavelength of the television signals they receive is far greater than the wavelengths of visible light. For electromagnetic radiation of even longer wavelengths, like the longest radio waves, the receiving parabolic reflectors can be even less smooth, but they must be very wide. You see an example of a large radio telescope in Concept 3.

Mirrors having a precise parabolic shape are difficult to manufacture. Some modern optical telescopes, called mosaic telescopes, combine the best features of both spherical and parabolic mirrors. They consist of a number of spherical mirror segments arranged in an overall parabolic shape. The mirrors are cut into hexagons so that they fit together neatly with no gaps. In the photograph above you see such a mirror.

This arrangement works well because the individual spherical segments are small enough to have negligible aberrations of their own and to be easy to assemble, and like all spherical mirrors they are easy to manufacture. Yet each small mirror can be positioned as part of a large overall parabolic shape that optimizes the net image quality produced by the reflector.

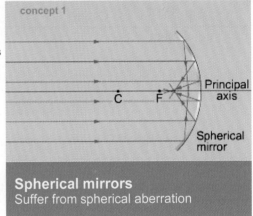

concept 1

Principal axis

Spherical mirror

Spherical mirrors
Suffer from spherical aberration

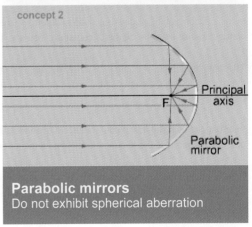

concept 2

Principal axis

Parabolic mirror

Parabolic mirrors
Do not exhibit spherical aberration

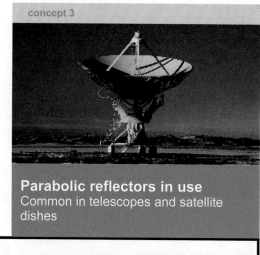

Parabolic reflectors in use
Common in telescopes and satellite dishes

concept 3

31.11 - Ray-tracing fundamentals

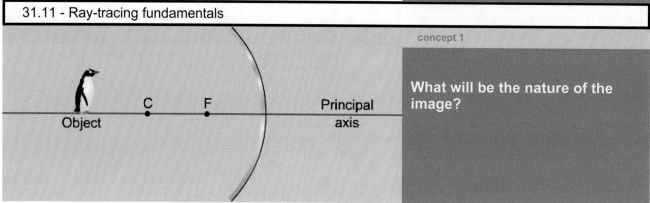

concept 1

Object

C   F

Principal
axis

What will be the nature of the image?

Ray tracing enables you to determine the fundamental properties of an image: Is it upright or inverted? Smaller or larger than the object? Real or virtual?

Ray tracing also provides an effective tool for verifying the computational results you get from applying the mirror and lens equations. It is easy to drop a sign, forget a reciprocal, or make other errors when applying these equations; ray tracing allows you to subject your answers to a "reality check."

In this section, ray tracing will be used to determine the basic attributes of an image that is produced by an object located farther from a concave mirror than the center of curvature. You see this configuration above.

To locate the image, we start with three rays emanating from the top of the object: in this case, the top of the penguin's head. The rays reach the mirror at three different points. They then reflect and converge. The point at which they converge is the location of the top of the image penguin's head.

With hand-drawn ray-tracing diagrams, we use the working approximation that the incident rays are paraxial, so that they converge at one point. In the simulations in this chapter, you can observe accurate ray-tracing diagrams that display the effects of spherical aberration.

Below, we show each ray separately; all three rays and the image are shown in Concept 5.

Ray 1 starts as an incident ray that is parallel to the principal axis. It reflects off the mirror and passes through the focal point after it reflects.

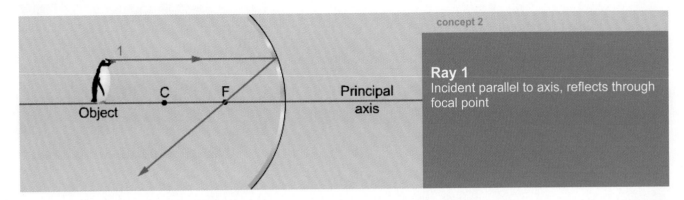

Ray 2 starts as an incident ray that passes through the focal point and then reflects parallel to the principal axis.

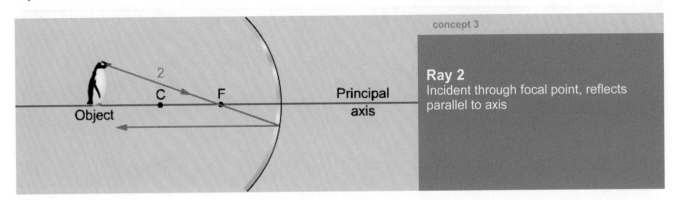

Ray 3 begins as an incident ray that passes through the center of curvature, strikes the mirror perpendicularly, and reflects back, moving along the same line as the incident ray.

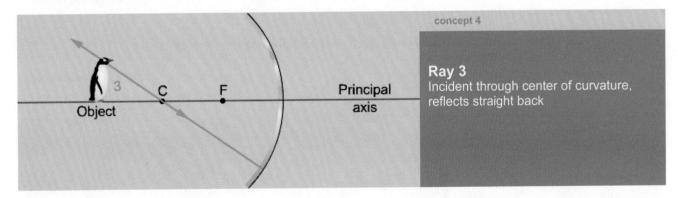

Why do these rays reflect in the way they do? The first incident ray is parallel to the principal axis. By definition, the reflection of this ray passes through the focal point.

The second ray is parallel to the principal axis **after** it reflects. The definition of focal point applied "in reverse" explains why this should be so: Since the ray passes through the focal point before it reflects, it is parallel to the axis after it reflects.

The final ray reflects straight back because, like a radius of the sphere, it meets the spherical surface perpendicularly. Its angle of incidence is zero degrees, so its angle of reflection will be the same.

Now that the three rays have been drawn separately, we draw them together in Concept 5. They converge at the head of the image. The image is both inverted (upside down) and smaller than the original object. It is located between the focal point and the center of curvature. The image is real, being located on the same side of the mirror as the object. Since it is real, if a piece of paper were placed at the point of intersection of the reflected rays, a small inverted image would be projected onto it.

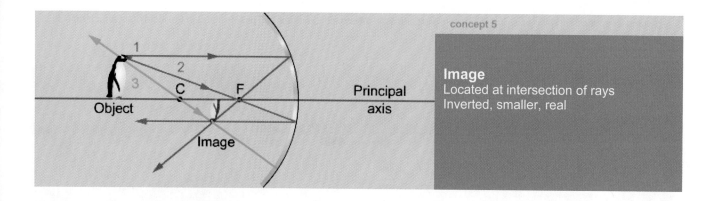

Image
Located at intersection of rays
Inverted, smaller, real

31.12 - Ray tracing: a second example

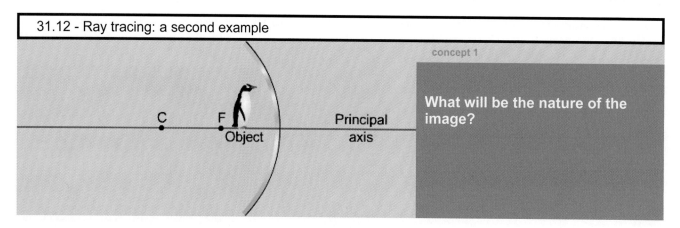

concept 1

What will be the nature of the image?

We will use ray tracing to determine the nature of the image created by an object that lies within the focal point of a concave mirror. As with the rays in the prior example, the incident rays all start or pass through a point at the top of the object, the penguin. They also have the same basic properties as the previous rays: One is parallel to the principal axis, one passes through the focal point, and the third passes through the center of curvature.

In contrast to the prior example, the reflected rays do not converge. We will need to use virtual rays to locate the image.

Ray 1 starts parallel to the principal axis, reflects, and passes through the focal point. Note that we extend the reflected ray backward through the mirror surface as a virtual ray (dashed line).

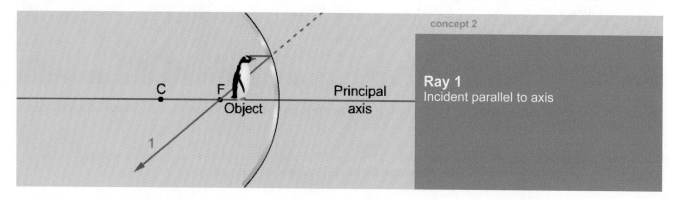

concept 2

Ray 1
Incident parallel to axis

Ray 2 must pass through the focal point before reaching the mirror. We draw it as passing through the focal point before intersecting the penguin's head. It then strikes the mirror and reflects parallel to the principal axis.

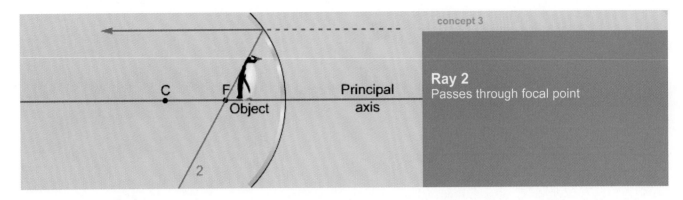

Ray 3 starts at C. It passes by the penguin's head and reflects back through C.

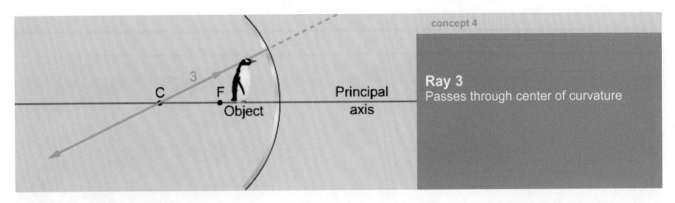

In Concept 5, you see all three rays in the same diagram. The real rays do not converge; to locate a point of convergence we must use the virtual rays shown in the illustration.

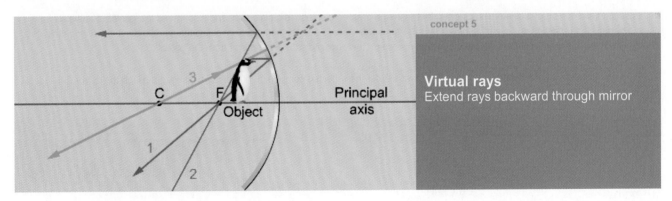

The point where the virtual rays converge, behind the mirror, is where the top of the image is located. We show the image in Concept 6. It is upright, larger than the object, and virtual.

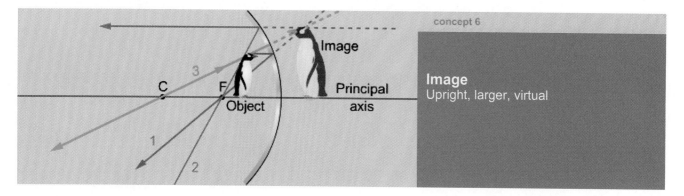

concept 6

Image
Upright, larger, virtual

When you look at yourself in a concave makeup mirror, you put your face within its focal point to see a magnified image of yourself.

31.13 - Ray tracing: a convex mirror

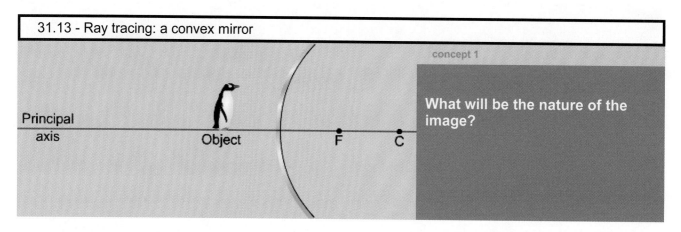

concept 1

What will be the nature of the image?

In this section, we construct a ray-tracing diagram for the image created by a convex mirror. The focal point and the center of curvature are always **behind** the reflecting surface of a convex mirror. We use three rays with the same essential properties as before, modifying their construction to compensate for the fact that the two points are on the opposite side of the mirror from the object.

Ray 1. Ray 1 is incident parallel to the principal axis. If we extend the reflected component of this ray backward through the mirror, the virtual ray will pass through the focal point.

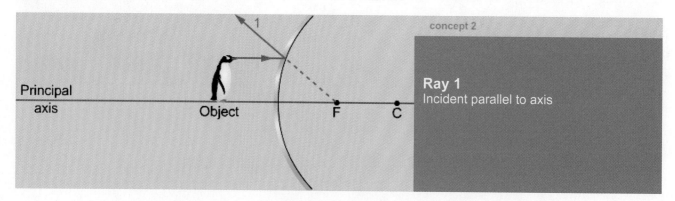

concept 2

Ray 1
Incident parallel to axis

Ray 2. Instead of passing through the focal point, the incident part of ray 2 is directed toward it. Before it can reach the focal point behind the mirror, it reflects parallel to the principal axis. Its virtual extension behind the mirror is also parallel to the axis.

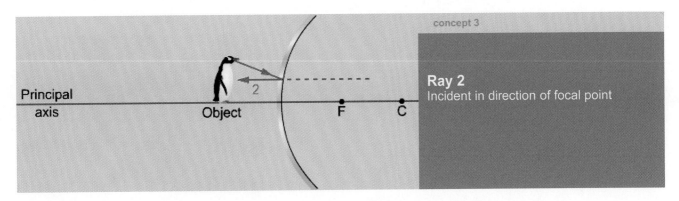

Ray 3. The incident component of Ray 3 is directed toward the center of curvature on the far side of the mirror and reflects back along the same line. The virtual extension of the reflected ray passes through the center of curvature.

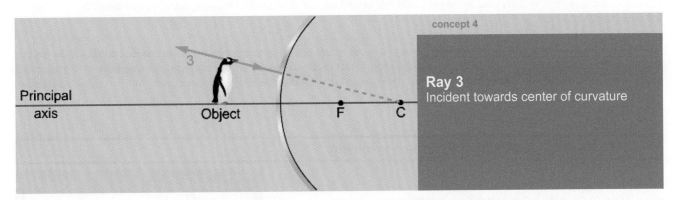

In the following illustration we draw all three rays together. There is no intersection of the actual reflected rays in front of the mirror, but their backward virtual extensions intersect behind the mirror.

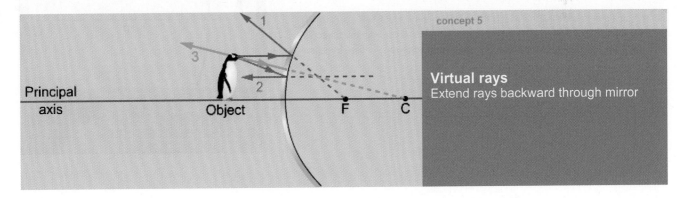

Finally, in Concept 6, we show the image as determined by the convergence point of the virtual rays. The image formed is upright, smaller than the original object, and virtual. Note that this is the only possible result for a convex mirror.

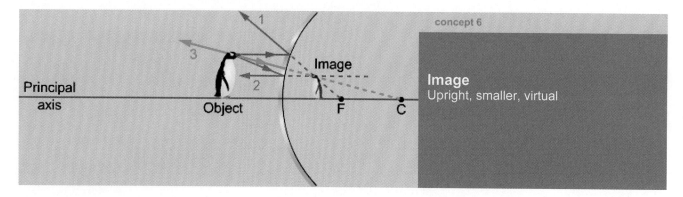

This ray-tracing diagram can be used to explain why security and automobile passenger-side mirrors are often convex. The mirror forms viewable images when the corresponding objects extend quite far above (or below) the principal axis, providing a very wide field of view. As you know, mirrors like this, typically used on the passenger side of vehicles, are often labeled with safety warnings that state, "Objects in mirror are closer than they appear."

However, if you look at concept 6, you will note that the object is actually *farther* from the mirror than the virtual image is, and this is always true for images formed by a convex mirror. So are the warnings wrong? No, the convex mirror's virtual image is always smaller than the image that would be produced by a planar mirror. Since the human brain relates size to distance, the image **appears** distant: We do interpret the object as being farther away than it really is.

31.14 - Interactive problem: image in a convex mirror

Here you use an interactive simulation to view the image produced by a convex mirror. You drag the object farther from and closer to the mirror and observe its image. You can turn on ray tracing with the SHOW RAYS button, and see how the rays can be used to determine the location of the image.

Some questions to consider include: Is the image ever inverted? Is it ever larger than the object? Is it ever real? Is it ever farther from the mirror than the object is? The object can be moved to positions that allow you to answer all these questions.

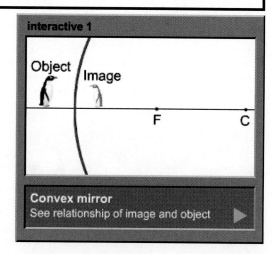

31.15 - Mirror equations

Quantity	Positive sign	Negative sign
Focal length, f	Concave mirror	Convex mirror
Image distance, d_i	In front of mirror (real)	Behind mirror (virtual)
Object distance, d_o	In front of mirror (real)	Behind mirror (virtual)
Magnification, m and height, h	Image upright	Image inverted

Variables in the mirror equations
Interpretation of signs

In this section, we discuss several equations used to determine the nature of images produced by mirrors. Before doing so, we will review and explain the mathematical sign conventions used in these equations.

Some of the notation we have already introduced: d is used for distance, f for focal length, and h for height. More specifically, d_o represents the distance of the object from the mirror and d_i the distance of the image from the mirror. Also, h_o is the height of the object and h_i is the height of the image.

With a single mirror, the object distance is always positive, although it can be negative in the more complex optical systems discussed below. The image distance is positive when the image is real, on the same side of the mirror as the object from which the image is created. The image distance is negative when the image is virtual, on the opposite side of the mirror. Remember that the focal length is positive for concave mirrors and negative for convex mirrors. The image height is positive for upright images and negative for inverted ones.

The magnification, represented by m, equals the image height divided by the object height. When the magnification is positive, the image is upright; when it is negative, the image is inverted relative to the object. Sometimes, the magnification as defined here is called *lateral magnification* to make it clear that it represents the change in height. When m is greater than one, then the image is larger than the object: what people ordinarily think of as "magnified."

Now, on to the equations. The mirror equations are very useful for designing equipment such as cameras and telescopes because they enable engineers to correctly focus an image at a required point (for example, at the surface of a photographic film, or in a digital camera, at the surface of a "charge-coupled device"). The formula in Equation 1 shows the relationship of object and image distance to the focal length of a mirror. It is valid when the incident rays from the object are paraxial.

The next two equations, shown in Equation 2, are used to define and calculate magnification. The first equation defines magnification: It is the ratio of the image and object heights. The magnification can also be calculated as the negative of the ratio of image distance to object distance.

If you now refer back to the table in Concept 1 for signs, you may see one entry that surprises you: an object with a negative distance. Such a "virtual object" can be created by a configuration of two mirrors, or by a lens and a mirror, as shown in the illustration below.

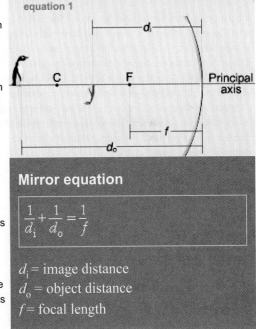

equation 1

Mirror equation

$$\frac{1}{d_i} + \frac{1}{d_o} = \frac{1}{f}$$

d_i = image distance
d_o = object distance
f = focal length

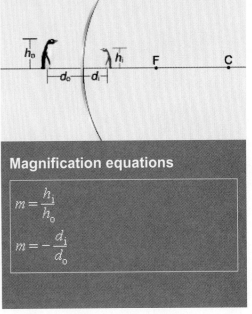

equation 2

Magnification equations

$$m = \frac{h_i}{h_o}$$

$$m = -\frac{d_i}{d_o}$$

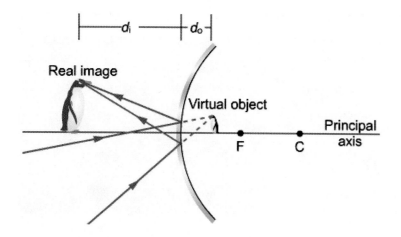

Real image

Virtual object

Principal axis

F   C

Incident rays from the original real object first reflect off some mirror, or pass through some lens, which is not shown in the illustration, being off screen to the left. As a result, converging rays come in from the left and strike the convex mirror in the diagram. The image they create would be a real image "behind" the location of the mirror if the mirror were not there. Since the mirror is there, the convergence point of the virtual rays on the right defines the location of a virtual object, whose distance from the mirror is negative. The incident rays reflect off the front of the mirror to create a real image, with a positive image distance, as shown. Since optical instruments such as telescopes and microscopes often rely on a combination of lenses and mirrors, negative object distances are not rare.

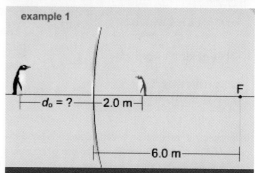

m = magnification of image
h_i = height of image
h_o = height of object

example 1

$d_o = ?$ ——— 2.0 m

6.0 m

What is the distance to the object?

$d_i = -2.0$ m, $f = -6.0$ m

$$\frac{1}{d_i} + \frac{1}{d_o} = \frac{1}{f}$$

$$\frac{1}{d_o} = \frac{1}{f} - \frac{1}{d_i}$$

$$\frac{1}{d_o} = \frac{1}{-6.0 \text{ m}} - \frac{1}{-2.0 \text{ m}}$$

$$\frac{1}{d_o} = 0.33 \text{ m}^{-1}$$

$$d_o = 3.0 \text{ m}$$

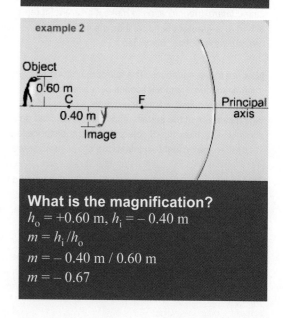

example 2

Object
0.60 m
C
0.40 m
Image
F
Principal axis

What is the magnification?

$h_o = +0.60$ m, $h_i = -0.40$ m

$m = h_i / h_o$

$m = -0.40$ m $/ 0.60$ m

$m = -0.67$

31.16 - Interactive checkpoint: mirror equations

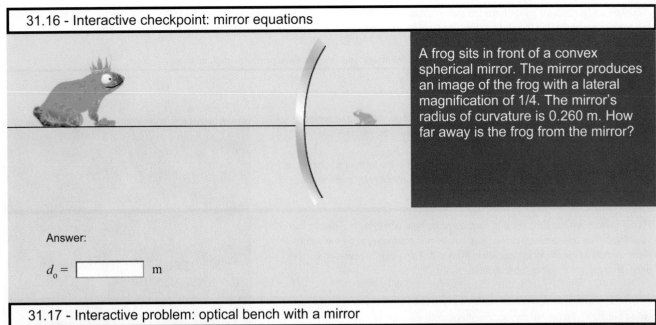

A frog sits in front of a convex spherical mirror. The mirror produces an image of the frog with a lateral magnification of 1/4. The mirror's radius of curvature is 0.260 m. How far away is the frog from the mirror?

Answer:

$d_o = $ [   ] m

31.17 - Interactive problem: optical bench with a mirror

The simulations here challenge you to use the mirror equations. In the first, you are asked to create an image 13.7 cm from the mirror's surface as shown in the illustration and in the simulation. The object is 11.2 cm from the mirror.

You set the focal length of the mirror by dragging the focal point F, or by setting its value in the control panel. As you change the focal length, you will also be changing the curvature of the mirror. Once you believe you have set the focal length correctly, press the CHECK button to test your answer. Be careful with signs!

Your mission in the second simulation to the right is to create a mirror that will have a magnification of +0.470 for the same object at the same position. Again, you control the focal length, and to test your answer, press the CHECK button in this simulation. As a hint: First, determine where the image must be using one formula, then use another formula to determine the required focal length.

If you have trouble with either of these tasks, review the prior section on the mirror equations.

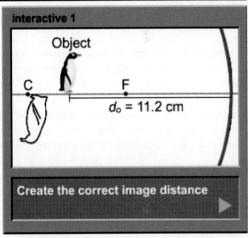

interactive 1

Object

C   F

$d_o = 11.2$ cm

Create the correct image distance

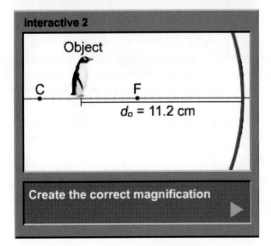

interactive 2

Object

C   F

$d_o = 11.2$ cm

Create the correct magnification

31.18 - Gotchas

Virtual images do not exist. This may be a philosophical question. They do exist in our minds. They cannot be touched, or projected onto a piece of paper. In contrast, real images can be projected onto a screen or a piece of paper.

A convex and a concave mirror have the same radius of curvature. This means their focal lengths are identical. The magnitudes of their focal lengths are the same, but the signs differ. The focal length is positive for a concave mirror and negative for a convex mirror.

A virtual image has a negative image distance. Yes. Conversely, real images have positive image distances.

31.19 - Summary

Reflection occurs when light bounces back from a surface, rather than passing through it or being absorbed. Reflection causes objects to be visible.

In optics, it is often useful to represent the path of light in the form of a light ray, a straight line that can be used to determine how light is affected by mirrors and lenses.

Planar mirrors are the simplest and most common type of mirror. In a planar mirror, your image has the same dimensions as you do and it appears to be the same distance behind the mirror as you are in front of it. The image is reversed front to back, but not right to left or top to bottom.

When you see your image in a planar mirror, you are seeing a virtual image, so called because you cannot project this image onto a screen at its perceived location. A virtual image appears to be on the opposite side of a mirror from the object it is created from, and its image distance is negative.

In contrast, a real image **can** be projected onto a screen, and it occurs on the same side of a mirror as the object it is created from. Its image distance is positive. Curved mirrors can create virtual or real images.

The law of reflection states that for a light ray reflecting off a mirror, the angle of incidence equals the angle of reflection. These two angles are measured between the light ray and a line normal to the surface of the mirror.

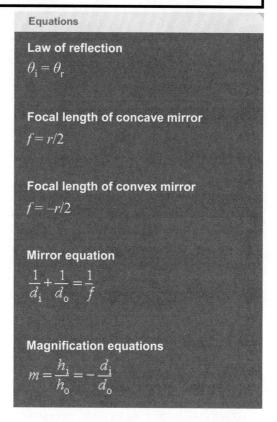

Equations

Law of reflection

$\theta_i = \theta_r$

Focal length of concave mirror

$f = r/2$

Focal length of convex mirror

$f = -r/2$

Mirror equation

$$\frac{1}{d_i} + \frac{1}{d_o} = \frac{1}{f}$$

Magnification equations

$$m = \frac{h_i}{h_o} = -\frac{d_i}{d_o}$$

A ray diagram can help you determine the location of the image an object casts in a **planar** mirror. Draw two incident rays from any point on the object to the mirror. Draw the reflected rays using the law of reflection, and trace their virtual extensions backward behind the mirror as dashed lines. The point of the image corresponding to the point source of the incident rays on the object is located where these virtual rays intersect.

Spherical mirrors have a constant curvature. A mirror is called concave if it curves toward (around) the object it reflects. A convex mirror curves away from the object it reflects.

All points on a spherical mirror are equidistant from its center of curvature. The principal axis is a line through the center of curvature and the midpoint of the mirror. Paraxial rays are incident rays close to the principal axis of a mirror. The reflections of these rays converge at the focal point if the rays are parallel to the principal axis. The height of an image is negative if the image is inverted.

The focal length of a curved mirror is the distance between a mirror and its focal point. By convention, it is positive for a concave mirror where the focal point is on the same side of the mirror as the object. It is negative for a convex mirror where the focal point is on the opposite side.

Spherical mirrors exhibit spherical aberration because only paraxial incident rays converge at the focal point. With a parabolic mirror, **all** incident rays that are parallel to the principal axis converge at the focal point.

Ray tracing for concave and convex mirrors is more complicated than for planar mirrors, but it can help you determine the orientation, relative size, and location (or type) of an image.

The mirror equation relates the distances of an object and its image from a mirror to the focal length of the mirror. The magnification equations define the magnification of an image created by a mirror. If the magnification is known, we may calculate the image height from the object height or the image distance from the object distance, or vice versa.

32.0 - Introduction

Light can refract − change direction − as it moves from one medium to another. For instance, if you stand at the edge of a pool and try to poke something underwater with a stick, you may misjudge the object's location. This is because the light from the object changes direction as it passes from the water to the air. You perceive the object to be closer to the surface than it actually is because you subconsciously assume that light travels in a straight line.

Although refraction can cause errors like this, it can also serve many useful purposes. Optical microscopes, eyeglass lenses, and indeed the lenses in your eyes all use refraction to bend and focus light, forming images and causing objects to appear a different size or crisper than they otherwise would. Where a lens focuses light, and whether it magnifies an object, is determined by both the curvature of the lens and the material of which it is made. Scientists have developed quantitative tools to determine the nature of the images created by a lens. We will explore these tools thoroughly later, "focusing" first, so to speak, on the principle of refraction underlying them.

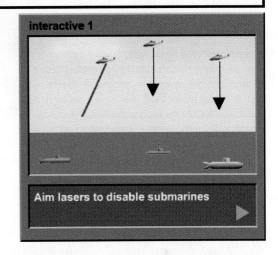

interactive 1

Aim lasers to disable submarines

To begin your study of refraction, try the simulation to the right. Each of your helicopters can fire a laser − a sharp beam of light − at any of three submarines lurking under the sea. The submarines have lasers, too, and will shoot back at your craft. Your mission is to disable the submarines before they disarm your helicopters. When you make a hit, you can shoot again. Otherwise, the submarines get their turn to shoot until they miss.

You play by dragging the aiming arrow underneath any one of your helicopters. Press FIRE and the laser beam will follow the direction of this arrow until it reaches the water, where refraction will cause the beam to change direction.

In addition to hitting the submarines before they get you, you can conduct some basic experiments concerning the nature of refraction. As with reflection, the angle of incidence is measured from a line normal (perpendicular) to a surface. In this case, the surface is the horizontal boundary between the water and the air. Observe how the light bends at the boundary when you shoot straight down, at a zero angle of incidence, or grazing the water, at a large angle of incidence. You can create a large angle of incidence by having the far right helicopter, for example, aim at the submarine on the far left.

You can also observe how refraction differs when a laser beam passes from air to water (your lasers) and from water to air (the submarines' lasers). Observe the dashed normal line at each crossover point and answer the following question: Does the laser beam bend toward or away from that line as it changes media? You should notice that the laser beams of the submarines behave differently than those of the helicopters when they change media.

As a final aside: You may see that some of the laser beams of the submarines never leave the water, but reflect back from the surface between the water and the air. This is called total internal reflection.

Refraction: The change in the direction of light as it passes from one medium to another.

A material through which light travels is called a *medium* (plural: *media*). When light traveling in one medium encounters another medium, its direction can change. It can reflect back, as it would with a mirror. It can also pass into the second medium and change direction. This phenomenon, called refraction, is shown to the right. In the photo, a beam of light from a laser refracts (bends) as it passes from the air into the water.

Refraction bends water waves into line with the shore.

Light refracts when its speeds in the two media are different. Light travels faster through air than in water, and it changes direction as it moves from air into water, or from water into air.

Although we are primarily interested in the refraction of light, all waves, including water waves, refract. Above, you see a photograph of surf wave fronts advancing parallel to a beach. Deep-ocean swells may approach a coastline from any angle, but they slow down as they encounter the shallows near the shore. The parts of a wave that encounter the shallow water earliest slow down first, and this causes the wave to refract. Sound waves can also refract. During a medical ultrasound scan, an acoustic lens can be used to focus the sound waves. The lens is made of a material in which sound travels faster than in water or body tissues.

concept 1

Refraction
Change in wave direction at interface
Caused by change in speed of wave

The surface between two media, such as air and water, is called an *interface*. As with mirrors, light rays are often used to depict how light refracts when it meets an interface. Lasers are often used to demonstrate refraction because they can create thin beams of light that do not spread out. These light beams are physical analogues of light rays.

Index of refraction of a material: The speed of light in a vacuum divided by the speed of light in the material.

Light travels at different speeds in different materials. The index of refraction of a material provides a measure of the speed of light in that material. The symbol n represents the index of refraction. The equation used to calculate the index of refraction for a material is shown to the right. The table to the right shows the indices for some common materials.

In the equation for the index of refraction, the speed of light in a vacuum is in the numerator. Light travels at its maximum speed in a vacuum, so the index of refraction for other materials is always greater than one.

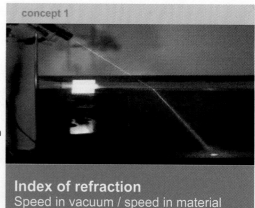

concept 1

Index of refraction
Speed in vacuum / speed in material

The index of refraction depends on the wavelength of the light. The table in Equation 2 is for yellow light with a wavelength of 589 nm. The index depends on the wavelength because the speed of light in a material depends on its wavelength. The speed of light in any material is slower for shorter wavelengths, so the index of refraction is greater for light of shorter wavelengths. For example, for a type of glass called crown glass, $n = 1.50$ for red light, and $n = 1.53$ for violet light, which has a shorter wavelength than red light.

The index of refraction of a material also depends somewhat on its temperature. For certain crystalline materials, it also depends on the angle at which the light travels through the crystal lattice. This is why the index of refraction for corundum is indicated as approximate in the table.

The index of refraction for visible light in the Earth's atmosphere is about 1.0003 at standard temperature and pressure. Since we typically use two or three significant figures, we treat that index as 1.00. At the same level of precision, the speed of light is 3.00×10^8 m/s.

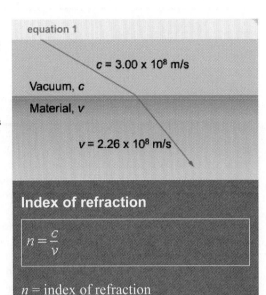

equation 1

$c = 3.00 \times 10^8$ m/s

Vacuum, c

Material, v

$v = 2.26 \times 10^8$ m/s

Index of refraction

$$n = \frac{c}{v}$$

n = index of refraction
c = speed of light in vacuum
v = speed of light in material

equation 2

	Index of refraction
Air	1.0003
Water	1.33
Vegetable oil	1.47
Crown glass	1.51
Salt	1.54
Flint glass	1.61
Corundum (ruby, sapphire)	1.77*
Diamond	2.42

At 20° C, λ = 589 nm   *Approximate value

Indices of refraction

example 1

Vacuum, $c = 3.00 \times 10^8$ m/s

Crown glass, $v = 1.99 \times 10^8$ m/s

Green light travels at 1.99×10^8 m/s in crown glass. What is the index of refraction of the glass for this light?

$$n = \frac{c}{v}$$

$$n = \frac{3.00 \times 10^8 \text{ m/s}}{1.99 \times 10^8 \text{ m/s}}$$

$$n = 1.51$$

32.3 - Snell's law

Snell's law is used to quantify refraction. In doing so, it uses some of the same terminology as the law of reflection. As with reflection, angles are measured between a ray and a line normal (perpendicular) to a surface. You see this illustrated in Concept 1, with both the angle of incidence (θ_i) and the angle of refraction (θ_r) shown.

Snell's law, shown in Equation 1, expresses the relationship between these angles. This law was discovered empirically by Willebrord Snell and written in its current form by René Descartes. It states that the product of the sine of the incident angle and the index of refraction of the incident medium equals the product of the sine of the refraction angle and the index of refraction of the refracting medium.

We also show the same equation in an alternate formulation: The ratio of the sine of the incident angle to the sine of the refracted angle is the **reciprocal** of the ratio of the first to the second index of refraction.

To put it more concretely, light bends **toward** the normal when it slows down, for instance, when it passes from air to water. You see this in Concept 1 to the right. It bends **away** from the normal when it speeds up, as from water to air.

If light passes through several media, Snell's law can be applied at each interface. You see this occurring in Concept 2. The light's direction changes toward the normal at the first interface as it slows, and then away from the normal as it crosses the second interface. It bends away because light moves faster in the third medium, which has a lesser index of refraction than the second.

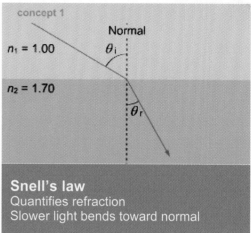

concept 1

$n_1 = 1.00$ Normal θ_i

$n_2 = 1.70$ θ_r

Snell's law
Quantifies refraction
Slower light bends toward normal

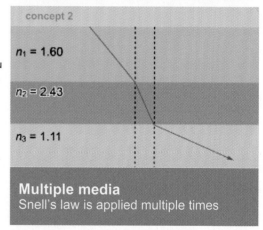

concept 2

$n_1 = 1.60$

$n_2 = 2.43$

$n_3 = 1.11$

Multiple media
Snell's law is applied multiple times

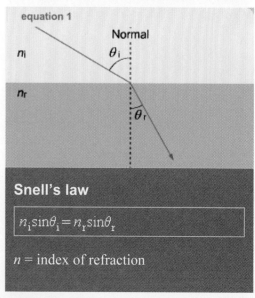

equation 1

n_i Normal θ_i

n_r θ_r

Snell's law

$$n_i \sin\theta_i = n_r \sin\theta_r$$

n = index of refraction

θ_i = incident angle from normal
θ_r = refracted angle from normal

$$\frac{\sin\theta_i}{\sin\theta_r} = \frac{n_r}{n_i}$$

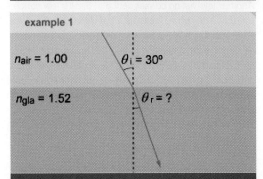

example 1

n_{air} = 1.00

n_{gla} = 1.52

θ_i = 30°

θ_r = ?

What is the angle of refraction here?

$n_{air} \sin \theta_i = n_{gla} \sin \theta_r$

$\sin \theta_r = (n_{air} \sin \theta_i) / n_{gla}$

$\theta_r = \arcsin [(n_{air} \sin \theta_i) / n_{gla}]$

$\theta_r = \arcsin [(1.00 \sin 30°)/1.52]$

$\theta_r = 19°$

32.4 - Interactive checkpoint: Snell's law

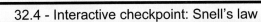

n_1 = 1.68 n_2 = ?

25.0°

30.5°

What is the index of refraction of the second material?

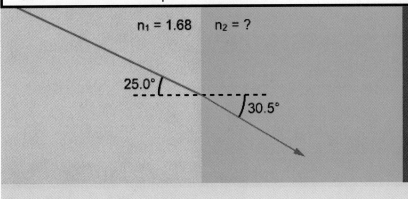

Answer:

$n_2 = $ [   ]

32.5 - Everyday effects of refraction

The refraction of light can cause interesting and sometimes confusing results as the brain interprets the position of objects it sees via refracted light. For instance, in the upper illustration to the right, you see an ancient Egyptian fisherman trying to spear a fish. The solid line indicates the refracted path of the light traveling from the fish to his eyes. Since his brain expects light to travel in a straight line, he projects the fish to be in the position indicated at the end of the dashed line, which causes him to think the fish is nearer to the surface than it is. Experienced spear fishermen know how to compensate for this effect.

The fisherman is not the only one to experience the effects of refraction. The fish does, too. The light from the world above seen by the fish also refracts. Light coming straight down will pass through the water's surface unchanged, but light at any angle will refract, in the process giving the fish a wider field of view of the world above than it would have if there were no refraction. In essence, the fish sees a compressed wide-angle view of the scene above. Certain camera lenses, appropriately called fisheye lenses, can create the same effect, as illustrated in Concept 2.

Another interesting consequence of Snell's law concerns light passing through a window. The light refracts as it travels from air to glass. After passing through the glass, it refracts again at the second interface. The ratio of the indices of refraction is now reversed, so the initial change in angle is cancelled out. The light ray that emerges is parallel to the initial ray, but displaced a small amount. The amount of displacement is small enough that we ordinarily do not notice "window shift." However, if you place a newspaper page on a tabletop and cover half of it with a flat pane of glass, you will be able to observe the displacement effect.

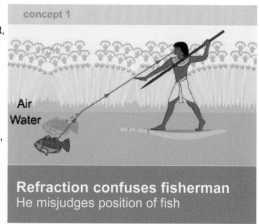

concept 1

Air
Water

Refraction confuses fisherman
He misjudges position of fish

concept 2

A fisheye view
Wide-angle view compresses images

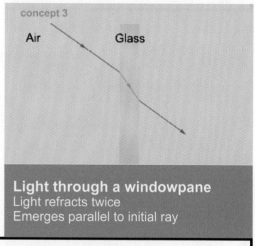

concept 3

Air   Glass

Light through a windowpane
Light refracts twice
Emerges parallel to initial ray

32.6 - Why refraction occurs

Why do waves change direction when they change speed? Here we offer a mechanical analogy to explain this phenomenon.

Consider the diagram in Concept 1 to the right. It uses the example of a car encountering ice on the side of a road. If this has ever happened to you, you know that the car can dangerously change direction when one (or more) of its wheels encounters ice, as shown in the diagram. Why is this so? The wheels on the ice provide less traction, so the right side of the car moves more slowly. The left side of the car continues to move at the same speed as before, which causes the car to rotate and veer off the road. When all the wheels supplying power are on the ice, the car will once again move straight ahead because both sides will be moving at the same speed.

Why light refracts can also be explained using Fermat's principle of least time. This principle, developed by French mathematician Pierre de

Fermat (1601−1665), states that light will travel the path between two points that requires the least amount of time. This may seem like it should be a straight line, but it is not when the speed varies along the path between two points.

This timesaving "technique" is similar to what you would intuitively do if you were standing on a beach and saw a swimmer floundering desperately in the water some distance down the shore. Instead of taking a direct straight-line path to the rescue, you would run along the beach for some distance, counting on your greater land speed, before taking to the water.

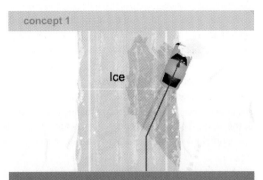

concept 1

Ice

Car hits ice
Speed change on one side changes direction of car

32.7 - Interactive problem: helicopter and submarines

The simulation on the right is similar to the one in this chapter's introduction. As before, submarines lurk under the waves, but now you have only a single helicopter.

As before, you have a laser you can aim in an attempt to disable two submarines before they disable you. You keep shooting as long as you keep making hits. To shoot your laser, aim it by dragging the aiming arrow and fire it by clicking on FIRE. The angle of incidence is shown in an output gauge.

As soon as you miss, it is the submarines' turn. Warning: The computer has been set to be far more accurate in this game than in the introductory one. Unless you are very precise with your shots, it is unlikely you will win.

However, there is good news: Now you have more intellectual firepower because you have the aid of Snell's law. You are also given some assistance from an able comrade; she has computed the angles of refraction required for your laser to reach the submarines, as shown in the diagram. You should use 1.33 for the index of refraction of water, and 1.00 for the index of refraction of air. If you correctly set the angle of incidence when you aim each of your shots, you can make two straight hits and disable the submarines before they disable you.

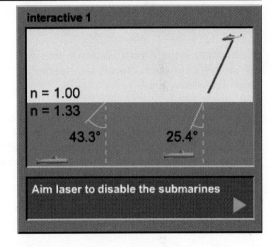

interactive 1

$n = 1.00$
$n = 1.33$

43.3°   25.4°

Aim laser to disable the submarines

32.8 - Total internal reflection

Total internal reflection: Light reflects completely at an interface, back into the medium with the higher refractive index.

Critical angle: The minimum angle of incidence at which total internal reflection occurs.

Total internal reflection means no light passes from one medium to another. On the right, we show how this occurs using the example of an underwater flashlight shining a beam at the interface between water and air. As the diagram shows, all the light reflects back into the medium with the higher refractive index, the water. No light passes into the air above the water.

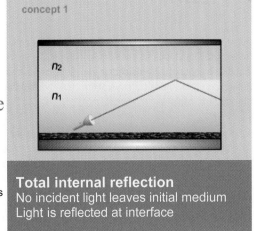

concept 1

n_2

n_1

Total internal reflection
No incident light leaves initial medium
Light is reflected at interface

Why does this occur? Consider what happens when light is directed from water into air. Water has a greater index of refraction than air. At relatively small angles of incidence, light passes from the water into the air, and as it does so, it refracts away from the normal. The angle of refraction is greater than the angle of incidence.

As the angle of incidence increases, the angle of refraction will increase as well, and it will always be greater than the angle of incidence. At a sufficient angle of incidence, the angle of refraction reaches $90°$, perpendicular to the normal and parallel to the surface of the water. The light no longer crosses the interface but remains in the water. The minimum angle of incidence at which this occurs is called the critical angle.

Even at angles of incidence less than the critical angle there is some internal reflection along with refraction. But when the critical angle is exceeded, there is no refraction at all: All of the light is internally reflected.

Total internal reflection is shown in Concept 1. All the light is reflected back into the water. Concept 2 shows the situation when the angle of incidence is equal to the critical angle. The critical angle depends on the ratio of the indices of refraction of the two media. You see this as the equation on the right, which is obtained by setting $\theta_r = 90°$ (so $\sin\theta_r = 1$) in Snell's law.

Diamonds rely on total internal reflection to achieve their sparkle. They are cut so that light entering them reflects internally and emerges only at certain points, giving the effect of scintillating light.

If you happen to have a diamond ring handy, you can demonstrate this dependence on the ratio of indices by placing the ring in water. The sparkle disappears; this is because the indices of refraction of diamond and water do not differ as significantly as those of diamond and air, so the geometry of the ring no longer causes the same internal reflection.

Engineers use total internal reflection in many different applications. For instance, right isosceles prisms are used in binoculars to redirect light, as in the illustration below.

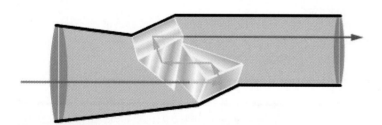

Fiber optic cable is used to transfer information (in glass or plastic) using total internal reflection. Data (such as speech) is first encoded as modulations of a beam of laser light. The light remains inside the transparent cable as it travels due to its total internal reflection off the inner surfaces of the cable walls. In this way, light is transmitted through the cable with little loss.

Using light instead of electricity to transfer information has several benefits. Light can be used to encode much more information than electric oscillations because of its extremely high frequency (more than 10^{14} Hz for red light), and fiber optic cable is immune to interference problems from nearby electrical applications.

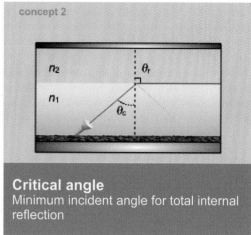

concept 2

Critical angle
Minimum incident angle for total internal reflection

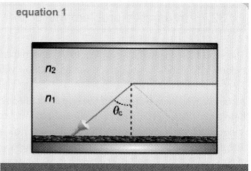

equation 1

Critical angle

$$\sin\theta_c = \frac{n_2}{n_1}$$

θ_c = critical angle
n_1, n_2 = indices of refraction ($n_1 > n_2$)

example 1

You are cutting a sapphire to make it as brilliant as possible. Find the critical angle for the sapphire in air. The index of refraction of a sapphire is 1.77.

$$\sin\theta_c = \frac{n_{air}}{n_{sap}}$$

$$\theta_c = \arcsin\left(\frac{n_{air}}{n_{sap}}\right)$$

$$\theta_c = \arcsin\left(\frac{1.00}{1.77}\right)$$

$$\theta_c = 34.4\,^\circ$$

32.9 - Dispersion and prisms

Dispersion: Refraction that causes light to separate into its various wavelengths.

Humans perceive different wavelengths of light as different colors. When we see light of a single wavelength, we perceive it as a pure color such as red, green or violet. The light that comes from the Sun and from standard light bulbs, which we perceive as white light, consists of a mixture of many different wavelengths of electromagnetic radiation.

A rainbow provides an example of dispersion.

Prisms, such as the one shown to the right, separate white light into its many wavelengths. This is called dispersion, or to be more specific, *chromatic dispersion*, since dispersion can also occur with non-visible electromagnetic radiation and mechanical waves as well. Sir Isaac Newton famously used a pair of prisms to disperse white sunlight into colors and recombine the colors into white light.

Prisms disperse light because the index of refraction depends on the light's wavelength. The index of refraction for a given material is greater for waves of shorter wavelength, so blue and violet light refract more than red or orange light. When white light is incident upon a prism, the different wavelengths that make it up are refracted at different angles, resulting in a rainbow of colors.

The rainbows we see in the sky are also caused by dispersion. Light disperses as it enters a spherical raindrop. Total internal reflection occurs inside the raindrop, and the light then refracts again when leaving the drop, dispersing even more. You see this illustrated in a raindrop to the right.

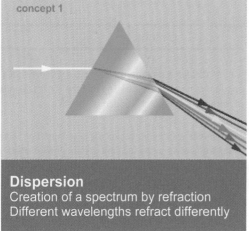

concept 1

Dispersion
Creation of a spectrum by refraction
Different wavelengths refract differently

Why does this process cause rainbows? Raindrops reflect back nested "cones" of light of different colors. In Concept 3 you see how red light reflected back from every drop in the outermost portions of the rainbow reaches the observer, but the violet light from those drops passes him by. You also see how the violet light from the innermost portions of the rainbow reaches him, but not the red light. Other topics in rainbow theory are still being researched. For instance, physicists, although vaguely alluding to quantum effects and the promise of string theory, have to date offered no convincing explanation for the pot of gold at the end of the rainbow.

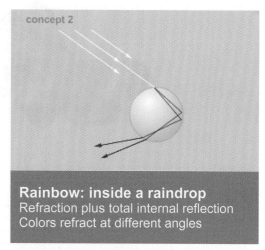

Rainbow: inside a raindrop
Refraction plus total internal reflection
Colors refract at different angles

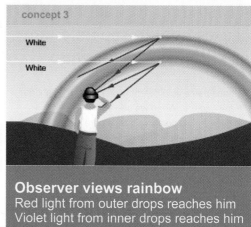

White

White

Observer views rainbow
Red light from outer drops reaches him
Violet light from inner drops reaches him

32.10 - Gotchas

You calculated a material as having a refractive index of 0.76. Oops! This is not possible. The speed of light in a vacuum is greater than its speed in any medium, meaning that the refractive index of the material must be greater than 1.00. Remember that when calculating the index of refraction, you put the speed of light in a vacuum in the numerator, not the denominator.

Light strikes water in a placid lake at an angle of 30° from the horizontal, so its incident angle is 30°. No, the incident angle is 60°. It is measured between the incident ray and the interface's **normal line**. This line is perpendicular to the interface.

All wavelengths (colors) of light refract at the same angle when crossing the interface between different media. No, the angle of refraction varies by wavelength.

32.11 - Summary

Refraction is the changing of a wave's direction due to a change in its speed. It occurs when a wave, like light, passes from one medium into another.

A material's index of refraction is the ratio of the speed of light in a vacuum (c) to its speed in the material. The index of refraction is represented by the letter n.

Snell's law quantifies how much light bends when it crosses an interface. Light bends towards a line normal to the interface between the media as it slows down (passes into a medium with a higher index of refraction). When light passes through multiple media its path can be calculated by applying Snell's law at each interface.

Total internal reflection occurs when no light is refracted at an interface; it is all reflected. This is only possible as light encounters an interface with a medium having a smaller index of refraction, at a large enough incident angle. The critical angle is the minimum angle of incidence at which total internal reflection occurs.

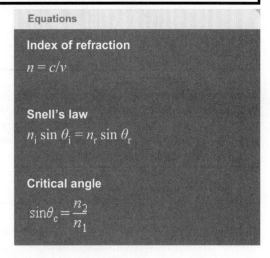

Equations

Index of refraction

$n = c/v$

Snell's law

$n_i \sin \theta_i = n_r \sin \theta_r$

Critical angle

$\sin \theta_c = \dfrac{n_2}{n_1}$

The index of refraction for a material varies somewhat by the wavelength of light being refracted. Light composed of many wavelengths, such as white light, can be separated into a spectrum by refraction. This effect is called dispersion. Prisms exhibit dispersion.

33.0 - Introduction

Lenses may be the application of refraction with which you are most familiar. Lenses of glass or plastic, fashioned into eyeglasses and contact lenses, are worn by about 60% of the population of the United States, and this percentage is projected to increase as the population ages. Even people who do not require visual correction are "wearing" lenses anyway, since the eye itself contains an organic lens.

The human eye has the ability to refract light and focus it on the retina at the back of the eye, where signals are then transmitted to the brain. If the focusing is not precise enough, glasses or contact lenses can improve the results. These days, the eye itself can be tuned via laser surgery as well.

Lenses augment vision in other fashions as well. Lenses in magnifying glasses, telescopes, and microscopes allow you to see things that would otherwise be too small or too far away to see in detail.

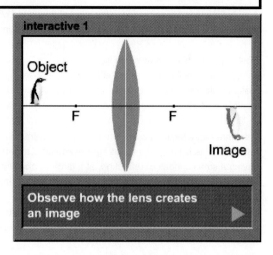

interactive 1

Object

F   F

Image

Observe how the lens creates an image

At the right, you can begin your experimentation with lenses. The convex lens will produce an image of the penguin. You can move the penguin left and right to see how its distance from the lens changes the resulting image. Where must the object be relative to the focal point F to create an image on the same side of the lens as the object? Where must it be to create an image on the far side? Can you make the image appear right-side up (rather than inverted, as it is in the picture on the right)? A note: When the object is very near the focal point, the image will be too far away from the lens to be shown in the simulation's window.

33.1 - Lenses

Lens: A device that uses refraction to redirect and focus light.

Light changes direction – refracts – as it passes from air to a lens material and back to air. Lenses take advantage of refraction to create images.

In general, lenses are made of a transparent material with a curved surface or surfaces. Although lenses are typically curved, we will use two prisms, as shown to the right, to introduce the fundamental functioning of lenses.

Lenses are used in eyeglasses to focus images.

In the upper diagram, you see two prisms placed so that their flat bases are touching. Three parallel rays of light strike the prisms. Because of the sloping surfaces of the prisms, the rays are refracted in different directions.

As you can see, after passing through the prisms, the three rays converge on the far side. This first set of prisms serves as a model for a *converging lens*. Converging lenses are thickest at their centers. With a two-prism lens, all the incoming rays would not converge at one point like the three we have chosen to show, which is why prisms do not make good lenses: The image they create will be blurry. A curved surface will focus the rays more precisely.

In the second diagram, we invert the prisms, so they touch tip to tip. The rays diverge after passing through them; they will not intersect on the far side of the prisms. This configuration provides a model for a *diverging lens*. The image created by a diverging lens is a virtual one. By extending the paths of the rays that have passed through the prisms backwards, we could locate the virtual image on the same side of the lens as the object that creates it.

In this chapter, we focus on lenses that are both spherical and thin. A spherical lens has two surfaces, each of which is a section of a sphere. The curvatures of the two sides of a lens can differ. Saying it is "thin" means the distance across a lens is small relative to the distance to the object that is the source of the image. Thin lenses provide an accurate model for optical equipment ranging from contact lenses to telescopes.

Much of the terminology and many basic concepts coincide for mirrors and lenses. A line that passes through the center of a lens perpendicular to its surface is called the *principal axis*. Parallel rays from an object infinitely far away refract through a lens and converge at the lens's *focal point*. The *focal length f* is the distance between the lens's center and its focal point. In contrast to mirrors, lenses have two focal points, one on each side of the lens, since incident rays can originate on either side of a lens. Rays that are close to the principal axis and converge at the focal point are called *paraxial rays*.

Lenses produce real and virtual images, just as mirrors do. As with mirrors, a real image can be projected onto a piece of paper, while a virtual image cannot. However, the locations of virtual and real images are reversed for lenses and mirrors. With lenses, virtual images occur on the **same** side of the lens as the object. Real images occur on the **opposite** side of the lens as the object.

The prisms in Concept 1 – the ones stacked base to base – produce a real image on the opposite side from the object. The ones placed tip to tip create a virtual image, one on the same side as the object.

As with mirrors, incoming rays that are far from the principal axis of a lens do not converge precisely at the focal point. This blurs the image and is called spherical aberration.

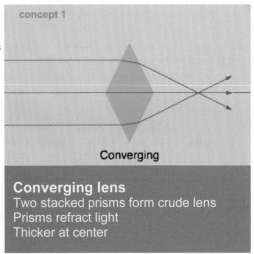

concept 1

Converging

Converging lens
Two stacked prisms form crude lens
Prisms refract light
Thicker at center

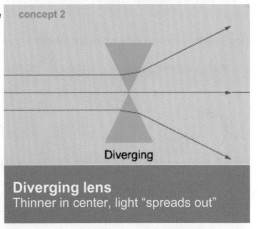

concept 2

Diverging

Diverging lens
Thinner in center, light "spreads out"

33.2 - Converging lens: ray-tracing diagram

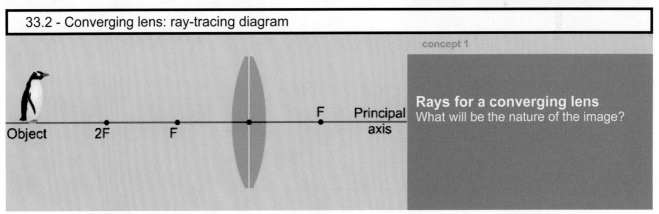

Object   2F   F   F   Principal axis

concept 1

Rays for a converging lens
What will be the nature of the image?

As with mirrors, ray-tracing diagrams are used to determine the orientation, and approximate size and location, of an image produced by a lens. The diagrams in this textbook employ a convention to make them easier to understand: Objects are shown fairly close to lenses that are relatively thick compared to the distances shown. For the approximations in the theory of thin lenses to hold true, the objects should be quite far from the lenses and the lenses should be much thinner than shown. Being literal would make for illustrations that would stretch far across the page or computer screen, so the diagrams are not drawn to scale.

Light that strikes the lens at an angle refracts twice, once upon entering the lens, and again while exiting. However, with a thin lens, we simplify things by modeling the light ray as changing direction just once as it passes through the lens.

Physicists use three specific rays to analyze the behavior of a lens; these rays differ somewhat from those used to analyze mirrors. A single converging lens can create different image types based on the position of the object relative to the focal point. In this example, we discuss the image created by an object more than twice the focal length away from a converging lens.

Ray 1 begins as a horizontal line, parallel to the principal axis, starting at the top of the object. It refracts at the lens and passes through the focal point on the far side of the lens. (We use "near" to describe the object's side of the lens, and "far" to describe the other side. We will typically place objects on the left side of the lens. Images can be created on the near or far side of the lens.)

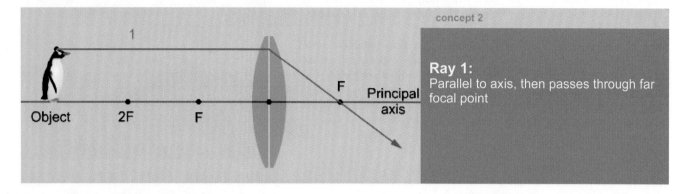

Ray 1:
Parallel to axis, then passes through far focal point

Ray 2 starts at the top of the object and passes through the center of the lens. It does not change direction.

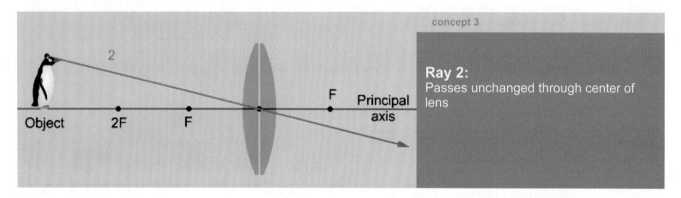

Ray 2:
Passes unchanged through center of lens

Ray 3 starts at the top of the object, passes through the focal point on the near side of the lens, is refracted by the lens, and continues parallel to the axis on the far side of the lens.

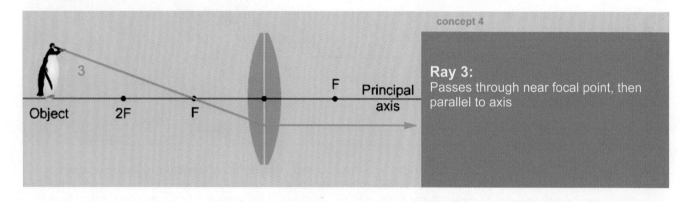

Ray 3:
Passes through near focal point, then parallel to axis

The image created by the lens is shown in the diagram below, where all three rays are combined together. The point at which the rays converge indicates the location of the top of the image. The image is inverted, smaller than the object and real.

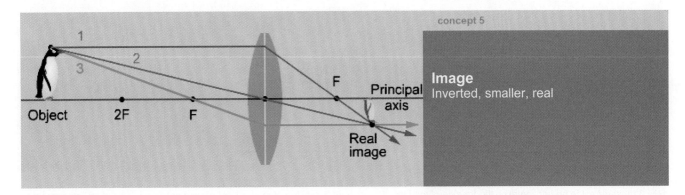

This example provides a model for a typical camera lens, which creates an inverted real image on the film or digital recording device on the far side of the lens.

33.3 - Diverging lens: ray-tracing diagram

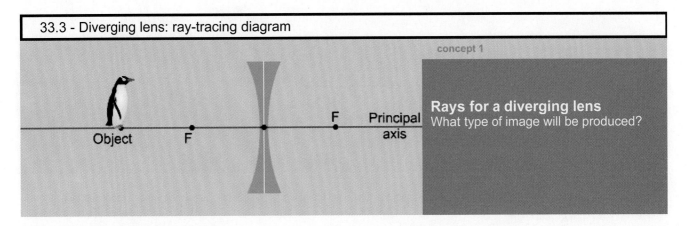

Like a convex mirror, a single diverging lens produces only one kind of image. The image is always upright, smaller than the object, and virtual. We use three rays to analyze the image.

Ray 1 starts parallel to the principal axis. With a diverging lens, it refracts away from the principal axis. To have the ray pass through a focal point, we must extend it backward using a virtual ray as shown in the diagram.

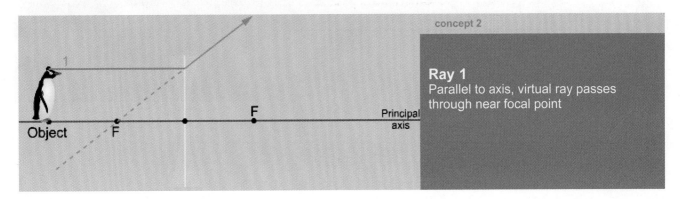

Ray 2 passes through the lens without changing direction.

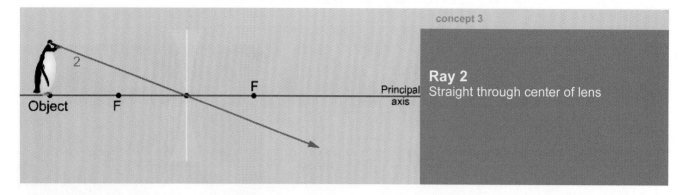

concept 3

Ray 2
Straight through center of lens

Ray 3 must refract to be horizontal on the far side of the lens. The forward extension of the incident portion of this ray is a virtual ray passing through the focal point on the far side. The backward extension of the refracted portion of the ray is a virtual ray parallel to the principal axis on the object side of the lens.

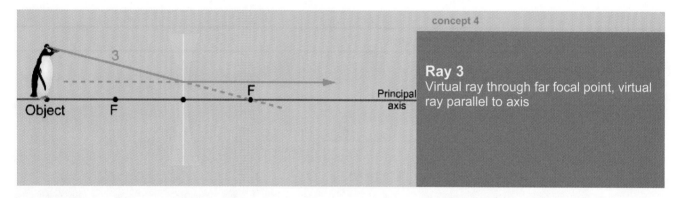

concept 4

Ray 3
Virtual ray through far focal point, virtual ray parallel to axis

As the illustration below shows, the image is upright, smaller than the object, and virtual. This is the case for all images produced by a single diverging lens.

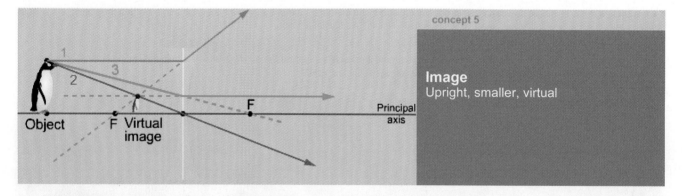

concept 5

Image
Upright, smaller, virtual

The example to the right leads you through another ray tracing exercise for a diverging lens. The object in the example is closer to the lens than the one above.

example 1

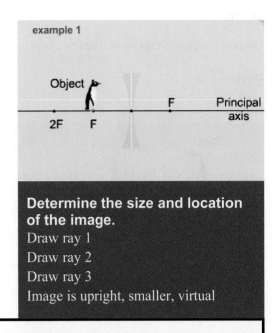

Determine the size and location of the image.
Draw ray 1
Draw ray 2
Draw ray 3
Image is upright, smaller, virtual

33.4 - Interactive problem: image with a diverging lens

This simulation lets you experiment with a diverging lens. You can drag the object toward and away from the lens, and note how the image changes. Also note which properties of the image remain consistent.

You can press "Show rays" to use the simulation to create a ray diagram. Pressing "Hide rays" turns off the rays.

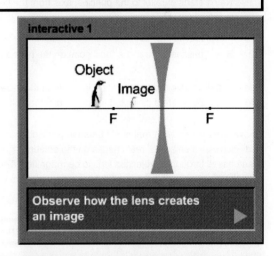

Observe how the lens creates an image ▶

33.5 - Sample problem: object outside the focal point of a converging lens

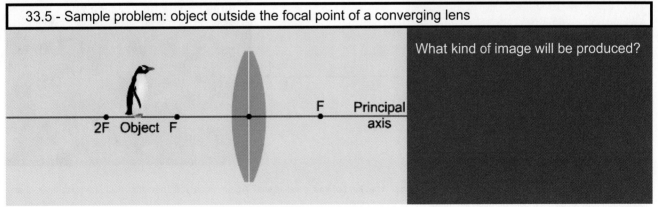

What kind of image will be produced?

As shown above, the penguin is between the focal point and a distance twice the focal length. What kind of image will result? Once you know the result, can you think of any application that relies on a configuration like this?

Strategy

Use ray tracing to establish the nature of the image.

Diagram

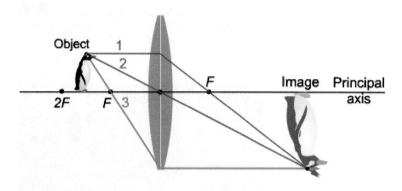

Step-by-step solution

1. Ray 1 starts parallel to the principal axis from the head of the penguin, refracts and passes through the focal point on the far side of the lens.
2. Ray 2 passes through the center of the lens without changing direction.
3. Ray 3 passes through the focal point on the near side and refracts at the lens to be parallel to the principal axis on the far side.

The result is an inverted image that is larger than the initial object. It is a real image, since light rays pass through the position of the image, and they would create a projected image on a screen placed there.

Above, we also asked: What might be an application that relies on a configuration like this? A movie theater projector is one example. The audience views enlarged, real images on the screen. Light is projected through the film, creating a luminous object from a tiny likeness, and then passes through a projection lens to be magnified. The real image appears on the movie screen. The "object" is upside down on the film, so when the lens inverts the image, it appears upright to the audience.

33.6 - Sample problem: object inside the focal point of a converging lens

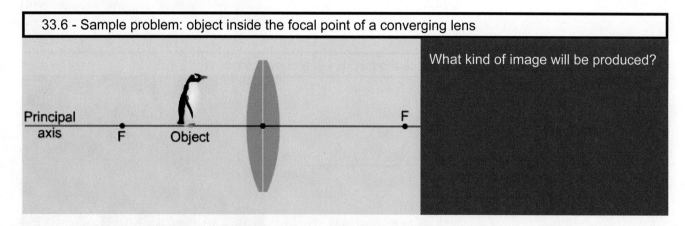

The penguin is inside the focal point of a converging lens. What kind of image will result? Again, once you know the result, can you think of any application that relies on a configuration like this?

Copyright 2000-2007 Kinetic Books Co. Chapter 33

Strategy

Use ray tracing to establish the nature of the image.

Diagram

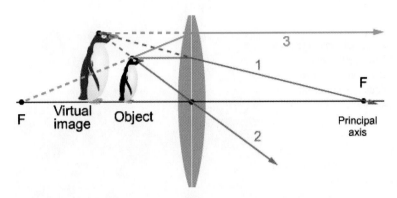

Step-by-step solution

1. Ray 1 starts parallel to the principal axis. It refracts at the lens and passes through the focal point on the far side. To obtain a convergence point for the image, we extend the ray backward, showing this extension with a dashed line.

2. Ray 2 passes through the center of the lens without changing direction. We again extend a virtual ray backward.

3. Ray 3 must be horizontal on the far side of the lens and it must also pass through a focal point. Here, it starts at the top of the object, directed upward so that its backward extension passes through the focal point on the near side. It refracts at the lens, becoming horizontal on the far side. By extending the horizontal portion backward, we create a virtual ray that passes through the convergence point.

The result is an upright, virtual image that is larger than the object. This configuration is typical of objects being viewed in a magnifying glass. The magnifying glass enlarges objects, making it easier to view their fine detail. The image cannot be projected, but it is upright, a matter of great convenience to physicists and textbook authors over 40 who may use a magnifying glass to see fine details!

33.7 - Lens equations			
Quantity	**Positive sign**	**Negative sign**	*concept 1*
Focal length, f	Converging lens	Diverging lens	**Lens and magnification equations** Interpretation of signs
Image distance, d_i	Far side (real)	Object side (virtual)	
Object distance, d_o	Real	Virtual	
Magnification, m and height, h	Image upright	Image inverted	
Radius of curvature, R	Center on far side	Center on object (near) side	

Ray diagrams provide a qualitative technique for establishing the nature of an image created by a thin lens. The image's position and size can be quantified with a set of three equations called the lens equations. These are the focus (we could not resist) of this section.

The *thin lens equation* is shown in Equation 1. It states the relationship between object distance, image distance, and focal length: The sum of the reciprocals of the object distance and the image distance equals the reciprocal of the focal length.

For instance, suppose you want to calculate the location of an image created by placing an object 0.50 meters away from a lens with a focal length of 0.33 meters. The thin lens equation and a little arithmetic reveal that the image distance is 1.0 meters. (We solve this problem in Example 1.) The positive value for the image distance places it on the far side of the lens, which means the image is real. These values also confirm the answer to a question posed in an earlier section, where the nature of the image of an object between F and 2F was determined using ray tracing.

The formulas in Equation 2 deal with *lateral magnification*, which is defined in the same way for lenses as it is for mirrors: the ratio of the image height to object height. It can also be computed using distances: The lateral magnification equals the negative of the ratio of image distance to object distance. This is the second equation. For instance, in the example just discussed above, this ratio is −2.0: the image is twice as tall as the object. The negative sign means the image is inverted.

The equation in Equation 3 is the *lensmaker's equation*. It relates the focal length of the lens to some of its physical properties, specifically its index of refraction and the radius of curvature of each surface of the lens. The equation enables a lensmaker (or physics student) to calculate the focal length for a lens that has differing curvatures on the two sides of the lens, or to create a lens with a particular focal length.

We show the version of the equation for a lens in air. If the lens is immersed in another substance, say water, then the variable n has to be replaced by the ratio of the index of refraction of the lens to the index of the surrounding material (for example, $n = n_{lens}/n_{water}$). The object side of a microscope objective lens is often immersed in a special optical oil, as with the German "Oel Immersion" objective lens shown below.

The equations can be tricky to apply because various values like image distance can be either positive or negative. You need to use the table in Concept 1 above, or perform the more difficult task of memorizing the conventions.

To review perhaps the trickiest sign convention, the radius of curvature R in the lensmaker's equation is negative when the center of curvature is on the near (the object) side of the lens and positive when it is on the far side. If this sounds confusing, consider each lens surface as part of a sphere. If the sphere's center of curvature is on the object side, so the sphere would enclose an object relatively near the lens, then R is negative.

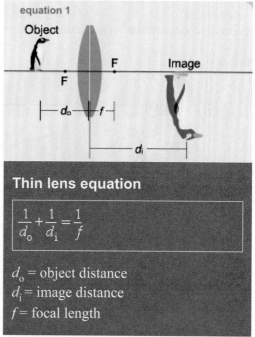

Thin lens equation

$$\frac{1}{d_o} + \frac{1}{d_i} = \frac{1}{f}$$

d_o = object distance
d_i = image distance
f = focal length

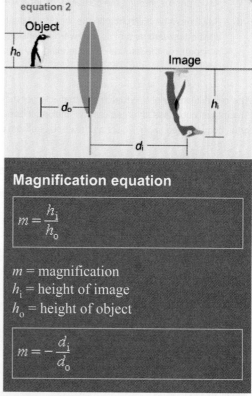

Magnification equation

$$m = \frac{h_i}{h_o}$$

m = magnification
h_i = height of image
h_o = height of object

$$m = -\frac{d_i}{d_o}$$

With a converging lens that is convex on both sides, like the ones used in the illustrations to the right, the radius of curvature for the near surface, R_1, is positive, and the radius of curvature for the far surface, R_2, is negative. As the diagram illustrates, with a lens that is convex on both sides, the center of curvature for each surface is on the opposite side of the lens from the surface. With a diverging lens made up of two concave surfaces, the signs are reversed and the centers are on the same side as the lens surfaces. Remember, we said this was tricky!

There are additional conventions: Focal lengths are positive for converging lenses and negative for diverging lenses. Object distances are positive when the object is real and negative when it is virtual. (Virtual objects can arise when there are multiple lenses. A virtual object is on the side of a lens opposite to the source of the light.) Image distances are positive when the image is real and negative when it is virtual. Magnification is positive for an image that is upright relative to the object and negative for one that is inverted relative to the object.

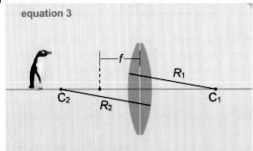

equation 3

Lensmaker's equation, air

$$\frac{1}{f} = (n-1)\left(\frac{1}{R_1} - \frac{1}{R_2}\right)$$

n = index of refraction
R_1 = radius of near surface
R_2 = radius of far surface

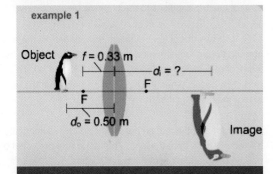

example 1

Find the distance to the image.

$$\frac{1}{d_o} + \frac{1}{d_i} = \frac{1}{f}$$

$$\frac{1}{d_i} = \frac{1}{f} - \frac{1}{d_o}$$

$$\frac{1}{d_i} = \frac{1}{0.33\,\text{m}} - \frac{1}{0.50\,\text{m}} = (3.0 - 2.0)$$

$$d_i = 1.0\,\text{m}$$

33.8 - Interactive problem: optical bench with a lens

Your mission here is to create the image at the location shown in the graphic at the right. The image is 13.5 cm tall, and 15.0 cm from the lens. The object is 9.0 cm tall. (Note: We are deliberately being ambiguous about mathematical signs here!)

You set both the object location and the lens's focal length to the nearest 0.01 cm in this simulation. Press CHECK to test your answer.

A hint: Start this problem by determining the magnification required for the specified image height, and then consider how that helps you to specify the object distance. If you need help with this problem, consult the section on lens equations. You will need to apply three equations from that section.

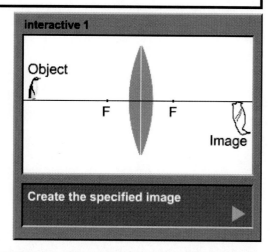

interactive 1

Object

F   F

Image

Create the specified image

33.9 - The human eye

The human eye contains a variable lens. This organ – a remarkable product of evolution – employs the lens to focus images on the *retina* at its back surface. Special cells called rods and cones line the retina. Light stimulates these cells, and they send signals in the form of electric impulses to the brain via the optic nerve.

Light passes through four different components of the eye on its way to the retina: the cornea, the aqueous humor, the lens, and the vitreous humor. Each has a different index of refraction, ranging from about 1.30 to 1.40. This means the greatest amount of refraction occurs when the light first crosses from the air ($n = 1.00$) to the cornea, where the indices differ the most.

In order for an object to be perceived clearly, its image must be focused on the retina, at a fixed distance from the lens. The real image projected on the retina is upside down, but the brain automatically corrects for this.

The eye must be able to create crisp images of objects that are located at varying distances. It accomplishes this by changing the shape of the lens, a process called *accommodation*. By causing the lens to contract or expand, the eye changes the radius of curvature and the focal length of the lens. On the right, you see the lens in both a relaxed state for viewing objects far away, and tensed as its curvature has been changed to focus on a nearer object.

The closest distance at which an object can be brought into focus is called the *near point*. A young adult with a fully tensed lens can clearly see objects that in some cases are as close as 15 cm, with an average near point for this age being 25 cm. By the time a person reaches her early forties, the near-point distance increases to an average of 40 cm. By age 65, the average near-point distance is 400 cm. Changes in the eye that occur with aging explain this increase. In fact, this progression is so predictable that the distance to the near point can pinpoint age to within a few years.

The *far point* is the greatest distance at which an object can be seen clearly. For people who do not need glasses for distance vision, this point is effectively infinitely far away. For those who are nearsighted, it can be much closer.

If you have 20/20 vision, you are lucky: You perceive objects crisply without the use of prescription lenses. If you have 20/60 vision, it means that you must be as close as 20 feet to see what a person with typical vision can see at 60 feet. Baseball players are noted for having acute vision, such as 20/15 vision. This means they see at 20 feet what most people need to be within 15 feet to see clearly.

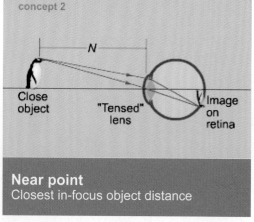

concept 1

Iris

Aqueous humor

Vitreous humor

Lens

Cornea

Retina

Ciliary muscle

Optic nerve

Human Eye
Contains variable lens
Image forms on retina

concept 2

N

Close object

"Tensed" lens

Image on retina

Near point
Closest in-focus object distance

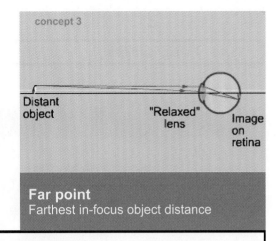

Far point
Farthest in-focus object distance

33.10 - Nearsightedness

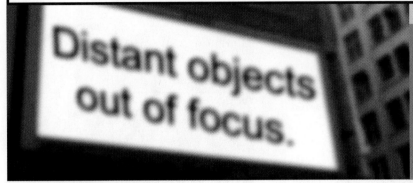

concept 1

Nearsightedness
Distant objects out of focus

Nearsightedness: Ability to focus on nearby objects but not distant objects.

To people with nearsightedness, or *myopia*, faraway objects are blurry and look like the image above.

To view an object that is far away, the eye's ciliary muscle completely relaxes, causing the lens to be as flat as possible. In a nearsighted eye, the eye is too long, causing images of faraway objects to form in front of the retina, even when the lens is completely relaxed. You see this in the conceptual diagram in Concept 2.

To correct this problem in focusing, a diverging lens can be placed in front of the eye. As illustrated in Concept 3, the lens spreads out the parallel rays before they reach the eye, so that the rays do not come to a focus quite so soon, but farther back upon the retina where they should.

More recently, laser surgery has become a popular method for correcting nearsightedness. A laser directed at the eye reshapes the cornea, causing its outer surface to be flatter so that an image can form more crisply on the retina. The angle of incidence for incoming light rays is less, causing them to converge farther back in the eye, at the retina.

Contact lenses can also correct nearsightedness; they change the radius of curvature of the front surface of the eye. Since the contact lenses are thicker at the edges than the center, they work by flattening the eye's surface.

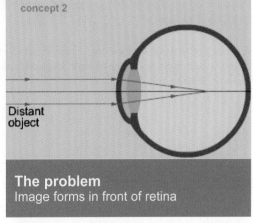

concept 2

The problem
Image forms in front of retina

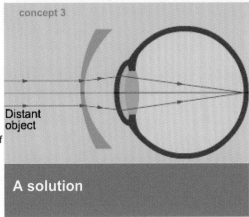

concept 3

A solution

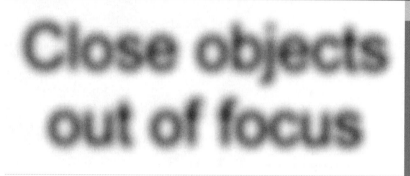

Corrected with diverging lens

concept 1

Farsightedness
Close objects out of focus

Farsightedness: Inability to clearly see objects that are relatively close.

With farsightedness, or *hyperopia*, the image of a nearby object forms behind the retina. The eyeball is too short, and no matter how hard the ciliary muscle strains, it cannot contract the lens enough to focus the image on the retina. You see this shown in Concept 2.

People with hyperopia have difficulty reading things that are close and often use reading glasses as a result. A related condition called *presbyopia* ("old vision") occurs in many people starting in their forties. With presbyopia, the eyeball is not too short, but the lens itself has become stiff with age and is unable to contract enough to focus images on the retina.

A converging lens can compensate for this problem by creating a virtual image beyond the eye's near point, so that the lens can focus an image on the retina. This solution is shown in Concept 3.

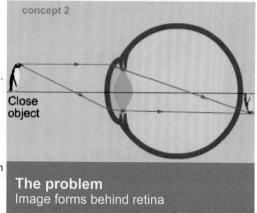

concept 2

Close object

The problem
Image forms behind retina

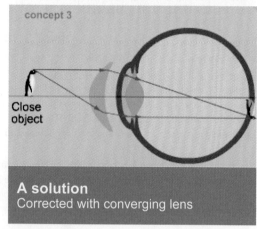

concept 3

Close object

A solution
Corrected with converging lens

Laser eye surgery, a procedure now quite popular, provides a way to alter the shape of the cornea so that glasses or contact lenses are not needed, or are required less frequently. It has proven quite popular amongst both celebrities (such as Tiger Woods) and non-celebrities.

To explain how the procedure works, we first review some fundamentals of how the eye focuses an image. The eye has two components that are most responsible for the location of the image it creates: the cornea (its outermost surface) and an internal variable lens. Light refracts as it passes through both of these components.

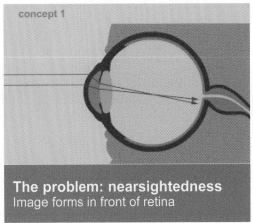

The problem: nearsightedness
Image forms in front of retina

Although one might think most of the refraction occurs at the lens, in fact about two-thirds of the refraction occurs at the cornea. It occurs there because the index of refraction of the cornea differs substantially from that of air. This difference is much larger than differences in the indices of refraction within the eye. The cornea and the lens combine to focus the light at the retina, which is at the back of the eye. The eye adjusts the curvature of the lens in order to alter its focal length, enabling it to focus objects at various distances. When the eye can change the lens shape enough so that light converges crisply at the retina for objects both near and far, a person has no need for glasses.

However, many people need glasses or contact lenses in order to see clearly. Nearsightedness and farsightedness occur when the lens's shape cannot be changed enough to sharply focus images on the retina. Eyeglasses and contact lenses compensate for this by providing a second lens that assists in the process of focusing the image at the proper position.

The solution
Cornea flattened to correct vision
After surgery – image forms on retina

Laser eye surgery takes a different tack: It changes the eye itself. The surgery changes the shape of the cornea in order to correct for the limitations of the lens. The procedure does not alter the lens inside the eye; rather, it "tunes" the cornea.

Currently, a type of laser surgery called *LASIK* (*laser in situ keratomileusis*) is the most widely used. To begin the process, medical personnel first determine how the cornea's curvature must be modified in order to improve vision. Then, a surgeon temporarily peels back the epithelium (the thin outermost layer of the eye) and trains a laser on the eye to remove small amounts of the cornea. The epithelium is then put back to cover the eye's surface.

Laser surgery can be used to treat both nearsightedness and farsightedness. Nearsightedness occurs when the lens cannot become sufficiently flat, resulting in an image formed in front of the retina. This is shown in Concept 1. To compensate for this, the surgeon flattens the cornea. This reduces the angle of incidence for light entering it, and the angle of refraction as a result. Concept 2 shows the eye after laser eye surgery for nearsightedness. The dashed line shows the original curvature of the eye.

The problem: farsightedness
Image forms behind retina

With farsightedness, the muscles of the eye cannot contract the lens enough. Close objects are focused behind the retina, again causing blurring. This problem is shown in Concept 3. To address it, the surgeon increases the steepness of the cornea. Since the angle of incidence of incoming light rays is increased, they refract more. The bottom illustration shows a farsighted eye after laser eye surgery. Again, the dashed line represents the initial shape of the eye.

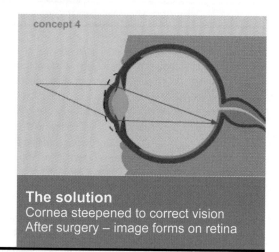

The solution
Cornea steepened to correct vision
After surgery – image forms on retina

33.13 - Angular size

Angular size: How much of the field of vision is filled by an object or image.

Sizing up the Needle.

Imagine yourself in Seattle, standing two kilometers from the Space Needle. You look at the structure, and then raise your hand so that your thumb is a half-meter from your eyes. Your thumb now appears to be about the same size in your field of vision as the Space Needle, although you know that the Space Needle is much bigger.

This effect occurs because of the relative angular sizes of your thumb and the Space Needle. The angular size refers to the angle, measured in radians, *subtended* by an object when viewed from a particular distance. The subtended angle is perhaps as well explained with a diagram as in text. The subtended angle is labeled θ in Concept 1 to the right. It measures the angle of your vision "blocked out" by the object.

Trigonometry can be used to determine angular size when the height h of the object and the distance d to the object are known. The angular size can be approximated as the height divided by the distance to the object. This approximation uses a small-angle approximation, $\theta \approx \tan \theta$ for small angles, where the angle must be measured in radians. This approximation for angular size is very good (within one percent) for angular sizes less than 0.17 rad (about $10°$). Approximations like this can be useful in astronomy to approximate distance or size. For instance, it can be useful to know that the Moon subtends about $0.5°$ (0.009 radians). If you know its distance, you can quickly approximate its diameter using this fact and some trigonometry.

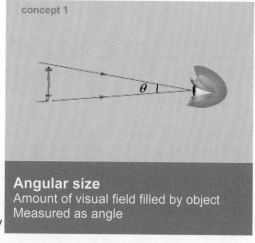

Angular size
Amount of visual field filled by object
Measured as angle

To leave space and return to Seattle: The thumb in the photograph above is 5 cm or so tall and 60 cm away. It has an angular size of 5 cm divided by 60 cm, which equals 0.08 rad. At a distance of 2 km, the Space Needle, which is 184 meters tall, would subtend an angle of about 184 m/ 2000 m, or 0.09 rad. These values confirm that the thumb is about the same angular size as the Space Needle.

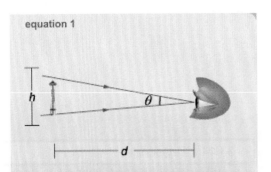

equation 1

Angular size

$$\theta \approx \frac{h}{d}$$

θ = angular size (in radians)
h = height of object
d = distance to object

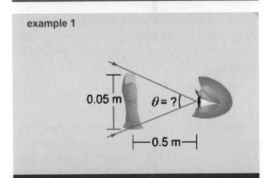

example 1

What is the angular size of this person's thumb at the given distance?

$\theta_{\text{Thumb}} \approx 0.05 \text{ m} / 0.5 \text{ m}$
$\theta_{\text{Thumb}} \approx 0.1 \text{ rad}$

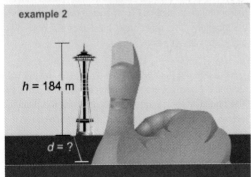

example 2

$h = 184$ m

$d = ?$

How far is this person from the Space Needle? She measures the angular size of her thumb

33.14 - Telescopes

concept 1

Refracting telescopes
Objective lens gathers light
Eyepiece magnifies image

Simple refracting (lens-based) telescopes have two lenses. A clever configuration of these lenses enables the telescope to serve three purposes: to gather as much light as possible from the object, to magnify the object and to provide as relaxed viewing of the image as possible.

The first lens encountered by incoming light rays, the objective lens, is used to gather as much light as possible. Light is at a premium in telescopes since faraway objects are typically faint. You cannot see most of the stars in the sky because they are too dim, not because they are too small (in angular size). Astronomers are willing to pay high prices to obtain telescopes with large objective lenses. Amateur astronomers purchasing their first telescope are often advised to pay more attention to its light gathering capability than to its magnifying power.

The eyepiece of a telescope performs two important tasks: It magnifies the real image created by the objective lens and creates a virtual image whose image distance is essentially at infinity. Creating a distant image is useful because the human eye is most relaxed when viewing objects at a distance.

At the right, you see the combination of lenses that constitutes a basic refracting astronomical telescope. To analyze how this system functions, you must first determine the location of the real image created by the objective lens. This image serves as the object for the eyepiece.

Telescopes are pointed at faraway objects, so the light rays entering the telescope are essentially parallel. Both the objective lens and the eyepiece are converging lenses. The objective lens creates a real image of the distant object at its focal point. The lenses are arranged so that this point is also at the focal point on the incident side of the eyepiece. Putting the object here causes the virtual image created by the eyepiece to be at infinity. The length of the telescope between the two lenses equals the sum of their focal lengths. You see all this in the sketch to the right.

concept 2

Parallel rays from distant object

Refracting telescope

F_{ob}, F_{ey}

Objective

First image

Eyepiece

Virtual rays from final image

How it works
Two converging lenses
Focal points at same location
Final image inverted, at infinity, virtual

concept 3

Eyepiece

Parabolic mirror

Mirror

Reflecting telescope

Reflecting telescope
Uses mirror in place of objective lens

As you can see in Concept 2, the image produced by the objective lens is inverted, smaller than the object, and real. The image produced by the eyepiece from this real image subtends a larger angle than the object, and it is virtual. The larger angle is an example of angular magnification, provided by the "magnifying glass" of the eyepiece. In this case it is being used to view the real image created by the objective lens, rather than a concrete object. The eyepiece does not invert the real image created by the objective lens, so the final image is inverted compared to the original object.

The telescope configuration we have been discussing works well for astronomy. The image it produces is inverted, but this typically poses no problem for astronomers, since they are accustomed to seeing telescope-rendered views of the objects they study. However, telescopes used to study terrestrial objects (like birds) use other configurations, including perhaps a diverging lens or a set of prisms, in order to avoid presenting an inverted image to the eye.

A different type of telescope designed for astronomy is called a *Newtonian reflector*. "Newtonian" refers to the developer of this type of telescope, Sir Isaac Newton, and "reflector" refers to the use of mirrors. In a reflector, a relatively large concave mirror performs the "light collecting" and first image creation duties that the objective lens performs in a refracting telescope. You see a diagram of a reflector to the right. Light passes down the tube, is collected by a curved mirror, redirected by a flat mirror and then passes through the eyepiece.

Why mirrors? Consider the reflecting telescope at California's Mount Palomar Observatory, which is famous for its 200 inch reflector. A glass objective lens of the same diameter would have a mass of about 40,000 kg (and weigh about 50 tons), more than three times the mass/weight of the mirror actually used. The weight of the mirror is still huge, but reducing the mass by more than two-thirds is a worthwhile accomplishment. In addition, lenses are subject to chromatic aberration (different colors of light focusing at different distances), while mirrors are not. A mirror is also easier to support (since it can be supported from behind), and only one side of the mirror needs to be manufactured with optical precision, versus the two sides of a lens. These factors play out in the construction of large research telescopes: The largest refractor in existence, at the Yerkes Observatory in Wisconsin, is only a little over one meter in diameter, while the largest reflectors, the Keck telescopes, are nearly ten meters in diameter.

33.15 - Lens aberrations

Lens aberration:
Imperfection in the images formed by a lens.

Spherical aberration: Image blurring due to the spherical contour of the lens.

Chromatic aberration: Image blurring due to differing refraction of various wavelengths (colors) of light.

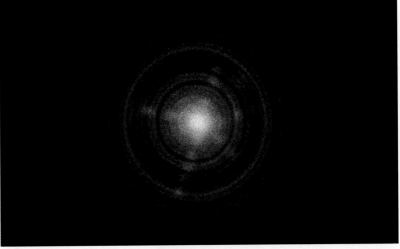

Spherical aberration.

You may have noticed that even when an image created by a lens is focused as sharply as possible, it is still somewhat blurry. The blurriness results from lens aberrations. Blurring means that the light rays from a single point on an object do not precisely converge at one point in the image, as the examples to the right illustrate, using horizontal rays from a point on a very distant object. A well-crafted lens causes little blur; lower quality lenses can suffer from substantial blurriness.

There are several types of aberration. Some aberrations may be caused by imperfections in the manufacturing of the lens, but one type arises unavoidably from the nature of a spherical lens. The lack of focus arising from spherical aberration most affects rays that strike a lens near its periphery. *Spherical aberration* means the light rays refract at an undesired angle; rather than converging to a single point, they converge to a larger region. The spherical nature of the lens causes this problem.

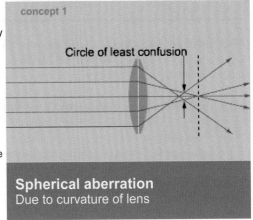

concept 1

Circle of least confusion

Spherical aberration
Due to curvature of lens

Instead of a single point of focus for incoming parallel rays, the lens creates a *circle of least confusion*, a region in which the rays approximately converge and an image is most satisfactorily viewed. This is diagrammed in Concept 1.

A typical image created by a spherical lens is shown above. The paraxial rays focus sharply in the center of the real image. Nonparaxial rays, having already passed through their closer focal points, are beginning to spread out again. Their contribution to the image shows up as a set of concentric rings. The outermost ring corresponds to rays passing through the outermost portions of the lens which have the shortest focal lengths.

Spherical aberration can be counteracted in a variety of ways. For instance, photographers are aware of this phenomenon, and when precise focus is important, they "stop down" the aperture of the iris that lets light into the camera lens, restricting the remaining light to the center portion of the lens. Mirrors are also subject to spherical aberration: In large astronomical telescopes, the problem is avoided by using parabolic or other non-spherical reflectors.

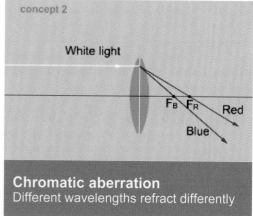

concept 2

White light

F_B F_R Red

Blue

Chromatic aberration
Different wavelengths refract differently

Chromatic aberration occurs because the refractive index of a material is a function of the wavelength of light. For instance, since blue light refracts more than red light when it passes from air into glass, a ray of white light disperses into its component colors when refracted by glass. This notably occurs in prisms, although there it is often the desired effect. You see a diagram illustrating chromatic aberration in Concept 2.

The photo below provides an example of chromatic aberration. There is a noticeable purple halo around the circular windows on the left side of the image. The right side of the image is actually the center of a larger cropped image. The chromatic aberration is less noticeable in this area, which corresponds to the center of the lens. Chromatic aberration worsens toward the edge of the lens.

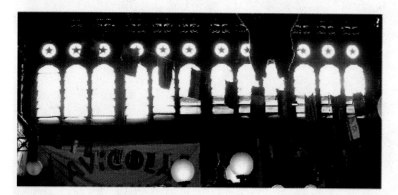

A compound lens made with lenses of different indices of refraction can counteract this effect. This type of *achromatic lens* is found in high quality optical equipment.

33.16 - Gotchas

"Real" means the same thing with lenses as it does with mirrors. On the one hand, yes. Real images can be projected onto paper with both lenses and mirrors. On the other hand, no. With lenses, a real image is on the opposite side of the lens from the object. With mirrors, a real image is on the same side of the mirror as the object.

Signs. You need to be careful with signs when using the lens equations, and we have provided a table to help you do so.

The ray diagrams for lenses are entirely accurate and represent physical reality. The diagrams in this (and other textbooks) employ a few conventions in order to make them easier to understand: Objects are shown fairly close to lenses that are relatively thick compared to the distance to the objects. For the approximations inherent in the theory of thin lenses to hold true, the objects should be quite far from the lenses and the lenses should be much thinner. Applying these changes to diagrams would make for illustrations that stretch far across the page or computer screen.

Lenses redirect light by refraction. Converging lenses are thicker in the middle and bring light rays together. Diverging lenses are thinner in the middle and spread light out.

Lens terminology is very similar to that of mirrors. An important difference is that when we consider a single lens, virtual images appear on the same side of the lens as the object, and real images appear on the opposite side. Another difference is that lenses have a focal point on each side.

Ray diagrams for converging and diverging lenses are also similar to those for mirrors.

And like mirrors, lenses have equations that quantify the relative size, orientation and distance of the images they produce. In addition, the lensmaker's equation determines the focal length of a lens with differing radii of curvature on its two sides. Sign conventions can be trickier for lenses, so pay special attention to them.

Several lenses can be used together to enhance their magnification properties, such as in a refracting telescopes.

The human eye contains a lens that can change shape in order to create a focused image on the light-sensitive retina at the back of the eye. A person's near point and far point are the closest and farthest distances on which she can focus.

Lenses can exhibit spherical aberration just as mirrors can. They also exhibit chromatic aberration due to the differing refractive indices of different wavelengths of light. Both kinds of aberration can cause an image to look blurry.

Equations

Thin lens equation

$$\frac{1}{d_o} + \frac{1}{d_i} = \frac{1}{f}$$

Lateral magnification

$$m = \frac{h_i}{h_o} = -\frac{d_i}{d_o}$$

Lensmaker's equation, air

$$\frac{1}{f} = (n-1)\left(\frac{1}{R_1} - \frac{1}{R_2}\right)$$

34.0 - Introduction

Light is a particle. Many of the great scientists of the 17th and 18th centuries who made fundamental contributions to the study of optics, including Isaac Newton, thought that light consisted of a stream of "corpuscles," or particles. In the 20th century, Albert Einstein explained the photoelectric effect. His explanation, for which he was awarded the 1921 Nobel Prize, depended on the fact that light acts like a particle. This property of light led to the coining of the term "photon" for a single particle of light by the chemist Gilbert Lewis.

Light is a wave. Between the 18th and 20th centuries, physicists discovered many wave-like properties of light. They found that a number of phenomena they routinely observed with water waves they could also observe with light.

For instance, the English scientist Thomas Young (1773-1829) showed that light could produce the same kinds of interference patterns that water waves produce. At the right, you see examples of interference patterns formed by light and by water waves. The similarities are striking. In this chapter, you will apply to light some of what you have studied about the interference of sound waves and traveling waves in strings.

Let there be light. Is light a particle, a wave, or both? Perhaps an Early Authority had it right. Light is light. It is a combination of electric and magnetic fields. Trying to classify light as a particle or as a wave may be a fruitless effort − better to revel in its unique properties. In this chapter, we will revel in its wave-like properties, and discuss the topic of interference. Your prior study of electromagnetic radiation modeled as a wave phenomenon will prove useful.

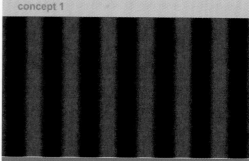

concept 1

Interference of ligth waves
Pattern of bright and dark on screen

concept 2

Interference of water waves
Expanding circular ripples
Pattern of disturbance and calm

34.1 - Interference

In Concept 1, you see an *interference pattern* created by causing a beam of light to pass through two parallel slits to illuminate a viewing screen. Constructive interference of light waves accounts for the bright regions (called bright *fringes*) while destructive interference causes the dark fringes.

In this section, we review some of the fundamentals of interference, and discuss the conditions necessary for light to make the pattern you see to the right. You may have already studied the interference of mechanical waves; for instance, what occurs when two waves on a string interact. In this chapter, you will study what happens when electromagnetic waves meet. Some of the same principles and terminology are used in discussing both kinds of interference.

Grass is green because it selectively absorbs nongreen colors. In contrast, the shimmering "color" of a peacock's feathers is due to interference effects.

When two light waves meet, the result can be constructive or destructive interference. In the following discussion, we assume that the waves have equal amplitude. Constructive interference creates a wave of greater amplitude and more intensity than either source wave; destructive interference results in a wave of smaller amplitude and less intensity than either source wave. At any point in a two-slit interference pattern such as that to the right, light waves from the two sources meet and interfere constructively, destructively, or partially (exhibiting a degree of interference somewhere between complete constructive and destructive interference).

To create an interference pattern, a physicist needs light that is:

1. *Monochromatic.* This means light with a specific wavelength. For instance, experimenters can produce the pattern you see in Concept 1 by using pure red light.

2. *Coherent.* This means the phase difference between the light waves arriving at any location remains constant over time.

The first condition, monochromatic light, means that all the light passing through the slits must have the same wavelength. White light, which is a mixture of many wavelengths (colors), does not produce distinct interference patterns. We often used a similar condition when analyzing the interference of mechanical waves, restricting our attention to what occurred when two waves of the same wavelength met.

We also implicitly used the second of the two conditions stated above with waves on a string. The phase difference between the waves sometimes remained constant throughout the string, and over long time periods.

For light waves, coherence can be achieved by causing light from a single point source to pass through two narrow slits, separating an initial beam of light into two beams with a constant phase difference. You see what happens when coherent light emerges from two slits and falls on a surface in Concepts 2 and 3.

If the light were not coherent, we would not be able to see interference. If the phase differences varied over time, then there would be constructive, partial, and destructive interference occurring at every particular spot at different times, and no overall pattern of interference could be readily observed. For example, if the coherent light from the two slits were replaced with incoherent light emanating from two light bulbs, only a uniform glow of illumination would be visible on the viewing screen.

For complete constructive interference to occur, two light waves have to be in phase, meaning there is zero phase difference (or else the phase difference is an integer multiple of 2π radians, or $360°$). At the point shown in Concept 2 the waves have no phase difference, peak meets peak and trough meets trough, and there is complete constructive interference. This causes the maxima, or regions of maximum intensity in the interference pattern.

In Concept 3, you see the result at a different location on the viewing screen where light waves from the two slits meet out of phase, with a phase difference of π radians, or $180°$ (the phase difference could also be an odd integer multiple of π radians, such as 3π radians, -5π radians and so on). With this phase difference, the result is complete destructive interference. Peak meets trough, trough meets peak, and the waves cancel. Complete destructive interference causes the minima, the stripes of darkness in the interference pattern.

The regions in between the lightest and darkest points are the result of partial interference. Here, the waves are somewhat out of phase, so they do not reinforce each other completely, nor do they completely cancel. The visual result is a progression of shades of intensity between the bright fringes caused by complete constructive interference and the dark fringes caused by complete destructive interference.

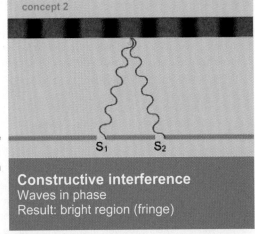

concept 1

Interference pattern
Bright and dark fringes

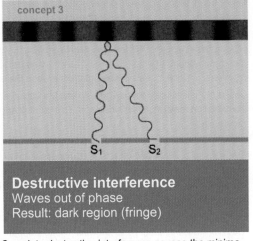

concept 2

S_1 S_2

Constructive interference
Waves in phase
Result: bright region (fringe)

concept 3

S_1 S_2

Destructive interference
Waves out of phase
Result: dark region (fringe)

The English scientist Thomas Young explored interference and diffraction in a series of experiments that demonstrated the wavelike nature of light. Young performed his first, crucial experiment in 1801. Here, we provide a summary of what he did. His actual procedure was slightly more complex than the description below due to the pioneering nature of his equipment.

Young shined light at a pair of barriers containing slits to create the interference pattern you see on the right. The first barrier had a single slit that acted as a coherent point source of light. (This single-slit barrier is not shown in the diagrams.) The coherent light then traveled through two parallel slits in the second barrier, each the same distance from the single slit, and then reached a viewing screen. In the diagrams you see the double-slit barrier and the pattern of interference he observed on the screen.

The pattern was one of equally spaced bright and dark fringes. Young knew that water waves passing through a pair of slits could cause a similar interference pattern. The fact that both water waves and light produced exactly the same type of pattern supported his hypothesis that light acted as a wave. Young further reinforced his position when he demonstrated that he could use interference patterns to calculate the wavelength of the light that he used in the experiment.

Why do waves create the interference pattern you see here? To answer this question, let's consider the diagram in Concept 2. Two rays of light meet at a point that is the same distance from each slit. The drawings of the rays emphasize their wavelike nature.

In this case, the two rays intersect the center of the screen in phase because both travel the **same distance** to this point. They were in phase when they passed through the slits, and since they traveled the same distance, they remain in phase at their point of convergence. They constructively interfere and produce a bright area of illumination. Other bright fringes occur to either side of the central fringe where the path difference between the waves is not zero, but one full wavelength, two wavelengths, and so on.

Now look at Concept 3. The rays of light reaching the viewing screen intersect at the first dark fringe to the left of center. They travel **different distances** to the surface: The ray from S_2 travels a half wavelength farther than the one from S_1. Because they start in phase at their respective slits, this means the waves are $\pi/2$ radians $(180°)$ out of phase when they arrive at the screen. This causes destructive interference, and darkness.

The pattern of bright and dark fringes extends to both the left and the right on the screen. The light is interfering constructively at the bright fringes, and destructively at the dark fringes, because of different path lengths to these regions and the resulting phase differences.

There are a few limitations to showing Young's apparatus in a compact diagram. First, the diagram is far from being drawn to scale. The screen should be much farther from the double-slit barrier than we show here, and the slits should be narrower and closer together. In actual interference experiments, the interfering rays from the two slits are practically parallel. Second, we vastly exaggerate the wavelength of the light.

You may have a question about what you would see if you conducted this experiment yourself. What if, at some instant, two waves meet at the screen and are in phase, but their electric and magnetic fields both happen to be zero at that point? Would you see "flickering" as the two reinforcing waves moved from peak to trough and back again? The answer is no: The frequency of light is so great that you only perceive the average brightness of a region; the human eye does not perceive changes in intensity due to the oscillation of a light wave.

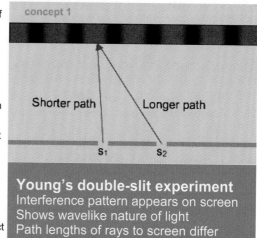

concept 1

Shorter path | Longer path

S_1 | S_2

Young's double-slit experiment
Interference pattern appears on screen
Shows wavelike nature of light
Path lengths of rays to screen differ

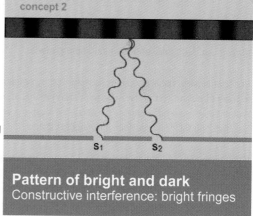

concept 2

S_1 | S_2

Pattern of bright and dark
Constructive interference: bright fringes

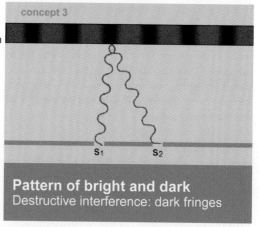

concept 3

S_1 | S_2

Pattern of bright and dark
Destructive interference: dark fringes

You do not even perceive flicker in systems oscillating at far lower frequencies, much less than the frequency of visible light, which is on the order of 10^{14} Hz. For example, a computer monitor refreshes its display 60 times a second, but you do not ordinarily perceive any flicker when you look at it.

34.3 - Michelson interferometer

Interferometer: A device that uses the interference of two beams of light to make precise measurements of their path difference. Historically used to study the nature of light.

Michelson interferometer. In this view the telescope is on the left, the adjustable mirror is on the right, and the fixed mirror is in front.

Albert A. Michelson, an American physicist, is famous for conducting an experiment that helped Albert Einstein to develop his theory of special relativity. Michelson's experiment helped to disprove the existence of the "ether," an invisible medium that many scientists believed was required for the transmission of light waves. In this section, we discuss the design of one piece of equipment he used, now called the Michelson interferometer, and how it uses the interference patterns of known wavelengths of light to measure minute differences in the path lengths of two beams of light.

You see a photograph of an interferometer above, and a conceptual diagram to the right. We use compass directions like "north" to explain the directions of the various beams. In the center of the diagram is a *beam splitter*. It is a plate of glass whose back is coated with a thin layer of silver. The beam splitter reflects half the light that falls on it, and lets the rest pass through.

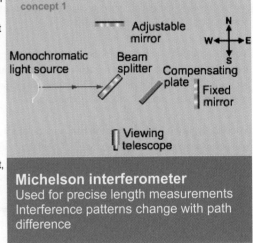

Michelson interferometer
Used for precise length measurements
Interference patterns change with path difference

The interferometer works in the following fashion:

1. Monochromatic, coherent light strikes the beam splitter from the west side.
2. The initial beam splits into two at the beam splitter. The silver coating reflects beam N to the north, and the splitter refracts beam E, which passes to the east.
3. Beam N travels to an adjustable mirror, reflects back, and then passes back through the splitter to a viewing telescope.
4. Beam E goes through a compensating plate of glass, reflects off a fixed mirror, passes through the compensating plate again and then reflects directly off the back of the splitter to reach the viewing telescope.

This system causes two mutually coherent beams of light to travel by different paths. An operator can control the length of the north-south path by changing the location of the adjustable mirror. The compensating plate ensures that both beams pass through the same amount of glass, which is important since light slows down in glass.

The purpose of this equipment is to control and detect with extreme precision changes in the path length difference between the two beams of light. Michelson knew the relationship between path length differences and interference patterns. A path difference of half a wavelength would cause the beams to interfere destructively, and a path length difference of an entire wavelength would cause complete constructive interference.

To measure a tiny increment of path length, Michelson could place a bright fringe at the center of the image created in the viewing telescope by setting the distance of the adjustable mirror. When he then moved the adjusting mirror a very small distance using a finely threaded screw adjustment, the image in the telescope would shift so that a dark fringe would be at the center. He knew he had moved the mirror one-quarter wavelength because the light traveled that additional distance to the adjusting mirror and then traveled back, making for one-half wavelength difference in total. A half wavelength path difference is the difference between complete constructive and complete destructive interference. In actual practice, Michelson's experiment had a few more "tricks" to it than we have described here, but this section conceptually summarizes how it worked.

34.4 - Thin-film interference

Thin-film interference: The interference caused by light waves reflecting off the two different surfaces of a thin film.

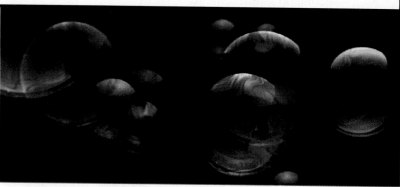

Thin-film interference in soap bubbles.

In soap bubbles and in thin layers of gasoline or oil floating on water, you sometimes see "rainbows," light of all the colors of the spectrum. The causes of rainbows in the sky and rainbows in soap bubbles are quite different. Those celestial "Pot-of-gold" rainbows are caused by refraction and reflection. Soap-bubble rainbows are caused by a phenomenon called thin-film interference.

To understand thin-film interference, we start with the fact that when light reflects off a material with a higher index of refraction than the medium it is traveling in, it changes phase by $180°$. When it reflects off a material with a lower index of refraction than the medium it is traveling in, there is no phase change.

Specifically, when light reaches the front surface of a thin film surrounded by air, some of it reflects, and changes phase by $180°$. Some of the light passes through this first surface, and then reflects off the far surface of the film. No phase change occurs here. As the light moves between the two media, it refracts as well.

This combination of reflection and refraction is illustrated in Concept 1. You see a downward ray striking the film from the upper left. Some of it reflects when it reaches the film's top surface, and we call that reflected ray 1. Some of the light passes into the film, reflects at the bottom surface, and passes back through the film again. We call that ray 2.

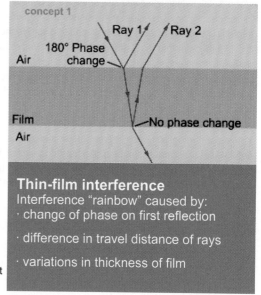

concept 1

Ray 1   Ray 2

Air   180° Phase change

Film   No phase change
Air

Thin-film interference
Interference "rainbow" caused by:
· change of phase on first reflection
· difference in travel distance of rays
· variations in thickness of film

The initial ray of light becomes two rays that have a somewhat complicated relationship in terms of their phase difference. Ray 1 changes phase $180°$ as it reflects, and ray 2 does not change phase as it reflects but it travels an extra distance through the film that ray 1 does not. Depending on the path length difference, which equals roughly twice the thickness of the film, the two rays could end up completely in phase, completely out of phase, or somewhere in between.

Interference depends not just on path difference but on wavelength as well. The type of interference occurring at a specific point in a thin film will differ by the local thickness of the film and the wavelength, or color, of the light. White light has components consisting of many colors, and in a film of variable thickness these components will interfere differently at different points.

What about the rainbow of colors you can observe on a soap bubble or oil sheen? The film of a soap bubble can be thicker or thinner at various locations. The path length difference at a certain point on a soap bubble may cause destructive interference for red light, but constructive interference for blue light. This means you perceive this region as blue. At another point, the bubble will have a different thickness, and the path length difference may cause the opposite result, and you see red there. These patterns can change quickly. A slight breeze or the flow of soap to the bottom of the bubble will cause parts of it to change thickness, resulting in a new pattern.

A region of a bubble that is about to burst is often thin enough that all wavelengths of light destructively interfere there, and the bubble appears dark. The path length difference through this part of the film is essentially zero, so the change of phase accompanying reflection at the front surface, which affects all wavelengths equally, causes destructive interference.

34.5 - Diffraction

Diffraction: The expansion or spreading of a wave front.

In this section, we switch from light to sound waves to discuss the important phenomenon of diffraction. We briefly switch to sound waves because they provide a way to describe diffraction using an everyday experience.

In Concept 1, we show the diffraction of wave fronts of a sound wave as they pass through a doorway. Only a section of each wave front can pass through the doorway. If this section of the wave front did not expand, it would move straight along the gray path. Instead, it expands spherically after passing through the doorway. The spherical expansion of the sound wave allows the person in the picture to hear the sound.

When you hear a friend down the hallway calling you, even though she is out of your line of sight, you hear her in part because the sound waves diffract as they emerge from the doorway. For a given size opening, waves of longer wavelength diffract more than those of shorter wavelength. Because light has a much shorter wavelength than sound, it would spread out far less after it passed through the doorway. This is why you can hear the voice of your friend, even when you cannot see her. However, even though you cannot observe light diffraction for doorway-sized openings, scientists have long observed it for smaller openings.

The debate over the cause of diffraction created a tale of considerable irony. The story starts with a competition sponsored by the French Academy on the subject of diffraction. The Frenchman Augustin Jean Fresnel (1788 - 1827) submitted a paper to the judges in 1818 discussing diffraction that was premised on considering light as a wave.

A noted mathematician, Simeon-Denis Poisson, had earlier mocked Fresnel's theories, pointing out that Fresnel's theory predicted that the shadow of a circular opaque object subjected to a bright light would exhibit a bright spot in its center. Since the circular object blocks the center portion of a screen from the light source, this result is highly surprising.

Noted mathematicians can be wrong (or should trust their mathematics). The Fresnel/Poisson debate was resolved by experiment. In Concept 2, the reddish image on the screen was created by shining a bright light at a small ball bearing. You can see the expected bright light surrounding the circumference of the ball, but – surprise! – there is also a bright spot at the center of the shadow caused by light diffracting around the ball's perimeter.

Fresnel was right, and Poisson unintentionally helped to confirm his theory. The irony is that though Fresnel did all the work, and Poisson initially ridiculed the theory, the bright center today is often called the *Poisson spot*. Others call it the *Fresnel spot*, perhaps a more appropriate name, with *Arago spot* yet another name (François Arago was the judge of the competition).

Waves also expand around sharp edges into regions that would otherwise be in shadow if the wave traveled only in a straight line. This type of diffraction causes an interference pattern. The photograph in Concept 3 shows *straight-edge diffraction*. Light from a point source passes by a sharp, well defined edge, and the resulting diffraction causes a pattern on a screen behind the object.

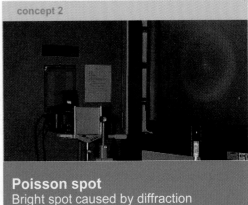

concept 1

Diffraction
Wave fronts "expanding"

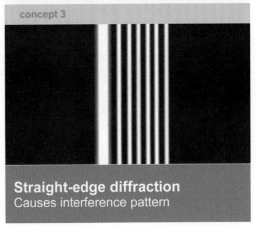

concept 2

Poisson spot
Bright spot caused by diffraction

concept 3

Straight-edge diffraction
Causes interference pattern

The Dutch scientist Christian Huygens (1629 - 1695) concluded that light was a wave, made up of tiny points that emit spherical *wavelets* like the ones you see in Concept 1 to the right. Although his model has its limitations, it provided a basis for explaining many phenomena that scientists observed, and his model was usefully employed and expanded. Here we explain his fundamental principle, and show how his model can be used to explain diffraction.

As Huygens wrote:

> …each particle of matter in which a wave spreads, ought not to communicate its motion only to the next particle which is in the straight line drawn from the luminous point, but that it also imparts some of it necessarily to all the others which touch it and which oppose themselves to its movement. So it arises that around each particle there is made a wave of which that particle is the center.

In Concept 2, you see the wave front created by the wavelets moving toward a barrier with a gap in it. Before the wavelets reach the barrier, each wavelet has another wavelet adjacent to it.

Huygens' principle states that the position of the wave front at any time can be found by drawing a line tangent to the leading surface of each wavelet. As each wavelet moves forward, the wave front moves forward as well.

Let's consider what happens when the wave front meets the barrier. The barrier prevents most of the wave front from moving forward (for simplicity's sake, we ignore the reflection of the wave). One section of the wave front (and the wavelets that make it up) passes through the opening. They continue to move forward after passing through.

As Huygens mentions in the quote above, you can think of the sources of the wavelets as a set of vibrating particles. After the wave front passes through the slit, the oscillating particles that now make up the wave front are free to interact with other particles above and below them. The interaction of the particles with their formerly stationary neighbors and the spherical form of the wavelets account for the spherical expansion of the wave front. This is illustrated in Concepts 3 and 4.

If you like, you can think of the wavelets as a group of subway passengers exiting a subway car. Their "wave" is constrained by the width of the subway doors, but when they exit the subway and enter the subway station, their wave can expand amongst the people awaiting the subway.

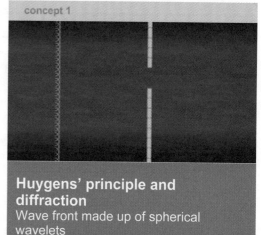

Huygens' principle and diffraction
Wave front made up of spherical wavelets

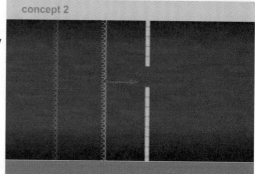

Huygens' principle
Wave front tangent to wavelets, same speed

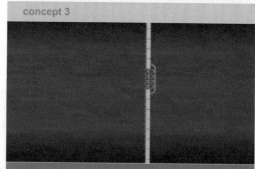

Diffraction
Portion of wave passes through slit
After the slit, particles at edges interact with nearby particles

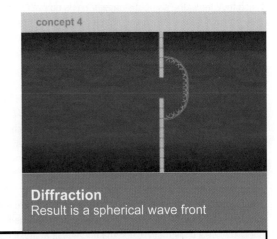

Diffraction
Result is a spherical wave front

34.7 - Single-slit diffraction

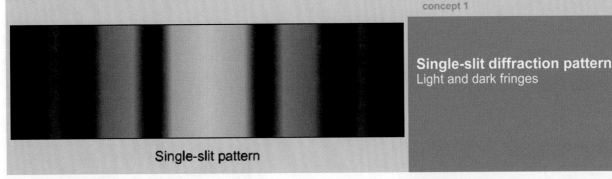

Single-slit pattern

Single-slit diffraction pattern
Light and dark fringes

Waves, including light waves, diffract as they pass through a single narrow slit. When a screen is placed on the other side of the slit, a *diffraction pattern* will be created on the screen. This pattern arises from interference among light waves coming through different portions of the slit. We will assume that the screen is far enough away from the slit that the rays that pass through are approximately parallel to each other. This is called *Fraunhofer diffraction*. (*Fresnel diffraction* occurs when the rays cannot be treated as parallel, and is discussed in more advanced texts.)

The result of Fraunhofer diffraction is a pattern of light and dark bands (often called *fringes*) on the screen, as shown above. The black-and-white image emphasizes the light and dark pattern.

This pattern of light and dark can be explained using the concept of interfering waves. As with double-slit interference, bright fringes result from constructive interference of waves and dark fringes from destructive interference. The intensity of the bright fringes diminishes the farther they are from the midpoint. The first bright fringe is located straight across from the single slit. The other fringes are located in a symmetric pattern on both sides of the center.

Use Huygens' principle
Model light as emanating from point sources

In the illustrations, we simplify the configuration necessary to produce the diffraction pattern shown. A lens is typically used to focus the light, making the diffraction pattern clearer.

To explain the source of the interference, we use Huygens' principle and treat the light passing through the slit as though it were made up of individual waves (wavelets) emanating from a series of point sources, as shown in Concept 2. We focus on the waves emanating from just two of those point sources to simplify the drawings and explanations. As with double-slit interference, the difference in the waves' path lengths to the screen (and any resulting phase difference) determines whether they interfere constructively, and create a bright fringe, or destructively, to create a dark fringe.

First, we show constructive interference. In Concept 3, we consider two waves from the edges of the slit. They meet at the center of the screen.

Since they travel the same distance, there is no path length difference, which means they arrive in phase. Any point source within the slit can be matched to a corresponding "mirror point" that is an equal distance from the midpoint, but on the other side. The interference is completely constructive, and the result is the central bright fringe, which is the brightest in the entire diffraction pattern.

In Concept 4, we show how completely destructive interference creates a dark fringe. In this case, we consider a wave on the left edge of the slit and a wave from the center of the slit. The wave on the left travels one-half wavelength less to reach the screen than the wave on its right. This means they will be completely out of phase when they meet at the screen. In fact, every wave has a corresponding wave exactly half a slit away that will cancel it at that screen location.

The regions between the lightest and darkest points are the result of intermediate interference. In these regions, the overall interference is neither completely destructive nor completely constructive, and the brightness at these points is between that of the points just discussed.

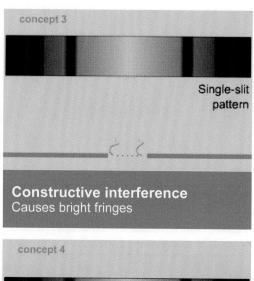

concept 3

Single-slit pattern

Constructive interference
Causes bright fringes

concept 4

Single-slit pattern

Destructive interference
Causes dark fringes

34.8 - Resolving power

Resolving power: Ability to distinguish between two objects.

Resolving power expresses the capability of an optical system to show the separation of objects that are close together. This correlates to the instrument's ability to show fine detail. A microscope is one example of an instrument that needs a good deal of resolving power. To be effective, a microscope must enable you to distinguish very small, close details. Telescopes also must supply great resolving power to allow the viewer to separate distant objects.

In concept 1 we show the importance of resolving power. The image of galaxy M100 on the left was taken by the Hubble Space Telescope before a defect in its mirror was corrected; the image on the right was taken after the defect was fixed. The right-hand image shows much more detail, and many more distinct objects are visible due to the greater resolving power achieved.

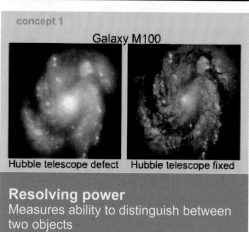

concept 1

Galaxy M100

Hubble telescope defect   Hubble telescope fixed

Resolving power
Measures ability to distinguish between two objects

The Hubble telescope can resolve light sources that are less than $0.00003°$ (≈ 0.0000005 rad) apart. What does that mean on a human scale? It could resolve a pair of headlights roughly 3000 km away, approximately the distance from Denver to Miami. A great conceptual design, some repairs and ongoing maintenance, and the fact that the telescope is above the blurring effects of the Earth's atmosphere, all contribute to this mind boggling capability.

You do not need a telescope to understand what is meant by resolving power. You can experience it simply by looking at a car's headlights at night. At a large distance, the car's lights look as if they come from a single source, in one blur of light. As the car comes closer, the blur resolves into two separate sources of light.

Copyright 2000-2007 Kinetic Books Co. Chapter 34

Diffraction causes the stars and the headlights to "blur" together. Concept 2 shows the diffraction pattern created by two sources that are far enough apart that their diffraction patterns do not significantly overlap. Concept 3 shows what occurs when the diffraction patterns overlap. One "blurry" central image is the result.

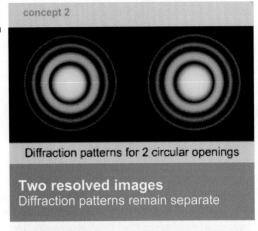

Diffraction patterns for 2 circular openings

Two resolved images
Diffraction patterns remain separate

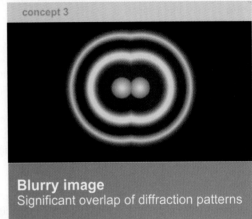

Blurry image
Significant overlap of diffraction patterns

34.9 - Resolving power of the eye

Human eyes, and those of other animals, resolve objects. From ten meters away, a person with good eyesight can resolve two objects separated by only three millimeters. Some animals can do far better. At the same distance, an eagle can resolve two objects that are only 0.8 mm apart. This ability allows eagles in flight to pick out potential prey on the ground with amazing accuracy. For example, an eagle can distinguish a rabbit from its surroundings from as far as a mile away.

Painters and other artists sometimes exploit the limitations of the human eye to create their effects. The style of painting known as Pointillism was famous for this. To the right, we have created our own Pointillist art. The "zoom-in" shows that the picture is composed of many small "dabs" of color. As you step back, your eye can no longer resolve the individual dabs, and you see the collective image.

Lack of resolution leads to art

If your school lacks a first rate collection of Post-Impressionistic paintings, the same effect is demonstrated in your daily newspaper. Look closely enough at a picture and you will see the dots that compose it.

34.10 - Physics at play: CDs and DVDs

Most computers today contain a CD-ROM drive and many contain a DVD drive. A CD or DVD can hold a great quantity of information. The drive relies on the principles of interference to "read" the disc.

A CD or DVD contains a long spiral track with *pits* in it. These pits are formed in a disc by an injection molding process, and represent some of the smallest mechanically manufactured objects. A thin layer of metal such as silver or aluminum covers the pits. This layer in turn is covered by a thin layer of plastic.

The pits are created on the top of the CD or DVD but the disc is read using a laser that is projected up from the bottom. From the bottom of the disc, the pits appear to be raised areas. Non-pitted areas of the disc are called *land*. (An incidental fact: The pits are nearer the top of the disc than the bottom, so scratches on its top are more likely to damage the CD than scratches the bottom, or "reading" side!)

CDs or DVDs created by *burners* do not create pits in the fashion described above, but rather change the color of a layer within the disc.

The CD or DVD reader contains a laser diode that emits a beam of light that reflects off the disc. The intensity of the reflected light varies as the disc rotates and the light reflects off pits and land. The intensity is measured and interpreted as a series of ones and zeros (digital information) by photodetectors. This information is then relayed to other systems that interpret it.

How does interference factor in? The laser beam reflects off of the CD. If all of the beam hits a land or a pit, then the path length difference back to the photodetector is essentially the same, and the result is constructive interference: bright light. You see this case in Concept 1.

On the other hand, when the disc moves and laser light is half on a pit, and half on the land, the path length difference is significant. The two parts of the laser beam have a total path length difference of one-half a wavelength, and the result is destructive interference: darkness.

You see this in Concept 2, where we emphasize "sides" of the same laser beam, and how one side reflects off of a pit and the other off a land.

DVDs contain more data than CDs and employ a variety of strategies to do so. For instance, DVD drives use lasers with shorter wavelengths. A shorter wavelength means smaller pits are possible, and these smaller pits can be placed more closely together, allowing more data to be stored.

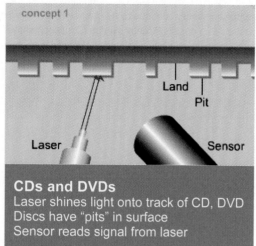

concept 1

Land
Pit
Laser   Sensor

CDs and DVDs
Laser shines light onto track of CD, DVD
Discs have "pits" in surface
Sensor reads signal from laser

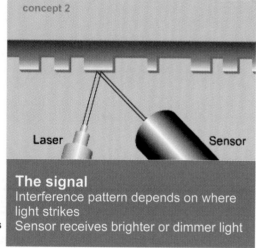

concept 2

Laser   Sensor

The signal
Interference pattern depends on where light strikes
Sensor receives brighter or dimmer light

34.11 - Gotchas

In a string, complete destructive interference occurs when the peaks of one wave meet the troughs of another wave with the same amplitude. The same is true with light. This is correct. With a string, the result is zero displacement. With light, the result is darkness.

In an interference pattern, bright fringes occur at peaks. Dark fringes occur at troughs. No. Any individual light wave continually oscillates from peak to trough. The bright and dark fringes occur because of the interference of two light waves. Bright fringes occur at locations of constructive interference, and dark fringes occur at locations of destructive interference.

A double-slit interference pattern is caused by differences in the path lengths traveled by the light emanating from each slit. This is true.

If the path length difference in a double-slit interference pattern equals one wavelength, the result is complete destructive interference. No, the result is complete constructive interference. When the path difference is one wavelength, the waves are in phase: Peak meets peak, and trough meets trough. A half wavelength path difference will cause destructive interference.

Light exhibits the properties of both a particle and a wave. The interference patterns created by light can be explained by treating it as a wave.

Interference patterns consist of alternating bright and dark bands called fringes. To create an interference pattern, you need at least two sources providing light that is both monochromatic (having only one wavelength) and coherent (light from the different sources has a phase relationship that does not change over time). You also need a screen on which to view the pattern.

The bright fringes in a two-slit interference pattern are the result of completely constructive interference of the light from the two sources, while the dark fringes are created by completely destructive interference.

Whether a given point on a viewing screen will be a point of constructive, destructive, or intermediate interference depends on the difference in the path lengths from each of two slits to that point.

An interferometer is an instrument that takes advantage of interference to make precise measurements of length. It relies on the fact that a specific difference in the path lengths of two monochromatic coherent beams of light causes a specific interference pattern at a point where the beams meet, and a microscopic change in the path difference causes an easily visible change in the interference pattern.

When a light wave reflects from a material with a higher index of refraction than the one in which it is traveling, it experiences a $180°$ phase change. When a light wave reflects from a material with a lower index of refraction, there is no phase change. This affects the nature of thin-film interference, where waves that reflect from the front surface of a thin film interfere with other waves that refract through the front surface and then reflect from the back surface.

Diffraction is the expansion or spreading of a wave front as it passes through an opening or past a sharp edge.

Huygens' principle is a model to explain diffraction. It says that a wave front is made up of a series of spherical wavelets.

Diffraction is most often discussed in terms of light waves. When light passes through a slit in a mask, it diffracts. We can model the light passing through the slit as coming from a series of point sources which each emit a spherical wave front. The light from each point source interferes with light from the others. This creates an interference pattern of dark and light fringes.

Diffraction limits the ability of optical systems to distinguish between two objects, to resolve them.

35.0 - Introduction

With a pair of brilliant papers published in 1905 and 1915, Albert Einstein inaugurated a revolution in physics. Scientists still are happily grappling with the implications of his work in these and other papers. His special theory of relativity and his later work predicted a range of phenomena from the amount light is "bent" by gravity, to time passing at a different rate for a passenger in a moving airplane than for an observer on the ground. To their great delight, when scientists went looking for these effects, they found them.

This revolution was all the more surprising since a distinguished scientist, Lord Kelvin, had not long before remarked: "There is nothing new to be discovered in physics now. All that remains is more and more precise measurement." Today's physicists are more realistic, which certainly makes their research more interesting!

Strange and wonderful ideas emanate from Einstein's work. His special theory of relativity predicts that an identical twin could leave her sister, fly off into space at nearly the speed of light and, upon her return, have aged 20 years less than her sibling. Other parts of his work, outside the realm of this chapter, have led to the discovery of black holes, objects with mass so concentrated and possessing such strong gravitational fields that even light cannot escape them.

Einstein himself found some of the implications of his research and that of his peers too incredible to believe. For instance, his work predicted that the universe is endlessly expanding. He found this idea troubling enough that he added a "cosmological constant" so the equations would predict a universe of a constant size. Subsequently, when the astronomer Edwin Hubble introduced evidence that the universe is indeed expanding, Einstein gladly removed the constant from his work, saying it was the biggest mistake he had ever made. Today, the debate about the merits of the cosmological constant continues as physicists continue their research.

Although at times seemingly "incredible," Einstein's essential theories have been tested and proven by scientific experiments. The results have confirmed his work to a level of precision of about one part in 10^{15}. Physicists believe that with advances in equipment and approach, they can confirm that the data conforms to his theories to even higher levels of precision.

This chapter focuses on Einstein's special theory of relativity, as opposed to his later and more complex general theory. Einstein's special theory of relativity is based on two postulates.

The first states that the laws of physics are the same in any inertial reference frame. What constitutes an inertial reference frame merits more discussion; briefly, you can consider any system moving at a constant velocity to be an inertial reference frame. In such a reference frame, the "classical" or Newtonian laws of physics hold true. Let's say you are either in a train moving at a constant 125 km/h, or standing on the ground. In either situation, you can throw a ball up in the air, and predict where it will land. (Note: the Earth itself is not truly an inertial reference frame because its rotational motion means that supposedly "fixed" objects are actually accelerating. However, we typically ignore this because of its minor impact.)

In sum, the laws of physics hold true in the train and on the ground, in France as well as in Germany. This is a postulate you likely assumed: that the physics you study do not vary by location. They hold true for any inertial reference frame. You could not use Newtonian mechanics in a bumpy truck as it drove along a winding country road, but this would be a quite atypical location for you to conduct lab experiments.

Einstein's second postulate states that the speed of light in a vacuum is the same in all inertial reference frames: It does not change due to the motion of the source of the light or the motion of the person observing the light. This insight is surprising, and does not accord with observations of everyday events.

For instance, if someone in a train moving toward you at a high speed throws a tennis ball out a window, you expect the tennis ball to be moving toward you. You intuitively add the velocity of the train to the velocity with which the ball was thrown to determine its overall velocity. You combine the velocities.

Einstein correctly stated that this is not true with light: Its speed does not change. If someone flashes a light at you from the train, whether the train moves toward you or away from you, the speed of light you measure **remains the same**.

With these two postulates, Einstein started a revolution. This chapter covers these two postulates in more depth, and then summarizes many of their amazing implications.

Reference frame: A coordinate system used to make observations.

We discussed reference frames many chapters earlier, in the context of motion in multiple dimensions. Since that was many chapters ago, we reprise the section here, though we have changed the examples and some of the discussion in order to make this section more appropriate for this chapter. Reference frames are a crucial element of special relativity.

A reference frame is a coordinate system used to make observations. If you stand next to a lab table and hold out a meter stick, you have established a reference frame for making observations. Your choice of a reference frame determines your perception of motion.

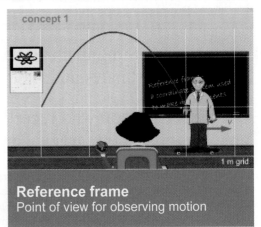

Reference frame
Point of view for observing motion

We use the classroom shown on the right to discuss reference frames. The classroom shows a professor on a skateboard and Katherine, a student in the professor's class. The professor conducts a demonstration in the class: He throws an eraser up, and catches it in the same hand. The professor does all this while moving across the classroom on a skateboard. Both the professor and Katherine have stopwatches to measure the time interval between "the throw" and "the catch".

In Concept 1, we show what Katherine observes. She sees the professor moving by at a speed v. The blue arc shows the path of the eraser from her reference frame. It moves both vertically and horizontally in projectile motion. A grid is shown in the illustration. Each side of the grid is 1.0 meter. Katherine sets the position of the "throw" at $(x = 0, y = 0)$ m, and the catch at (3.00, 0) m. The eraser reaches its peak at (1.50, 1.50) m in her reference frame.

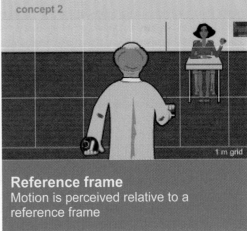

Reference frame
Motion is perceived relative to a reference frame

Katherine can also establish the time coordinates of these events. She starts her stopwatch when the professor throws the ball, so the throw is at $t = 0$ s. He catches the ball at $t = 1.11$ seconds.

In Concept 2, we show the exact same series of events as observed in the professor's reference frame. He considers himself as stationary and views the class as moving by. It is the same experience as looking out the window of an airplane: You consider yourself stationary as you sit in a seat, and the ground is passing by.

In his reference frame, the eraser travels solely vertically. Its initial and final positions are (0, 0) m. Its peak position is (0, 1.50) m. He also has a stopwatch, which he also starts when he tosses the eraser. His observations of the time (to the precision of this stopwatch) are identical. He throws the ball at $t = 0.00$ s, and catches it at $t = 1.11$ s. To describe the catch, he could describe its space time coordinates as (0 m, 0 m, 0 m, 1.11 s). The first three coordinates state its x, y and z position, and the last states the time.

The conclusion of all this: Reference frames determine the observations made by observers. Katherine observes the eraser moving horizontally as well as vertically; the professor sees it move only vertically.

You may object: But does the professor not know he is moving? Should he not factor in his motion? Consider throwing an eraser up and down and catching it. Did you catch it at (roughly) the same position? In your reference frame, perhaps your classroom, the answer is "yes". But to an observer watching from the Moon, the answer is no, since the Earth is moving relative to the Moon.

There is no correct inertial reference frame. Katherine cannot say her reference frame is better than the reference frame used by the professor. Measurements of position, time and other values made by either observer are equally valid.

In your earlier studies, you were asked to assume that the time intervals in each reference frame were identical. At the speed the professor is moving, and to the hundredth of the second, the two observers measure the same time interval. However, if the professor were moving at, say, 75% of the speed of light, the time intervals would be quite distinct. Discussing how measured time intervals change as the observers' relative speeds approach the speed of light is a major topic in this chapter.

35.2 - Events and observers

Event: Something that can be pinpointed using position coordinates and time.

Observer: Person who records where and when an event occurs in a particular reference frame.

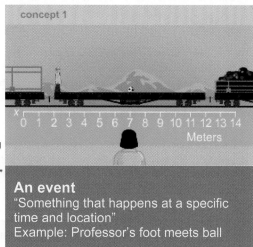

An event
"Something that happens at a specific time and location"
Example: Professor's foot meets ball

The definition of an event may accord with your own sense of the word – it is something that occurs at a specific place and time. A bat striking a ball is an event; the ball striking the glove of a fan in the bleachers is another event. In physics, a "Saturday night dance" is **not** an event, since it does not occur at a specific time or a specific enough location.

In the illustrations to the right, we consider a single event: The professor on the train kicks a soccer ball. He is standing on a train that is moving at a constant velocity on the track. Another observer, Sara, stands on the ground and observes the same event, the professor kicking the soccer ball. An observer is someone who records when and where something occurs in a reference frame.

Both agree that the professor kicked the soccer ball, and that it rolls along the train. But they use different reference frames to describe where and when the soccer ball was kicked.

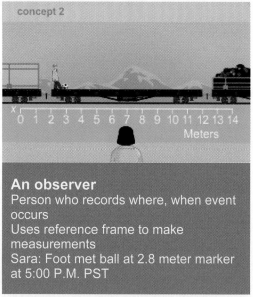

An observer
Person who records where, when event occurs
Uses reference frame to make measurements
Sara: Foot met ball at 2.8 meter marker at 5:00 P.M. PST

In Concept 2, you see the position and time of the event described using Sara's reference frame. She uses a set of position markers on the ground. (You can see markers like this, though at a scale greater than meters, on railroad tracks and highways). In her reference frame, the ball was kicked at the position 2.8 meters, and her watch tells her it was kicked at 5:00 PM Pacific Standard Time.

In Concept 3, we show the same event, but now the professor describes it using his reference frame. He measures position using a scale on the train. Using that reference frame, he states that he kicked the ball at the position 0.7 meters. He also has not changed his watch since he set out on his journey, so his watch tells him that he kicked the ball at 8:00 PM Eastern Standard Time.

These two sets of observations can be reconciled, but they illustrate how the reference frames of the two observers determine the coordinates of the observations they make. Both sets of observations are equally valid, given the reference frames of the observers, but they do differ. They provide a starting point in special relativity: Reference frames play an essential role in the observations made by observers.

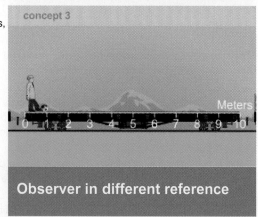

Observer in different reference

frame
Observers in different reference frames make different observations
Professor: Foot met ball at position 0.7 meters at 8:00 P.M. EST

35.3 - Light can travel through a vacuum

As the 20th century dawned, the topic of how light travels generated much debate in the physics community. The evidence brought to bear on this debate helped Einstein to confirm one of his central insights: The speed of light in a vacuum is constant. The speed of light does not depend on the motion of its source or of the observer. This conclusion is one of Einstein's two postulates; the experiments that enabled him to deduce this are an interesting story in the history of science.

The primary experiment that propelled Einstein toward his conclusion was not intended to lead to conclusions about the speed of light. Rather, it was an experiment about the existence and nature of the medium through which light travels. Earlier observations had convinced scientists that light acted as a wave. Experiments had shown that a beam of light spreads out (diffracts) in the same manner as a wave of water, and that light produces interference patterns that are consistent with the patterns caused by waves as well.

Since physicists knew light acted as a wave, they went in search of the medium in which it traveled. They reasoned that waves always move through some form of medium − water, the wire of a Slinky®, the strings of a violin. However, the medium for light was mysterious. Scientists were puzzled by the fact that light travels through the near vacuum of space, where there apparently is no medium. Physicists assumed there must be a medium, and called this elusive medium the *ether*. They assumed the ether permeated the universe, including the Earth's atmosphere.

Some physicists were skeptical about the existence of the ether. Nonetheless, they looked for ways to measure its attributes. Two clever American physicists, Albert Michelson and Edward Morley, conducted an experiment that played a key role in proving that ether did **not** exist.

Michelson and Morley reasoned: If light travels in a medium, it should move faster when traveling in the same direction as that medium and slower when traveling against it. In other words, light should act like a swimmer in the ocean: An observer on the ground would see the swimmer moving faster when swimming with the current and slower against it.

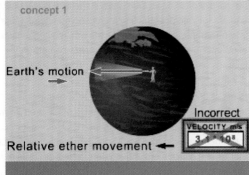

concept 1

Earth's motion

Relative ether movement ←

Incorrect
VELOCITY m/s
3.1 * 10⁸

Light travels through vacuum
If light traveled through ether
· It would travel faster when moving with the ether

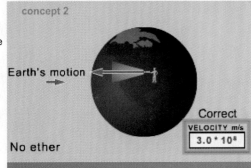

concept 2

Earth's motion

Correct
VELOCITY m/s
3.0 * 10⁸

No ether

Light travels through vacuum
No difference in speed measured
· There is no ether. The speed of light is constant

The most prevalent theory of ether stated that it was stationary and the Earth moved through it. An object stationary on the Earth would be moving through the ether. Michelson and Morley decided to measure the speed of light when the light was moving in different directions relative to the Earth's motion around the Sun. If ether existed, the speed of light would be different, and would be slowest when it moved in the same direction as the Earth's motion through the ether.

Here is an analogy that may make this clearer. Imagine two birds flying at the same speed in opposite directions, while you observe them from a slow-moving train, with the train's motion causing you to feel air in your face. If the train is moving in the same direction as one of the birds, that bird will appear to fly slower than the other bird. The birds are like light, the air is like the ether, and the train is like the Earth.

The two physicists searched for changes in the speed of light using an apparatus now known as a Michelson interferometer. Michelson estimated that the Earth's motion through the ether would cause a change in the speed of light on the order of 30,000 m/s. The interferometer was capable of detecting this 0.01% change in the speed of light.

Michelson made multiple observations, measuring the speed of light with different orientations relative to the Earth's rotation and motion around the Sun. He observed no changes in its speed. As he tersely summarized: "The result of the hypothesis of a stationary ether [with respect to the Earth] is thus shown to be incorrect." (Michelson also considered the case that the ether was dragged along with the Earth; this possibility was later shown to be false as well.)

Michelson's conclusion was correct. His experiment indicated that the effects expected when waves propagate through a moving medium did **not** occur. Despite some efforts to revive the theory of ether, the clarity and simplicity of Michelson's experiment was a major and conclusive blow to the theory of ether.

If this experiment had proven only that light could travel in a vacuum, disproving the existence of the ether, it would have been a landmark in the history of science. But Einstein realized that something even more interesting was being shown by the experiment: The motion of the equipment was not affecting the observed speed of light in the way classical physics predicted it should. As the light moved in the interferometer, the equipment itself was moving, which according to the physics as Einstein had learned it should alter the effects of the experiment. In other words, even without an ether, the equipment itself was moving, and that should have affected the measurement of the light.

In his 1905 paper on special relativity, Einstein wrote, "...the unsuccessful attempts to discover any motion of the Earth relative to the 'light medium,' suggest that the phenomena of electrodynamics as well as of mechanics possess no properties corresponding to the idea of absolute rest." Michelson's experiment helped Einstein to formulate his second postulate: The speed of light is absolute; it does not depend on the reference frame. It also supported Einstein's first postulate. If the ether frame existed, the laws of light propagation would have been different in that frame, which would have contradicted the requirement that the forms of the laws of physics be the same for all observers in inertial reference frames.

35.4 - Simultaneity, or the lack thereof

concept 1

Simultaneity
Events perceived as simultaneous in one reference frame
Not simultaneous in another

Einstein's simultaneity thought experiment: The relative motion of two observers determines whether they perceive two events as simultaneous.

One of the consequences of Einstein's postulates is that the perception of "simultaneous" events is relative to an observer's reference frame. Einstein demonstrated that his postulates proved that two observers would disagree on how much time elapsed between two events, or on whether two events occurred simultaneously. In this, he disagreed with Sir Isaac Newton. Newton had stated: "Absolute, true and mathematical time, of itself, and from its own nature, flows equably without relation to anything external." Einstein was to prove this wrong.

To make his point, he used a specific means to define simultaneity, noting that if an observer sees two events that are the same distance away occurring at the same moment in time, she thinks the two events occurred at the same moment in time. It

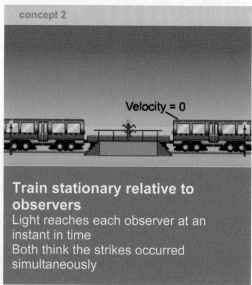

concept 2

Velocity = 0

Train stationary relative to observers
Light reaches each observer at an instant in time
Both think the strikes occurred simultaneously

seems a commonsense conclusion that another observer, also equidistant from the events, would see them occurring simultaneously. Einstein's genius lay in challenging this conclusion. He created a scenario showing that the relative motion of two observers influenced whether they perceived two events as occurring simultaneously, or as occurring one after the other.

Einstein made his case in part with a famous "*gedanken* experiment," or "thought experiment." A thought experiment is one that is conducted in the mind, as opposed to in a laboratory. Einstein used his thought experiment to make the following revolutionary point: *The measured length of time intervals differs when observers are in motion relative to one another.*

To state Einstein's thought experiment, we use a train and a platform beside the train. A professor stands still on an open railcar at the middle of the train. Another observer, Katherine, stands still at the middle of the platform. Two lightning rods, shown as gray towers in Concept 2 and Concept 3, are equidistant from Katherine and the midpoint of the platform.

We start this experiment with the train not moving, and the professor directly across from Katherine, so he is also equidistant from the lightning rods. A lightning bolt strikes each lightning rod. These lightning strikes cause flashes of light that will be visible to the observers. Photons − packets of light − move from each lightning rod toward them. Each lightning strike counts as one of the two spatially separated events we are analyzing. We draw the photons from one rod in blue, and the photons from the other rod in red, so that you can more easily distinguish them.

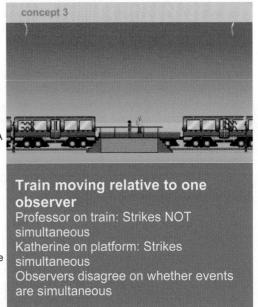

concept 3

Train moving relative to one observer
Professor on train: Strikes NOT simultaneous
Katherine on platform: Strikes simultaneous
Observers disagree on whether events are simultaneous

When will an observer conclude that the two events are simultaneous? The professor concludes that the bolts struck simultaneously **only** if two photons reach him at exactly the same moment. Why? Since both travel the same distance, the events are equidistant from him. The professor reasons that if the photons reach him simultaneously after traveling the same distance at the same speed, they must have started their journey simultaneously.

Katherine also concludes that the bolts struck simultaneously **only** if two photons reach her at a single instant in time. She too believes the events occurred simultaneously if two photons, traveling the same distance and the same speed, reach her simultaneously.

All this is "as expected". Two lightning bolts strike rods, photons from the strike reach each observer simultaneously, and they conclude that the two bolts struck simultaneously because the photons traveled the same distance to each observer at the same speed. This situation is shown in Concept 2, as the photons reach Katherine and the professor.

Now, Einstein changed the scenario: He put the train in motion. Einstein asked again: would they both say that the lightning bolts struck simultaneously? That the time interval between the events was zero?

The answer, as illustrated by Concept 3 is: No. In the scenario we show, Katherine still states that the lightning bolts struck simultaneously because both photons reach her simultaneously. However, as you can see, the photons from the strike on the right have reached the professor, but those on the left have not. His conclusion is that the strike on the right occurred before the strike on the left.

Although they cannot be readily seen in the illustration, this time we have the strikes make slight scorch marks on the train. The professor can later walk up and down the train and reassure himself that the distance between each strike and his position as an observer is the same.

Einstein's thought experiment with the train showed that the perception of the time interval between events depends on the observer's frame of reference. Specifically, he showed how two events that are perceived as occurring simultaneously in one reference frame would be perceived as occurring at two different moments in time (non-simultaneously) in another reference frame that is in motion with respect to the first.

Both observers were correct, based on observations in their own reference frames. This phenomenon is called the **relativity of simultaneity**. It means that time intervals between events − something that Newton assumed was absolute − are actually relative, that is, they vary depending on an observer's state of motion.

As Einstein wrote: "Are two events (e.g. the two strokes of lightning A and B) which are simultaneous *with reference to the railway embankment* also simultaneous *relatively to the train*? We shall show directly that the answer must be negative."

An observer's measurement of time intervals depends on his or her frame of reference. Time is relative. Motion alters time. This is a strange conclusion, but it is true, and it changes our view of the universe. Few thought about it before Einstein, because in his day, the effect was inaccessible to measurements at the low speeds humans were accustomed to observing. For instance, for a jogger moving at several meters per second past a stationary observer, the difference is negligible (about one part in 10^{16}), but the effect becomes much more significant as the relative speed between two observers increases.

Since Einstein's time, technological advances have made it necessary to factor this effect into the design of certain systems. You may have seen or used a Global Positioning System (GPS) unit, which receives signals from a network of orbiting satellites to pinpoint its location on the Earth's surface. The lightning strikes we considered are analogous to the signals that are emitted by satellites. The GPS unit works by interpreting the time delays in the electromagnetic signals that are received from these fast-moving satellites whose positions are precisely known. Relativistic considerations play a central role in making the system work.

35.5 - Interactive problem: Conduct Einstein's simultaneity experiment

There are two simulations to the right. In the first, the professor, Katherine and the train are all stationary. In the second, the professor and the train move.

As discussed before, lightning bolts strike each lightning rod. These lightning strikes cause flashes of light that will be visible to the observers. Photons − packets of light − move from the position of each lightning rod toward them. Each lightning strike counts as one of the two spatially separated events we are analyzing. We draw the photons from one rod in blue, and the photons from the other rod in red, so that you can easily distinguish them.

The lightning bolts also scorch the sides of the train as they hit the rods. The professor can use these scorch marks to confirm that the two events are equidistant from the train's center where he is standing.

Press GO to launch the lightning strikes. The simulations run in extreme slow motion. We have slowed time down by a factor of more than fifty million to clearly show what is happening.

The first simulation is in Katherine's reference frame. The second simulation starts in Katherine's reference frame. You can view the same events in the professor's reference frame by pressing the "Professor's reference frame" tab.

Try each simulation. Do Katherine and the professor observe the lightning bolts as striking the lightning rods simultaneously when the train is stationary? When the train is moving?

In order to let you experiment further with this thought experiment, both simulations contain a feature on the control panel that allows you to adjust the interval of time that Katherine observes between the lightning strikes. You can use this controller to see how she and the professor observe the events as this interval changes. For instance, you can cause there to be a five-nanosecond interval of time between when one photon reaches her and the next photon reaches her. This lets you go beyond Einstein's thought experiment, where the time interval in Katherine's reference frame was always zero and she observed the lightning strikes as occurring simultaneously.

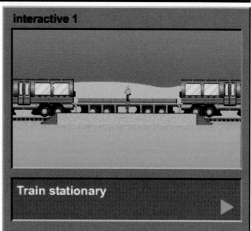

interactive 1

Train stationary

interactive 2

Train moves past Katherine

In the second simulation, can you adjust the time interval in Katherine's reference frame to cause the photons to arrive at the same instant at the professor's location? If you cause this to happen, what does Katherine now observe? Can you cause them to both believe the strikes occurred simultaneously when the train is moving? (Hint: Do not spend too much time trying!).

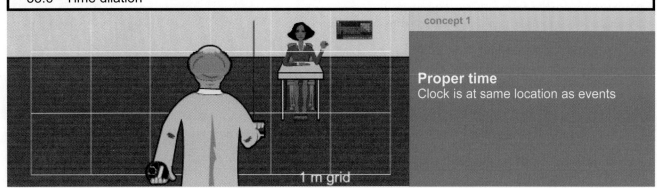

1 m grid

concept 1

Proper time
Clock is at same location as events

Time dilation: A clock moving relative to an observer runs more slowly, measuring longer time intervals, than clocks at rest relative to the observer.

Einstein pondered: If the speed of light is constant, what does this imply? He concluded that it means that things we think of as absolute – like the time interval between events – must be "relative."

Consider the professor and the student, Katherine, in the diagrams above and on the right. The professor moves rapidly through the classroom on his skateboard. He throws and catches the ball, using his stopwatch to measure the time interval between the throw and the catch. You see this illustrated in Concept 1.

Katherine watches all this and measures the time between the throw and the catch using her stopwatch. This is shown in Concept 2.

If they compare their observations afterwards and had incredibly precise equipment, Katherine will discover that she measured more time passing between the two events than the professor does with his stopwatch. If the professor moves at everyday speeds as we show above, the effect will be very small, far too small to be measured on any typical stopwatch. But if the professor were moving past at 87% of the speed of the light, Katherine would measure over twice as much time between the two events as the professor does.

The professor's time is said to be "dilated", which means it is passing more slowly. This is not due to some malfunctioning nor change in functioning of his clock. Any clock in his frame, including the professor's "biological clock", will record less time passing.

Time dilation can be quantified, as the equation at the right shows. To understand the equation you must understand another term: *proper time*. The proper time between two events is the time measured by a clock in the reference frame where the two events occur in the same place. "Proper" comes from the German for the events' "own time". The proper time is measured with a single clock, which is at rest in the reference frame in which the events occur at the same *xyz* coordinates. The professor's stopwatch measures the proper time.

Another observer, the student Katherine in this case, watches the professor (and his stopwatch) pass by at a velocity *v*. On the right side of the equation is the proper time interval, t_0. Katherine measures an interval of time *t* between the events.

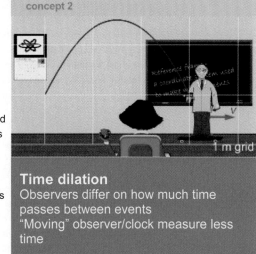

concept 2

1 m grid

Time dilation
Observers differ on how much time passes between events
"Moving" observer/clock measure less time

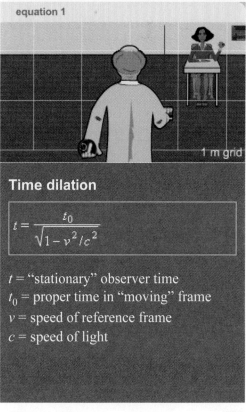

equation 1

1 m grid

Time dilation

$$t = \frac{t_0}{\sqrt{1 - v^2/c^2}}$$

t = "stationary" observer time
t_0 = proper time in "moving" frame
v = speed of reference frame
c = speed of light

We also present the equation in another way. The term that multiplies the proper time, that is, the reciprocal of the square root term, is frequently used in relativity. It is represented by the Greek letter γ (gamma) and is called the *Lorentz factor*.

Physicists have confirmed the principle of time dilation by many methods, such as studying muons. *Muons* are subatomic particles that have an average *half life* of about 2.2 microseconds. That is, in a sample of muons that are stationary relative to an observer, half of them will decay (change) into other particles during this interval of time.

Fast-moving muons are produced when cosmic rays enter the Earth's atmosphere and collide at high speeds with atoms there. The muons travel toward the ground at about $0.999c$. Scientists observe that these moving muons decay more slowly than stationary muons.

Why? The fraction of muons that decay is a function of time, and less time elapses in the reference frame of the moving muons. In fact, time passes about 22 times more slowly in the moving muons' reference frame. If 2.2 μs have passed according to the scientists' clock, then only 0.1 μs have passed in the moving muon reference frame, which is a time interval much shorter than the half life of the muons. The scientists see that far less than one-half of the muons have decayed in 2.2 μs, and conclude that the moving muons decay more slowly. In the reference frame of the muons, the decay rate is unchanged. Time dilation explains the discrepancy.

You can confirm the "22 times" ratio using the time dilation equation. The proper time is being measured by the muons' "clock", which is observed via their decay rate.

Experiments with highly precise clocks have also confirmed Einstein's conclusions concerning the effect of motion on time. For instance, scientists have measured a difference in the time interval measured by a clock in a plane to that measured by a clock on the ground. Einstein's general theory of relativity and its predictions figure prominently into the results, but his two theories account for the discrepancies between the time intervals measured by the clocks.

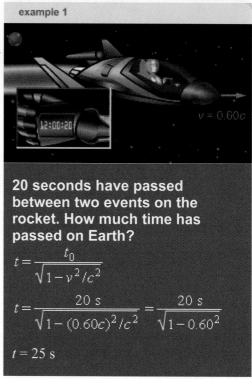

$$t = \gamma t_0$$

$$\gamma = \frac{1}{\sqrt{1 - v^2/c^2}}$$

example 1

v = 0.60c

12:00:20

20 seconds have passed between two events on the rocket. How much time has passed on Earth?

$$t = \frac{t_0}{\sqrt{1 - v^2/c^2}}$$

$$t = \frac{20 \text{ s}}{\sqrt{1 - (0.60c)^2/c^2}} = \frac{20 \text{ s}}{\sqrt{1 - 0.60^2}}$$

$$t = 25 \text{ s}$$

Do you experience time dilation? Yes, but very small amounts of it, given how slowly you move compared to the speed of light. Using the equation to the right, you could determine that if you travel for an hour in an airplane flying at 1000 km/h, you would have aged about 0.0000000015 (that is, 1.5×10^{-9}) seconds less than a person who remained stationary on the ground. To provide another sense of the magnitudes, if you moved at a speed of 90 km/hr away from a twin for a 100-year lifespan, you would have lived 11 microseconds less. On the other hand, if you could move at one-tenth the speed of light during a century of his life, you would be six months younger, and if you moved at 90 percent of the speed of light, 270,000,000 meters every second, you would be 44 years old when he was 100.

35.7 - Exploring and deriving time dilation

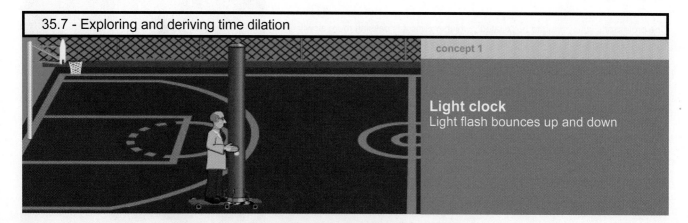

concept 1

Light clock
Light flash bounces up and down

We will use the experiment portrayed on the right to derive the equation for time dilation. Following the steps of the derivation may also help you to understand how Einstein's postulates lead inescapably to the conclusion that time dilation occurs.

The experiment uses a light-based clock mounted on a high-speed skateboard. Ordinary clocks use periodic mechanical or electric processes, such as the oscillation of a pendulum or a timing circuit, to establish a unit of time. A *light clock* uses the amount of time it takes a pulse of light to travel a particular distance. The light clock is convenient to use in this scenario, but any clock would record the same result.

A light pulse is emitted from the base of the clock. The pulse reflects off the top of the clock and returns to the bottom. The clock measures time by using the relationship of time to distance and speed. The elapsed time for the up-and-down journey equals the distance the light pulse travels, divided by the speed of light.

In our experiment, let's consider one "tick" of the clock. The light rises from the bottom of the clock, reflects off the top, and returns to the bottom. The professor, who is also on the skateboard, sees the light pulse moving straight up and down, and he measures the distance it travels as being twice the height of the clock.

Now, let's consider what another observer sees. Katherine is standing on the ground and watches the professor and the clock pass by. She also watches the light pulse as it moves. However, she measures a different value for the distance traveled by the light pulse. She sees it not only moving up and down, but also forward. She measures the light pulse moving through the distance indicated by the two lines labeled s in Concept 3.

If this seems confusing, just think of a friend riding a train, throwing a ball straight up and down. From your friend's perspective, the ball just travels up and down. From a vantage point on the ground outside, you would see the ball moving horizontally at the same time it is moving up and down.

The clock uses light, which according to Einstein's second postulate has a **constant speed** independent of any frame of reference. Einstein's first postulate states that the **laws of physics are the same** in any inertial reference frame. That is, in our scenario, both observers can use the same equation: Time equals the distance traveled by the pulse, divided by the speed of light.

Having explained the experiment, we will now analyze it algebraically, calculating the distance traveled by the clock and the time interval required for one tick of the clock in each frame of reference. This will enable us to derive the equation for time dilation shown in Equation 1.

Variables

We will use the triangle shown to the right in Equation 1 to relate displacement, speed and a time interval. The triangle reflects half of one tick of the light pulse, as it moves from the bottom to the top. The clock moves L horizontally during half of one tick, and Katherine observes the light moving a distance s.

Professor's reference frame
Light moves strictly up and down

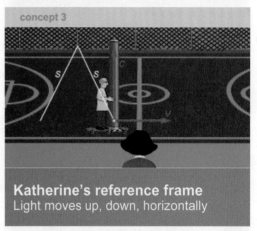

Katherine's reference frame
Light moves up, down, horizontally

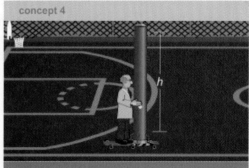

Time measurements differ
Time = distance / speed of light
Katherine, professor measure different distances
Speed of light is constant
Katherine, professor measure different time

	measured by Katherine	measured by professor
clock's horizontal displacement, half tick	L	0 m
distance light pulse moves, half tick	s	h
clock's speed	v	0 m/s
height of clock	h	h
elapsed time	t	t_0
speed of light	$c = 3.00 \times 10^8$ m/s	

Strategy

1. Use the Pythagorean theorem to determine the distance the light pulse moves in one tick as measured by Katherine.

2. Use the fact that distance equals the product of speed and time to replace the distances in the diagram.

3. Simplify the equation.

Mathematics principle

We will use the Pythagorean theorem

$$c = \sqrt{a^2 + b^2}$$

Step-by-step derivation

In Katherine's reference frame, the light traces out the hypotenuses of two right triangles. We use the Pythagorean theorem to calculate the hypotenuse. The triangle's height is calculated using the speed of light and the time measured by the professor. Its base is calculated using Katherine's measurement of the clock's speed.

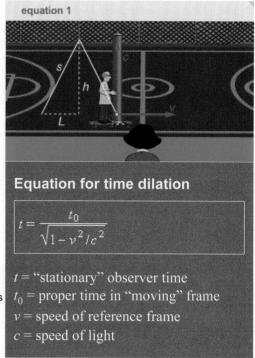

equation 1

Equation for time dilation

$$t = \frac{t_0}{\sqrt{1 - v^2/c^2}}$$

t = "stationary" observer time
t_0 = proper time in "moving" frame
v = speed of reference frame
c = speed of light

Step		Reason
1.	$s = \sqrt{h^2 + L^2}$	Pythagorean theorem
2.	$2s = \sqrt{(2h)^2 + (2L)^2}$	light travels two hypotenuses
3.	$2h = ct_0$	definition of speed
4.	$2L = vt$	definition of speed
5.	$2s = \sqrt{(ct_0)^2 + (vt)^2}$	substitute equations 3 and 4 into equation 2

We have one last distance left, and again we substitute for it using the speed equation. Then a series of algebraic steps yield the equation for time dilation.

Step	Reason
6. $2s = ct$	definition of speed
7. $c^2 t^2 = (ct_0)^2 + (vt)^2$	substitute equation 6 into equation 5; square both sides
8. $c^2 t^2 - v^2 t^2 = c^2 t_0^2$	expand and re-arrange
9. $t^2 = \dfrac{c^2 t_0^2}{(c^2 - v^2)} = \dfrac{t_0^2}{(1 - v^2/c^2)}$	divide both sides by $c^2 - v^2$; simplify
10. $t = \dfrac{t_0}{\sqrt{1 - v^2/c^2}}$	take square root

35.8 - Interactive problem: Experiment with the light clock

In this simulation, you experiment with a light clock. The professor rolls across a basketball court with a light clock on his skateboard, while Katherine watches from the side. You will view the light clock in operation from the professor's reference frame, and from the student's reference frame. You are asked to calculate the time measured by each observer for the professor to cross the basketball court.

The simulation launches in the professor's reference frame, where the light clock is stationary. Press GO and watch the basketball court and the background pass by. A counter will record the number of light clock cycles, the number of round trip journeys made by the light pulse. The clock is 3.0 m tall.

Then press the tab labeled "Student's reference frame" and press GO again. You will see the same series of events from Katherine's reference frame. The simulation displays the path of the light and indicates some key distances in a fashion similar to the derivation of the prior section.

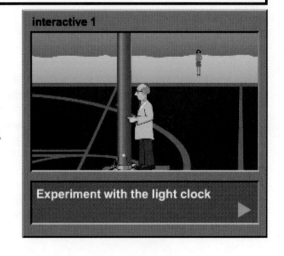

interactive 1

Experiment with the light clock

If you asked the professor how long it took him to cross the basketball court, what would he say? What if you asked Katherine the same question? Check your answers by entering them in the simulation.

Now a thought question for you, foreshadowing a future topic. Katherine measures the length of this court as 24.0 m (alas, she does not have an NBA standard court). You can use this length and the time she measures to determine the professor's speed. This is the same speed the professor would measure of the ground moving beneath him.

Let's say the professor decided to use the time he measures and this speed to determine how long the court is. How long does he think the court is? Does he think it is shorter or longer than 24.0 m?

Length contraction: The length of an object is less when it is moving relative to an observer than when it is stationary.

Einstein's postulates require that time dilates – observers measure different time intervals between two events when their reference frames are in relative motion. The postulates also require that length "contract". The length of an object will be less when it is moving relative to an observer than when it is stationary. (You will see that the effect is far too small to measure for everyday speeds, which is why you do not notice this effect.)

Consider the train scenario on the right. The train is moving rapidly past an observer at $0.8c$. This is not an everyday speed for even a bullet train. The professor is onboard the train, at rest relative to it. He measures the length of his car as 10 meters. This is the car's *proper length*, the length measured by an observer stationary relative to the length being measured. The use of proper here is analogous to the use of proper in "proper time".

Sara, standing on the ground, measures a different value. She measures the train car as being just six meters long. The relative motion of the two observers causes the differing measurement.

The equation on the right quantifies length contraction. This equation converts the proper length measured by an observer who is stationary relative to the length being measured, to the length observed by an observer who views the object as moving.

As with time dilation, you face two challenges: First, believing it to be true, since it defies your intuition and experience, and second, understanding the notation for the equation. We are not sure how much we can change your intuition, but at the least we can work on the notation. To stress the notation once more: The proper length (L_0) on the right side of the equation is the length measured in a reference frame stationary relative to the object being measured. In the illustration, it is the professor measuring the length of the car.

The quantity L on the left-hand side of the equation represents the length that will be measured by a person who views the object (and its reference frame) as moving. This person observes the object as moving at velocity v.

Length contraction occurs only along the direction of the relative motion. In the scenario in this section, only the car's length changes, not its height nor depth. If the train were carrying a light clock, the **vertical** dimension of the clock, used by onboard travelers to measure time intervals, would not be affected by length contraction.

Does the moving object "really" contract? Well, to pose an analogous question from everyday life, do faraway objects really get smaller, as they appear to our eyes? The observations and measurements made by different observers do differ. In discussions of relativity, much focus is placed on observers and measurements, since experiments show effects such as time dilation and length contraction are real.

On the other hand, we are taking liberties in showing the object's contraction in these illustrations. If the train car were photographed from a station as it passed by, it would appear rotated. The rear of the car is farther away from the stationary observer, and light from the rear will take longer to reach her than light from the front of the vehicle.

concept 1

Length contraction
Observer stationary with respect to object measures one length

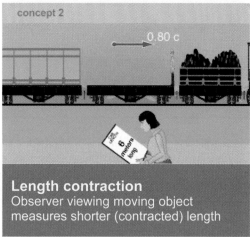

concept 2

0.80 c

Length contraction
Observer viewing moving object measures shorter (contracted) length

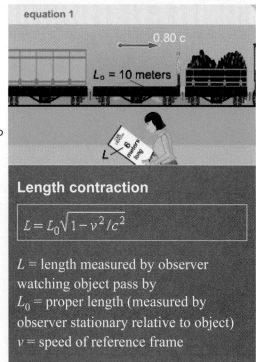

equation 1

0.80 c

L_0 = 10 meters

Length contraction

$$L = L_0 \sqrt{1 - v^2/c^2}$$

L = length measured by observer watching object pass by
L_0 = proper length (measured by observer stationary relative to object)
v = speed of reference frame

The light that arrives simultaneously for the observer is emitted at different instants in time from the car, which moves during that interval of time. Using geometrical arguments, it can be shown that this effect creates the perception of rotation.

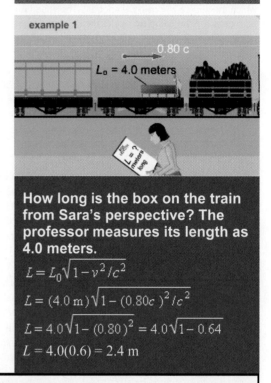

c = speed of light

example 1

How long is the box on the train from Sara's perspective? The professor measures its length as 4.0 meters.

$$L = L_0 \sqrt{1 - v^2/c^2}$$

$$L = (4.0 \text{ m}) \sqrt{1 - (0.80c)^2/c^2}$$

$$L = 4.0 \sqrt{1 - (0.80)^2} = 4.0 \sqrt{1 - 0.64}$$

$$L = 4.0(0.6) = 2.4 \text{ m}$$

35.10 - Doppler shift for light

concept 1

Doppler shift: light
Motion changes light frequency (color)
Shift depends on velocity between source, observer

The Doppler effect is frequently thought of in terms of sound. The siren on a police car heading toward you will sound different than when it is moving away from you. This effect occurs because the motion of the siren changes the frequency of the sound waves that reach you.

The change in the frequency depends on whether you move toward the source of a sound, or the source moves toward you. There is an asymmetry because sound travels through a medium, and it matters which reference frame – yours or the source's – is stationary with respect to the medium.

In contrast, light requires no medium. With light (and other electromagnetic radiation), the Doppler effect depends solely on the relative motion of the source of the light and the observer of the light. In some ways, this makes the Doppler shift "easier" to calculate with light.

concept 2

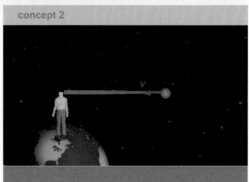

Light source closing in
Blue shift

On the right, we show equations for calculating the change in perceived frequency due to the Doppler shift. The symbol f_0 represents the frequency of the light as it is emitted from the source (or as it would be perceived by an observer stationary relative to the source). This is called the *proper frequency*. The symbol f represents the frequency perceived by an observer in a reference frame in which the source is moving at speed v. The speed is always positive. The two equations are the same except for the signs; the signs differ for the reasons discussed below.

When the observer and the source are moving toward one other, the frequency of the light seen by the observer will increase. The speed of the wave – the speed of light – must remain constant. Since the wavelength equals the speed of light divided by the frequency, then as the frequency increases, the wavelength decreases. When the source is moving away from the observer, the opposite effect occurs: The wave frequency decreases and the wavelength increases.

With light, decreasing wavelength due to the approach of the light source is called a *blue shift* since shorter wavelengths occur near the blue end of the visible spectrum. Increasing wavelength due to the recession of the light source is called a *red shift*. Almost all distant stars and galaxies, in whatever direction you look, exhibit red shift. In fact, the farther away they are, the greater the red shift. This is used as evidence that the universe is expanding.

The Doppler effect proved to be crucial to astronomers trying to understand the nature of the universe. Einstein's work provided grounds for believing that the universe was expanding, an implication that proved quite troubling to Einstein himself, who "corrected" his equations to provide for a static universe. But several years after Einstein performed this correction, the American astronomer Edwin Hubble (1889–1953) showed that distant stars and galaxies exhibit a red shift.

Astronomers like Hubble were trained to expect certain patterns in the light emanating from stars. Elements like calcium in the atmospheres of stars absorb certain wavelengths of light; these show up as "gaps" – *spectral lines* – in the light emitted from stars. Hubble expected those spectral lines to occur at certain wavelengths. Instead, he found them "red shifted" to different wavelengths. Although Hubble knew that the Doppler shift could account for these changes, he and his colleagues were astonished that stars in every direction were moving away.

The debate about the nature and fate of the universe continues; but the red shift of starlight provided crucial data to scientists that caused them to further examine the possibility that the universe is expanding. The second sample problem to the right challenges you to compute the speed at which a galaxy is moving away from the Earth based on the shift in its observed wavelength.

concept 3

Light source moving away
Red shift

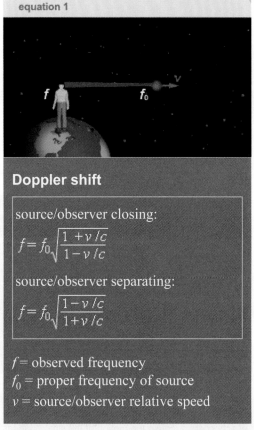

equation 1

f f_0

Doppler shift

source/observer closing:

$$f = f_0 \sqrt{\frac{1 + v/c}{1 - v/c}}$$

source/observer separating:

$$f = f_0 \sqrt{\frac{1 - v/c}{1 + v/c}}$$

f = observed frequency
f_0 = proper frequency of source
v = source/observer relative speed

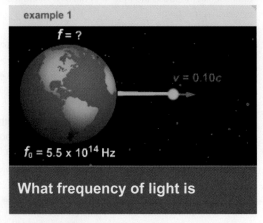

example 1

$f = ?$

$v = 0.10c$

$f_0 = 5.5 \times 10^{14}$ Hz

What frequency of light is

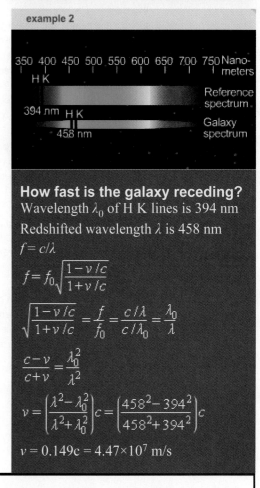

observed on Earth?

$$f = f_0 \sqrt{\frac{1 - v/c}{1 + v/c}}$$

$$f = (5.5 \times 10^{14}) \sqrt{\frac{1 - (0.10c)/c}{1 + (0.10c)/c}}$$

$$f = (5.5 \times 10^{14}) \sqrt{\frac{0.9}{1.1}}$$

$$f = 5.0 \times 10^{14} \text{ Hz}$$

example 2

350 400 450 500 550 600 650 700 750 Nano-meters
H K

394 nm H K   Reference spectrum

458 nm   Galaxy spectrum

How fast is the galaxy receding?

Wavelength λ_0 of H K lines is 394 nm

Redshifted wavelength λ is 458 nm

$$f = c/\lambda$$

$$f = f_0 \sqrt{\frac{1 - v/c}{1 + v/c}}$$

$$\sqrt{\frac{1 - v/c}{1 + v/c}} = \frac{f}{f_0} = \frac{c/\lambda}{c/\lambda_0} = \frac{\lambda_0}{\lambda}$$

$$\frac{c - v}{c + v} = \frac{\lambda_0^2}{\lambda^2}$$

$$v = \left(\frac{\lambda^2 - \lambda_0^2}{\lambda^2 + \lambda_0^2}\right) c = \left(\frac{458^2 - 394^2}{458^2 + 394^2}\right) c$$

$$v = 0.149c = 4.47 \times 10^7 \text{ m/s}$$

35.11 - Relativistic linear momentum

In discussing relativistic linear momentum, and the equations that describe it, we start with three premises.

First, the same laws of physics hold true in any inertial reference frame. This is Einstein's first postulate. If a property like momentum is conserved in one inertial reference frame, it must be conserved in any other inertial reference frame.

Second, Einstein's second postulate, that the speed of light is constant. These two postulates were used to deduce equations for time dilation, length contraction and so on.

Third, we expect that at much lower speeds, the equations in this section will essentially reduce to the "classical" ones that work perfectly well at low speeds. For instance, the momentum of an object moving at say 30 m/s should very, very closely equal mv. This has held true with prior equations in this chapter. At speeds much less than the speed of light, the equations predict results that accord with "classic" mechanics equations.

These three premises are satisfied by the relativistic equation for momentum at the right. This extended equation for momentum is required because it can be shown that if Newtonian, or classical, momentum is conserved in one reference frame, then when the velocities are converted to the values that would be observed in another frame, the total momentum is never conserved in that second reference frame.

Specifically, if a collision occurs in a moving reference frame S', and the velocities are converted to the values that would be observed in S, the quantity mv before and after the collision is changed by the collision. Using the equation shown to the right ensures this will not occur, and that momentum is conserved when the collision is observed from any reference frame.

The larger the relative speed of the frames, the greater the discrepancy between the classical momentum and the relativistic momentum will be. It turns out that the Lorentz factor γ appearing in the definition of momentum shown in Equation 1 provides exactly the right corrective factor for momentum to be conserved in both S and S', no matter how fast the frames move with respect to each other. (The variable u in the formula refers to the speed of an object in its frame, not the speed of one frame with respect to another.)

The extended momentum equation obeys the first two premises stated above. It also obeys the third. At velocities much less than the speed of light, momentum approaches mv, since dividing the square of a velocity like 300 m/s by the square of speed of light means the relativistic effect is near nil.

As the example on the right shows, at half the speed of light, relativistic effects increase momentum by 15% over its classical value. The effect increases significantly as an object moves at speeds closer to the speed of light: At 99% of the speed of light, momentum is about seven times its classical value.

This phenomenon is of great importance in the modern physics research done with large particle accelerators, such as the Fermilab accelerator in Illinois, or the CERN accelerator in France and Switzerland. Objects move near the speed of light in these accelerators, and calculating their momentum requires the use of the equation shown in this section.

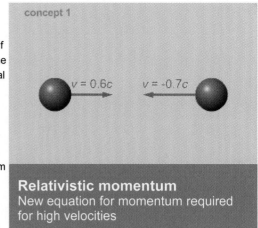

concept 1

Relativistic momentum
New equation for momentum required for high velocities

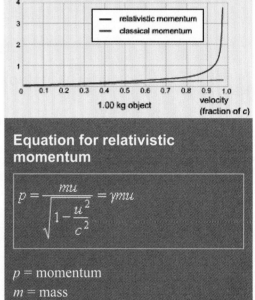

equation 1

Relativistic and classical momentum

Equation for relativistic momentum

$$p = \frac{mu}{\sqrt{1 - \dfrac{u^2}{c^2}}} = \gamma mu$$

p = momentum
m = mass
u = velocity of object
c = speed of light
γ = Lorentz factor

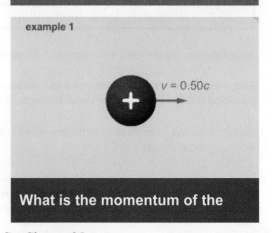

example 1

$v = 0.50c$

What is the momentum of the

proton? Its mass is 1.67×10⁻²⁷ kg.

$$p = \frac{mu}{\sqrt{1 - \dfrac{u^2}{c^2}}}$$

$$p = \frac{(1.67 \times 10^{-27}\ \text{kg})\,(1.50 \times 10^8\ \text{m/s})}{\sqrt{1 - ((0.500c)^2/c^2)}}$$

$$p = 2.89 \times 10^{-19}\ \text{kg·m/s}$$

(Relativistic effects add 15%)

35.12 - Mass and energy

The world's "most famous equation" is shown in Equation 1: *Rest energy* (also known as *mass energy*) equals mass times the speed of light squared. By "rest energy", we mean the energy equivalent of its mass.

If a mass is moving, its total relativistic energy can be calculated as the sum of this value and its kinetic energy. The equation for calculating this total energy is shown in Equation 2. The equation factors in relativistic effects when calculating KE.

It is interesting to consider Equation 1 in the context of the Sun. The Sun becomes less massive as its mass is transformed by fusion reactions into the energy it radiates. It radiates 3.91×10^{26} joules of energy per second, and as a consequence, it "loses" more than four billion kilograms per second! (But do not worry! Its total mass is 1.99×10^{30} kg).

Earlier scientists had proposed the conservation of mass in chemical reactions. This textbook has discussed the conservation of energy. At non-relativistic speeds, these principles hold true to a high degree of accuracy. Einstein showed both mass and energy must be considered when applying conservation principles.

Thermonuclear processes inside the sun convert a very large quantity of mass into a stupendous quantity of energy every second. Much more comprehensible amounts of matter yield tremendous amounts of energy as well. For example, if one gram of matter were converted entirely to energy, it would produce the energy equivalent of combusting fifteen thousand barrels of oil. On the dark side of things, converting into energy a tiny fraction of the 2 kg of matter in a nuclear bomb can produce a blast equivalent to the chemical energy released from the explosion of 50 billion kilograms of dynamite.

Atomic particles are often subject to relativistic effects because of their high speeds. For convenience, the energy and mass of such particles is often measured in units other than joules and kilograms. An electron volt (eV) equals the change in the potential energy of an elementary charge (1.60×10^{-19} C) when it moves through a potential difference of one volt. Electron volts are convenient measures of particle energy. Particle mass is often measured in units of eV/c^2, or energy divided by the speed of light squared. The fact that these are mass units follows from the equation $E = mc^2$.

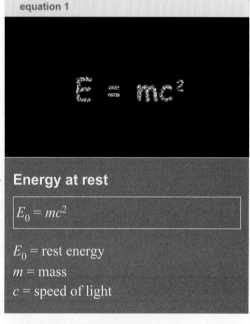

equation 1

$$E = mc^2$$

Energy at rest

$$E_0 = mc^2$$

E_0 = rest energy
m = mass
c = speed of light

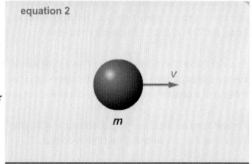

equation 2

v

m

Total energy

$$E = \gamma mc^2$$

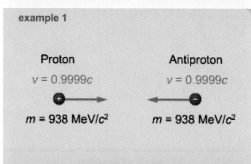

E = total energy
γ = Lorentz factor
m = rest mass
c = speed of light

example 1

Proton
$v = 0.9999c$

⊕ →

$m = 938 \text{ MeV}/c^2$

Antiproton
$v = 0.9999c$

← ⊖

$m = 938 \text{ MeV}/c^2$

When a proton and antiproton collide, they annihilate each other and their mass energy is converted into a pair of gamma ray photons. Calculate the total energy of the gamma rays.

$$\gamma = \frac{1}{\sqrt{1 - u^2/c^2}}$$

$$\gamma = \frac{1}{\sqrt{1 - (0.9999c)^2/c^2}} = 70.7$$

$$E = \gamma m c^2$$
$$E = (70.7)(938 \text{ MeV}/c^2)c^2$$
$$E = 6.63\times10^4 \text{ MeV}$$
$$2E = 1.33\times10^5 \text{ MeV}$$

35.13 - Gotchas

If you measure the speed of light from a star that is moving toward you, you will get a higher value than if you measure the speed of light from a star that is moving away from you. No! You will measure the same speed. The speed of light does not change based on motion of source or observer. This is one of Einstein's postulates.

You are flying from Earth to Alpha Centauri at a constant speed of 150,000,000 m/s. Given your incredible speed, you should expect some of the laws of physics to change. No, Einstein's other postulate is that the laws of physics are the same in any inertial reference frame. You are moving at a constant speed, so you are in an inertial reference frame.

I'm watching an airplane flying overhead at 400 km/hr. The pilot throws and catches a ball, measuring the time with a stopwatch. Her stopwatch measures the proper time. Yes, that is correct.

Since you are standing still as you watch the plane pass by, you measure its proper length. No. You have to be at rest relative to an object to measure its proper length. However, in the case of an airplane, the difference is negligible – not so for relativistic speeds!

Einstein was very smart. Yes.

Einstein radically changed our perception of space and time with his two postulates of special relativity. The first postulate states that the laws of physics are the same for observers in any inertial reference frame. The second postulate states that the speed of light in a vacuum is the same in all inertial reference frames.

An event is specified by giving its space and time coordinates. Observers who are in different inertial reference frames will assign different coordinates to the same event.

Observers in a reference frame where two events occur at the same place measure a time interval between those events called the proper time. Observers moving relative to that frame will always measure a longer time interval. This effect is known as time dilation.

The inability to agree on time intervals led to Einstein's thought experiment about the concept of simultaneity. In this thought experiment, he showed that observers in reference frames moving relative to one another would **not** agree that there was zero time interval between separated events − in short, they would disagree about whether events occurred simultaneously or not.

Special relativity also correctly predicts that different observers may not agree on the spatial interval between two events. The length of an object at rest in an inertial reference name is known as its proper length. Observers who are moving relative to that frame will always measure a shorter length than the proper length. This effect is known as length contraction.

The Doppler effect applies to light. The astronomer Hubble used this effect to argue that the universe is expanding.

The intertwining of space and time means that a relativistic definition of linear momentum must be accepted if consistent relations among them are to be retained at both low and high speeds, and for observers in all inertial reference frames.

Special relativity reveals a previously unseen connection between two fundamental concepts: mass and energy. A mass has a tremendous amount of rest energy locked up, ready to be released either in a terrifying chain reaction or in a controlled, useful manner. Meanwhile, the converse is also true: Energy has a mass equivalent and may be transformed into matter.

Equations

Time dilation

$$t = \frac{t_0}{\sqrt{1 - v^2/c^2}}$$

$$t = \gamma t_0$$

Lorentz factor

$$\gamma = \frac{1}{\sqrt{1 - v^2/c^2}}$$

Length contraction

$$L = L_0 \sqrt{1 - v^2/c^2}$$

Doppler shift

Source/observer closing:

$$f = f_0 \sqrt{\frac{1 + v/c}{1 - v/c}}$$

Source/observer separating:

$$f = f_0 \sqrt{\frac{1 - v/c}{1 + v/c}}$$

Relativistic momentum

$$p = \frac{mu}{\sqrt{1 - \frac{u^2}{c^2}}} = \gamma m u$$

Rest energy

$$E_0 = mc^2$$

Total energy

$$E = \gamma mc^2$$

36 Quantum Physics Part One

□ Conceptual

36.0 - Introduction

Quantum physics is the branch of science required to fully explain the behavior of light, its interaction with matter, and the behavior of exceedingly small particles such as atoms and electrons. As scientists began to discover in the late 19th and early 20th centuries, certain principles and techniques of classical physics fail utterly when applied to light and to atomic-scale systems.

Although "quantum physics" often connotes mystery and difficulty, its applications are very real. You may be pleasantly surprised at how much you can understand when you are equipped with just a few fundamental concepts from this science.

In particular, you can learn the principles governing the functioning of two of the most pivotal technologies of the last half-century: semiconductors and lasers.

interactive 1

Study the photoelectric effect
Observe electron emission

Why are these two technologies so important? Without semiconductors, there would be neither transistors, nor the microprocessors built from them. Semiconductor-based microprocessors serve as the "brains" of computers and are found in digital cameras, cell phones, and automobiles: wherever engineers want "smart" behavior. Semiconductors are also used in various types of computer memory, such as random access memory (RAM). Semiconductor chips not only "think," they also "remember."

In recent years, **connecting** all these semiconductor devices has become the central thrust of the information processing industry. The Internet, cell-phone "fixed-rate calling plans", video on demand, downloadable music, and even the Web-based version of the textbook you are now reading all rely on the cheap and rapid transmission of information over wired or wireless networks. The two technologies most responsible for creating this networking revolution of rapidly decreasing costs and dramatically increasing bandwidth have been the microprocessor and the laser.

How do these two technologies enable networking? Communication networks use devices like *routers* and *high-speed switches* to transmit data. These devices rely on microprocessors to determine where to send their information and they form parts of extended physical systems that use lasers to move the information at light speed over fiber-optic cables.

Lasers give you access to data from sources both distant and nearby. In addition to sending data around the world, they are used on your desktop or in your home to read the data stored on CDs and DVDs (not to mention their use in stores to read data codes on your purchases). Without lasers, vinyl records and "floppy disks" might still be the primary means of storing audio and digital data. Believe us: If you have never used a floppy disk, you haven't missed much.

How does quantum physics relate to the working of these devices?

Explaining what is meant by "quantum" is the place to start. A key tenet of quantum physics is that particles in some systems, like the electrons in hydrogen atoms, exist only at certain energy levels. Physicists say the energy levels of the electrons in an atom are *quantized*.

It may be easiest to explain a quantum property by first considering its opposite, a property that is *continuous*. Consider the potential energy of a bucket that is raised or lowered by a rope. You can raise it 1.000 meters off the ground, or 1.001 m, or 1.002 m, or however much you like. By controlling its height, you can make its potential energy whatever you like. The range of possible energy values is continuous: say 10.00 joules, 10.000017 J, 10.027 J and so forth.

Electrons prove not to be as flexible. The electrons around a hydrogen (or other) atom exist only in states with certain discrete energy values; for instance, two possible energy levels for the hydrogen electron are −1.51 eV (electron volts) or −3.40 eV (−2.42×10⁻¹⁹ J or −5.44×10⁻¹⁹ J respectively). Between these two values lies a forbidden gap, and a hydrogen atom's electron is never observed with energies in that range. Physicists say an electron's energy is quantized, that it only exists at certain levels. In the example of the hydrogen electron mentioned above, you will **never** observe an energy of −1.6 eV or −2.9 eV, since those are forbidden.

Copyright 2000-2007 Kinetic Books Co. Chapter 36

You may ask: How does an electron change between energy levels? How can it "move" across a "forbidden gap" to a higher or lower energy state, if intermediate energy values are forbidden? You may not be satisfied with the answer, but it is most straightforward to say: Those are simply the only values that have ever been measured. Any time a scientist measures a property of an atomic electron (such as its energy, or its angular momentum), she only observes results from a particular set of values that can be predicted with extreme accuracy by quantum physics. It is impossible to "catch" an electron in any in-between state.

The simulation at the right reproduces one of the key experiments that led to the widespread acceptance of the ideas of quantum physics. Einstein explained data from a more sophisticated version of the same experiment, known as the photoelectric effect, to earn his Nobel Prize.

Describing the experiment is simple. Scientists had noticed that when they shined a beam of light on a metal, electrons were released from the illuminated surface. From their perspective, this was not particularly surprising: The energy of the light was transferred to the electrons, allowing some of them to escape their bonds to the atoms of the metal.

The emission of electrons could be explained by classical physics. Light was a wave with energy, and that energy could provide a "kick" to electrons as the metal absorbed the light.

Although the experiment and the expected outcome are simple in concept, the detailed results were quite surprising and could **not** be explained by classical physics. Some colors of light, such as red, could not eject electrons from the surface, no matter how bright the beam was. On the other hand, other colors, such as violet, were effective at ejecting electrons from the metal surface, even when the beam intensity was very low. It was the frequency of the light, and not its intensity, that determined whether or not electrons were ejected.

What the scientists observed does not make sense if light is conceived of solely as a wave. Let's compare their observations in terms of water waves crashing against a wooden dock. It is as if low-frequency waves (with their crests arriving, say, every five seconds) could **never** rattle the dock enough to knock free the timbers that make it up, even if they were giant waves 50 meters tall.

Now imagine centimeter-high waves arriving more frequently, say every second. Imagine that these small but frequent waves could knock loose pieces of the wood from the dock. Water waves with these effects would be confusing to observe, and you might be as confused as the scientists who observed dim but high frequency light freeing electrons from samples of metal.

Einstein successfully explained the photoelectric effect. He argued that light has both a wave nature and a particle nature. Electromagnetic radiation, he said, consists of small packets called photons. Photons are small "chunks" of light energy. More energetic light consists of more photons, **not** larger, more energetic waves. In addition, he stated that the higher the frequency of light, the more energetic the photons that make up the light. Dim but high frequency light can eject electrons because of the interaction between the energetic photons that make it up and the atoms of the metal. It is the energy of the individual photons that matters, not the overall energy of the light.

Conceiving of light as consisting of photons could explain another mysterious result: More intense light of a certain color caused more electrons to be emitted, but their maximum kinetic energy was exactly the same. The classical physicist would expect the "larger wave" of the more intense light to cause higher-energy electrons to be released, but this did not happen. Einstein's theory explains why: more intense light consists of more photons, each with the same energy as before. Again, it is the interaction between an individual photon and an individual atom that matters.

You just read a brief summary of some crucial points in quantum physics. You will become familiar with the photoelectric effect by using the simulation on the right. In your experiment with this effect, the flashlight can shine red or violet light. It can be set to emit either low or high intensity light.

When you press GO, you will see photons moving in slow motion from the flashlight toward the metal. When appropriate, we show electrons escaping from the metal.

Start the simulation with the light set to LOW. One color of light will cause electrons to escape the metal being used in our simulation; another will not. Red light has a longer wavelength but a lower frequency than violet light. Which of the two colors of light do you think will cause electrons to be emitted?

Now set the intensity of the light to HIGH, and try both colors again. What do you expect will change when you make this change? What do you think will stay the same?

Quantum: The smallest amount of something that can exist independently.

Quantum refers to the fundamental or least amount of something. For instance, the quantum of money in the U.S. is the penny. Your net worth will be a multiple of that quantum. You can be a pauper worth one penny, a millionaire with a worth of 100,000,000 pennies, or a starving college student with a net worth of −5,012 pennies. However, you cannot legally use three-quarters of a penny, or 1.45 pennies, or $3\pi/4$ pennies. There are many similar examples of things that come in discrete amounts: the number of siblings you have, the number of eggs you can purchase at a store, and so on.

A physicist would say that things like money or siblings or eggs are *quantized*. Calling something quantized means that it is grainy; it is the opposite of continuous. Using the example mentioned in this chapter's introduction, one would say that the height and energy of a bucket being raised by a rope are continuous quantities, as are the height and energy of an elevator car. In contrast, the height and energy of elevator **stops** are quantized; they occur solely at discrete points. You only see buttons for the first, second and third floors, not for the 1.75th floor.

A mathematical example of something that is continuous is shown on the right: real numbers. Examples of real numbers are 3, or 3.1, 3.01, 3.001, 3.002 and so forth. The set of real numbers is continuous, **not** quantized.

Although the idea of quantization may seem intuitive for money, it is much less obvious in some areas of physics: Scientists now know that many things once thought to be continuous are in fact quantized. Albert Einstein, for instance, showed that the energy of any precise color of light is quantized.

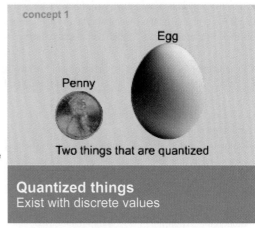

concept 1

Penny   Egg

Two things that are quantized

Quantized things
Exist with discrete values

concept 2

3   3.0001   3.001   3.01   3.1

Real numbers

Opposite of quantized
Continuous
· Real numbers are an example

Prior to Einstein scientists expected properties of light, such as its energy, to be continuous. Why? In the 18th and 19th centuries, a series of discoveries had led most scientists to conclude that light was a wave. They knew very well that the energy of a mechanical wave is continuous, not quantized. An ocean wave, for instance, can have a height (amplitude) of 1.01 meters, or 1.04 meters, or any value in between, and its energy will depend on that amplitude. Since light was believed to be a wave, scientists concluded that its energy would be continuous as well, and that for example, they could create a beam of a certain frequency of blue light with any desired energy simply by making the light brighter or darker.

However, as the next sections discuss, in the early 20th century it became increasingly clear that light is quantized: It consists of small chunks or packets of energy. The energy of a beam of a particular color of light must be a multiple of the energy of the packets that make it up. This realization had profound implications for the understanding of both light itself and the atoms that emit the light.

"The most important result of the application of quantum mechanics to the description of electrons in a solid is that the allowed energy levels of electrons will be grouped into *bands*." So wrote Andy Grove, then an employee of the Intel Corporation and a faculty member of the University of California at Berkeley, in his text on the physics and technology of semiconductor devices. Grove became the chairman of Intel during its rise to power, prestige and profitability.

The electrically excited neon gas in this sign emits light at several sharply defined red-orange wavelengths.

Grove cites two quantum principles. First, the concept that there are "energy levels" for electrons, and second, that these are grouped into bands (the emphasis in the quote is his).

For now, we will simplify our discussion by focusing on energy levels. Bands refer to the fact that certain electrons exist at energy levels that are close to one another. In practical applications, the distinction between a band and an energy level is often dropped.

Grove's words convey how important the ideas of quantum theory are for semiconductor science and technology. We use these words to motivate the next few sections of this book. One might wonder: How did physicists discover that atomic electrons had discrete energy levels? In other words, how did they first learn that the energy levels of electrons are quantized, not continuous?

Physicists advanced the theory as their observations forced them to. The story begins in 1666 when Newton showed that a prism could disperse sunlight into a spectrum of colors. Today, one would say Newton showed that sunlight comprises light of many wavelengths: Light perceived as white is in fact made up of a rainbow of components of various hues. When it was first discovered, the spectrum of sunlight seemed to be a continuous gamut of colors.

A series of later experiments convinced scientists that light had a wavelike nature. They could create interference patterns with light that were conceptually identical to patterns created by water waves. Physicists even found that they could measure the wavelengths of various colors of light. One mystery of science seemed to be solved: Light was a wave.

However, in 1814, the German physicist Joseph von Fraunhofer made careful observations using a thin slit, and discovered that the spectrum of sunlight contained many narrow dark lines, or gaps. In other words, certain wavelengths of light were not present in the spectrum he was observing. He discovered that the spectrum of sunlight was not continuous.

Throughout the 1800s, scientists studied the light emitted and absorbed by various gases. They discovered that a gas like hydrogen only emits or absorbs light of specific wavelengths. By 1880, the wavelengths of the *spectral lines* of various elements, including most famously hydrogen, were well known. In Concept 1 you see an illustration of the spectral lines in the *emission spectrum* of excited hydrogen gas.

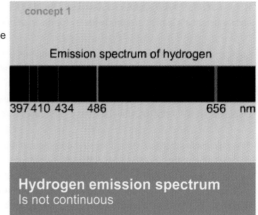

concept 1

Emission spectrum of hydrogen

397 410 434   486   656   nm

Hydrogen emission spectrum
Is not continuous

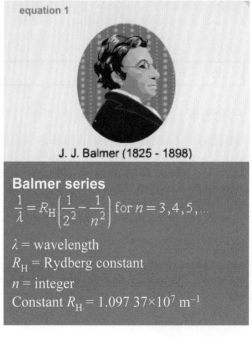

equation 1

J. J. Balmer (1825 - 1898)

Balmer series

$$\frac{1}{\lambda} = R_\mathrm{H}\left(\frac{1}{2^2} - \frac{1}{n^2}\right) \text{ for } n = 3, 4, 5, \ldots$$

λ = wavelength
R_H = Rydberg constant
n = integer
Constant $R_\mathrm{H} = 1.097\,37 \times 10^7 \text{ m}^{-1}$

The distinct colors and wavelengths of light you see are characteristic of light emitted by this element. Similar lines, but with different colors − wavelengths − can be found when the light of a neon sign, or the glow of a fluorescing ruby, is analyzed. (Each element has a corresponding *absorbtion spectrum*, consisting of dark lines at exactly the same wavelengths, against a rainbow background.)

As you can see, the spectral lines of hydrogen are sharp and distinct, not blurred. For instance, the red light you see has a wavelength of 656.3 nanometers, the blue-green light has a wavelength of 486.1 nm, and the violet light has a wavelength of 434.1 nm. Hydrogen atoms emit this light after being "excited" by an electrical discharge through the gas, caused by a potential difference of 5000 volts applied between two electrodes.

The discrete nature of the hydrogen spectrum puzzled and intrigued physicists. Why did the light emitted by hydrogen only exist at certain wavelengths, rather than being continuous like a rainbow? And why at these particular wavelengths? Was there any way to predict the wavelengths?

A Swiss high school teacher, J. J. Balmer, analyzed the pattern. He determined that the wavelengths were not random, but could be determined using the formula in Equation 1. The constant R_H that appears in Balmer's formula is called the *Rydberg constant*.

Intriguing mathematical patterns did not stop with the set of spectral lines known as the *Balmer series*. There are also wavelengths emitted by hydrogen that lie outside of the visible spectrum, which are predicted by formulas very similar to the one in Equation 1.

Later scientists determined that similar relationships existed for the spectral lines of other elements, as stated by the *Rydberg-Ritz combination principle*. Although the hydrogen atom is often used to discuss this principle in order to keep things simple, it applies to all atoms. For instance, the neon sign you see in the photograph above is displaying red light at the wavelengths of several of its spectral lines.

The physicists who determined these mathematical relationships did not know **why** the wavelengths of the spectral lines followed the patterns they did. These data were just too far ahead of the theory of atomic structure. Scientists could observe the discrete spectral lines of the emitted and absorbed light, and note the mathematical relations that predicted their wavelengths, but could only speculate as to the cause.

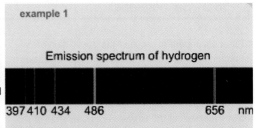

example 1

Emission spectrum of hydrogen

397 410 434   486   656   nm

What is the lowest visible frequency of light emitted by hydrogen?

$$\frac{1}{\lambda} = R_H \left(\frac{1}{2^2} - \frac{1}{n^2} \right)$$

$$c = f\lambda \text{ so } \frac{1}{\lambda} = \frac{f}{c}$$

$$\frac{f}{c} = R_H \left(\frac{1}{2^2} - \frac{1}{n^2} \right)$$

$$f = cR_H \left(\frac{1}{2^2} - \frac{1}{3^2} \right) = cR_H \left(\frac{5}{36} \right)$$

$$f = \frac{5}{36} (3.00 \times 10^8 \tfrac{m}{s})(1.097 \times 10^7 \tfrac{1}{m})$$

$$f = 4.57 \times 10^{14} \text{ Hz}$$

However, the work was underway. The light emitted by hydrogen was found to have a discrete spectrum, one that could be predicted by a formula. It was a tantalizing clue about the quantized nature of atoms.

36.3 - Photons

Photon: A packet of light. The fundamental unit or quantum of light.

Max Planck showed how the radiation emitted by an ideal object in thermal equilibrium with its surroundings could be explained if the radiation emitted or absorbed by the body was quantized. His theory had a somewhat marginal existence for four years until Albert Einstein, then employed as a Swiss patent clerk, began to consider it in depth.

Planck's theory stated that the energy (radiation) **absorbed or emitted by an object** had to be taken up or released in discrete chunks, as quanta. However, he still conceived of the radiation itself as a wave. His theory simply stated that matter absorbed or emitted the radiation in discrete amounts.

Einstein took the next bold step: He stated that the radiation itself was quantized. He saw that what Planck had been studying was not just how matter absorbed and emitted radiation, but the basic nature of the radiation itself.

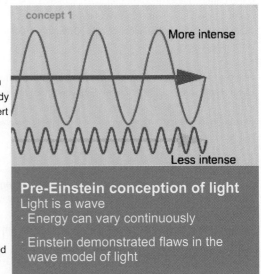

concept 1

More intense

Less intense

Pre-Einstein conception of light
Light is a wave
· Energy can vary continuously

· Einstein demonstrated flaws in the wave model of light

Einstein stated that light of any frequency is quantized in units now called *photons*. The energy of a photon is proportional to its frequency f.

He wrote, "The energy in a beam of light is not distributed continuously through space, but consists of a finite number of energy quanta, which are localized at points, which cannot be subdivided, and which are absorbed or emitted only as whole units." (This was in the same year that he published his special theory of relativity; not a bad year.)

This new model challenged the previous concept that light behaved solely as a wave. Instead, it stated that light could also be conceived of as a stream of packets of energy, almost as particles.

The energy of each photon could be calculated with the equation $E = hf$. In other words, red light of frequency 4.60×10^{14} Hz cannot have just any energy level; its energy is always an integer multiple of hf. One photon of red light of frequency 4.60×10^{14} cycles per second has 3.05×10^{-19} J of energy, two photons of this frequency red light have 6.10×10^{-19} J of energy, and there is no such thing as 1.5 photons of red light, any more than there can be 1.5 electrons.

It was not easy for scientists to accept Einstein's new theory. When four elite scientists – including Planck – nominated Einstein to the Prussian Academy of Science they wrote, "That he may have missed the target in his speculations, as, for example, in his hypothesis of light quanta, cannot really be held too much against him, for it is not possible to introduce fundamentally new ideas, even in the most exact sciences, without occasionally taking a risk."

One year later, the American physicist Robert A. Millikan reported a precise confirmation of Einstein's equation for the energy of the photon, $E = hf$.

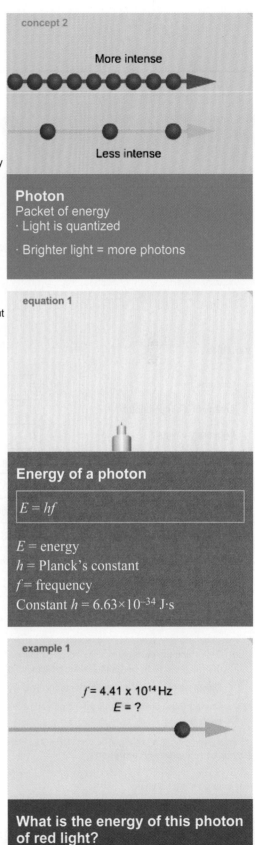

concept 2

More intense

Less intense

Photon
Packet of energy
· Light is quantized

· Brighter light = more photons

equation 1

Energy of a photon

$$E = hf$$

E = energy
h = Planck's constant
f = frequency
Constant $h = 6.63 \times 10^{-34}$ J·s

example 1

$f = 4.41 \times 10^{14}$ Hz
$E = ?$

What is the energy of this photon of red light?
$E = hf$

$$E = (6.63 \times 10^{-34} \text{ J} \cdot \text{s})(4.41 \times 10^{14} \text{ s}^{-1})$$
$$E = 2.92 \times 10^{-19} \text{ J}$$

36.4 - Sample problem: solar radiance

Take the "typical" wavelength of light to be 550 nm. What is the energy of a photon of that light? If you were to stare into the Sun (a very bad idea!), how many photons per second would enter one of your eyes? Use 7.85×10^{-7} m² for the surface area of the pupil and assume that the intensity of sunlight on the Earth's surface at your location is 1000 W/m².

Variables

total energy	E
energy of a single photon	E_p
frequency of light	f
wavelength of light	$\lambda = 550 \times 10^{-9}$ m
Planck's constant	$h = 6.63 \times 10^{-34}$ J·s
intensity of light	$I = 1000$ W/m²
surface area of one pupil	$A = 7.85 \times 10^{-7}$ m²
speed of light	$c = 3.00 \times 10^8$ m/s
number of photons per second	N

What is the strategy?

1. Determine the energy of each photon by using Einstein's equation for the energy of a photon. To determine the photon's frequency, use the relationship between the speed of light, its wavelength and its frequency.

2. Calculate the power of the light entering your eye by using the relationship of intensity, power and surface area.

3. Compare the power of sunlight hitting your eye to the energy of a single photon and calculate how many photons are hitting your eye each second.

Physics principles and equations

The energy of a photon is

$$E = h f$$

The relationship between wave speed (in this case, c), wavelength and frequency is

$$c = \lambda f$$

Intensity can be calculated as

$$I = \frac{P}{A}$$

Power equals

$$P = \frac{\Delta E}{\Delta t}$$

Step-by-step solution

We first compute the energy of a single incident photon, answering the first part of the question above.

Step	Reason
1. $E_p = hf$	energy of a photon
2. $c = \lambda f$	wave speed, wavelength and frequency
3. $f = \frac{c}{\lambda}$	solve for frequency
4. $E_p = \frac{hc}{\lambda}$	substitute step 3 into step 1
5. $E_p = \frac{\left(6.63 \times 10^{-34} \text{ J} \cdot \text{s}\right)\left(3.00 \times 10^{8} \frac{m}{s}\right)}{\left(550 \times 10^{-9} \text{ m}\right)}$ $E_p = 3.62 \times 10^{-19} \text{ J}$	evaluate

Next we calculate the power of the sunlight entering your pupil. To do so, we use the intensity equation above, the given intensity of the light and the area of the pupil.

Step	Reason
6. $I = \frac{P}{A}$	intensity
7. $P = IA$	solve for power
8. $P = \left(1000 \text{ W/m}^2\right)\left(7.85 \times 10^{-7} \text{ m}^2\right)$ $P = 7.85 \times 10^{-4} \text{ W}$	evaluate

We have determined the power of the light entering your pupil and the energy of a single photon. Now we will relate these two values to find the number of photons per second that enter your eye.

Step	Reason
9. $\quad P = \dfrac{\Delta E}{\Delta t}$	definition of power
10. $P = NE_p$	power and photon rate
11. $\quad N = \dfrac{P}{E_p}$	solve equation 10 for N
12. $\quad N = \dfrac{(7.85 \times 10^{-4}\ \text{W})}{(3.62 \times 10^{-19}\ \text{J})}$ $N = 2.17 \times 10^{15}$ photons per second	evaluate

Note that N is a very large number of photons per second. Sensors in the eye's retina can actually respond to just a single photon. A single molecule in one "rod" cell in your eye can absorb one photon, triggering a chemical reaction that sends a signal to the optic nerve. However, neural filters only let a signal go to the brain if approximately five to nine photons arrive every 100 ms. This limit prevents the visual fuzziness or "noise" that would exist under conditions of low intensity light if the eyes were too sensitive.

36.5 - Photoelectric effect

Photoelectric effect: The ejection of electrons from a material due to light striking it. Aspects of this effect were used by Einstein to demonstrate the quantization of light.

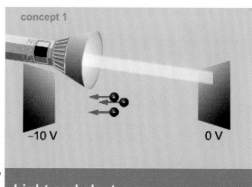

concept 1

Light and electrons
Shining light on metal causes it to emit electrons

-10 V   0 V

What caused Einstein to believe that light was quantized? In the year 1905 he used a quantum model of light to explain the results of an experiment that could not be explained using classical electromagnetic theory. In fact, Einstein won the 1921 Nobel Prize in Physics "for his services to Theoretical Physics, and especially for his discovery of the law of the photoelectric effect."

In 1887, Heinrich Hertz had shown that shining light on metal could cause electrons to be ejected from the metal. You can think of this process as analogous to evaporation. When light shines on water, it can cause some of the water molecules to escape as a gas. When light shines on metal, some of the electrons can escape the metal.

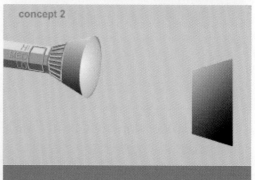

concept 2

Incorrect expectation

We illustrate this phenomenon in Concept 1, with electrons escaping from the metal electrode on the right. The "ejected" electrons could be readily explained by the classical model of light as a wave composed of electric and magnetic fields. These waves transported energy, and it made sense that some of the electrons in the metal could absorb enough of this energy to escape the attractive force binding them to atoms in the metal.

In Concept 1, you also see parts of an apparatus used to conduct experiments whose results were not so readily explained using classical theory. It consists of two electrodes enclosed in a vacuum. The left electrode has a lower electric potential than the right electrode, which means it will repel electrons. You may also think of the apparatus in this way: an electric field is established between the electrodes that points from the right to the left. This field "pushes" the electrons to the right, back toward the electrode they have escaped from.

Shining light on the right-hand electrode causes electrons to be ejected from it and to move to the left. The faster they are moving, the more negative the electric potential of the left electrode has to be to keep them from reaching it. By adjusting the electric potential on the left electrode so that the electrons "just fail" to reach it, an experimenter can determine the maximum kinetic energy of the electrons.

An expected result of this experiment would be that, the more intense the light shining on the right electrode, the more energy its electrons would absorb, and the faster they would move when ejected from the metal. It would be like chopping wood with an ax. As you chop the wood, the harder you strike, the faster you expect some of the chips to fly off.

However, to the surprise of the experimenters, this proved **not** to be the case. There is **no** correlation between the intensity of the light and the maximum kinetic energy of the electrons. Rather, when the intensity of the light is increased, more electrons are emitted. Instead of the kinetic energy of the escaping electrons increasing, only their number increases. The incorrect "classical" expectation is shown in Concept 2, and the actual observed behavior in the experiment is shown in Concept 3 (refresh your browser to restart these animations). In terms of the ax analogy: It is as if hitting the log harder results not in more energetic chips, but in more chips of the same energy flying off.

Another surprising result was that when the frequency of the light was below a certain value, known as the *cutoff frequency*, the light could be of great intensity, but no electrons at all would be ejected. Classical physics cannot explain these phenomena. To use the ax example one more time: If you strike a log very infrequently, but with great force (energy), you would expect chips to fly off. However, if the photoelectric effect applied to wood chopping, then when you chop at a slow rate, no chips will fly off, no matter how hard you strike the log. Very odd!

Quantum theory, however, explains both these results quite neatly. Considering light as packets of energy means that with more intense light more packets are striking the metal each second. The energy of each packet does not change with intensity; the number of packets does. More photons (each having the same energy) striking the right electrode each second increases the rate at which electrons are ejected from the metal, but not their maximum kinetic energy.

This can also be likened to knocking over bottles with bullets from a rifle. In classical theory, more "intensity" means switching to a bigger, more powerful rifle, so that each bullet will hit a bottle with more energy. The same number of bottles will still be hit; they just go flying off the target faster.

In quantum theory, more "intensity" does not mean switching to a larger caliber, more powerful rifle. More intensity means firing more bullets per second from the same rifle, which means more bottles get knocked over. The increased intensity does not involve changing the energy of the bullets, so the bottles always get struck with the same amount of energy.

Quantum theory also explains why low-frequency light cannot cause any electrons at all to be emitted. The energy of each photon equals hf. Using intense light of low frequency means that many low-energy packets of light are striking the metal, but no individual packet has enough energy to raise an electron to an energy level high enough for it to escape.

Speed/energy of an electron corresponds to light's intensity??

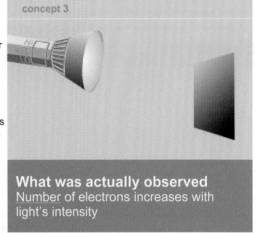

concept 3

What was actually observed
Number of electrons increases with light's intensity

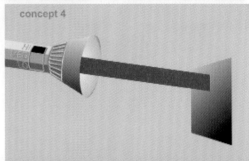

concept 4

Relationship of frequency and electrons
No electrons emitted
· For colors below a certain frequency
· No matter how intense the light

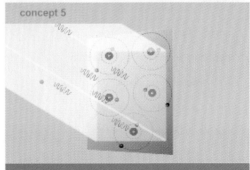

concept 5

Quantum theory (and Einstein) to the rescue
More intense light → more photons
More photons → more ejected electrons

The minimum energy an electron needs to escape the metal is called the *work function*, and low-frequency photons have less energy than this. To use the rifle analogy: Employing low-frequency light is like changing from bullets to spitballs. No spitball alone has enough energy to knock over a target. In quantum theory, increasing the intensity of light means the number of spitballs increases, **not** the energy of a spitball. Just as no spitball is energetic enough to knock over a bottle, no low-frequency photon in the experimental apparatus is energetic enough to free an electron.

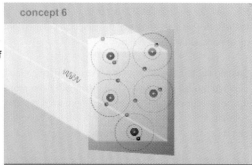

Frequency/energy of light and electrons

Lower frequency light → photons less energetic

Less energetic photons cannot free electrons

36.6 - Sample problem: photoelectric effect

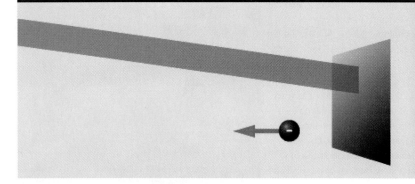

Ultraviolet light with a frequency of 1.03×10^{15} Hz is incident on a metallic sodium surface. The work function, the minimum amount of energy required for an electron to be ejected from this material, is $\varphi = 2.36$ eV. What is the maximum kinetic energy an escaping electron can have?

The electrons in a particular metal have a range of different energies and require various amounts of additional energy in order to be "freed" when the metal is struck by a photon.

The *work function* of a material is the least amount of energy required to release any electron from it. In other words, it is the amount of energy required to free the "least attached" electron.

Variables

energy of photon	E
maximum kinetic energy of electron	KE_{max}
work function for sodium	$\varphi = 2.36$ eV
Planck's constant	$h = 6.63\times10^{-34}$ J·s
frequency of ultraviolet light	$f = 1.03\times10^{15}$ Hz

What is the strategy?

1. Use the conservation of energy. This means that the energy of the incoming photon must equal the energy required to free the electron plus the kinetic energy of the electron as it flies away from the surface. (Ultraviolet light does have enough energy to free an electron in this case.)

2. Observe that the electrons that are least bound to the metal will be the electrons that leave it with the maximum kinetic energy. The less energy that is "spent" by a photon to free an electron, the more energy there is "left" that can go to increasing the electron's kinetic

energy.

Physics principles and equations

Energy is conserved.

The energy of a photon is

$$E = hf$$

Step-by-step solution

Step	Reason
1. $E = KE_{max} + \varphi$	conservation of energy
2. $KE_{max} = E - \varphi$	solve for KE_{max}
3. $E = hf$	energy of a photon
4. $KE_{max} = hf - \varphi$	substitute equation 3 into equation 2
5. $hf = \left(6.63 \times 10^{-34}\ \frac{J}{s}\right)\left(1.03 \times 10^{15}\ s^{-1}\right)$ $hf = 6.83 \times 10^{-19}\ J$	photon energy
6. $hf = 6.83 \times 10^{-19}\ J\left(\dfrac{1\ eV}{1.6 \times 10^{-19}\ J}\right)$ $hf = 4.27\ eV$	convert units
7. $KE_{max} = 4.27\ eV - 2.36\ eV$ $KE_{max} = 1.89\ eV$	evaluate

We converted to electron volts in step six because in quantum physics, energies are commonly stated in electron volts rather than joules. An electron with kinetic energy $KE_{max} = 1.89$ eV would be moving at a speed of 8.19×10^5 m/s, which is approximately 0.27% of the speed of light. At this speed, relativistic effects do not play a significant role and are ignored in the solution above.

The equation derived above, $KE_{max} = hf - \varphi$, was an important result that was used to confirm the particle-like nature of light. Einstein first stated it in 1905, and Robert A. Millikan experimentally verified it shortly thereafter.

36.7 - Interactive problem: photoelectric effect

Laser engineers use the principles of quantum physics. In the simulation on the right, you will experiment with one of the fundamental phenomena that underlie the working of a ruby laser. Rubies are crystals of aluminum oxide with chromium impurities that give them their distinctive red color. More importantly for engineers, chromium is primarily responsible for ruby's lasing properties.

The simulation focuses on one of the outermost electrons of a chromium atom. The initial step to make a laser work is to excite the electron so that it is in a high energy state. The electron starts at a low energy state called E_1. Your first goal is to increase this electron's energy, and cause it to jump to a higher energy state called E_3.

How can you boost the energy of the electron from E_1 to E_3? Here, you may fire at the atom either photons of red light with a frequency of 4.32×10^{14} Hz, or photons of green light with a frequency of 5.45×10^{14} Hz. One photon of the red light used in the simulation has an energy of 1.79 eV, and a photon of the green light has an energy of 2.26 eV. These photon energies are calculated using the formula $E = hf$, where h is Planck's constant and f is the frequency of the light.

Conduct a few experiments by selecting photons of different colors (energies) and then pressing GO. Do photons of both frequencies have an effect on the outermost electron of the chromium atom, or just one frequency? After testing the photons, can you deduce what the energy difference is between E_1 and E_3?

After you fire the appropriate photon, the electron will have energy E_3, but this energy level is highly unstable. The electron will rapidly and spontaneously fall to an intermediate energy level E_2. This new state is relatively stable compared to the higher state, and we will pause time in the simulation when it reaches this "metastable" state. (A photon is emitted when the electron drops from E_3 to E_2 but that photon is irrelevant to the operation of the laser.)

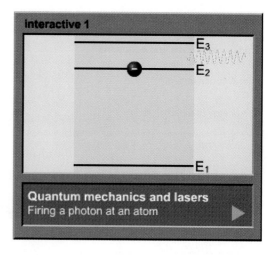

Your final goal is to stimulate the chromium atom to emit another photon, which it will do when the electron drops from energy E_2 to E_1. You do this by firing a new photon at the chromium. Which color do you think will cause the emission of an additional photon?

If you see two photons moving to the right and the electron in the chromium atom returns to energy level E_1, you have successfully simulated the workings of a laser. Congratulations! The second photon you fired by pressing GO has been "amplified" since it results in two photons moving through the ruby. It has taken advantage of the energy stored in the atom to do this.

As you conduct your experiments, you may note that the details of the laser process differ from material to material. With neon, the crucial transition is from the highest metastable level to a middle level. With chromium, the material used for this transition, the crucial transition is from a middle metastable level back to the lowest energy state.

36.8 - Bohr atom

Bohr atom: The atom consists of a nucleus surrounded by electrons orbiting it at specific radii and energy levels.

Einstein showed that light was quantized. The Danish physicist Niels Bohr proposed a model of the atom in which the energy of electrons was quantized, and could only exist at certain values. Together, these theories explained the frequencies of spectral emission and absorption lines.

Before discussing Bohr's theory, we will briefly explain some work that preceded his, and then explain his crucial hypotheses.

In 1897, the scientist J. J. Thomson showed that the "rays" often observed flowing between charged electrodes in a vacuum were streams of negatively charged particles. In other words, he discovered the electron. His discovery caused scientists to update their model of the atom. Some theorized that atoms consisted of a "mix" of negative particles and positive regions, like negatively charged chocolate chips embedded in positively charged cookie dough. (In fact, Thomson called it the *plum pudding model*, after the plums scattered throughout a pudding.)

However, in 1910 Ernest Rutherford conducted experiments that led scientists to reject the plum pudding model. He fired alpha particles at a thin gold foil, expecting them to sail through. (An alpha particle consists of two protons and two neutrons, and is positively charged.)

Rutherford discovered that although most of the particles passed through the foil with minimal deflection, a few had violent collisions. These particles were deflected at extreme angles, or even rebounded straight back.

Only a dense, positive nucleus could explain this result. Rutherford's subsequent analysis led him to conclude that this tightly packed nucleus must be surrounded by electrons that were orbiting the nucleus at relatively great distances, a model eerily similar to the solar system. In short, he developed the basis of a model that is still commonly used today to describe the atom.

During the period of these discoveries, the physicist Robert Millikan measured the magnitude of the elementary charge, which is the amount of charge of an electron or a proton. In a little over a decade, the basic model of a positively charged nucleus orbited by negatively charged electrons had been established, as had the charge of an electron.

The model of the atom was radically advanced by the work of Thomson, Rutherford and Millikan. However, physicists remained puzzled by a paradox stemming from their understanding of electromagnetic theory and orbital mechanics.

Electromagnetic theory predicts that accelerating charges emit electromagnetic radiation. Electrons circling around the nucleus of an atom are constantly accelerating because they are constantly changing direction; this is similar to how the electrons in an antenna repeatedly accelerate back and forth as they oscillate over its length in simple harmonic motion. If orbital electrons were emitting radiation due to their acceleration, they would be losing energy, and they should eventually crash into the nucleus. The analogous effect is witnessed with a satellite orbiting the Earth: If it continually loses energy due to atmospheric resistance, its orbital radius decreases, and it eventually crashes.

However, since most atoms are stable (phew!), electrons are not "crashing" into nuclei, but rather are maintaining orbits of a constant radius. Bohr could not explain why the electrons acted as they did, but he formulated a theory that was consistent with what physicists were observing. He stated that electrons in atoms could only exist in certain orbits called *stationary orbits* or *stationary states*. Bohr postulated that in these states the size and energy of an electron's orbit is stable and constant. (By using the term stationary, Bohr did not mean that the electrons stood still, but rather that their orbital radii and energies remained constant.)

In Bohr's model, both the orbital radius of an electron and the total energy of its orbit are quantized. Electrons can only exist at certain distances from the nucleus that correspond to certain energy levels. (Bohr used the concept of angular momentum to determine the sizes of the orbits.) His model also led to the conclusion that an electron in such an orbit does **not** radiate energy continuously and that its orbital radius cannot gradually decay, but remains constant unless it is disturbed.

In Concept 2 we show a table of energy levels for a hydrogen atom. The lowest energy level is called the *ground-state energy level*. At this level, the electron is at its closest to the nucleus, and this distance is called the *Bohr radius*. This is the smallest possible orbit of the electron. The ground-state energy of a hydrogen atom is −13.6 electron volts.

Note that the value is negative. Physicists liken this to an electron being placed in a well. It takes 13.6 eV to remove the electron from the atom so that it is free, no longer bound to the proton that is the nucleus of the hydrogen atom. The closer it is to the nucleus, the more negative its energy. This is akin to measuring the gravitational potential energy of, say, a rock at the bottom of a well. Its gravitational potential energy is stated to be negative there, and it becomes less negative as it approaches the top of the well at the surface of the Earth.

concept 2

Table of energy states of hydrogen electron

n	Energy of electron (eV)
1	-13.6
2	-3.40
3	-1.51
4	-0.85

Energy levels of hydrogen atoms

equation 1

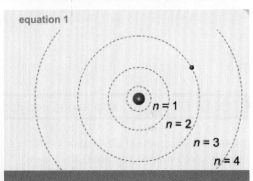

Energy levels of hydrogen atoms

$$\Delta E = E_f - E_i$$

ΔE = change in energy of atom
E = energy of an electron's orbit

example 1

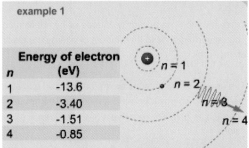

n	Energy of electron (eV)
1	-13.6
2	-3.40
3	-1.51
4	-0.85

When an electron moves from N_3 to N_2, what happens to its energy? Calculate the change in energy of the atom.

$\Delta E = E_f - E_i$

$\Delta E = (-3.40 \text{ eV}) - (-1.51 \text{ eV})$

$\Delta E = -1.89 \text{ eV}$

Today, electrons are not considered to be particles moving like satellites in orbits around the nucleus, and a quantum-physics *electron cloud model* of the atom has replaced the Bohr model. Nevertheless, many of Bohr's ideas have proven to be very useful, and his model greatly advanced the understanding of the atom.

How does Bohr's work relate to spectral lines? His model provided the first steps toward a quantized view of the atom. As an electron moves between specific energy levels, it emits or absorbs a quantized amount of energy in the form of a single photon of a specific frequency.

The spectral lines that result when a gas emits or absorbs energy are thus also quantized. Bohr's work provided a model on the atomic side of why this should be the case.

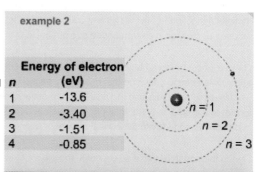

example 2

n	Energy of electron (eV)
1	-13.6
2	-3.40
3	-1.51
4	-0.85

By how much does the atom's energy change when the photon strikes, moving the electron from N_1 to N_3?

$\Delta E = E_f - E_i$

$\Delta E = (-1.51 \text{ eV}) - (-13.6 \text{ eV})$

$\Delta E = 12.1 \text{ eV}$

36.9 - Energy levels, photons and spectral lines

The Bohr model, combined with Einstein's and Planck's work, explained the discrete spectral lines that physicists were observing.

Why does excited hydrogen gas only emit light at certain frequencies? When it is excited, say by heat, or by an electric current, its atoms absorb energy. When a hydrogen atom absorbs energy, its electron jumps from one orbit to another, from a lower energy level to a higher one. The change in energy is quantized because electrons can only exist at the specific energy levels prescribed in Bohr's model.

Hot, excited metal atoms emit light at characteristic frequencies. For example, fireworks packed with copper salts radiate blue light when they explode.

When the atom loses energy, it does so by releasing a single photon. The energy of the photon corresponds to the amount of energy the electron loses as it returns to a lower-energy orbit.

The energy of the photons emitted by excited gas atoms must be quantized because the electron energy levels are quantized. The frequency of a photon is proportional to its energy, $f = E/h$. We perceive a given frequency (or wavelength) of light as a specific color.

For example, consider the red-colored line having wavelength 656 nm and frequency 4.57×10^{14} Hz in the emission spectrum of hydrogen. A photon of this color must have energy 3.03×10^{-19} J, or 1.89 eV.

It is possible to calculate the orbital change of the electron in a hydrogen atom that creates light of this frequency. An electron in the $n = 3$ orbit has −1.51 eV of energy. An electron in the $n = 2$ orbit has −3.40 eV of energy. An electron that drops from N_3 to N_2 gives up 1.89 eV of energy: exactly the energy of the red-color photon. A mystery solved! Some Nobels won!

In sum, in the first decades of the 20th century, scientists had already discovered the physics that Andy Grove and his peers would need in order to create semiconductors

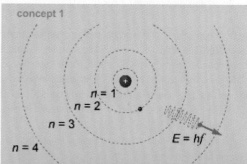

concept 1

$E = hf$

Bohr, photons and spectral lines
Orbits (and energy levels) are quantized
· Only certain energy changes possible

Photons of light are quantized
· Energy = Planck's constant times frequency
· Observed spectral lines match energy differences

and lasers. In fact, the first patents for basic semiconductor transistors were granted in Germany and the United States in the 1920s and 1930s. The practical manufacture of these devices required progress in the material sciences, but transistors were manufactured in the late 1940s, and the first modern-day field effect device, a type of transistor, was proposed in 1952 and built in 1953.

36.10 - Interactive checkpoint: photons and electron energy levels

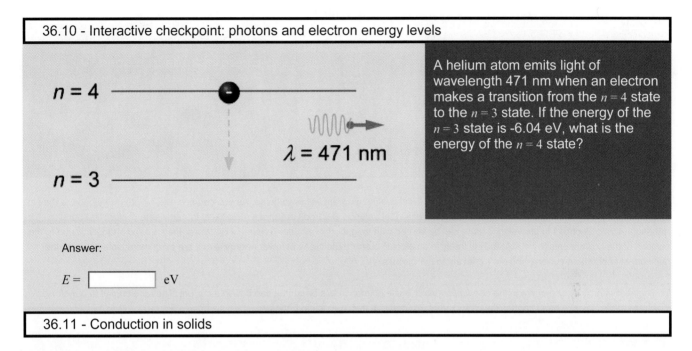

A helium atom emits light of wavelength 471 nm when an electron makes a transition from the $n = 4$ state to the $n = 3$ state. If the energy of the $n = 3$ state is -6.04 eV, what is the energy of the $n = 4$ state?

Answer:

$E = $ [   ] eV

36.11 - Conduction in solids

This chapter started off by noting that the development of semiconductor-based devices, such as transistors, has been one of the most important technological advances of the past 50 years. We also promised that understanding their functioning would require only a basic understanding of some principles of quantum physics. With your introduction to quantized energy levels and photons essentially complete for the purposes of this chapter, we can now start the discussion of semiconductors, and shortly, lasers.

To explain semiconductors, we need to discuss the conduction of electrical currents in solids. In terms of conducting electricity, semiconductors lie between the extreme cases of conductors and insulators (hence the "semi" in their name). The ability of engineers to influence how readily semiconductors conduct a current is a key to their utility.

To review some terminology: Some substances (like copper or aluminum) are considered conductors; current flows relatively easily in a conductor. Others (like silicon laced with impurities) are considered semiconductors. Others, like silicon dioxide, are insulators, where it is very difficult to cause a current to flow.

In this section, we discuss why current flows more − or less − easily in conductors, semiconductors and insulators. We start with an energy diagram of two electrons in a single atom, as you see below. The electrons exist at distinct energy levels.

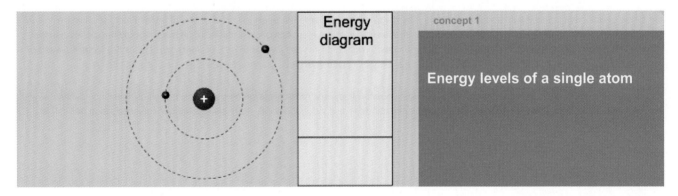

Energy diagram

concept 1

Energy levels of a single atom

To understand the relative ease or difficulty of causing a current to flow, we need the concept of *energy bands*. Below we show what happens when many atoms are brought together, say atoms that have crystallized into a solid. When atoms are brought very close together, their energy levels interact and merge into a set of broader energy bands. Instead of the electrons of an individual atom being restricted to particular energy levels that are so sharp and distinct they are represented with lines, the electrons now can exist with their energies in ranges of values, or bands.

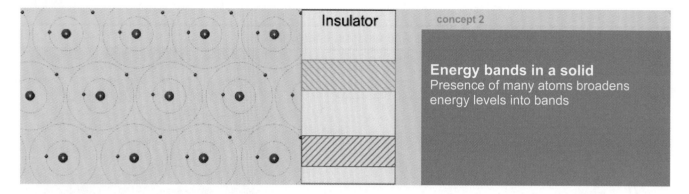

In fact, we can get more specific about these bands. We will use the diagram below to do so. As you can see, the lower energy band is the *valence band*. If you have studied chemistry, you may recall that valence electrons are those most likely to participate in chemical bonds. Although atomic electrons in the valence band can be shared with neighboring atoms in chemical reactions, they are too strongly bound to the nucleus of their own atoms to be able to flow freely in an electric current. Electrons at lower energy levels are even more closely tied to the nucleus, cannot flow in current, and are irrelevant to our discussion.

The highest-energy electrons are in the *conduction band*. It is electrons in this band that can flow in a current. They are crucial to our story: Electrons in the valence band cannot flow in a current; electrons in the conduction band can.

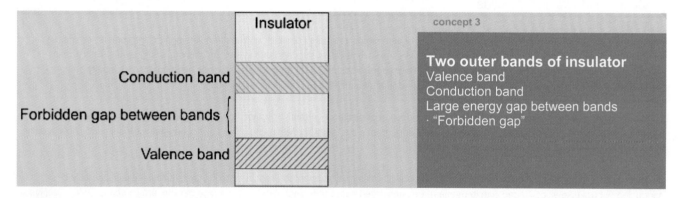

It takes energy to move from one band to another, just as it takes energy for an electron to move from one energy level to another in an isolated atom. When energy is added to an atom, its electrons can be promoted from the valence band to the conduction band, where they are free to move and become part of a current. How much energy it takes to accomplish this determines whether the material is classified as a conductor, a semiconductor or an insulator.

Let's now discuss this concept with specific materials. The diagram above shows the *energy band diagram* of an insulator, say silicon dioxide, for the valence and conduction bands. As in the prior illustration, the valence electrons occupy states in the lower energy band shown in the diagram. The conduction band is the upper band. Between these two bands lies the *forbidden gap, or band gap*. This is the Mojave Desert of electrons. They are not allowed to exist there. Electrons can only exist with energies in ranges like the valence or conduction bands.

As you see, the forbidden gap is comparatively large in an insulator. It takes a relatively large amount of energy (8 eV for silicon dioxide, if you like specifics) to cause an electron to move from the valence band to the conduction band. With few electrons in the conduction band, it is extremely difficult to produce a current.

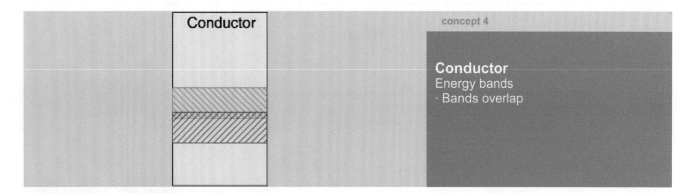

concept 4

Conductor
Energy bands
· Bands overlap

Now we consider the other extreme: a conductor. Its energy diagram is shown above. Note how the energy bands overlap; in a conductor, this overlapping region is only partially filled with electrons. It is "easy" for an electron to move from the valence to the conduction band when a potential difference is introduced. This means a conductor like copper can provide a ready supply of conduction electrons, ready to rumble when the slightest electric field from a source like a battery is applied.

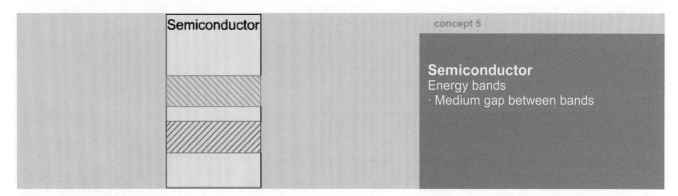

concept 5

Semiconductor
Energy bands
· Medium gap between bands

Above, you see the energy level diagram for the third type of material, a semiconductor. (We use silicon; purists may rightly complain that pure silicon is not truly a semiconductor, but we hope they will let us slide for a moment.) Its properties lie between those of insulators and conductors. As the diagram suggests, it takes less energy than with an insulator for an electron to move from the valence to the conducting band. At room temperature, it takes 1.12 eV.

To contrast the differences, the diagram below shows energy band diagrams for the three types of material side by side by side. You can see how the energy gaps differ by the type of material.

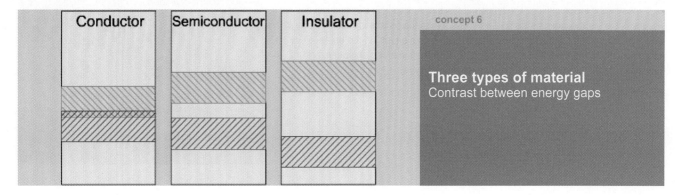

concept 6

Three types of material
Contrast between energy gaps

A hole: is caused by the departure of an electron and is positive.

In a physics topic like direct current circuits, an electric current is described as a flow of electrons, since it is moving electrons that are the charge carriers in a copper wire. However, semiconductor engineers think about the flow of current slightly differently. We will use a silicon atom or two to explain.

Here is a traditional discussion of *covalent bonds* as taught in first-year chemistry: A single silicon atom has four electrons in its valence band, but it "wants" to have eight there. When it is part of a solid piece of silicon, it forms covalent bonds with neighboring atoms. It "shares" electrons with neighboring silicon atoms, and by sharing, it fills its valence band with eight electrons. You see a symmetrical, "satisfied" silicon atom in the diagram of Concept 1.

Now let us consider what happens when an electron makes a jump from the valence band to the conduction band. It might do so as the silicon increases in temperature and the internal energy of the material increases.

When an electron makes this jump, a silicon atom has lost its valence electron. The valence band now has an opening, called a hole. The diagram in Concept 2 shows the "missing" electron as a hole. A hole is positive since it is caused by the departure of an electron. The number of protons in the region now exceeds the number of electrons by one.

Holes are crucial in semiconductors. Why? Because they provide a place for electrons to flow to. They provide natural "landing spots" for mobile electrons.

However, there is more to it than that. When considering semiconductors, the flow of electrons is crucial, as electrons constitute the electrical current in a conductor. However, equally important and real in the eyes of semiconductor engineers is the flow of holes. In the animation in Concept 3, we illustrate some moving electrons and the resultant motion of a hole. Refresh your browser screen if you did not see this animation yet and wish to do so.

You may consider hole movement as being akin to a bubble moving through a fluid. A bubble is the absence of fluid. The motion of the bubble can be described more concretely as a movement of the fluid around it. When the bubble moves one way, there is a flow of fluid in the other direction. However, the "movement" of the bubble is much more noticeable than the motion of the fluid itself. Semiconductor engineers and physicists treat holes as though they were particles as real as electrons.

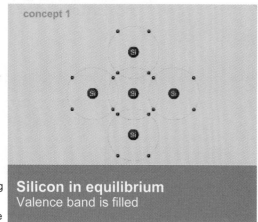

concept 1

Silicon in equilibrium
Valence band is filled

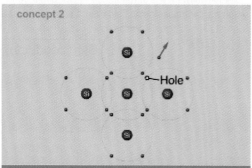

concept 2

Silicon with an electron in the conduction band
Valence band is "missing" an electron
A hole is created
· Holes are positive

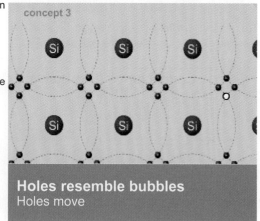

concept 3

Holes resemble bubbles
Holes move

Doping: Increasing the availability of conducting electrons or holes by adding impurities to a material like silicon.

Commercial semiconductors are *doped*. This is thoroughly frowned upon in the Olympics, but quite a desirable thing to do in a semiconductor foundry. Adding impurities to a substance like silicon allows engineers to tailor its electrical properties and makes it more useful in building devices like diodes and transistors.

We start with the diagram in Concept 1 showing silicon atoms in an ideal or equilibrium state, perhaps at a temperature near absolute zero. The atoms fill their valence bands by sharing electrons.

Now let's consider the same pure silicon, but at room temperature. The average thermal energy of the atoms has increased. This increase in energy means some electrons will have enough energy to spontaneously make the energy jump from the valence to the conducting band.

In fact, in absolute terms, a large number of electrons will make the jump. A cubic centimeter of silicon contains 5×10^{22} atoms, and 2×10^{23} valence electrons. At room temperature (293 K), you will find about 1×10^{10} electrons in the conducting band in this volume of silicon. Since they have left the valence band, you will find an identical number of holes. On the one hand, this is a vast number ($10,000,000,000$ electrons and an equal number of holes). On the other hand, it is extremely small compared to the total number of electrons: About one electron out of every 10^{13} valence electrons has become a conducting electron.

One out of 10^{13} is a small fraction, less than semiconductor engineers desire. To increase the number of conducting electrons and holes, the silicon is doped. In doping, impurities are added to the silicon to increase its ability to conduct current. Arsenic and phosphorus are common elements that are added to increase the number of available conducting electrons, while hole-increasing elements include gallium and boron.

Arsenic and phosphorus atoms both have five valence electrons, one more than silicon has. When an arsenic atom takes the place of a silicon atom in the atomic lattice, four of its valence electrons fit easily into the covalent bonds and in essence become members of the valence band of the adjacent silicon atoms. The fifth electron, however, enters the conduction band since there is no room for it in the valence band.

In Concept 2, you see an arsenic (As) atom and its "fifth" electron. When it is doped with an element like arsenic, the semiconductor is called an *n-type* semiconductor. The "*n*" stands for negative, since the charge carriers supplied by the dopant are negative. The "extra" electrons are called *donor* electrons.

To facilitate the flow of current, an engineer may want a material with holes: places for those electrons to flow to. She would use an element like gallium or boron whose atoms have just three valence electrons. When such an element replaces silicon in the atomic lattice, it is one electron short. The result is a hole, as shown in Concept 3.

When it is doped with an element like gallium (Ga), the semiconductor is called a *p-type* semiconductor. The "*p*" stands for positive, representing the fact that holes act like positive charges when they move.

Arsenic is used to supply carrier electrons and gallium is used to supply holes. In quantitative terms, the band gap separating the "fifth" arsenic

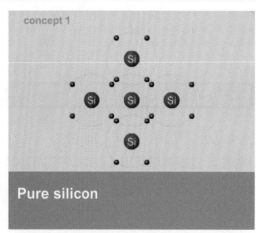

Pure silicon

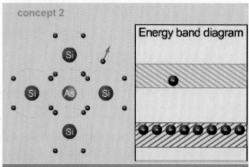

Energy band diagram

Doping
Adding a different material to silicon
n-type: inserts extra electron
"Extra" electron readily moves to conduction band

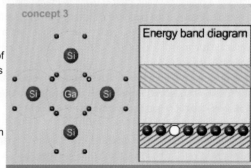

Energy band diagram

Creating holes with doping
p-type: an electron "short"
Provides destination for mobile electrons

valence electron from the conduction band is about 1/20th the size of the band gap for the silicon valence electrons.

In sum, an *n*-type semiconductor has a set of electrons ready to move, while in contrast a *p*-type semiconductor has a place ready for valence electrons to go, freeing up holes that can then move. When an external electric field is applied to a doped semiconductor, current will flow much more readily than in a pure semiconductor.

36.14 - p-n junction

p-n junction: *p*-type and *n*-type semiconducting materials placed adjacent to one another. This type of junction is the basis of devices like diodes and transistors.

Diode: A component that readily allows the flow of current in one direction, and is highly resistant to current in the other.

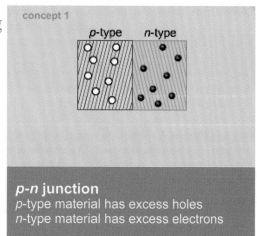

concept 1

p-n junction
p-type material has excess holes
n-type material has excess electrons

In this section, we discuss what happens when *p*- and *n*-type materials are placed in contact with one another. One result is a useful device, the diode.

Consider the *p-n* junction shown in Concept 1. A junction refers to the region or a device where the two types of semiconducting material are touching. Remember that the *n* section has excess electrons that can flow fairly readily, while the *p* section has excess holes that could accept those electrons.

When these two types of material are placed next to one another, some holes flow from the *p* to the *n* material, and some electrons flow from the *n* to the *p* material.

This is called a *diffusion current*. The electrons diffuse from the *n*-type material, where there is a higher concentration of them, to the *p*-type, where they are relatively scarce. The holes move in the opposite direction, from the *p*-region where they are abundant to the *n*-region where they are scarce. They diffuse, just as perfume molecules diffuse across a room.

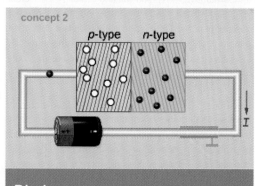

concept 2

Diode
Allows current to flow in one direction

The *p-n* junction is the essential element of a diode. When it is connected in a circuit in the fashion shown in Concept 2, the net flow of current is relatively great at low voltages. This is called a *forward-bias connection*.

Why does the current flow easily? Electrons flow from the *n*-region of the semiconductor rather readily to fill holes on the *p* side. The negative terminal of the battery acts to replenish the supply of electrons in the *n*-region and the positive terminal replenishes the holes in the *p*-region.

Now we reverse the orientation of the battery, as shown in Concept 3. The diode will block nearly all the current for low applied voltage: It acts as a resistor of great resistance. This is called a *back-bias connection*.

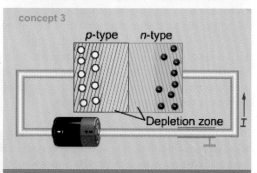

concept 3

Battery reversed
Creates depletion zone
Prevents flow of current

Why does this orientation prove so resistant to current? As Concept 3 shows, the battery causes a significant *depletion zone*. Holes in the *p*-region are moved away from the junction as they move toward the negative terminal of the battery, and free electrons in the *n*-region move away from the junction toward the positive terminal. The region around the junction on both sides loses its mobile charge carriers; it becomes depleted. The battery can "pull" harder and harder, but in effect, all it does is expand the depletion zone, instead of causing a continuing current.

The two graphs on the right show current versus voltage curves for forward bias and reverse bias connections. In the forward bias case, the current increases with potential difference. The diode acts roughly like a resistor. In the reverse bias case, the diode acts almost like a break in the circuit, and even relatively large potential differences cause negligible currents.

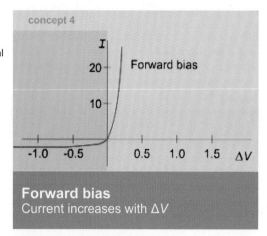

Forward bias
Current increases with ΔV

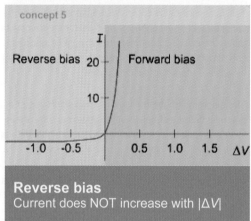

Reverse bias
Current does NOT increase with $|\Delta V|$

36.15 - Physics at work: MOSFET transistors

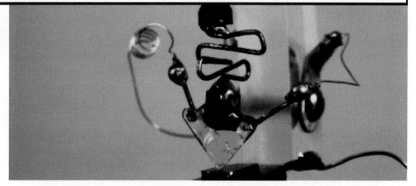

Transistor: A three-terminal semiconductor device that forms the basis of random access memory and microprocessors.

The physicist William Shockley proposed the first modern-day transistors in 1952, although earlier scientists had devised conceptual prototypes. In a circuit, transistors can be controlled so that they work

The first transistor, built at Bell Labs in 1947. The semiconductor substrate is a germanium crystal. The three electrical leads are the source, gate and drain.

either as strong resistors or effective conductors, which is what makes them important in electronics applications, such as electronic on/off switches (in computers), or as part of signal amplifiers (in your stereo).

The transistors discussed in this section are called *field effect transistors*, since the conductivity (or resistance if you like) of such transistors is regulated by an electric field. The first transistors, developed earlier, were of a type called *junction transistors* or *junction field effect transistors*, but *MOSFET* transistors dominate many applications today.

MOS stands for metal-oxide-semiconductor and FET stands for field-effect transistor. MOSFET transistors are crucial in microelectronics, forming the basis of random access memory (*RAM*) and of *charge-coupled devices* (CCDs). A *CCD* is used to record images in digital cameras and digital video cameras.

Enough acronyms: There are many more! (Other acronyms were suggested for MOSFET, including MISFET...) Let's move to the design of an *n channel* MOSFET transistor. The basic design is shown in Concept 1.

Silicon is lightly doped to form a *p*-type semiconductor, which is the bottom layer you see in the diagrams on the right. This layer, the *substrate*, is deliberately very lightly doped so that it will be a poor conductor, but the holes it contains are necessary for a reason you will soon learn. Then two much more heavily doped *islands* of *n*-type semiconductor, which are shown in green in the diagram, are formed on top of the substrate. One island is the *source* S and the other is the *drain* D.

A thin channel of *n*-type material, called appropriately enough, the *n channel*, connects the two islands. A layer of insulating material (such as silicon dioxide, whence the "O" in MOSFET), mere nanometers thick, is deposited on top and penetrated by the two metal leads (whence the M) shown in the diagram. On top of the insulating material lies a third deposit of metal, called the *gate* G. Because of the insulating layer, no charge can flow from the gate to the rest of the transistor.

This is a reasonably complex configuration. It is all the more impressive when you consider that semiconductor manufacturers are now building transistors where the gates measure 65 nanometers across, and that a single microprocessor chip can contain 500 million or more transistors. (It is a safe bet that humans have manufactured more transistors than any other device.)

The diagrams on the right show a transistor as part of a circuit. There is always a potential difference between the source and the drain. The key to how the transistor functions resides in whether there is a potential difference between the source and the gate. We will call this difference the gate voltage.

Let's consider what happens when there is no potential difference at the gate: In this case it has no effect on the other parts of the device. The illustration in Concept 2 shows this state. Electrons flow from the negative lead to the source island, then across the *n* channel to the drain island and the positive lead, because of the potential difference between the source and the drain. In short, a current flows through the transistor when the gate voltage is zero.

Now we assume that there is a negative gate voltage. This is illustrated in Concept 3. (A signal from another circuit might "turn on" this potential difference.) When it is turned on, we show the gate as negatively charged. Electrons repel each other, so the field caused by the electrons in the gate drives the *n* channel's electrons into the *p*-doped substrate where they find holes to occupy.

The channel is said to be *depleted*: The *n* channel has less *n*, electrons. Another way to put it is that the channel becomes narrower. This increases its resistance, and with a strong enough electric field from the gate, no electrons can flow from the source to the drain at all. This is where the "field effect" in MOSFET comes into play. (The substrate is too lightly doped and too poor a native conductor to allow current to flow there.) The entire process can be likened to stepping on a flexible garden hose to cut off the flow of water.

With a variation of the electric field of the gate, the transistor can be turned from ON to OFF, from allowing current to flow to preventing it. This simple idea, enabling circuits to be set to "ON" or "OFF", to represent "1" or "0", "true" or "false", underlies the design of computer memories and microprocessors.

After all this, you may think: It just turns on and off. Indeed. Just repeat that 500 million times or so and you have a microprocessor! The sophistication of the manufacturing process allows many transistors to be packed into a very small region.

The transistor also can function as part of an *amplifier*. Imagine that the potential

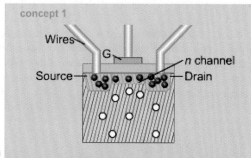

Structure of a MOSFET transistor
Substrate is lightly doped *p*-type semiconductor
Two islands of *n*-type material sit atop substrate
· One island is source S, one is drain D

n channel connects islands
Insulator covers substrate, islands
Metal gate G is above insulator

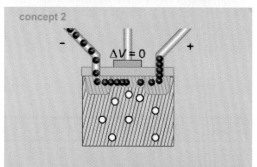

How a transistor functions (ON)
When gate voltage = 0 with
Potential difference between source and drain
· Electrons flow from source to drain

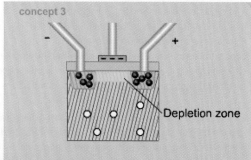

How a transistor functions (OFF)
When gate has negative voltage
Electrons driven out of *n* channel
· *n* channel is depleted of electrons

difference between the source and the drain is very large: This is the "power" part of the amplifier. We show this in Concept 4.

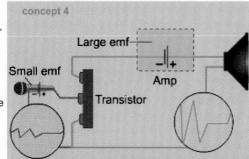

Current cannot flow

concept 4

Large emf

Small emf

Amp

Transistor

A transistor at work
Source/drain emf is large
Gate emf is small (signal)
Signal determines output of amplifier

When there is no sound, the microphone creates a negative gate voltage, depleting the *n* channel and preventing current from flowing through the transistor. Although the voltage from the "large emf" source is much greater than the voltage of the microphone, the microphone is preventing any current from flowing.

Now imagine that a singer starts her song. As the sound of her voice becomes louder, the microphone creates a smaller negative gate voltage, or even a positive one, and current is allowed to flow from the drain to the source, unleashing the power of the large emf and driving the loudspeaker. The transistor functions as a variable resistor that is controlled by the microphone signal.

The strong current flowing through the channel from the source to the drain is in perfect synchronization with the amount of charge on the gate, which depends on the voltage applied by the microphone. The large signal mimics the small one.

36.16 - Physics at work: photovoltaic cells

Photovoltaic effect: Electron flow caused by photons.

Solar cells are semiconductor devices that absorb light and convert its energy into electricity. Since sunlight is free and the operation of the cells has no environmentally hazardous side effects, there is an obvious appeal to their use. The challenge for researchers and manufacturers is to lower their cost and to raise their efficiency so that they may effectively compete with oil, coal and other traditional energy sources.

Banks of photovoltaic cells populate a "solar energy farm"
that can produce hundreds of kilowatts of electric power.

How do solar cells work? In Concept 1 we show a typical *n*-on-*p* junction solar cell, the most common type of cell. A wafer of *p*-type silicon has an element such as phosphorous diffused into its upper surface. This results in an *n*-type material, one with mobile electrons, being located above a *p*-type material, whose charge carriers are mobile holes. In short, this is a *p-n* junction, or diode.

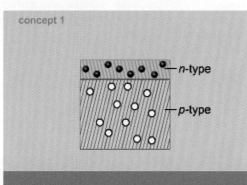

concept 1

n-type

p-type

Structure of photovoltaic cell
p-substrate with *n*-type material diffused into surface
· A *p-n* junction

With solar cells, the concept of diffusion current is important. Near the junction, mobile electrons from the *n*-region diffuse into the *p*-region, leaving positively charged donor ions (holes) in their wake. These holes remain there and form a positive region.

Mobile holes also diffuse from the *p*-region in the other direction, into the *n*-region. This flow of charge, a *diffusion current*, occurs for the same reason perfume diffuses across a room, from where the concentration is higher to where the concentration is lower. The result is a depletion zone near the junction. That is, the *n*-region is relatively depleted of mobile electrons and the *p*-region is depleted of the same number of holes.

The effects of this diffusion are shown in Concept 2. After enough charges move, equilibrium is reached: The result in the depletion zone is a built-in electric field that points from the *n*-region toward the *p*-region. This field opposes any further motion of charge, and the diffusion current quickly stops.

In an earlier section, we discussed how placing a *p-n* junction in a circuit with a battery could create a depletion zone. The point here is that a depletion zone also forms spontaneously when the materials are simply placed adjacent to one another.

Now let's consider what happens when a photon strikes the solar cell. The only photons relevant to our story are those that are energetic enough to promote an electron from the valence to the conduction band. When such a photon strikes a valence electron in the semiconductor, it increases the energy of the electron, promoting it to the higher band.

The electron will flow toward the *n*-type semiconductor, since that side of the depletion zone is positively charged, and the hole will flow to the negatively charged *p*-type semiconductor. To put it another way, the electric field caused by the diffusion current "pushes and pulls" the holes and electrons freed by photons striking the semiconducting material. Press the refresh button in your browser to see this occur in Concept 3.

Since many photons will strike the material, many electrons and holes will flow: A current is born. By placing metallic contacts on either side of the junction, this current can be used to power a load. In Concept 4, you see the solar cell in a circuit powering a home. There is a flow of negatively charged electrons out of the *n*-region into the circuit, and a flow of positively charged holes out of the *p*-region into the circuit.

The price of photovoltaic cells has been steadily decreasing over the past 30 years. However, the electrical power produced by such cells still costs more than power from fossil fuels (coal and oil), or wind-generated power. To cite some approximate numbers (since energy prices fluctuate), a kilowatt-hour produced by burning a fossil fuel costs from 3.5 to 4.5 cents. Wind power costs just 4.5 to 5.5 cents per kilowatt-hour, although there are issues with it: What do you do when the wind is not blowing?

In contrast, the cost of solar power is approximately 25 to 45 cents per kilowatt-hour. Solar power costs more money, although it could be cost effective for supplying power to remote locations, since power lines would not have to be run from distant power plants.

Analysts in the environmental community do raise issues about the "true" costs of different energy sources, such as the costs of environmental side effects, including health issues, pollution and global warming. Fair enough! With those costs factored in, different conclusions can be drawn about which power source really is the cheapest. However, the numbers above reflect the costs that companies and consumers pay in the short term for power from different sources, and they help to explain the current dominance of fossil-fuel energy.

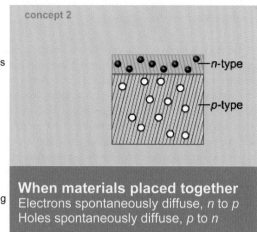

When materials placed together
Electrons spontaneously diffuse, *n* to *p*
Holes spontaneously diffuse, *p* to *n*

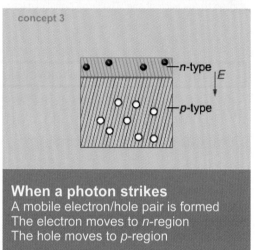

When a photon strikes
A mobile electron/hole pair is formed
The electron moves to *n*-region
The hole moves to *p*-region

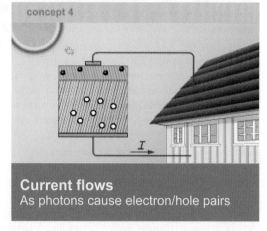

Current flows
As photons cause electron/hole pairs

Laser: Light Amplification by the Stimulated Emission of Radiation.

Laser emitting coherent red light.

Semiconductor transistors rely on physics that was pioneered in the early 20th century, and so do lasers.

Lasers amplify electromagnetic radiation. They can be used to amplify radiation at frequencies ranging from infrared to x-rays. To simplify the discussion, we will simply say that they amplify light, not worrying about whether or not the radiation is visible to humans.

The light that emanates from a laser has three crucial properties. It is (1) coherent, (2) monochromatic, having one frequency, and (3) highly directional. *Coherent* means that the emitted waves are all in phase with one another: The light can be considered as a single wave. In contrast, the light waves that emanate from a light bulb are out of phase, or incoherent. Such light is often described as consisting of a collection of finite *wave trains*, and the trains are not synchronized.

In Concepts 1 and 2, you see light emanating from a flashlight and from a laser. The light from the flashlight consists of many wave trains, which as you can see have different wavelengths and frequencies, and are traveling in different directions. The wave trains from the flashlight are not in phase: The locations of peaks and troughs vary by wave train. The contrast with laser light is clear: its waves are in phase, have one frequency, and travel in a single direction.

A working laser has three essential parts: a laser medium, a pumping process, and a feedback mechanism.

The *laser medium* can be manufactured from a wide variety of materials. The first operational laser used a ruby crystal. Today, the laser medium can be a gas (such as helium-neon), a liquid, or a solid, as is the case with diode lasers, the type you would find in a DVD player.

The laser has a *pumping process*, during which the atomic electrons of the medium are excited to high energy levels. This can be done by means such as electric discharges, flash lamps, or even light from other lasers.

The pumping process increases the energy of the atoms of the medium. Once these atoms are excited, photons injected into the medium cause it to emit other photons: Light shined into the laser medium generates additional light.

concept 1

Light from flashlight
Incoherent, multi-colored, divergent

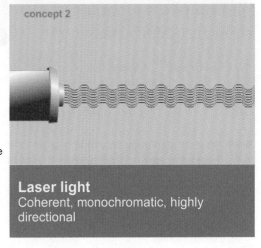

concept 2

Laser light
Coherent, monochromatic, highly directional

The container has silvered reflective walls, so that photons in the medium are reflected back into it. The process repeats as these photons cause even more in-phase photons to be emitted, and the original light is amplified.

This basic system is illustrated in Concept 3. (Press the refresh button in your browser if you want to see the animation.) The laser medium is inside the container. All the photons reflect off of the mirror on the left, back into the medium, and most of them reflect off the mirror on the right, while some are allowed to pass through. The mirrors form an *optical feedback mechanism*.

This feedback mechanism can be likened to the *audio feedback* that may occur with a sound amplifier. If you have ever winced at the loud squeal as someone experiments with an amplifier, you have heard the unintended consequences of feedback: Too much of the amplified sound is feeding back into the microphone, and is amplified again, and again, until a high-amplification runaway reaction occurs. In a laser, the mirrors reflecting light back into the laser medium provide the feedback. When the system is properly configured, coherent oscillation occurs, and a highly monochromatic, highly directional output beam is created.

Above, we have described the fundamentals of a laser. There remains a basic question, however: Why should the light emanating from the laser be of one color, or frequency? In a laser, you pump energy into the medium, and then use that energy to create an intense beam of light. But why is that light all of the same wavelength, say 633 nm? To explain why, we have to turn to quantum theory.

Fundamental laser components
Laser medium: accepts energy, emits light
Pumping process: how electrons get excited
Feedback mechanism: enhances and focuses the signal

36.18 - Laser pumping and stimulated emission

Pumping: Exciting atoms into higher energy levels.

Stimulated emission: An "excited" atom emits a photon when a photon of the right frequency passes by.

Illumination with ultraviolet light makes these minerals fluoresce with characteristic colors. A sample of calcite, in the middle, glows orange.

The core of a laser's functioning is its pumping process, followed by the stimulated emission of radiation. In this section, we describe three types of interaction between radiation and matter. The first, where matter absorbs radiation, is relevant to pumping. The second and third are processes in which matter emits radiation.

Below, we show absorption. An atom in its *ground state* absorbs a photon and one of its electrons changes states, moving to a higher energy level. These levels are typically described with subscripts; so, for example, the atom might go from energy level E_0 to level E_1.

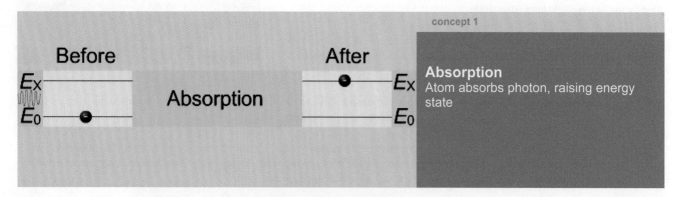

concept 1

Absorption
Atom absorbs photon, raising energy state

After an atom is excited, how does it return to its ground state? One answer is shown in the illustration below, which illustrates *spontaneous emission*: An atom can spontaneously, with no outside influence, lower its energy state by emitting a photon in a random direction. (This may not seem spontaneous since the atom first had to be "excited," but this is the terminology, and it contrasts with what will be described below.)

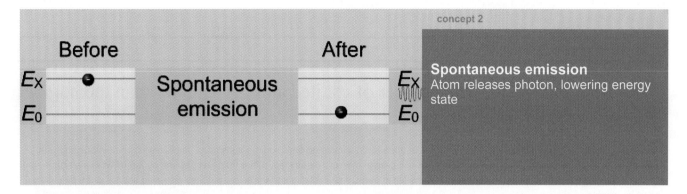

If you shine ultraviolet light upon certain minerals, such as calcite, they *fluoresce*, that is, they glow as long as the energizing ultraviolet radiation continues. A mineral absorbs high-energy photons of radiation and then spontaneously emits photons in a series of steps. These minerals only absorb and emit certain wavelengths of light, due to the quantized nature of their energy levels, so they glow a particular color.

Spontaneous emission is an interesting topic but not the controlled process desired in lasers. If all the laser medium did was to absorb light and then spontaneously re-emit it in random directions, there would be no amplification of the light.

Stimulated emission is the key to lasers. Below, you see an atom that has already been excited to a higher energy state.

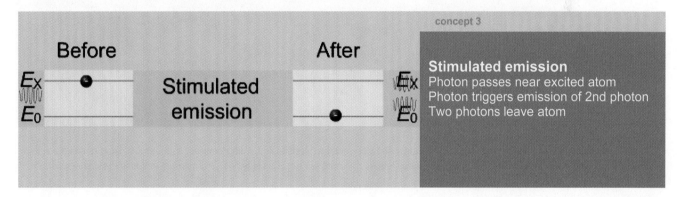

A photon of the appropriate frequency passes close to the excited atom. The result: The atom emits its own photon of the same frequency and returns to its initial energy state. Here is the "gain" produced by lasers: One photon of light causes a net result of two: the process of **l**ight **a**mplification by the **s**timulated **e**mission of **r**adiation. The presence of one photon causes another to be emitted.

We use words like "passes close" and "presence" because photons do not "collide" with atoms during stimulated emission, but they do cause the atom to emit a second photon when the energy of the stimulating photon corresponds to a difference in energy levels allowed in the atom. In sum, with stimulated emission, you start with one photon, and end with two.

To explain further what is occurring in a laser medium, we will use two analogies. The simpler one is mechanistic. Imagine a pool ball that has been raised off the ground and placed on the surface of a flat kitchen table. This increases its gravitational potential energy and corresponds to an atom that has been excited. A second pool ball is rolled at the first and both of them fly off the table. The combined kinetic energy of the two balls as they reach the ground is greater than the original kinetic energy of the ball that was rolled. The collision has "unleashed" the potential energy of the pool ball that was resting on the table.

There is a limitation here, perhaps an issue that concerned you as you considered this metaphor and applied it to a large number of pool balls, in order to make it more similar to the many atoms in the laser medium. The process would not produce a coherent stream of pool balls. If you did this experiment with many pool balls, they would fly off the table in many directions.

It is better to think of the light as a wave and to consider the phenomenon of resonance, as exhibited by mechanical or electromagnetic waves. Quantum physics states that atoms act like electromagnetic oscillators with particular resonant frequencies. The passing light wave causes the atoms in the medium to begin vibrating in a resonant, coherent relationship. The oscillations are driven by, and in phase with, the stimulating light wave. The atoms respond to the incoming light and reradiate like tiny antennae. The reradiated waves reinforce the waves that cause them.

36.19 - Population inversion

Population inversion: The number of excited atoms is greater than the number of lower-energy atoms.

Stimulated emission is required for lasers to function. For there to be stimulated emission, photons must be passing by and interacting with excited atoms in a medium, from which they can cause coherent photons to be emitted, rather than just passing by atoms whose electrons are at lower energy levels. Not only do the low-energy atoms fail to participate in stimulated emission, but they may also sabotage the process by absorbing photons.

Under normal circumstances, more atoms in a medium will be in lower energy states than in higher energy states. A population inversion is required: The majority of the atoms must be pumped to a higher energy level. When photons strike a medium with an inverted population, stimulated emission is more likely to occur.

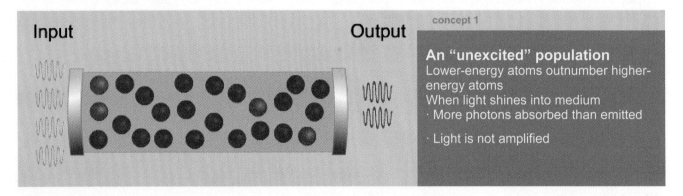

concept 1

An "unexcited" population
Lower-energy atoms outnumber higher-energy atoms
When light shines into medium
· More photons absorbed than emitted

· Light is not amplified

To illustrate the need for an inverted population, we start by showing you the opposite in the diagram above: photons striking a material with a normal population. Some of the atoms are at higher energy levels, but most are not. This is typical of a material that is in thermal equilibrium with its surroundings, such as one at room temperature.

When photons strike the material, most of them are absorbed. This raises the energy levels of some of its atoms, which then spontaneously emit photons in random directions. Occasionally, there is stimulated emission when a photon encounters an atom that already contains an excited electron, but this is rare. This is no way to run a laser!

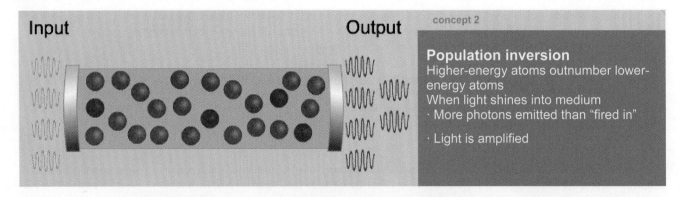

concept 2

Population inversion
Higher-energy atoms outnumber lower-energy atoms
When light shines into medium
· More photons emitted than "fired in"

· Light is amplified

In contrast, the medium above has a population inversion. A photon is far more likely to strike an excited atom, and stimulated emission becomes commonplace. Placing the medium in a reflecting container can further aid this process. Photons will reflect off the container walls and strike other excited atoms, causing a "chain reaction" of stimulated emissions. Energy can be continually added by pumping the medium, ensuring a ready supply of excited atoms.

36.20 - Physics at work: operating a laser

Today, there is a variety of ways to create a population inversion that enables light amplification. To discuss one, let's consider a type of laser that was developed early on, in 1960 and 1961, and remains common, the helium-neon (He-Ne) laser. A glass tube is filled with helium and neon gases. An electric current passes through the tube, and its electrons collide with helium atoms, raising their energy levels from their ground state E_0 to an elevated state E_A.

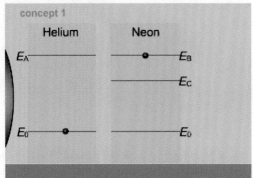

He-Ne laser in a laboratory.

In this state, the helium atoms are said to be at a *metastable* level. They will stay there for a relatively long period of time, as opposed to quickly and spontaneously emitting photons and falling back to a lower energy level. (Relatively long, in this context, means on the order of a thousandth or a ten-thousandth of a second.)

The helium atoms, including those at the metastable level E_A, are continually colliding with neon atoms in the gas mixture. The energy level of a metastable helium atom is very close to that of a high-energy neon atom. In a collision with a ground-state neon atom, a metastable helium atom causes the neon to rise to energy level E_B while the helium atom itself returns to the ground state. This is shown in Concept 1. Neon atoms at E_B are also metastable; they will persist for a relatively long time at this elevated energy level.

Laser process: part 1
Energy of helium atoms raised
Energy transferred to neon atoms
Population inversion results

Why not just let the electric discharge excite the neon atoms, and skip the helium? Helium is required since neon atoms do not respond readily to electron bombardment by the current that excites the helium atoms.

So far, we remain in the dark, so to speak. Many neon atoms have had their energy raised to E_B. The population has been inverted: There are more neon atoms at E_B than at E_0. The next goal is to stimulate the neon atoms to emit photons, dropping to the intermediate energy level E_C in the process. To accomplish this, light is beamed into the laser medium consisting of photons having an energy corresponding precisely to the difference between E_B and E_C. These photons interact with neon atoms whose electrons are at energy level E_B, causing stimulated emissions: The E_B neon atoms each emit a photon of the same frequency, and drop to energy level E_C. The atoms undergo what is called a *laser transition*.

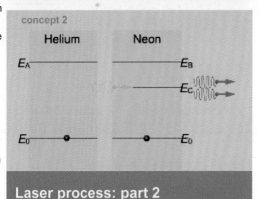

Laser process: part 2
Photons enter laser medium
Stimulated emission occurs
· light is amplified

Neon returns to initial state

It is important to note that the energy of each stimulating photon must equal the energy difference between E_B and E_C in order for the laser to function. Here is where quantum physics comes into play. A precise understanding of the energy levels of helium and neon atoms is required to design a successful He-Ne laser, as is knowledge of the relationship between the energy and frequency of a photon.

The additional photons that are emitted interact with other energized neon atoms, causing further stimulated emissions. Mirrors on both ends of the laser reflect these photons back into the laser medium, along the axis of propagation. The distance between the mirrors is crucial since it ensures the constructive interference of the light. They require extremely precise fabrication, and reflect more than 99.5% of the photons that hit them.

One last detail: How about the neon atoms that are now at energy level E_C? They rapidly and spontaneously decay to their ground state, emitting photons in all directions in the process. Those photons are in essence "noise" while the stimulated emission photons are "the signal." The spontaneous emission occurs after about 10^{-8} seconds, ten thousand or so times faster than it occurs with metastable states.

This rapid transition is important. It means that not many neon atoms linger in the E_C state. They quickly return to the E_0 state where collisions with helium atoms can excite them back to E_B, and the lasing process can begin anew. And there is another reason why it is important that few atoms have energy E_C: If there were too many of these around, then they would absorb photons and return to energy E_B, which would thwart the lasing process. (Neon atoms at E_0 cannot absorb photons and rise to either E_B or E_C, since the required energy differences do not match the energy of the photons being used.)

He-Ne lasers are inexpensive and common. The laser tubes can be purchased for less than $100. These may yield a power output of 1.0 mW when connected to a DC power input of 10 W. This means they are about 0.01% efficient. Such lasers have been used for purposes ranging from supermarket scanners to laser printers, but semiconductor lasers, which are cheaper to fabricate, are rapidly superceding them.

36.21 - Sample problem: ruby laser

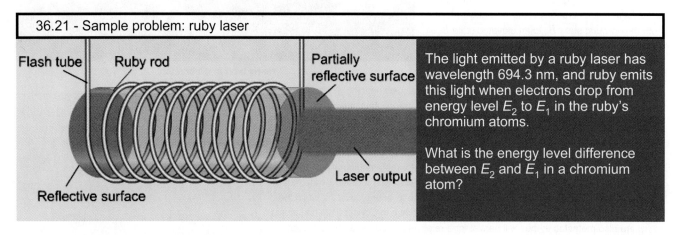

The light emitted by a ruby laser has wavelength 694.3 nm, and ruby emits this light when electrons drop from energy level E_2 to E_1 in the ruby's chromium atoms.

What is the energy level difference between E_2 and E_1 in a chromium atom?

Theodore Maimann built the first operational laser in 1960, a flash-pumped ruby laser. Maimann placed a cylindrical ruby rod inside a flash pump. The flash pump excited the chromium atoms in the ruby to a metastable state using an intense burst of light. Then the ions fluoresced back to the ground state, releasing light of wavelength 694.3 nm. Carefully aligned mirrors were placed at either end of the ruby to produce a coherent laser oscillation.

Variables

energy	E
wavelength	$\lambda = 694.3$ nm

What is the strategy?

1. Calculate the energy of a photon of the light emitted from a ruby laser.
2. Use the energy of the light to calculate the energy level difference between E_2 and E_1.

Physics principles and equations

Energy of a photon

$$E = hf$$

Energy level difference

$$\Delta E = E_f - E_i$$

Copyright 2000-2007 Kinetic Books Co. Chapter 36

Step-by-step solution

Step	Reason
1. $E = hf$	energy of photon
2. $f = \dfrac{c}{\lambda}$	frequency, wave speed and wavelength
3. $E = \dfrac{hc}{\lambda}$	substitute equation 2 into equation 1
4. $\Delta E = E_1 - E_2$ $\|\Delta E\| = E_2 - E_1$	energy difference
5. $E_2 - E_1 = \dfrac{hc}{\lambda}$	substitute equation 4 into equation 3
6. $E_2 - E_1 = \dfrac{\left(6.63 \times 10^{-34}\ \text{J} \cdot \text{s}\right)\left(3.00 \times 10^{8}\ \frac{m}{s}\right)}{\left(694.3 \times 10^{-9}\ \text{m}\right)}$ $E_2 - E_1 = 2.86 \times 10^{-19}\ \text{J} = 1.79\ \text{eV}$	evaluate

---

36.22 - Gotchas

An atom's electrons can exist at any energy level. No, this statement contradicts one of the key tenets of quantum physics. The electrons can only exist at specific energy states, and will not be found with energies between those levels.

A friend says: an electron falls from an energy level of −4.5 eV to −7.2 eV. It emits a photon with 2.7 eV of energy. Has he learned his quantum physics? Yes, he has. The energy of the photon equals the amount of energy given up by the atom.

All photons have the same energy. No, all photons of electromagnetic radiation (for example, light) of a **particular frequency** have the same amount of energy. The energy of a photon increases with the frequency of the radiation.

Something is quantized if it has a smallest, indivisible unit. The opposite of quantized is continuous. The eggs you buy in a carton at the grocery store are quantized; the amount of milk you pour into a glass is effectively continuous.

The Balmer series formula predicts the wavelengths of visible light that are present in the emission spectrum of excited hydrogen gas. When discovered, it revealed a mathematical pattern in the spacing of the spectral emission (or absorption) lines of hydrogen that strongly hinted at an underlying order.

The physicists Max Planck and Albert Einstein showed that radiation is quantized. The quantum of light is called a photon. The energy of a photon of electromagnetic radiation equals Planck's constant times the frequency of the radiation. Einstein cleared up the mystery behind the photoelectric effect by making the assumption that light is quantized.

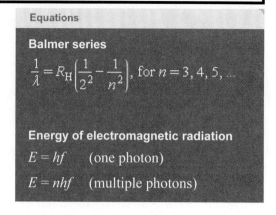

Equations

Balmer series

$$\frac{1}{\lambda} = R_H \left(\frac{1}{2^2} - \frac{1}{n^2} \right), \text{ for } n = 3, 4, 5, \ldots$$

Energy of electromagnetic radiation

$E = hf$ (one photon)

$E = nhf$ (multiple photons)

Niels Bohr developed the basis for the modern-day quantum view of the atom. He stated that the orbits of electrons around the nucleus of an atom are quantized: Electrons can only exist at orbits of specific radii and energy levels. When its electrons jump between levels, an atom emits or absorbs photons whose energy corresponds to the change in electron energy.

Quantum theory is used in the design of semiconductors. Semiconductors are doped – mixed with impurities – to alter the nature of the resistance they offer to currents. Doping creates more mobile electrons and holes than exist in pure semiconductor material.

Key components of transistors include p- and n-type semiconductors. A p-type material has mobile holes that act as charge carriers; an n-type material has mobile electrons. An external potential difference can increase the supply of these charge carrriers near a p-n junction in a transistor, allowing current to flow more readily. However, if the potential difference is changed in magnitude or reversed, it can cause mobile charge carriers to move away from the junction, reducing the flow of current or stopping it altogether.

Laser designers also rely on insights from quantum theory. Some agent such as an electrical discharge excites the laser medium, for example a helium-neon gas mixture. This elevates the medium's electrons to higher energy states. When photons of light are injected into the medium, the excited atoms are stimulated to emit identical, in-phase photons, increasing the flux of photons in the medium and amplifying the light.

For a laser to work, there must be a population inversion: there must be more excited atoms than unexcited ones in the laser medium. If there is no population inversion, then any photons injected into the medium will be absorbed, increasing the energy of the atoms, rather than causing additional photons to be emitted.

37.0 - Introduction

Richard Feynman (1918 − 1988) was an American physicist best known to the general public for his leading role in the commission that investigated the destruction of the space shuttle Challenger in 1986. His bestselling memoirs delighted millions with his irreverence and tales of bongo drum-playing.

In the physics community, Feynman was known for his insight into quantum mechanics and the brilliance of his lectures. The "Feynman Lectures in Physics," still in print today, show his timeless ability to clearly and memorably explain fundamental aspects of physics.

We start this chapter by giving you a chance to conduct a thought experiment that Feynman described as "impossible, absolutely impossible, to explain in any classical way, and which has in it the heart of quantum mechanics." In this thought experiment, Feynman emphasized the shortcomings of considering matter solely as composed of particles, and the need to adopt a vision where matter has both a particle and a wave nature. This is known as the wave-particle duality.

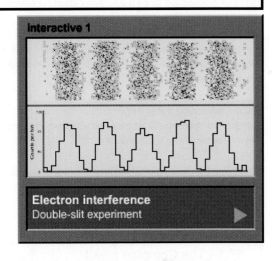

interactive 1

Electron interference
Double-slit experiment

Feynman first asked the reader to consider classical particles, that is, those for which the physics of Newton completely predicts the motion. Feynman used bullets in his experiment; we will be slightly more pacific and ask you to imagine throwing baseballs at a picket fence. The picket fence is missing two of its slats. The missing slats provide gaps that the baseballs can pass through. The balls will stop when they strike a wall behind the fence.

If you conducted this experiment yourself, you would find that most of the baseballs hit the wall directly behind the missing slats. A few baseballs would hit slightly to the sides of those areas, corresponding to the balls that went through the gaps at an angle. You would see two piles of baseballs that accumulated behind the gaps in the fence.

Feynman used this first thought experiment to remind his audience how they expect the world to "work" based on everyday experience. This experiment provided the contrast with another experiment, one you can conduct for yourself using the simulation to the right.

In the simulation, you are conducting a similar experiment, but with particles of far smaller scale. Instead of baseballs being fired, electrons are fired one at a time toward a barrier with two slits. The slits are very narrow and very close together.

The electrons pass through the slits and reach a screen, which is a photographic material that records where they land. The electrons cannot be observed as they move from the source to the barrier, or from the barrier to the screen. Only the final position is marked, by using black dots.

Press FIRE to launch a single electron. Then, hold the FIRE button down to fire a stream of electrons so you can see the pattern of where they land.

Look at the pattern of where the electrons accumulate. Instead of accumulating in two piles, like the baseballs did in Feynman's first thought experiment, you see regions where many electrons accumulate, alternating with regions where very few electrons land. The pattern should remind you of the dark and light fringes that are created on a screen when light shines through a pair of slits.

In the theory of optics, physicists explain the pattern of light and dark fringes by modeling light as a wave, with wave-like properties such as frequency and wavelength. This simulation shows that something which you have solely considered to be a particle, an electron, also displays wave-like properties in a similar experiment. This is the essential point of Feynman's second thought experiment: Particles such as electrons have wave-like properties. A single particle can travel from a source to a screen and demonstrate interference effects due to the presence of the two slits. The wave that is associated with a moving particle is called a *matter wave*.

Now you can use the simulation again to see another fundamental aspect of quantum mechanics. Reset the simulation. Press the FIRE button a few times and note the locations of the first three or four electrons. Then press RESET again, fire a few more electrons, and note their locations. In your two experiments, did the first three or four electrons show up at the same location each time?

The answer to the question is "no". In both this simulation, and in the real experiments that this simulation is recreating, the location of a single electron cannot be predicted. Although the overall pattern of light and dark fringes as you fire hundreds of electrons can be predicted, where a particular electron will strike the screen cannot be determined in advance.

This is the second point of the animation: The locations of the electrons can be stated in terms of likelihoods, like the probability of drawing an ace from a deck of cards. The pattern of light and dark fringes provides a "map" of where an electron is likely to strike the photographic paper behind the slits. However, you cannot predict in advance where any one electron will land, any more than you can state with certainty that one particular card will be an ace.

You are witnessing a major point of quantum mechanics in this simulation. Scientists have performed the experiment with electrons, and the results have been exactly as depicted. Electron after electron can be fired through slits, and the interference of their matter waves will create a pattern like the one you see here.

The simulation shows the wave-like properties of particles. Scientists like Einstein had also postulated the particle-like nature of light, which had been considered a wave. This chapter will start with that topic, the particle nature of electromagnetic radiation, before returning to the topic that the experiment in this section illustrates.

37.1 - The Compton effect

Compton effect: Considering x-rays as composed of particles explains why their frequency diminishes as they are scattered by a material.

Einstein stated that light was composed of indivisible packets of energy. His theory was rooted in experiment. By treating light as a particle he could explain the photoelectric effect and make successful predictions: Calculating the energy of the photons that make up light of a particular color allowed Einstein to predict whether shining that color light on a given material would cause it to emit electrons.

This opened up another question: Did light have other particle properties, such as momentum? In 1916, Einstein derived an equation quantifying a photon's momentum. As shown in Equation 1, the momentum equals Planck's constant divided by the photon's wavelength. However, it remained to be shown experimentally that photons actually had momentum. Some scientists believed that the photoelectric effect might be explained by updating the wave theory of light, but if light could be shown to have momentum then it would be hard to deny its particle-like nature.

Physicists such as W.H. and W.L. Bragg − a famous British father-and-son pair − had been using x-rays to analyze the structure of matter, particularly crystals. The small wavelengths of x-rays, compared to the atomic spacing in the crystals, meant that the scattered radiation would exhibit diffraction patterns, that is, the radiation would be strong in particular directions. The diffraction pattern could be used to analyze the regular, periodic layout of atoms within crystals, and this technique was later used to deduce the double-helix structure of DNA. Since diffraction is a property only of waves, you might think that x-ray diffraction experiments could not provide any support for a particle view of electromagnetic radiation − but as it turned out, they did.

Scientists experimenting with x-rays scattering from target materials started to observe some disturbing data. To explain their discomfort, we first have to explain what they expected.

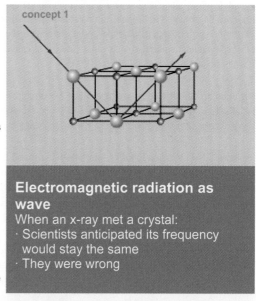

concept 1

Electromagnetic radiation as wave
When an x-ray met a crystal:
· Scientists anticipated its frequency would stay the same
· They were wrong

concept 2

Compton effect
Consider x-ray as a photon (particle)

Their expectations were based on the view of light as an electromagnetic wave, consisting of oscillating electric and magnetic fields. In this classical picture, when an electromagnetic wave encounters an atom, it causes the atom's electrons to oscillate at the same frequency as the wave. Accelerating charges emit radiation, so these oscillating charges then radiate their own electromagnetic waves. This process is called *scattering*; some waves would be re-emitted in the same direction as the initial wave, while others would be re-emitted in other directions.

The critical point to focus on is the frequency of the re-radiated waves. Classical electromagnetic theory, used by scientists like the Braggs, predicted that the outgoing waves should have the same frequency as the incoming waves. Scattering would change the direction of the incoming radiation, but scientists were confident that it should **not** change its frequency.

Alas, observations did not accord with theory. Scientists observed that atoms being subjected to x-rays were re-emitting radiation of lower frequency than the initial radiation, and the effect depended on the angle at which the radiation was scattered. Something was diminishing the frequency (and the energy) of the scattered radiation.

At first, the data were not taken seriously. However, in 1923 the American physicist A. H. Compton published two papers that argued conclusively that if radiation were quantized, one should expect the frequency to be reduced. The problem was not with the experimental data; the problem was with a theory that regarded light solely as a wave.

How did Compton explain the discrepancy? He assumed that the electromagnetic radiation was made up of photons that had momentum. He proposed that instead of picturing a light wave shaking electrons up and down, scientists ought to picture the interaction as akin to a collision between two particles, a photon and an electron. Like Einstein, he was asking his peers to expand their conception of radiation to include properties usually associated with particles, such as momentum.

He then used classical mechanics, applying the laws of conservation of energy and momentum to the collision. He applied the same principles that would be applied to a collision of two billiard balls. (His analysis had to be more complex than that for two balls, because he had to relate the quantized photon energy to wavelength and frequency, and relate its energy and momentum.)

Compton stated that when the photon in question collides with an electron belonging to an atom in the target, the electron gains some kinetic energy from the collision. Energy must be conserved, and the photon loses that same amount of energy. The energy of a photon equals hf, the product of Planck's constant and its frequency. When its energy is diminished in the scattering process, so too is its frequency.

Not only did Compton's work explain the reduction in frequency, but his analysis of the collision also correctly relates the direction of the scattered x-rays to their change in frequency. When a moving particle strikes a stationary target, its change in momentum and the angle at which it scatters are related. Consider the photon-electron collision. If the direction at which the photon comes out is virtually unchanged from its original direction, then its change in momentum is small, and very little momentum (and energy) will be given to the electron. In other words, the two particles just suffered a glancing blow.

When Compton observed x-ray photons whose direction was barely changed, he saw that their frequency was also practically unchanged. Again, the basics of collisions held true.

As the angle between the emitted and incident radiation increased, the change in momentum increased. More momentum (and energy) is transferred to the electron. Radiation that was *backward scattered* suffered the largest reduction in frequency.

Compton's work with x-rays confirmed that electromagnetic radiation possesses momentum, a property that had been classically associated with particles. It was increasingly hard to argue that light should only be considered a wave when it could be demonstrated that it had momentum, and its interaction with matter could be modeled using a classical explanation of collisions. It became necessary to admit that under certain conditions the wave nature of light is observed while in different experiments the particle nature is needed to explain the results.

A photon "collides" with an electron in the crystal
Photon loses energy in collision
Less energy means lower frequency ($E = hf$)

equation 1

Momentum of a photon

$$p = \frac{h}{\lambda}$$

p = momentum
λ = wavelength
h = Planck's constant, 6.63×10^{-34} J·s

After Compton's observations, physicists were forced to confront the fact that light, which had been thought of as solely an electromagnetic wave, also has properties of a particle. This new viewpoint enabled them to understand the experimental data they were confronting.

However, there still remained many enigmas. For instance, Bohr had constructed his model of the hydrogen atom, which successfully predicted observed emission and absorption spectra. Bohr proposed quantized energy states for the electron, starting with a classical view of the electron as a negatively charged, point-sized particle circling the positive nucleus, and using Planck's work. However, Bohr was not able to demonstrate why his model was correct.

In 1923, a French doctoral student named Louis de Broglie proposed a simple idea to help to rescue the physicists from their intellectual tar pit. Recognizing that light has both wave and particle properties, he reasoned that nature is symmetrical, and that the same is true for matter. De Broglie asserted that particles such as electrons have both particle and wave properties.

To quote de Broglie: "…I had a sudden inspiration. Einstein's wave-particle dualism was an absolutely general phenomenon extending to all physical nature…"

Although it was a simple idea, it propelled the next revolution in physics.

De Broglie conceived of the electron in an atom as a standing "matter wave" vibrating around the nucleus. In other words, the electron is "smeared out" instead of being a single point-sized particle. Let's consider the implications of representing an electron with such a wave, as shown in Concept 2.

As you may recall, a standing wave results from waves that interfere with one another. For there to be constructive interference, peak must meet peak, and trough must meet trough. In contrast, if at a given location, the peak of one wave meets the trough of another, the result is destructive interference − a flat line, in essence.

Here, the string is looped into a circle, and the length of the string is the circumference of the circle. A wave begins its circular path around the string, and when it makes a loop, it meets up with itself.

If as it makes a second journey around, peak meets peak, the result will be a standing wave. On the other hand, if peak meets trough, the wave will cancel. The relationship between the circumference of the circle and the wavelength determines whether there is constructive interference. In Concept 2, we show an example where there is constructive interference.

The wave shown to the right does not represent the actual path of the electron through space. It is a matter wave − a way to visualize the likelihood of finding the electron at a given location. If the amplitude of the wave is zero, then the likelihood is zero, and there will be no electron.

This provides one piece of the puzzle. Only certain wavelengths are possible for a given orbit, but that doesn't prevent any orbit being possible − it just dictates possible wavelengths.

The other piece of the puzzle comes from considering the angular momentum of the electron. De Broglie showed why Bohr's quantization argument could be justified by considering the angular momentum of the electron and the relationship between momentum and wavelength.

To quantify the wavelength of a matter particle such as an electron, de Broglie proposed that the same equation that describes the momentum

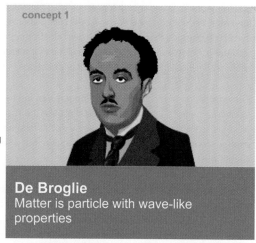

concept 1

De Broglie
Matter is particle with wave-like properties

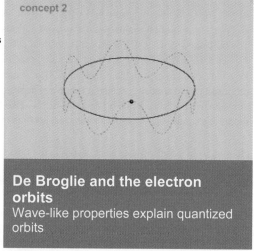

concept 2

De Broglie and the electron orbits
Wave-like properties explain quantized orbits

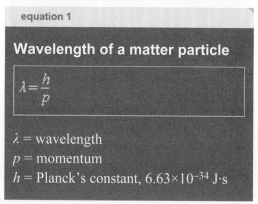

equation 1

Wavelength of a matter particle

$$\lambda = \frac{h}{p}$$

λ = wavelength
p = momentum
h = Planck's constant, 6.63×10^{-34} J·s

of a photon, $p = h/\lambda$, could also be applied to matter. A particle's wavelength, sometimes called the de Broglie wavelength, is related to its momentum by $\lambda = h/p$, as shown in Equation 1.

De Broglie's insight provided a crucial step in the understanding of the atom. He and other physicists used the idea to write down equations for the standing waves corresponding to any particle confined to a small space. The form of the matter waves (also known as the wavefunction of the particle) leads to predictions about the behavior of the particle. This is the principle behind quantum mechanics, also called wave mechanics.

37.3 - Observing matter waves

When light is shone through a pair of small slits, an interference pattern results. We show a light interference pattern in Concept 1.

If electrons can act like waves, they should also display interference patterns, and they do. The slits used should be of a width comparable to the wavelengths of the electrons in the experiment, which are moving at a speed such that their wavelength is on the order of 10^{-10} meters. You see the interference pattern caused by sending electrons through slits in Concept 2.

At the time that de Broglie proposed his theory of matter waves, it was not possible to make slits small enough to demonstrate electron diffraction. However, in 1927 two physicists named Clinton Davisson and Lester Germer inadvertently produced electron diffraction using a crystal of nickel. The spacing between atoms in the crystal happened to be on the order of the electron wavelength, causing the electrons' matter waves to interfere.

After witnessing this and the diffraction of other particles such as neutrons and whole hydrogen atoms, scientists began to take the wave-like nature of particles for granted, or perhaps better put, to marvel at it as a fact of nature. They called it the *wave-particle duality*.

Once they finished marveling, they also concluded that they could take advantage of the wave properties of matter. Wave diffraction imposes a limit on how small of an object can be resolved when it is probed with radiation of a certain wavelength. For example, an ordinary microscope uses visible light and glass lenses, and cannot resolve objects much smaller than 10^{-6} m, which is on the order of the wavelength of visible light.

To gain increased resolution, a *transmission electron microscope* (TEM) employs electrons instead of light. The wavelengths of those electrons are about ten thousand times smaller than that of light, which allows the TEM to resolve objects down to a size of about 10^{-10} m. Just as the light in an ordinary microscope passes through a sample that is fixed on a glass slide, the electron beam (think of it as a wave) passes through the thin sample on the way to a detector. An ordinary microscope uses a glass lens to focus light rays; the TEM uses magnetic fields to focus the charged electron beam.

In Concept 3 is an artificially-colored image captured by a transmission electron microscope. It shows a salivary gland of a mosquito infected by the Eastern equine encephalitis virus (red dots). The individual viruses are about 60 nanometers in diameter, and even smaller details than this are visible in the image. In comparison, the best optical microscopes can only resolve details as small as 200 nanometers.

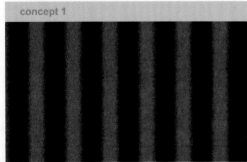

concept 1

Finding the wave in light
Light's wave-like properties visible in interference patterns

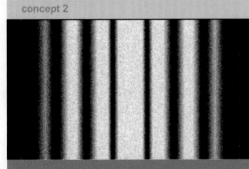

concept 2

Matter waves
Electron interference pattern
Pattern also created by projecting electrons at crystal

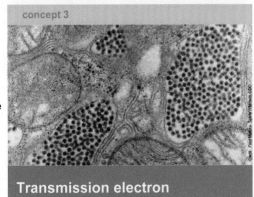

concept 3

Transmission electron

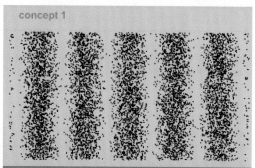

microscope
Takes advantage of small wavelengths of electrons
Resolves details at a scale of 10^{-10} meters

37.4 - Matter waves are probabilistic

De Broglie correctly asserted that electrons and other particles can be described as matter waves. Physicists, being quantitative types, wanted to know: How could they mathematically describe the location of a wave-particle like an electron?

In classical mechanics, when the net force exerted on a particle of a certain mass is known, the equation $F = ma$ is used to calculate the acceleration of the particle. If the initial position and velocity are also known, then other equations can determine the particle's location and velocity at any time.

Quantum physicists found that applying classical equations to atomic-sized particles led to paradoxes. For instance, the equations could be interpreted to predict that a quarter photon, or half an electron, should be present at a given location. This was in contradiction not only to the tenets of quantum physics, but to experiments, which showed that photon and electrons were indivisible.

Another conundrum can be discussed using the double-slit experiment. Electrons are fired through a pair of slits toward a barrier, as shown in Concept 1. A photographic plate records where the electrons strike the barrier. The pattern recorded on the plate (and shown in Concept 1) looks the same as that created by shining light through the slits.

Although physicists can state in advance what the overall pattern will look like based on factors such as how wide the slits are, they cannot predict in advance where any given electron will land on the photographic plate. They can only state the probability that it will land near a given location − for instance, the probability is much higher in the areas of the plate that contain the most dots.

You can liken this to a game of cards. You know that on average, one out of four cards will be a spade. However, given a shuffled deck and asked to state for sure whether a spade will be the first card you draw, or the second, you cannot. You can only say that there is a one in four chance that it will be a spade.

If 12 cards are dealt from a shuffled deck of cards, the probability is greatest that 3 cards will be spades, but from observing the repetition of many such trials, you could conclude that it is fairly likely that the actual number will be 2 or 4, and it is possible that there will be 1 or 5 spades, or even 0 or 12. All you can do is describe the probability of a given number of spades that will emerge when you deal 12 cards.

The section started with a question: How can the location of a particle like an electron be described? Quantum physicists describe such a particle with a *wavefunction*. The value of a wavefunction at a particular point and time is related to the **probability** of finding the particle near that point, at that time. To be more precise, the absolute square of the wavefunction is a probability density, a concept we discuss next.

Quantum physicists use the idea of probability density to describe the likelihood of finding a particle in a given region of space. *Probability density* is the probability per unit volume and is the absolute square of the wavefunction. (In one-dimensional problems, probability density is the probability per unit length, and in two-dimensional problems, it

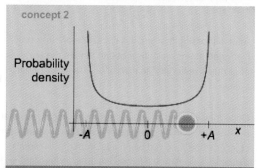

Electron fired through slits
Create interference pattern
Where a single electron will land can only be stated as likelihood

Position
Can be stated as a probability for "classical" objects

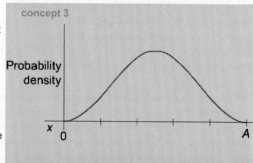

Particle in a box
Probability density describes likelihood that particle will be found in a given

Copyright 2000-2007 Kinetic Books Co. Chapter 37

is the probability per unit area.)

The term "absolute square" covers the case when the wavefunction has complex values (containing the imaginary number i). The absolute square equals the wavefunction multiplied by its complex conjugate. If the wavefunction contains only real values, so that its complex conjugate is the wavefunction itself, then the absolute square of the wavefunction is the same as the "ordinary" square of the wavefunction.

What is meant by probability density? It is a concept that can be applied to objects typically described with classical mechanics. For instance, someone could create a graph of your probability density at midnight. It is relatively likely that if someone is looking for you at that time, they would find you in bed. This means that the probability density function has a relatively high value there. The probability density function at midnight would also have smaller peaks at other locations in space, such as the chair in front of your computer, or in front of the refrigerator. Since the probability is zero to find you on Mars at midnight (or at any other time), the probability density function would be zero there.

The same idea can be applied to the position of a mass on a spring that is moving back and forth in simple harmonic motion with a certain total energy (or, physicists say that the system is in a particular state). You could graph the probability density function for the location of the mass. In fact, we did so, and that graph is shown in Concept 2.

How do you interpret this graph? Again, the locations where the graph is higher are the locations where it is more likely you would observe the mass. If you were only allowed to take photographs of the mass at random times, you would create a graph like this. (This is the situation in which quantum physicists find themselves.) The graph is higher near the endpoints of the mass's motion because it is moving more slowly there, which means it spends more time there and you are more likely to observe it there. Taking a snapshot at a random time, you are least likely to find it near the center because it moves the most quickly through that region.

In Concept 3, we move more to the realm of quantum mechanics. One intellectual construct that quantum physicists use to describe particles is the concept of a particle moving in a one-dimensional rigid box. We use the concept of waves and a wavefunction to describe that particle, which in this case is in its lowest energy state. We then construct a probability density graph. It shows that the particle is more likely to be found in the center of the box. The walls of the box are at 0 and A, and the particle never escapes the box. This means the particle is always present within the box, that is, the probability of finding it outside this region is zero.

The probability density that describes the position of an actual particle is rarely as simple as the one shown in Concept 3. In Concept 4, you see the graph of the probability density function for the electron in the ground-state in a hydrogen atom (the electron has the lowest energy that it can have). You can see that the electron is most likely to be found at the Bohr radius, but that it is possible for the electron to be found at radii other than this value. For large values of the radius, the probability density approaches zero. The very low probability density at large radii means it is possible, but highly, highly unlikely, that a bound electron can be found, say, one meter from the nucleus. Quantum physicists can use the Schrödinger equation to create a wavefunction that yields the graph you see in Concept 4. This is one of the fundamental equations in quantum mechanics.

The graph in Concept 4 tells us about the behavior of an electron in the ground-state of a hydrogen atom. If you measured the distance of the electron from the nucleus, and then did so again and again, each time charting its location, you would create a graph (a *radial probability density*) similar to that. You would note that the largest number of your observations have the electron at a distance equal to the Bohr radius, but you would find it at other locations as well.

Along with Einstein's theories of relativity, quantum mechanics has changed the world's conception of reality. Einstein showed that time and length cannot be treated as absolutes, but that the motion of the observer affects these properties. Physicists have now shown that concepts as common as the location of a particle must be stated in terms of probabilities. The work of these physicists has set the direction of physics for the last 100 years or so.

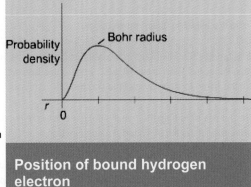

region

concept 4

Probability density

Bohr radius

r

0

Position of bound hydrogen electron
Height of graph reflects likelihood of finding particle in given region

37.5 - Interactive exercise: observing the probabilities of a particle

The simulation on the right is used to show how an interference pattern emerges as more and more electron waves pass through a pair of slits.

You are asked to observe two things.

First, press the FIRE button a few times and observe the location of the first five or six electrons. Then press RESET, and do this again. Do you observe each electron at the same location every time you run the simulation?

At the risk of ruining the punch line, the answer is no. If this is not clear, just fire one electron, press RESET, and fire one electron again.

You cannot predict in advance where a given electron will land on the screen. You can predict the probability of it landing near a certain spot, but not where it will land for sure.

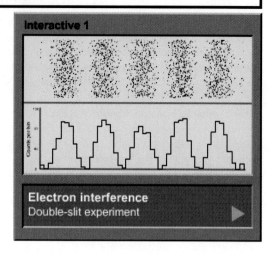

Interactive 1

Electron interference
Double-slit experiment

Although you cannot predict the location of any given electron, after enough electrons pass through, the overall pattern is visible as predicted by the intensity function.

After you fire 200 or so electrons, look at the graph. (Depress and hold down the FIRE button.) It will very closely resemble the graph of the intensity function for the interference of two electromagnetic waves passing through a pair of slits. Where the function is greater, you will see more photons accumulate over time. The smaller the function at a point, the fewer the number of particles (be they photons or electrons) that will accumulate nearby. Try firing 500 electrons, and you will see that the graph resembles the intensity function even more as the number of particles increases.

What you are observing here is in contrast to what one would expect using classical physics. If you toss a ball with a speed of exactly 25.0 m/s at an angle of 30.0 degrees from a height of exactly 1.50 m in a vacuum, classical physics states that you can exactly predict its trajectory and where it will land. If you again throw it with the same velocity from the same height, it will always land at the same location. Classical physics would claim the same certainty and reproducibility for an electron launched in the same way.

No such luck with quantum physics – or maybe one should say "it's all luck" with quantum physics? If you fire two consecutive electrons at the double-slit system, under identical conditions, you do not know for sure that the particles will land even remotely near the same spot. You can only observe where they land this time.

The more electrons that are fired, the more accurately you can predict the overall pattern. But you can no more predict the outcome of a single spin of a roulette wheel than the landing point of any one photon or electron.

37.6 - Heisenberg uncertainty principle

In prior sections, we discussed the interpretation of a matter wavefunction as relating to the likelihood that a particle will be found in a particular location.

Now we will turn to what happens when you try to measure the location of a particle. We will keep things simpler by assuming that the particle moves along a line, namely the x axis.

In general, if you want to know where a particle is, you make a measurement. All measurements are imperfect and have some uncertainty. Δx represents the uncertainty in position. If you were making a measurement of the momentum of the particle in the x-direction, there would also be some uncertainty of momentum Δp_x.

A classical physicist would agree there is some uncertainty in all measurements, just as you may have learned while doing lab assignments. Better procedures and instruments

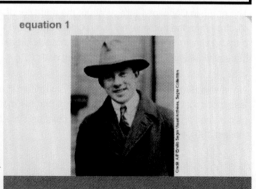

equation 1

Heisenberg uncertainty principle

can reduce the uncertainty. For example, if you were trying to measure an electron's position and momentum 5.00 seconds after it had been propelled by a given electric field, you might set up 1000 identical trials, use the best instruments available, and average the results for momentum and for position.

$$(\Delta x)(\Delta p_x) \geq \frac{\hbar}{2}$$

Δx = uncertainty in position
Δp_x = uncertainty in momentum
$\hbar$ = Planck's constant/2π

According to classical physics, these uncertainties can in principle be reduced to zero. There are no limits to knowledge about a classical particle. A classical physicist considering the theoretical uncertainty of position and momentum could write an equation like:

$$(\Delta x)(\Delta p_x) = 0 \quad \text{(classical physics)}$$

The German physicist Werner Heisenberg, in contrast, made the bold statement that knowledge is limited. He related the uncertainties in the particle's position and momentum along the same axis:

$$(\Delta x)(\Delta p_x) \geq \frac{\hbar}{2}$$

This inequality is a statement of the *Heisenberg uncertainty principle*. It states that there is a tradeoff between reducing the uncertainty in position and trying to do the same for momentum. One can find situations where Δx is relatively small, but this low uncertainty in position comes at the price of a higher uncertainty in the particle's momentum. Or if the momentum can be well determined, then the particle's location will be less precisely known.

Heisenberg's principle does not describe an "equipment problem". The problem cannot be solved with a better microscope, or more expensive lab equipment, or any other technique. Physicists hold that it is a fundamental property of reality: A particle's position and momentum must reflect a certain minimum amount of uncertainty because the particle simply cannot have both a definite position and a definite momentum. The wave/particle is spread out in space.

One important implication of this principle is that a particle can never have zero kinetic energy. If it did, it would be stationary (and have zero momentum), and then both its position and momentum could be determined. Consistency with the uncertainty relation requires that the particle must have at least some amount of kinetic energy, even at zero temperature.

Again, as with much quantum physics, the departure from classical physics becomes apparent only when the mass of the particle is very small.

37.7 - Gotchas

More massive particles always have shorter de Broglie wavelengths than less massive particles. Not necessarily. A particle's wavelength depends on its momentum, which equals its mass multiplied by its velocity. A more massive particle may have a longer wavelength than a lighter particle, if its velocity is small enough.

Only particles like protons and electrons have a de Broglie wavelength associated with them. "Matter waves" do not apply to larger things like baseballs. No. The wavelengths of objects with relatively large momenta, such as moving baseballs, are so small that experiments do not reveal their wave-like properties. But these objects are still subject to the laws of quantum physics. For large objects moving at ordinary speeds, the predictions of quantum physics and those of Newtonian mechanics are identical for all intents and purposes, much as special relativity essentially agrees with Newtonian mechanics at slow enough speeds.

37.8 - Summary

Further evidence that light has properties of particles − in addition to properties of waves − is provided by the Compton effect. When a photon and an electron collide, they behave much like two colliding billiard balls. The photon's frequency is reduced, because it has transferred some energy to the electron. The Compton effect provides evidence that though photons do not have mass, they **do** have momentum.

One of the basic tenets of quantum physics is that matter, like light, also exhibits wave-particle duality. The wave nature of matter explains why the energies of electrons in an atom are quantized.

The equation $\lambda = h/p$ relates a particle's wavelength to its momentum, and applies to particles of matter or of light.

Matter wave interference can be observed using an experiment similar to the double-slit experiment for light. However, in the case of matter waves, the wavelengths of even the smallest particles (generally those with the least momentum), such as electrons, are very small and so require very small slits to observe. Such small, closely-spaced slits are difficult to manufacture, but certain crystals naturally have atomic spacing similar to the required slit spacing. Matter waves were first observed using such crystals.

Matter waves are probabilistic. The wave- and particle-like properties of matter are reconciled in the form of the particle's wavefunction. The value of the wavefunction is related to the probability that the particle will be found at a given location at a given time. Mathematically speaking, a particle is described by a probability density function that tells the probability of observing the particle in any region.

One consequence of the wave-particle duality is that it is impossible to know both the position and momentum of a particle to infinite precision at the same time. In fact the product of the uncertainties in position and momentum has a precise lower limit: half of $\hbar$. This is the Heisenberg uncertainty principle.

Equations

Momentum of a photon

$$p = \frac{h}{\lambda}$$

Wavelength of a matter particle

$$\lambda = \frac{h}{p}$$

Heisenberg uncertainty principle

$$(\Delta x)(\Delta p_x) \geq \frac{\hbar}{2}$$

38.0 - Introduction

"Turn off the lights when you leave the room." "Don't buy that gas guzzler." "Turn the thermostat down a few degrees in winter." These phrases are all about saving energy, a worthwhile topic, but this chapter is about where that energy comes from.

The energy powering your computer and lights is electrical, but that electricity was likely generated from the burning of oil or coal. In turn, these fossil fuels came from the remains of ancient animals and plants, which derived their energy from sunlight. If your power was generated from hydroelectric sources – letting water stored behind a dam spin a turbine as it falls to a lower height – it was sunlight that evaporated the water, which later turned into rainwater which was stored behind the dam.

Nuclear power plants convert the energy stored in atoms into energy humans can use.

Ultimately, the source of our energy here on Earth is the Sun, and nuclear fusion is what powers the Sun. The fusion process takes lighter chemical elements such as hydrogen, and forms helium and heavier elements, in the process releasing energy.

In that respect, we owe our very existence to nuclear energy. However, to some, the term "nuclear physics" brings darker images to mind. For better or worse, the world learned what nuclear fission was in 1945 at Hiroshima, although the exact same physics principles behind atomic bombs are used peacefully every day.

In this chapter, you will learn about the nature of atoms, which is a field of study called *nuclear physics*. You will become more familiar with protons, neutrons and alpha particles. You will learn what occurs when atoms are split apart (fission), or when they are forced to merge (fusion).

You will also learn about many peaceful applications in the field of atomic physics such as radioactive dating (no, this does not mean that two radioactives go out for dinner and a movie) and energy production in nuclear reactors.

38.1 - The atom and the electron

Nobel Laureate Richard Feynman posed a hypothetical situation in which our entire base of scientific knowledge was destroyed, and we could pass on just one sentence to our descendants. What would we choose to tell them, in order to convey the most information in the fewest words?

In the famous "Feynman Lectures", his choice was to tell the post-apocalyptic population that all matter is composed of atoms, which are tiny particles that continually move around, attracting each other when they are fairly close together, but strongly repelling when they are pressed even closer together.

How did scientists arrive at this modern picture of the atom? In fact, what is an atom?

Humans have spent many millennia asking the question "What is the world made of?" We have come a long way from the ancient Greeks, who believed that the cosmos was composed of four elements: water, earth, air, and fire. Now, we know of over 100 chemical elements, which are the fundamental building blocks of matter. You have heard of many of the elements: hydrogen, oxygen, carbon, gold, lead, and so on.

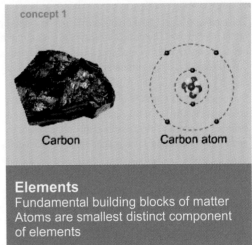

concept 1

Carbon   Carbon atom

Elements
Fundamental building blocks of matter
Atoms are smallest distinct component of elements

The modern definition of an *element* is a substance that cannot be divided or changed into another substance using ordinary chemical methods. Each element has different physical and chemical properties such as density, specific heat, and the way in which it bonds with other elements. You can see an example of a common element, carbon, in Concept 1.

An atom is the smallest piece of an element that still has its chemical and physical properties. Atoms consist of electrons circling a nucleus composed of protons and neutrons. This is illustrated in Concept 2. The next few sections will discuss the inner structure of the atom.

The modern theory of the atom began with the discovery of the first subatomic particle, the electron, in experiments performed over the course of about 40 years in the late 1800s. Physicists found that when they applied a high voltage across a low-pressure gas, an electric discharge was produced. They used a device called a *cathode ray tube* to achieve this effect. Today, you can witness a similar discharge in a neon sign or a fluorescent light bulb.

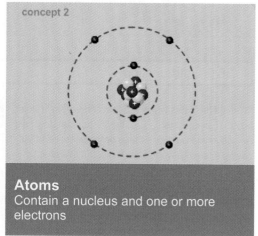

concept 2

Atoms
Contain a nucleus and one or more electrons

The physicists determined that the gas in the tube was conducting electric charge. The tube's negative electrode, also called a *cathode*, emitted a type of "invisible ray" that could cause a glow in the treated glass wall of the tube. Later experiments showed that the rays could be deflected by electric and magnetic fields. This suggested that the rays were charged particles, and not a form of electromagnetic radiation.

Today, scientists would say that an electric current is flowing through the gas, and the current consists of electrons. The discovery of the electron is credited to J.J. Thomson in 1897. He showed that these rays were small, negatively charged particles. Thomson also made the first measurement of the ratio of their charge to their mass.

As with many scientific discoveries, this discovery raised more questions. Scientists had long known about electric charge. Since most matter is neutral, they knew there must be positive charges to balance the negative charge of the electrons. To put it at the microscopic level: Atoms must contain positive charges to balance the negative electrons. But how were these positive and negative charges arranged in an atom? Answering that question is the topic of the next section.

38.2 - Rutherford's discovery of the nucleus

Nucleus: A relatively small region in the center of an atom where the positive charge - and most of the mass - of an atom is located.

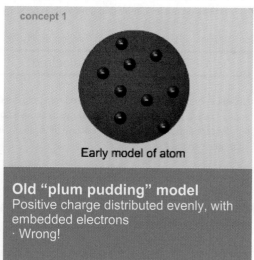

concept 1

Early model of atom

Old "plum pudding" model
Positive charge distributed evenly, with embedded electrons
· Wrong!

The modern model of the atom describes it as a small positive nucleus, surrounded by orbiting electrons. The radii of the orbits are far larger than the size of the nucleus. How did scientists create this model of the atom? For instance, what led them to believe that the nucleus was small compared to the size of the orbital radii?

Scientists in the early 20th century struggled to understand the nature of atoms. They could not directly see the structure of atoms, but knew that they contained negatively-charged electrons. They reasoned that atoms must contain equal amounts of positive and negative charges since matter tends to be electrically neutral.

Without other data, most scientists thought that the positive charges that make up matter were evenly distributed throughout the atom – why not? Since electrons have so little mass, scientists knew that the positive charges carried almost all the mass of the atom. Their mental picture of the atom looked like a blob of positively-charged cookie dough with small chocolate chips (electrons) embedded in it. The model actually bore the name of a more popular dessert at the time: The *plum pudding model* consisted of negatively-charged electrons (plums) scattered throughout a massive cloud of positive charge (pudding) that was distributed uniformly throughout the volume of the atom. This model is shown in Concept 1.

Lord Rutherford made a major breakthrough in this area, winning the 1908 Nobel Prize in Chemistry for his experiments. As a good scientist, he wanted data to support (or contradict) the plum pudding model of the atom. At the time, Rutherford was studying *alpha particles*, which are massive, positively charged particles that are emitted at high speed from some radioactive substances (such as radon). He realized that a beam of alpha particles might serve as a tool to probe the atomic interior.

In his experiment, he aimed a beam of these particles at a thin gold foil, and measured the distribution of the outgoing alpha particles. This is known as a *scattering experiment* – observing how the particles scatter – and it is a now-common technique to probe the details of atomic-sized systems.

A mechanical analogy to what Rutherford did would be to probe the interior of a box by shooting a high-powered BB gun at it. If the box were filled with sponge cake, the BBs would pass through. If it had a metal plate inside, the BBs would rebound back. Or if there were a small metal sphere inside, a small fraction would rebound or scatter sideways, with a distribution of angles.

Rutherford initially assumed that the alpha particles would be passing through a "pudding" of positive charges spread uniformly throughout the foil. Relying on this model, Rutherford predicted that most of the alpha particles should just pass straight through or be only minimally deflected.

This was not what he observed. Much to Rutherford's surprise, a small fraction of the particles were scattered by $90°$ or more. Occasionally, an alpha particle even rebounded from the foil, straight back at the source. He concluded that the atom must not have a uniform distribution of positive charge inside. Instead, the large force necessary to cause such scattering of the positively charged alpha particle could be provided only if the atom's positive charge (and mass) were highly concentrated within the atom, in a region called the nucleus.

After analyzing the data and seeing how few of the alpha particles actually scattered, Rutherford concluded that the nuclear radius must be about 10,000 times smaller than the atomic radius, a figure that is still accepted today. Rutherford's groundbreaking experiment proved that the atom is mostly empty space. His atomic model is shown in Concept 3. Note that the diagram is not even close to being drawn to scale; the atomic diameter is far too small compared to the nuclear size. If the diagram were drawn so that the nucleus were 1 cm wide, roughly the width of your pinky, the atom would have to be drawn about 100 meters wide, about 10% longer than the length of an American football field.

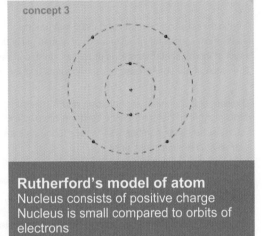

concept 2

Gold foil

Rutherford's experiment
Fired alpha particles at gold foil
Some particles scattered by a large amount
Implied compact, massive nucleus

concept 3

Rutherford's model of atom
Nucleus consists of positive charge
Nucleus is small compared to orbits of electrons

38.3 - Components of the nucleus

Rutherford proved that atoms consist of a compact, very dense positively-charged nucleus surrounded by negatively-charged electrons. In this section, we take a deeper look at the parts of the nucleus, and introduce some common terminology and notation that scientists use when talking about elements and nuclei.

The positive charge of the nucleus comes from particles called protons, which are about 1800 times more massive than electrons. The simplest nucleus consists of a single proton, and the simplest atom is hydrogen, which consists of a proton and an orbiting electron.

What distinguishes an atom of hydrogen from an atom of gold? A chemical element is defined by the number of protons in its nucleus. For an atom of a particular element, the nucleus consists of Z protons, where Z is called the *atomic number* of the element.

Hydrogen has a single proton, so for hydrogen, $Z = 1$. Gold has 79 protons, so its

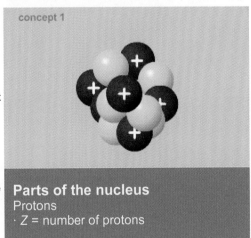

concept 1

Parts of the nucleus
Protons
· Z = number of protons

atomic number is 79. Protons and electrons have equal but opposite charges. This means that an electrically neutral atom has the same number of electrons as protons, so for example a gold atom has 79 protons and 79 electrons.

There can be more to a nucleus than just protons; there may also be other particles present, called *neutrons*. These are uncharged particles that are just a bit more massive as the proton (about 0.1% more massive). Protons and neutrons are known as *nucleons* because they make up the nucleus.

The *neutron number*, N, states the number of neutrons. Any atom of an element always has the same number of protons, but it can have different numbers of neutrons. Two forms of an element with different numbers of neutrons are known as *isotopes*. Hydrogen, for instance, **always** has a single proton, but it can have either zero neutrons ("common hydrogen"), one neutron (an isotope called deuterium), or two neutrons (called tritium). Deuterium and tritium are shown in Concept 2.

Different isotopes of an element will have different atomic masses because of the differing numbers of neutrons. The table in Concept 3 summarizes the charge and mass properties for protons, neutrons, and electrons.

Atomic masses can be measured using instruments such as the mass spectrometer. Masses are commonly given in terms of atomic mass units, u, defined such that the mass of the most abundant kind of carbon atom, carbon-12, has a mass of exactly 12 u. The value of an atomic mass unit in kilograms is given in Equation 1.

The sum of Z, the number of protons, and N, the number of neutrons, is called A, the *mass number* of the atom. Since electrons have little mass compared to protons and neutrons, the mass number is very close to the entire mass of the atom when it is expressed in atomic mass units.

An atom with a particular combination of Z and N is called a *nuclide*. A particular nuclide always has the same type of nucleus. A widely adopted notation to identify a nuclide is to write the chemical symbol of the element, with its atomic number subscripted to the left and its mass number superscripted to the left. This is shown in Equation 2, as applied to the most common carbon nuclide which has six protons and six neutrons.

Neutrons
· N = number of neutrons

concept 2

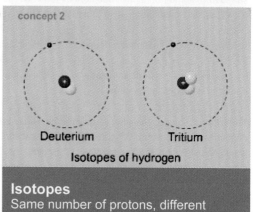

Deuterium   Tritium
Isotopes of hydrogen

Isotopes
Same number of protons, different number of neutrons

concept 3

	Mass	Charge
Proton	1.673×10^{-27} kg	$+1.602 \times 10^{-19}$ C
Neutron	1.675×10^{-27} kg	0 C
Electron	9.109×10^{-31} kg	-1.602×10^{-19} C

Neutrons and protons have similar mass
Protons far more massive than electrons

equation 1

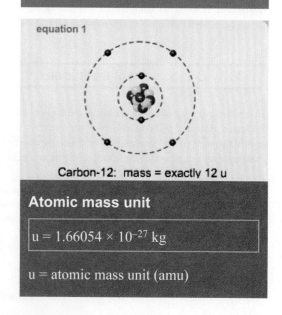

Carbon-12: mass = exactly 12 u

Atomic mass unit

$$u = 1.66054 \times 10^{-27} \text{ kg}$$

u = atomic mass unit (amu)

equation 2

Carbon-12 has 6 protons and 6 neutrons

$$^{12}_{6}C$$

Atomic number = 6
Mass number = 12
Carbon-12: mass = exactly 12 u

Mass number

$$A = Z + N$$

A = mass number
Z = atomic number
N = neutron number

38.4 - Interactive checkpoint: using Z, N and A

A neutral atom of sodium-23 has 11 protons and a mass number of 23. How many electrons does it have? How many neutrons does it have?

Answer:

Number of electrons = [   ]

Number of neutrons = [   ]

38.5 - The strong nuclear force

Atoms contain positively-charged nuclei that attract the negative electrons, and the nuclei contain closely packed protons and neutrons. These conclusions bring up a major question about the nucleus. Since protons are positively charged, and positive charges repel, why do the protons in the nucleus not fly away from one another? In this section, we will explore the nature of the force that holds nucleons together.

One good hypothesis would be that the force of gravity attracts them. This is a good hypothesis, but incorrect: It turns out that gravity is far too weak. (For two protons, by using Newton's law of gravity and Coulomb's law, you can calculate that the attractive force of gravity is about 10^{36} times weaker than the electrostatic repulsive force.)

One hypothesis down. Since gravity cannot explain the stability of the nucleus, the only alternative is that there must be another attractive force. This fundamental force is called the *strong force*.

The strong force has several important properties. It is "strong;" it manages to hold together the protons in a nucleus despite their electrostatic repulsion. It always binds particles together, even if their electric charges are the same, or if they are uncharged.

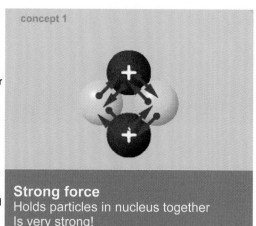

concept 1

The strong force causes protons to attract protons, protons to attract neutrons, and neutrons to attract other neutrons. The strong force acts only over a very short range. For example, once two protons are separated by more than about 10^{-15} m (roughly their own diameter), there is hardly any attraction due to the strong force, though the electrostatic repulsion is still substantial.

Although much has been learned about the properties of the strong force from experiments, there is no simple formula to relate its strength to distance. With the electrostatic and gravitational forces, the amount of force is inversely proportional to the square of the distance between the particles. In contrast, no simple formula can be stated for the dependence of the strong force on distance, though there are complicated numerical approximations.

Strong force
Holds particles in nucleus together
Is very strong!
Always attractive, regardless of charge
Acts only over a very short range

How have physicists studied the strong force? They experiment by bombarding target nuclei with high energy particles, which are influenced by the nuclei via the strong force or the electrostatic force. These forces can change the paths of the incoming particles. By observing the distribution of the outgoing particles, and comparing it to the predictions of theoretical models, scientists can test these models.

38.6 - Nuclear properties

Are the nucleons rigid objects, or soft, compressible ones? In other words, do they behave like hard marbles that are clumped together, or is there some flexibility to them, like cotton balls being crammed into a bag? These questions can be answered if we can determine how the size of the nucleus depends on the number of nucleons in the nucleus.

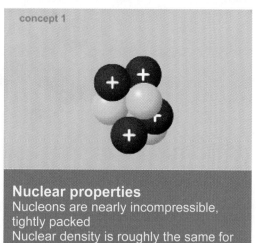

concept 1

It turns out that nucleons are nearly incompressible. This conclusion can be drawn by looking at how the radius of the nucleus relates to the number of nucleons inside. The same experiments that physicists perform to study the strong force, where they fire particles at nuclei, have also allowed them to measure other properties of the nucleus, such as its size.

Nuclear properties
Nucleons are nearly incompressible, tightly packed
Nuclear density is roughly the same for all atoms

They have determined that the radius of an atom's nucleus is proportional to the cube root of its mass number. As shown in Equation 1, the radius equals the cube root of the number of neutrons and protons, multiplied by 1.2×10^{-15} m.

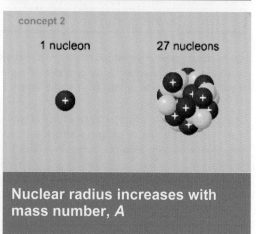

concept 2

1 nucleon   27 nucleons

There are some striking implications of this simple-looking formula. It holds the answer to our question about the rigidity of nucleons, and implies other facts about the nucleus. Consider how the radius of a sphere relates to its volume. The volume of the spherical nucleus is equal to $4\pi/3$ times the radius cubed. If you cube the radius, using the equation to the right, you are cubing $A^{1/3}$, which equals A. In other words, the volume is proportional to A, the number of neutrons and protons: Each time you add a nucleon, you are adding roughly the same amount of volume to the nucleus.

The equation also allows one to conclude that the neutrons and protons must be tightly packed. If there were large spaces between nucleons, then as their number increased, the volume would increase at an even faster rate; for example, the volume would more than double when you doubled A. (If this is not obvious to you, consider the change in the volume of adding a tenth planet beyond Pluto, versus adding another marble to a bag of marbles. Adding another planet would increase the volume of the Solar System by more than the volume of the planet itself; but as you add hard marbles to a cluster of marbles, the volume of the cluster increases by about the volume of a single marble

Nuclear radius increases with mass number, A

each time.)

The equation tells scientists that the density of all nuclear material is constant. How do we know this? Density equals mass divided by volume, and since the mass and volume increase at the ratio of 1:1, the density does not change.

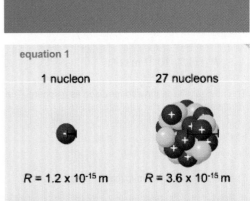

equation 1

1 nucleon   27 nucleons

$R = 1.2 \times 10^{-15}$ m $R = 3.6 \times 10^{-15}$ m

Dependence of radius on A

$$R = (1.2 \times 10^{-15} \text{ m})A^{1/3}$$

R = nuclear radius
A = mass number

38.7 - Sample problem: nuclear density

Calculate the density of the hydrogen nucleus ($A = 1$, mass ≈ 1.0 u) and of an aluminum-27 nucleus ($A = 27$, mass ≈ 27 u). Express the answer in kg/m³, to two significant figures.

Variables

mass of hydrogen nucleus	m_H
radius of hydrogen nucleus	R_H
volume of hydrogen nucleus	V_H
mass of aluminum nucleus	m_{Al}
radius of aluminum nucleus	R_{Al}
volume of aluminum nucleus	V_{Al}

What is the strategy?

1. Convert the mass of each nucleus from atomic units to kilograms using the conversion factor stated below.
2. Find the radius of each nucleus using the relationship between radius and mass number.
3. Calculate the volume of each nucleus using the radius just calculated.
4. Divide mass by volume to find the density.

Physics principles and equations

The nuclear radius grows as the cube root of the mass number.

$$R = (1.2 \times 10^{-15} \text{ m}) A^{1/3}$$

The nuclear shape may be modeled as a sphere. The volume of a sphere in terms of its radius is

$$V = \frac{4\pi}{3} R^3$$

The definition of an atomic mass unit is

$$u = 1.66 \times 10^{-27} \text{ kg}$$

Mass density

$$\rho = m/V$$

Step-by-step solution

We begin by converting the mass of the hydrogen nucleus into kilograms, then we calculate the radius of the nucleus. Using the radius, we calculate the nuclear volume. Finally, we divide the mass by the volume to determine the density.

Step	Reason
1. $m_H = 1u = 1.66 \times 10^{-27} \text{ kg}$	hydrogen nuclear mass, definition of u
2. $R = (1.2 \times 10^{-15} \text{ m}) A^{1/3}$	apply nuclear radius equation
3. $V_H = \frac{4\pi}{3} R_H^3$ $V_H = \frac{4\pi}{3} (1.2 \times 10^{-15} \text{ m})^3$ $V_H = 7.2 \times 10^{-45} \text{ m}^3$	calculate volume of hydrogen nucleus
4. $\rho_H = \frac{m_H}{V_H}$ $\rho_H = \frac{1.66 \times 10^{-27} \text{ kg}}{7.2 \times 10^{-45} \text{ m}^3}$ $\rho_H = 2.3 \times 10^{17} \text{ kg/m}^3$	definition of density

Now perform the same calculations for aluminum.

Step	Reason
5. $m_{Al} = 27\ u = 27(1.66 \times 10^{-27}\ kg)$	aluminum nuclear mass, definition of u
6. $R = (1.2 \times 10^{-15}\ m)A^{1/3}$	apply nuclear radius equation
7. $V_{Al} = \dfrac{4\pi}{3} R_{Al}^3$ $V_{Al} = \dfrac{4\pi}{3}\left(3.6 \times 10^{-15}\ m\right)^3$ $V_{Al} = 2.0 \times 10^{-43}\ m^3$	calculate volume of aluminum nucleus
8. $\rho_{Al} = \dfrac{m_{Al}}{V_{Al}}$ $\rho_{Al} = \dfrac{4.48 \times 10^{-26}\ kg}{2.0 \times 10^{-43}\ m^3}$ $\rho_{Al} = 2.2 \times 10^{17}\ kg/m^3$	definition of density

The densities are nearly identical. This is further confirmation that nucleons are tightly packed and incompressible.

The nuclear density is far beyond the density of materials in our experience. For example, consider gold, which is 19.3 times denser than water and almost 1.7 times as dense as lead. A nucleus is 12,000,000,000,000 times denser than gold. (In case you were wondering, no, the zero key did not get stuck down while we typed that number.) Recall that Rutherford found that the atomic radius was on the order of 10,000 times the nuclear radius. The volume of a sphere scales as the cube of the radius, so the ratio of atomic to nuclear volume is approximately (10,000)[3]. Since the mass of an atom mostly resides in the nucleus, and so much of an atom is empty, this explains the incredible density of a nucleus.

38.8 - Stable nuclei

What are the rules for the number of allowed protons and neutrons in a nucleus? Is any combination of protons and neutrons possible? Could there be a hydrogen atom whose nucleus has 1 proton and 7 neutrons? What about a silver atom with 47 protons and no neutrons? Could there be an element with 150 protons and any number of neutrons?

The nuclei described above do not exist. You could not even momentarily create nuclei with such extreme imbalances of protons and neutrons, or in the last case, a nucleus with so many protons. Only certain combinations of protons and neutrons can form nuclei, and even fewer combinations can form stable nuclei.

By *stable*, we mean elements that will not spontaneously decay. Gold-197 is the only stable isotope of gold, while there are several stable oxygen isotopes: oxygen-16, oxygen-17 and oxygen-18.

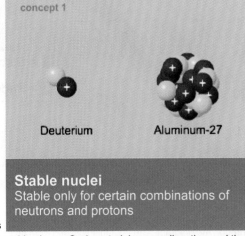

concept 1

Deuterium   Aluminum-27

Stable nuclei
Stable only for certain combinations of neutrons and protons

Some nuclides are *unstable*, meaning they have a limited lifespan. An unstable nucleus is called a *radionuclide*, and it will spontaneously and rapidly *decay* or split up into more stable pieces. Such materials are *radioactive*, and the details of the decay process are the subject of another section.

In this section, we discuss what makes for a stable nucleus. The question of stability is of fundamental importance. If all elements were unstable, then life would as we know it would not exist − the carbon, oxygen and other elements that make up your body would be constantly changing into other elements. Life is complicated enough!

On the other hand, if all elements were equally stable, then the nuclear fusion process that powers stars (including the Sun) would never happen, and the universe would be almost all hydrogen, with none of the heavier elements that make life possible.

To explain why some atoms are stable and others are not, it helps to consider a diagram of stable and unstable nuclides where Z is plotted against N. For example, even though isotopes of silver with its 47 protons ($Z = 47$) have been created with mass numbers as low as 96 and as high as 124, just two of these nuclides are stable ($A = 107$ and 109). In other words, there must be 60 or 62 neutrons along with the 47 protons.

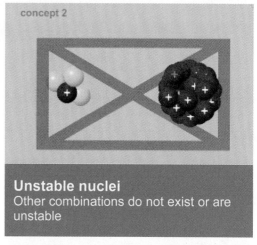

Unstable nuclei
Other combinations do not exist or are unstable

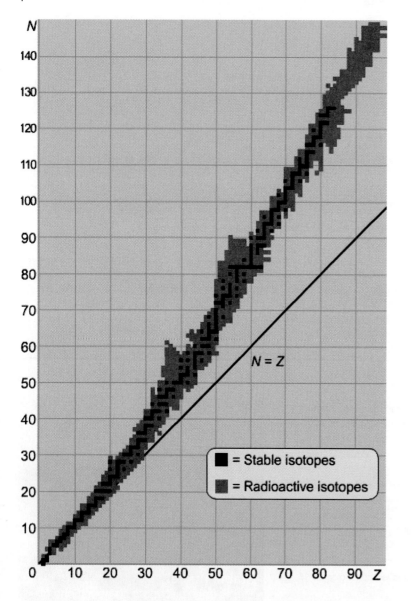

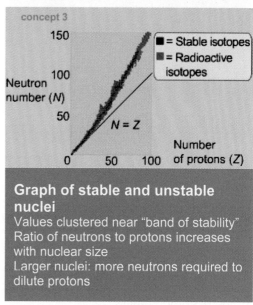

Graph of stable and unstable nuclei
Values clustered near "band of stability"
Ratio of neutrons to protons increases with nuclear size
Larger nuclei: more neutrons required to dilute protons

We would like you to observe three important features of this diagram. First, note that the stable nuclides are clustered around a band running through the diagram. The unstable nuclides exist on either side of this band. Second, you can see how the stable nuclei are distributed. Roughly speaking, for less massive nuclei, the number of protons and neutrons is approximately equal: They cluster around the line $N = Z$. In contrast, for more massive nuclei, the number of neutrons exceeds the number of protons, $N > Z$. Third, observe that there are no stable nuclei beyond bismuth ($Z = 83$).

Since neutrons are effective at diluting the repulsive electric force between protons (by spacing them out more), and the strong force binds neutrons effectively to protons and other neutrons, it seems like having more neutrons can only bind the nucleus more tightly. You may be wondering why an atom cannot have an extremely high ratio of neutrons to protons. For instance, why are there no hydrogen isotopes with eight neutrons, or even just seven neutrons? Quantum mechanical principles dictate why.

In contrast, explaining why very large nuclei are unstable, even if N is closer to Z, only requires considering the nature of the strong and electrostatic forces, not quantum mechanics.

Heavy elements like uranium have a large number of protons, which all repel one another. As the number of protons increases, the repulsive force keeps growing and growing, making the nucleus more and more unstable.

Neutrons counteract this growing instability by increasing the distance between protons, which decreases the electrostatic forces, and by attracting each other and the protons with the strong nuclear force.

However, there comes a point when the nucleus gets too large, and will be unstable no matter how many neutrons are present. This can be understood by considering the relative ranges of the strong and electrostatic forces. The strong force only acts between very close neighbors, while the repulsive electrostatic force acts between all protons regardless of their position within a nucleus. When there are lots of protons already present, and one more proton is added, it will be subject to repulsive electrostatic forces from every proton that is already there, while the attractive strong force will only be exerted by a few very close neutrons or protons. Eventually, it becomes impossible for the nucleus to "hold in" an additional proton because the strong force cannot overcome the electrostatic force.

38.9 - Nuclear binding energy

Binding energy: The energy that must be added to disassemble, or unbind, a nucleus into the protons and neutrons that make it up.

You may have heard of radioactivity, and know that uranium atoms will spontaneously decay into other elements, while other elements such as common iron (iron-56) are stable. Stable nuclei such as iron all have one thing in common: Their nucleons are tightly bound. Unstable atoms are not as tightly bound. What does it mean to be "tightly bound"?

Note that the term "stability" in nuclear physics is not making a statement about the tendency of an atom to enter into chemical reactions. For example, we say that iron is "stable" in the nuclear sense, even though it rusts. When iron combines with oxygen to form iron oxide, it is a chemical reaction, not a nuclear reaction. The iron remains iron when it becomes iron oxide; it shares electrons with oxygen but the element's nucleus remains unchanged.

What makes the protons and neutrons in a radioactive uranium atom less tightly bound than the nucleons in an extremely stable iron atom? Can we quantify and compare the stability of nuclei?

As it turns out, we can. One way to measure the stability of a nucleus is to try and rip the nucleons apart, overcoming the strong force. When physicists conduct such experiments, they find it takes energy to break the nuclear bonds (which the strong force is responsible for), that is, to take apart a nucleus into separate protons and neutrons. (This makes sense, because if no energy was required to separate them, they would fall apart on their own.)

The particles that emerge when the nucleus is forced apart can be analyzed. Careful measurements show that the sum of the masses of the separate nucleons is always *greater* than the mass of the nucleus when it is whole.

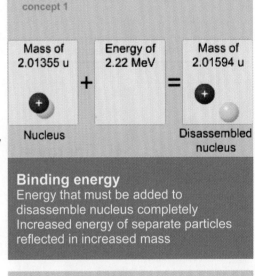

concept 1

Mass of 2.01355 u	Energy of 2.22 MeV	Mass of 2.01594 u
Nucleus		Disassembled nucleus

Binding energy
Energy that must be added to disassemble nucleus completely
Increased energy of separate particles reflected in increased mass

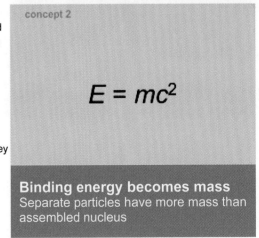

concept 2

$$E = mc^2$$

Binding energy becomes mass
Separate particles have more mass than assembled nucleus

Concept 1 shows this, using an isotope of hydrogen, deuterium, as an example.

Why should the mass of the nucleus **increase** when it is broken up? To a classical physicist, unacquainted with Einstein's theory of special relativity, this would be a surprise since mass is assumed to be conserved.

However, we know that another conservation principle applies here: the total of mass and energy (or mass-energy) must remain the same, though the individual terms may vary. Einstein's principle of mass-energy equivalence, summed up by the equation $E = mc^2$, applies. This is shown in Concept 2. It takes energy to separate the particles, and the energy added to the nucleus to fragment it into nucleons shows up as the "extra" mass. (We will assume for the sake of simplicity that the kinetic energies of the particles and of the nucleus are negligible.)

The energy that must be **added** to completely disassemble the nucleus is known as the *binding energy*. This works in both directions. The binding energy is **released** when the protons and neutrons come together to form a bound nucleus. This is illustrated in Concept 3.

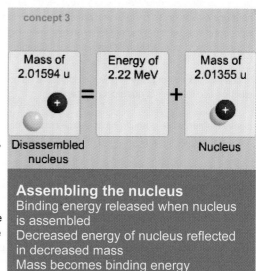

concept 3

| Mass of 2.01594 u | Energy of 2.22 MeV | Mass of 2.01355 u |

Disassembled nucleus   Nucleus

Assembling the nucleus
Binding energy released when nucleus is assembled
Decreased energy of nucleus reflected in decreased mass
Mass becomes binding energy

The terminology could be a little confusing. You can think of it like gravity: You must "add" energy to pull apart two particles, or lift a rock farther from the surface of the Earth. That is analogous to the binding energy.

Because of the equivalence of energy and mass, the binding energy may also be related to mass. When energy is added to a nucleus to disassemble it, the mass of the parts increases. On the other hand, when a nucleus is assembled, the **release** of binding energy from the system shows itself as a corresponding **reduction** of mass in the assembled nucleus. This is sometimes called the "missing mass".

38.10 - Interactive checkpoint: calculating the binding energy

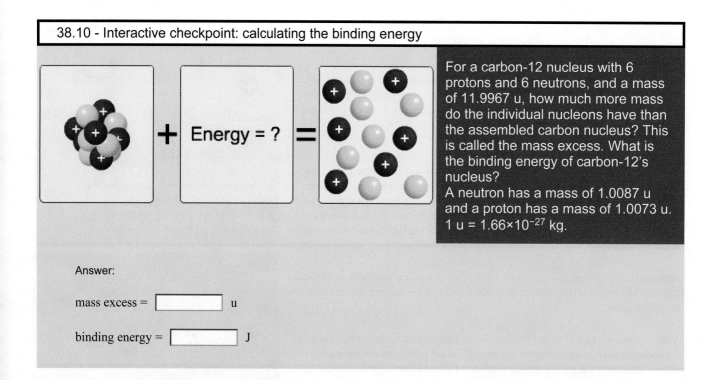

For a carbon-12 nucleus with 6 protons and 6 neutrons, and a mass of 11.9967 u, how much more mass do the individual nucleons have than the assembled carbon nucleus? This is called the mass excess. What is the binding energy of carbon-12's nucleus?
A neutron has a mass of 1.0087 u and a proton has a mass of 1.0073 u.
1 u = 1.66×10⁻²⁷ kg.

Answer:

mass excess = [   ] u

binding energy = [   ] J

The binding energy is a measure of stability for a nucleus, since the binding energy is how much energy it takes to completely disassemble a nucleus. Roughly speaking, the higher the binding energy, the harder it is to pull all the nucleons apart.

However, determining which nuclides are stable is not as simple as calculating the binding energy. In this section, we discuss how the stability of a nuclide can be determined.

We will use two nuclides as examples: $^{56}_{26}\text{Fe}$ (iron-56), and $^{235}_{92}\text{U}$ (uranium-235). Using a table of nuclear data, one may find that the binding energy of an iron-56 atom, which has 26 protons and 30 neutrons, is 492 MeV. The binding energy of a uranium-235 atom ($Z = 92$, $N = 143$) is 1784 MeV.

Does this mean that the uranium nucleus is more stable since it has a greater binding energy? Not necessarily. To compare the stability of different nuclei, a useful number to consider is the binding energy **per nucleon**. To calculate this ratio, divide the binding energy of the nucleus by the mass number, the total number of protons and neutrons. This provides a metric to compare the binding energy per nucleon in the iron isotope with the binding energy per nucleon in uranium.

The binding energy per nucleon in uranium-235 is 7.59 MeV and the binding energy per nucleon in iron-56 is 8.79 MeV. The binding energy per nucleon is a good measure for stability; the fact that the binder energy per nucleon is higher for iron than uranium correctly predicts that iron-56 is more stable than uranium-235. (In fact, the binding energy per nucleon for iron-56 is among the highest for all nuclides.)

The graph in Concept 2 shows the binding energy per nucleon for naturally occurring isotopes, plotted against the mass number A. This is called the binding energy curve.

concept 1

	Total binding energy	Mass number, A	Binding energy per nucleon
Uranium-235	1784 MeV	235	7.59 MeV
Iron-56	492 MeV	56	8.79 MeV

Stability and binding energy
Stability determined by binding energy per nucleon

concept 2

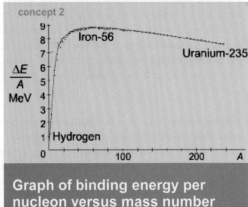

Graph of binding energy per nucleon versus mass number
Graph peaks near iron-56

example 1

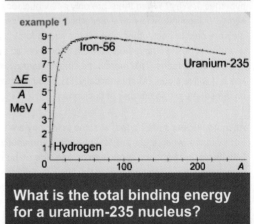

What is the total binding energy for a uranium-235 nucleus?

$$\text{binding energy} = \left(\frac{\Delta E}{A}\right) \times (A)$$

$$\text{binding energy} = (7.59 \text{ MeV}) \times (235)$$

$$\text{binding energy} = 1784 \text{ MeV}$$

The graph of binding energy per nucleon versus mass number has a distinct shape that proves to be very important. The higher on the graph an element is (indicating more binding energy per nucleon), the more stable it is.

The most stable elements are at the highest points, with iron-56 in this region, as you can see in Concept 1.

Very light nuclei (on the left of iron-56 in the binding energy curve) can become more stable if they combine to form larger nuclei through a process called fusion. By this process, the binding energy per nucleon is raised, which means that energy is released. This is the process by which stars, like the Sun, continually transform their mass into energy. In a multistep process within the Sun, hydrogen nuclei fuse together to become helium-4 nuclei.

As mentioned, the most stable locations on the curve represent elements such as iron and nickel. Heavier, radioactive nuclei to their right can increase their binding energy per nucleon and become more stable by "moving to the left and up" on the curve. For instance, you can see in Concept 3 that uranium is less stable than iron. A heavy nucleus could become more stable by emitting particles and becoming slightly smaller (the process of radioactive decay) or, in extreme cases, by splitting into two medium-sized nuclei (a process called fission). This is the principle behind radioactivity and nuclear power.

The shape of the graph also illustrates the relative distances at which the strong and electrostatic forces effectively operate. The argument that follows is reasonably complex but provides a good example of how graphical data can be analyzed. The difference between these two forces can be used to explain why the graph first shows a rapid increase of binding energy per nucleon, then levels off, and finally declines.

Earlier, we discussed the short-range nature of the strong force. It is so short-range that it acts only between a nucleon and its nearest neighbors. The graph supports this hypothesis. Why? When there are only a few nucleons, they are all very close and every nucleon interacts with every other. For instance, when there are two nucleons, they are next to each other, and exert a strong force on one another. As a third nucleon is added, it has two neighbors to exert a force on, so the force increases faster than the number of nucleons. This means the binding energy per nucleon increases, so the line has a positive slope. (Mathematically, the binding energy of the smaller nuclei increases as the square of the number of nucleons.)

As more nucleons are added, at some point they are too far apart to all be "neighbors". For instance, when there are 100 nucleons, and another is added, it can only interact with its close neighbors. A nucleon on one side of the nucleus is too far away to exert a significant strong force on one on the far side. Adding a nucleon does not increase the binding energy per nucleon. This means with larger nuclei, the additional binding energy per nucleon becomes constant. The sharp increase in binding energy per nucleon ceases.

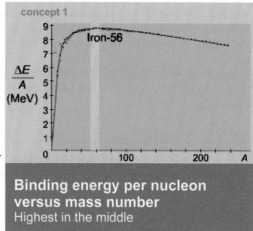

Binding energy per nucleon versus mass number
Highest in the middle

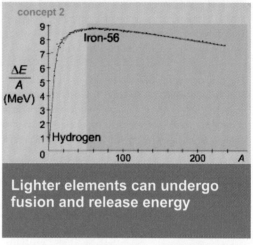

Lighter elements can undergo fusion and release energy

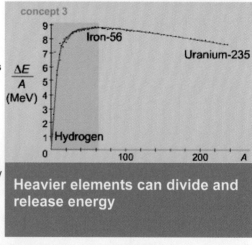

Heavier elements can divide and release energy

The strong force needs to be contrasted with the electrostatic force, which acts to push apart the protons, and which acts at a greater distance than the strong force. When a new proton is added, it is attracted only to its nearest neighbors via the strong force, but is repelled by every other proton that is already present because the electrostatic force acts at a greater range. This, in turn, makes it easier to disassemble the nucleus when more of the protons want to be separated.

In sum, at first the strong force dominates, causing the increase in binding energy per nucleon. But as the nucleus grows in size, the electrostatic force plays a larger role, causing an eventual decrease in binding energy per nucleon.

Fission: A heavy nucleus breaks up into two smaller ones, releasing energy.

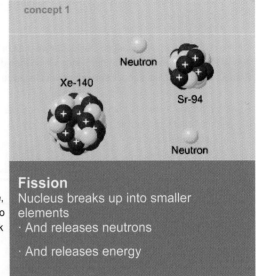

concept 1

Fission
Nucleus breaks up into smaller elements
· And releases neutrons

· And releases energy

You may have heard the term "splitting the atom" as something that humans first accomplished in the 20th century. In this section, you will learn what it means to "split" an atom. Fission is the process used both in *nuclear reactors* to produce electrical power and also in the first *atomic bombs*.

When a nucleus breaks up into smaller, more stable pieces, this is known as *fission*. Some unstable nuclei, such as uranium-236, do this spontaneously. When an atom undergoes fission, it changes identity, as the new nuclei it breaks into have different numbers of protons. There are many ways that the nucleus can break up. For example, the uranium-236 nucleus can break into Xe-140 and Sr-94, in the process releasing two neutrons. To see this fission process, press the refresh button in your browser and look at Concept 1.

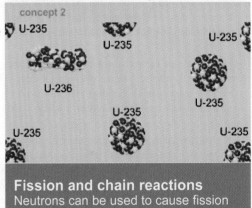

concept 2

Fission and chain reactions
Neutrons can be used to cause fission
Fission can be self-sustaining
Releases energy

However, being the impatient race that we are, humans learned to induce the process to happen at a greater rate. Induced fission, also known informally as "splitting the atom," was first performed by Otto Hahn and Fritz Strassmann. They bombarded uranium with neutrons and found that lighter elements (such as barium) were produced.

Why are neutrons effective at inducing fission? Was it not stated earlier that the strong force they supply is crucial to holding a nucleus together? Yes, but it is possible to have too much of a good thing. For a given number of protons in a nucleus – for a certain element – the band of stability is quite narrow. Too few neutrons or too many neutrons make the nucleus unstable.

In fact, neutrons are a natural choice to induce fission. Since they are electrically neutral, they can easily approach and hit the nucleus without being repelled by electrostatic forces. If the incoming neutron has the right speed, the nucleus captures it and becomes even more unstable. The nucleus has one neutron too many for the number of protons, and that immediately causes the new compound nucleus to fission into various elements.

Energy is released during fission; in the above process, roughly 200 MeV. You can understand why this happens by returning to the concept of binding energy per nucleon, which is lower for very heavy nuclei than it is for intermediate-size nuclei.

The binding energy is the amount of energy that is required to separate a nucleus into its separate nucleons, or it is the energy **released** when separate nucleons are brought together to form a nucleus. The more tightly bound a nucleus is, the higher the binding energy, that is, the more energy is released. Since the intermediate-size nuclei have the highest binding energy per nucleon, this means that heavier nuclei will release energy as they split apart and become medium-sized.

We have discussed fissioning a single atom with the release of energy. This is a crucial scientific achievement, but in order for this to be useful (for example, in a nuclear reactor), the process needs to be self-sustaining.

What makes fission a practical process is that in a fission reaction, one or more neutrons may be released, which can then induce more fission reactions in nearby atoms, which produce more neutrons, and so on. Why are there "extra" neutrons? Recall that for heavier nuclei, the number of neutrons exceeds the number of protons, while for lighter nuclei, the number of neutrons and protons tends to be nearly equal. This means there are usually some neutrons left over after the nuclear re-arrangement.

When there are enough uranium atoms so that at least one neutron, on average, is captured by another uranium atom, the *critical mass* has been reached. The process is self-sustaining, and it is called a *chain reaction*. Press the refresh button to see the fission process occur in

Concept 2.

Since humans learned to split the atom in the 20th century, the process has been put to great use. The most well-known application was the use of nuclear fission in the "atomic" bomb. A runaway chain reaction happens very fast, releasing a lot of energy in a burst which can be used to devastating effect.

On the positive side of the ledger, nuclear power has been used as an energy source. A slowly progressing chain reaction produces a steady flow of heat that can be used to boil water, which then drives steam turbines to generate electricity. The poster-child for nuclear power is France, which supplies about three-quarters of its electrical needs with nuclear reactors.

However, nuclear power is not without its risks or costs. Some of the byproducts of the fission process are highly radioactive and remain dangerous for tens of thousands of years. A typical way to dispose of these wastes is to bury them deep in the Earth. If they leak, they contaminate water sources.

38.14 - Fusion

Fusion: Two light nuclei fuse into a heavier one, releasing energy.

Fusion is a process in which nuclei join together to become a single, larger nucleus. This process also releases energy. Because positively charged nuclei repel one another, fusion does not occur spontaneously under normal conditions on Earth.

However, fusion is commonplace in the Sun and other stars where hydrogen atoms fuse into helium atoms. Fusion provides the energy to keep the star going, which Earth ultimately experiences as light and heat. Fusion occurs in the Sun because of the high temperature within the star; its interior is at about 100 million Kelvin.

At this high temperature, the atoms are in an ionized state of matter called *plasma*. While normal matter consists of distinct neutral atoms, plasma is a "soup" of positive nuclei and negative electrons. In the interior of the Sun, nuclei are hot enough and moving quickly enough to overcome the electrostatic repulsion of their positive nuclei. They move close enough to be bound by the attractive strong force between them, then fuse into a single nucleus.

concept 1

Deuterium + Deuterium = Helium-3 + Energy of 3.27 MeV

Fusion
Light nuclei fuse into larger, more stable pieces
Releases energy

Why is energy released in the process? For light elements (atoms to the left of the peak on the binding energy curve), the binding energy per nucleon increases with atomic number. As smaller nuclei are fused into larger ones, the result is a more efficient arrangement of nucleons; one that is harder to break apart. Since the new nucleus is more efficient – more tightly bound – than the previous ones, there is energy to spare.

It may be tempting to think that fusion and fission are opposite processes, since one combines nuclei and the other splits them. It may seem confusing as to how two "opposite" processes can release energy. The key is that fission with energy release occurs only when very heavy nuclei break apart into medium-size nuclei, and fusion with energy release occurs when very light nuclei fuse into heavier ones. The answer again resides on the curve of binding energy; "mid-sized" elements have the highest binding energy per nucleon. As predicted by the curve, it requires energy to combine two medium-sized nuclei into a single large nucleus, just as it requires energy to split a medium-size nucleus into smaller nuclei.

Fusion is critical to the universe we observe. Without it, there would be no stars, and in fact no elements heavier than Lithium ($Z = 3$). However, there is also a practical reason for scientific interest in fusion. If we could create and control fusion, we could use it as an energy source. Using fusion as an energy source has two huge appeals: the fuel (hydrogen isotopes) is present in the oceans in essentially unlimited quantities (compared to the relative scarcity of, say, uranium) and fusion creates no radioactive byproducts.

However, before fusion reactors become commonplace, some daunting engineering challenges will have to be solved. Recreating the conditions inside the Sun, with its enormous temperatures, is no easy feat. Furthermore, simply getting the atoms hot is not sufficient; there is a minimum plasma density that must also be achieved so that collisions between nuclei will occur frequently enough to release energy, which keeps the plasma hot and keeps the fusion reaction going. The combination of high temperature and high density requirements necessarily means that the pressure must also be very high, to hold all of the reactants together.

Copyright 2000-2007 Kinetic Books Co. Chapter 38

As in the case of fission reactions, early work on fusion was directed toward nuclear weapons. Scientists solved the problem of achieving the ultrahigh temperature and pressure conditions necessary for fusion by using a fission ("atomic") bomb as a trigger, to both heat up and compress the fusion fuel. Some trigger! Using atomic bombs to power a nearby fusion reactor is not a very popular proposal.

There are two less-explosive schemes that are currently being pursued to keep the superhot plasma together for fusion to occur. *Magnetic confinement* uses electromagnetic fields to hold the charged particles together. *Inertial confinement fusion* uses a solid pellet of deuterium and tritium that is crushed by the light pressure of perfectly timed, short-duration, high-powered laser beams from all directions. The term comes from the fact that the particles' own inertia keeps them in place during the laser pulse.

38.15 - Radioactivity and radiation

Radioactive decay: A nucleus spontaneously emits particles or high-energy photons and either changes identity or becomes less excited.

Transmutation: Changing of one element to another after α or β radiation is emitted.

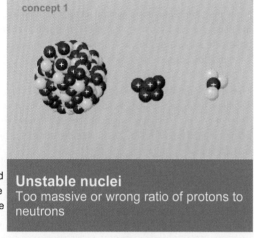

Unstable nuclei
Too massive or wrong ratio of protons to neutrons

Fission is not the only way that a nucleus with an unstable combination of protons and neutrons can change into a more stable configuration. An unstable nucleus may instead spontaneously emit a charged particle or a high-energy photon in order to reach a more stable state. It changes via a *nuclear reaction*. Isotopes that change (decay) like this are said to be *radioactive*. It is possible for the isotope to become a different chemical element after the decay, a process known as *transmutation*.

The outgoing radiation can be classified as *alpha rays*, *beta rays*, or *gamma rays*. (They are represented by the Greek letters α, β, and γ.) Different decay processes result in different forms of radiation. Alpha and beta rays consist of matter particles, while gamma rays are photons (light particles).

In an alpha decay, the initial radioactive isotope decays into a different element by emitting an α particle. An α particle is made up of two protons and two neutrons. It is a helium-4 nucleus.

The initial isotope is known as the *parent*. Because it loses two protons, its atomic number is reduced by two (the mass number is reduced by four). Since the nucleus now has a different number of protons, it becomes another element − it has transmuted. The newly-formed nucleus is known as the *daughter*.

Alpha decay occurs most commonly in heavy nuclei whose ratio of protons to neutrons, Z/N, is too large, making them unstable. An α particle is a very stable particle, and the daughter nucleus that is left behind is more stable (tightly bound) than the parent. To put it another way, the net result of the radioactive decay is a reduction of the ratio Z/N.

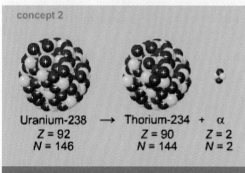

Uranium-238 → Thorium-234 + α
$Z = 92$ $Z = 90$ $Z = 2$
$N = 146$ $N = 144$ $N = 2$

Radioactive decay with α or β ray
Nucleus decays by emitting charged particle
· Radioactive element has transmuted (changed to another element)

Beta decay is characterized by the emission of an electron or antielectron. There are two types of beta decay, negative and positive. Negative β emission is represented in Concept 4. This occurs when a neutron inside the nucleus decays into a proton, an electron (the beta ray), and an almost zero-mass, uncharged particle known as an *antineutrino*. The antineutrino's interaction with matter is so weak that it is very hard to detect, and so it is customarily left out of nuclear equations.

The emitted electron did not exist in the nucleus beforehand, and is not one of the orbital electrons in the parent nucleus. When a neutron inside the nucleus turns into a proton, electron, and neutrino (and then emits the electron as a negative beta ray), its number of protons increases by one. The mass number stays the same. The released electron usually zips away, leaving behind a daughter atom with a net positive charge.

In positive β emission, the nucleus emits an antielectron (also called a positron). Antielectrons are essentially the same as electrons, except they have a change of **positive** e. The decay process is shown in Concept 5. A proton inside the atom decays into a neutron, an antielectron (the beta ray), and a neutrino. Like an antineutrino, a *neutrino* has no charge and almost zero mass. Its interaction with matter is also weak and it too is customarily left out of nuclear equations.

In emitting either type of β ray, the initial isotope changes atomic number, so β decay results in transmutation.

In *gamma decay*, the radioactive isotope emits a high-energy photon, also known as a γ ray.

Since the atomic number stays the same, the atom is the same chemical element after the decay. In this case it is the nuclear energy that changes in the decay. A nucleus can have different energy states. When a nucleus changes from an excited, high energy state to a lower one, a photon is emitted.

This is similar to the case when an electron falls from one energy level to another. A notable difference is that nuclear energy levels are much more widely spaced, on the order of millions of electron volts as opposed to say five or ten. This means the emitted photon, called a gamma ray, is much more energetic than the photon emitted by an excited atom.

A gamma decay is represented in Concept 6. An excited nucleus is denoted by an asterisk "*" after the usual symbol. How does the nucleus get into an excited state? This usually happens after another kind of decay. In many cases of α and β decay, the product nucleus is in an excited state, after which it emits a γ ray and transitions to a lower state or to the ground state. Because the photon is electrically neutral, transmutation does not occur during gamma radiation.

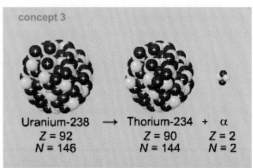

concept 3

Uranium-238 $\longrightarrow$ Thorium-234 $+$ α
$Z = 92$ $Z = 90$ $Z = 2$
$N = 146$ $N = 144$ $N = 2$

Alpha radiation
Nucleus emits alpha particle (2 protons, 2 neutrons)
Number of protons in nucleus decreases by 2
· Transmutation

Mass number decreases by 4

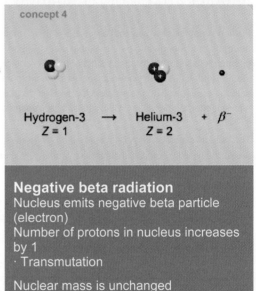

concept 4

Hydrogen-3 $\longrightarrow$ Helium-3 $+$ β^-
$Z = 1$ $Z = 2$

Negative beta radiation
Nucleus emits negative beta particle (electron)
Number of protons in nucleus increases by 1
· Transmutation

Nuclear mass is unchanged

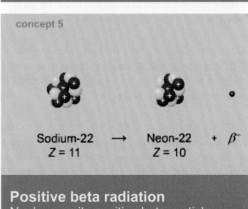

concept 5

Sodium-22 $\longrightarrow$ Neon-22 $+$ β^-
$Z = 11$ $Z = 10$

Positive beta radiation
Nucleus emits positive beta particle (antielectron)
Number of protons in nucleus decreases

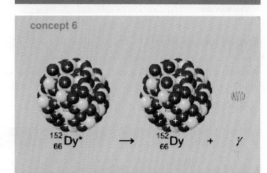

by 1
· Transmutation

Nuclear mass is unchanged

concept 6

$$^{152}_{66}\text{Dy}^* \longrightarrow \ ^{152}_{66}\text{Dy} + \gamma$$

Radioactive decay with gamma ray
Nucleus emits gamma ray (high-energy photon)
· Becomes less excited

· No transmutation

· Nuclear mass is unchanged

38.16 - Sample problem: radioactive decay

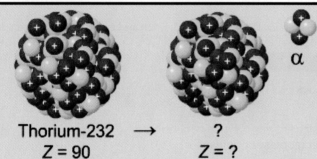

Thorium-232 $\rightarrow$?
$Z = 90$ $Z = ?$
$A = 232$ $A = ?$

A thorium-232 nucleus ($Z = 90$, $A = 232$) is radioactive and decays by first emitting an alpha particle, then two negative beta particles. What are the atomic number and the mass number of the daughter nucleus after each of these three decay steps?

Variables

atomic number, number of protons	Z
mass number, total number of protons and neutrons	A

What is the strategy?

1. The α and β particles have known charge and known mass number. Subtract these from the atomic number and the mass number of the parent nucleus to determine the daughter nucleus's values of Z and A.

Physics principles and equations

An α particle consists of 2 protons and 2 neutrons. Its mass number is four.

A negative β particle consists of one electron. When the parent nucleus emits it, the number of protons increases by one and its mass number is unchanged.

Step-by-step solution

We will use the notation Z_0 and A_0 to denote the initial values of the proton number and the mass number, Z_1 and A_1 to denote their values after the first decay step, Z_2 and A_2 to denote their values after the second decay step, and Z_3 and A_3 to denote their values after the third and final decay step.

Step	Reason
1. $Z_0 = 90$ $Z_0 = 232$	initial values
2. $Z_1 = Z_0 - 2$ $Z_1 = 90 - 2$ $Z_1 = 88$	α emission decreases nuclear charge
3. $A_1 = A_0 - 4$ $A_1 = 232 - 4$ $A_1 = 228$	α emission decreases nuclear mass

After the first decay process, the nucleus has 88 protons and 228 nucleons in total. This is radon-228, which then emits a negative β particle.

Step	Reason
4. $Z_1 = 88$ $A_1 = 228$	initial values
5. $Z_2 = Z_1 + 1$ $Z_2 = 88 + 1$ $Z_2 = 89$	β emission increases nuclear charge
6. $A_2 = A_1$ $A_2 = 228$	β emission does not affect nuclear mass

Copyright 2000-2007 Kinetic Books Co. Chapter 38

After the second decay process, there is a nucleus with 89 protons and 228 nucleons in total. This is actinium-228, which then decays by emitting another negative β particle.

Step	Reason
7. $Z_2 = 89$ $A_2 = 228$	initial values
8. $Z_3 = Z_2 + 1$ $Z_3 = 89 + 1$ $Z_3 = 90$	β emission increases nuclear charge
9. $A_3 = A_2$ $A_3 = 228$	β emission does not affect nuclear mass

After the third decay process, the nucleus has 90 protons, and a total of 228 nucleons. The end result after the three decays is again thorium because the number of its protons is again 90. After the three decays, the element is thorium-228. This lighter thorium isotope then continues to decay in a series of α and β decays until it becomes the stable isotope lead-208.

38.17 - Radioactive decay and half-lives

Half-life: The time it takes for half of a group of radioactive atoms to decay.

We have discussed the methods by which radioactive isotopes decay, by emitting α, β, or γ rays. What can be said about the rate at which they decay? If you have a sample of radioactive atoms, how many of them will decay in, say, the next minute?

The answer depends on the radioactive isotope. For any isotope, the fraction of atoms that will decay in a minute can be determined. A quantity of particular interest is the half-life, which is the average time it takes for one-half of the radioactive material present to decay.

For example, let's consider 16.00 mg of a parent nuclide, ^{131}I, which is a radioactive isotope of iodine. Its half-life is 8.04 days. You would find that after 8.04 days, one-half of the parent nuclei have decayed, and 8.00 mg of ^{131}I remains. After another 8.04 days, one-half of the remaining iodine will have decayed, and 4.00 mg remains. After a third 8.04 days, only 2.00 mg would remain, and after 8.04 more days, 1.00 mg would remain, and so on. Half of the remaining iodine decays every 8.04 days.

If it is possible to know how many atoms in a sample are going to decay within a certain time interval, is it possible to know when a particular atom will decay? Numerous experiments have shown that the answer to that question for a particular atom is no. This is similar to the situation of flipping one thousand coins and making a prediction of "50% heads." The prediction will be quite accurate, though you cannot reliably predict the outcome of any particular coin. The process of radioactive decay provided evidence of the statistical nature of quantum mechanics, which governs processes on a subatomic scale.

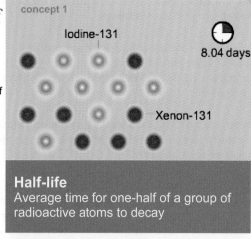

concept 1

Iodine-131

8.04 days

Xenon-131

Half-life
Average time for one-half of a group of radioactive atoms to decay

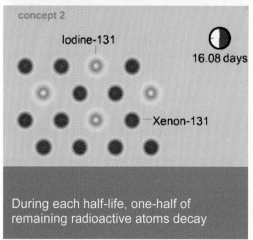

concept 2

Iodine-131

16.08 days

Xenon-131

During each half-life, one-half of remaining radioactive atoms decay

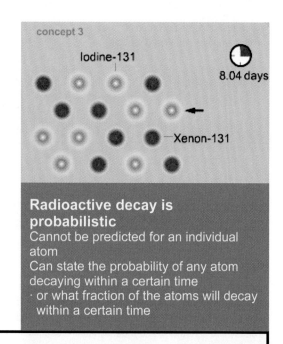

concept 3

Iodine-131

8.04 days

Xenon-131

Radioactive decay is probabilistic
Cannot be predicted for an individual atom
Can state the probability of any atom decaying within a certain time
· or what fraction of the atoms will decay within a certain time

38.18 - Interactive problem: radioactive dating

Carbon-14 is a radioactive isotope of carbon that has six protons and eight neutrons in its nucleus. It is commonly used to establish a date for organic specimens. In the first simulation, you will observe the decay of carbon-14 (C-14), and determine the half-life of that radioactive isotope.

You are equipped with a digital timer and a gauge that reports the number of parent atoms that are present. Before the simulation starts, there are 32 billion parent atoms. Each of the spheres on the screen represents a billion atoms. A sphere changes color when a billion atoms have decayed.

When you press GO, the timer starts and the carbon begins to decay to nitrogen by emitting β rays, and the number of daughter nitrogen atoms begins to grow. The daughter atoms are stable.

In the simulation, time is sped up and passes in thousands of years. The number of carbon atoms is shown both graphically with a "thermometer"-type gauge as well as numerically. When half the initial number of parent atoms has become daughter atoms, press PAUSE and note the elapsed time. (That is, at this moment, 16 billion of the carbon atoms remain present, and the rest have decayed.)

After noting the time, restart the process by pressing GO to resume the simulation and press PAUSE when half of the remaining parent atoms have become daughter atoms − in other words, when about eight billion carbon atoms remain. How does this second time interval compare to the first interval of time, when the number of parent atoms changed from 32 billion to 16 billion?

Repeat this process once more (or as many times as you like), each time pausing when the number of parent atoms has fallen in half. Do you see a pattern? You are measuring the half-life of the material, which is the average time needed for half of the parent atoms in a radioactive sample to decay. Enter your measurement for the half-life of carbon-14 by selecting the appropriate amount of years. Press CHECK to see if you are correct.

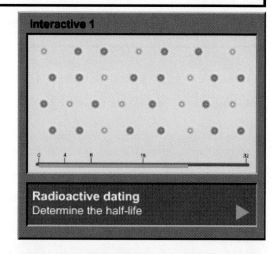

interactive 1

Radioactive dating
Determine the half-life

interactive 2

Physics Crime Scene Investigation
Measure the half-life and find whodunit

In the second simulation, you will use your newly acquired skills at measuring half-lives to investigate a crime scene. You are an environmental investigator and a criminal is once again dumping pure samples of a radioactive lead isotope, $^{209}_{82}\text{Pb}$, into a vacant lot. Holy ecological disaster!

You have been unable to catch the perpetrator in the act, but a security camera filmed three suspicious-looking characters in the vacant lot at different times. If you can determine when the radioactive waste was dumped in the lot, you will know which of these three suspects is guilty.

The factory that creates the waste is cooperating with you. They tell you that the isotope was pure lead-209 samples that initially contained 192 billion atoms. When you find the waste, it is about midnight. At midnight, 24 billion lead atoms remain, which means 168 billion of the lead atoms have decayed into bismuth atoms. In other words, one-eighth of the original lead-209 is left.

Your mission has three parts. First, determine how many half-lives have elapsed since the pure lead-209 sample was dumped. If you are having trouble with this piece of your detective work, return to the first simulation and calculate how many half-lives it takes for seven-eighths of the carbon atoms to decay.

Second, measure the half-life of lead-209 using a technique similar to what you used in the first simulation. You have the same tools as you had before.

Third, you can use the evidence from the security camera. The camera filmed Anna in the lot 6.51 hours before you obtained the sample. Sara was loitering in the area about 9.76 hours before this time, and a third suspect, Katherine, was filmed there 13.0 hours before the sample was found.

To put this all together: You use the value you determined for the half life of lead, and multiply that by the number of half-lives that have passed since the lead was dumped. That tells you how long the lead was there, so you can nail the suspect. To confirm your conclusion, drag the handcuffs in the simulation to the dastardly dumper. The simulation (and perhaps the suspect's reaction) will let you know if you are correct.

38.19 - Particle physics and GUTs

With this section, we come to the end of our discussion of the atom and the nucleus. It seems appropriate to take a peek ahead to the current state of nuclear physics, and to discuss what you and others may be learning in the decades ahead.

Particle physics, also known as high-energy physics, is one of the largest subfields of current physics. Essentially, it tries to answer the question "What is everything made of?" Ordinary matter is composed of the particles you have encountered so far – protons, neutrons, and electrons – and in the early 1900s, that seemed to be all that was needed to answer the big question. However, starting in the 1930s, particle physicists began discovering new, exotic particles that were created in an energy-to-mass conversion during collisions between the known particles. Several hundred other particles have since been discovered, most of which are unstable. Some of the particles are stable if they are left alone, but are composed of *antimatter*, which annihilates ordinary matter upon contact.

Early experimenters relied on cosmic rays (high-energy particles that permeate our galaxy) to initiate reactions. (The exact source of cosmic rays is still an open question. Stars emit them during intermittent flare-ups, but supernova explosions, when stars die, are thought to be responsible for much of the cosmic ray output.)

Later, more controlled experiments were carried out in particle accelerators, also known as atom-smashers, where particles are made to collide with higher and higher energies. Physicists now recognize that many of the heavier particles are made up from smaller building blocks called *quarks*. They understand that the smorgasbord of particles is due to the fact that when particles collide, newly-created quarks can combine with those already present to form systems of bound quarks.

The ultimate goal of physicists is a theory of everything (how is that for ambition?). Historically speaking, great breakthroughs in physics have often resulted in a simplification of our view of the universe. For example, Newton's universal law of gravity showed that the laws governing celestial orbits were the same as those governing the motion of objects falling under earth's gravity. Maxwell and his generation showed how electricity and magnetism, long thought to be unrelated, were really aspects of the same force. Physicists optimistically believe that the universe has an underlying simplicity, and that the number of fundamental forces can be reduced further.

We have discussed gravity, the electromagnetic force, and the strong force. (There is also the weak force which we have not discussed.) Albert Einstein spent a lot of his working life trying to interpret these forces as different aspects of a single "superforce". Historically, electricity and magnetism were united in the 1800s, and in the latter part of the 20th century, the weak force and the electromagnetic force were also joined theoretically. The goal of further reduction with the ultimate prize of unification still continues today.

As far as high-energy physicists are concerned, the goal is a *Grand Unification Theory*, or *GUT*. The current dream is to unify gravity with the strong, weak, and electromagnetic forces. You may have heard of attempts such as *superstring theory*, which interpret particles, such as electrons, as being modes of oscillation of unimaginably small "strings". Acceptance of superstring theory demands the idea that the universe may not consist of four dimensions (three spatial dimensions plus time), but instead ten or more dimensions. Bizarre as these ideas may seem, they are no less bizarre than relativity, nuclear theory, and quantum physics would have seemed to a scientist of the 19th century.

38.20 - Gotchas

All carbon atoms are the same. Not true: While carbon atoms all have six protons in their nucleus, different carbon atoms may have different numbers of neutrons. Nuclei with six protons but different numbers of neutrons are isotopes of carbon.

The nucleus is so small that an atom is about 99.99% empty space. No, but you are on the right track if you think this. Since the atomic diameter is about 10,000 times larger than the nucleus, the atom is more like 99.9999999999% empty space.

Protons and neutrons have different charge but approximately the same mass. Yes. A proton has a charge of 1.60×10^{-19} C and a neutron has no net electrical charge. The neutron is about 0.1% more massive than the proton, and they are each about 1800 times as massive as the electron.

The energy that is required to disassemble a nucleus into its constituent parts is the same amount of energy that is released when the same nucleus is assembled from separated nucleons. Yes; the **amount** of energy is the same and is called the binding energy. It requires energy to break apart a stable nucleus, and energy is released when the nucleus is assembled.

If half of a radioactive isotope decays during one half-life, then after two half-lives, it will all be gone. No, a half-life is the average time it takes for one-half of the radioactive material that is present to decay. After two half-lives, there will be one-quarter of the original amount left. After three half-lives, there will be one-eighth, and so on.

Elements are substances that cannot be divided or changed into other substances using ordinary chemical methods. An atom is the smallest piece of an element that still has its chemical and physical properties. An atom consists of electrons orbiting a very small, very dense nucleus. The nucleus contains both protons and neutrons, which collectively are called nucleons.

The number of protons in an atom is the atomic number, Z. The number of neutrons is the neutron number, N. The total is known as the atomic mass number, A. Atomic masses are measured in terms of atomic mass units. The mass of a carbon-12 atom is defined to be exactly 12 u.

Isotopes are forms of an element with the same atomic number (which makes them the same element) but different numbers of neutrons (and hence different atomic mass numbers).

A fundamental, very short-range interaction called the strong force holds the nucleons together, counteracting the electrostatic repulsion between protons.

The nucleons are nearly incompressible and are tightly packed in the nucleus. The nuclear radius grows roughly as the cube root of the mass number.

Equations

Z = atomic (proton) number

N = number of neutrons

Atomic mass number

$A = Z + N$

Atomic mass unit

$u = 1.66054 \times 10^{-27} \text{ kg}$

Nuclear radius

$R = (1.2 \times 10^{-15} \text{ m})A^{1/3}$

Mass-energy equivalence

$E = mc^2$

Nuclei are stable only for certain combinations of protons and neutrons. On a plot of neutron number versus proton number, stable nuclei are represented as a band of stability that passes through the center of the diagram. For small nuclei, the numbers of protons and neutrons are roughly equal, but for large nuclei, the neutrons outnumber the protons by about 50%. Heavy nuclei need an excess of neutrons to dilute the proton concentration.

Binding energy is the energy that must be added to disassemble, or unbind, a nucleus into the protons and neutrons that make it up. The same amount of energy is released if the nucleus is assembled from nucleons that are initially separated.

The sum of the masses of the separate nucleons is always greater than the mass of the nucleus when it is whole. The mass difference is related to the binding energy by Einstein's equation for mass-energy equivalence.

When the binding energy of one nucleus is greater than that of another, this means the particles are more tightly bound. For comparing how tightly bound two nuclei are, the binding energy per nucleon is the important figure.

The shape of the binding energy per nucleon vs. mass number curve is important. The curve is highest in the middle. This means that light nuclei can undergo the fusion process and release energy as this will increase their binding energy per nucleon. Similarly, heavy nuclei can undergo the fission process and release energy as this also will increase their binding energy per nucleon.

In the process of radioactive decay, an unstable nucleus spontaneously emits particles or high-energy photons. If the parent nucleus emits a charged particle such as an α particle, negative β, or positive β, then the number of protons in the nucleus changes. Transmutation is the changing of one element to another. If the parent nucleus emits gamma rays, which are uncharged photons, then transmutation does not take place, because the number of protons in the nucleus has not changed.

The half-life of a radioactive isotope is the average time it takes for the decay of one-half of the atoms that are present in a sample.